RADICAL EQUALITY

Cultural Memory
in
the
Present

Hent de Vries, Editor

RADICAL EQUALITY

Ambedkar, Gandhi, and the Risk of Democracy

Aishwary Kumar

STANFORD UNIVERSITY PRESS

STANFORD, CALIFORNIA

Stanford University Press
Stanford, California

Printed in the United States of America on acid-free, archival-quality paper

Library of Congress Cataloging-in-Publication Data

Kumar, Aishwary, author.
  Radical equality : Ambedkar, Gandhi, and the risk of democracy / Aishwary Kumar.
    pages cm
  Includes bibliographical references and index.
  ISBN 978-0-8047-9195-3 (cloth : alk. paper)
  1. Ambedkar, B. R. (Bhimrao Ramji), 1891-1956—Political and social views.
2. Gandhi, Mahatma, 1869-1948—Political and social views. 3. Anti-imperialist movements—India—History—20th century. 4. Equality—India—History—20th century. 5. Democracy—India—History—20th century. 6. Nonviolence—India—History—20th century. 7. Nationalism—India—History—20th century. 8. India—Politics and government—1919-1947. I. Title.
  DS481.A6K86 2015
  954.03'5—dc23

                              2014033656

ISBN 978-0-8047-9426-8 (electronic)

Typeset by Bruce Lundquist in 11/13.5 Adobe Garamond

For my parents
Chitralekha and Amulya Kumar Ghosh

Contents

Acknowledgments

The moment of a book's completion, if there is one, marks perhaps the moment of greatest difficulty for its author. In completion, not only must the author marshal that final rush of belief that he has something meaningful to say, he must also face the end of his work with a realization that what has been put to paper, even in the most solitary recesses of thinking, might have no meaning without those who made it possible. Chris Bayly is foremost among those, lending me conviction and helping me cultivate what I hope will be a sustained humility of thought. One rarely has the fortune of being trained by someone who does not merely speak about our many invaluable liberties but who also gives them. For that immeasurable gift, which Chris has given me without reserve, no acknowledgment might ever be enough. This study began in Cambridge but it was able to become what it is now at Stanford. I cannot remember a time over what is now close to a decade when I had an idea, a sentence, or just a splinter of thought, and Keith Baker was not there to unconditionally nourish and infinitely complicate it. With probing intelligence, uncompromising rigor, and an elegance of speech and prose that remains unmatched, Keith has made not just this book possible but framed, with characteristic generosity and patience, the very terms and dimensions of my thinking.

I thank Sugata Bose and David Washbrook for being the first to push me beyond what eight years ago they called, in perhaps a deliberately ironic Malthusian quip, the overpopulated world of *Hind Swaraj*, thus opening a new horizon for the work that was still trying to find its arc. To the four interlocutors who know that world better than most, I have no words to express my gratitude. Karuna Mantena, Uday Singh Mehta, Rajeswari Sunder Rajan, and Ajay Skaria have been readers, critics, guides, and friends of the kind one dreams of. Shahzad Bashir, Dipesh Chakrabarty, Vinayak Chaturvedi, Robert Crews, J. P. Daughton, Rochona Majumdar, and Simona Sawhney have seen this book grow from the very beginning, patiently nourishing it with graceful criticism, ready wit, and unfailing thoughtfulness, all expressed in a manner that is singularly theirs. Joel Benin, Jessica Riskin, Paul Robinson,

James Sheehan, and Steve Zipperstein have given, well beyond the limits of what I deserve, the gift of their insights, mentorship, and time. Étienne Balibar, Fredric Cooper, Andreas Eckert, Martin van Gelderen, Jürgen Kocka, Martti Koskenniemi, and Jyotirmaya Sharma, masters of warm conversations and penetrating insights, have as thoughtfully shepherded ideas and challenged my formulations as they have helped bring them to their realization here. Uttam Piyush taught me how to love more than two languages at once. Praveen and Rita Ghosh introduced me to the pleasures of reading. Anand Teltumbde gifted me one of the earliest compact discs of Ambedkar's writings. Ajay Skaria shared with me his copy of the Gujarati *Hind Swaraj*. And in Berlin, Shalini Randeria read Gujarati with me well into the nights, lending her time and insight to the minutest aspects of this work. Along with them, I owe a note of gratitude to Dipesh Chakrabarty, Bo Strath, Sanjay Subrahmanyam, and Henning Trueper for inviting me to join the Working Group Teleology in Europe from the autumn of 2011 onward.

Over the years, I have incurred many more debts, both of people and the exemplary institutions of which they have been part. In the history department at Stanford University, Phillip Buc, David Como, Zephyr Frank, Sean Hanretta, Yumi Moon, Jack Rakove, Richard Roberts, Peter Stansky, and Jun Uchida have made this path truly worth traversing. At Trinity College, Cambridge, the late Rajnarayan Chandavarkar, Joya Chatterjee, Jean Khalfa, Anil Seal, and Amartya Sen ensured the most supportive, and often the most spectacular, conditions for writing and research. At the faculty of history, Cambridge, Richard Drayton, Tim Harper, Rosalind O'Hanlon, Quentin Skinner, and Megan Vaughan, in their distinctive ways, set me on a journey that I had least expected to undertake, opening horizons in global histories of legal and political thought that had, at that time, only begun to unfold. At Jawaharlal Nehru University, New Delhi, Aijaz Ahmad, Neeladri Bhattacharya, Gopal Guru, Indivar Kamtekar, K. N. Panikkar, Prabhat Pattnaik, Tanika Sarkar, and Radhika Singha opened for me, as they still do, the deep and vast provinces of their own thinking. By way of beginnings, I could not have asked more from them. I must thank Felicitas Hentschke and Dominik Huenniger, and with them, the terrific group of fellows and staff at the Lichtenberg-Kolleg: Göttingen Institute of Advanced Study at Göttingen University; Re:Work, IGK at Humboldt University, Berlin; and Research Project Europe, 1815–1914 at the University of Helsinki for providing historic settings, unstinting care and generous resources that made the final stages of the book's completion such a pleasure.

For many memorable conversations, exchanges, and mediations, without which none of this would have been possible, I am indebted to Sunil Amrith,

Rachel Berger, Baidik Bhattacharya, Akeel Bilgrami, Ritu Birla, Arindam Chakrabarti, Partha Chatterjee, Brinda Dalmia, Rohit De, Faisal Devji, Arvind Elangovan, Leela Gandhi, Raymond Geuss, Kaveri Gill, Priyamvada Gopal, Pamila Gupta, Humeira Iqtidar, Kriti Kapila, Shruti Kapila, Bodhisattva Kar, Sudipta Kaviraj, Riyad Koya, Udaya Kumar, Sangeeta Mediratta, Dilip Menon, Jisha Menon, Barbara Metcalf, Thomas Metcalf, Srijana Mitra Das, Nitya Mohan, Mithi Mukherjee, Angus Nicholls, Neha Paliwal, V. Narayana Rao, Nasreen Rehman, Nate Roberts, V. Sanil, Sumit Sarkar, Andrew Sartori, Siddharth Satpathy, Sharmila Sen, Mishka Sinha, Mrinalini Sinha, Gitanjali Surendran, Ananya Vajpeyi, and Milind Wakankar. Parts of the book have been presented in Berlin, Budapest, Cambridge, Chicago, Göttingen, Harvard, Helsinki, Johannesburg, London, Madison, Minnesota, Mumbai, New Delhi, New York, St. Gallen, Stanford, and Vancouver. I am grateful to the audiences at these places and to the participants of the workshop on Civility, Cruelty, Truth that I have run at Stanford since 2011 for their engagement, which has helped me refine the materials presented there.

For the home this book has found, I am most thankful to Hent de Vries and Emily-Jane Cohen. Anne Fuzellier Jain and Friederike Sundaram have seen the book through production with a remarkable combination of insight, energy, and patience. A warm note of thanks is due to the two anonymous readers at Stanford University Press. I am also indebted to John Rawlings at Stanford University Libraries, the archivists at the British Library in London, and the Nehru Memorial and Museum Library and National Archives of India in New Delhi, along with the staff of the libraries at University of California at Berkeley and University of Texas at Austin, who opened many trails into the labyrinthine world of early twentieth-century materials and editions. Utathya Chattopadhyay, Smaran Dayal, and Pujya Jennifer Pascal have provided thorough assistance and engaging insights. To my students who have endured the making of this book and breathed life into it, in the classroom and outside, especially Madihah Akhter, Kristen Alff, Anubha Anushree, Maria Hafeez Awan, Ahoo Najafian, Nitya Rajeshuni, Henri Stern, Jacob Stern, Neel Thakkar, Derek Vanderpool, and Anand Venkatkrishnan, I can express my gratitude only in the most inadequate manner.

My parents, Chitralekha and Amulya Kumar Ghosh, have set examples—through the impeccable conduct of their lives, richness of thought, and ability to give and listen unconditionally—that I aspire to achieve in my own life every single day, and falter. This book is a small gesture of trying to return to them what remains quite simply unreturnable. Its only solace is that it comes in a form that they will deeply cherish and appreciate. My sister, Smriti, and brother, Kunwar (and only an ocean or two away—in Bombay and Brisbane—

our angels Shreya, Shresth, and Darsh), are the heart and soul of my endeavors. There is nothing that I have written—and will ever write—that does not carry the mark of their warmth, intelligence, and humor. In Honolulu and Irvine, the Senguptas and Irvings have given me home away from home. But for their immense affection and love of ideas, the solitary labor that writing a book demands would have been an exercise of a very different order. Closer in space, there are those who complete one's life in ways unknown and unpredictable! Nancy Hill, Inga Pierson, Margaret Sena, thank you for the winding conversations, charming evenings, and fantastic journeys.

Finally, there are those that must not be thanked. Parna Sengupta, the immeasurable love of my life, has shouldered the responsibility for all of it with such forgiveness, belief, and brilliance that it leaves me frequently speechless. All I can say is that only her unconditional sacrifice gives this work—and the apparitional nature of its author's existence—the little semblance of justice that it has managed to retain through the years of its making. That this book is here at all is because she has nourished not just my work but also the source of all our happiness. That is Arjun, who alone makes my craft and life worth my while. To him and my grandfathers, Sirish Chandra Ghosh and Rabindranath Sinha, who taught me so much and whom I miss every moment, this book might finally give some justification, even if little compensation, for my long absences.

Early versions of some materials in Chapter 3 have appeared under the title "Ambedkar's Inheritances," in *Modern Intellectual History* 7, no. 2 (2010). A small part of Chapter 4 has appeared as "The Ellipsis of Touch: Gandhi's Unequals," in *Public Culture* 23 (no.2, 2011). A fragment of Chapter 7 appears in *Seminar* 641, January 2013, under the title "Force and Adoration: Ambedkar's *Maitri*." I am thankful to Cambridge University Press, Duke University Press, and *Seminar* for their permission to reproduce the materials here.

RADICAL EQUALITY

Of Faith in Equality

Toward a Global Measure

"Modern India," apart from naming a time and place, has come to stand in for an interminable struggle with history—the struggle to formulate, despite the violence of its antiquity, an ethics of justice for the present; the struggle to affirm, in spite of the exclusions of its modernity, a belief in democracy that is still to come. This book examines the intellectual and political history of the encounter between Bhimrao Ramji Ambedkar (1891–1956) and Mohandas Karamchand Gandhi (1869–1948), two of the most formidable non-Western thinkers of the twentieth century, whose visions of moral and political life have left the deepest imprints on that struggle and the paradox that sustains it. One was a prodigious "untouchable" who, lifting himself against the exclusion and violence that surrounded him, became a revolutionary constitutionalist, a thinker whose laborious draftsmanship and exegetical rigor produced a new constitution for the free republic in 1950. The other, born in a community of Hindu Vaishnava merchants, was an inept lawyer who galvanized through the sheer force of his convictions and prose—and often through his commitment to the virtues of such quotidian and solitary practices as spinning and weaving—an as-yet-unformed people against the most powerful empire of his time. Never had the colonial world's right to justice been formulated in such proximity by two thinkers who had otherwise struggled so ceaselessly, with such scruple and hostility, against each other. But perhaps more crucially, never had this right to justice been sought in the shadows of a religion known to be so persistently oppressive and violent toward those it claimed as its very own. Ambedkar's and Gandhi's struggle was waged as much over the modern and secularist "faith in equality" as it was around the place and boundaries of faith in secularist notions of equality itself.[1] *Radical Equality* reconstructs the morals and methods of that formidable struggle for justice and its consequences for a global genealogy of democratic ethics.

The struggle for an egalitarian India, even in their own time, was not reducible to the impasse between Ambedkar and Gandhi alone. Yet the complexity of their kinship anticipated and amplified the paradoxes of the "mentality of democracy," as Akeel Bilgrami calls it, in the colonial world in a manner few other relationships did.[2] With the arrival of Gandhi and Ambedkar within the first two decades of the twentieth century, the nationalist demand for freedom from empire, which had until then driven liberal and revolutionary anticolonialisms of various hues, was for the first time integrated into a rigorous pursuit of equality. For both Gandhi and Ambedkar, political life—the sense of belonging to a community and constituting a people—was inconceivable without an unconditional equality in moral and social relations. The right to live equally, even and especially in the shadows of imperial unfreedom, was the indispensable mediating force between the otherwise sequestered existences of the colonized and colonizer, Shudra and Brahmin, "untouchable" and "touchable." It was this egalitarian commitment, which was never afraid of embracing a certain hierarchy (of suffering, skills, traditions, and faiths), never shy of expounding the virtues of sovereignty and force, even segregation, which would bring Gandhi and Ambedkar together and pull them apart in a remarkable kinship forged during the three most decisive decades of India's anticolonial struggle.

A distinctive notion of equality was thereby placed at the moral center of India's incipient democracy. This was not the seed of an imperfect and faltering democracy, as liberal proponents of the empire since the nineteenth century had often predicted the rule of the people in the non-Western world might be. Such people's ruling themselves without adequate institutional and psychological preparation, the colonizers had warned, would lead to a democracy bound by a morally corruptible and socially unequal structure whose idioms, imported from the language of European political thought, would be deployed in the colonies for mere rhetorical effect, even as democracy's substantive essence, its European spirit, would be compromised beyond recognition.[3] A sustained attention to Ambedkar's and Gandhi's ethics and politics—their attempt to imagine a people bound together not as much by institutions and the law as grounded in shared moral and fraternal commitments—reveals, however, that anticolonial political thought came to be rooted not so much in the compromised democracy that metropolitan intellectuals such as John Stuart Mill had feared that the colonized, in the absence of the tutelage of their masters, might end up with. What emerged instead is a democracy of antinomies, a democracy whose matrices reflect an unremitting and radically original approach to the modern egalitarian imperative. And yet beneath its great striving for a community of equals, this approach also nourished a self-oriented, self-conserving—indeed, conservative—"spirit of democracy" peculiar to the history of twentieth-century anticolonialism,[4] one in which the concern with sovereignty (whether of the self or of the collective), the essence of being free and human, came to be articulated just as often without a commitment to inclusion and equality. No two thinkers in the modern non-West would struggle with this risk of an inegalitarian democracy, this sacrifice of equality in the very name of an ethical and political community, more productively than Ambedkar and Gandhi.

In this chapter, covering a wider and deeper ground than a conventional introduction, I turn toward the political and philosophical conditions, the complex set of interwar moral, theological, and republican attitudes, under which this sacrificial politics took its originary form. I do not intend to recuperate the lives of Ambedkar and Gandhi in the mode of intellectual biography, each of them either placed on the terrain of his own moral psychology and convictions or rehabilitated into a world of argument where the entire sum of his thought might be seen merely as response to the other's claims and maneuvers. Instead, I trace their conceptual innovations and linguistic choices to delineate the symptoms of what otherwise looks like an irreparable disjuncture in the colonial world's attempt to fashion a society of equals.[5] For many, I accept, the claim of a discursive and structural disjuncture between European and anticolonial formulations of the political (and almost as a corollary, the seeming irreparability of the relationship between Ambedkar and Gandhi) might well be tenable, even ideologically necessary. But such a claim still leaves untouched the task of explaining why and in what forms equality, in the wake of twentieth-century struggles waged for the emancipation of society (national and international), became at once global in its rhetorical and moral reach and hierarchical in its institutional and political form. Conceived as an archeology of this egalitarian commitment, *Radical Equality* seeks to shed light on the conjoined ethics of justice and exclusion that has given global democratic thought its paradoxical form.

But a study of the global life of democracy—the tension between popular sovereignty and civic virtue, the struggle for balance between insurrection and constitution—entails not simply an inquiry into the processes by which the meanings, values, and practices of "the political" (or theologico-political) came to acquire their ambiguous universality (spreading outward from Europe since the late eighteenth century until they were rendered at different moments and under varying conditions into a universal language of political ideas and ideals). Such a study also requires an archeology of the limits—

conceptual, rhetorical, material, and symbolic—lodged at the center of the political as such, limits at which the founding norms of democracy exclude its most insurrectionary practitioners, just as, in a moment of striking unity between force and justice, the excluded turn against those norms and rules of democracy that structure their oppressive existence.

It is at this limit, in a moment of risk at once classical and radical, even constitutive of democracy, that I mine the depths of what Gandhi, in his response to Ambedkar's 1936 treatise *Annihilation of Caste*, had called his aloneness—indeed, attributed a political and ethical singularity to it.[6] As a way to put Ambedkar's aloneness in its time and place, one that he would steadily, deliberately, and sensitively transform into a political and philosophical attitude singular to him, I begin with two texts and a history—*a* history because I am interested not so much in the insurmountable discontinuities between the texts and their authors as I am in those practices of reading and reception that betray, despite the history of mutual hostility that surrounds Gandhi and Ambedkar, their ambivalent and silent affirmations. This is less a history of enunciations and universality of meaning, then, than it is a history of rarity and exception, a history of depths.

Two Strikes at Freedom

In December 1935, the Jat Pat Todak Mandal, an organization dedicated to the abolition of caste and untouchability, invited forty-five-year-old Bhimrao Ambedkar to deliver its annual keynote lecture in the northern Indian city of Lahore. Born in Mhow, a cantonment in Madhya Pradesh, into the family of a military schoolteacher, Bhimrao began his public life in the 1920s as an anticaste crusader in Bombay Presidency. By the 1930s he had emerged, in the wake of his galvanizing and widely publicized speeches at the Round Table Conferences in London in 1930–1931, as one of the leading authorities on colonial franchise and republican constitutions—an authority, however, who would develop a rather conflicted relationship with the norms and rationales of interwar nationalist and republican thought. Ambedkar would in many ways mature into a republican thinker in the classical sense of the term, condensing in his thought all the rigor and tension that constitute that formidable tradition in Europe and elsewhere. He would, despite his affinities for republican ethics and ideals of citizen virtue, remain uncompromisingly resistant to the oppressive national-spiritual rhetoric in which anticolonial thinkers couched their own struggle for sovereignty. His decision in December 1927 to publicly burn a copy of the *Manusmriti*, the ancient work of Indic jurisprudence considered unimpeachable in Hindu moral and political culture, had endeared him neither to liberal social reformers nor conservative nationalists of his time. As the Jat Pat Todak Mandal would soon realize, once they were confronted by Ambedkar's uncompromising faith in equality, an encounter with sacrilege was always round the corner.

Despite serious misgivings about the Mandal's liberal reformist methods and susceptibility to conservative Hindu opinion, Ambedkar accepted their invitation. Having by now freed himself decisively from the fundamental impasse of his time—the claim of abstract equality between India and Europe on which nationalists of various persuasions had mounted their demand for freedom from the empire for more than two generations—Ambedkar envisioned the lecture giving him a proper stage to formulate the conditions of another freedom, another equality, perhaps another politics for colonial India altogether. As news of his imminent visit to the Punjab spread, however, office bearers of majoritarian and extremist organizations such as the Arya Samaj and Hindu Mahasabha mounted pressure, rebuking the Mandal for having chosen Ambedkar as the speaker for their annual event and asking it to withdraw the invitation. The Mandal initially resisted the reactionary offensive. But by April 1936, it began to insist that Ambedkar allow copies of his lecture to be printed in Lahore, where they could potentially limit its impact and distribution, rather than in Bombay, where they would have no control over the text's circulation. Ambedkar, already put off by a series of ambiguous messages from the Mandal, refused to concede ground.[7] By May 1936, his presidential lecture had been successfully killed. Its theme would have been the annihilation of caste.

The death of the lecture in the British Punjab marked the birth in Bombay of a treatise unparalleled in the history of anticolonial emancipation, a treatise that promised to emancipate not simply politics but the moral psychology of freedom itself from the dialectic of nation and empire. As soon as the invitation to lecture was rescinded, Ambedkar went ahead and published the text of his speech as a slim volume of less than hundred pages, composed in a fashion that defied all standards of genre, dissent, and circulation. Within the first two months of its publication, *Annihilation of Caste* sold more than 1,500 copies. By the end of its first year, translations into Gujarati, Tamil, Hindi, Malayalam, and Punjabi were under way or already published. The second edition of the English original was published in 1937, and a third edition in 1944. Like much of Ambedkar's prolific writing spread over four decades of public life (including the republican constitution of free India, which he helped author between 1947 and 1950 as the elected chairman of its drafting committee), *Annihilation of Caste* drew disengaged criticism and sometimes deafening silence in nationalist and reformist circles.

Much of the response, when it came, was predictably derogatory and hostile.[8] But foremost among those who responded to it with any degree of rigor and reserve was Ambedkar's political antagonist and philosophical peer, M. K. Gandhi.

Annihilation of Caste was published just a year before the general elections of 1937 and a year after the Government of India Act of 1935. It came, then, at the crest of a democratic wave swelled with dreams of Indian franchise. Yet for millions of religious minorities and outcastes, justice and even freedom still looked like a receding horizon. It was this receding tide of freedom (in both its moral and political sense) that Ambedkar perhaps sought to stem. The work must therefore be approached, first and foremost, as a conceptual event in the philosophical history of Indian democracy. It certainly facilitated the most potent and decisive philosophical encounter between Ambedkar and Gandhi, an encounter that amplified in as clear a manner as possible the kinship and difference between the two. In fact, *Annihilation of Caste* revealed those impulses in their thinking of transformative action, those elements in their critique of force, which would remain unbridgeable. And if nationalists would henceforth refuse to associate Ambedkar with their good conscience and pursuit of freedom, it was not because he had renounced his commitment to freedom but rather because he alone had thought courageously of the possibility of such sovereignty in the most egalitarian and forceful fashion—a sovereignty whose earliest expression could be traced back to Gandhi's own masterwork composed earlier in the century, *Hind Swaraj* (1909).

Annihilation of Caste and *Hind Swaraj* are discordant constituents of a shared moral psychology that had begun to coalesce in early twentieth-century India. Although the two texts attempt to think anew the conditions of resistance and truth in the ineradicable shadows of force, they were equally out of joint with their times. For neither simply poses questions about the efficacy of abstract ends such as freedom, to which nationalists of their time were so fervently and blindly committed. On the contrary, they both shift nationalism's obsessive interest in ends and seek to reformulate the means and force proper to justice. What kind of force—routine, infinitesimal, even invisible—constitutes a free and equal life? Could the people's commitment to civic duty and practical knowledges alone—say, the art of spinning, spending time on cleaning up public spaces, or forging a weapon—retrieve such life? What might such minutiae of practices—which Gandhi often assembled under the term "sacrifice," thereby investing in routine activities the power to acquire a state indifferent to the inequities of everyday life—prepare one for? Could death, at war or through self-sacrifice, be the ground of equality? Could suffering, especially when mandated by religious injunctions and inflicted by the involuntary force of law, be transformed into ameliorative acts of justice through a voluntary embrace of pain, even mortality? Might the return in any simple sense to religion—and there has never been a religion (or state) that has not demanded sacrifice—restore the irreducible dignity of life?[9] Could sacrifice, in other words, bring justice to those who were already most poor, most untouchable, and irreparably violated by the law? And what form, if vulnerability and death might be construed as the ground of equality at all, might the sacrifice of the already sacrificed take?

As figure, metaphor, ritual, and skill, "sacrifice," for both Ambedkar and Gandhi, referred to the art of offering one's own life before taking another's. It entailed the disciplinary rigor and method of self-dissolution, one that could be cultivated only in a firm and fearless knowledge of life's inevitable and incurable mortality. But this understanding, when translated into the idiom of mass politics, could not have been immune to ethical regressions. In fact, "sacrifice," which frequently appears in Ambedkar's and Gandhi's speeches and writings in one form or another, in terms such as "fearless sacrifice" or "limitless sacrifice," only accentuates the difficulty of this moral and political ontology. Few classical concepts, after all, have been as essential to the practices and aspirations of modern politics and as elusive in their connotations and meanings. Its origins rooted in ancient religion and myth and its logic grounded in the fears and trepidations of an enchanted and even "broken world," sacrifice has long been replaced by those exigencies of modern politics that now extract life (and demand death) from citizens and strangers under other names and for causes other than the pacification of divine wrath: security, liberty, democracy, civic duty, protection and prolongation of life, even freedom of the republic.[10] The burden of Ambedkar's political philosophical struggle was precisely to reveal how profoundly sacrifice, whether ordinary or spectacular, ancient or modern, demanded in segregated towns or offered at war, continues to shape—and yet possesses the capacity to transform nonviolently, bloodlessly, and if need be, by force—the moral reflexes and material exclusions of modern democratic politics. "My definition of democracy is," Ambedkar would argue in an address delivered at the district law library in Pune, "a form and a method of Government whereby revolutionary changes in the economic and social life of the people are brought about without bloodshed."[11]

If sacrifice of life is the price of freedom that a people must pay, if sacrifice of self and family is the metaphysical foundation of social citizenship that might be safely secured only by the sovereign state (as has been argued since the seventeenth century, when modern political thought began to acquire its identifiable form, one strand within it culminating in Hegel's 1821 treatise

Philosophy of Right), then something is profoundly unjust, untruthful, even cruel, in the way freedom has been conceptualized since Europe's first modernity. Freedom itself, then, must be reconceived, and with it "martyrdom," which, Ambedkar would insist in 1943, nationalists had appropriated and trivialized, confusing it with their willingness to simply go to prison.[12]

Yet Ambedkar, who would scrupulously pursue the logic of exclusion that inhered in the juridical construction of freedom-as-sacrifice down to its classical origins (while himself mobilizing it, against the nationalist ethos of his time, as a figure of responsibility and justice), is rarely seen to be a thinker of what Thomas Nagel has called "mortal questions."[13] The relationship between finitude, force, and justice—which is to say, the relationship between action and death—has never been seen as clearly belonging to the province of his moral imagination. Such a reservation is all the more striking because the mode of theologico-political thinking of which Ambedkar became a formidable twentieth-century practitioner and rhetorician has had a distinctive genealogy within dissident social and religious traditions of precolonial South Asia. In fact, the dialectic of passivity and resistance, death and justice, were part of the lower caste "idea of the social" even before the advent of colonialism.[14] These mentalities and practices have since the nineteenth century given lower caste protest both a remarkable ability to cross-pollinate with other traditions of the Indic and Indo-Islamic millennium and a ceaseless—at once strategic and critical—energy driven toward entering the electoral spaces of postcolonial democracy. If there was one impulse among these that was discernible in *Annihilation of Caste*, it was Ambedkar's insistence on reclaiming politics as the shared space of belief, which is to say, the right to hold something just as being true. Justice is the only irreducible truth, the only indivisible ground of faith whose expanse exceeds the theater of electoral interest and calculation. It was perhaps appropriate, then, that the more electoral ground Ambedkar lost, the more unavoidable the force of his revolutionary critique appeared; the more difficult his electoral survival seemed, the more indispensable the rigor of his constitutional imagination for the new republic became.

This constitutional imagination had never been never separate from Ambedkar's belief in the insurrectionary duties of the citizen, one that he begins to articulate with unprecedented clarity in *Annihilation of Caste*. Indeed, the treatise forges a galvanizing (and at times poignant) relationship between the ethics of revolutionary annihilation and the creative energies of the people, between a people's immeasurable, destructive force and their spiritual capacity to constitute themselves anew. "Annihilation," the gesture, concept, and metaphor for force, signals this range and depth of Ambedkar's rhetorical and conceptual ambitions. In fact, with its creative energies in ceaseless struggle with its origins in nihilism and Indo-European negative theology, the term renders Ambedkar's resistance against the caste order as a graded and gendered servitude of faculties (which, he insisted, needed to be annihilated without any love for its juridical and material rules) inseparable from his affinity for religion as such (which had to be destroyed precisely to be created anew). Always aware of those who are left behind and cast out, always a gleaner of semblances and essences, *Annihilation of Caste* thus sets in motion two dueling impulses. On the one hand, there was the imperative to recuperate the materiality and practice of an ethical religion through the act of individual and collective heresy. On the other hand, there was the need to posit a revolutionary subject through the "general mobilization" of the multitude. The reclamation of authentic belief, the right to truth, and the ability to mobilize a shared and general will, Ambedkar insists, are inseparable from one another; together they constitute a people's movement toward a free and revolutionary democracy. This freedom to believe, which underwrites the right to a just religion, not only exceeds the organized, hierarchical, and ecclesiastical limits on faith, it exceeds even the practice of mysticism that had lent lower caste protest in the precolonial period its emancipatory charge. It is in this rupture from premodern genealogies of emancipatory mysticism and humanistic pieties of modern nationalism alike that Ambedkar would emerge as the thinker of the theologico-political in its classical and insurrectionary sense.

When I invoke "the classical," I do not intend to refer to a mode of argument and thought that is classical simply because it adheres to the paradigms and languages of politics that were gradually set in place and consolidated worldwide, beginning at least since the late eighteenth century, by Europe's global ascendancy. Rather, whenever I discern in an argument and thought a classical bent, I have in mind the tension that arose from an acute awareness among dissident thinkers across a range of religious and humanistic traditions in India, Europe, Africa, and elsewhere—the awareness that the recovery of freedom anywhere, whether from its ancient or modern loss, in its religious or republican dimension, in the capital or the colony, demands an engagement with the incurable universality of human suffering everywhere. This was no vicarious universalism of the European liberal type, which would often postulate an abstract equivalence between popular struggles for justice in Europe and the colonies, struggles that were otherwise waged in the shadows of immiscibly different and often insurmountable forces and conditions. When I refer to "the classical," then, I have in mind a tradition of grappling with the inextricable relationship between force and justice, a tradition whose lineage Ambedkar would himself trace to the Rousseauist strand within modern revolutionary thought.

But why do I insist on Ambedkar's struggle for an ethical and political religion? And what does the "theologico-political," that intractable concept-figure constituted by the triad of faith, force, and sovereignty, have to do with this insistence? As a brief illustration of what might be gained by placing Ambedkar within the theologico-political problem, let me turn to the final pages from *Annihilation of Caste*. This is where Ambedkar argues, most decisively, that the right to have justice requires the multitude, caste Hindus and those designated "untouchable," to cultivate a fidelity to force. Justice always demands a religious resistance. It calls for violence against violence of the scripture. In such moments, Ambedkar is never far from predilection for security and sovereignty, force and sacrifice. "In my opinion," he states near the end of *Annihilation of Caste*, "only when the Hindu Society becomes a casteless society . . . can hope to have strength enough to defend itself." Then, in the final sentences of the first edition, comes an unequivocal warning from a thinker who, just a moment later, would cease to think of himself as a Hindu: "Without such internal strength, Swaraj for Hindus may turn out to be only a step towards slavery."[15]

To affirm religion not for its own sake but to affirm it in order to make what was just strong and what was strong just; to acquire the "means of defense" for the weak without lapsing into hostility and militarism;[16] to refuse, above all, the nationalist bait of freedom that came without justice, for the simple reason that such freedom was enslavement by merely another name—this was the moral logic at work in *Annihilation of Caste*. Ambedkar had no interest in the various "species of reform" in its liberal sense, he claimed.[17] His was a treatise on the taking the difficult path to reform, one that involved the purity of means and force alone. And this belief in force, which sustained his formulations on the egalitarian sovereignty of the people, was never far from a certain religiosity. "The moment it degenerates into rules it ceases to be Religion, as it kills responsibility, which is the essence of a truly religious act," Ambedkar declares in a pivotal passage in *Annihilation of Caste*. "I have, therefore, no hesitation in saying that such a religion must be destroyed and I say, there is nothing irreligious in working for the destruction of such a religion."[18]

I will return more than once to this search for a pure means, this immeasurable freedom of force whose essence Ambedkar is able to grasp in terms only of a "truly religious act," and which he calls "annihilation" (*ucched*). My point here simply pertains to the place this work occupies in Ambedkar's moral and political convictions. In fact, *Annihilation of Caste* can be regarded as the Archimedean point at which Ambedkar's politics acquires its exemplary and precarious balance, the moment of revolutionary action when force is rendered most unconditional, immeasurable, and egalitarian. Religion, he argues, has to be destroyed so that a faith without intermediaries and mediation by the law, freed from ecclesiastical and juridical injunctions, might be reclaimed by the multitude for itself. Indeed, to not destroy a religion bound by rules, to not resist the historic alliance between theology and the majoritarian will to domination (to which any unvigilant love of democracy might easily lapse), to not revolt against the mystical permanence of the theologico-political bond, becomes in Ambedkar's schema the most irreligious instance of the multitude's complicity with its own subjugation and defeat. And it is in this willingness to see the complicity of the colonized in their oppression where others had seen their innocence that Ambedkar and Gandhi would remain most intimate and irreconcilable.

In November 1909, almost three decades before *Annihilation of Caste*, Gandhi, onboard a ship sailing from London to Cape Town, composed his own masterwork in a fit of spiritual possession. Published originally in December 1909 in *Indian Opinion*, a Gujarati newspaper he had established in 1903 in Johannesburg, the English translation of *Hind Swaraj, or Indian Home Rule* appeared on 20 March 1910. It generated among imperial officials an anxiety similar to that later generated among nationalists by *Annihilation of Caste*. The British Government in Bombay confiscated copies of the work almost immediately after they hit Indian shores.[19] *Hind Swaraj* is written in deceptively simple style, constructed as a dialogue between a "reader" and an "editor." The Reader in that dialogue ventriloquizes the standard extremist rhetoric of the day. He repeatedly dismisses, at various points in the dialogue, the liberal method of petitioning the British parliament, as if, he observes, Indians were ever going to be treated as equal citizens of the empire even if they were to remain its most loyal subjects. He argues instead for the overthrow of the British rule in India by "force of arms."[20] The Editor, in response, ventriloquizes Gandhi's arguments, equally averse to the forceless petitioning of the liberals, yet committed to and elaborating on the virtues of nonviolent passive resistance, or "truth-force" (*satyagraha*).

The distinctive gesture Gandhi makes in *Hind Swaraj*, one that places the work within the classical discourse of politics, is its institution of force as the principal category of moral and political action. The expression "force of arms" alone, for example, appears in the second part of *Hind Swaraj* eight times, an indication of the struggle that had, by the turn of the century, ensued between satyagrahic and extremist thought, on the one hand, and within satyagraha itself, on the other.[21] Like *Annihilation of Caste*, *Hind Swaraj* is written partly as a moral treatise on responsibility, partly as a political essay on sovereignty. Both works were equally untimely, addressed to an audience that was yet to be born, galvanizing in less than a hundred pages each the existing languages of moral and political action in the colonial world. Trying to bring into existence a new political community whose time and space had yet to be rendered determinate by a triumphant nationalism, each speaks in the language of a universal praxis that had to be imagined afresh. Breaking from the dichotomy between violence and nonviolence that had plagued the early twentieth-century debate between Indian liberals and extremists over the tactics proper to their battle for national sovereignty, both treatises, above all, transform the language of anticolonial emancipatory struggles.

Force would become the fulcrum of this transformative gesture, the site of a moral, interpretive, and performative (but not always nonviolent) *coup de force*. In its simplest theoretical sense, the figure and category of force condenses the most decisive departure from an ends-bound politics to a means-oriented one. About the need to formulate a new ethics of means and responsibility, Ambedkar is unequivocal: "I have emphasized this question of the ways and means of destroying caste," he argues, "because I think that knowing the proper ways and means is more important that knowing the ideal."[22] Three years later, Gandhi echoes the point: "If one takes care of the means, the end will take care of itself. Nonviolence is the means, the end for every nation is complete independence."[23]

Despite, or perhaps especially because of, their attempt to reposit the relations between means and ends (while rendering their political struggle against Britain secondary to that task), both *Hind Swaraj* and *Annihilation of Caste* were actively ignored or dismissed by the leading nationalists and reformers of their times. In fact, *Hind Swaraj* was read with greater interest in Europe among the continent's anarchists, socialists, pacifists, and animal rights activists than it was by Gandhi's early followers in India. Latter-day Congress nationalists, among them Gandhi's chosen heir Jawaharlal Nehru, found it a distraction from the more important task of creating a sovereign and modern republic.[24] Indeed, few would read *Hind Swaraj* as carefully as Ambedkar, who kept returning to it well until the 1940s. He detected in the text a mercantile and usurious impulse that would show itself in Gandhi's irrefutable bias toward big business, which in the 1940s began to look even more ironic in light of the unequivocal denunciation of machinery and railways that a younger Gandhi had launched in *Hind Swaraj*. For Ambedkar, *Hind Swaraj* bore the seeds of Gandhi's cognitive inability to understand the insidious operations of national ideology, his lasting failure to grasp the alliance between private property and exclusion of entire communities from civic spaces and rights, his unwillingness to examine the religious foundations of everyday violence. A pernicious extension of which was the ancient, caste-based division of labor on which modern industrial and finance capital in India had come to thrive, and which no degree of friendship and trust between the oppressor and oppressed might ameliorate. Gandhi's profound prejudice against labor and caste reform, Ambedkar insisted, emerged from this refusal to appreciate the nature of "interest" in both its social and financial dimension that had come to structure the civic norms and practices of nationalist politics. But interest also had a moral dimension, one that involved a slow, insidious, and willful exclusion of the poor and untouchable from the political realm of civil disobedience. "Interest, interest on interest, he adds on and on, and thereby draws millions of families perpetually into his net," Ambedkar writes in 1945 of the usurious Bania, the moneylender caste to which Gandhi belonged.[25]

There were resonances too, echoes of which would reverberate with varying intensity through the first half of the twentieth century. Both *Hind Swaraj* and *Annihilation of Caste* formulate a theory of action in which resistance is considered political and just only inasmuch as it is also grounded in the sovereignty of the people. Both are discourses, in the final instance, on (and against) the theologico-political foundations of nationalist and republican sovereignty in its classical sense. By the time the second edition of *Annihilation of Caste* was published, it began to bear a striking resemblance, even in its architecture, to *Hind Swaraj*. Composed as a revolutionary monologue on justice and force (what is "annihilation," we might ask again, if not a radicalization of the concept of force?), *Annihilation of Caste* soon turned into a dialogue between Ambedkar and Gandhi. Only now, in an ironic reversal, Ambedkar seems like the editor and Gandhi, the fanatical reader. By 1944, then in its third edition, *Annihilation of Caste* began to appear with an appendix containing Gandhi's criticisms of the treatise culled from his newspaper *Harijan* and another appendix carrying Ambedkar's counterresponses to Gandhi. Resolutely averse to reducing the price of his massively circulating newspapers, *Young India* and *Harijan*, in the midst of the mass movements of the 1920s and 1930s (on the ground that readers must also bear the responsibility for what they get to read[26]), Gandhi, in a dramatic opening moment in his dialogue with Ambedkar, betrays the worst, most unequal, perhaps most banal among satyagraha's moralizing impulses. "He has priced it at 8 annas," he writes of Ambedkar's pricing of *Annihilation of Caste*. "I would suggest a reduction to 2 annas or at least 4 annas."[27]

Is Gandhi putting a price on Ambedkar's critique? Is he insinuating that this critique is irresponsible, unnecessary, perhaps worthless, even if it is unavoidable? Or is he, in some peculiar way often known only to him, trying to ensure that his antagonist's treatise reaches more people? If that is the case, why might the upper caste Hindu not be expected to pay for a copy of *Annihilation of Caste*, why would the reader not be responsible for its ideas and material in the same manner that such a reader might be for Gandhi's newspapers? Is Gandhi reducing Ambedkar's call for justice to that which it was not, that is, a certain calculation, a utilitarian quibble? Why this strange lapse into calculability at the very moment when *Annihilation of Caste* has lodged a demand for a justice, a force, a truth beyond measure?[28] Seeking a higher moral sense and ground of judgment, Gandhi here begins increasingly to sound like the Reader, that archetypal conservative nationalist of *Hind Swaraj* that he had battled with such temerity earlier in the century. In fact, the argument between Ambedkar and Gandhi around *Annihilation of Caste* reveals a radical conservatism, a war against equality, which undercuts anti-colonialism's emancipatory promise. For Ambedkar's undelivered lecture had not simply challenged the foundations of anticolonial ethics. It had imparted the relationship between ethics and politics itself an unprecedented insurrectionary tenor—an insurrection detached from abstractions of national sovereignty and grounded, for the first time, in the complexities of colonial India's social relations. There was a vision of democracy that had existed before *Annihilation of Caste*, and there was one that came after it. *Radical Equality* is an archeology of that interminable tension between two visions of democracy, two ways of grasping at sovereignty, in the colonial world.

The Strange Distinction of Anticolonial Morals

The relationship between Ambedkar and Gandhi has been archived in the annals of anticolonial nationalism as a story of antagonism generated by their irreconcilable views on empire, untouchability, and popular franchise. In one strand of this powerful historical consensus, Gandhi is projected as an unwavering thinker of nonviolent ethics in a world saturated by violence. Oblivious to such pervasive structures as those of the state and law, as indifferent to the violence of his own moral practices as he apparently was to the political contingencies and temptations around him, Gandhi is celebrated for having stoically inhabited an austere moral and sacrificial world that belonged only to him.[29] By the time he returned to India in 1915, he was already widely known within the British empire for his two decades of struggle against the white supremacist regime in South Africa, a country he had arrived in 1893 as an employee of a Muslim trading company (traveling the oceanic route charted by the Gujarati merchant caste he was born into). His notorious ineptness with legal language and his failure as a lawyer had by then been converted into a prose of remorseless moral clarity, even unapologetic pietism, which could as frequently turn into a display of his quintessentially colonial love for petitioning (an activity to which he devotes a brilliant chapter in *Hind Swaraj*).

Both an imperial nuisance and celebrity, an astute mobilizer of men who could often be monumentally indifferent to their emotions, Gandhi soon emerged as the unchallenged successor to both liberal and militant strands of anticolonial politics in India. His acute sense of timing, his knack for words, sounds, and neologisms, and his rigorous attentiveness to scripture and assorted theological texts (which may have reminded his followers of the great nineteenth-century political hermeneutists he had replaced), helped Gandhi produce in the 1920s and the 1930s a series of religious commentaries and public writings. It is a body of work as attuned to the realities of politics of its time as it is courageously discontinuous with it. By 1919, the year he launched his first major noncooperation movement in opposition to the mistreatment of Turkey by the Allies in Europe and a British Army massacre of 1,500 civil protesters in the Punjab, Gandhi had laid the groundwork for a moral philosophy of struggle unprecedented in its sincerity (if still too experimental to be coherent)—a philosophy that was at once unapologetically civilizational in rhetoric and spirit, committed to the sanctity of religious institutions and spiritual capitals such as the Caliphate and subsequently Jerusalem, immersed in the tactical nuances of imperial geopolitics and colonial franchise, and yet, was acutely sensitive to the benefits of being perceived as heterodox, heretical, and anarchist. These very attributes would institute a radical limit in Gandhi's moral and political practice. His courageous embrace of the spiritual vulnerability that accrues from being seen, for instance, could lead Gandhi to believe that the experience of being touched is merely corporeal and thus secondary to one's humanity. His capacity to listen to the urges of his convictions and intuitions, which propelled him in a flash of genius to launch his second mass movement in 1930 by simply plucking an illicit pinch of salt off India's western coast, might, on another day, lead Gandhi into the most coercive and unilateral fasts unto death against friends and opponents. His ability to renounce practices that might even remotely resemble in their secretiveness the tendencies of the modern state could, at its worst, edge out from his vision the many ways in which transparency itself often conceals the most insidious forms of interest and cruelty.

If Gandhi had managed, at any rate, to dream of sovereignty for a civilization without a state, his most formidable interlocutor could apparently dream only in the language of the state, never of the ethics of sovereignty proper. Ambedkar, born in 1891 into the family of an "untouchable" Mahar military schoolteacher in Bombay Presidency, is identified as the iconic leader of more than 50 million untouchables who had lived on the margins of social, juridical, and political life in the Indian subcontinent for more than two millennia. As the early studies by Eleanor Zelliot, Gail Omvedt, and others emphasize, Ambedkar was not simply a rights theorist, even though his sympathizers and critics alike often prefer to view him as such.[30] He might even be, by some accounts, the greatest thinker of the Indian subcontinent (and chronicler of its complex relationship to the past) to be so little known to scholars of constitutional and republican thought outside India.[31] After studying with Edward Seligman, the pioneering theorist of public finance and taxation, and John Dewey, the doyen of American pragmatism, both then at Columbia University in New York (where on scholarship he earned an MA and a PhD in economics in 1916–1917), the prodigious Ambedkar established himself over the next decade as a leading logician, lawyer, constitutionalist, anticaste radical, and scholar of religion, one gifted with an unsparing intellect and unparalleled powers of theorization and synthesis.

Stigmatized for being an outcaste even at the peak of his critical powers and political visibility, his return to public life in India, in contrast to Gandhi's, was famously difficult. "The Untouchables," he writes in a fragment titled "Frustration," "are a spent and sacrificed people."[32] In his unfinished autobiography, *Waiting for a Visa*, Ambedkar observes that this forced expenditure and exhaustion, which clung to one's skin like death, was wiped off his consciousness by "five years of staying in Europe and America."[33] But it returned to haunt him the moment he set foot on his homeland. Ambedkar never explains which visa he was waiting for, but he knew—given his immense interest in the Old Testament themes of exodus and exile (*deshantar*), his weakness for the classical Buddhist ethics of statelessness and wandering (*parivraja*), his formidable understanding of the exclusionary and even racial foundations of modern citizenship—that people had been sacrificed or were dying at that very moment for the lack of entry and exit papers. "Gandhiji," he had grimly declared to his peer a few years earlier in August 1931, "I have no homeland."[34] This frustration, or shall we say, cognitive homelessness (which could never possibly find its fullest political expression), would produce a radical formula for justice, one drawing on idioms of both vulnerability and force. In fact, Ambedkar would wager the very future of the nation form on this militant formula. In his inflammatory and underexamined republican classic, *Thoughts on Pakistan* (1941), in a chapter titled "National Frustration," he would ask, "Is there any new force that remains to be harnessed?"[35]

The search for a new grammar and logic of force was to strongly mediate Ambedkar's approach to colonial and national questions. It would wedge him into the interwar theoretical and theological debates in an exemplary fashion, pulling him closer to historians and philologists he admired, such as Ernest Renan (with Renan's principle of spiritual nationalism giving *Thoughts on Pakistan* its dramatic and utopian candor), and, at the same time, drawing him into an engagement with revolutionary strands of Rousseauist heritage.[36] In *Thoughts on Pakistan*, for instance, the idea of possessive interest that underpins modern theories of individualism is subsumed decisively within the logic of general will, or what Ambedkar calls, in a Rousseauist vein, a people's "right of insurrection."[37] By 1930, Ambedkar had established himself as an authoritative voice on matters of restitution, franchise, and devolution of colonial power. Much of this reputation was hard earned, consolidated through a series of lectures, among them his *Lectures on the English Constitution*, and books published between the 1920s and the late 1940s. Perhaps because of this ability to understand the logic of constitutional power in all its promise and risk, Ambedkar came to develop an almost antagonistic relationship with mainstream versions of anticolonial nationalism and their absolutist commitment to political sovereignty. One year, he could write a treatise on the problem of constituent power in its irreconcilable tension with Indian visions of the state, such as *States and Minorities* (1947), and in the next, he could recede into studies of antiquity and myth, producing a work such as *The Untouchables* (1948). It is perhaps fitting that Ambedkar—generally seen as a thinker who just could not envision the conditions of egalitarian citizenship outside the juridical and institutional languages of the state—was appointed the first law minister of independent India in 1947. He was elected soon thereafter by India's Constituent Assembly to preside over the drafting committee of the world's longest written national constitution.

This foundational relationship with the republican constitution of free India has come to overdetermine Ambedkar's entire intellectual history, effectively mainstreaming the recalcitrant dimensions of his thought and curtailing the insurrectionary possibilities—and duties—of citizenship that his thinking otherwise sought to open up.[38] His trajectory, one that presents the most dramatic non-European instance of a turn in revolutionary political thought and its theory of general will, has thus come to framed as a locus of meditations on caste and constitution.[39] The intricacies of this constitutionalist impulse, its unsettling entanglement with questions of sovereignty, insurrection, and virtue, entanglements that together form (even at their best) the most intractable issue in the history of modern political thought, have come to be reduced to a story that has been much easier to tell, that of Ambedkar's draftsmanship.[40] It is as if in his figure the tensions of constituent power—a people's sovereign right and faculty to act and to institute itself as a political community—can be seamlessly appropriated into the history of India's Constituent Assembly. The contradictions of the anticolonial movement for sovereignty might then be resolved by consecrating the national social state and sanctifying its constitutional success, of which Ambedkar could be positioned

as a liberal democratic champion. A thinker par excellence of the relationship between philosophy and government, Ambedkar thus stands outside the
classical debates on the relationship between action, obedience, and truth,
his conceptual scruples and struggles circumscribed within the framework of
what Hannah Arendt, distinguishing it sharply from the realm of the political, calls "the social question" (on which more later).[41]

The impact of this circumscription of Ambedkar as a theorist of social amelioration—and his evacuation from the realm of insurrectionary
politics—has been subtle and sustained; its effect on the history of radical democracy, impoverishing. Thus, the history of the late nineteenth-century emergence among the colonized of "a new science of politics" (in Eric
Voegelin's classic terms) now lies centered around figures such as Bankim
Chandra Chattopadhyay of Bengal and Bal Gangadhar Tilak of Bombay.[42] It
was within this strand of nationalist thought that the spiritualization of politics, which is to say, the consolidation of religious identity and emotion into
a moral psychology of resistance, had found its early impetus. By the 1890s,
the question of home rule, or *swaraj*, had been rendered into the language at
once of existential risk and spiritual survival. This was the period when con-
certed efforts to secure freedom from the empire (or some degree of autonomy within it), which had since the 1860s centered around activities of liberal
political associations, landholders' lobbies, reform groups, and community
petitioners, began to align with rhetorics of civilizational transcendence and
spiritual restitution. *Dharma*, which in its classical sense refers to an intricate
and diverse set of social and ethical obligations mandated by moral law, now
became, in its more popular English rendering as "religion," the locus classi-
cus in emerging theories of action. From the end of the nineteenth century
onward, calls for political sovereignty, backed by newer tactics of mass mobilization, would become increasingly difficult to separate from the rhetoric of
religious renewal and spiritual force of the majority.

In his treatise *Hindutva: Who Is a Hindu?* (1923), the extremist nationalist Vinayak Damodar Savarkar (1883–1966), whose shadow looms large over
Gandhi's *Hind Swaraj*, would eventually give this majoritarian and terrifying vision of politics its most eloquent name. The term *hindutva*, which had
earlier appeared in Bengali in Bankim Chandra Chattopadhyay's nationalist novel *Anandamath* (1882), does not merely refer to the religious substance
of sovereignty, personal or political. Instead, it separates, through a civilizational and war-bound division, a Hindu's very being from those of other
faiths. "Forty centuries, if not more, had been at work to mold [*hindutva*] as
it is," claims Savarkar in an epochal tone. "For indeed, is it not the resultant
of countless actions—now conflicting, now comingling, now cooperating—

of our whole race? Hindutva is not a word but a history. Not only the spiritual or religious history of our people as at times it is mistaken to be by being confounded with the other cognate term Hinduism, but a history in full." More than Hinduism, in other words, *hindutva* represents a fully natural, ontological history of a people. "Hinduism," writes Savarkar, "is only a derivative, a fraction, a part of Hindutva."[43] Gandhi's own ethics of spiritual fortitude and historical fullness was unequivocally suspicious of this rhetoric and politics of difference that Hindu nationalists of his time gave themselves over to. And yet the formula and force of his own nonviolence, his own conviction that social violence and cruelty might be redressed only from within the ontological closure and confines of being, never succeeded in fully distancing itself from *hindutva*'s militantly expansive nationalism.[44]

India's political modernity, then, was not simply a radical experiment in the politics of faith, as both Gandhi and Ambedkar would come to insist just a few decades later. Rather, it was theologico-political at its source. The enchantment with the idea of the state among the earliest and most sophisticated proponents of Indian modernity would never be easily distinguishable from their prescriptions on religious conduct and spiritual affirmation. Equality, the founding concept of the social question within traditions of modern thought and ethics, would come to be sharply demarcated from this new religious and political theory of sovereignty that opened up and gathered unprecedented popular support during the struggle against imperial rule. In fact, the lack of nationalist commitment to equality became starkly evident during the religious antagonisms and riots endemic to the period of transition to anticolonial mass politics. *Hind Swaraj*, which Gandhi constructed as a dialogue with extremist nationalists of the time, addresses the alarming resurgence of fratricidal conflict between Hindus and Muslims with great tact. Against the grain of the times, the work articulates the need to cultivate respect for other people's faiths—and the necessary steadfastness of one's own—as the only force proper to India's struggle for *swaraj*. But Gandhi's absolute silence on caste inequality and the peculiar absence of the "untouchable" in the rich economy of metaphors that gives much of *Hind Swaraj* its rhetorical power, is revealing. The silence offers an early glimpse of the distinctions that would not only underwrite Gandhi's moral ontology, his "experiments with truth," but also tactically sustain, in the most concrete situations, the hard realism of his political decisions and measures.[45]

It was this ambiguity in Indian imaginaries of the nation form—the juridical and religious exclusions inseparable from the triumphant proclamations of anticolonial nationalism—that Ambedkar had in mind, when, in the second edition of *Thoughts on Pakistan* (1941), issued as *Pakistan, or the Partition of India* (1945), he coined, in a moment of seeming casualness, that distinctive expression, the "Indian Political."[46] Ambedkar was not the first critic of these exclusions, even if he was the most exacting. Although the beginnings of this other tradition of critique can be traced back to the late nineteenth century and dated most decisively to the publication of the militant anticaste reformer Jotirao Phule's *Gulamgiri* (*Slavery*, 1873), a work inspired by the American Civil War, it has never seemed (to historians of the Indian political) to belong to the anticolonial order of things. For the likes of Phule concerned themselves with the institution of society, with the problem of coexistence among Indian society's diverse, unequal, and mutually untouchable constituents. Their conception of freedom foregrounded those everyday prohibitions—indignity, segregation, untouchability—that seemed too mundane, too constrained by an obsession with the ethics of social life, especially on the scale of a nationalism concerned with grander projects of spiritual well-being. Their social theory apparently reduced the idea of freedom—and justice itself—to questions of spatial mobility, occupational dignity, physical noninterference, and social security.[47]

This other vision of freedom, in other words, was not concerned with the ethics of civilizational mastery and national spirit. Nor did its universalism associate itself expressly with the humanist desire for liberation from imperial domination.[48] In fact, this struggle seems to have never belonged to the governing rules and shared expectations of the political at all. Instead, its "small" insurrections have been consigned to the realm of the social, a domain concerned with the spatial and material dimensions of everyday stigma, suffering, poverty, and labor relations. Its demands for restitution were, after all, articulated in terms of constitutional safeguards and juridical regulations against caste cruelty and religious oppression alone. With an incurably anthropological and statist understanding of ideals such as citizenship, advocates of this struggle aligned themselves with the abstract reason of the "rights of man," looking toward the egalitarian zeal of democracy in America while disavowing the spiritual rigor and love of tradition that would need to be embraced for a political restoration of the Indian self. It is most probably in this irresponsibility toward the transcendence of tradition, this act of instituting in tradition's place an immanent sense and sensibility of equality, that Ananya Vajpeyi has discerned the limits of Ambedkar's "moral imagination."[49]

A fine distinction between the political and social, the spiritual and material—and in Gandhi's Platonic world, the intelligible and sensible—sustains the wide variety of judgments and consensuses on this insurrectionary (but always patient and attentive) vision of politics within which Ambedkar would place himself. This distinction, a peculiarly Indian iteration of Hannah Arendt's separation of the political from the social, has had a long life in anti-colonial historiography. "The whole record of past revolutions demonstrates," Arendt cautioned in *On Revolution* (1963), "that every attempt to solve the social question by political means leads into terror."[50] One can interpret this cautionary distinction in several ways. Suffice it to note here that it was for-mulated and put into work in the colonies by those seeking liberation from European domination much before Arendt gave it philosophical heft in the af-termath of twentieth-century totalitarianisms. In India, it appears clearly in a series of categorical hierarchies in which, beginning in the late nineteenth cen-tury, the anticolonial demand for liberation from the empire was formulated: freedom before equality, unity before justice, territorial safety before social se-curity, and as Ambedkar would often wryly remark—most powerfully in *An-nihilation of Caste* itself, as he took on the Brahmin liberal S. Radhakrishnan (subsequently the second president of free India)—claims to civilizational cer-titude before a commitment to civic virtue.[51] In a distinctive act of sequester-ing, the political is wrested away from those who think about its truth, value, and mentality, its relationship to ethics, in terms less hierarchical and exclu-sionary, more dispersed and decentralized (or, in Ambedkar's constitutional parlance, more "federal") than the vision of politics instituted by anticolonial nationalism could safely allow. Such sequestering not only ensures the exclu-sion (from the genealogy of the Indian political) of thinkers such as Phule, the man who first formulated the idea that the collective cultivation of virtue is a question of *satyashodh* (researches and experiments in one's own truth), half a century before Gandhi would monumentalize this idea in his autobi-ography *My Experiments with Truth* (while maintaining a lifelong silence on Phule).[52] It has also meant that Ambedkar is himself reduced to an enigmatic, if not troubling, figure. As if by the very nature of this prehistory of exclu-sion, Ambedkar was destined, as he put it himself, to remain a "part apart," his Atlantic inspiration often considered embarrassing for those who position twentieth-century anticolonialism as a doctrine of spiritual freedom mounted against Eurocentric paradigms of political thought and practice.

The contrast between Ambedkar and his younger contemporary from Martinique, Frantz Fanon (1925–1961) is instructive.[53] By the last quarter of the twentieth century, Fanon, despite his Hegelian, Nietzschean, and Freud-ian affinities and his great faith in European humanism, had not only been in-stalled as a theorist par excellence of colonial servitude and emancipation. He had also emerged, within the framework of postcolonial critique of Europe, as a thinker whose faith in "colonial wars" as a spiritually cleansing route to lib-eration could be considered intimate with Gandhi's famed commitment to nonviolence itself. The philosophical underpinnings of Fanon's and Gandhi's

struggles, regardless of the profound difference in their methodological commitments, were shared, inasmuch as their horizons were cognitive, geared not
merely toward the physical emancipation of the colonized but toward freedom
from the mentality of servitude. For, it could be argued, they were both engaged in "the slave's recovery."[54] Even a cursory glance at the moral psychology of *Annihilation of Caste* would have complicated this attempt to canonize
the great texts of twentieth-century anticolonialism. But perhaps its sensitive approach to alienation (which, insisted Ambedkar, plagued the oppressor as much as the oppressed and which always preceded more material forms
of cruelty), its reclamation of liberty as the freedom to "reason," its braiding of
civic virtue with the firmness of faith, might have enriched the global political tradition itself, one to which *Annihilation of Caste* righteously belonged.

Not only, however, has *Annihilation of Caste* (for even the most sophisticated theorists of anticolonial praxis) seemed too distant from what they
think are the core values of global anticolonial struggles. The reception of
Ambedkar's thought itself—often closely engaged with strands of Roman,
Florentine, and French republicanism—has been hemmed in by a series of
overdeterminations, a result perhaps of the generalized aversion toward Enlightenment categories within the field of postcolonial inquiry, his trajectory
perceived neither universal enough nor national-spiritual in the anticolonial
sense of the term. Either he is a thinker emblematic of what Uday S. Mehta
calls the "absolutism of politics," a figure in whom the appropriation of the
social question by political excess found its germinal form (a tendency that
Arendt associates with the Jacobin heritage of European revolutions), or he
is a theorist of justice whose preoccupation with legal safeguards and fairness, tethered to a strong national social state, are symptoms of what Sudipta
Kaviraj identifies as the "enchantment of the state" in India.[55] It all comes
back to Ambedkar himself, a constitutionalist whose faith in the law threatened to obliterate and at the same time render him irrelevant to the spiritual
convictions that had fashioned anticolonial visions of politics.

Excessively instrumental in his political decisions on the one hand, then,
and morally indifferent to the spiritual task of the political on the other: the
logic of this splitting of Ambedkar is doubly paradoxical, considering that
Ambedkar had himself noted the risk of obfuscating the distinction between
political and social reform (with one then appropriating the other) three decades before the brutal reality of European totalitarianism lent Arendt her
fundamental insight.[56] In the most careful hands, such as those of political scientist Gopal Guru, whose call for an "archeology of untouchability" mounts
a formidable challenge against genealogical modes of writing the history of
human experience, Ambedkar's critique of Brahminic reason is shown to con-

tain the seeds of an egalitarian social science in India.[57] Yet the conceptual nuances of his moral psychology, the richness of rhetorical turns in his writings and speeches, all of which carry a charge and exactitude proper to the province of political philosophy, still remain only obliquely acknowledged.

I use the term "political philosophy" not to strengthen the claims of universality, let alone intensify the methodological dogmatism, of the anthropological mode of thinking about politics whose consolidation in its humanist form is traced back to the rise of early modern commercial society in Europe (the so-called classical period or first modernity of political thought). It is against the hegemony of this framework and (of its inability to comprehend the distinctively Indian experience of untouchability), after all, that Gopal Guru has mounted his careful critique. Nor do I bring up "political philosophy" to buttress the stability of European categories and persistent "habits of thought" that they have tended to engender in those touched by European empires, as Dipesh Chakrabarty has put it.[58] "Political philosophy," it is even more important to note, is not a term that Ambedkar himself often uses to describe his theoretical endeavors. For him, as for someone like Arendt, "politics" and "philosophy" belong to two separate orders. They signify two modes of understanding and being in the world that even in the best of times share a strained relationship. Arendt, after all, was reluctant to be called a philosopher because she saw it as too anthropological a designation to capture the essence of being political. Being political, in her view, demanded responding to the shifting and uneven realities of individuals rather than being imprisoned by the categorical rights of man. Politics—and political understanding—is the condition of being quick in one's thinking in relation to the plurality of life-worlds. A *political* thought arises, then, only from one's openness to an event in its multiplicity.[59]

When I use the expression "political philosophy" in reference Ambedkar's thinking, then, I do so with the sole purpose of recalling the logic and burden of transformative force that Ambedkar had himself made that term carry in *Thoughts on Pakistan* or in essays such as "Ranade, Gandhi, and Jinnah" (1943). I have in mind his conviction that any understanding of politics must be necessarily insurrectionary in its articulation. Politics can be philosophical—and philosophy political—only inasmuch as it requires a moral groundwork, a theory of action, which would both be realistic and prompt in its response to lived experience and its uncertainties. This responsiveness—and ethics of responsibility—would mold Ambedkar's thinking when he engaged such classical categories as "the state" and "the multitude" (or such ontological categories as "truth"), or even "social reform," refusing to constrain them within the boundaries of nations, traditions, and theologies.

Even in "Ranade, Gandhi, and Jinnah" (composed as a tribute to Mahadev Govind Ranade, the nineteenth-century social reformer from western India), where Ambedkar brings up the term "political philosophy" on almost half a dozen occasions, he does so to probe not simply the history of social reform in India, clearly, but what he suggests are its political philosophical foundations—of which Ranade becomes in this essay an exemplary yet fraught figure, a figure whose social revolutionary courage is constantly imperiled by his political commitments, a figure in whose biography, above all, one gets the chance to probe not just the moral psychology but moral ontology of reform in India (and its decisive failure). The problem, as Ambedkar suggests, is not that Ranade, like Gandhi and Jinnah, does not have a political philosophy. The problem is that he only has a political philosophy, neither a social nor a moral one.

My point is not simply, then, that Ambedkar was as important a thinker of the political as he was of social relations or that Gandhi's vocabulary was as crucial for Ambedkar's grasp of truth as his grammar of justice was decisive for Gandhi's. Any such claim of commensurability or reciprocity is susceptible to lapsing back to the same distinctions whose history and economy I have delineated in the preceding pages. Instead, my argument is that Ambedkar experienced the political—and its relationship with the ethical—at its limit; that he inhabited, probed, vacillated, thought, and made demands on it at the extremities of its conceptual and methodological norms; that, above all, a global genealogy of democratic ethics becomes possible only by attending to those moments when his conceptual and rhetorical choices transform the limits of the political in its specificity and universality. And such choices include those instances and elements of risk in which Ambedkar condenses the totality of politics into the logic, demands, and materiality of single events and figures.

Coup de Force

At the heart of this study, then, is the tenuous distinction between the social and political, between aspiration and action, which sustains the internal exclusions of anticolonial moral and political culture. One might arrange these distinctions, in a more classical vein, under the founding tension of modern political thought, that between equality and freedom—that is, the tension between measure and counting (which permits each person to be abstracted into a number and rendered equal to another) and immeasurability and incalculability (which the empirical and incommensurable state of a person's freedom implies). Equality requires mechanisms, legislation, and limits; freedom refuses such foundations. Equality is constituted; it makes "a people" possible and brings them together. Conversely, people make equality possible by instituting an abstract and anonymous commensurability among themselves. Freedom, in contrast, is revolutionary and constituent; it promises to condense the incommensurable force of the multitude into collective acts against domination, acts that are meant to annihilate, separate, and reconstitute moral relations.

Whereas anticolonial thought from the late nineteenth century onward is seen as having invented a science of politics for the colonized aspiring to a free world, and Gandhi in the early years of the twentieth century is seen as recovering its authentic spirit through, in his own words, "love-force, soul-force, or, more popularly but less accurately, passive resistance [*satyagraha*],"[60] Ambedkar has come to be seen as interested in the science of constituting the state as the guardian of civic rights and egalitarian spaces alone. This tension between freedom and equality, underwritten within modern political thought by an already fragile separation of *constituent power* (which posits the lawmaking force of the multitude at the moment of its greatest creativity, the moment that a people founds a sovereign, constitutional polity) from *revolutionary force* (which posits the multitude's spiritual freedom to annihilate all extant structures of rule, representation, and office), with Ambedkar placed firmly in the social legislative domain of constitutional authority as opposed to the transformative realm of revolutionary action, remains profoundly delimiting. For not only does this framework obscure the full measure of Ambedkar's ability to take politics back to its foundation in the egalitarian sovereignty of the multitude; an ability that, by its repudiation of the idea that freedom and equality both suffer whenever they are sought together, had interfered with the most fundamental of tensions in modern political thought.[61] It also suppresses the effects of Ambedkar's resistance against the separation of freedom from equality, which lent him (as did his rise in the 1940s as the republic's foremost constitutional authority) a unique perspective for grappling with this classical problem, often in the most unexpected ways. His strategies derived their form and content from the specific demands of India's anticolonial struggle but also, as *Annihilation of Caste* and *Thoughts on Pakistan* would show in quick succession, militantly exceeded them. Ambedkar's ability to exploit the unresolved relationship between revolution and constitution, popular sovereignty and shared vulnerability, collective action and the irreplaceability of individual life, lent his thought its immense rigor. Indeed, it shaped his distinctive relationship to the theologico-political underpinnings of sovereign power itself.

To trace the lines and angles of this political thought is to write another history of equality, a history that in the modern non-West often runs against the grain of global liberal constitutionalism. It is, of course, true that even in the most classical versions of political thought, the conceptual and historical line between a people's constituent power and the constituted domain of authority (the state) to which that power gives rise has rarely been straightforward. But in Ambedkar, the thinker of force par excellence, this line would take unprecedented turns in relation and response to the vicissitudes of India's anticolonial struggle. In fact, by refusing the strict demarcation between constituent power and constituted norm, between revolutionary force and civic fairness, his language and method would depart from both the Jacobin and Communist traditions whose genealogy Antonio Negri has traced in his work *Insurgencies*.[62]

Studies of political thought, however, when they have engaged with Ambedkar at all, have found it more convenient to leave out the moments of dissidence that punctuate his thought (and the place of revolution within them). They certainly ignore his resistances against the certitudes of the law—indeed, his withdrawal from the juridical, moral, and political certainties of the modern self itself.[63] Ambedkar's constitutionalism has in fact eclipsed any acknowledgment of the revolutionary force of his ideas, which have instead been grafted onto a narrative of his derivative liberalism in much the same way that Gandhi's commitment to nonviolence has overshadowed his complex relationship to justice, a category he mobilized for arguments and positions that were often visibly unjust. This remains the case despite a sustained engagement with Gandhi's politics by scholars across several generations, from Romain Rolland and Richard Gregg in the 1920s and 1930s, to Joan Bondurant and Raghavan Iyer in the decades right after India's independence in 1947, down to important recent studies by Akeel Bilgrami, Faisal Devji, Karuna Mantena, Uday S. Mehta, and Ajay Skaria.[64] Their influence on my own work as well as my differences and departures from them should become clearer as the argument in this book progresses.

Here, I only want to re-emphasize that *Radical Equality* is neither a study of an important figure and his corpus in its integrity nor is it a social and historical biography of an encounter between two thinkers at war. It is a history of an antinomy in anticolonial political thought, a history that seeks to consider Ambedkar and Gandhi together as exemplars of a shared philosophical conviction that was as radically new in its prescriptions as it was classical in its problematic. This conviction rarely lends itself to the popular hope of bridging the ethical divide between them (a bridge otherwise strongly desired by chroniclers of India's unitary foundations, who see the difference between Ambedkar and Gandhi as merely a local disagreement over caste reform). Nor does this conviction give itself to the safety and complacency of fixed battle lines (across which, since their own time, a veritable industry of polarizing polemic has thrived). Rather, this was a shared and strained conviction that was locked in a ceaseless struggle to formulate a new political and moral ontology.

I say "ontology" because both Ambedkar and Gandhi believed that freedom requires a new language of truth, a new order of conceptuality, a semantic, interpretive, and performative *coup de force* in thought and action that might wrest the truth of existence at its barest back from the obfuscations of juridical, civilizational, and political theologies. Identity and difference, even in the face of India's centrifugal diversity, had to be reclaimed first as psychological possibilities, their moral scope and value determined before they could be rendered into the abstract language of political rationality and social collectivity. This was not a battle against one empire, but a war on an entire structure of linguistic, conceptual, and religious exclusions on which servitude had acquired the status of an everyday moral relation among Indians themselves. Under such conditions, freedom could be apprehended only within the ontological order of truth, its force intensified (through a rigorous ethics of everyday life) and stripped of its mystical attributes, its articulation and practice taken to the extremes of cognitive and material clarity. The task of reclaiming the concept of freedom from absolutist visions of imperial and nationalist sovereignty was thus rendered inseparable from the freedom to challenge the concept (and to invent it anew). Ambedkar's ceaseless and visibly Deweyan emphasis on the need to "educate, agitate, and organize" stems from this commitment to renewing the language, access, history, skill, and boundaries of conceptual thinking within which categories such as freedom and equality had been hitherto confined.

Authentic freedom, after all, also means the liberty to turn freedom against its own injunctions and norms, to delve into its ontological secrets and historical excesses, its conceptual and rhetorical exclusions.[65] There would be no freedom if every person, nourishing his belief in his own individual way, did not have the space (cognitive and physical) to think about freedom freely and equally, experience its truth without interference, and give it a new name. With all its promise and risk, there is nothing greater at stake in Ambedkar's thought than this egalitarian and immeasurable thinking of freedom.[66] The search for a free and just existence, at the same time, did not follow the same course for Ambedkar and Gandhi. Nevertheless, both place the imperative of an interpretive and conceptually transformative *coup de force*—indeed, the notion of force (whether the "force of law" or "force of arms," "soul-force" or that of the hand)—at the core of moral relations. Force lends an immanent materiality, a concrete and often vehement realism, an empirical counterpoint to the "imaginary institution of India."[67] Force contains a people's right to reinstitute their conceptual, spatial, and cognitive order, in which the plurality and incommensurability of everyday experience might be militantly rethought and reclaimed, but in which the singularity of each person's existence and finitude might still be generalized through sacrifice toward a just universalism. From the late 1920s onward, Ambedkar would seek to condense this logic of equality within singularity into the classical Buddhist term *samata*.[68]

In the chapters that follow, I explore the multiple meanings and material contexts of these three categories—incommensurability, singularity, and sacrifice—as they are mobilized, translated, and renounced in Ambedkar's and Gandhi's thinking of freedom. In advance of the fuller discussion, let me briefly introduce the most ubiquitous of satyagrahic concepts that Gandhi wrested from extremist iterations of his time and made his own: sacrifice. Sacrifice began to appear with noticeable frequency in Gandhi's thinking from 1907 onward, often in deceptively lucid combinations of tropes and neologisms, each alluding to a complex and austere set of obligations mandated by moral law (*dharma*). Directly, it appeared in terms such as "self-sacrifice," "limitless sacrifice," "fearless sacrifice," and "spirit of sacrifice." Indirectly, it invoked a certain notion of force through such formulations as "ethics of destruction" and "mastery over passions." And as spiritual mandate drawn from the tradition of Hindu negative theology, it appeared in expressions such as "living by dying." In satyagraha's political moments, at its most public and prescriptive, Gandhi's formulations on sacrificial obligation and duty came to address a series of limit figures to which the satyagrahi had to respond, listen, and take care of (if need be to the point of his own dissolution and death), such as the pauper, the untouchable, and the unequal as such.

By the 1920s, *dharma* had come to mean for Gandhi a plethora of rigorous everyday rules, methods (*sadhana*), and responsibilities, each of which Gandhi believed contained the seeds of genuinely emancipatory possibilities. There emerged from these experiments, for instance, his mandates on *shudradharma*, which laid out the duty and responsibilities of the Shudra, the fourth and lowest order of Hindu society, whose physical suffering the satyagrahi would now reproduce and steadfastly endure within the precincts of the *ashram*; *kshatriyadharma*, which invoked the duty of the warrior, the second order of ancient society and constitution, whose skills with instruments and famed willingness to die for the good cause the satyagrahi had to strive to emulate and master; *dayadharma*, which established the satyagrahi's obligation to be compassionate toward the oppressor and oppressed, the dominant and unequal, equally, without distinction; and *maryada dharma*, the imperative of observing disciplinary limits, injunctions, and generosity, especially in the satyagrahi's encounter with those who were irreconcilably different and un-equal. *Maryada dharma* included the duty to make exceptions to the moral law, to sacrifice the classical rules of pollution and nonsacrifice (say, the law of nonkilling of the animal for food), such as in the satyagrahi's readiness to serve meat to Muslim guests in the otherwise vegetarian *ashram* or to touch the untouchable during specific hours of the day.

For a thinker so sensitive to the emancipatory possibilities of sacrifice, so committed to rescuing its meanings from the monopoly of the state (where modern political thought had placed it) and rehabilitating it in the rhythmic effort of ordinary occupations and people (spinning, weaving, prayer, and the like), it is suggestive that Gandhi rarely questioned the originary exclusions, divisions, and sacrifice that were foundational to the many forms of *dharma* that satyagraha would come to embrace and improvise on. Only a careful ar-cheology of this concept, a consideration of its relationship to such satyagra-hic concepts as fearlessness, limit, war, and spirit (terms Gandhi often couples with his conception of sacrifice) might reveal why, beneath satyagraha's ethics of austerity and nonviolence, an equally potent structure of force and exclu-sion would come to mediate its obligations toward the unequal and unfree.

It is important to bear in mind that for neither Ambedkar nor Gandhi is the concept of "force" simply another substitute for collective action, popu-lar sovereignty, or even unconditional individual autonomy. Even when they speak in the conventional idiom of war and mobilization, which is often, force remains for them distinct, so that it can never be collapsed into other forms of power, whether military, legislative, or executive (although it often func-tions that way in the classical traditions of political thought). Instead, force is the condensation of the subject's experience and intense will to act, even at the risk of death, in a moment of unrestrained creativity and immeasurable freedom. Force is the moral firmness (Gandhi's *agraha*) that constitutes the inalienable truthfulness of being; it is existence that is irreducibly free, equal, and fearless (Ambedkar's *samata*). As concept and act, force makes visible (and reclaims) the experience of freedom in its most indivisible form. "It is Swaraj when we learn to rule ourselves," writes Gandhi in a deceptively simple for-mulation of freedom.[69] The closeness of this articulation of self-rule to the classical notion of indivisibility that underwrites the theory and practice of sovereign power cannot be overstated. Once unleashed, Gandhi's ethics of rig-orous and sacrificial practice, the obsession with mastery over a skill or truth, even over sleep (that *sadhana* demanded), would be hard to delimit within the disciplinary obligations and duties of the self alone.

Rearranged within the bounds of the ideal and striving self, never-theless, there was (unlike in categories such as "power," "authority," and "violence"), something profoundly democratic about force.[70] Of all these classical categories, force alone could be posited as not only available to everyone, even and especially under conditions of gravest inequality and servitude, it could also be imparted a spiritual-linguistic power, one that breached the exclusions of conceptual language itself. Force encapsulates a mode of truthful thought and action in the realm of which the weakest and the strongest might exchange places. Given the ubiquity of this concept in their writings, any history of equality in the colonial world remains incomplete without a sustained account of Ambedkar's and Gandhi's struggle with this elusive and mystical concept.

This struggle would often take classical form, its interest in civic virtue and justice mediated strongly by a sustained passion for religiosity and sacrifice. But the struggle was also shaped by the demands and contingencies of the interwar period. The crisis of parliamentary democracy in Europe and the resurgence of religious extremism at home put immense pressure on Ambedkar's and Gandhi's theoretical resources and abilities. Neither would remain untouched by this remarkable and protracted moment, with the violent unraveling of republican democracy in the 1930s and 1940s in Europe—or what Ambedkar, citing the fate of the Weimar, would call its slowness—matched only by the capacity of republicanism to continue promising a world free of mastery in which a community of shared values might be secured. This language of community, which was never too far from their belief in the virtues of force and mastery, even sacrifice, would pitch Ambedkar and Gandhi endlessly against various moral and political strands in interwar India and Europe, ranging from revolutionary anarchists to Atlantic pragmatists, from Zionists to pacifists and fascists, from classical thinkers of popular sovereignty and general will to scriptural hermeneutists and nationalist theologians. It was against these interlocutors that, in the most extraordinary interwar decades, Ambedkar and Gandhi brought together a constellation of theories of justice—and a language of equality—that still sits uncomfortably on the structures and practices of modern republican democracy (or sometimes, as I hope to show, sits terrifyingly well, which is much the same problem). Beyond a study of identity and difference between two thinkers, this book is, then, an archeology of the decisive and precarious turn in anticolonial thought toward the question of equality, an archeology that attempts to determine not merely the context but the order of conceptuality—the origins, structures, and modulations of concepts—within (and in excess of) which the contours of modern political thought were redrawn in twentieth-century colonial world.

Theologico-Political Dilemmas

Before I outline the method and architecture of this study, it is necessary to place my work in relation to what has come to be called, since and following Ambedkar, "Dalit politics," inarguably one of the most important arenas of emancipatory struggles in modern India. The term *dalit*, which derives from the Sanskrit root *dal* and literally means "spilt" or "broken open," has in its more political rendering come to stand for the condition of being "ground down." It is now understood as referring to ancient India's "broken men" and the memory of their defeat and enslavement. Ambedkar would devote two rigorous studies on the history and myth of this subjugation, *Who Were the Shudras?* (1946) and *The Untouchables* (1948). By the 1970s, *dalit* had been sequestered from its negative connotation and instituted as an affirmative political self-description that India's formerly "untouchable" communities would mobilize in the expanding electoral and legislative arena. The expression "Dalit politics," however, has never been delimited by the calculus and interest of electoral competition. Over the last four decades, it has come to refer to a complex set of political, institutional, ethical, and aesthetic practices that constitute a radical "rejection of rejection," as Gopal Guru formulates their repudiation of caste taboos and exclusions.[71] The Dalit is one who morally, politically, and corporeally rejects the ancient and modern norms of invisibility, unapproachability, and untouchability. The word itself dates to the 1830s, when it was recorded in the western Indian state of Maharashtra, and was subsequently radicalized by the militant reformer Jotirao Phule in the third quarter of the nineteenth century.[72] Ambedkar was aware of this genealogy, one that was grounded not only in the history of reformist and anticaste sentiments in western India but also in a rich tradition of warrior mythography in the region.[73]

In crucial ways, Ambedkar's engagement with the concept of force, which brought his thought even closer to Gandhi's than either was willing to concede, emerged from this profound knowledge of the western Indian warrior and sacrificial traditions that underlie Phule's insurrectionary grammar. In her study *The Caste Question*, Anupama Rao has given significant theoretical heft to the term *dalit*, attributing its moral-linguistic energies to lower caste attempts to formulate the conditions of an emancipatory minority politics beyond the name's original allusions to defeat, humiliation, and negativity.[74] Rao's contribution, along with the more recent work of historians Ramnarayan Rawat and Dwaipayan Sen on the northern and eastern parts of the subcontinent respectively, is to illuminate the inextricable relationship forged, by the late nineteenth century, between caste identities, religious belief, and emerging languages of rights-based politics.[75] This process was complicated further (and violently so) by the expansion of colonial franchise in the interwar decades and then by the partition of India in 1947, amplifying at once the emancipatory and exclusionary energies of movements for restitution and representation that would leave an indelible imprint on the emerging postcolonial political field. Quite apart from electoral competition and contests over ritual spaces such as temples, wells, and town squares (and even the right to offer prayer and sacrifice in public areas), these movements would become integral to the very framework of the new democratic consciousness. Often in urban India, caste contests and violence manifest themselves not just in the physical defacement and desecration of Ambedkar's and Gandhi's statues by groups designated in secularist parlance as "fringe." They also entail preprogrammed and organized killing, evidence as much of volatile caste fault lines that the perpetrators inhabit as of the participants' shifting religious, political, and sectarian commitments. Sectarian violence in India, in other words, has never been confined within the stable limits of—and identification grounded in—religion alone. In fact, such violence, its causes, sites, and methods, have forced a continuous reassessment of the secularist understanding of citizenship and its value itself.

Even if Ambedkar, the first to probe in a sustained fashion the alliance between the political, juridical, and religious spheres in the Indic traditions, was to be seen as a theorist of rights and restitution, as he often is, I think it is impossible to ignore the religious foundation of his political thought and practice. This foundation was not built over a dialectical relationship with religion, as if his religiosity simply moved between moments of negation and affirmation, or worse, made a secularist peace with religion in the cause of civic order. Instead, I have in mind here a nondialectical, "nonnegative negation" of religion,[76] which is to say, an affirmation of faith that seemed to work precisely through (and intensify during) Ambedkar's calls for the relinquishment—indeed, the annihilation—of religious rules and injunctions.[77] In Ambedkar's thought and writing, neither the radical mobilization of belief nor his resistance against ecclesiastical authority, neither his defacement and sacrifice of the gods nor the endless fascination with divinity's transcendental and imperishable being, remain wholly separable. Nor, above all, can they be easily extricated from his attempt to craft a new political imagination, a timeless (if not immortal) republic on which authentic freedom—the freedom of equals—might be grounded.

The insights from contemporary studies of Dalit politics, perhaps most productively condensed in Gopal Guru and Sundar Sarukkai's *The Cracked Mirror*, are indispensable to the kind of archeological work I undertake in

Radical Equality. My interest, however, is in a specific moment in the pre-history of an antinomy in modern India's early experiments in democracy, one that precedes the emergence of Dalit politics and theory in the later de-cades of the twentieth-century, especially the rich and complex electoral, in-stitutional, and literary sensibilities that begin to thrive within it after India's independence in 1947. In fact, throughout his political career, Ambedkar himself used the term *dalit* sparingly. There are a few fragments of private correspondence in which, writing in English, he describes himself as a "bro-ken man"—for instance, in a tragic, almost Biblical, letter on suffering and death he wrote in memory of his children, whom he had buried.[78] Ambedkar, as Gopal Guru argues, was nevertheless bound to use a range of linguistic and terminological strategies, given the variety of institutional imperatives he faced. He would use different categories and expressions in different settings to allude to those who were most oppressed by the caste order, sometimes re-ferring to them in imperial constitutional terms, such as "depressed classes," at other times using Sanskrit-derived terms, such as *bahishkrit*, translatable as "boycotted," "outlawed," or "banned." He would periodically deploy terms such as "untouchables" and "unapproachables," and, most frequently, in his explicitly theologico-political writings on Vedic religion and its rituals of sac-rifice (whose violence, he showed, was inseparable from the Indic theory of sovereignty and state), he would mobilize the term *Shudra*.[79]

Critics who argue that "religion" is a Latin category imported into the colonies during the high noon of Orientalism might ask, in the same vein, whether the notion of the "theologico-political" also emanates from (and must therefore be analytically limited to) the history of the emergence of the modern secular state in Europe. Does placing Ambedkar within the prob-lem of the theologico-political—and approaching him, as I do, as its critic and thinker—further reinforce the idea that he was not indigenous enough, not in the least because he was prone to thinking in categories derived from the European Enlightenment? Trapped in the epistemological warp produced by the eighteenth-century Orientalist "invention of religion"[80] as a globally relevant category (a warp from which he could never free his thought), was Ambedkar prone to drawing unreflexively on analytical categories whose provenance actually lay in those traditions of European intellectual history that were not only alien but indeed antithetical to the nationalist project of recovering the Indian self? Was he, in other words, drawn precisely to those traditions within which "religion," as system, concept, and discipline, had been given birth and disseminated in the service of European colonial power, even as he turned a blind eye to the need for pulling non-Western thought out from the shadows of European intellectual and theological—indeed,

Christian humanist—frameworks?[81] Why otherwise, some might ask, would an Indian thinker, unless he were thoroughly derivative, use such terms as "scheme of divine governance"[82] when all there was to Hindu *dharma* was a constellation of everyday moral obligations and self-sacrificial practices rather than a political theology?

Matters—and the reception of Ambedkar's thought—have been further complicated by the Christian roots of political theology itself. Claude Lefort shows, for instance, that whenever democracy as a system of people's rule is placed within, against, or in alignment with the theologico-political discourse, it is the history of Christianity's troubled movement toward secularization that is scrutinized.[83] John Dunn makes a case, equally convincingly, for focusing on the theocentrism of liberal thought, showing how Locke's conception of civil society hinges on his firm belief in human dependence on the "direction of God."[84] Pierre Manent's genealogy of French liberalism begins, in its very first chapter, with an account of "Europe and the Theologico-Political Problem."[85]

Of course, what Lefort has so sensitively called the "permanence of the theologico-political" in the history of Europe's—which is, in the final instance, Christianity's—secularization (or, indeed, its failure), cannot be merely a Christian story. On the contrary, any history of Christianity's failure to fully secularize (and secularism's failure to rid itself of its Christian past), already makes the nexus of faith, force, and sovereignty a global phenomenon, given the foundational relationship among European empires, colonial catechism, and Christian humanism.[86] Nevertheless, the alliance between theological mandates and earthly sovereignty—in which the modern head of state, even if legally elected by popular vote, remains but a worldly analogue of an unconditional divine authority whose decisions (and suspensions of the law) stand outside the purview of the laws of the people—has been viewed largely as a problem and paradox internal to the monotheistic traditions alone.[87] Even Hegel, while warning in *The Philosophy of Mind* (1817) that looking on such "inseparables" as religion and state as "separable" would be a "monstrous blunder," had in mind a distinctively European tendency that emerged after the French Revolution, namely, the zeal to visualize a secular, nonreligious state (which did not actually exist anywhere, according to Hegel).[88]

No thinker understood the Abrahamic specificity of the alliance between divine will and profane violence, between sacrifice and exclusion, as well as Ambedkar, which is precisely why, despite his own taste for a certain kind of "religion of the book" and notwithstanding the nationalist argument that has since the nineteenth century regarded Hinduism as a set of ethical obligations (*dharma*) radically different from "religion" of the Abrahamic and evangelical sort, he had still gone ahead and tactically placed Hinduism as the fourth among the three monotheisms of the world.

The fundamental characteristic of *positive* Religions is that they have not grown up like primitive religions, under the action of unconscious forces operating silently from age to age, but trace their origin to the teaching of great religious innovators, who spoke as the organs of a divine revelation. Being the result of conscious formulations the philosophy of a religion which is positive is easy to find and easy to state. Hinduism like Judaism, Christianity and Islam is in the main a positive religion. One does not have to search for its scheme of divine governance. It is not like an unwritten constitution. On the Hindu scheme of divine governance is enshrined in a written constitution and any one who cares to know it will find it laid bare in that Sacred Book called the *Manu Smriti*, a divine code which lays down the rules which govern the religious, ritualistic and social life of the Hindus in minute detail and which must be regarded as the Bible of the Hindus and containing the philosophy of Hinduism.[89]

Was this attribution of monotheism to *dharma*'s capacious logic—matched only by the *Manusmriti*'s intricate laws that enforced it—meant to make way for Ambedkar's critique of the organized juridical and ecclesiastical authority that otherwise remains, unlike the rich legacy of martyrdom of the Roman Catholic Church, pernicious and invisible in Hinduism? Was the structure of *dharma* inseparable for Ambedkar from the corruptions of force and latitude for violence that is permissible within Indic theories of the state? Did he view the sacred triad of force, faith, and sovereignty (or, in classical terms, the alliance between rule, obedience, and office) as an Indo-European problem?[90] What if the category of the theologico-political were viewed not simply as a notion that accounts for the Judeo-Christian theory and institution of sovereignty but as a category that makes possible, in the manner of that other tradition that derives its energy from Spinoza's *Theological-Political Treatise* (1670), a critique of priestly influence on civic institutions? What if the theologico-political were to refer to the force mobilized on the side of general will, the multitude's action, rather than on the side of executive power? What if it were, as Ambedkar believed it was, a seed of belief, a place for politics, opened up by the inseparable bond between force and justice, one that contained the possibility of a democratic faith? And if that were the case, was not the theologico-political, beyond the distinction between "natural religion" and "revealed religion" (which Ambedkar calls out as a false contradiction very early on in *Philosophy of Hinduism*), not an unavoidable knot in the universal history of religion and government, one that needed to be disentangled and recovered everywhere if democracy were to have a chance anywhere?

These questions bring us back to Ambedkar's and Gandhi's shared belief that freedom requires a new force, a sovereignty without theology. But insofar as any attempt to constitute a sovereign people unburdened by ecclesiastical injunctions seeks to purge the worst impulses of scriptural religion, it also remains under the constant threat of the worst of those impulses. Ambedkar, at any rate, dramatically redraws the boundaries of the Catholic sense of the theologico-political, uprooting it from its origins in Christianity and deploying it to analyze the collusion between theology and government, scripture and office, in Indic traditions. In fact, by placing Hinduism unequivocally among the great "religions of the book," he opens a capacious set of polytheistic beliefs to theologico-political systematization, a gesture that would in turn clear the ground for the fierce critique of Hinduism's "spiritual content" (which was for him never distinct from the state) that he would mount in his unfinished *Essays on the Bhagavad Gita*. One might even argue that the contours of Ambedkar's own engagement with the concept of force (in all its richness and originality) would emerge only from his critique of the mystical foundation of Hinduism's political authority.[91] With all its emancipatory and extremist possibilities, then, the theologico-political turn in his thought would turn out to be a difficult but productive passage, classical in framework yet radical in scope, a passage through which not only his religious convictions but also his mortal ontology passed. Committed to denouncing the violence of positive religions, he nevertheless sought another religion of the book (or, indeed, a book for *his* religion), a desire that would culminate in his masterwork, *The Buddha and His Dhamma* (1956).

In the section that follows, I retrace the global movement of texts and contexts, influences, and resistances within which Ambedkar's thought acquired its exceptional form, in the process elaborating on my reasons for placing him within the tradition of classical politics, recovering him as a figure confronted with the founding antinomies of the modern political tradition at their limit. Among these antinomies are those between revolution and constitution, sovereignty and freedom, belief and truth, unmediated general will and mediated (or parliamentary) representation—the last of which he found necessary in the face of the religious and juridical disenfranchisement of India's "untouchables," even if philosophically, he remained, like Gandhi, unconvinced about political representation as the adequate solution to moral and social disenfranchisement. Rehabilitating Ambedkar as a classical thinker should in no way imply that I am making a case for rendering secondary the most formative and decisive dimension of his politics and ethics—that is, the annihilation of caste and its system of juridically sanctioned servitude. On the contrary, it is the sheer longevity of caste—its invisible, cryptic exclusions—that presses on the necessity of recovering Ambedkar's formidable moral ontology, his ability to pursue the most intractable dilemmas of politics and subjectivity, his indomitable struggle to exceed the norms, rules, and distinctions of his times. His ability to delve into conditions of cognitive servitude and passivity (from which, he believed, the multitude's insurrectionary force might emerge) requires that meticulous attention be paid to both the breadth of his political thought and depth of his moral commitments, that the threads of his innovations and influences be traced beyond the contextual limits imposed by nationalist and reformist reason, that problems Ambedkar saw himself confronting be recovered in all their promises, richness, and risk.

Such attentiveness might not only illuminate those dimensions in his vision of politics that were closest to classical ideals of revolutionary action and popular sovereignty. It might also bring into view another imagination of freedom itself—an imagination ceaselessly struggling against the norms of its times—amplifying, in the process, the obstacles that it encountered in its movement through the powerful discourses of anticolonial sovereignty, against which Ambedkar (and in his own way, Gandhi) would contend for much of his political life. D. R. Nagaraj's essays in the 1990s had laid the groundwork for all future investigations into the monumental confrontation that occurred in the 1930s between the two thinkers.[92] In this book, I am interested less in retelling the story of that clash than in the divergence of presuppositions and methods in Ambedkar's and Gandhi's intersecting priorities. This is a history of the disjuncture—within the shared egalitarian imperative—in their grasp and reconfiguration of classical idioms. Their kinship or difference is central to this book only inasmuch as the microhistory of their encounter contains within its rich linguistic, conceptual, and rhetorical details the nuances of a struggle of which they were exemplary theorists: the struggle of colonized Indians to formulate the conditions of a democracy within the structure of a religion known to be singularly hierarchical and exclusionary among religions.

Classical at a Distance

At the time of the Gandhi's return to India in 1915, a twenty-five-year-old Ambedkar was still polishing his rhetoric and style in the graduate seminar rooms of Columbia University. Both spent a crucial part of their formative years in London less than three decades apart, Gandhi as a law student at Inner Temple between 1888 and 1891, Ambedkar as a doctoral candidate in economics at the London School of Economics between 1916 and 1917, from which he was forced to return after his scholarship expired, taking up service, as the terms of the scholarship stipulated, in the bureaucracy of the princely state of Baroda.[93] While the young Gandhi, handed a copy of *Theory of Utility* by a friend in London, found Bentham unreadable,[94] Ambedkar immersed himself in the traditions of natural and positive law, going on to deliver his *Lectures on the English Constitution* in the early 1930s in Bombay.

Despite this adeptness with the nuances of political and legal argument, neither Ambedkar's nor Gandhi's critique of social hierarchies, their attempt to fashion a new moral subject, remained untouched by their sustained engagement with vernacular literatures and epistemologies. Gandhi's emerged from within Gujarati linguistic and literary history; Ambedkar's arose from the Mahar warrior traditions of Maharashtra in western India and the juridical traditions of Gangetic statecraft in eastern India, whose greatest (and Ambedkar's most favored) text was Kautilya's *Arthashastra* (regarded in the early decades of the twentieth century as a theoretical precursor to the classic of Florentine republicanism, Niccolò Machiavelli's *The Prince* (1532)).[95] Gandhi's understanding of belief and truth emerged from his distinctive engagement with the *advaita* (nondualist) strands of classical Hinduism; Ambedkar's, from the Madhyamika tradition of Buddhist negative theology.[96] At his best, Gandhi would have little hesitation in finding in classical monarchy the ethical foundations of government, which he would call, from the 1920s onward *Ramarajya*, or the reign of Rama, considered in Hindu political culture to be the highest ideal and expression of just rule. Ambedkar, at his most insurrectionary, on the other hand, would in his Rousseauist moments find even parliamentary representation to be a corruption of democracy, a fiction of national sovereignty, a false civility secured by the alienation and rightlessness of the non-citizen.

Apart from the complexity of their relationship to religious and humanistic traditions, a third, and in my view, decisive force shaped their moral and political convictions: its timing during the decades spanning the two world wars. War formed the crucible of their encounter, and not just the world wars or the genocidal civil war that preceded the formation of free India and Pakistan in 1947, but also war as the theater of action where ethics—the capacity to be a moral agent, the ability to keep faith, the skill of mastering fear, the ability, above all, to become an example for another—approached its greatest (and, as we shall see, terrifying) purity. War gave this intellectual kinship its language, its urgency, and its force. War refracted not merely Ambedkar's and Gandhi's interpretations of such classical texts as the *Bhagavad Gita*. It also offered an exemplary context to put their ideas into practice. "What am I to advise a man to do who wants to kill but is unable owing to his being maimed?" Gandhi would ask in 1918, defending his decision to support Britain's war effort. "Before I can make him feel the virtue of not killing, I must restore to him the arm he has lost."[97] As if pushing this rhetoric of armament and the arm to its extreme, demanding that Gandhi stand by his sacrificial truth, Ambedkar offers his own militantly republican formulation: "To take a catastrophe like war, society must mobilise all its resources for militarization. Everyone must do war. Everyone must be a soldier."[98]

At once extremist in tone and civic in the virtues they marshal, the force lines of Ambedkar's influences, provocations, and citations acquire labyrinthine form by the late 1930s, each thread spun to create a tension between two distinct traditions of thinking about knowledge and politics, craft and action, legislation and force. John Dewey, his teacher, provides one strand. *The Public and Its Problems* (1927) and *Individualism Old and New* (1930), both published in the decade before *Annihilation of Caste*, would open Ambedkar's thought to the conceptual and pedagogical richness of Atlantic radical democracy. The much more classical and powerful Rousseauist lineage within modern republican thought provides the other strand, one that would strongly mediate Ambedkar's struggle with the paradox of popular sovereignty and constituent power.

Both the vocabulary and tone of *Annihilation of Caste* bear the strong imprint of Dewey's 1927 expression, "eclipse of the public." After all, Ambedkar speaks there not of franchise for the most oppressed and untouchable alone but of India's collective failure to imagine a morally rigorous and just public life, its failure to create a political community guided by the force of the soul. This is not the "soul-force" of Gandhi's *Hind Swaraj*, grounded in the heroic privations and "privacies of inner life," to use another Deweyan expression, which the teacher deploys in *Human Nature and Conduct* (1922). Rather, Ambedkar insists, this is the force of collective feeling and love for community, a shared freedom that had been numbed by Hinduism's entrenched indifference to its own cruelties. It was not surprising that *Annihilation of Caste* itself ends with a melancholic flourish, its closing pages recounting mournfully what Dewey had called in *Individualism Old and New* the "tragedy of the lost individual."[99]

Focusing solely on Dewey's influence, however, obscures many untraced supplements of Ambedkar's thought, for there were figures from different, often irreconcilable, traditions that he was engaged with during the interwar years, and with whom his relationships were far from settled. Often, he would refuse to choose one thinker over the other. As he would put it in his most enigmatic reading of the legacy of Marx on modern political thought, "What remains of Karl Marx is a residue of fire, small but still very important."[100] With the exception of Rousseau, no other thinker could take Marx's place for Ambedkar. Even if there were a substitute, no other thinker could have occasioned a tribute of this kind. Indeed, in Ambedkar's remorseless diagnoses of modern politics and its relationship to private property, only Rousseau would

be read more attentively (and cited more rarely) than Marx. Despite his qual-
ification then (stemming from his belief that Marx fails to understand the
revolutionary force of religion), there are elements in Ambedkar's critique of
alienation that carry strong Marxian resonances, resonances that were themselves redolent of Marx's adjacency not only with Rousseau but also with
Romanticism. There were, for instance, in his early seminar papers in New
York in the 1910s the first glimpses of Ambedkar's sensitivity to the "ghostli-
ness" of force, a notion that he derives, as did Marx, from his early readings of
Shakespeare and Hegel. Rousseau's *Social Contract* (1762), along with Marx's
Communist Manifesto (1848), Mill's *On Liberty* (1859), and Pope Leo XIII's
encyclical *Rerum Novarum* (On the Condition of Labor) (1891), Ambedkar
would declare in 1943, were the indispensable primary texts for a laboring
multitude that now, more urgently than ever, needed to read in order to grasp
the insidious relationship between parliamentary democracy, private property, and nationalist ideology.[101]

It was around this time, roughly between 1935 and 1945, that Ambedkar
would begin to develop a distinctive understanding of freedom, at once republican in its vision, ontological in its depth, and phenomenological in its sensitivity to the morals—or rather, religiosity—of everyday life. For Ambedkar,
only a democratization of the innermost recesses of faith could transcend—
if need be, by force—the artificial division between civic virtue and personal
conviction, between the political and religious. In fact, if there was a central
lesson in *Annihilation of Caste*, if there was an irreducible "principle" that
underpinned its formula of a "truly religious act," it was its author's conviction that the democratization of religion—the duty to make faith accessible
to everyone freely and equally—was a people's highest obligation toward itself. Not surprisingly, given this enormous faith in the transformative promise
(and risk) of religion, Ambedkar perennially worried about religion's violent
past, ceaselessly interrogating its transcendental truths and everyday exclusions. Precisely because, unlike Marx, who saw in religion the ultimate source
of all human alienation, Ambedkar never let go of his belief that religion had
a spirit, a responsibility, a future in the democracy to come.[102]

Gandhi too, from the very beginning, had been ambivalent about the
ideals of liberal democracy, finding its secularist separation between public
commitments and private beliefs too constraining. In fact, he would invoke,
often without irony, the "spirit of democracy" especially when he was at odds
with its enumerative logic, which he believed reduced people to abstract and
faceless numbers. And yet he was equally susceptible to speaking of democracy's horrors when he was closest to its majoritarian—and exclusionary—
impulses. Like Ambedkar, at any rate, he would refuse to relinquish the

paradoxes of republican democracy.[103] In *Hind Swaraj*, he notoriously com-
pares the British Parliament to a "prostitute"[104] and cautions colonial Indians
against the perils of harboring belief that the majority is necessarily right just
because the first principle of democracy—numerical might—says so.[105] But
Hind Swaraj is the last time that Gandhi mounts that critique in such strong
terms. Subsequent developments in his thought and practice suggest a more
tactical approach, one as reminiscent of his pragmatic affiliations as his anarchist past in England. In his prolonged engagement with the Anglophone
tradition, Gandhi had carefully skirted Mill, Bentham, and Spencer, turning
instead to the transcendentalism of Emerson and Thoreau. Closer to the spirit
of satyagraha were the moral theories of Tolstoy and Raychandbhai Mehta, a
Gujarati Jain thinker whom Gandhi regarded as his religious mentor. If his
appetite for philosophical traditions distant from his own was voracious, the
reasons for his choice of particular texts were idiosyncratic and opaque. But
never were they easily separable from his political commitments. Even before he composed *Hind Swaraj*, Gandhi had translated into Gujarati, for his
newspaper *Indian Opinion* in South Africa, American theologian William
Macintyre Salter's *Ethical Religion* and English philanthropist John Ruskin's
Unto His Last.[106] His encounter with American pragmatist William James's
Varieties of Religious Experience, which James had delivered as the Gifford Lectures in Natural Religion in Edinburgh in 1901–1902, occurred, most likely
for the first time, a decade and a half later, during his internment at the Yeravda Prison in 1924.[107] Such influences might appear to be at cross-purposes,
but seemingly irreconcilable differences in method would soon be hemmed
in by a commitment to reinstitute the relationship between ethics and politics, belief and meaning, means and ends.

Given over to revolution in its most spiritual sense, yet suspicious of
the pernicious alliance between religion and authority in all its ecclesiastical
forms, Ambedkar meanwhile walked carefully around Hegel and Marx before
finding other resources for his moral psychology of resistance (and, often, his
belief in the unmediated and unrepresentable sovereignty of the people) in
Rousseau and Nietzsche, even as he remained ambivalently drawn to Georges
Sorel's fin-de-siècle syndicalism and his theory of the "general strike," which
had influenced important strands of interwar thinking on action and sovereignty (both on the left and right).[108] But Ambedkar drew and molded into
shape his most fundamental, enduring, and revolutionary insights first from
Durkheim's *Elementary Forms of Religious Life* (1912), written in the long aftermath of the Dreyfus affair in France,[109] and then, from the late 1930s onward,
from Henri Bergson's milestone in the philosophy of immanence, *Les deux
sources de la morale et de la religion* (*The Two Sources of Religion and Morality*,

1932).[110] While he might have drawn from Rousseau the distinction between sacred, mythical, and civic purposes of religion, especially in his mature meditations on the relationship between theology and government, it was Bergson who provided him the vocabulary of religion's "two sources," which was to become so crucial to the moral theology of *The Buddha and His Dhamma*.[111] *Annihilation of Caste* itself was published in 1936, just a year after *Two Sources* became available in English, and even though Bergson appears more explicitly in Ambedkar's later writings, in those moments, for instance, when he attempts to reconcile the universal resurgence of religion with the force of modern science (neither of which he was willing to give up), the vitalist resonance in his formulation of "general mobilization" had already appeared. The similarities between Ambedkar's "general mobilization" and Sorel's "general strike" were not incidental either, even if, as we shall see, there were immense differences that need to be approached carefully. Yet both Sorel and Ambedkar, while separated by a generation, may have been equally close observers of the turns and shifts in Bergson's vitalist philosophy.[112]

Ambedkar's sensitivity to the porousness between religion and morality, at any rate, would owe much to Bergson's *Two Sources*, as would his privileging of a nonmasculine notion of fraternity and brotherhood over abstract theories of equality. "A force of unvarying direction, which is to the soul what the force of gravity is to the body," Bergson argues in *Two Sources*, "ensures the cohesion of the group by bending all individual wills in the same direction. Such is moral obligation."[113] This idea, that the moral obligation of one's soul, in its primordial and secluded authenticity, is grounded in the shared values and quotidian sacrifices of collective life alone, would appear in Ambedkar's later writings in various permutations. In fact, in *Philosophy of Hinduism*, civic consciousness tethered to individual souls and selves would be connected, in an especially Bergsonian fashion, with the insurgent and constituent power of the multitude.[114] This would be, then, a theory of Bergsonian immanence of the subject that would be strongly mediated by the Rousseauist emphasis on "full common force . . . by means of which," as Rousseau puts it in *The Social Contract*, "each uniting with all, nevertheless obey only himself and remain free as before."[115] As figure, concept, and metaphor, "force" in Ambedkar's own thought stood for this act of positing moral and political relations (with oneself and others, in dissidence and sympathy, with measure and yet immeasurably) anew.

There was, of course, a tension running through these strategies of reading and affiliation, one best reflected in Ambedkar's reservation toward Durkheim. Durkheim's *Elementary Forms*—and with it, *Religion of the Semites* (1889) by William Robertson Smith, the Cambridge theologian and scholar of

Arabic[116]—may have cleared the philosophical ground for Ambedkar's enduring engagement with (and reconfiguration of) the concept of force. But there
was one significant departure: he would refuse to adhere to Durkheim's (or
Robertson Smith's) purely anthropological view of sacrifice as a set of formalis-
tic, predictable, and visible rites and forces, focusing instead on its pernicious,
mythic, and invisible circulation through the body politic. Yet the close attention paid to force (as category and fact) in *Elementary Forms* must have stuck
a chord with Ambedkar. "The notion of force," Durkheim claims, "is religious
in origin. First philosophy, and then the sciences borrowed from religion."
And then, in a pivotal chapter on "The Idea of Force," Durkheim, in a manner
reminiscent of Hegel's *Phenomenology of Spirit*, blurs the distinction between
metaphor and effect, spirit and materiality, performance and reality. "When
we say that these principles are force, we are not using the word in a metaphorical way: they behave like real forces." Durkheim ends the chapter in the
most decisive manner: "The same is true of the concept of force in general."[117]
Comte may have prophesized that force would disappear from science because
of its roots in myth. But that seeming disappearance, Durkheim promises to
show, is the very ground of the mystical endurance of force. In fact, it is this
intrinsic mutability, this capacity to change itself, change hands, change its
order, change relationships between things and people even at the moment
of its greatest weakness—an attribute that force shared with religion—that
makes force and religion so difficult to separate from each other. Religion's
spirit, its capacity to promise life and incite horror simultaneously—*horror re-
ligiosus*—is not simply inextricable from the operations, violence, and exclusions of force, Durkheim argues. It is constitutive of it. How, then, might one
bring into existence another force, another belief, one that would be proper
to justice, one that would be less elusive, less duplicitous? How, as Ambedkar puts it with an unmistakable Bergsonian resonance, could one restore to
religion "its force as a governing principle of life" without reducing it to a
theology of government? How could one affirm life in the inescapable (and
sometimes, necessary) shadows of theologico-political rules and obligations?[118]

In the section that follows, I turn to one specific instance that might
help illuminate what I have called the disjuncture in Ambedkar's and Gandhi's shared struggle to affirm life in its irreducible equality. Or what can
be called, in another way, their desire to impart to equality the status of
an inalienable condition, equality as a moral faculty—indeed, as force—
necessary not only for being free from the domination of others but for
being truthful to one's own vulnerable and mortal self. Equality comes to
be formulated, then, as a risky condition between freedom and vulnerability, mastery and weakness, the political and the social. When Ambedkar and

Gandhi mobilized this risk (each using different names for it), they broke away most decisively from that determining sense of measure and fairness that classical conceptions of politics have brought to ideals of a just society. Both believed that an equal life—which was always a matter of providing the conditions for shared, approachable, and touchable lives—could not simply thrive under the injunctions, mandates, and rules of national sovereignty. Nor could constitutional safeguards by themselves secure such a life. Rather, for such inalienable equality to come into existence, the constituents of the nation would have to accept difference, even vulnerability and nonsovereignty, as the moral basis of everyday freedoms. Equality had to be viewed as a set of everyday relationships formed, simultaneously, from one's attentiveness to the other's incurable finitude and one's reclamation of force—accentuation of difference, even distance—as the condition of a just world. Equality was a relationship as much with one's own life as it was with the other's vulnerability. It was, for Ambedkar and Gandhi, one might argue, a *place* between force and justice.

Of Presence: Between *Samadarshita* and *Samata*

By the middle of the 1930s, their disagreement over the question of caste equality had caused a permanent breach between Ambedkar and Gandhi. And yet the questions they struggled with were strikingly similar. How can one think of equality within the reality of India's centrifugal difference? How might one be just rather than simply equal in the abstract sense of the term? How could a just force, the right to have justice, be retained when sovereignty too often, too quickly, almost inevitably lapsed into violence? How might moral relations be grounded in an ethics of nonsovereignty without renouncing the value of legislative and constituent power, which is the only means of sustaining an egalitarian sovereignty, a people's republic?

After the failure of his first noncooperation movement, which he had unilaterally suspended in the winter of 1922 after a violent crowd in the United Provinces burned down a police station and killed close to two dozen colonial constables trapped inside, Gandhi began reading and lecturing on that classic Indian text on ethics and fratricide, the *Bhagavad Gita*. In his *Discourses on the Gita*, Gandhi formulates, for the first time and in the most careful fashion, his moral vision of equality:

When can we say of a person that he is *samadarshi*? Can we say so of that man who would give equal quantities to an elephant and an ant? Indeed no. We can say it of him who gives to each according to his or her need. A mother will give nothing to her child who is ill and will give another who is well as much as he can eat. A person who is filled with the spirit of non-violence, with compassion, will so act that the world will say of him that he behaved toward all as if they were himself, did justice to all; that he gave water to him who needed water and milk to him who needed milk. No one can be like God, absolutely free from impurity and equal toward all. One can, therefore, become *samadarshi* only by losing oneself in Him. . . . Let us describe some instances of equal regard for all. One is that of the elephant and the ant. Second, if an enemy and a friend arrive at his place together, both hungry, the *samadarshi* will offer food first to the enemy. He would feel that to be justice. He would be afraid lest there be some hatred for the enemy lurking in his heart, and he would satisfy him first.[119]

Key terms and figures of the satyagrahic lexicon appear in this critique of abstract egalitarian norms: compassion, nonviolence, place, God, and, above all, spirit, each mediated by the fact of difference, which is also what often leads, Gandhi admits in his writings elsewhere, to situations of conflict and war. Indeed, as the Lord Krishna tells the supreme warrior Arjuna throughout their dialogues that constitute the *Bhagavad Gita*, equality, even compassion—the duty (or sudden urge) to treat the other, enemy or brother, as equal—is always at war with itself. And it is at war not only because it is most fragile and demanding when the choice turns out to be one between the friend and enemy—that is, when the need to be egalitarian manifests itself in the moral urgency of the battlefield, as it does when Arjuna is faced with the fratricidal prospect of annihilating his cousins in order to recover for his brother Yudhishthira his usurped kingdom. Equality is at war also because, to be just in its most uncompromising sense, to avoid lapsing into an abstract regime of substitution and sameness, it must always be open to exclusion and selectiveness, to discrimination between brothers and friends, between countrymen and aliens, between insects and mammals. The satyagrahi's equality is subject to the irreducible difference of opinion, filiation, and species, and, at the same time, indifferent to distinctions between oppressors and oppressed, friend and foe. In this simultaneous awareness of difference (between the needs of various others) and the need to remain indifferent (to the fact of the other's viewpoint in relation to one's own), Gandhi's equality comes to be founded on the sensitive act of privileging one over another, excluding one in face of the other. In fact, the proper rendering of Gandhian *ahimsa*, as I argue in Chapter 4, is not "nonviolence" but "nonindifference," an ethics of compassion acutely aware of, even vested in, difference and distance, an ethics in which nonviolent compassion itself remained inseparable from (or constantly in tension with) the exercise of force. The exemplar that perfects this difficult moral balance between difference and indifference is Gandhi's *samadarshi*.

Samadarshi is a polyvalent compound, in no small measure because it refers—or attaches itself—simultaneously to a cognitive principle or ideal (*adarsh*) and a moral empiricism that can be grounded only in the concrete act of witnessing and sight (*darshan*). Thus, the *samadarshi* is one who at once believes in the principle of the other as equal (*sam*) and one whose sense of equality ensues from the empirical experience of witnessing, judging, and giving oneself to the other's difference and differential need. The *samadarshi* does not, therefore, give as much to a hungry friend as he does to the enemy. But nor does every enemy or unequal become, in a moment of fraternal universalism, a brother. Rather, equality flows from a firm moral principle that emphasizes clarity of vision and appreciation of heterogeneity over abstract sameness of the kind instituted by liberal humanistic discourses of ability, distribution, fairness, and access to goods. Depending on the specific circumstance, one's sense of equality becomes contingent, reversible, and porous, taking the form in one instance of equanimity; in another instance, gift; in yet another, charity; and in some others, service. Each instance is regulated by a disciplinary and punitive limit—which Gandhi calls *maryada dharma*—imposed on the egalitarian gesture itself.

Punishment (especially of the self, and yet never easily confined within the limits of the self alone), was crucial to this egalitarianism. And it was a propensity that pushed the ideal of *samadarshita* perilously close to the classical ideals of the state. For if not everyone shares the ability—indeed, the right—to see the same thing in order to make the same or even equally moral judgments, how can the logic of *samadarshita* escape a certain discriminating idealism? How can it escape rendering the act of discrimination itself into an ideal? And could anyone but an absolutely sovereign self, one whose motivations are indifferent to the needs of the unequal and wagered instead on the ability to discriminate and judge those needs based on his innermost truth alone, a self grounded in mastery but oblivious to the force that makes the self the center of judgment in the first place, be a *samadarshi*? Equality would thus be produced more as an exception, a decision, as an instance of self-mastery. The principle of *samadarshita*, grounded thus in the apotheosis of the exception, would not be so much as divorced from the empirical and everyday content of inequality (to which Gandhi was profoundly sensitive) as its vision and practice would be founded on—and draw moral substance from—those practices of cruelty and injustice that remain materially invisible, mystical, and ordinary. Injustice, after all, could equally often be hidden or obscured by the laws of seeing and not-seeing. Cruelty could as easily be nonmanifest, spiritual, invisible, or so ordinary that it escapes the *samadarshi*'s line of vision and sense of judgment.

An equality grounded in the practice of witnessing and judging for oneself, a principle rooted in the empiricism of being present (and how else could the difference of the other be given its due respect), was thus always susceptible to recoil in the face of—or at worse, turn indifferent to—internal exclusions, exclusions that haunt the social from within, inequities that are, as Ambedkar called them, ghosts, everywhere yet nowhere.

As Ambedkar, meanwhile, sets himself the task, from the 1940s onward, of unearthing and scrutinizing Indic etymologies in such works as *Philosophy of Hinduism, Riddles of Hinduism,* and the unfinished *Essays on the Bhagavad Gita,* he rarely formulates the principle of equality in representational or visual terms. In a crucial passage in *Annihilation of Caste,* for instance, he mounts a challenge against the humanist emphasis on presence and vision most clearly. "Caste is not a physical object like a wall of bricks or a line of barbed wire which prevents the Hindus from co-mingling and which has, therefore, to be pulled down." On the contrary, caste is an empty crypt at the heart of India's moral psychology. "Caste is a notion, it is a state of the mind. The destruction of Caste does not therefore mean the destruction of a physical barrier. It means a notional change."[120]

For Ambedkar, too, equality is an ontological condition, a question of judgment grounded in the idea of a sovereign and autonomous being (different from the other). But it is also one that is not simply available in those places and species that one chooses to see it in. To become a truth proper to humanity, equality must be seen as a work of ontological production. To be made and remade, wrested and reclaimed, true equality required autonomy and freedom, a renunciation of measure and limits that politics imposes on it. After all, Ambedkar's is a society of the immeasurably unequal, of those whose servitude remains difficult to apprehend and arrange within an order of determinate jurisdictions and barbed wires. In this society, unequals were not simply "untouchable." They were also declared "invisible." Often, their shadows were barred as "unapproachable," permanently consigned beyond the presence of the caste Hindu. If each of these unequals is unequal in a different way than the other; if each existence is regulated within an economy of nearness and distance that functions differently from the other (one forced by the law to be invisible, another unapproachable, still another barred from touch and light), how could equality between these unequals be viewed within the framework of presence and substitution? A general equality under these conditions would only be a delimited and conditional equality, abstract and indifferent at best. In such a conditional world, there would always be someone unequal, living at the mercy of masters who themselves would be divided by grades, offices, capacities, and authority. For Ambedkar, therefore, untouchability is not one inequality among others, not one more form of slavery among others. Rather, it is a nonviolent art of physical and cognitive enslavement, a structure of dispersed and "graded sovereignty" perfected over millennia. It is, he argues, the greatest vulnerability, the most fatal and exceptional, the most sovereign among all inequalities.

With this radical search for equality within the framework (and constant risk) of sovereignty, Ambedkar's democratic ethics arrives at the center of his "methodological extremism," as I call it in Chapter 5. Let me re-emphasize that his critique of presence is not a plea for the abstract equality promised by the liberal contract, let alone a bargaining space for restitution and redress. Instead, it intimates a difficulty, a struggle to conceptualize equality as the ontological ground where the weakest alone might lay claim over democracy, where the defeated alone might nourish a just and insurrectionary sense of being wronged. There is a radical empiricism at work here, but one that is rooted neither in the ontology of mere vision and principled judgment (*samadarshita*) nor in the phenomenology of mere touching (*sparsyata*). Instead, Ambedkar seeks equality in the dignified authenticity of finitude invoked by the thoughtfully chosen and judiciously deployed term *samata*. When translated precisely, taken back to its Buddhist theological roots, *samata* yields not "equality" as a passive condition (*samaanta*) but rather the "equal-ness" of a living being grasped at the moment of its coming into the world. *Samata* is not a moral precept or constitutional principle, like the one encapsulated in the formula "all men are born equal," an abstraction that Ambedkar expressed dissatisfaction with more than once. Rather, it refers to an equal-ness grounded in a person's inalienable right of being and becoming, in the knowledge, the *samatajnana*, of every creature's unique way of living and dying.

Samata draws attention to the ineradicable difference in the nature and experience of death—the finitude common to all beings that otherwise live incommensurably—in two senses. One is historical, in which it is acknowledged that death could be passive, suffered under historical conditions of involuntary and voluntary servitude, even devotion (*bhakti*). The other is ontological, in which death is seen as representing an insurrectionary possibility, a moment of war and combat, embraced as a gift of freedom for the "untouchable." Between these two senses of death, the term *samata* suggests both authenticity and vulnerability, in which a person becomes aware of being capable of inalienable force and irreducible equality (with oneself and others) at his weakest and most vulnerable. In his Marathi autobiography *Vasti*, Vasant Moon, one of the most important editors of Ambedkar's works, writes of how, at the assemblies in the 1930s and 1940s of the Dalit militant group, Samata Sainik Dal (loosely translatable as "Soldiers for Equality"), chants of blood and sacrifice, composed as salutation to Ambedkar's piercing intellect, became extremely popular among the young members.[121] Equally suggestive is the choice of the name Samata Samaj Sangh (translatable as "League for the Society of Equals") for the organization that Ambedkar founded in 1927 to campaign for intercaste marriages and dining, activities to which Gandhi was stridently opposed. A year later, he helped found the radical reformist fortnightly *Samata*.

One moment deployed as an ethical demand to free from the injunctions of moral law the most quotidian activities of civic life—eating together, drawing water from shared wells, walking on common roads, reading the same books and newspapers—that constitute the empirical content of the social, *samata* might, in another moment, conjure visions of blood, force, and insurrection. This was equality ceaselessly under production then: singular and shared, exposed and resolute, insurgent and nonsovereign. One might even argue that *samata* suggests a certain condition of being at war with oneself, at war with the constraints and boundaries of the self itself, often on behalf of others with whom one shared nothing but mortality, nothing but an exposure to force. Ambedkar's public pronouncement in 1935 on the kind of death he desired—a desire that would be reformulated more than once during the often hostile debates in the Constituent Assembly in the late 1940s—is a poignant expression of this self at war with itself: "It was my misfortune to be born a Hindu. I do not have the capacity to eliminate this defect in me. However, I do have the strength to not accept the humiliating practices that I was subjected to as an Untouchable. It is within my capacity to reject the Hindu religion. I will say this publicly, that even though I was born a Hindu, I will not die a Hindu."[122]

Here Ambedkar institutes a politics grounded not in the amplification but secession of the mortal self. The secession of self does not, however, amount to a secession of force. It simply proclaims the coming of a politics conscious of the deep history of appropriations and rejections, privileges and cruelties, that constitute, in a manner that is forever indelible and irresolvable, one's relationship to one's self. Within one swift declaration, Ambedkar shifts from defect to resolve, from birth to death. For a subject humiliated by his own religion and forced to see himself as an embodiment of lack, he insists (using his own person), must be most resolute when he is most violated. And this resolve is given not at or by birth (which is already appropriated by a religion that too must be destroyed); rather, it comes as the gift of death to oneself, as a permanent dissidence against the self itself. A just life might emerge, then, only from the shadows of everyday experience and mortality, its existence punctuated by the fecund tension between the untouchable's vulnerable finitude and his sovereign vulnerability: a suffering, a sacrifice, a death—and therefore, a freedom—highest among all the known structures and laws of suffering and sacrifice. "I am not a part of the whole," Ambedkar responded during a debate in the Bombay Legislative Assembly in 1939, when another representative questioned his loyalty to the nation. "I am a part apart."[123]

This was a remarkable declaration of independence, especially because it was articulated at the moment of gravest exposure to accusations of irresponsibility toward the nation. But what is even more significant is how Ambedkar forges a relationship between a condemned self (condemned by birth to be defective) and its absolute sovereignty, its vulnerability and its force, its weakness and its freedom. This affirmation of life when it is most vulnerable, this ability to resist the demands of sameness and fidelity lend the language of *samata* its insurrectionary charge. There was a search for primordial purity, an ethics of antisovereignty even, at work in these insurgent acts of naming and founding; an ethics of force that might at the same time, Ambedkar hoped, resist the temptation to dominate those who experienced the world (and left it) differently. It was this consciousness of difference that freed Ambedkar's *samata* from the classical distinctions on which humanist thought has come to be founded—distinctions between vision and touch, intelligibility and sensibility, absence and presence, friend and enemy, human and animal.

A Philosophical History of the Indian Political

Radical Equality writes a history of this distinction—the working and reworking of the tension—between classical humanism and the global life of its categories. It attempts to reclaim what I call, following Pierre Rosanvallon, a "philosophical history of the political,"[124] a history that allows us to shift the analytical lens away from the dialectical logic of nation and empire, from the narratives of glorious struggle between Europe and colony, and instead probe the tension between the just and unjust that remains unthought in these narratives. This can be done not by looking at the anticolonial tradition simply from another lens, whether international, cosmopolitan, oceanic, or post-European (none of which fully escapes the prejudices it inherits from the imperial and nationalist past of political philosophy),[125] but only by placing at the center of modern political and legal thought those whose ideas of justice and citizenship, whose nonnationalist conceptualizations of the social question, often at odds with histories centered on independence and state, are excluded from anticolonial and postcolonial formulations of the political as such. As Ambedkar quickly realized during his attempts to write the counterhistory of the modern nation-form (such as in his essay "The Untouchables and *Pax Britannica*," which retells the story of the Indian Mutiny of 1857 from the perspective of its outcaste foot soldiers), the rehabilitation of the tension between the just and unjust—right in the middle of the heroic accounts of a nation's arrival into modernity—is an extreme measure, one that puts under a cloud one's commitment to freedom from imperial domination itself, opening one to accusations of complicity and collaboration with empire. But it is a risk that any free and democratic thinking—any democracy that considers neither empire nor nation to either be its first principle or final word—must unconditionally take.

As I show in the chapters that follow, this risk has both rhetorical and conceptual dimensions. And it is only by tracing the mutations of classical concepts at the moment of their clearest theoretical articulation, by isolating radical exceptions and extremities at the moment of their enunciation (Gandhi's *harijan* and Ambedkar's *ucched* [annihilation] will serve as my entry points into these extremes of thought), that a philosophical history of the political is made possible. "Classical" in this context does not mean forcing the political history of the non-West to yield to the norms and languages of the Western political tradition, reducing them to what Partha Chatterjee cautions is the logic of "elemental sameness."[126] Rather, "classical" refers to that which lies beyond the simple negation of the norm, whether Indic or European. It refers to that which appears in Ambedkar and Gandhi as the negation of negation. Certainly the relationships between government and people, constituent power and the juridical state, the multitude and sovereignty, justice and the law, constitute an inextricable antinomy of the modern political universe, regardless of—indeed, amplified further by—the uneven and troubled global trajectory of modernity. But the universality of this antinomy is not reducible to the conflict between imperial and national humanisms alone. Instead, this antinomy is constituted by what I would like to call an "affirmative negativity" (or, as in Ambedkar's relationship with religion, a nonnegative negation). An antinomy constituted, in other words, by active, even insurrectionary engagement with the task of conceptual innovation that makes the fundamental tensions of modern political thought (and European modernity) unavoidable for anticolonial thinkers engaged in such a task, and simultaneously, by active resistance of the oppressed against the violence of abstraction and conceptual thinking.

Viewed in these terms, Ambedkar's and Gandhi's originality would seem to reside in neither the formidable theoritical task they took on nor the vernacular solutions they proposed but rather in their awareness of blindness, which their conceptual and linguistic worlds, their prose and syntax, would need to address in order precisely to overcome the abstract and violent aspects of European (and nationalist) habits of conceptual thinking—the exclusions, hierarchy, and difference built into visions of politics as such. This awareness explains why their writings are replete with expressions of dissatisfaction with concepts such as equality, revolution, constitution, representation, parliament, and even democracy; why they push the normative boundaries of moral and political thought to extremes, opening pathways that were to remain irreconcilable with the intentions that their intellectual trajectories have themselves come to be associated with. The fundamental task of a philosophical history of the political must be to recuperate the problems that Gandhi and Ambedkar (among many others in the colonial world) saw themselves confronting.[127] There is a distinct tradition of intellectual history that comes close to the task Rosanvallon sets for a philosophical history, despite his own reservations about that tradition. This tradition includes, for instance, Quentin Skinner's intellectual biography of Machiavelli, which I take to be an important example of attentiveness to obstacle as an integral part of a thinker's originality, as I do Keith Michael Baker's systematic reconstruction of the discursive and institutional inventiveness (never separate from the struggle to find a language proper to the new political culture) of the revolutionary moment in France. In his sustained and careful retrieval of an Indian history of liberalism, C. A. Bayly has examined the effects of these conceptual mutations on a global scale, placing the idealistic universalism of modern liberal thought, its desire to preach to the colonized, at the center at once of its social promise and cognitive limit.[128] I depart from Bayly's central thesis in the second part of this book, examining not the limits of liberalism in the empire, which he has accomplished in an exemplary and sympathetic fashion, but instead probing, after Ambedkar, the moral limit that constitutes liberal idealism in general and its belief in the fairness of constitutional norms in particular.

My departure from this tradition of writing the history of political thought (often called the "Cambridge School") is not grounded in a dispute about the meanings, salience, and universality of such categories as "revolution" and "liberalism." Rather, I probe the definition and frontiers of the "classical" itself, the intelligibility and certainty of meanings that historians impute to classical categories, the teleological and overdetermined trajectory within which the logic and context of their mutation is understood. I ask, in other words, whether an archeology of these concepts, the excavation of those structures of feeling and grammar that the concepts are tethered to—sometimes by their authors, often by the social and political context of their production—might also illuminate the moral reflexes that do not succumb to and indeed aggressively resist the very order of intelligibility that the thinker (and his time and place) seeks to impose on them. Rather than judging a thinker on his integrity or coherence—a gesture that, Skinner warns, might yield a mythology, not a history—a philosophical history of the political must be awake to the obstacles that thought creates for itself as it moves through the body of work from which it has emerged.[129] Only by retracing the path along which those obstacles were encountered can the historian approach democracy as a *problem* in the history of modern ideas.

This problematization involves resisting the logic of "formal deduction," as Claude Lefort calls it.[130] It involves a refusal to reduce a work to the sum total of its theses alone. It requires tracing the unconscious movements of thought whose effects go beyond the margins of declared intent. In fact, only when viewed within the global and imperial conjuncture when democracy seemed more an exception than a norm, only when placed in the cognitive context from which treatises such as *Hind Swaraj* and *Annihilation of Caste* emerged, do Gandhi's and Ambedkar's works begin to reveal an insurrectionary element at the limit of politics, an insurrection that sought to extract the political itself—and the social question—from the doctrinal prescriptions and certitude of its European past. I use "insurrection" not in a casual vein, but to amplify the claim that I made at the beginning of this chapter: a certain critique and recovery of force for the multitude, a certain vacillation between revolutionary force and juridical power, a certain thinking of transformative and (in Ambedkar's favored terms) "direct action" was at stakes in both texts, whose moral psychology and consequences remain to be examined.

Part 1 of the book, "Beginnings," traces the early anticipations of Ambedkar's and Gandhi's shared interest in the category of force. Both chapters in this part begin with elements of their critique that took form outside India at the turn of the century. Chapter 2 examines the thought and method behind Gandhi's potent neologism *satyagraha*, which, since its coinage and induction into his political language in South Africa, he often rendered as "truth-force" or "soul-force." I attempt a substantive departure in this chapter, shifting the emphasis away from truth (*satya*), which has been the dominant way of understanding Gandhi's politics, toward the other term in the pairing—firmness, steadfastness, or force (*agraha*)—which I argue is the structuring concept of satyagraha, its very "spirit." But *satyagraha* was not simply a spiritual discourse. It was also a phenomenology of spirit, one in which Gandhi's immense discourse on the ethics of working by hand—his conception of sovereignty of (and acquired through) the rhythmic force of human hand—coalesced into a philosophical anthropology with grave consequences for the social question in India. Chapter 3 engages Ambedkar's critique of force from his early days in New York. It pursues the thread of his attraction to classical texts on sovereignty (which had by the early twentieth century also become the sovereign texts of Indian nationalism) through to his mature postwar engagement with the notion of authority and the moral law (*dharma*), the violence of which he saw most mystically condensed in the *Gita*. The effects of Ambedkar's and Gandhi's sustained and irreconcilable fascination with force, even in its most quotidian manifestations (and especially in their own practical philosophy), would be momentous. Indeed, two distinct conceptions of moral and political action, two distinct articulations of justice, would emerge from this encounter, the effects of which would play out with greatest intensity in the 1930s and 1940s.

Part 2, "Interwar," engages the two extraordinary decades during which India's experiments with franchise and constitution reached an abrasive highpoint. Chapter 4 examines the sacrificial demands of Gandhi's *maryada dharma*, a term that condenses his conception of social obligation within the disciplinary and punitive limits of moral law. I place this logic of discipline and limit (*maryada*) at the center of Gandhi's militant phenomenology or "touchability," examining how it sustained and challenged his perception of untouchability. The political stakes of Gandhi's understanding and critique were high: his consecration of the "untouchable" as *harijan*—the gesture that set the tone of social and political schisms in the 1930s—would leave a profound imprint not only on the constitution of "the people" (*jan*), but on all future conceptualizations of social question in India. It was also in the 1930s, on either side of the Government of India Act of 1935, that Ambedkar, outflanked by Gandhi after the Poona Pact of 1932, finally found that rigorous and unrelenting voice on matters relating to freedom and sovereignty with which he would be associated (and by Nehru, grudgingly admired) until his death in 1956. Indeed, by refusing to think of equality without freedom—contrary to the prescriptions of classical liberalism, in which one, almost by moral necessity, compromises the other—Ambedkar recovers for Indian democracy a classical ethics of citizen virtue and autonomy that would transform not only his own intellectual history but the very framework of debates on popular sovereignty and dissidence in modern India.

Placing Ambedkar within a global constellation of republican ideals of citizenship centered on virtue and sovereignty, Chapter 5 focuses on the ethical and political demand mounted in *Annihilation of Caste*, turning the historian's lens away from "caste," which has until now grounded all analyses of Ambedkar's politics, toward the category of "annihilation," the figure, trope, and concept that conjures the vision of immeasurable and transformative force. Doing so illuminates a prehistory of Ambedkar's relationship with constitutionalism (and eventually, independent India's Constituent Assembly) that looks rather different from what is conventionally assumed about his understanding of political and social relations. *Thoughts on Pakistan*, his most troubling work of political philosophy, a text in which his understanding of constituent power—the people's "right of disruption"—reaches its climax, was published at the end of this dramatic interwar period. Departing from established protocols and periodization, which treat *Thoughts* as an aberration, I place it at of the heart of Ambedkar's ambivalence toward the classical republican tradition, from which his thinking of force and virtue emerged.

Part 3, "Reconstitutions," focuses on Ambedkar's final considerations on the paradox of a politics grounded in sacrifice. Could there be a sacrificial politics that is not unjust? Might there be a politics that, measuring itself against nothing but sacrificial death (heroic or involuntary), had not already fallen into the vortex of violence? Could the pursuit of responsibility—or, for that matter, justice—through sacrifice, stripped of its moral consequences, be an egalitarian or political virtue all by itself? Chapter 6 returns to 1936 and examines Gandhi's engagement with *Annihilation of Caste*. My ambition in this chapter is limited and precise: to ask how Gandhi's moral ontology of action, transformed by the pressures and exigencies of mass politics over two decades before he encounters a text like *Annihilation of Caste*, mediates the sacrificial ethics of Gandhi, the reader. Chapter 7, the book's last, reconstructs the mature Ambedkar's most radical gesture yet toward a religious politics. Examining closely his explicitly religious—indeed, theologico-political—works, especially "Buddha or Karl Marx" and *The Buddha and His Dhamma*, both completed in 1956, in conjunction with his critiques of religion as they appear in *Annihilation of Caste* and *Philosophy of Hinduism*, the chapter probes Ambedkar's struggle to formulate the conditions of autonomy and justice—the will to dissidence—within the framework of a classical religion.

The later Ambedkar, I argue, refuses to take the secularist route of democratizing religious belief by reclaiming it simply as a civic morality. He does not, like Locke and the civic religious tradition that followed him, attempt to reformulate faith as an ensemble of municipal practices that might be made available to everyone equally by being fashioned as a public norm.[131] Nor does he reduce religious morals to a set of monastic and ritual practices aimed at freeing the subject from the burdens of a world otherwise saturated by unbearable suffering and destitution. Instead, Ambedkar seeks to radicalize the idea of religion's transcendence itself, turning its obligation toward the mortal subject—and all religions worthy of the name, he argues in *Philosophy of Hinduism*, promise life and health to mortals—into the foundation of an immortal justice. This justice was immortal because it thrived within the precincts of a revolutionary fraternity (*maitri*) alone, one whose ethics were unmoored from its naturalistic roots in birth, brotherhood, and family, and reoriented toward a democratic bond forged through ordinary virtues, compassions, and duties; toward those aspects of shared life that eschewed the primacy of a sacrificial death and instead affirmed life in its infinite difference; toward those lives that were born again and again, as Ambedkar's Buddha insists, through acts of sympathy, selflessness, and gift. As Ambedkar's later attempts to render fraternity into a nonhumanist conception of *maitri* would show, such democracy could be rooted only in the citizen's responsibility toward the finitude and impermanence (*sunnyata*) of *all* life, touchable and untouchable, citizen and noncitizen, friend and enemy, animal and human. In such a democracy not only must everyone have equal faith in the other but everyone must have the equal right to keep faith as such. It is in this ontological sense that Ambedkar had spoken, as early as *Annihilation of Caste*, of "the essence of a truly religious act." What kind of relationship between justice and force, between a people's sense of belief and its insurrectionary power, did the mature turns of this thought leave behind for the society of equals that was still to come? I end the book with this question at hand.

PART I

BEGINNINGS: ELEMENTS OF A CRITIQUE OF FORCE

Spirits of *Satyagraha*

A History of Force

In January 1908, in the midst of his movement in South Africa and less than two years before composing *Hind Swaraj*, Gandhi confessed to being uncomfortable with the English term "passive resistance." Dissatisfied with it partly because the name was "foreign," he invited readers of his newspaper *Indian Opinion* to suggest names that might stay faithful to the Indian provenance of the political and moral method that had come to be associated with his struggle. Among the many unsatisfactory suggestions he received from his readers was one that partially attracted Gandhi. "The word is *sadagraha*," he disclosed in his column. But as would usually be the case henceforth, he improvised on the suggestion, replacing the reader's stress on doing good (*sad*) with his own emphasis on being true (*sat*). "I think *satyagraha* is better than *sadagraha*. 'Resistance' means determined opposition to anything. The correspondent has rendered it as *agraha*. *Agraha* in a right cause is *sat* or *satya agraha*. The correspondent therefore has rendered 'passive resistance' as firmness in a good cause. Though the phrase does not exhaust the connotation of the word 'passive,' we shall use *satyagraha* till a word is available. Satyagraha, then," Gandhi declared, "is at high tide at present."[1] In this shift of accent from the agent's goodness onto his truth and righteousness, from the agent's receptivity and openness to others onto his ability to "give himself away" as gift to a world marked by servitude, emerged Gandhi's distinctive conceptualization of freedom (*swaraj*).

Crucial to this conceptualization was the category of force. For even before his return from South Africa in 1915 had transformed India's struggle against the empire, Gandhi had introduced a singular category in the language of twentieth-century anticolonialism. Helping him avoid, with greatest vigilance, the normative distinction between force and nonviolence, the category of firmness, or *agraha*, would in fact become the defining neologism in the moral and political landscape of the colonial world, quickly subsuming the passivity associated with Gandhi's early struggles in South Africa. "Firmness" was a very potent term, very strategically chosen. And Gandhi would deploy it in myriad iterations over the next four decades to underscore both the tactical necessity of force and the imperative of observing a moral measure in its exercise. For the Sanskrit term *agraha* could be rendered both as firmness and as request, a moral appeal. A constitutive civility was attached to the force mobilized through the use of this term. But *agraha* did not simply imply a negative resistance whose only efficacy might lie in withstanding the prohibitions imposed on the colonized by the empire. It also deployed, in its positive sense, a force capable of action and initiation, and if need be, vows (*vrat*) of a sacrificial and war-bound kind. "Whether you secure freedom by the use of physical force or spiritual force, i.e., through self-suffering, the price to be paid must be heavy," Gandhi warned in 1926. "Bravery and perseverance in the face of odds are as necessary, if not more, to the man of spirit as to the man of the sword. . . . Pratap reduced himself to penury. . . . Prahlad delivered his body for free destruction for what he believed to be his freedom."[2] Within the limits of a word, then, *agraha* marshaled both the sacrificial firmness of the satyagrahi's spiritual autonomy and his manual "grasp."[3] And this grasp, this ability to hold, wield, turn, and scribble, was not simply a matter of spirit and symbol, *bhaav* and sentiment. On the contrary, with its profoundly material aspirations, arenas, and effects, it was to push Gandhi's radical empiricism, his commitment to the social itself, to its breaking point.

By 1917, around the time of his campaign against the indigo planters of Champaran district in Bihar, Gandhi was ready to dissociate himself from the term "passive." Uncomfortable now with the English term "passive resistance" and its Hindi equivalent, *nishkriya pratirodha*, he stressed *satyagraha's* affirmative, positive force. Satyagraha was founded not simply on disobedience of a passive kind, he insisted, but on the force of "active" resistance.[4] Two years later, he reasserted his preference, claiming, "civil resistance describes the struggle perfectly." As with most ideas that appeared to him by way of epiphany, Gandhi outlined the inadequacy of the term "disobedience" for the kind of action he wanted to perfect. "The phrase occurred to me by chance only a few days ago. . . . Civil Resistance is wider in meaning than 'civil disobedience,' though it suggests less than 'satyagraha.'"[5] Despite the growing popularity of the term "civil disobedience," which he would retain for much of his political career, Gandhi continued to favor the more forceful term "civil resistance." "Civil resistance is a complete substitute for violence," he declared in 1934. "Through it everyone has to achieve his own *swaraj*. This weapon has given spirit and new strength to the masses."[6] This spirit of the people, its value and place in Gandhi's reclamation of a force whose laws were, he insisted, at once new and natural, will be the focus of this chapter. At its center will be Gandhi's relationship to the spirit of the law itself.

A Transcendentalism of Limits

The philosophical and philological struggle that ensued after his return from South Africa notwithstanding, Gandhi held on resolutely to the term *satyagraha*. Unlike other related neologisms, he now considered it inexhaustible and untranslatable, even if, beginning with *Hind Swaraj* in 1909, suggestive equivalents, such as "soul-force" and "truth-force," had begun to appear in his writings. He wrote one of satyagraha's earliest biographies himself, first in Gujarati in 1923 while he was in prison, then had it translated into English, titling it *Satyagraha in South Africa* in a revealingly partial rendering of the Gujarati title, *Dakshina Africana Satyagrahano Itihas*, which, if fully translated, might have instead yielded *A History of Satyagraha in South Africa*. But approving Valji Desai's translation of the original (and the redaction of *A History* from the title), Gandhi assured the readers that "the spirit of the original has been very faithfully kept by the translator."[7] There was for him an element of newness and promise in the word *satyagraha*, then, whose radiant spirit gleamed in its full force only when it was unmoored from its originary history in South Africa, proclaimed untranslatable, and left islanded in a sea of colonial English discourse.

This emphasis on the untranslatability of the word was not meant to underscore satyagraha's linguistic peculiarity or Indic specificity. Instead, it was meant to posit a new universalism, a moral ontology of action indifferent to the particularities of history, a manner of social and ethical life whose transformative force lay not in the instrumentality (or even rationality) of the political but in the inalienable being (*sat*) of the principled agent. As redolent of an austere Sanskrit high culture as it was a bid for the vernacular-popular, *satyagraha* allowed Gandhi to conceptualize force as a fulcrum of everyday virtue and action distinct from its association with institutions and discourses of sovereignty. Unburdened by idioms of English and colonial political thought, this was a word, Gandhi hoped, that might potentially enter the universal history of resistance on a colonized people's terms: on terms of civility set by the oppressed rather than their masters; on terms of equality in which Europe's will to rule would be overcome by a principled vow and refusal of the colonized to be governed.

This belief required a moral firmness, a refusal to comply, and an active, indeed virulent, use of resistance. "But we lack the spirit of satyagraha to such an extent," Gandhi rued in *Hind Swaraj*, "that when ordered by the Government, we do more degrading things than dance naked before it."[8] A decade later, this lack of firmness in his people—as much against their own temptations as against external domination—would press against Gandhi with even greater vehemence. "Civility, good manners and humility—these virtues are at such discount these days that they seem to have no place at all in the building of our character," he lamented in December 1921, less than two months before his followers, in a moment of indiscriminate retaliation, would burn down a police station in north India, killing twenty-three colonial constables trapped inside. "It may be safely asserted that a person deficient in good manners lacks discrimination and that, lacking discrimination, he lacks every thing else. Vishvamitra's *tapascharya* was considered incomplete till he had learnt civility. Civility and humility are expressions of the spirit of nonviolence." The "non-violent non-cooperator," that is to say, the satyagrahi, Gandhi finished, "should regard civility as a distinct virtue." Only then might the exacting corporeal and spiritual sacrifices (*tapascharya*) of satyagraha provide the true "measure of an individual's or nation's culture."[9]

Satyagraha, clearly then, was not reducible to etiquette, equanimity, or even fairness. At its heart, on the contrary, was a search for measure (especially in one's fairness and equanimity toward others). It was an experiment in truthful discrimination, one in which the egalitarian promise of politics had to be tempered by the insuperable vow of self-sacrifice, in which the immanence of being had to be circumscribed by a transcendentalism of disciplinary limit (*maryada*) on the self. In this enforcement of limits, the satyagrahic conception of freedom—its "greatest force"—came closest to religion. "Freedom, both individual and religious, has always had and will always have many limits," Gandhi wrote during his second civil disobedience in 1931. "Religion does not hanker after rights, it hungers for restraints and restrictions."[10] If there was any text that would seek to forge another relationship between religion and freedom, a religion free of rules and limits, a religion with a moral obligation to democratize belief beyond measure, it was the one that would come just five years later. A religion unable to open itself unconditionally and immeasurably, Ambedkar would argue in *Annihilation of Caste*, was a myth, an economy of exchange and sacrifice. Such religion might have a spirit; it might even be a ghost. But it would be incapable of a truly "religious responsibility."

As words appeared and disappeared in a series of moral and philological experiments, meanwhile, and as Gandhi continued to express reservations about the passivity invoked by such terms as "passive resistance" and "civil disobedience," the concept of force in its positive firmness gradually became an irreplaceable constituent of his moral and political thought. Coupled with truth (*satya*), the concept of firmness (*agraha*) had perhaps come to affirm for Gandhi an ontological fact: that force exists even and especially when it is invisible, that the firmness and authenticity of force lie precisely in its capacity, like a mystical and secretive spirit—indeed, like God himself—to escape history. It was in this sense that force was spiritual, and spirit, force. Such force was available not for moral judgments as if it were a self-evident virtue or manifest vice. Rather, like nonviolence, this "force of spirit" belonged to the ontological order of being as such, to the order of absolute truth, and could therefore be thought only in terms of a transcendental principle. Hence, let us note, Gandhi's emphasis on "truth-force" as one of the primary virtues of the satyagrahi's personhood. When force became the constitutive part of one's being, when its ethics was mastered solitarily, immovably, invisibly, then it made nothing short of "true civilization" possible. A strong enunciation of such mastery appears in the thirteenth chapter of *Hind Swaraj*. "Civilization is that mode of conduct," writes Gandhi, "which points out to man the path of duty. Performance of duty and observance of morality are convertible terms. To observe morality is to attain mastery over our mind and our passions. So doing, we know ourselves. The Gujarati equivalent for civilization (*sudharo*) means 'good conduct.'"[11]

Moral firmness against passion—mastery—nourished not only the seeds of civility in conduct toward others but also one's ability to know "oneself." The firmness of the satyagrahi's egalitarianism, thus, was both relational (its form dependent on the presence and condition of the unequal), and ontological (its deepest truths so profoundly immersed in personal convictions that it was opaque to that very unequal whose presence generated its need). Firmness did not merely amplify the fact of one's difference from others; its very force emanated from the untouchable sovereignty of the deepest recesses of the soul. Gandhi considered this knowledge—and the will and ability to acquire it through exacting practice—to be the source of "soul-force." In 1919, in a letter he wrote to the Danish missionary Esther Faering, he elaborated on the significance of punitive vows and practices of self-purificatory sacrifice for satyagraha.

Body is matter, soul is spirit, and there is internal conflict between matter and spirit. Triumph of matter over the spirit means destruction of the latter. It is common knowledge that [this is] in the same proportion that we indulge the body or mortify the soul. Body or matter has undoubtedly its uses. The spirit can express itself only through matter or body. But that result can be obtained only when the body is used as an instrument for the uplifting of the soul. The vast majority of the human family do not use the body in that manner. The result is triumph of the body or matter over the spirit or the soul. We who know the soul to be imperishable living in a body which ever changes its substance and is perishable must by making fixed resolutions bring our bodies under such control that finally we may be able to use them for the fullest service of the soul. This idea is fairly clearly brought out in the New Testament. But I have seen it nowhere explained as fully and clearly as in the Hindu scriptures. You will find this law of self-denial written in every page of the *Ramayana* and the *Mahabharata*.[12]

Now, clearly, the language of courage, steadfastness, "resolution," and vow had taken a theological charge here. Gandhi would often locate the sources of the most truthful and impassioned form of these virtues in scripture. In the section that follows, I trace the early modern (and global) history of this supplanting of passion by interest, theology by ontology, and perhaps most crucially, mysticism by truth, within which I locate Gandhi's conception and rhetoric of spirit. The supple shift in the rhythm of this passage itself, however, warrants attention. What had begun with a sense of conflict between matter and spirit culminates in a proclamation of hierarchy between body and soul. The related gesture, namely, setting up a moral equivalence between the soul and spirit was even more significant. For in effect, this equivalence had allowed the institution of a hierarchy between and among a people, a sovereignty of those virtuous persons who use the body as merely a steadfast instrument of the soul over those who failed to do so. Elsewhere, coming close to the Platonic distinction between the sensible and intelligible, Gandhi would call this ability to use the body as instrument of spirit an "intelligent sacrifice."[13] In the final part of this chapter, I turn to the consequences of this satyagrahic investment in the faculties and instruments of mastery, one that mediated Gandhi's commitment to the quotidian rhythms, tact, and touchability of the human hand. And the hand, among all the human organs, would not remain just another instrument. In Gandhi's moral ontology, it would be positioned as a faculty proper to the soul of the satyagrahi alone, an organ of distinction between those who had spirit—that is, those who had firmness and force, *agraha* and *bal*—and those who did not, those who worked (and died) with a steady hand and those who failed, lacking by their very constitution the faculty to cultivate a relationship with their own death.[14]

Despite its affinity with traditions of ascetic solitude and mastery, this logic of firmness did promise to make possible a community of equals, a community—the ethical and social form of which Gandhi had outlined in the tenth chapter of *Hind Swaraj*, devoted to the relationship between "Hindus and Mahomedans"—in which individuals must be aware of the ineradicable difference that separates them as humans and species, a community in which the need for equality and the desire for happiness even of the greatest number must never be allowed to overcome the requirements of measure and civility.

The conduct of force was truly egalitarian, insisted Gandhi, only as long as its wielder was aware of difference, only as long as force itself was possessed differentially and unequally. It was this ironic egalitarianism—the demand for measure and fairness on the grounds of mastery and difference—that Gandhi often condensed in the term "spirit." This spirit (which had to be cultivated even in face of absolute subjugation) was radical in its universality. Even the weakest, most oppressed, most unequal, could not be seen as being completely devoid of spirit. In fact very often, the weakest might be the greatest spiritual exemplars of satyagraha. As a satyagrahi, Gandhi exhorted his followers during his first noncooperation movement in 1920:

My duty is to lay down my life. I can be called a true Kshatriya [member of a traditional caste of rulers and warriors] only if I can lay down my life in defending myself, my wife or my country. The weakest among the weak, even a woman, can cultivate the true Kshatriya spirit within himself or herself—that is, can tell an enemy, "I will stand firm—do your worst." Otherwise, even a murderer would have to be called a Kshatriya and a man who raised his hand to strike a woman could also be called a Kshatriya. That is why I proclaim to the people of India ever so loudly, that whatever they do, they should do in the true Kshatriya spirit.[15]

In the interest of the more limited task of retracing Gandhi's historiography of force that I have set myself in this chapter, I will pass over for now the immense provocation that Gandhi delivers by way of this anachronistic neologism, "Kshatriya spirit," which, even as it speaks of the weak as exemplary, invokes a very classical, hierarchical, and institutional history of force. Less than two decades later, as India was about to be dragged by Britain without her consent into the Second World War, Gandhi would lament again that there were no warrior Kshatriyas left in India; in fact, this was why, in his eyes, the nation's spirit had been so easily colonized by Britain.[16] I will return to the consequences this spiritualism in the later chapters. What strikes me as worthy of inquiry in these exhortations, given especially Gandhi's attentiveness to words and their rhythms, is the apparent looseness, even irresponsibility, with which he frequently conjures the idea of spirit. There seems, at first sight, to be little organization or pattern in the frequency with which this figure appears in his speeches and writings. And yet, despite the haphazardness, when spirit appears—as it frequently does during the years of his mass movements around 1920–1922 and 1930–1932—it acquires the form of an apparatus, an illocutionary and material scaffolding that imparts to the morals of satyagrahic action their immense and dogmatic resilience.

Thus, in Gandhi's attempt to reclaim the firmness of being for satyagraha's battle against the empire, spirit comes fundamentally to stand in for duty or obligation laid down by the moral law (*dharma*). "Kshatriya spirit," therefore, could be rendered in Gandhian parlance as *kshatriyadharma*. Spirit in such cases did not always reiterate the limits set by custom and birth. Sometimes it appealed, in a genuinely democratizing gesture, to the universal responsibility and right—if not ability—of everyone to become a Kshatriya worthy of the name. Two inseparable impulses in this institution of spirit-as-*dharma* are of interest then: first, Gandhi's braiding of spirit with the agent's sacrificial firmness and force, with his capacity to stare at his own death; and, second and more crucially, the alignment of this spirit (otherwise grounded in the autonomy of the fearless agent) with a transcendental—indeed, theologico-political—notion of civility, with the civility of rulers and sovereigns. Unpacking gradually what I mean by the "theologico-political" in Gandhi, I begin in this chapter with an examination of the relationship he forged between force, nonviolence, and spirit, placing his experiments in a global context within which the modern humanist discourse on "spirit" itself had first emerged. In anticipation of the chapters that follow, I will also delineate the enduring moral and political consequences of Gandhi's spiritual experiments for the emergence of a democratic ethos in modern India. My interest is not so much in providing a new genealogy of satyagraha as much as it is in examining the strategies and effects of Gandhi's attempt formulate a new mode of action for colonial India, an attempt from which emerged both the conceptual militancy and conservative energies of his politics.

When, in the second chapter of *Hind Swaraj*, the Reader, who ventriloquizes the anarchist views of the time, asks the Editor about the effects of the British decision to partition Bengal, Gandhi elaborates at some length on this new mode of action: "Hitherto we have considered that for redress of grievances we must approach the throne, and if we get no redress we must sit still, except that we may still petition. After the Partition, people saw that petitions must be backed up by force, and that they must be capable of suffering. This new spirit must be considered to be the chief result of the Partition."[17]

To probe this coupling of newness and spirit—newness *of* spirit—is to already place oneself within the economy of Gandhi's immense transactions (material and semantic) in force; economy because the problem of force, for him, was not as much a problem of violence as it was of measure and austerity, of reserve and discrimination; economy also because of the rhetorical profusion and polyvalence of "force" in his own thought; economy, above all, because satyagraha was always a matter of force against force in a battle for spirit. For apart from passages such as these, which appear throughout *Hind Swaraj*, Gandhi would devote two key chapters toward the end of the work to the category of force (and its relationship to satyagraha) alone. Despite bringing to the grammar of twentieth-century mass politics an unprecedented philological complexity, moreover, he would draw generously from a preexisting and ever expanding constellation of Indic and European metaphors and concepts. Categories such as nonviolence, or ideals of obligation grounded in the self (*swadharma*), visions even of self-rule (*swaraj*), had existed in the Indian imagination for decades before he arrived on the scene. It was his induction of firmness (*agraha*) and force (*bal*), his radical coupling of these two terms with the moral ontology of subjective being, which set his thought apart from the liberal and extremist thinkers of his time with a distinctiveness that would eventually transform colonial India's struggle to find a language of moral and political action proper to its struggle for sovereignty.[18]

But force also remained Gandhi's greatest, perhaps decisive, theoretical challenge. "These views are mine, and yet they are not mine," he had famously conceded in the foreword to the first edition of *Hind Swaraj*. "They are mine because I hope to act according to them. They are almost a part of my being. But, yet, they are not mine, because I lay no claim to originality."[19] Reorienting the introductory interpretation offered in the bilingual edition of *Hind Swaraj* by Suresh Sharma and Tridip Suhrud, who see in this gesture a Gandhian humility at work, one might insist that it was precisely in this self-effacing renunciation of "originality"—in the act of giving oneself up to another's force, potential, thought, or creativity—that Gandhi's most affirmative, self-conserving, and conservative ontology of being lay hidden.[20] Giving oneself up to another, after all, might also involve the extenuation of a profoundly originary, primitive, even indifferent, self: the self, Gandhi would say, in the absoluteness of its spirit.

Deeply aware of histories of words and names, Gandhi, at any rate, developed a productive relationship with them, mutating their definitions when he could not find appropriate replacements. In the period preceding him, for example, among the most influential users of the term *swaraj* were thinkers he had found "frightening" in his early years: the extremist Bal Gangadhar Tilak and the Hindutva theorist V. D. Savarkar, both conservative Brahmins from the Bombay Presidency, a region from which their radical critic Bhimrao Ambedkar would also emerge less than a generation later. But where Tilak and Savarkar had attached *swaraj* to visibility, upsurge, and spectacle (even though preparations for such seditious activity against the colonial state were to remain highly secretive), Gandhi appropriated *swaraj* for his moral theory of invisible, slow, and measured action. It was around his insistence on measure, in fact, that Gandhi's difference from revolutionary socialists and Ambedkar in the 1920s and the 1930s would curve toward an irreconcilable disjuncture.

But to say "irreconcilable" is not to say indifferent, let alone invulnerable. *Hind Swaraj* was not a treatise on the phenomenology of force in any simple sense. It was an ethical demand lodged with Europe and India alike for thinking, on global scale, the concept of force anew, even and especially in the shadows of that which Gandhi considered to be its spiritual antithesis: domination. Force against domination, in other words: this is perhaps why he arranged a pair of pivotal chapters in *Hind Swaraj*, titled "Brute Force" and "Passive Resistance," in such tight theoretical sequence. Each title named the other's antinomy, their author forging a paradoxical kinship between passivity and force, compassion and mastery, a paradox on which satyagraha's universalism—its spirit, or *bhaav*—would itself come to be founded. It has, of course, come to be taken as axiomatic since at least Raghavan Iyer's groundbreaking study appeared in 1973—and acknowledged in Gandhi's own wartorn times by figures as diverse as Romain Rolland, Rabindranath Tagore, and Martin Buber—that the apostle of nonviolence had spiritualized politics in an unprecedented manner, that he had brought back to political practice a "moral force" that had for long gone missing from the affairs of the human world. Rarely, however, is the value and consequence of this moralization or spiritualization—by which I mean Gandhi's ceaseless struggle for justice, his attempt to conceptualize equality at its limit—probed. Rarer still are interrogations of what the discourse of spirit made possible—and occluded—within satyagraha. To ask a classical question, which will exhaust neither the best nor the worst of Gandhi's experiments with truth, What was spirit?

Gandhi loved to reveal, often immediately after coining a neologism or announcing the tactics of a new political campaign, that he was gripped, inflamed, and possessed by spirit, that it had forced itself on him and revealed the truth to him, many a time in a dream. Often, he visualized this enlightenment in deeply religious hues; at other times, he was straightforward and unequivocal. "For me, there is no politics without religion," he declared in 1924.[21] But even though in the early years he spoke of spirituality as the religious core of satyagraha, the rhetoric of spirit increasingly appeared at the limit of Gandhi's religion, at the limit of his own religious pledge—and all religious traditions are constituted by this pledge—to maintain the dignity and equality of life; hence, what I call, after the moral tradition engaged with the question of justice (whose conceptual and rhetorical extremities Jacques Derrida has traced along the line that runs from Pascal to Benjamin), satyagraha's radical conservatism.[22] At its most militantly egalitarian and inclusive, satyagraha conserved inequality, a spiritual virulence, at its very source, which perhaps explains why Gandhi resorted to "spirit" not always at the moment of greatest ethical clarity but rather during moments of greatest (and gravest) moral ambiguity. Tracing the ambiguities of Gandhi's spiritual politics in this chapter, I offer a genealogy of satyagraha as an ontology of force, a genealogy that places force, or *bal*, at the center of Gandhi's metaphysics of morals. I turn away from an entire tradition of thinking about satyagraha that has developed around Gandhi's experiments with truth, seeking to illuminate instead the meanings and consequences of that other term in the couple, the equally spiritual if more intransigent concept, firmness.

First, I argue that beneath Gandhi's attempt to render politics into a moral ontology—that is, politics as an activity whose means, ends, and consequences were inseparable from the nature (and essence) of one's very being ("the mind is a restless bird," he had cautioned the "impatient" extremist nationalists in *Hind Swaraj*[23])—the rhetoric of spirit allowed him to think of satyagraha both as an ethics of extraordinary resistance and as a tactical instrument of the more realist obligations of politics. An ethics of complicity with those injunctions of the moral law that had sustained the classical idea of state and rule (*rajadharma*), in other words, was inscribed at the heart of satyagraha. It was this vigilant complicity with idioms of rule (*rajya*), with idioms of a transcendental sovereignty, whether of God or king, that I refer to as Gandhi's sensitive affinity with the theologico-political tradition. One might argue that the morals even of satyagrahic compassion for the unequal were mediated by this cautious affinity, a caution (or hesitation) most revealingly condensed in that ingenious and typically Gandhian term, "force of compassion" (*dayabal*). Other variations of this neologism, each of which accreted around Gandhi's struggle to overcome the distinction between sacrifice and nonviolence, were equally suggestive: "force of soul" or "force of self" (*atmabal*) and "force of character" (*charitrabal*).[24] Then, there was his attempt to attach the people's spirit to the idea of the warrior's obligation or sacrificial duty itself, whose example we have seen at work in the expression "Kshatriya spirit" or *kshatriyadharma*.[25] There was another if more stringent equivalent, which Gandhi simply called "discipline," or *maryada*, better rendered as "limit." In Chapter 3, I examine in some detail the logic and practice of Gandhi's *maryada dharma*, which developed specifically around his phenomenology of touching the untouchable.

Second, I propose that the rhetoric of spirit condensed Gandhi's articulation of satyagraha as a praxis of distinction, an awareness of difference between political actors and moral agents, and in the most fundamental way, as an articulation of sacrifice centered on the subject's ability to live and die differently. To have spirit, to be a nonanimal, according to Gandhi, not only demanded that one be aware of death. It demanded that one make death, with civility and fearlessness, the very foundation of one's existence or being.

This ability to die properly was not in itself adequate to satyagrahic discipline. The satyagrahis had to supplement it with their resolve to make the unequal equal; their sacrifice was to be tempered by a commitment to turn their finitude into an ameliorative force. Nothing other than this egalitarianism might differentiate the true satyagrahis—their "spirit of sacrifice"—from other humans and species. In that sense, force was the natural foundation of both the satyagrahis' egalitarianism and the discrete separateness of their being. For instance, animals, while exemplary, could not wield "soul-force." Around the category of force, Gandhi thus came to arrange not only the everyday practices of satyagrahic measure and limits but also the moral ontology of being in its transcendental sense. From this transcendentalism of limits, emerged his experiments in democracy, his attempts to spiritualize equality, in their greatest salience and equivocation. But to retrace the intricate steps of this equivocation is to follow not only the visible movements of Gandhi's thought, it is to also retrieve those interwar impulses and forces that pressed on his imagination in enduring and irresolvable ways. Spirit offers a potent opening into that history of Gandhian equivocation.

Spirit, Commerce, Politics

The rehabilitation of satyagraha within a philosophical history of spirit in its global form illuminates the contours of satyagraha's radical universalism—that is, its efficacy as a mode of action and resistance, its promise of a freedom whose radiance, Gandhi insisted, remained undiminished by, even indifferent to, the time, place, and nature of oppression against which it was mobilized. But a philosophical history also amplifies what was distinctively hierarchical in Gandhi's frequent lapses into the language of spiritual universalism itself. Approaching satyagraha through Gandhi's immense discourse on spirit, above all, illuminates a counterhistory of the relationship between religion and freedom in the colonial world, one in which the equivalence between the "religious" and "spiritual" realms is revealed in all its limits. Within the humanist tradition, this confusion of the "spiritual" with the "religious" produces another equivalence, that between "spirit" and the citizens' mystical, emotional, or psychological states (which must all be privatized and sequestered away from civic and political concerns such as public safety and freedom).

Yet, historically, the term "religion" has hardly ever exhausted the ambiguities that have materially, morally, and rhetorically constituted (especially in its interwar form) the idea of spirit and spirituality. Even a brief genealogy of "spirit," which I undertake in this section, will reveal that in its modern form "spirit" emerged neither as the equivalent of a compassionate and egalitarian religiosity nor as a consequence of the subversive energies of medieval cults and the oppositional rhythms of early modern mysticism, whose social worlds in Europe and India have been traced by historians ranging from Michel de Certeau to Sumit Sarkar and Eleanor Zelliot, among others.[26] Those emancipatory strands of popular and lower caste devotion in the Indian subcontinent, brought together under the name of *bhakti*, had always had a complex relationship with mainstream Indic traditions and their sacrificial theologies. While late medieval *bhakti* had rejoiced in an egalitarian turn of belief inward and had celebrated the mystical communion of the devotee with God unfettered by prohibitions of religion and caste, modern spiritualism had come to attach itself to a politics of cognitive and corporeal asceticism that belonged to a radically different universe, a decidedly hierarchical order of belief. In fact, the classical faith in God's transcendence into which all life must finally merge had mutated, by the early modern period, into a political—indeed, very often punitive—language of sacrifice and sovereignty. By the middle of the nineteenth century, the emancipatory energies of *bhakti* had shifted strongly toward the strident theologico-political nationalization of spirit (we might even call it the entrenchment of punitive humanism in modern religions), a shift exemplified by the emergence of figures such as Dayananda Saraswati in the Punjab and Swami Vivekananda in Bengal. The political theorist Jyotirmaya Sharma finds in this shift nothing short of a "restatement of religion."[27]

In a late essay, Ambedkar had discerned, almost as an aside, this susceptibility to the nationalization of theology inherent in anticolonial political thought and practice, its spirit curving outward into a demand for political equality with Europe all the while it came to hinge itself on a conformist, homogenizing, even monotheistic desire for mastery at home. How was this desire for mastery—this will to dominate—legitimized within the framework of the demand for freedom? It was sensitively done, Ambedkar argued, by positing a unity between religion and theology, between everyday injunctions on civic life and the insuperable moral law of government. "To understand the function and purposes of religion," therefore, wrote Ambedkar, "it is necessary to separate religion from theology. The primary things in religion are the usages, practices and observances, rites and rituals. Theology is secondary. Its object is merely to nationalize them."[28] If nationalists and theological humanists had since the nineteenth century cited the intricate variations in—and individual liberty to improvise on—norms of ritual, rule, and duty as a testimony to the freedom that Hindu *dharma* granted its practitioners, it was only because this freedom (without civic and social equality) could be explained in terms of a political theology, a transcendental law and economy of government, one in which the citizen's gaze could be turned away from punitive exclusions and cruelties of a highly practical religion and aligned along the spiritual demands and destiny of the Indian political.

This partially explains Ambedkar's enigmatic decision, right at the beginning of *Philosophy of Hinduism*, to place Hinduism among the "religions of the book," by which he did not mean that Hinduism was even close to being Abrahamic in its sacrificial consciousness, whose force he in fact deeply admired. He meant instead that as a "positive religion," Hinduism easily lent itself to dogmatic and ecclesiastical violence. In its modern form, indeed as a perennially modern religion that was improvised on and codified anew every time a new empire (Buddhist, Hindu, Muslim, or European) established itself in the subcontinent, the spirit of Hinduism was the spirit of complicity with the rules and injunctions of government (which he distinguished from the civic association and municipal values of Roman and Buddhist vintage). For Ambedkar, Hinduism embodied the spirit of the state in its unambiguously colonizing and psychic form, a property that had also lent it, paradoxically, its resilience under conditions of invasion, defeat, and statelessness.[29] It was perhaps in this sense that Gandhi remained a nineteenth-century figure, embodying an affinity simultaneously for law and spirituality, property and austerity, mastery and civility, in a balance of virtue and interest, but one that was itself redolent of a major strand within the European Enlightenment. It was a calibrated moral-juridical strategy that had helped European and colonial bourgeoisie consolidate itself through a potent mixing of theological rules and legislative improvisation (spiritual tutelage for the oppressed, claimed Ambedkar, as an alibi for their political representation).[30]

Spirit, one might argue, of course, had always had a theologico-political foundation rather than a purely mystical one. But by the middle of the nineteenth century, it had divided and separated itself decisively from its heterodox prehistory. In its modern iteration, restored to its philosophical place and seriousness by Hegel's *Phenomenology of Spirit* (1807), "spirit" came to denote not the sapient meanderings of mysticism but rather the actualization of reason. Transformed into a figure of antimystical rigor, the figure of spirit now instituted an experimental but stable measure—Hegel's "sense-certainty"—of means and ends. It is revealing that the *Phenomenology*, in its discussion of "consciousness," devotes so much space to elaborating on the relationship between "force" and "understanding." What philosophical work did this attentiveness to force, this placement of its rhythms at the center of the modern agent's subjective consciousness, do for Hegel? It established that the cognitive structure of the modern autonomous self, the self's freedom and spirit—that is, the self's moral psychological capacity to understand the conditions of its own existence, shaped and reshaped continually as it was by the struggle between servitude and autonomy—could have acquired its true form in the shadows of force alone. Spirit and force, freedom and sacrifice, will and mastery were conjoined at the very origin of the modern subject, their kinship emerging not from the antinomy but from the affinity between the religious ideal of the ethical self and the transcendental ambitions of the modern state.

There was a tension here, one that would open a fissure in Gandhi's own moral ontology. For if ethics had a co-creative relationship with the state, then the grounding of ethical life in rules of sacrificial self-dissolution, the extenuation of the self to the point of its perishing (*tapascharya*), could not be seen simply (or only) as a sign of the agent's heroic recession from the order of modern institutions. On the contrary, such a recession of the individual into spirituality was as likely to provide the state with its most invincible moral and political legitimacy. Indeed, no virtue of the citizenry has been seen, at least since Machiavelli, to be as fundamental to the endurance of the state in its republican form as the citizens' willingness to offer—and the state's right to demand—their life for the sake of collective liberty and security. "A soldier who disobeys an order to fire breaks the oath which he has taken and renders himself guilty of criminal disobedience," Gandhi wrote after a regiment of the famed Royal Garhwali Rifles of the British imperial army, in perhaps the most daring instance of civil disobedience, refused to open fire on unarmed and peaceful civil resisters in the city of Peshawar in April 1930. But speaking to the French newspaper *Le Monde* two years later, Gandhi was unequivocal in his denunciation of the soldiers' discriminating sense of ethics. What was improper was not only their transgression against the sovereignty of military rules. What was wrong was the soldiers' belief that the right of *decision* (to fire or not) lay with them. "I cannot ask officials and soldiers to disobey, for when I am in power, I shall in all likelihood make use of those same officials and those same soldiers. If I taught them to disobey I should be afraid that they might do the same when I am in power."[31] In laying down this punitive principle of what he called, in his *Discourses on the Gita, sattvik* sacrifice (sacrifice within the limits of the moral law of obedience and humility), Gandhi was not in opposition but perhaps in greatest proximity to a certain spirit of European humanist and nationalist thought.

Spirit ran into the rough weather of empire nevertheless. Less than a century after the youthful adventures of *Phenomenology of Spirit* and the mature certainties of its sequel, *Philosophy of Right*, had transformed the moral and juridical framework of Western thought, spirit had begun to return to Europe in a new form. Its Hegelian rigor had now acquired the form of a philosophical anxiety. This was not the moral anxiety of empire and slavery, which had been neither new nor irrelevant to Hegel's own analytical apparatus. As Susan Buck-Morss has shown, the violent (and dialectical) structure of plantation labor and colonial resistance, which became for Europeans difficult to avoid once the Haitian Revolution had stamped itself on the continent's humanist consciousness, may have already left deep imprints on Hegel's theoretical analysis of the master-slave relationship.[32] But in its second coming, the anxiety of spirit was as thoroughly existential, as much a question of Europe's interiority and singularity, as it had been territorial and world-historical in Hegel's time. In this second coming, spirit's return was facilitated by the inner anxiety of Europe's own decline and decay, by the wariness set in by its unbridled capitalist expansion abroad and concomitant cultural alienation and persecution at home, and by the worry, above all, that not merely its imperial headlands and marketplaces but Europe's very spirit, its exemplary destiny, was in crisis.

By the end of the First World War, spiritual anxiety had turned into brute pessimism. Faced with a continent destroyed irreversibly by colonial offensives and the grim technological war waged on nature and species alike, intellectuals such as Martin Heidegger, Edmund Husserl, Max Scheler, Oswald Spengler, and Paul Valéry, among others, closed philosophical ranks.[33] Their plea for Europe's cosmopolitan generosity turned into an obsessive focus on Europe's provincial authenticity, and sometimes, as in Scheler's case, into an obsession with the spiritual distinction between the Germans and the English themselves. The desire to vouchsafe the continent's dignified smallness (the original Europe, according to Valéry, had been a small cluster of marketplaces on the Mediterranean) mutated, in time, into a categorical inability to see beyond Europe. Rather than a sustained questioning of Europe's capitalist and colonial foundations, the crisis forced an anxious and mournful return of intellectuals to that very spirit, with a cryptic, almost Burkean adherence to national peculiarity-as-national tradition in tow. "Instead of casting away all our old prejudices," Burke had written in his *Reflections on the Revolution in France* (1790), "we cherish them to a very considerable degree, and to take more shame to ourselves, we cherish them because they are prejudices."[34] A century later, the conservative tradition of celebrating prejudice as national virtue (that needed to be preserved from the corruptions of imperial hubris), the indomitable ability to express glee and scoff in the same breath at the peculiarity of one's culture, had given way to—and indeed formulated—a global system of national-commercial states. By the late nineteenth century, imperial anxiety, at the heart of which in Burke's time had been the corrupt trading companies threatening to all but dissolve the rich essence of domestic mores and traditions, had aligned itself with the quasi-religious rhetoric, simultaneously, of Europe's spiritual smallness (the self-sufficient austerity of its being) and its world-historical destiny (backed by an expansionist geopolitical and technological force). The return to Europe's dignity, its purity and responsibility grounded in the care of the soul and being, was accompanied, in other words, by an aggressive universalism abroad. Spirit had returned this time not exactly as a supplement to eighteenth-century evangelical religion or Christian humanism, commerce or sociability, although the rhetoric of neither would be spared. Instead, it had reemerged as a shelter for the alliance between national markets, individual asceticism, and imperial force. Most important, it had returned as a moral theory of those little freedoms afforded by everyday reciprocity, provincial solitude, and ascetic practices of the self that would least trouble the unconscionable violence of the European markets overseas and at home.

"Spirit came first," argued Valéry in 1939, "and it could not have been otherwise. It is the commerce of spirits that was necessarily the first commerce in the world, the very first, the one that started it all, necessarily the original: for before swapping goods, it was necessary to swap signs, and consequently a set of signs had to be agreed on. There is no market, no exchange without language; the first instrument of all trade is language. . . . Consequently, in saying that the word is identical with spirit," Valéry concluded, "I am not uttering a heresy."[35] Valéry's attempt to return spirit—and the European mind—to the language of ordinary commerce—and rehabilitate commerce as spiritual in the most ontological-cognitive sense—was symptomatic of the intellectual disengagement and disenchantment that had ensued in the wake of the violence of European states. But it was an ambivalent disenchantment, an incomplete and complicit one. It thrived precisely in proximity to that which the European state and its marketplaces had made possible over the preceding two centuries. For what Valéry's celebration of trade as the first moral language between people (law not only as the language of humanity but its very spirit) revealed was not simply the disavowal, even forgetting, of the empire that lay at the heart of European attempts to imagine a cosmopolitan world, a world where responsibility—the obligation to freedom and justice, not to forget democracy—would still be a "European responsibility." It also revealed a paradox fundamental to the new spiritual dispensation: the interwar turn toward the provincial richness of everyday life, the nostalgic belief in the spiritual authenticity of ordinary people, the plea to return to the smallness of Europe, which offered—according to Valéry—an ethical escape from the technological and materialist degradation of European spirit, had not so much facilitated a break from the reason of imperial commerce as it had come to thrive on the artifice of colonial commerce itself. Spirit had returned not in crisis (despite the rhetoric of its destitution) but rather in stridently universal-izing form, bringing back with its melancholic Zeitgeist the very hierarchies and exclusions that had constituted the modern world in the first place.

Anticolonialism was not any more innocent of this exclusion—albeit, in its case, it would be an internal exclusion—than Europe was. In fact, the mutually nourishing relationship between empire and nationalism, each fos-tering the other, ensured that the spirit of theologico-political humanism returned everywhere. As I have argued in Chapter 1, an aggressive rhetoric of political resistance, articulated around the discourse of civilizational en-durance and backed by ideals of moral courage and sacrificial theology, had already begun to take shape in colonial India by the last quarter of the nine-teenth century. Religion could now be understood, in a Kantian sense, within the limits of reason alone. So that while truth could be reasoned about in dif-ferent ways, sought in multifarious activities and faiths, the most authentic and sovereign truth could be sought only in the Vedas and Upanishads. Love of God in no way mandated a nonhierarchical communion with the divine and human others. Instead, love was rehabilitated in the empirical ability to see God. Needless to add, only a few were gifted with this spiritual fac-ulty. Thus, *bhakti*'s radical rejection of the hierarchical four-fold caste system (*varnashramadharma*) as the foundation of moral obligation was decisively reversed. In its place, political theologists such as Vivekananda returned to the Kshatriya kings of antiquity as exemplars of just action. Like Gandhi, who arrived on the scene less than quarter of a century later, Vivekananda too had latched onto the monarchical idea of *kshatriyadharma* as the founding ground of moral responsibility. Everyday morals, thus understood in terms of a perpetual sacrifice, could be firmly positioned as the vehicle of national destiny, one in which theology might be muscled into and blended seamlessly with projects of spiritual restitution and territorial sovereignty. Hinduism was not merely nondualist anymore, in that it required one to be equally indif-ferent to sorrow and joy, life and death, being and nonbeing. Nondualism (*advaita*) itself became a theological system in which others could be judged, ranked, asked to conform, barred, and mastered. In figures such as Tilak and Vivekananda, the spirit of an ancient faith had acquired a moral ontology of everyday life appropriate to the pursuit of sovereignty in its most expansion-ist and aggressive modern form.

Gandhi, who returned to India in 1915, by which time both liberal and extremist nationalists had seemingly exhausted their moral arsenal (against the empire and each other), remained at once supple and resistant to these theologico-political realignments. In fact, he would not have fully read Tilak's magisterial *Gitarahasya* (1915), a call to arms veiled behind a dazzling 1,200-

page commentary on a fratricidal text that Tilak authored during his imprisonment in Burma, whose first edition in Gujarati and Hindi appeared only two years later in 1917. Gandhi had deep affinities with the subject-centered faith of the *bhakti* tradition, from which emerged in 1931 perhaps the most inventive and significant of his neologisms, *harijan*, a name he chose in 1931 for the Hindu untouchable (*asprishya*). Yet, while his pantheon of *bhakti* saints included Tukaram, a poet belonging to the Kunbi community, traditionally a low caste of peasants and grocers, satyagraha's kinship with emancipatory *bhakti* remained ambiguous. If Tilak's politics based on "birthright" frightened Gandhi, his hermeneutic mastery and disciplinary style resonated with Gandhi's own literary-philosophical ambitions. In fact, with its insistence on scriptural authority, its dogged emphasis on reading scripture only in a disciplined way, its assertion that truth ensued (and might be found) only in the groundlessness of the transcendental being (*brahman*), satyagrahic spiritualism marked a distinctive break within *bhakti*'s mystical religiosity. *Bhakti*'s celebration of ecstasy, mirth, and madness as ways to escape the oppressiveness of human existence was replaced, in a series of interpretive and juridical measures, by another—more Kantian—universalism, in which moral duty was extracted from the particularities of social and sensual worlds. Satyagraha's sacrificial rules and obligations (*dharma*) would draw its legitimacy, in the final instance, only from nondualism's disciplinary proprieties.

In an essay on the *Gita* composed in the mid-1920s, Gandhi revealed his closeness to *advaita* Hinduism's negative theology, his attraction to its world of transcendental truth and meaning, in the most unequivocal manner. And this transcendental truth was a question of limits, a question of faithfulness to the laws of genre, a fidelity to the law as such.

Anyone who offers to interpret the Shastras must have observed prescribed disciplines in his life. Those, however, who are devoid of this spirit and lack even faith, are not qualified to explain the meaning of the Shastras. . . . The Shastras are not meant for those who question the validity of the principle of truth itself, or rather, the Shastras are no better than ordinary books for such a person. No one can meet him in argument. Anyone, on the other hand, who does not find the principle of non-violence in the Shastras is indeed in danger, but his case is not hopeless. Truth is a positive value, while non-violence is a negative value. Truth affirms. Non-violence forbids something which is real enough. Truth exists, untruth does not exist. Violence exists, non-violence does not. Even so, the highest *dharma* for us is that nothing but non-violence can be. Truth is its own proof, and non-violence is its supreme fruit. The latter is necessarily contained in the former. Since, however, it is not evident as truth is, one may try to discover the meaning of the Shastras without believing in it. But the spirit of non-violence alone will reveal to one the true meaning of the Shastras.[36]

This is a demanding passage, with Gandhi, in the classic manner of *advaita*'s negative theology, trying to affirm the transcendental ground of nonviolence in its very groundlessness and nonexistence. The most immediately noticeable aspect of this formulation is that it discovers the "spirit of non-violence" in the truth imparted by the Shastras, a move that is reminiscent of that deep tradition in Hindu political theology whose modern lineaments we have just traced. But Gandhi also broke from that conservative tradition of political theology and its propensity to impute universality to its own scripture, which had veered so aggressively since the late nineteenth century toward a tendency to dominate other creeds, faiths, and truths. The biggest wave of cow-protection riots, instigated by the militant Hindu Gaurakshini Sabhas, had engulfed northern India in 1893, the same year that Gandhi landed in Durban to work for a Muslim trading company. In contrast to the violently revivalist strand whose resurgence he had witnessed at home at the beginning of his oceanic itinerary, it is not surprising that Gandhi's belief in the ultimate authority of the Shastras was not so much universal in an institutional and territorial sense—in that everyone who was a member of the political community must be bound to believe in them—as it was ontological, that is to say, related to the person's being (*sat*). One had to be proper (*sattvik*), that is to say, even-minded toward pleasure and pain, life and death, given over to a humility of being that only one's awareness of limits and mortality might impart, to understand that there was a lesson on nonviolence in even those scriptures that otherwise seem to be inextricable from histories of war and sacrifice. One could not stand outside this logic (as a nonbeliever or nihilist) and judge the moral principles (*niti*) enshrined in the scriptures. On the contrary, the subject could bear witness to the scripture's spirit of nonviolence only when its truth had become the "moral fiber" of his being.

Belief in nonviolence, in other words, stemmed not from empirical evidence of the existence of God but from a transcendental groundlessness in which the locus of even one's own being remained unseen like a seed beneath the ground, a being whose truth could be grasped only through infinite practice and experimentation. As Gandhi puts it in his remarkable enunciation of this invisible spirit of nonviolence (*ahimsa*), "violence exists; non-violence does not." In fact, this entire passage, taken from "The Meaning of the Gita," an essay he published in 1925, exhibits an astonishing continuity with the seventeenth chapter of *Hind Swaraj*, titled "Passive Resistance," with one significant distinction: in that early work, as we shall see in the next section, this nonexistence and invisibility of being was attached to force. Sixteen years later, it is nonviolence that provides Gandhi the foundation for his moral ontology. Force and nonviolence, perhaps, shared an inalienable property: they both emerged from a truth that was invisible, which did not exist, and which was therefore constituted, like spirit—Ambedkar would say, like myth—in its very negation.

Gandhi was most modern, even if not decisively humanist, in ascribing this spiritual invisibility to force. For he had placed himself, consciously or otherwise, within an early modern tradition in which the discourse on spirit had returned not as a substitue for religiosity in an everyday sense but as a set of meditations on the ethics and politics of sovereignty and the state. After all, inasmuch as truth was now spiritual and situated in the groundless recesses of a transcendental being in which all life was seen to merge, inasmuch as the search for a truthful self had receded into the minutiae of everyday practices regulated by scriptural injunctions, did not this truth bear striking resemblance—indeed, tendencies of complicity—with precisely those discourses of sovereignty in which the state had been given, at least since Hegel, a spiritual sanctity? Had not this moral ontology of satyagrahic being, even if grounded in the little rhythms and freedoms of the everyday, somewhere veered too close to that other spirit, the spirit of the laws? Is that why thinkers as diverse as Valéry and Gandhi could come to press the rhetoric of spirit as easily into the service of their pronouncements about the crisis of civilization as they could press it into the service of their affirmations of the moral responsibility (and thus, quasi-transcendental sovereignty) of their own civilizations?[37]

Despite the significant philosophical and rhetorical overlap between their antimaterialist energies, which Leela Gandhi has recently reconstructed, both these tendencies—affirmations of civilizational crisis and calls for the recession of the agent into the everyday minutiae of self-fashioning as an act of spiritual resistance against capital and empire—were to remain inseparable from the transcendental logic of the modern state (that had, in turn, secured the early modern discourse on civic virtue, sacrifice, and liberty).[38] Interwar phenomenology itself, its deep sensitivity to the texture and richness of everyday life notwithstanding, tended to swerve toward an ontological essentialization of—and was even coeval with—that sacrificial logic. In the "Postscript" (1943) added to his 1929 essay "What is Metaphysics?," Martin Heidegger installed sacrifice as the essence of the very "truth of being," locating its courage and incalculability in the "neighborhood of the indestructible." "Sacrifice tolerates no calculation," wrote Heidegger. It refuses the "obsession with ends," which only distorts "the essence of sacrifice." Sacrifice was freedom in "action," perhaps the only way of "preserving the favor of being."[39] Heidegger was not alone. The striking resonance between Husserl's phenomenology outlined in the middle of the 1930s in his *Crisis of the European Sciences* and the classical Indic doctrine of the transcendence of soul found in the Upanishads—in which death in its barest and most corporeal form is sanctified as a

mere passage to the worldly subject's merging with infinite and transcendental being (*brahman*)—was but one more example of this theologico-political
or ontotheological (indeed, Indo-European) configuration. Measure or moderation—a certain mastery over the passions of the self, a merchantlike austerity—was crucial to the ethics of what Gandhi would, on his part, call the
"*mantra* of living by dying." For, measure (limit, control, restraint, juridically
enforced impediment even) calibrated the exorbitant practices of sacrificial
self-intensification with the imperative of ordinary commerce and municipal
life fundamental to civic humanism. The "spirit of commerce," wrote Montesquieu in a suggestive passage on democracy in *The Spirit of the Laws* (1748),
"brings with it the spirit of frugality, of economy, of moderation, of work, of
wisdom, of tranquility, of order, and of regularity. In this manner, as long as
this spirit prevails, the riches it creates do no have any bad effect."[40]

It is astonishing how much of this spirit of measure, this critique of passion, could come to permeate a text like *Hind Swaraj*. At any rate, a less militant
framework within which Gandhi's *kshatriyadharma* acquired its disciplinary
form, or rather, a *kshatriyadharma* closer to humanist interest than religious
disinterest, becomes visible when anticolonial morals are refracted through
this philosophical history of spirit. In fact, historians of anticolonialism have
tended to ignore this other history altogether. This has happened not the least
because of an easy conflation of spirit with religiosity (and from a related consensus that has developed around Gandhi's politics); namely, that his spiritualism, centered on the mastery of the self—to be attained through solitary
practices such as celibacy, spinning, fasting, voluntary poverty—was meant to
clear for the colonial subject a morally thick, deliberate, and exacting route for
escaping a world where all action had been contaminated by the calculative demands of politics in its modern form.[41] But did the spirit of satyagraha belong
to the order of the mystical proper? Was the mystical itself, let alone the act of
refusing to attach it to politics, ever autonomous of the moral law?

Gandhi's resistance against calls for a return to subversive and heterodox
forms of spiritual pursuits, exemplified at the turn of the century, for instance,
by theosophy's engagement with the occult, was suggestive. He had, he said,
little time for such mystical experiments with ghosts and specters.[42] He did
retrieve the grammar of spirituality from the politico-religious mobilizations
of the late nineteenth century, even as he courageously disavowed the desire
for a modern state that lay at the heart of those majoritarian movements.
"The State," he argued in a 1935 interview, "represents violence in a concen-
trated and organized form. The individual has a soul, but as the State is a soulless machine, it can never be weaned from violence to which it owes its very
existence."[43] And yet the idea of spirit—indeed, of the soul, which Gandhi

had coupled with force to create that defining neologism, "soul-force," or *at-mabal*—had itself, since Locke's *An Essay Concerning Human Understanding* (1694), never ceased to be an inextricable part of the modern "invention of consciousness."[44] What came to be called, somewhat loosely, "the spiritual," then, was not the same as that which had been called, in an earlier epoch, "the mystical." The spirit invoked in Montesquieu's *Spirit of the Laws*, which strove to establish such categories as good government, legitimate force, and general obedience as universal norms for democracy was, after all, a figure that encapsulated the ambitions of liberal morality. Hegel's *Phenomenology of Spirit* itself cannot be extricated from this struggle to grasp the logic of collusion between force, consciousness, and autonomy, which modern capitalist society was faced with. Even in the young Hegel's *The Spirit of Christianity* (1798–1799), spirit was not as much the constituent matter of religion as it was a trope for Christianity's successful institution of the family at the center of the ethical world. This early induction of the family into juridical discourse only anticipated some of the more fundamental passages on sovereignty, property, and kinship that would eventually emerge in the *Philosophy of Right*. And then Max Weber's *The Protestant Ethic and the Spirit of Capitalism* (1905) finally connected, in the most unequivocal fashion, the inwardness of Protestant Christianity with the brutal aggression of its capitalist spirit. It was Weber who warned that spirit actualized not the triumph of the mystical but rather its defeat, ushering in a carefully structured system of appropriation of human and natural resources, of which spirit as such was a constitutive part, not an enchanting antithesis.

Gandhi's writings bear an unmistakable imprint of his enthusiasm for the spiritual ethos and civic sociability of commercial society, even if it was expressed in muted terms and given other names. His sustained critique of the state, his repudiation of revolutionary action, and his institution of the *ashram* as a nourishing ground for regulated and measured equality seemed at times to be coming from this attraction to the classical theory of liberty as liberty from ecclesiastical and governmental interference rather than from his moral and political commitment to—if his attitude can be called at all—a philosophical anarchism.[45] Satyagraha, he insisted, was a struggle for the civic right to (and gift of) noninterference. It was as much a science rooted in the moral law and rules that depended on the "government's civility" as it was an ethics of measure and sacrifice. "It is my firm conviction," he cautioned, "that if the State suppressed capitalism by violence, it will be caught in the coils of violence itself, and will fail to develop nonviolence at any time."[46]

Under the figure of spirit, then, reemerged not merely the plea for restoring the transcendence of the soul to its moral, political, and philosophical seriousness (in the common manner of Husserl's phenomenology and the theological mandate of *advaita* Hinduism). In the name of spirit also emerged a brilliantly reoriented theory of freedom as obligation to the law (if not reducible to its sovereignty alone), one that would both resist and collude with the most dogmatic injunctions of classical religion. Viewed in the light of a global and philosophical history of spirit, *Hind Swaraj*, mounting as it had a formidable ethics of force and measure, seems not as untimely as it appears to be at the first glance. Rather, it fit right into the spiritual anxiety and imperative of the times. Gandhi, as I show in the sections that follow, would emerge both as a radical dissenter within this tradition and its most rigorously conservative theorist.

Crypt of Faith

Pervasive, infinitesimal, differential, and undetectable its very nature, force (*bal*), and its counterpart, resistance (*agraha*), were to become the foundation of satyagraha's moral ontology. And while this force was constituted by one's effort in the most solitary, heroic, and corporeal sense, it left no evidence, history, or trace. The force of nonviolence was "cryptic" in the strongest sense of the term, at once aligned with a religious universalism and charged with an irrevocable secrecy. Of this invisible, mystical, and infinitesimal force, Gandhi spoke for the first time at length in *Hind Swaraj*.

The fact that there are so many men still alive in the world shows that it is based not on the force of arms but on the force of truth or love. Therefore, the greatest and most unimpeachable evidence of this force is to be found in the fact that in spite of the wars of the world it still lives on. Little quarrels of millions of families in their daily lives disappear before the exercise of this force. Hundreds of nations live in peace. History does not and cannot take note of this fact. History is really a record of every interruption of the even working of the force of love or of the soul. Two brothers quarrel; one of them repents and reawakens the love that was lying dormant in him; the two again begin to live in peace; nobody takes note of this. But if the two brothers, through the intervention of solicitors or some other reason take up arms or go to law—which is another form of the exhibition of brute force—their doings would be immediately noticed in the Press, they would be the talk of their neighbors and would probably go down to history. . . . History, then, is a record of an interruption of the course of nature. Soul-force, being natural, is not noted in history.[47]

Setting aside the counterintuitive formulation of force as a symptom, or even extension, of love, it is clear in this passage that Gandhi was bringing an unprecedented rigor to reconceptualizing what is perhaps the most overused and least textured category in the modern political tradition, "force." Indeed,

Gandhi's world, natural and human, was built around the minutiae of force. And satyagraha, much like the world it wanted to transform, multiplied its own force among ordinary brothers and families. Its effects could only be spiritual, for only spirit was everywhere yet invisible, only spiritual force remained unrecorded and "immeasurable."[48] Elsewhere in *Hind Swaraj*, Gandhi spoke of this force in the name of justice and dignity, as an instrument of India's emancipation from colonial slavery. But this force, while profoundly material, was also cognitive, a faculty grounded in the belief that humanity's potentiality (and intrinsic justness) was beyond measure. "To believe that what has not occurred in history will not occur at all is to argue disbelief in the dignity of man."[49] By the late 1920s, he had begun to connect this idea of justice with the state of *Ramarajya*, the spiritual kingdom or rule of the epic hero-king Rama.[50] It was on the seemingly anachronistic question of Rama's resplendent and transcendental heroism that his argument with Ambedkar gathered its force in the 1930s.

Authentic "truth-force" or "love-force," Gandhi argues meanwhile, escapes history. He marks out and separates this force from the meanings generally associated with the general conceptions of force. In those conventional iterations, "force" denotes practices such as coercion, bomb making, revolutionary assassinations, police action, military violence, and even the litigious spectacle of the district, national, and international courts, whose perverse ability to muster "brute force," as much in the name of the law as against it, imparts to them the status of historical events. In contrast, satyagraha attempts to move not simply beyond the "law of nations" but beyond the metaphysics of humanist history itself. Passive resistance, Gandhi argues elsewhere, is filial, ancestral, and "natural."[51] And clearly in this passage, this force is posited as belonging neither to the state nor the transcendental sovereignty of God. This force belongs only to the realm of civility between ordinary actors, a civility that requires not juridical arbitration but moral firmness and equality.[52] Yet for Gandhi, this courageous and early attempt to work out the idea of firmness proved difficult to keep separate either from the logic of transcendence or from institutional-scriptural foundations of sovereignty.

Let me put the difficulty in even stronger terms: it was precisely Gandhi's attentiveness to the egalitarian possibilities of force, which he sought to retrieve otherwise and outside its normative meanings and valences, his promise to the people of a force spiritualized, that released the most insidious energies in his program of justice. In its coupling of an experimental and contingent force grounded in everyday practices with an ontological, transcendental, and spiritual truth, was not satyagraha making a call to a certain sovereignty? Was this call only for a militant amplification of the self's capacity to master itself? In another sense, how strongly, how successfully, could this affirmation of mastery be kept within the confines of the self? More important, how discrete was this sovereign self from those laws and theories of juridical rule and the moral realm of the state with which it had come to share, consciously or otherwise, the discourse of spiritual transcendence?

Perhaps it was not an accident that the various linguistic renderings of satyagraha that Gandhi experimented with over the following four decades invariably mobilized visions of strength and mastery, whether such mastery was grounded in the satyagrahi's soul, his compassion, his abilities with the hand, or simply his "inner struggle" with spirit. It was perhaps not happenstance either that *Hind Swaraj* itself was written in the midst of its author's visceral, feverish, and self-confessed possession by spirit. I will return to this state of possession. Let us note for now that Gandhi would come to conjure the image and metaphor of spirit prolifically, first in South Africa in the years leading up to the composition of *Hind Swaraj*, and subsequently in India around the years of his three major civil disobedience movements against the empire. But unlike the concept of force, he never got down to elaborating on it. At the peak of his first noncooperation movement in 1921, in the wake of his promise of "swaraj within one year," he nevertheless revealed his immense interest in spirit in the most unequivocal fashion.

I know that opposition stares you and stares me in the face even today. We have just broken the ground, but it is true that if we are going to win this great battle that you, the people of Calcutta, commenced in September of last year we shall have to continue as we have begun in full faith. I am not ashamed to repeat before you who seem to be nurtured in modern traditions—who seem to be filled with the writing of modern writers, I am not ashamed to repeat before you that this is a religious battle. I am not ashamed to repeat before you that this is an attempt to revolutionize the political outlook—that this is an attempt to spiritualize our politics. . . . My faith has never burnt as brightly as it burns tonight, as I am talking to the young men of Bengal. You have given me greater hope, you have given me greater courage—you have given me greater strength.[53]

Clearly, this call to civilization and spiritualization of the people was not a call for absolute unity, a remission of difference, an absence of discrimination. Rather, spirit was conceived here in terms of a "fullness of faith," a cultivated and measured brimming over, a movement toward a "religious battle" in which religion's ontotheological truth could be understood only by renouncing all extant universalisms; by overcoming all the demands of identity and sameness that the modern tradition compresses under the terms "nation" and "secularism"; by reclaiming politics, above all, as an extension of religious belief, everyday social mores, and, if need be, shared prejudices. From within the fecund diversity of this "full faith," as Gandhi had insisted in *Hind Swaraj*, grew a new spirit, a new practice and rhythm of transformative force, one that renounced the universalism of European and imperial humanism without relinquishing the faith in universalism as such, which makes any religion possible in the first place. As this inflamed and hyperbolic speech, delivered in Calcutta as "the honor of Islam trembled in balance," shows, there was much in Gandhi's speeches and writings that might suggest a synergy between his conceptualization of religion and his rhetoric of spirit, both aligned against the oppressive materialism and incivility of "modern civilization." It was in this sense that he often mobilized the category of "simplicity," which like firmness, or *agraha*, he described as his "faith in the inborn religious instincts of every Indian—be he a Hindu or be he a Mohammedan, Christian, Parsi or a Jew—it is that faith in me which has sustained me throughout all the dark days of scoffing, of skepticism, and of opposition."[54]

A "full faith" brimming with force was also, in Gandhi's view then, the simplest. But it was so not because such faith was easy to adhere to. No creed, Gandhi would warn Ambedkar, was easy, shorn of violence and myth, free of punishment, absolutely egalitarian. Instead, a faith was simple despite its fullness and complexity, despite its exposure to (and cultivation of) difference, because it was firm. For Gandhi, the universality of true religion lay in its awareness of the irreconcilable and necessary difference in beliefs, in its resoluteness against the conversion of the world into one and homogeneous faith, in its resistance against a world aspiring to sameness and identity. Satyagraha's universality (and its opposition to *conversion*—the act of leaving one faith for another—in which Ambedkar saw the seeds of authentic freedom) was constituted around this paradoxical ethics, an ethics of fullness grounded in insurmountable and desirable distinction.

But what was insurmountable could not just be let off, it had to be outflanked. Fullness as ethics required, on the one hand, an intensification of otherness and distinction and, on the other hand, a trivialization, even forgetting of conflict and exclusion. At its worst, this ethics, its inclusive and discriminating universalism, quickly lapsed back into a mode of theological appropriation, a habit of claiming or stealing that which was not satyagraha's own, a gesture of celebrating those religions whose birth and history, theology and politics, pitched them in nothing short of a revolutionary opposition to the spirit of satyagraha. One could discern in these satyagrahic gestures the false act, even pretense, of merging with—without converting its own principles in the light of—that faith that was separated from its own by an abyss. And this appropriative tendency, whose target was often classical Buddhism, appeared rather early in Gandhi's writings. Two years before he coined the word *satyagraha*, he betrayed this secret in his *Lectures on Religion*.

Lord Buddha was moved to pity when he saw his religion [Hinduism] reduced to such a plight. He renounced the world and started doing penance. He spent several years in devout contemplation and ultimately suggested some reform in the Hindu religion. His piety greatly affected the minds of the Brahmins, and the killing of animals for sacrifice was stopped to a great extent. It cannot, therefore, be said that the Buddha founded a new or different religion. But those who came after him gave his teachings the identity of a separate religion. King Ashoka the Great sent missionaries to different lands for the propagation of Buddhism, and spread that religion in Ceylon, China, Burma and other countries. A distinctive beauty of Hinduism was revealed during this process: no one was converted to Buddhism by force. People's minds were sought to be influenced only by discussion and argument and mainly by the very pure conduct of the preachers themselves. It may be said that, in India at any rate, Hinduism and Buddhism were but one, and that even today the fundamental principles of both are identical.[55]

This passage has taken us to the fanatical extremities of Gandhi's conception of firmness. A profoundly appropriative and insidious force is set to work here, one that credits even the worst of Hinduism with giving birth to the best of that which had emerged against it. And, that faith that had emerged against Hinduism, argues Gandhi, was no revolution, no spiritual insurrection, no inauguration of religious newness. It was a mere extension of a religious fraternity, an expansion of the Indic family of creeds, a different way of living an ethical and nonviolent life that had sprung from an unfortunate feud over ecclesiastical decadence and sacrificial excess (both at war and in ritual). But perhaps most important in Gandhi's appropriation was his attempt to wrest back the revolutionary force of Buddhism for (and within) Hinduism's theological universality. This involved a sublation of theological conflict through the language of moral and aesthetic force. "A distinctive beauty of Hinduism was revealed during this process: no one was converted to Buddhism by force." It was because of Hinduism's aesthetic generosity, then, that Buddhism spread among converts without force, remaining nonviolent, attuned to a compassionate universality, awake to love for the human and animal alike. The moment it aligned itself with an imperial and proselytizing state (an alliance Gandhi believes was alien to the spirit of Hinduism), Buddhism risked losing not merely its Indic character, its radiant and fraternal dwelling. It had imperiled its very identity, its claim to tradition, its ontological being as an autonomous religion. For there was no Buddhism unless the "distinctive beauty" of Hinduism illuminated it for posterity. Within the length of a passage, Gandhi had turned around an entire history of Hinduism's sacrificial excess into a proposition of its firmness and beauty. The ethics of fullness had mutated into a discourse of oneness, the language of distinction and simplicity giving way to that of geopolitical identity and mastery. If one was born in that land, one was always already Hindu in spirit.

One does not need to know the religious history of classical India (and its terrifying resolutions in modern times) to see how deeply mired Gandhi's appropriation of heterodox and insurrectionary religious traditions was with a certain strand of centralizing nationalist, even secularist, theology. This logic of appropriation, which we have seen implicated since the nineteenth century in the philosophical discourse on spirit, was most adjacent with the language of compassionate universality precisely when it was most colonizing and hierarchical. In the colonies, among the nationalists, of course, this logic (and the spiritual sovereignty that ensued from it) was not necessarily articulated in the sensitive language of religious difference. Instead, this claim to political and religious sovereignty had come to insinuate itself in the rhetoric of spiritual oneness and civilizational identity. The spirit of satyagraha, still two years away from being given its name, had itself emerged in Gandhi's 1905 *Lectures on Religion* at its most mystical. And I insist on "mystical" not merely in the religious sense, but in the sense of a fanatically safeguarded crypt, a tradition, and, above all, a civilizational authority, at the heart of which Buddhism—that other (equally theological and political) discourse on nonviolence—had to be appropriated, silenced, avoided. Nothing could have been more historicist, more centralizing, more virulent, than this vision of firmness that lay at the foundation of satyagraha's "soul-force."

Gandhi's letter to his friend C. F. Andrews, right in the midst of their most serious disagreement over the incendiary methods of his first noncooperation movement in 1920–1921 was symptomatic of this firmness that would underwrite satyagrahic fanaticism in the heyday of Indian anticolonialism. "The picture of your lighting that great pile, including beautiful fabrics, shocked me intensely," Andrews complained to Gandhi. "We get into the vicious cycle from which Europe is now trying so desperately to escape. . . . It shocked me and seemed to me a form almost of violence; and yet I know how violence is abhorrent to you. . . . Lighting bonfires of foreign cloth and telling people it is a religious sin to wear it, destroying in the fire the noble handiwork of one's fellow men and women, one's brothers and sisters abroad, saying it would be 'defiling' to wear it . . . you are doing something violent, distorted, unnatural."[56] Carefully evading his friend's critique, Gandhi simply declared to Andrews, "You are ever with me in spirit."[57] Three months later, he supplanted this gift of friendship with an ethics of belligerence. "The warmth generated by bonfires will last for the coming winter," he wrote in the midst of the massive public burning of Manchester cloth by the satyagrahis, while the underclothed poor among Gandhi's followers stared nervously at the impending winter of 1921. But firm and remorseless, Gandhi pressed on. "If the bonfires are kept up till the last piece is burnt, the warmth will last for ever, and each successive winter will see the nation more and more invigorated."[58]

The perverse symbolism of warmth apart, it was revealing that in seeking to impart to satyagraha the luminosity of a spiritual universalism, Gandhi had actually receded into the private warmth of the domestic fire. "I like to light an oven. I am a believer in nonviolence. There is nonviolence and love in every fiber of my being," he reiterated less than a month later, connecting his "ethics of destruction" with the morals of nonviolence. Satyagraha sought equality with Europe through destructive sacrifice, and although it was nonviolent, it was hardly shorn of a punitive impulse. "Love is the epitome of strength." And "punishments of the loved ones," wrote Gandhi, "are like balm to the soul."[59] For Gandhi, love, filiation, and brotherhood, even in their absolute generosity, could never swerve too far from a measure (or touch) of punitive—which is to say, juridical—austerity. "Why should we not so conduct ourselves that any conflict between India and Pakistan becomes impossible?" he would ask in 1948, as violence across north India in the aftermath of the country's partition worsened. "We must be brave and trust the Muslims. If later they violate the trust you can cut off their heads. But you cannot say that if anyone refuses to go to Pakistan his head should be cut off."[60]

This ambiguous compassion, always tempered by a retributive form of rationality, laid the groundwork for Gandhi's moral ontology, or what he might have called the fullness of force, one that aligned satyagraha with the sacrificial faith of a very modern sort. This is the alignment that I have called, following Lefort, Manent, and others, satyagraha's "theologico-political problem"; a problem (or difficulty) that rendered its very spirit or *bhaav* inextricable from the classical discourses of rule, ability, and obedience. Although he described himself as "rationalist in spirit," especially when he was speaking on religious matters,[61] Gandhi frequently conceded that in his negotiation between reason and religion, he was guided by the Christian injunction, "the letter killeth, the spirit giveth life," as he was, for instance, during the defense of his own readings of the *Gita* and *Ramayana*.[62] But he was equally prone to evading the more brutal and apologetic side of spirit. "The less said about the spirit the better," he once asserted. Because the task of nourishing spirit required extraordinary exactitude and practice—indeed, silence.[63] Grounded in truth (*satya*) and nonviolence (*ahimsa*), a spirit proper to the human—thus the link between being (*sat*) as such and being proper in sacrifice (*sattvik*)—required mastery not only over the art of the soul in the religious sense but also, in the most ontological sense, over crafts and abilities of the hand. Satyagraha's emphasis on spinning, scavenging, knitting, writing, and other manual activities, as Gandhi frequently reiterated, was hardly incidental. Rather, the obligation and ability to work by hand was the fulcrum of ethical life, the possibility of actualizing spirit. And through this rhythmic, slow, and patient actualization of spirit by hand, *ahimsa* was rendered into something more (and something less) than nonviolence. It became a gift of nonindifference, a force of ameliorative humility and compassion, offered both to the incurably unequal (*asamaan*) and the extraordinary and exceptional (*asamaanya*) sovereign.

There was a tension, I am suggesting then, between Gandhi's religiosity (which he considered to be an irrefutably private matter) and his spiritualism (which was militantly interventionist and couched in the rhetoric of democratization of craft). Satyagraha's natural and invisible force accrued from the people's sacrifices alone, from their renunciation of interest, incivility, and perjury. "Any secrecy," Gandhi warned them, "hinders the real spirit of democracy."[64] In these moments, when the rhetoric of renunciation took on the classical language of civic humanism, spirit was aligned not with religions of antiquity but with the emancipatory universalism of a modern politics. And at its most egalitarian, satyagraha observed no limits in its attempt to touch, learn, and disseminate the most obscure, impure, and degraded manual crafts, those whose practice was forced as hereditary occupation on the most oppressed among India's multitude. Yet, at its heart, the spirit of satyagraha, its *dharma*, its sense of obligation toward the unequal, retained an ambiguous affinity for the most punitive institutions and hierarchies of the moral law.

Before I turn to the originality and suppleness of that affinity, its sensitive and insidious logic, we must stay just a little longer with a set of fundamental questions about the origin of the "spirit" itself, which Gandhi often used interchangeably with more classical terms, such as feeling (*bhaav*), sacrifice (*yajna*), soul (*hriday*), and perhaps most crucial for a society risking its collective life for a democracy whose form and future was at best nebulous, spirit as obligation to the injunctions of the moral law (*dharma*). Why did Gandhi speak so frequently of spirit? What conceptual and rhetorical work did such a capacious figure do for him? Where did its force—which he conjured by relentlessly invoking different cognitive and corporeal states, such as dream, restlessness, risk, possession, epiphany, struggle, and haunting, or simply by calling into presence a masculine God—come from?[65] Was the source of this force the satyagrahi's soul, from which Gandhi had derived at least one powerful translation of satyagraha, "soul-force"? Or was he invoking love, the infinitesimal and quotidian "love-force" emanating from the passive resister's purity of heart? Was the spiritualization of resistance a purely religious affair, his conjurations of the "spirit of self-sacrifice" signaling Gandhi's withdrawal into the groundlessness of *advaita* alone, away from the realities of political action and obligation? That could not have been the case in any simple sense, for as we have seen, Gandhi often mobilized spirit in order to emphasize the imperative of truth and virtue between political antagonists and friends. Spirit, in fact, demanded from the moral agent a radical selflessness, the dissolution of his very self in his encounter with oppressor and oppressed alike. But the question was, did this exemplary principle of self-dissolution, the assimilation of one's own self into the transcendent Being—a sacrifice that alone secreted the possibility of freedom—become proper to satyagraha precisely by remaining mystical, its epistemology and practice restricted to the innermost rationales and reasons of the masterly human (and God) alone? In this demand for the dissolution of the subject in the interest of equality, did a certain inequality, a transcendentalism of limits, insinuate itself at the heart of Gandhi's spiritual experiments?

Barely a year after the 1932 Poona Pact with Ambedkar on the question of separate electorates for the "untouchables," for instance, Gandhi asserted the value of knowledge within limits in clearest terms. "A true Brahmin is one who possesses the attributes of a Kshatriya, a Vaishya, and a Shudra, and has, in addition, learning [*vidya*]. . . . Shudras are not, of course, devoid of learning but service is their main characteristic." And just a sentence later, came a singularly ontotheological gesture, attaching the essence of untouchable existence to the figure of God himself. "How can a religion that sees the whole universe as a manifestation of Vishnu treat the Harijans as apart from Vishnu?"[66] This apotheosis of the unequal, which otherwise bookends Gandhi's immense compassion toward the untouchable, is riveting. Especially because it comes moments after the *harijan* and the Shudra have been excluded from the knowledge, practice, and laws of faith itself. An anthropological exclusion swiftly mutates into a plea for the sacredness of the excluded; the law of restricting knowledge and faculty to the few is consolidated into an ontological essence, such as in the expressions "a *true* Brahmin" or "a *true* Shudra." It is precisely the imposition of limits on the unequal's faculties, in other words, that enables satyagraha's immeasurable reverence toward the unequal's existence, so that measure, limit (*maryada*) as such, can be imparted the force of a spiritual and disciplinary obligation (*maryada dharma*) whose fulfilment is the duty both of the satyagrahi and unequal.

It was when satyagraha was most passionately spiritual and ameliorative, saturated by its devotion toward the unequal, then, that it was also most dogmatically anthropological and unjust. Spirit underwrote this philosophical anthropology, or rather this theologico-political humanism, one in which the autonomy of the human, which Gandhi deeply valued and which is common to all humanistic traditions, nevertheless remained within satyagraha a function of the transcendental will, a higher purpose, an ethical demand rooted in the innermost, even groundless, recesses of belief (or worse, the mythic and juridical force that acted in its name). As word, metaphor, and effect, only "spirit" could capture the moral ontology of this groundlessness.

In the section that follows, returning briefly to *Hind Swaraj*, I focus on two turns in this spiritual thread that occurred within a decade of the composition of that important text. The first was generated by Gandhi's encounter with fin-de-siècle liberal nationalism and revolutionary extremism, as he tactfully negotiated the two strands leading up to his first major movements in the late 1910s. The second turn found its axis in Gandhi's increasingly prolific and accretive moral ontology of the hand: hand both as organ and spirit; hand as a marker of force, ability, and difference; hand, above all, as an instrument of contact and touch in the most material and everyday sense, which acquired an even stronger political and ethical charge from the early 1920s onward. One specific conceptual event would come to be inscribed at the heart of this moral ontology or manual ethics: the introduction into the grammar of satyagraha of the term *sadhana*, loosely translatable as "practice," "method," or "exactitude" in a sense that was both deeply aesthetic and vehemently sacrificial. But perhaps most suggestively, *sadhana*, which is etymologically linked to the Sanskrit term *sadhan* (means), would come to encapsulate in one word Gandhi's enduring struggle to formulate a theory of transformative and measured force. These two turns between 1900 and 1930 formed the context in which he came to reconceptualize the relationship between force and obligation, between *bal* and *dharma*, distilling much of it in the 1920s through his *Discourses on the Gita*.

Resistances: Of *Yugadharma*

It was during his transcontinental journey between Britain and South Africa in November 1909 that the distinctive kinship between truth and resistance, which Gandhi had the year before condensed in the neologism *satyagraha*, began to receive its most sustained treatment. In a letter dispatched a month earlier from London to his theosophist friend Henry Polak, Gandhi had already confessed to being violently possessed by the spirit of passive resistance. He wrote to Polak how the pace of London's public transport had been inflaming his sense of truth. "Every time I get into a railway car, use a motor-bus, I know that I am doing violence to my sense of what is right." The unbridled desire to live longer, the striving for infinitude and mastery, which had destroyed Europe's soul, perturbed Gandhi. "India's salvation," he was now convinced, "lies in unlearning what she has learnt during the last fifty years." And then came the affirmation of spirit as truth: "It is the true spirit of passive resistance that has brought me to the above definite conclusions."[67] This letter, written in a "state of possession," is the only recorded instance of Gandhi attempting to impart a "concrete form" to his spiritual critique of Europe, as if this visceral enragement of the soul were a preparation for the eccentric masterwork to come.[68]

Onboard the *Kildonan Castle* on his way back from London to Cape Town in November 1909, Gandhi composed the body of *Hind Swaraj*. As the indifferent nationalist reception of the work would eventually show, it was an untimely intervention. In fact, barring Ambedkar—who, in a moment of dramatic self-projection (and in the midst of his own classically Rousseauist critique of property as interest), would see in Gandhi's moral and political convictions a return to Ruskin, Tolstoy, and Rousseau himself—*Hind Swaraj* was nearly lost in the busy world of anticolonial activity.[69] The Indian National Congress was suspended in December 1907 after liberal and extremist nationalists had failed to agree on a common course of action against the colonial government. Months later, a young revolutionary terrorist from the Punjab assassinated a British official in London. Written in the shadows of these ideological splits and assertive extremisms, *Hind Swaraj* was where Gandhi's theory of measure, his critique of both the sacrificial zeal of young revolutionaries and liberal misunderstandings of sovereignty found its singular idiom. Responding to the extremist Reader who advocates the use of violence against Britain, Gandhi tries to conceptualize, in the most sustained and supple fashion, another mode of action against the empire. Cleverly, he takes up the innocuous example of petitioning, the most prolific activity of Indian liberals in the early decades of their struggle for imperial citizenship. Let us note in the following passage the emphasis on force, a category whose immense polyvalence and heterogeneity—its relationship to equality—Gandhi illuminates and multiplies by brisk repetition.

It is a fact beyond dispute that a petition, without the backing of force, is useless . . . a petition of an equal is a sign of courtesy; a petition from a slave is a symbol of his slavery. A petition backed by force is a petition from an equal and, when he transmits his demand in the form of a petition, it testifies to his nobility. Two kinds of force can back petitions. "We shall hurt you if you do not give this," is one kind of force; it is the force of arms, whose evil results we have already examined. The second kind of force can thus be stated: "If you do not concede our demand, we shall be no longer your petitioners. You can govern us only so long as we remain the governed; we shall no longer have any dealings with you." The force implied in this may be described as love-force,

soul-force, or, more popularly but less accurately, passive resistance. This force is indestructible. He who uses it perfectly understands his position. . . . The force of arms is
powerless when matched against the force of love or the soul.[70]

This remains one of the subtlest yet most decisive passages in *Hind
Swaraj*. Gandhi does not so much disengage from his commitment to the
norms of empire—that is, from the liberal belief in petitioning the Crown—
as much as he radically redefines the nature of force that underpins the nationalists' engagement with Britain. Petitioning as peaceful means is not
denounced, but it can be a ground for equality only if it is backed by force.
This new force accrues not from being better and more civil subjects of empire in any conventional sense. Instead, it accrues from the relinquishment of
imperial citizenship itself. It accrues, in other words, from the force of voluntary dispossession. Only in the possession of this "indestructible force"—one
that emanates from soul or spirit and might be perfected only through the
voluntary refusal to be governed—can the unequal be rendered equal. A year
earlier, we have seen, Gandhi had started to call such an engagement with India's inequality *satyagraha*, a moral firmness that transforms the armed force
of anarchists and imperialists alike into a force that structures a relation of
civility among equals. In another, more promising (if somewhat indetermi-
nate) sense, equality was neither the means nor the end of the satyagrahi's resistance. Instead, it was for him the irreducible ground of compassion toward
the sovereign and unequal alike.[71] Equality, Gandhi insisted, had to be pre-
supposed rather than viewed as something that had to be fought for; equality was a civic virtue rather than a political claim. Thus, in sharp opposition
to the revolutionary energies of young India, against which *Hind Swaraj* was
composed, satyagrahic action remained firmly within the limits of a prohibi-
tive equality, regulated by a firm ethics of measure. Gandhi would subsequently call this obligation to limit *maryada dharma*.

Guided as it often was by the truth of the moral law more than by a superficial affinity for sovereignty, *maryada dharma* would become the invisible
soul of Gandhi's vision of discipline. It would also produce, as we shall see in
Chapter 4, a reticence, a tendency to cede the ground of resistance in favor of
the oppressor himself, often in the interest of a methodical, demanding, and
scrupulous cultivation of skill and method (*sadhana*). But cessation into *sadhana*, or what Gandhi more often and more innocuously called "constructive program," even at its best, even at the moment of its greatest empathy
for those who were forced into degrading manual work, was not shorn of anthropological demarcations and distinctions. For it was often not all humanity but rather the human possessed with very dexterous, very exclusive skills
that belonged to the order and possibility of *sadhana*. In these moments,

spirit, distinct from the animal, the *atishudra*, the unequal as such, invariably made an appearance.

It was within this much deeper and difficult engagement with the question of method and rigor, with the ethics of mastery—and by implication, emancipation—within measure, that the *Gita*, the founding treatise on sovereignty in the Indic tradition, became so crucial to Gandhi's meditations in the 1920s. He was, of course, Gandhi insisted, committed to the *Gita* only in spirit. Or as he put it in a firmer fashion, he had committed himself only to the "spirit of the verse," thus rarely needing to encumber himself with its fratricidal content, whose violence he never denied either. These two gestures—a tactical ambiguity toward statemaking violence of which the *Gita* was the sanctioning verse within the Indic tradition on the one hand and a fidelity to the *Gita*'s spirit alone on the other hand—were not unrelated. "I never thought or said," Gandhi explained, "that the *Gita* was composed for expounding nonviolence. On the contrary, I have believed and have said that at the time of the *Gita*, war was accepted as normal, though they believed in the dharma of non-violence."[72]

For Gandhi, the *Gita* alone, among all canonical texts, had the potential to impart, with just the right measure of force, a lesson on righteous action. But if this lesson was to be taken in the right spirit (rather than being squandered away by too indignant an ethics), then accepting the obvious generality of violence in the age of tribal republics was necessary. Gandhi's *Discourses* begin, then, with this originary cessation of ground to the logic of obedience and office (ancient and modern). This is why to a true satyagrahi, Gandhi insists, Arjuna's resistance against the duty to kill his brothers in the interest of the state must stand for the warrior's immoral insurrection against the moral law. It was an act of uncivil disobedience of which, we have seen, Gandhi had declared the soldiers of Garhwali Rifles who refused to open fire on peaceful protesters in Peshawar guilty. For Arjuna was not being nonviolent so much as he was relinquishing his obligation as a warrior. "Had Arjuna's obstinate refusal to fight anything to do with non-violence?" Gandhi asked his followers in one of his shorter essays on the *Gita*. "In fact, he had fought often enough in the past. On the present occasion"—as the armies squared up for one final war that would bring the *Mahabharata* to a close—"his reason was suddenly clouded by ignorant attachment. He did not wish to kill his kinsmen. He did not say he would not kill anyone even if he believed that person to be wicked." It is Krishna, Gandhi says, who "understands the momentary darkening of Arjuna's reason" and dislodges the false nonviolence that has suddenly gripped the warrior. Krishna reinstills the moral imperative of force. "He, therefore, tells him: 'You have already committed violence. By talking now like a wise man, you will not learn non-violence. Having started on this course, you must finish the job.'"[73]

This passage amplifies the fecund extremities of Gandhi's spiritual politics, in which absolute violence and absolute nonviolence have merged in the most punitive way. Because you have already broken a neighbor's or brother's limbs, Gandhi's Krishna might suggest, why not break his neck too and free him from his suffering? But even here, an anthropological distinction and decisionism appears: satyagrahic euthanasia, indeed mercy, was offered to the animal alone, not to the human.[74] A few paragraphs later, anticipating Ambedkar's critique of the *Gita*, Gandhi clarifies:

I do not wish to suggest that violence has no place at all in the teaching of the Gita. The dharma which it teaches does not mean that a person who has not yet awakened to the truth of non-violence may act like a coward. Anyone who fears others, accumulates possessions and indulges in sense-pleasures will certainly fight with violent means, but violence does not, for that reason, become justified as his dharma. There is only one dharma. Non-violence means *moksha*, and *moksha* means realizing Satyanarayana [truth as God]. But this dharma does not under any circumstances countenance running away in fear. In this world which baffles our reason, violence there will then always be. The Gita shows the way which will lead us out of it, but it also says that we cannot escape it simply by running away from it like cowards. Anyone who prepares to run away would do better, instead, to kill and be killed.[75]

Spiritual action demanded resistance against fear, resistance, as Gandhi put it, against the wavering of spirit. His term for such a fearless resister, the warrior who possessed sovereign force and was "stable in spirit," was *stithiprajna* or *samadhistha*.[76] The *stithiprajna* was the one who remained unmarred by his circumstance (*stithi*); his knowledge and consciousness, and in the ultimate instance, his craft, remained resolute even and especially at war. The *samadhistha* was the meditative practitioner, the exemplar of equipoise, the moral agent capable of equanimity (and even equality), one who remained undeterred by the constraints of circumstance and inevitability of death. In its alignment with the *stithiprajna* and *samadhistha*, spirit marshaled a very precise responsibility: the duty to recover or maintain the truth of transcendence by amplifying (and in the final instance, dissolving) the self at the moment of its greatest force. At its best, satyagraha was constituted by this accentuation of the firmness of being in the face of mortality. Its truth was cast around the amplification of finitude (and, at its worst, around the disavowal of life's injurability itself) as the deathless ground of spirit. Hence, Gandhi's intensive and repetitive dwelling on the moment of Arjuna's equivocation. The Kshatriya warrior's dilemma, which arose from his inability to separate his obligations from their consequences, from his unwillingness to separate his ends from his means, illuminated, according to Gandhi, the necessity of extracting moral force out of its own worldly violence. From this extraction of force, this separation of force from its phenomenological manifestations and distracting ephemerality emerged the deathless spirit that stabilized the satyagrahi's obligation toward *yugadharma*, the "religion of the age."[77]

Although force, especially a warrior's force, was not to be construed as an alliance with the oppressor, it was, despite Gandhi's vigilance, ineluctably contaminated by it. I say "contaminated" because this alliance was rooted not in Gandhi's indifference to the violence of the state (to which he was singularly awake) but rather in his immense awareness of the uses of its mythic power (to which he remained susceptible). A brilliant interrogator of the effects of force (in no small measure of the way it moved within the apparatuses and jurisdictions of the modern state), Gandhi remained deliberately indifferent to its mythic and insidious operations—that is, to its ability to appear or represent itself as spiritual, or worse, righteous, precisely when it was most hierarchical. It is illuminating, for instance, that he refused to speak in any sustained manner of the moral failure that had caused the *Mahabharata*'s fratricidal war: the will to the state, one that the Pandava brothers shared with their manipulative cousins, the Kauravas, even as they went to war over it. If Gandhi was critical of the state, then his immersion in the *Gita* was also indicative of how profoundly attracted he was to those moral psychologies, emotions, moods, and decisions, for which the state—and the epic war at the center of the *Gita* itself—was a cipher. He mounted his resistance against the empire with no greater conviction and frequency, after all, than he did against his own people, deciding to withdraw his movements whenever they threatened to transgress against satyagrahic injunctions. What was this immense decisionism, this love of obedience, a symptom of? Of satyagraha's *coup de force*: the ability to inscribe nonviolence, indeed civil disobedience as the vehement extension of force itself. Force as the only truth that might as quickly recede (or be remade) into being an instrument of authority, a faculty of decision, an organ of mastery, as it might of popular resistance. Let us make the distinction again. Violence repelled him. Force, as the moral foundation of decisionism, did not. Gandhi's defense of his decision to recruit Indian men for Britain's war effort in 1918 was categorical:

Either we must renounce the benefits of the State or help it to the best of our ability to prosecute the war. . . . Indians have a double duty to perform. If they are to preach the mission of peace, they must first prove their ability in war. . . . A nation that is unfit to fight cannot from experience prove the virtue of not fighting. I do not infer from this that India must fight. But I do say that India must know how to fight. Ahimsa is the eradication of the desire to injure or to kill. Ahimsa can be practiced only toward those that are inferior to you in every way.[78]

To live one's life according to the hard truth of nonviolence, one had to master the rigor of sacrifice, even violent death. But what benefits endowed by the imperial state to its colonial subjects was Gandhi invoking, given that just a decade earlier, *Hind Swaraj* had proclaimed nothing short of a civilizational degradation at the heart of India's colonial relationship? He had in fact insinuated a civilizational distinction, a separateness of temperament and faculty, between England and India. Gandhi does not clarify the reasons for this shift of allegiance and judgment. What he does betray, however, is a certain predilection for mastery. Mastery of the self, an ethics of unflinching self-sacrifice, certainly, but one that despite all its vigilance lapsed into a desire for sovereignty over others. *Ahimsa*, insists Gandhi, was to be practiced not simply against the strong but also as the strong.

In itself, this was the most succinct definition of satyagrahic force. But this *coup de force* was to get riskier in 1919, because Gandhian duty and right to sacrifice oneself at war was not innocent of a long history of exclusion and hierarchy. Nor was it oblivious to the redaction of caste from the struggle and language of freedom, of the separation of the social (justice and access) from the political (sovereignty and autonomy) as such. Gandhi, we shall see in Chapter 4, would not give everyone the right to attain equality at war, the right to master the "force of nonviolence," the faculty adequate to discerning the cryptic "workings of nonviolence." If the temptation of violence was grave, then, in the same vein, not everyone was given equal latitude to succumb to it. In fact, it was in moments of gravest violence that satyagraha acquired its most decisionist and anthropological form, one whose exclusions would be articulated frequently around the most inalienably human of all faculties: the faculty of the hand.

A Hand Proper to Freedom

In February 1922, nationalist volunteers, radicalized by Gandhi's promise of "swaraj within one year," burned down a police station in the United Provinces, killing close to two dozen colonial policemen trapped inside.[79] Shocked and disappointed, Gandhi responded by ending the two-year-long Khilafat and noncooperation movement at the height of its influence. Sometime around this period, in the wake of endemic violence perpetrated in his name, the concept of *sadhana* entered his lexicon. His meticulously compiled bibliography suggests that he was, during his incarceration at the Yeravda Prison, reading Rabindranath Tagore's *Sadhana: The Realization of Life* (1915), a set of philosophical and aesthetic meditations on the self in its relation to action and evil (which was itself profoundly influenced by the Upanishads and Buddhist negative theology).[80] Thus began, within the precinct opened and circumscribed by a word, Gandhi's systematic elaboration on firmness, discipline, and rigor. The concept was to remain the most experimental, compassionate, and demanding—indeed, unresolved—knot in the satyagrahic discourse on spirit. Around it were to also become discernible in Gandhi's ethics and politics some important shifts away from the early insurgency of *Hind Swaraj*.

In its broadest sense, *sadhana* heightened the aesthetic dimension of satyagrahic sacrifice. It was not an artistic seclusion or pacifism of a conventional sort, even if a sense of meditative artistry and refinement, pushing toward an ascetic withdrawal into solitary practice, was attached to it. For Gandhi, instead, *sadhana* named a commitment to finding a proper measure between means and ends, to pursuing one's craft in the manner of the *stithiprajna*, unperturbed by the vicissitudes of circumstance. *Sadhana* demanded the satyagrahi's immersion in the inseparable and antinomic relationship between force and nonviolence.[81] Invoking by its very name a rigorous awareness of means (*sadhan*), *sadhana* expressed the demands of sacrifice with unflinching civility and measure, imparting to satyagrahic practice, even at its most exorbitant, a sense of limit. And it was profoundly spiritual too, inasmuch as it entailed a withdrawal from those senses that constitute the very being of the embodied subject—touch, speech, and even dream. Gandhi argued, for instance, that the true measure of an agent's *sadhana* was to be found in his ability to keep silence. "This morning," he wrote in January 1940, "I was not very careful and slipped into speech. This does happen, though it ought not to. All this reveals that my *sadhana* is quite imperfect. I have therefore decided to observe silence as far as possible. I need introspection."[82]

Sadhana was not, however, simply a call to spiritual steadfastness and rigor. It was also the satyagrahi's perfection and mastery of the hand. There was, in other words, both an ascetics and aesthetics of force, an intense manipulability and touchability, involved in it. Its moral force arose from touching and shaping physical materials. Consider thus the Platonic affirmation of pottery in *Hind Swaraj*: "A clay pot would break through impact, if not with one stone, then with another. The way to save the pot is not to keep it away from the danger point but to bake it so that no stone would break it. We have then to make our hearts of perfectly baked clay."[83] The metaphors were hardly fortuitous. Gandhi's mobilization of force by way of invoking a potter's mastery at the wheel had deep moral philosophical roots. In fact, the Platonism of this passage could not have been more revealing of Gandhi's humanist affinities. From Socrates on, after all, the kinship between the rhythms of the hand and malleability of the soul has been fundamental to classical thought. In that deep tradition of thinking about moral perfectionism, the soul's touchability and perfectibility has often been seen as being closest to—indeed, most authentically reflected in—the measured movements of a potter's hand.[84] In what was perhaps the most illuminating tribute to this engagement with Platonism, Gandhi had published in Gujarati a summary in five parts of Plato's *Apology* in his South African newspaper *Indian Opinion* some years before composing *Hind Swaraj*.[85]

There had always been a rhetorical energy in Gandhi's meditations, and as Simona Sawhney has argued, allegory as a literary-philosophical form was crucial to his reflections on nonviolence.[86] I see this rhetoric—the frequent recourse to animals, the fabulous use of species organs, the privileging of the circular and dexterous over the prehensile—as constitutive of Gandhi's deep pragmatism, his attempt to envision politics in the most material, realist, and yet always aesthetic, terms. His discourse on the hand was characteristic of this realism. "But by main force to snatch the salt from the poor, harmless satyagrahis' hands is barbarism pure and simple and an insult to India," he wrote after his subversive 200-mile Salt March from Ahmedabad to Dandi on the Gujarat coast in 1930. "Such insult can be answered only by allowing our hand to be fractured without loosening the grasp."[87] The disciplined hand, then, was not just any species organ. It was a hand capable of clenching—and from that very ability to clench, to refuse to let go, to guard and keep safe the future, emerged the dream of sovereignty, or *swaraj*. "If a fist containing salt be clenched, none dare to open it," Gandhi had written just a month before. He quickly moved on to the imperial hand, invoking its spiritually destitute movements. Both hands had force, but Gandhi made an attempt to differentiate imperial sovereignty from satyagrahic mastery. "They may open fire upon you. Men may come with bayonets and sticks and use them on you, but salt should not be taken out of your hands." Finally, the moment of *sadhana* found its apotheosis—*moksha*, or liberation from cycles of life and death—in the irreducible sovereignty of death. "Bodies may be lying dead, hands may have been cut off but still you keep to your promise. I will then understand that *swaraj* is approaching."[88] In the final instance, at the moment of the satyagrahi's death, Gandhi insisted, it was the hand, even under the threat of amputation, which must remain sovereign. In the hand's knowledge of its own finitude, satyagraha found its spirit, and in the fatal spilling of the satyagrahi's blood, nonviolence its "living force."[89]

This transformation of the manual into a faculty of autonomy and will—that is to say, into an intrinsic ability on whose cultivation now hinged the very distinction between freedom and servitude—was not limited to Gandhi's tactics of 1930–1931. The attempt to reveal the brutality of empire, even in the face of death, by clenching a fistful of salt along India's coastline, was part of an enduring ethical and political framework, grounded in judgments about what was proper to being human as such. "You have not yet got control over the pen," Gandhi reprimanded a translator of his works in 1940, summarily declaring that her inability to write legibly and correctly was a sign of her incomplete existence.[90] As late as 1947, even as the independence and partition of the subcontinent loomed barely months ahead, Gandhi, with his characteristic focus on the mundane, was still prone to reprimand himself over his misuse of the hand. "My handwriting has come out badly due to haste."[91] Biographers of satyagraha have conserved vignettes of Gandhi's obsessions with the manual. "He wrote with his right hand," goes a legend about the frantic and dexterous first draft of *Hind Swaraj*. "When the right hand got tired he wrote with his left hand! Thus 40 pages he wrote with the left hand."[92] Some of Gandhi's own pronouncements might have seemed as dramatic to his followers at the time as they seem to historians now. But whether or not they were rhetorical, they invariably touched the most material and phenomenal aspects of the everyday life of the satyagrahi. Not merely production, but an ontology of conviction, the giving over of one's innermost self to the other, was involved here. "My hand," Gandhi had written to Esther Faering in 1919, "is still too shaky for steady and continuous writing. But I feel I must make the attempt to give you something in my own hand."[93] And it was through this committing of the hand as gift, this making political of the hand, that, by the late 1910s and early 1920s, Gandhi began to find satyagraha, as he had until then theorized and practiced it, to be insufficiently attentive to the violence of untouchability and its degrading economy of manual work. Let us note for now that *Hind Swaraj*, composed barely a decade earlier, had been completely silent on the "untouchable."

Although the relationship between spirit and hand was central to satyagraha, this does not mean that Gandhi's conceptualization of *sadhana* can be reduced to a constellation of corporeal and sacrificial practices. On the contrary, dexterous mastery, the precise use of the weapon or spindle, the selfless acts of scavenging or weaving, were for Gandhi always more than simply moral forms of physical labor, more than simply the discrete parts of his idiosyncratic attempt to reform the passions of the flesh. The spiritual activation and activity of the hand were constituents of his profound egalitarianism; symptoms of his deep immersion in the everyday suffering and violations of the unequal (*asamaan*), the pauper (*daridra*), and the untouchable (*asprishya*), within which, precisely, satyagraha also reached its most conservative limit.

In a speech on ashram vows delivered two years before he would launch his first mass movement, Gandhi revealed both the generosity and limit of this egalitarianism most succinctly. "You may ask: 'Why should *we* use our

hands?' and say, 'the manual work has got to be done by those who are illit-
erate. I can only occupy myself with reading literature and political essays.'
I think that we have to realize the dignity of labor. If a barber or shoemaker
attends a college, he ought not to abandon the profession of barber or shoemaker."[94] The ambiguity of this militant egalitarianism—the radicalization
of the limit—was profound. There was, on the one hand, a formidable restoration of the manual, a promise to lift it from its imputed degradations and
social prejudices and impart it spiritual worth. On the other hand, the entire
horizon of emancipation was opened and circumscribed within the subject's
history—the subject's history with the hand—alone. A barber's son must remain a barber: this simultaneous circumscription of faculty and fetishization
of skill as the basis of moral perfection (and worse, authenticity of personhood), lent satyagraha its resilient dogmatism. One was spiritually equal not
simply when one had mastered the movements of the hand; rather, one was
equal only when one stayed within the rules, histories, and limits of the hand.

It was also in this spiritual sense, paradoxically, as I have argued, that
satyagraha remained profoundly humanist. "I saw in South Africa," Gandhi
recollected in 1919, "that our struggle had pure truth and justice in it and
the force we employed was not brute force but soul-force. In however small
a measure it may have been, it was yet soul-force. We do not find such force
employed by animals."[95] Why were animals devoid of force? Because animals,
Gandhi would insist, lack belief for no fault of theirs. They lack the capacity
to have faith; they remain perennially incapable of possessing the knowledge
of their own mortality—which is to say, they remain spiritually poor. But
perhaps most irrefutably, for Gandhi, animals were unequal in the satyagrahic sense because they were devoid of hands. "Have monkeys ever used weapons?" he asked his followers a year later.[96] Satyagraha's belief in the sovereignty
of the hand—its belief in its singularity and ability, its exclusive humanity—
was marked by this inequality and difference. Out of this need of maintaining
distinctions emerged Gandhi's formidable attempt to touch the untouchable
within limits in the 1920s and the 1930s. I will return to this ethical, political
and religious investment in touching as the fundamental gesture of emancipation in Chapter 4. For now, it is important to underline that these distinctions were ultimately ontological; that is, they instituted and systematized a
metaphysics of being and truth that was founded on the ability of the hand to
rotate, spin, discriminate, work, enforce, and think truthfully. The hand was
the instrument of thought, not merely an organ of touch.

Our education has to be revolutionized. The brain must be educated through the
hand. If I were a poet, I could write poetry on the possibilities of the five fingers.
Why should you think that the mind is everything and the hands and feet nothing?

Those who do not train their hands, who go through the ordinary rut of education, lack "music" in their life. All their faculties are not trained. . . . The brain gets weary of mere words, and the child's mind begins to wander. The hand does the things it ought not to do, the eye sees the things it ought not to see, the ear hears the things it ought not to hear, and they do not do, see, or hear, respectively, what they ought to. They are not taught to make the right choice and so their education often proves their ruin. An education which does not teach us to discriminate between good and bad, to assimilate the one and eschew the other, is a misnomer. . . . If I find a teacher who becomes dull to his students after a month's spinning, I should dismiss him. There will be newness in every lesson such as there can be new music on the same instrument. By changing over from one craft to another a child tends to become like a monkey jumping from branch to branch with abode nowhere.[97]

It is not simply the juridical idealism (which threatens punitive action against teachers for being dull) that lends density to Gandhi's thinking in this passage. Nor is it the physiognomic basis of aesthetic judgment (which sees poetry in the perfection of fingers) that illuminates the potential extremes and regressions of Gandhi's social thought. Nor, above all, is it the elevation of pedagogy into a moral law of discrimination (whose essence is condensed in the agent's ability to discern between good and bad and which in turn defines the person's very being) that implicates Gandhi's politics in an exclusively anthropological notion of life. Rather, I have in mind here something much smaller, much more sensitive, that slips away under Gandhi's deceptive lucidity: the gesture of wagering an entire spiritual struggle on the quotidian cultivation of the manual, a revolution of faculties hinged on the rhythms and touches of the hand, which lights the depths of Gandhi's radical conservatism. And for all its conceptual tightness and poetic lucidity, this spirit of the laws yet again lapses into a profoundly anthropological thinking of force.

After all, the hand, among all organs and limbs, recalls a history exclusive to humanity. History, the story of the movement of creaturely life from animal to man, from nature to society, originates, even in the strictest biological sense, with the development of the hand. There is no more humanist a history, no more fundamental a history of humanity, than that of the hominid's movement away from his primate past in the course of gradually developing more complex prehensile faculties: his ability to grasp, clench, and seize, slowly folding onto the ever more complex capacities to mold, rotate, potter, wield, weave, scribble, suture. The history of humanity is the story of the emergence among men and women of this knack for the fluidity and circularity of force, which Gandhi had found most perfectly conserved in the natural rhythms of spinning wheel. "Soul-force, being natural," we have seen Gandhi provocatively insist in *Hind Swaraj*, "is not noted in history." Soul-force, I submit, *was* history. Its very perfection and invisibility was grounded, after all, in a humanist perfection of force and rhythm. And the hand was the most egalitarian, most limiting, and irreplaceable constituent of this struggle for perfection; an instrument, one might say, of satyagraha's spiritualism—its philosophical anthropology—in its most radical and conservative form.[98]

During his first noncooperation movement in 1921, Gandhi instituted the value of this instrument in no uncertain terms, attaching it not only to his political and economic struggle against an empire whose power was founded on cheap, machine-produced cloth but to an ontology of sacrifice (*yajna*) itself. This rhetorical and conceptual fascination with the manual was part of satyagraha's moral ontology not simply because Gandhi was redefining the intrinsic meaning of sacrifice, which, by linking his "ethics of destruction" with an "indestructible" freedom, even death, he most audaciously was. He was beginning, in the years following *Hind Swaraj*, to also conflate the injunctions of the moral law with the very possibility of justice. Gandhi, as had been evident ever since his denunciation of the law courts and lawyers in his masterwork, harbored little faith in modern legal institutions. But his commitment to obedience (inscribed at the heart of his theory of civil disobedience), his obligation toward the moral law, which he rendered sometimes as *maryada* and more often as *dharma*, remained crucial to satyagraha's conservative egalitarianism. The noncooperation movement in 1920–1921 illuminated the repercussions of this slippage between justice and the law for the first time.

There can be many ways of interpreting *yajna*. For the Hindu householder, five *yajnas* are considered essential: the oven, the pestle, the quern [stone mortar], the pitcher and the spinning-wheel. The fewer there are of these the less substantial the household. A glance at them, however, will show that the important sacrifices are the first and the last and the middle three are their offshoots. The quern, the pitcher and the pestle presuppose the oven. The oven would not work at its best in the absence of the quern or the pestle in a home, but still it can pull on. But stop the spinning-wheel and you are without a principal organ. You have paralysis. A man who does no *yajna* for his food and clothing has no right to either. There should be a custom that he who does not work at his stove must go without food, and he who does not ply his spinning-wheel must go naked. We have discarded the spinning wheel without discarding clothes. He is a thief who wears clothes without doing any spinning, in the same way that he who consumes food without working for it is a thief. *Yajna* means an offering, a sacrifice of the self, which is what physical labor is. They who work at the oven and the wheel are engaged in an intelligent sacrifice.[99]

This is an extremely rich passage, given the manner in which Gandhi, invoking the rhythmic value of the spinning wheel, sets up a radical equivalence between sacrifice and "intelligence" in one breath, and in another breath lapses into the language of positive law, conflating equality itself with sacrifice, justice with guilt and punishment. One might pause at length over his immense interest in the spinning wheel, in whose calibrated pace and measured synchrony with the human hand he may have discerned (as Uday S. Mehta has argued) the possibility of a patient, nonvicarious, and spiritually embedded relationship with time.[100] Gandhi had come to associate this alternative temporality—to be rescued through the quotidian routine of spinning—most explicitly with *swaraj*.

My aim, however, is to highlight the moral and political ontology that sustained his interest in synchrony and movement of the hand; to probe why this attempt to bring into existence a new political subject through a practiced cultivation of measure, whether at the wheel or at war, at the hearth or altar, necessarily entailed a problematic spiritualization of force; to trace what this bond between force and spirit, action and the moral law, meant for satyagraha's commitment to justice; to ask, above all, how this sensitive thinker of equality came to mark out, through the corporeal traits of hand, the most dogmatic lines of spiritual difference between species. I intend to ask, in other words, not why and how Gandhi celebrated the circular rhythms of the wheel but rather what, in an ontological sense, drew him in the first place to its torque, to its underlying logic of *dharma*, its economy and history of force.

Answering this set of questions requires vigilance. Here too, here especially, this vigilance must keep a watch over Gandhi's own rules of vigilance that he followed while interpreting the meaning of *dharma* (a vigilance without which one might fall, he cautioned in his *Discourses*, into error, or worse, nihilism).[101] Inasmuch as grasping the law and spirit of this Gandhian vigilance is crucial to understanding the fecundity of Gandhi's history of force, I have made a beginning in this chapter, laying the groundwork for an archeology of its specific sites and articulations in the chapters that follow. The preceding passage on *yajna* makes it clear, meanwhile, that his consideration of morally permissible forms of labor and production was constituted around his fascination with artisanal austerity. And again this mastery was neither desired nor demanded in a metaphorical sense. Nor was it applied to satyagrahic life in a generic and universal form. Gandhi was clear that not every hand and every agent who possessed such craftsmanship was equally spiritual, and, that not all activities of the hand could be construed as equally sacrificial in any abstract sense. There was, within satyagraha's formidable universalism, a discriminating politics, a measure of skills and abilities, a transcendentalism of (and within) limits, that could not but compromise its best, most just impulses. Within this order of limits, working by hand, giving it a rhythmic synchrony with the soul, was instituted as the means of reclaiming not only national culture but also a cognitive freedom, and in the innermost sense, the moral ontology of being itself.

Certainly, by asking satyagrahis to destroy British fabric in piles across India, Gandhi had set in motion a movement against Manchester's industrial capacity to produce and flood the colonies with cheap cloth. But that strategy of undermining the empire by refusing to use its goods and producing one's own was hardly original. In its militant form, it dated back to the swadeshi movement of early 1900s Bengal, a movement long simmering but finally provoked by the British partition in 1905 of that province along religious lines, and one that inaugurated the era of sustained popular mobilization and boycott of colonial institutions, services, and goods.[102]

The newness of satyagraha lay in its punitive discourse on spiritual reparation, now aligned with the sacrificial obligations of the hand. A mere glance at the passage above reveals how strongly Gandhi's conception of duty was mediated by the categorical—indeed, absolutist—imperative of the moral law. It was this theology of obligation to work by hand—more often than not expressed in the language of command, guilt, and punishment—that would come to saturate Gandhi's war against untouchability from the 1920s onward. The hand, after all, is not simply an instrument of force; it is an organ of contact and touch in the most emancipatory (and when tactless, violating) sense. At any rate, by the end of Gandhi's first noncooperation movement in 1922, a punitive threat had insinuated itself into satyagrahic economy of the manual. One can argue, no doubt, that the discriminating use of the hand—Gandhi's endless invocation of dexterity, his institution of "intelligent sacrifice" as manual labor—was only one among the many aspects of *sadhana*. It was only one of the many constituents of his attempt to rethink the relationship between means and ends. But India's attempt to create the conditions of a just society, its attempt to formulate a democratic ethics of work, its struggle against (and indifference to) the brute fact of manual scavenging, was affected more strongly by few other spiritual innovations in its modern history.

Spirit against Itself

Composed in 1909, four years after Weber's *Protestant Ethic and the Spirit of Capitalism, Hind Swaraj*, despite its longing for an early modern version of civic virtue and measure, bore powerful imprints of the global return of "spirit." It was a return that would manifest itself in interwar moral and political thought in an antinomic combination of existential anxiety and spiritual affirmation. One fuelled the demand to return to ordinary commerce and provincial authenticity (of which Gandhi's own attentiveness to the phenomenological richness of everyday life was a part); the other propelled an aggressive universalism, even cosmopolitanism, couched in the language of civilizational purity and national destiny. Far from being religious in its emancipatory sense, the rhetoric of spirit thus reactivated humanist reflexes and an ever tightening exclusion of beliefs, tribes, castes, and even species from the realm of morals. "As a Mahatma," Ambedkar would write of Gandhi in 1936 in response to Gandhi's critique of *Annihilation of Caste*, "he may be trying to spiritualize politics. Whether he has succeeded in it or not politics have certainly commercialized him."[103] The fact that in its modern form, spirit had been inseparable—rhetorically, conceptually, and genealogically—from the spirit of the laws, embodying the best and worst of commercial interest and its new science of government, was clearly not inconsequential for anticolonial struggles. In the web of these spiritual pressures, many of which were still to come, Gandhi had begun to weave at the turn of the century an unprecedented theory of action. On the one hand, the spirit of satyagraha promised a turn in nationalist politics toward those who were most different, unequal, poor, and untouchable. On the other hand, when spirit appeared as measure, as an injunction of the moral law, as a transcendentalism of limits, it instituted within satyagraha a dogmatic indifference toward precisely those it had so profoundly touched (and those who had touched it).

If spirit was also a certain mood, then the soulful questioning, the fiery possessions, the restlessness and "terrible inner struggle" that it brought with itself—under whose spell Gandhi wrote *Hind Swaraj* in 1909 and sat on an epic fast unto death in 1931 against Ambedkar's demand for separate electorates for the "untouchables"—were not mystical states in the classical sense of the term.[104] Instead, spirit arranged Gandhi's deeply anthropological moral ontology—indeed, his ontotheology (that is, the theology of being)—in which only the firmness of grasp, only the ability to master the knowledge of one's mortality through rigorous sacrifice, might open the subject to the groundless being and invisible truth of nonviolence. It was from an affinity for this groundlessness of nonviolence that the phenomenology of the manual, the ethics of *sadhana* as transformative force, emerged. Faced with the perilous reality of atomic warfare in the late 1940s and the emergence of the new international order of states, Gandhi, rather than giving up on force, articulated in an even stronger fashion the ontological necessity of reclaiming force otherwise. "The force of the spirit is ever progressive and endless. Its full expression makes it unconquerable in the world. . . . What is more, that force resides in everybody, man, woman, and child, irrespective of the color of the skin. Only in many it lies dormant, but it is capable of being awakened by judicious training."[105]

Between Weber and Gandhi, meanwhile, a young Ambedkar in New York, less than a decade after *Hind Swaraj*, would begin to call into question this phenomenology of spirit. In a dramatic inversion of Gandhi's moral ontology, he would detect in spiritualism a certain triumph of the "irreligious" and in spirit the double of "brute force," the theologico-political "force of law," the invisible "ghost" of everyday violence masquerading as religious universalism. But Ambedkar was all too aware that the act of bringing into existence a revolutionary subject was nothing short of a spiritual act. And this act of creativity and foundation, this originary—and *an-archic*—gesture that must exceed all existent norms and concepts of politics, required force in its most rigorous, truthful, and primordial form. The force of "annihilation" might be nurtured in the immeasurability of the unequal's spiritual conviction alone. "My final words of advice to you," Ambedkar told his followers in 1942, "are educate, agitate and organize; have faith in yourself. With justice on our side, I do not see how we can lose our battle. The battle to me is a matter of joy. The battle is in the fullest sense spiritual. There is nothing material or social in it. For ours is a battle, not for wealth or for power. It is a battle for freedom. It is a battle for the reclamation of human personality."[106]

Keeping aside the insurrectionary morals of this pronouncement for the chapters that follow, one might discern (but there are dangers in doing this all too quickly) that *Hind Swaraj* had not only anticipated the young Ambedkar's ethical, political, and religious concerns. It had also opened an economy of moral precepts and concepts that he would take to its very limit. Ambedkar would move away from Gandhi decisively by the late 1920s. But force—the word and its spirit, its will and intensity, the unconditional love of truth that it sustained when wielded by the most vulnerable—would become no less crucial a constituent of his politics. It is to this other moment in anticolonial resistance, one that was beginning to acquire its distinctive form in New York of the 1910s, that I now turn.

Laws of Force
Ambedkar and the Mystical Foundation of Authority

In May 1915, four months after Gandhi's return from South Africa to India and six years after the publication of *Hind Swaraj*, a young Bhimrao Ambedkar submitted his master's thesis at Columbia University in New York. Admitted to the university's political science department, which he had joined in 1914 with the help of a scholarship awarded by the ruler of the princely state of Baroda, the prodigious student ultimately graduated in economics two years later. His thesis was titled *Administration and Finance of the East India Company*.[1] Its scholarly tenor and institutional context notwithstanding, the short work stood out as one of Ambedkar's earliest political essays in a prolific sequence of public writings that would last more than four decades. In fact, the thesis (and the unfinished papers around it) offer a glimpse of Ambedkar's emerging interest in the history of classical Rome and republicanism, themes and histories to which he would return more than once, more than ephemerally, in the 1930s and 1940s. As an anticipation of the work to come, then, what enduring conceptual and rhetorical threads were woven into the text of these early writings?

It is with this question at hand that I reconstruct in this chapter the central concerns of Ambedkar's moral, religious, and political thought, moving away from the overdetermined trajectory of his legislative commitments (as if his entire oeuvre from the very beginning was a preparation for India's Constituent Assembly) and stressing in their stead on the genealogy of his distinctive approach to the problem of constituent power—the multitude's right to revolutionary force beyond all norms and injunctions—and thus of constitutionalism itself. I begin by tracing the contours of his early writings, a small, sometimes fragmentary, but often important body of work whose preliminary ground was laid, like Gandhi's, away from India, first in New York, where Ambedkar lived for two crucial years at the beginning of the Great War (1914–1916), and then in London, where he arrived in 1916 for his doctoral and law studies at the London School of Economics and Political Science and at Gray's Inn, respectively, staying there for a year before his scholarship ran out. He subsequently returned to London for three years (1920–1923) to finish his degrees. This early escape, exposure, and training, this "freedom of beginnings,"[2] one might call it, laid the foundations of a moral and political thought that would come to develop as acute an awareness of the possibilities offered by revolutionary humanism in its modern sense as it would be attuned to the need to engage, exactingly and uncompromisingly, the Indo-European juridical and theological traditions of antiquity.

In the three interim years that he spent in India (1917–1920), the period of Gandhi's rise to prominence in India as well, a young Ambedkar had already begun to establish himself as a thinker of the political in the strongest sense of the term. In January 1920, for instance, he had launched his first publishing endeavor, a fortnightly that he evocatively named *Mooknayak*. The name must have already revealed to many a critical faculty, a strategic precision with words gradually beginning to rise to its full powers, bringing into relief a new moral psychology of politics that would henceforth thrive in the potent space between speech and silence, civility and force. *Mooknayak* could be translated either as "the silent hero" or "the leader of the mute." What shifts between the two renderings is not the emphasis on muteness. What shifts between them instead is the center of force from the individual to collective. The power of the term derives, in other words, from the belief and agency of the reader alone, its charge dependent on whether he understood the force of moral and political transformation to be embodied in the figure of a solitary hero—which the reader, despite the injunctions of *dharma* that barred him from reading, might himself become—or he perceived such force to be condensed in a revolutionary collectivity of those millions like him who felt they had been reduced to a fraction: a collectivity, in other words, of society's most vulnerable, most unequal, most untouchable (*atishudra*). *Mooknayak*, unlike Gandhi's *harijan* (on which more in Chapter 4), invoked a subject that was not merely a passive and unequal recipient of the gift of the name. Rather, it named a subject that was ceaselessly under production, reading, assembling, touching, and reclaiming its freedom to speech (and if need be, rebellious silence) beyond and before the law.

This polyvalence, if not open-endedness, in the meanings of freedom, with its ceaseless movement between individual and collective, between autonomy and general will, was to remain an enduring feature in Ambedkar's semantic and conceptual struggles. With his departure for London set for later that year *Mooknayak*, of course, was bound not to last long, and it folded by the end of October 1920. Yet its title had revealed, in the manner that *Annihilation of Caste* would reconfirm in 1936, Ambedkar's gifted ability to identify the limit on language imposed by colonial and nationalist norms of civility. But perhaps more crucially, it had offered an insight into his ability to push those limits to the extremities of public imagination itself, highlighting, by the use of a name, the unwillingness of an increasingly self-oriented (and self-righteous) nationalism to speak of the outcaste's finitude and experience on equal terms.

Two years earlier, in a brief review of Bertrand Russell's relationship with pacifism, Ambedkar had placed his most enduring rhetorical and conceptual wager in clearer terms. "Regarding the war, perhaps, the West may be blamed," he wrote in 1918 as the Great War ground to its end. "But it [the West] can retort and say, 'Life consists in activity. It is better to act even violently as in war than not at all for [it is] only when we act that we may hope to act well.'"[3] Love of life was worth its name, according to the young Ambedkar, only when it was greater than mere life, only when one's possession of mobility and craft, one's activity and skill, one's attentiveness to the demands of virtue—indeed, attentiveness as virtue—secured the ground of transformative action. Perhaps life was experienced in its authenticity in the alertness of the battlefield alone, when its movements were closest to sacrifice and death. Then, in a flash of suggestive insight into the attitudes of European pacifists and their failed efforts against the war, Ambedkar called for what he thought the European proponents of nonviolence had often lacked, the skill and rigor of "an intelligent control of force."[4] I want to stay with this fleeting invocation of force, not only because it is such a classical concept or because it has been so ubiquitous, at least since Machiavelli, across various traditions of modern political thought that it passes by without much questioning,[5] but also because Ambedkar joins force with another equally classical idea, that of "intelligence" and "faculty" as the ground for "acting well" and virtuously. What might this have meant, this demand that the young thinker had made for the arraignment of one force by another? What was this force that had compelled him to think of mobilizing force differently, more intelligently, more discriminatingly? Where might this other, more virtuous force come from? Could force, which he would come to associate with revolutionary belief and action of the people alone, be saved from the state, from the temptations of sovereign—indeed, conservative—power?

Any demand for rigor and control of force, we have seen in the previous chapter, is paradoxical. The very nature of force, both in its materiality and as a category of thought, is such that to control one force always requires the mobilization of another. Unlike violence, which may have unequivocal phenomenological or psychic manifestations, force, by its very existence, is equivocal: it itself releases that which opposes it. There is a ceaseless productiveness to this dialectic (a young Ambedkar, faced with the indomitable cruelty of the *Manusmriti*, would call it its deathless "spirit") that does not always appear retributive or reactive, or even visible, in the manner acts of violence and counterviolence appear toward each other. On the contrary, the very being of force is constituted by this invisible tension between the two impulses, between that which within force is active and emancipatory, that which posits its own movement and freedom, and that which, released by force itself, is reactive and conservative, and which posits a constraint or limit on its own freedom and movement.[6]

I reconstructed in Chapter 2 the conceptual and rhetorical work involved in Gandhi's distinctive attempt to compress this tension of force, or *bal*, within the rigor of *sadhana* and place it at the heart of his moral ontology. The tension in satyagraha arose from within the internal workings of what Gandhi called the "force of nonviolence." His critique of force was always an exercise in positing and repositing moral relations in their barest and often most vehement form, an attitude that allowed a radical distancing of satyagraha from the state and yet led it back to the same ontological and anthropological distinctions that assume the sovereignty of a specific kind of human agent to be the locus of action. The mere rhetoric of force, let alone the sacrificial routine and rigor of *sadhana*, as I have suggested, drew the satyagrahi into a theologico-political—Gandhi called it "spiritual"—world (something neither he nor Ambedkar would say was true of violence). There was, between the two thinkers, thus, a shared concern with the mysticism of the concept of force (as distinct from violence), one that had begun to acquire its peculiar form in the late 1910s and would last more than four decades.

The second edition of Ambedkar's *Thoughts on Pakistan*, released in 1945 in the shadows of the Second World War and strongly inflected, both in its grammar and theoretical ambition, by emerging concerns over unstable national borders, refugee populations, and stateless minorities, captured this shared fascination with force in the most dramatic fashion. *Thoughts on Pakistan*, in fact, placed force at the heart of civic virtue and citizenship, and it did so in terms of a moral ontology that involved, in no small measure, an interpretive violence of a very radical sort. This is what I have called in Chapter 1 Ambedkar's *coup de force*: an insurrectionary reclamation of the right to—and language of—justice whose own force, whose own rhetorical violence, could not be judged by any existing foundation, norm, or tradition of the moral law. Force was the immeasurable freedom of language, the irreplaceable right to interpretation, the moral psychology and speech of another equality. Let us recall that slightly more than a year after a young Ambedkar had published his 1918 review of Russell, Gandhi had launched his Khilafat agitation in India, the first mass movement in modern times organized in solidarity with Muslims around the world, who, the Indian leader felt, had been betrayed by the victorious Allies. In a salutary recollection of Gandhi's mobilization of Hindus and Muslims for that common cause in 1920–1921, Ambedkar now wrote:

Only during the Khilafat agitation did the waters of the two channels leave their appointed course and flow as one stream in one channel. It was believed that nothing would separate the waters which God was pleased to join. But that hope was belied. It was found that there was something in the composition of the two waters which would compel their separation. Within a few years of their confluence and as soon as the substance of the Khilafat cause vanished—the water from the one stream reacted violently to the presence of the other, as one does to a foreign substance entering one's body. . . . The velocity and violence with which the two waters have burst out from the pool in which they had temporarily gathered have altered the direction in which they were flowing. . . . Apart from any possible objection to the particular figure of speech, I am sure, it cannot be said that this is a wrong reading of the history of Hindu-Muslim politics. If one bears this parallelism in mind, he will know that there is nothing sudden about the transformation. For, if the transformation is a revolution, the parallelism in Hindu-Muslim politics marks the evolution of that revolution.[7]

What work does this highly performative "figure of speech" do for Ambedkar's political philosophy? How does a discourse on self-determination and citizenship, indeed, civic liberty, which *Thoughts on Pakistan* was by the admission of its author, come to be arranged around this unbridled and yet always self-conscious, almost hesitant language of force, one in which constitutional thought and revolutionary rhetoric, political ontology and moral psychology, natural force (or God's will) and human life have become inseparable? As we proceed, let us, as Ambedkar demands, bear this parallelism in mind: the relationship between Hindus and Muslims is understood best when it is approached in terms of the alignment and realignment of revolutionary force—that is to say, a force that belongs to the communities alone, a force that revolts against any attempt by the rulers to impose false unity or artificial difference between them. This is no minor or measurable force; it is beyond human calculation. In fact, Ambedkar has in place a geological scale for its measure. And there is something deeply unresolved, transgressive, and insurrectionary at its heart because not only does the force of one community constitute the other, each also reacts violently against that very constitution. Force at once unites the two communities and threatens to separate them. This ferocious and fraternal tension, this revolutionary immediacy that simultaneously makes a people into a community and splits them, this insurrectionary ethics, in short, constitutes for Ambedkar the essence of the political. The essence itself, at once revolutionary and fanatic, he concedes, requires a remorseless and patient analysis, an adversarial "figure of speech" even. The adversarial rhetoric does not mar the civic possibilities of political action and fraternity; on the contrary, it brings to the surface those forces that otherwise remain lodged within the body politic like specters and crypts. For true force, even when it is revolutionary (and true revolution, especially when it is forceful), works insidiously, slowly, invisibly, as if it belongs to the parallel and slowly evolving order of the natural world. Its sources are so preternatural that they escape the eye, as if they had divine roots. His own moral ontology, Ambedkar explains, makes no distinction between natural, creaturely, and human forces. Rather, it pursues them to their extremities, a place where the working of force is revealed in its insidious unity and grasped in its primordial essence. "I am sure burying Pakistan is not the same thing," he thus argues, "as burying the ghost of Pakistan."[8]

Although Ambedkar regrets his susceptibility to hyperbole, the categories he deploys here were meant to force open nothing short of a rhetorical and conceptual order in which the centrifugal diversity of the nation and the moral relations of its constituents might be approached, truthfully and without hostility, in the language of their abyssal difference. Force, velocity, energy, precipitation, spirit, faculty, these were not simply performative nodes in a series of insurgent critiques of nationalist politics. Rather, they bore revolutionary promise, carrying with them the marks of the struggle that, Ambedkar believed, had to be waged as much within the order of language, as much for honesty, honor, and ethics of thinking, as within the sphere of material and civic rights. Conversely, this critique of force, this vehement thinking of difference, this rhetoric of specters, scenes, and stages as the symbolic precondition of real politics was activated (and could be justified only) in pursuit of a radical equality open to the truth of absolute incommensurability between friends and neighbors. And even before a protective constitutional structure or state (Hindu or Muslim, authoritarian or democratic) could be put in place, this incommensurability had to be recognized (and the difference of the people secured) by giving it another language, another idiom of equality to think with.

Force, in all its conceptual, performative, and phenomenological dimensions, compressed within a word this struggle to reformulate the morals (and mentality) of a radical equality. For Ambedkar, this was a cognitive task, a task that involved both the education and agitation of senses and faculties.

It required a rigorous moral ontology, an ability to reclaim the most shared, fraternal, and incommensurable dimensions of experience (and the *atishudra's* sense of truth) that had been suppressed by the juridical and punitive demarcations of the moral law. It was in this context that in an exemplary moment (in the midst of his most galvanizing satyagraha in 1927), a young Ambedkar would audaciously reclaim the *Gita* from nationalist laws of reading and interpretation, proclaiming it as a treatise that mandated satyagraha not simply against this empire or that, not simply a moral struggle against one's inner temptations (*tamas*) or outer (*rajas*), but instead a treatise that made the unconditional democratization of truth the primary condition of any ethics— a democratization, in other words, of the multitude's sense of belief, its force, unconstrained by the exclusions of *kshatriyadharma*. As his struggle for an alternative language of freedom, a sovereignty without theology, would intensify in the 1940s and 1950s, Ambedkar himself, we shall see, would turn radically away from this early (and militant) interpretation of the *Gita*, growing increasingly uneasy with the debilitating consequences of its fratricidal will to the state on the one hand and its moral solipsism on the other. But there was unity of thought here nevertheless. In a society cleaved by hierarchies that rendered normative ideals of citizenship inadequate, force, he believed, was the only inalienable element of selfhood and community that was not contaminated in advance by the injunctions and exclusions of the moral law (*dharma*). With its promise of newness and technique, its ability to traverse the distance between the manual and the intellectual, the material and the semantic, force was not simply to be sought out. Force, he had exhorted somewhat melancholically, had to be harnessed.[9] Of course, the tension between the symbolic and real, between the people's constituent power and the sovereign state it brings into existence, has never been easily resolved, any such revolutionary attempt threatening to swerve into those propensities for exclusion that it had set out to annihilate.

I will return to this problem, which I identify as Ambedkar's equivocation toward constitutionalism, in Chapter 5. For now, I want to argue that the methodological extremism of *Thoughts on Pakistan*, the courage to take a certain conception of force to its limit, has tended to occlude what had been even in the young Ambedkar a remarkable understanding of this risk—indeed, an awareness of the mysticism of the concept. Conceptualizing force, he had conceded without a qualm, institutes its own circular logic: it places political and rhetorical demands on the critic and critique, it bears moral consequences for one's thought and action, it implicates the thinker in the spatial and temporal dynamic of faith, tradition, and nation. Ambedkar, we shall see, was neither always convinced of the ethical and political efficacy of force as concept nor always immune to its rhetorical and theologico-political intensity. Whenever deployed without adequate vigilance, he warned, force puts its own ethics at risk. And yet even a preliminary survey of his corpus reveals that this concept, word, figure, and (often) performance would become the fulcrum of his thinking on the morals and politics of action (as opposed to his concern with the social conditions of work alone).[10] In fact, force, with all its energy and polyvalence, is the only enduring category in Ambedkar's conception of the insurrectionary and virtuous citizen that might illuminate the complexities of his attempt to formulate the conditions of what Pierre Rosanvallon calls, in a radical coupling of two heterogeneous traditions, "revolutionary democracy."[11] In Ambedkar's final years, this force was reconfigured as the energy behind what might be called a "revolutionary civility" or even "hospitality" (*maitri*).

But evidence of both the early institution (and struggle) in Ambedkar's thought with force and its subsequent turns presents itself only when one is open to discerning in him a stylist and phenomenologist of action; a figure whose thought probed the deepest cognitive recesses, sensory effects, natural histories, and moral perils of revolutionary agency; a theorist of the political who saw himself, above all, as the annihilator of its limits and repairer of its truth; a thinker given over not simply to recovering the possibility of social agency but crafting a moral ontology of virtue and being as such. I map in the first half of this chapter the early intimations of this moral ontology, whose contours the young Ambedkar had begun to draw in New York in the 1910s. In the second half of the chapter, I pick up the threads of this early thought, which reappeared from the 1930s onward with even greater force in his meditations on a revolutionary and egalitarian faith, in his conviction that religion belonged to the political alone and was, at its best and worst, inseparable from it. It was during this period that the fundamental difference between Ambedkar and Gandhi began to acquire its distinctive form. While Gandhi would come to insist that there was "no politics without religion," Ambedkar would probe whether religion, especially with its claims to purity and transcendence, with its promise of a radiant and sacrificial bond between the oppressor and oppressed, had not always been an instrument of the founding exclusions of politics; whether the satyagrahic claim to imbue politics with a spiritual radiance did not at once mystify the worst and expropriate the most just aspects of religion.[12] Perhaps it was against this mysticism that Ambedkar's exasperation—against the Brahmanic refusal to acknowledge that the Vedas could not have come out of nowhere, that their authority had an origin other than the mouth of a being that did not exist, that the foundation of authority itself was not selfless but profoundly theologico-political—so crucial to the *Riddles of Hinduism*, emerged. "Why this circumlocution?" Ambedkar asked, as he probed the alliance between negative theology and the ancient constitution.[13]

Three Elements of a Critique

Running through the various seminar papers that Ambedkar prepared as a graduate student in New York—some with theoretical concerns that were beginning to show signs of his emerging affinities for Rousseau, Nietzsche, and Bergson—was that singular thread along which his moral and political thought over the next four decades would gather its decisive form, the thread along which he would conduct what I have called a "critique of force." It is a critique in its negative sense, but also in the sense of positive elaboration, a conceptual assessment, a semantic recuperation and augmentation of its emancipatory energies, a rigorous separation of the force of the weak from the corrupt violence of its institutional aura and mystical foundation, a critique, above all, in which Ambedkar would himself be most excessive, sacrificial, and religious. Even a trace of conceptual dishonesty or rhetorical haste, a political manipulation or willful mishandling of the concept, he would subsequently write in an apocalyptic tenor in the second edition of *Thoughts on Pakistan*, "may destroy the work of a whole century."[14]

Three distinct elements of this struggle to think force anew emerged in Ambedkar's thought. The first is the thread along which, through a painstaking pursuit of Indic texts on sovereignty and penology, he began to conceptualize force as that which lay at the source of all theologico-political articulations of tradition and authority—force, that is, as violence sanctioned by custom, but also, relatedly, force as the most authentic, immeasurable expression of the freedom of the subject that is corrupted by that other force, the "force of the strongest," one that emanates from the oppressive alliance between religion and sovereignty, the alliance between that which reserves the juridico-political right of taking life (the sovereign) and that which attributes sacredness to life (the theological) in the interest of a greater truth or immortality of being. This alliance not only lies at the heart of modern doctrines and practices of government. It also, Ambedkar would argue in such essays as "Why Is Lawlessness Lawful?" and "Untouchability and Lawlessness," secures through a circular logic its own institutional and ideological permanence. That is to say, theological injunctions and rules do not merely institute the authority of earthly sovereigns, they also acquire—through written statutes of the very government their law has legitimized—their own aura of truth and civility. They thus become "custom," that most deceptively ordinary, cryptic, and punitive of words used by the lawmakers.

Custom is not the antithesis of positive law; it is simply that which comes before the law. It is, Ambedkar argues in *Annihilation of Caste*, the ontological foundation of all authority. For custom, whose ubiquity gives it the appearance of an innocuous (and even civic) restraint, is in essence a regime of injunctions in which law takes its most surreptitious, enduring, and compelling form. Custom, he argues in a classically republican vein, is violence without the police, domination without interference. Custom gives the sovereign's wish the form of voluntary acquiescence; in truth, it is voluntary servitude maintained by the invisible threat of ostracism and (if need be) police power. In a discussion of the pernicious longevity of the *Manusmriti* or the "Dharma of Manu [ancient India's most significant lawgiver]," Ambedkar thus makes a subtle distinction between custom and law, between moral norm and police power. They are, he says, heterogeneous but inseparable. "Custom is no small a thing as compared to Law. It is true that law is enforced by the state through its police power; custom, unless it is valid is not. But in practice this difference is of no consequence. Custom is enforced by people far more effectively than law is by the state. This is because the compelling force of an organized people is far greater than the compelling force of the state."[15] Here, "the people" (in its organized, juridical sense) is a collective that acts surreptitiously, beneath and beside the state, without a display of force. And in this seeming nonforce of the juridical domain of everyday life are hidden the most visceral, intimate, and measured operations of law over life. Custom, its unsaid obligations and injunctions (*dharma*), is that through which law passes into life and life becomes inseparable from the law.

Ordinary ways and acts of being human are thus made to pass through a maze of punitive ordinances. Touching, the sensory and most radiant core of humanity, the source of its most mundane feelings and sympathies, its greatest gift, is circumscribed within norms of intimacy and distance, approachability and unapproachability, its ethics and humanity sequestered from the shared spaces of civic and municipal life and put under the invisible (but always threatening and compelling) watch of police power. One henceforth touches the other only in the threatening shadows of the law. In fact, writes Ambedkar in a tragic fragment of *Waiting for a Visa*, the "untouchable" and the Hindu are touched constantly, even (and especially) at death, albeit not by each other but by the law alone. The custom of "not touching," the norm of keeping distance, thus becomes sovereign among all Indic injunctions, an ironic marker of Hindu etiquette and civility (*sadachar*), at once mystical like the law and immeasurable like suffering. No God is sovereign enough to override this injunction, no mathematics precise enough to register this catastrophe.[16] "Firstly untouchability is not a legal term," Ambedkar writes in an essay suggestively titled "From Millions to Fractions." "There is no exact legal definition of untouchability whereby it could be possible to define who is an Untouchable and who is not. Untouchability is a social concept that has become embodied in a custom, and as custom varies so does untouchability. Consequently there is always some difficulty in the way of ascertaining the population of the Untouchables with mathematical exactitude."[17] In this radical awareness—that the exactitude of custom lay precisely in its apparitional nonchalance and cryptic ubiquity—Ambedkar is in classical company. After all, this critique of authority (which is always, by its very nature, at once numerical and resistant to mathematical reason) goes deep in the modern tradition. "Custom alone," writes Pascal in his *Pensées* (1670), "is the creator of equity, for the simple reason that it is accepted. It is the hidden foundation of its authority. He who tries to trace it to its first principles annihilates it."[18] In a work characterized as much by his poetic brilliance as by his exegetical rigor, Ambedkar calls this hidden foundation of authority the "riddle of Hinduism," the groundless beauty of divine utterance (*vach*) emanating not from God's gift of faith to ordinary mortals but from the masculine, devouring, and "mystical sacrifice of Purusha."[19]

Why is this transformation of the devouring mouth into the luminous face of divine justice mystical? By what means does divinity's gruesome and sacrificial mouth, its foul and "lawless" contagion, come to acquire an imperishable and "lawgiving" being (*purusha*)? How, Ambedkar would ask in a brilliant turn of dialectical thinking, did the lawlessness of *purusha* become the foundation of authority?[20] In the chapter that follows, we shall see a radically different understanding of this transcendental and imperishable being at work in Gandhi's conception of the limit (*maryada dharma*). There, the figure of *purusha* would be mobilized in Gandhi's thinking of a just and righteous sovereign, the highest of all exemplars (*maryada purushottama*) of virtue and love, the most impeccable of all lawgivers. For Ambedkar, too, the mystical function of *purusha* is to give the law. But this lawgiving, which occurs from a groundless source, serves another function: the concealment of juridical violence by the rhetoric of custom. The celebration of being as essentially nonbeing, in which suffering could be made bearable in the name of a transcendental being or immortal cosmic soul, ensues from this foundational violence. Ambedkar was possibly the one political thinker in modern India who had the conceptual and philological wherewithal to probe the political operations of negative theology (an epistemology to which he would arrive not through Upanishadic theology, which he critiques here, but though the alternative route of Madhyamika Buddhism). For him, not only was the insinuation of sacrificial custom as divine justice the essence of the theologico-political tradition (and the reason for its permanence), but also conversely, he argued, all rhetorics of civilizational, imperial, spiritual, or national-cultural permanence were already theologico-political. Theology, sacred or civic, made sense (and was deployed) only when the modes, operations, and entrenchments of sovereign power were under threat and needed to be secured by new laws. The true force of the law lay, then, not in its visible execution; it lay in its "artful" self-preservation and mystical permanence. Ambedkar remained concerned throughout with the irreducible elements of this tripartite alliance between religion and sovereignty, the third dimension of which was provided by the doctrine of the immortality of the soul in its classical as well as modern Indo-European forms.[21] Indeed, one might argue, at the heart of his moral ontology lay this very question. Why do certain traditions, certain faiths, certain rules, certain spirits, endure while others remain finite? And even more crucially, in the terms set by Pascal, What was the nature of force that sustained one custom and annihilated another?

In the most fundamental sense, Ambedkar's ceaseless thinking of the future, his belief in the imperative of newness, his commitment to the radical constitution and reconstitution of society until it was hammered to perfection, emerged from his consciousness of the historicity of force. By "historicity," I mean Ambedkar's unique skepticism about history's purported ability to tell everything about the deep past. His was not an interest in the history of force in its conventional senses, which reduce its potentiality to a function of power, and which, given one's own implication in the ceaseless logic of force, he believed, one could never write from the outside in the way that one might write a history of violence. Violence produced phenomenological and social effects and thus opened itself to analytical frameworks and categorizations. Force, by its very nature, remained hidden from such analytical and historical determinations. Historicity was this awareness of the manner in which force became invisible to history, the manner in which history itself was given over to force, the manner in which force became spiritual. In its spiritualization, force was sequestered from the morals of everyday life and mobilized in the interest of abstract and oppressive categories such as civilization and nation. Unless one reworked the mystical foundation of this relationship between force and spirit, unless one reclaimed the immeasurability (and destructiveness) of force as justice—a demand that was enshrined in the very title of *Annihilation of Caste*—the realm of action, the very language of freedom, was bound to remain unjust and hierarchical.

Here emerged the second thread of Ambedkar's critique of force, the thread of *his* force, one that might be called a nonviolent violence, but which he called, at three different moments, "annihilation" (in *Annihilation of Caste* in 1936), "general mobilization" (first in *Annihilation of Caste* and then again in *Philosophy of Hinduism*, among other works), and finally, in a brilliant radical-ization of the unequal's weakness and finitude, the force of "impermanence," or *sunnyata* (in *The Buddha and His Dhamma* in 1956). Indeed, a mature Ambedkar would attempt, in the shadow of the "weak force" of *sunnyata*, to recover another, equally classical mode of revolutionary action and belief. I will return to each of these conceptual turns and to the neologisms that they gave birth to in the chapters that follow. In this chapter, I would like to stay with Ambedkar's early critique, pursuing, in the final sections of the chapter, some of its recurrent motifs that came to be woven into his mature works. Force, as it emerged within (and as) an ethics of vulnerability and equal-ness, or *samata*, as a concept that sought to posit another freedom, will be my guiding thread.

It may be argued that Ambedkar's fascination with force was a result in some measure of the enduring memory of his childhood as the "untouchable" son of a Mahar who had served with pride in the colonial British army. Until the very end of his life, Ambedkar continued to plan to write the definitive history of the armed forces in India. Force and forces were the biographical fabric, one might say, of his moral and political thought. In the memory of a twentieth-century "untouchable," after all, Britain's colonial army had, ironi-cally, opened the horizons of a world in which the outcaste and untouchable (*atishudra*), conscripted as an imperial warrior-citizen (*Shudra*) in a way he had been not since antiquity, moved without ban and prohibition. This was a world in which spaces could be traversed freely (if only along the fronts of colonial conquest): towns could be explored in the rhythms of a soldier's can-tonment postings, food could be shared and touched without the threat of ex-communication or death, one could look at a Brahmin and in turn be seen by him. Senses could be reclaimed from the darkness of caste in the strange secu-rity of an alien and colonizing army. It was true too that the armed forces, in a sacrificial situation only they could create and justify by appealing to a greater cause, opened the ground of equality among soldiers willing (and forced) to die. Forces carried a breath of freedom, in other words, that transcended the empirical servitude of untouchable life.

Even at their best, however, the military and "military service" offered to Ambedkar only limited, if always poignant, moral and psychological resources for meditations on freedom.[22] The emotional and spiritual matrix of his thought—in which, ironically, freedom thrived in the movements of an alien and colonizing army alone—was so dense and vertiginous that nothing but a singular faith, indeed, a heretical reclamation of faith beyond all established norms of theological belief and nationalist fidelity, could alone have sustained it. "I am no worshipper of idols. I believe in breaking them. . . . That is the true faith of the nationalist," asserted Ambedkar in January 1943, just four years before India's independence, in a rather heterodox affirmation of his faithfulness.[23] That breakage, that force, whose truth Ambedkar loved and cared about, was no simple cognate of imperial or nationalist power. Nor was it reducible to its filial or paternal roots in soldiery, in the father's attempt to inculcate a reverential pride in the young Bhimrao toward texts of Indic vintage notwithstanding. Nor, above all, was the energy and intensity of this force delimited by what Ambedkar regarded as the theological instinct of nationalism, an instinct, he argued, which was but an obverse of the nationalization of theology—indeed, the nationalist appropriation of martyrdom and sacrifice itself.[24] Belonging in its authentic form to the multitude alone, true force in Ambedkar's sense opened the possibility of life shared by ordinary and equal mortals, bringing into existence an immeasurable love, which he would call, in a distinctive turn of thought, the "love of truth."[25]

I will spend some time examining what this remarkable expression might mean in the context of some crucial moral and political shifts in Ambedkar's approach to Indic texts on authority and sovereignty, especially the dramatic shifts in his engagement with the *Gita*. Because it is from these shifts that the third thread in Ambedkar's critique of force—which I call, in light of the radical reconceptualization of belief that it would involve in the later works, his "heretical empiricism"—would be woven with a complex religious sensibility. A radical love, then, one that renounced neither the radiance of collective solidarity nor the incommensurable singularity of individual sacrifice: this was both Ambedkar's greatest truth and greatest difficulty. A brief turn toward the broader implications of the argument I am making here is necessary before I begin to trace the trajectory of religion— or rather *dhamma*, a religion without religion—within this heretical politics. The turn to religion was not a detour taken from the late 1940s onward by the mature Ambedkar, who, it is often argued, moved toward categories such as belief and truth, even theology, only after an angry disillusionment with the electoral politics of the late colonial period and his limited success in it had begun to set in. On the contrary, this emphasis on the religious, this recuperation of the political and ethical as fidelity to a shared and egalitarian sovereignty of the people, had begun to emerge much earlier. *Annihilation of Caste* (1936), as I show in Chapter 5, was only the most radiant expression of this enduring concern with a democratic faith grounded in every individual's sovereign right to—and responsibility toward—belief, without which there would be no belief in democracy. And yet the truth of "that mysterious thing called conscience"[26] (an expression that pointed toward the taste for the mystical, or even the ungraspable, in Ambedkar's own thought) was often sought out without any subscription to the rhetoric of transcendence or belief in the groundlessness of God. Rather, the mystery of consciousness derived from the struggles immanent to the subject, a subject rebelling against limits, scouring the deepest recesses of its patience, seeking to find a free and unlimited self, and yet aware of its own finitude, always tragically near to— voluntarily or under the force of law—its own mortality. The empiricism of this belief, beyond all concept and idealism, thus remained as grounded in the truth of collective vulnerability—the immortality and ceaseless rebirth of the people as fraternity—as it did in visions of just force.

This belief was empiricist inasmuch as it was instituted neither around the abstract rules and transcendental truths of the moral law nor around the disciplinary demands and monastic abilities of sacrifice. Instead, it belonged to the finitude of everyday life, to the realm of popular energy and activities that a religious responsibility toward life alone might nurture. In a manner that was strongly reminiscent, perhaps even directly drawn, from the division between philosophy and religion that Nietzsche had proposed, Ambedkar wrote in the *Philosophy of Hinduism*: "The philosophers of Upanishads did not realize that to know truth was not enough. One must learn to love truth. The difference between philosophy and religion may be put in two ways. Philosophy is concerned with knowing truth. Religion is concerned with the love of truth. Philosophy is static. Religion is dynamic."[27]

Now, this rendering of philosophy as the static science of "knowing truth," sits uncomfortably, if it is not completely at odds, with Ambedkar's prolifically expressed taste for a dynamic political philosophy. A hasty reading might even suggest a contradiction here. Looked at closely, however, what seems to be at work in this separation, primarily, is not an argument for the distinction between philosophy and religion but a productive tension between the two. The emphasis is on two inseparable approaches to—and rhetorics of—truth. Philosophy (like theology), Ambedkar argues, has the stability of discipline and the law on its side; religion has dynamism, energy, and force. The philosophical (or metaphysical) approach claims for truth a moral universality, a moral reasoning on which transcendental ideals of duty, obedience, and the law are established. The religious approach, on the other hand, grounds truth in the empiricism of fraternity, feeling, and virtue. Clearly, one cannot be easily demarcated from the other. If, however, truth was to be grasped in its fullness, if it had to be imparted force, if it was to be loved in its contingency (and even failure), it could be recovered only from the rich variety of everyday activities, experiences, and faiths. Because love of truth could only be religious, belief had to be seen as an act of holding on to something true. Belief entailed the nourishment and guarding of the wholeness of truth beyond all disciplinary norms, limits, and measures of the moral law; it required not an ascetic withdrawal from the activities and abrasions of everyday life but a struggle with its newness and singularity each single day.

And yet (and this is where Ambedkar returns, through religion, to an insurrectionary ontology within moral philosophy), the unequal's belief, despite the shame, vulnerability, and humiliation inflicted by untouchability, had to produce—indeed, belief had to itself be—an act of force that posited a counteruniversality. Belief, which he elsewhere calls "faith in equality," had to be an act of reclaiming, by violence at once rhetorical and conceptual, the irrefutable generality of human suffering. Ambedkar's love of truth, one might argue, then, was the act of making political—which is also to say, making *universal*—the immanence and inalienability of the unequal's singularity through the amplification of his shared finitude. The most rigorous affirmation of this belief—"belief" as holding on to truth—came rather furtively in 1943, in a speech Ambedkar composed as a tribute to the social reformer from western India Mahadev Govind Ranade. Here, love of truth, the ability to speak without compromise, is separated from politeness and aligned instead with force. But note that what is renounced is politeness, not the irreducible civility that attaches to—and must be considered inseparable from—belief (in moral and political causes).

No one can hope to make any effective mark upon his time and bring the aid that is worth bringing to great principles and struggling causes if he is not strong in his love and his hatred. I hate injustice, tyranny, pompousness and humbug, and my hatred embraces all those who are guilty of them. I want to tell my critics that I regard my feelings of hatred as a real force. They are only the reflex of the love I bear for the causes I believe in and I am in no wise ashamed of it.[28]

Hatred as real force, force as a reflex of love for truth, and love, in turn, constituted through acts of force: we will have to follow these impulses carefully, for part of this thinking of force as love (and vice versa) would wind up in Ambedkar's mature works as well. This passage stands out, meanwhile, as a testimony to Ambedkar's never having given up on, either politically or philosophically, the category of truth. And this was despite his enduring suspicion regarding ontotheology—the belief that the authentic truth of being lay hidden in the mystical groundlessness of a supreme, transcendental being—and Gandhi's privative experiments in truth. On the contrary, he reclaims truth on this occasion as the freedom to believe, truth as the freedom of the subject to hold, embrace, and experience faith; truth, above all, as the willingness to accept, publicly and freely, one's own complicity in the agonistic and spiritual logic of force. This freedom was inseparable in turn, as we shall see in *Annihilation of Caste*, from the freedom to reclaim force, its historicity and generality, its very being. Freedom was not only the autonomy to nurture force when one was unequal and weak (for it was precisely the unequal and weak who prevented force from becoming an instrument of tyranny). Freedom was the space to nourish a "weak force" itself, an ethics of non-sovereignty and love—which the mature Ambedkar in the 1950s would call *maitri*, a politics of friendship, and which we might render as "revolutionary civility," a civility that exceeded not only the humanist ideals of nonviolence but the sovereignty of the human as such. The early suggestions and gestures of his New York seminar papers become salient in relation to this distinctive critique of sovereignty.

A Shakespearean Heresy

Despite its precocious engagement with the moral and material effects of empire, *Administration and Finance of the East India Company*, written when its author was in his twenties, was no *Hind Swaraj*. Ambedkar's response to Gandhi's fin-de-siècle treatise would come half a century later at the end of his own prolific life, in what would arguably be his own masterwork, *The Buddha and His Dhamma*. Yet the title of his M.A. thesis had already confirmed, despite perennial nationalist suspicion of his fidelities, that Ambedkar had come early to thinking about the empire. It was not merely his fascination with statistics—for which Gandhi's acolytes would come to so often chide him—that was at work there. Instead, the first chapter of the thesis was devoted almost entirely to the conceptual and rhetorical ground on which the British East India Company had come to establish its political sovereignty over its Indian dominions. At the end of the opening section of that thesis, after having detailed the corrupt procedures of the Company's court of directors, the young Ambedkar came up with a theatrical allegory to represent what in *Hind Swaraj* Gandhi had called the "pitiable condition of India." "The last chapter must have made it clear," Ambedkar declares, "how and why Western Europe was at a death grapple for the control of India. We followed the armies of the different leaders of different nations—fighting for a country the people of which had very little to choose in the final destiny—the Cama, the Albuquerques, the Busseys, the Lallys, the Clives, the Malcolms, the lakes and the shores, as though enacting the train of ghosts of Banquo's line all that terrified Shakespeare's Macbeth out of his senses."[29]

This is an intriguing formulation, and for someone like Ambedkar, who would eventually master the art of pithy prose, exemplary for the conjuring gesture it makes. This might have been, in fact, another Ambedkar altogether, whose own conceptual and mystical rhythm we must follow with greatest care, resisting the all too easy figures—lawmaker, constitution drafter, rights advocate, statistical moralist, reactive parliamentarian—in which nationalist and anticolonial historiography even at their most sympathetic have tended to confine him. His resort to Shakespeare illuminates not merely his formidable rhetorical preferences or his literary sources, among which are not only the Renaissance dramatist but also figures of English Romanticism, such as Shelley and Coleridge. It also exemplifies Ambedkar's ability to see the features of modern sovereignty, the very framework within which its juridical and political meanings had emerged, as inseparable from the history of representation. In fact, in this resort to ghosts, through which Ambedkar amplifies the combined operations of—and equality between—the symbolic and the real, it is his suspicion of the concept of representation itself, including his intermittent suspicion, in a Rousseauist vein, of the radiance of parliamentary democracy, that is given full force.

One can only quote Ambedkar telegraphically, for this remained a complex issue in his attempt to reconceptualize the problem of general will. "There is," he cautioned in 1945 against democracy's majoritarian and fascist impulses (which were also in his view the results of the aesthetization of politics), "a great need of some one with sufficient courage to tell Indians: Beware of parliamentary democracy, it is not the best product as it appears to be."[30] The influence of *The Discourse on Inequality* (1755) and *The Social Contract* (1762) on Ambedkar's thinking had been palpable even in *Annihilation of Caste*. But two decades earlier, in his Columbia University seminar paper, "Castes in India" (1916), Ambedkar had already, in a moment of brilliant comparativism, compared the "origin of caste" with "enclosure." "The study of the origin of caste," the student wrote, "must furnish us with an answer to the question—what is the class that raised this 'enclosure' around itself?" The resonance between Rousseau's early modern commercial society and Ambedkar's classical India was clear: in both, Ambedkar argued, resources that had belonged to everyone (and worked on by the common people) had been enclosed and expropriated as property by those who had no role in creating its value (except that caste, by the sheer contaminating power it attributed to a person's touch and hand, went much further than enclosure would in degrading both the worker and whatever property had been allowed to remain with him).[31] The pattern of Rousseauist themes and effects on Ambedkar's vocabulary meanwhile (Rousseau is quoted more directly in *Thoughts on Pakistan*, for example) remained diffuse.[32] It was a strong influence nevertheless, and one that Ambedkar retained throughout, most notably, as we shall see, in his emphasis on the civic-revolutionary force of the multitude as the instrument of authentic liberty.[33]

There was, of course, another distinctive genealogy of this suspicion of representation, this Shudra-Shakespearean ability to present as "scene" the usurpation of the multitude's speech by royal agents and ecclesiastical ventriloquists, by executives and lawmakers whose convincing stagecraft both enables and corrupts the possibility of civic life and politics proper.[34] To reconstitute the conditions of political civility, to recover what Ambedkar would call in 1941 the "love of politics," demands a struggle against these institutional, political, and theological usurpers, the mystical spirits and specters of classical jurists and lawgivers.[35] For despite all its rhetoric of liberal or democratic representation, sovereignty in either its imperial or nationalist form, Ambedkar argued, had been not less but more mystical, not less but more vindictive toward those in whose name it acts, not farther but closer to the language of transcendence and divinity. "It is useless to make a distinction between the secular Brahmins and priestly Brahmins," he wrote on the state of the body politic in 1936. "Both are kith and kin. They are two arms of the same body and one bound to fight for the existence of the other."[36] In New York two decades earlier, we shall see below, he had given indications of what would become an enduring resistance against this alliance, Indic and European alike, between sovereign, secular power and the deathless, mystical foundation of its authority.

Shakespeare had been crucial in Ambedkar's time to European thinkers in the French- and German-speaking world engaged with the religious, creaturely, and mystical dimensions of sovereignty.[37] In fact, his kinship with this cluster of moral and legal philosophers, which might include Georges Sorel, Georg Lukács, Walter Benjamin, Ernst Kantorowicz, and Carl Schmitt (all except Sorel born within six years of Ambedkar's birth), must be seen as being hinged not only on his equivocal encounter with early twentieth-century French syndicalism but also on his affinities with Marx and Nietzsche, whose influence on these later thinkers too, not to mention on Ambedkar himself, remained foundational.[38] One is immediately reminded of those memorable passages in Marx's *Economic and Philosophical Manuscripts of 1844* in which the figure of the ghost is brought to stand in as a description for the "real nature of money," a philosophical-anthropological gesture whose reverberations can be felt in the young Ambedkar's own critique of the East India Company.[39] Earlier and closer to home, in nineteenth-century western India, the militant Shudra thinker Jotirao Phule had seen in the colonized Brahmin the grey shades of Shakespeare's *Othello*: "The Brahmin of the present time," Phule wrote in his 1873 masterwork *Gulamgiri* (translated into English as *Slavery*), "finds to some extent, like Othello, that 'his occupation is gone.' But knowing full well this state of matters," Phule asks, "is the Brahmin inclined to make atonement for his past selfishness?"[40] It was as if in invoking *Macbeth* half a century later in New York—a gesture ironic yet appropriate to this formidable heritage, in that Phule had dedicated *Gulamgiri* to "the good people of the United States" for their "sublime" sacrifice against slavery—Ambedkar was answering his master's Shakespearean question.

Note, then, Ambedkar's pointed accent on the people who had "very little to choose in the final destiny." This was not, contra Gandhi, a multitude that had out of spiritual weakness and volition given India to Britain, succumbing to its own lack of firmness by having agreed to keep the English in India.[41] A different thinking was at work here, one that had actively refused the spiritual geography that Gandhi had mapped just six years earlier in *Hind Swaraj*. In this other thinking, agency and force were neither a set of natural attributes nor were they virtues cultivable by good conduct alone. The assumption that the space for such conduct was freely and equally available to everyone, that everyone was equally free to think about freedom as such, was itself the mystical foundation of hierarchy, a false and abstract equality. In truth, virtue and agency were uneven and even unfree, sequestered from the multitude and distributed among the few according to the moral law of obligation (*niti dharma*) that had been instituted through an alliance between priests and warriors. This was the multitude, then, that had little choice. Devoid of speech and representation, it was spoken for only by the mystical ventriloquists, by those conjurers of sacred aura and divine utterance whose own authority lay shrouded in secrecy. If the long line of European conquerors, like ghosts of Banquo, had chased the dream of sovereignty across India, the Brahmin ventriloquists who claimed to speak for India had not resisted. Instead, they had looked away, hiding behind their own gods and spirits, scared as they were, like Macbeth, "out of their senses." Macbeth always knew that the guilt lay with him. He knew well the evil and violence he harbored within himself. The empire, like Banquo's apparition, played its trick in a similar fashion. As if in a flash of dialectical justice, the violence of religion perpetrated against the multitude, the corrupt authority of warriors and priests that lay at the heart of Indic sovereignty, had now returned in the form of Britain's empire to haunt the Macbeth-like Brahmin ventriloquists themselves.

So relentless was Ambedkar's indictment of the Company's methods, its scandalous use of force and abuse of military dominance in service of its profits, that one might have already anticipated the birth of the inspired reader that he would soon become of that strident eighteenth-century critic of British corruption in Bengal, Edmund Burke.[42] Burke is not named directly in the thesis. He came to be quoted copiously in the work that Ambedkar did after his return to India, most notably *Thoughts on Pakistan* and his late essay

"Buddha or Karl Marx."[43] And suggestively, Burke was cited not so much in Ambedkar's critique of the empire as he was mobilized for his critique of authority, in his thinking of terror, coerciveness, and corruptions of force. By the end of his time in New York, at any rate, Ambedkar's fascination with spirits and specters had begun to acquire a certain pattern. Barely over a year after his invocation of *Macbeth*, in another Columbia University seminar for which he wrote his brilliant early paper "Castes in India" (he was 26 when it was published in May 1917 in *The Indian Antiquary*), the young Ambedkar speaks of force in the most unequivocal manner yet. His target is Manu, the classical Indic jurist, whose laws, are codified in a book of verses called the *Manusmriti*, which is considered to be the foundational text in Indic jurisprudence. Although the ghostly remnants of classical jurists appear in this essay too, it is also in many ways a decisive beginning of Ambedkar's enduring engagement with the theologico-political problem, a beginning of another equally significant impulse. This impulse was yet to be fully discernible. But it would form a strand that appears with greatest clarity in his more mature works, gathering strength around Ambedkar's insistence on force as weakness, force as an ethical nonsovereignty, force, above all, as the radical relinquishment of the state and its laws of sacrifice. In his struggle against the juridical and moral law of *Manusmriti*, meanwhile, a young Ambedkar had come up against the immensity of force in its absolute unity and permanence.

I first propose to handle the lawgiver of India. Every country has its lawgiver, who arises as an incarnation [*avatar*] in times of emergency to set right a sinning humanity and give it the laws of justice and morality. Manu, the lawgiver of India, if he did exist, was certainly an audacious person. . . . [However,] it is unimaginable that the law of caste was given. It is hardly an exaggeration to say that Manu could not have outlived his law, for what is that class that can submit to be degraded to the status of brutes by the pen of a man, and suffer him to raise another class to the pinnacle? Unless he was a tyrant who held all the population in subjection it cannot be imagined that he could have been allowed to dispense his patronage in this grossly unjust manner, as may be easily seen by a mere glance at his "Institutes." I may seem hard on Manu, but I am sure my force is not strong enough to kill his ghost. He lives, like a disembodied spirit and is appealed to, and I am afraid will yet live long.[44]

Among the many conceptual and rhetorical aspects that can be separated and probed in this brilliant and exasperated passage, I want to focus on Ambedkar's mindfulness of the elusive phantasm of juridical authority. Disembodied, invisible, and deathless, Manu's spirit was proving for the young student impossible to exorcize. The force of this phantasm accrued not merely from its disembodied life, which lent it, in the manner of the sovereigns of old, a mythic and sacrosanct aura. The force accrued from the specter's ability to insinuate itself, in moments of exception and crisis, as the embodied voice of sovereignty itself, its ability to simultaneously wield the pen in order to write the law and immunize those laws, of which the *Manusmriti* (also known as *The Institutes of Manu*) was a compendium, by gross force. Brutal sovereignty, the mobilization of power in its most material and punitive form, were inseparable, argued Ambedkar, from acts of lawmaking and legislation. Rather, law's force seemed most spiritual and egalitarian, most protective and generous, precisely when it was most punitive and its effects most visceral. This paradox marks the foundation of *Chaturvarnya*; indeed, it underlies the ontology of religion as such. As if in a violent irony, it is precisely the deathlessness of Hinduism's sovereign lawgiver, in contrast to the mortality of such figures as Christ, Paul, or Moses, that ensures the pernicious permanence of that religion's oppressive moral law.

In his discernment of an apparitional force at the heart of this theologico-political configuration, Ambedkar had also moved away from the classically materialist and anthropological analyses of religion, one that Indian Marxist historians such as D. D. Kosambi would clear the ground for in the middle of the twentieth century (and which Durkheim's *Elementary Forms*, with its chapter on "the idea of force," had done earlier in the century).[45] While Kosambi's interest developed around the everyday life of religion, and while he sought out the material nuance and logical arrangement of spaces, goods, and things that underlay religious practices, Ambedkar probed the ontological boundary of the religious where it turned spectral—that is, at the limit beyond which the religious became spiritual and ethereal; where the phenomenology of everyday life became inseparable from the conceptual and cognitive order of sovereignty; where, therefore, religion could not be understood within the limits of reason and materiality alone; where the operations of its mystical and masculine transcendence (*purusha*) could be revealed only through a spiritual analysis of the political, only by inhabiting the mystical rather than by cultivating an objective, secularist distance from it. If we identify the "mystical" in terms of its fundamental function, which holds true across religious traditions, monotheistic and otherwise—that of imbuing faith at once with an absolute, transcendental secrecy and an inseparable, immanent unity between the mortal subject and the transcendental being—then we begin to see the constitutive paradox at the heart of Hinduism's mystical discourse against which Ambedkar had begun to mount his struggle.[46] We can also sense why he remained equivocal with regard to secularist critiques (and anthropological morphologies) of religion; they did not go close enough to experience it.

After all, the foundation of *Manusmriti*'s authority is mystical not simply because it was corrupt, which is true of any authority that seeks its legitimacy in the groundless divinity of God. Rather, it is mystical because it had the ability to appear, at the moment precisely of its gravest violence, so generous and protective toward the subject. Ambedkar would subsequently find the sovereign example of this simultaneity of self-erasure and exclusion, the concealment of mastery behind the rhetoric of disinterest and custom, in the *Gita's* fratricidal ethics. And this struggle against the *Gita* was no evidence of his modernist disenchantment with the theologico-political as such. Instead, the struggle would reveal what was most religious, most given over to sacrifice, in Ambedkar's own thought. One might even argue that by the beginning of the 1920s, struggle itself had been instituted at the heart of his moral and political practice, just as its spiritual cognate, experiment, had been in Gandhi's.

Let me return briefly to Ambedkar's exasperated resistance against the *Manusmriti*: "I may seem hard on Manu," he concedes, "but I am sure my force is not strong enough to kill his ghost." This affinity for force and forcing—and the invocation of ghosts and specters—is not merely semantic or rhetorical. Its sources are Shakespearean, but for that reason alone its logic cannot be seen to be any less concerned with Ambedkar's politics and ethics than it clearly is with his literary and poetic sensibilities. Quite to the contrary, force was an irrevocable constituent of Ambedkar's emerging ethics. In 1927, four years after his return from London, he publicly burned at a Satyagraha Conference in Mahad, a town just over a hundred miles south of Bombay, a copy of the *Manusmriti*. The ghost was now being exorcized by fire in classic satyagrahic fashion. "The bonfire of *Manusmriti*," Ambedkar recalled, "was a very cautious and drastic step . . . taken with a view to forcing the attention of caste Hindus. If you do not knock at the door, none opens it. It is not that all parts of *Manusmriti* are condemnable. . . . We made a bonfire of it because we view it as symbol of injustice . . . because of its teachings we have been ground down under despicable poverty, and so we made the dash, staked all, took our lives in our hands and performed the deed."[47]

If we follow the thread of Ambedkar's moral ontology on its own terms, his emphasis on force as exactitude becomes immediately discernible— "forcing" is an act of freedom at once immeasurable and grounded in a cautious and measured civility, at once a revolutionary act of burning the moral law in its physical manifestation as a book and a heretical gesture of recalling the mystical or spectral attributes of the law that had rendered justice impossible to secure without force. It was in this sense that the burning of the *Manusmriti*—the act of forcing open (as Ambedkar puts it in a performative fashion) the door of the moral law behind which lay the freedom from juridical and cognitive servitude—exceeded the specificity of the gesture and instituted a new measure of insurrection itself. It was an interpretive and collective *coup de force* in the true sense of the term, no less momentous a revolt against Hinduism's "spirit of inequality," insisted Ambedkar, than the storming of Bastille had been against the monarchical order in France, precisely because no existing foundation or law had been ever witness to—or might be able judge—its insurrectionary virtues.[48] In such moments of revolutionary universalism, force was rhetorical, even performative, and yet always grounded in the empiricism of experience, in the pure will and specific materiality of the collective act. Above all—and it is at this point that the conditions of a revolutionary nonviolence emerge in Ambedkar's thinking—force was that which made the unequal's experience visible at its *weakest*, imparting to it a freedom and immortality that was grounded in the truth of shared mortality alone. That enigmatic concession made by a young New York student, "I am sure my force is not strong enough to kill his ghost," was but a consciousness of this limit and finitude. In fact, in its authentic form, force, unlike violence, was always "weak," aware of finitude and limit, resistant to declarations of transcendence and plentitude. Its transformative and emancipatory potential remained concealed and congealed in its very weakness and vulnerability, in its forcelessness and scarcity even.[49]

When distinctions between force and nonviolence, justice and sacrifice, heresy and belief—distinctions that are set to work and undone in the subtlest of ways in Ambedkar's corpus—are patiently scrutinized, they reveal Ambedkar not only as a thinker of sacrifice (with a place singularly his own among the ranks of contemporary classicists, such as Georges Dumézil, who were working during the same years in the interstices of Indo-European linguistic and political theology) but also as a sacrificial thinker.[50] They illuminate his concerns not only as a critical theorist of religion, one who might look radically different from the disenchanted theorist of rights he is often described as, but also as a formidably religious thinker. After all, it was a singular if heretical commitment to faith alone that allowed Ambedkar to reclaim the immortality of the soul—a figure irrefutably spiritual if not unambiguously religious in its provenance—as the ground for justice. Invoking Burke and Coleridge at the end of a remarkable passage in his 1943 tribute to Mahadev Govind Ranade, the eminent liberal reformer from western India, Ambedkar posits authentic force as belonging neither to the order of revolutionary terror nor the parliament and republic, but instead to the realm of soulful rhythm and action.

As experience proves, rights are protected not by law but by the social and moral conscience of society. If social conscience is such that it is prepared to recognize the rights which law chooses to enact rights will be safe and secure. But if the fundamental rights are opposed by the community, no Law, no Parliament, no judiciary can guarantee them in the real sense of the word. What is the use of the fundamental rights to the Negroes in America, to the Jews in Germany, and to the Untouchables in India? As Burke said, there is no method found for punishing the multitude. Law can punish a single solitary recalcitrant criminal. It can never operate against a whole body of people who are determined to defy it. Social conscience—to use the language of Coleridge—that calm incorruptible legislator of the soul without whom all other powers would "'meet in mere oppugnancy'—is the only safeguard of all rights fundamental or non-fundamental."[51]

This passage is uncharacteristic not for the soulful foundation of justice that Ambedkar lays claim over but rather for his mobilization of the soul (in whose empirical or spiritual existence he did not believe in the usual religious sense) as the immanent ground of a sovereign and egalitarian faith, soul as the moral and political foundation of a shared political community.[52] Calm and incorruptible, the soul breaks from all established ecclesiastical structures, replacing the punitive dictates of *dharma* with the virtues of *dhamma* as a collective obligation to be just. Indeed, this healing and just force, argues Ambedkar, overrides the mechanisms for restitution and reparation set in place by juridical and parliamentary injunctions themselves. Mere laws, if Germany and the United States were any indication, were worthless anyway until the political—that is to say, the multitude's power to constitute itself as a collective—was reclaimed as a realm of shared sacrifice and revolutionary concert. The pernicious universalism of untouchability, like that of racism and anti-Semitism, or even nationalism, could not be resisted by mounting a criminal investigation against it. Its mystical universalism could be countered only by reconstituting freedom as a collective and shared universality, by curing what Ambedkar had seven years earlier called the "disease of indifferentism."[53]

I will examine Gandhi's strikingly adjacent thinking of nonviolence as nonindifference in Chapter 4. But for now we must mark the end of this momentary resonance between Ambedkar's fidelity to the Coleridgean incorruptibility of the soul and Gandhi's spiritual formulations on "soul-force." Ambedkar's "soul" was neither an extension of the sacrificial principles of the moral law nor a disciplinary cognate of what Gandhi would in the 1930s call *maryada dharma*. Rather, this soul was the marker of the unequal's vulnerability and feebleness, his imperfection and fallibility, within which suffering and fear, the precarious knowledge of one's finitude itself, was experienced in its most unmediated form. Such a soul could not have been the ground of spiritual mastery; inseparable from mortality instead, it could only have been the source of a collective and revolutionary autonomy. In Ambedkar's hands, then, the soul becomes a heretical category, a space of weakness and force where servitude and freedom, courage and justice become inseparable, each rendered unthinkable without the other within the unequal's awareness. Freedom was authentic, *Annihilation of Caste* had repeatedly cautioned, only when the multitude was "moved" in *this* life, only when constituent power—that is, the multitude's rightful claim to seek immortality through action—sought its "letter and spirit" now, in the foundation of an egalitarian sovereignty.[54] "Spare us," Ambedkar had demanded as he finished his tribute to Ranade, "the tedium of idle clatter of liberals and liberalism."[55]

Immortal, Incommensurable, Equal

Some would argue that by 1943, when Ambedkar wrote the tribute to Ranade, he had been decisively outflanked by the Gandhian Congress. It was easy, therefore, for him to cultivate this tenor of antiliberalism, part of which also emerged from his affinity for certain strands of European revolutionary and conservative thought, not to forget the realities of the war that lent his rhetoric in these years a particularly insurrectionary tenor. But such contextualization, which reduces the rhythms of political thought to the vagaries of electoral fortune alone, risks losing the depth of Ambedkar's moral stance. Seven years before the Ranade essay, in which he had unequivocally refused the teleological "waiting room" of liberal caste reform, calling it "idle clatter" for its tactical slowness and willful deferral of justice, Ambedkar had published his undelivered lecture, *Annihilation of Caste*.[56] An extraordinary sense—and performance—of force saturates *Annihilation of Caste*. In fact, Ambedkar would never write more eloquently of force in its institutional, semantic, and theological senses, or warn more evocatively against the moral failures of republican government, Hellenic or Indic, than he would in one singular passage of that work. But the text of that lecture is a testimony also to his deeper conceptual hunger, as if he were grappling to pin down the elusive moral ontology of action, its historicity and truths, its mystical foundations and emancipatory potentialities, its strange movements between caste and class, Hinduism and Platonism.[57] In fact, *Annihilation of Caste* would have left little doubt—and one cannot but think of its only precedent in the colonial world, *Hind Swaraj*—that Ambedkar was trying nothing short of mastering the concept of force itself. There were two forces here too: the first with its source in *Chaturvarnya*, that most inauthentic, punitive, and violent of juridical frameworks, whose modern manifestations had been no less brutal and cruel; the second that derived from the multitude's will to annihilation, which had to be mobilized, with its immeasurable and even anarchic force—that is, the force that exceeded the law of limits and measure—against the first. For *Chaturvarnya* was not simply a social institution. It was a failure of thought, the death of heresy, the multitude's forgetfulness of force as such, one that had lent it the aura of a divine ordinance.

It is important to note that the rhetorical structure of *Annihilation of Caste*, which is in its own right the source of its immense performance and force, is not its only galvanizing feature. When the speech was published in 1936, just a year before national elections under the Government of India Act of 1935 were to be held for the first time in the subcontinent, the reformist sensibilities of liberals and satyagrahis alike were perturbed by Ambedkar's attempt to see in caste—with all its material exclusions, bodily violence, and spatial prohibitions—the concealed matter and cognitive servitude of an entire civilization. Did this civilization, Ambedkar asks, have any residual capacity for civility that might justify its imminent democratization? Would franchise or even "equalization of property" alone bring equality in its truthful sense?[58] Would the sacrificial atonement of a few among the oppressive majority secure the future of reason? Was "a Hindu," he asks, "free to follow his reason?"[59] Or, given that such a freedom of reason looked unlikely, might not a revolutionary force—the universalization of force—alone clear the possibility of justice?

Thus emerges a text punctuated by a series of incandescent bursts of mystical energy. For what Ambedkar had attempted to formulate (even if he had not yet fully succeeded), was a *non*-theologico-political possibility of force, a force that is immortal without being given over to mastery and transcendence. But in order to wrest such force, in order to think such force, one had to first reclaim an "understanding" of force, its attributes and foundations, its reasons and truth. One had to reclaim difference, the vulnerability, incommensurability, and singularity of life, from which the very facticity of force (in social and moral relations) emerged. This facticity was grounded not in the constitution of an individual but in the faculty of collective and constituent power. Force was the becoming political of vulnerability; it was a faculty taken away from the weakest, most unequal of the social order, which had to now be returned to them. But why was this faculty a faculty of force? Because force alone was singular, crafted and honed by every individual in the radiant specificity of his own personhood and civility. Force was the negation of all alienation that estranged man from himself, that reduced him into an abstract, negotiable number, that converted him from "millions to fractions" and back. In a brilliant critique of abstract notions of equality and commensurability, a tendency he dated back to the greatest texts of the republican tradition, Ambedkar writes:

Chaturvarnya pre-supposes that you can classify people into four definite classes. Is this possible? In this respect, the ideal of Chaturvarnya has, as you will see, a close affinity to the Platonic ideal. To Plato, men fell by nature into three classes. In some individuals, he believed mere appetites dominated. He assigned them to the laboring and trading classes. Others revealed to him that over and above appetites, they have a courageous disposition. He classed them as defenders in war and guardians of internal peace. Others showed a capacity to grasp the universal reason underlying things. He made them the lawgivers of the people. The criticism to which Plato's *Republic* is subject, is also the criticism which must apply to the system of *Chaturvarnya*, in so far as it proceeds on the possibility of an accurate classification of men into four distinct classes. The chief criticism against Plato is that his idea of lumping of individuals into a few sharply marked-off classes is a very superficial view of man and his powers. Plato had no perception of the uniqueness of every individual, of his incommensurability with others, of each individual forming a class of his own. He had no recognition of the infinite diversity of active tendencies and combination of tendencies of which an individual is capable. To him, there were types of faculties or powers in the individual constitution. All this is demonstrably wrong. . . . Chaturvarnya must fail for the very reason for which Plato's *Republic* must fail.[60]

For the sheer manner in which it marked Ambedkar's struggle to move away from the Platonic heritage within classical republicanism, this passage was a key moment in *Annihilation of Caste* (and in Ambedkar's corpus at large). The *Republic* and *Manusmriti*, he argues, are not theological texts on sovereignty in the usual sense of the term. For neither of them stops at—or is even interested in—propounding "a divine scheme of governance" alone.[61] Instead, they are treatises on the kinship between civility and enforcement, obligations and rules, life and law. Any classicist who has studied the philosophy of government— philosophy and government—knows, Ambedkar argues, that the interest of these two treatises lies in maintaining the balance between civic freedoms and legal prohibitions, between appetites and accesses. Each is an elaborate compendium of rules for prayer, feast, sacrifice, war, burials, and mourning; each contains elaborate laws for the regulation of life from the cradle to the grave. From injunctions on the movement of pregnant women to rituals for pacifying the ghosts of the dead, no spiritual or material fact of everyday life in ancient Greece and India remains untouched by their moral law. Both Plato's republic and *Chaturvarnya* "must perpetually face the problem of the transgressor." Thus emerge the immaculate laws of punitive counterviolence. "Unless there is a penalty attached to the act of transgression . . . the whole system will break down, being contrary to human nature. Chaturvarnya cannot subsist by its own inherent goodness. It must be enforced by law."[62] This was a world saturated by force, then, one where force had insinuated itself in the name of God and tradition, republic and theocracy, plutocracy and democracy alike.

Ambedkar's revolt was mounted against the alienating effects of this moral law. His problem was not with the intrusion of religiosity into these ancient political and juridical systems, nor, clearly, with the saturation of world by force as such. "History bears out the proposition," he had argued elsewhere in the lecture, citing the examples of Luther and Mohammad, "that political revolutions have always been preceded by social and religious revolutions," the absence of which in India explained the destitute and violent nature of belief in that country.[63] Nor was he unequivocally opposed to the satyagrahic rhetoric of the soul, with its force worthy of mobilization in pursuit of moral and political transformation. This was an ethics, on the contrary, to which Ambedkar was strongly drawn, even if he hardly believed in taking care of the soul in satyagrahic or Platonic fashion. Nor, above all, did he refuse the value of immortality—indeed, rebirth—for politics, even if for him the virtues of immortality could be grounded only in finitude, only in the belief that what endures, what is immortal, what must be kept alive, is not the transcendental idea of Being but rather the immanent truth of a material world formed through collective action.

Immortality worthy of a moral and political act, thus, could be grounded only in the freedom to affirm life in its infinite difference and finitude. This was a counterintuitive turn of thought, one that involved a distinctive engagement with various traditions of Indian and European nihilism. I will return to that moment later in the book. At this point, however, we must note that by grounding politics in affirmations of shared life rather than in the solitude of a sacrificial death, Ambedkar had reclaimed a very specific kind of immortality for politics. He had rendered the freedom of mortals itself immortal, a freedom founded not on attributes marked by birth, family, or even paternity but in the authenticity of groundlessness, in a singularity of incommensurable lives whose right to justice required no foundation. This freedom would be immortal inasmuch as its foundation would be laid in the empirical infinitude (or immeasurable richness) of each person's singularity, one that could nevertheless be brought to life only in the shared and unlimited space of collective action.[64] In such a world of singularities, each life would also be equal inasmuch as it would be equally free to exist in its "incommensurability" and difference. Without this freedom to exist, this autonomy to live out one's finitude in the world, this *equality of freedom*, this right, above all, to sacrifice oneself for justice, Ambedkar insists, equality itself would be "glaringly fallacious." Equality was but a "fiction" anyway, he claims in an intriguing interpretation of the French Revolution, if it were not sustained by the groundless and unconditional sharing of freedom among mortals. This sharing is what he often calls, in an anti-Platonic vein, "fraternity."

In his later works, especially the essays of the 1940s and 1950s, Ambedkar shows signs of recognizing the masculine impulses intrinsic to the language of fraternity, which had, in its French Revolutionary iteration, always invoked the sharing of the father's remains among the brothers alone. Thus, he frequently replaces "fraternity" with *maitri* ("friendship" or "fellowship") in his final writings and, in an All India Radio Broadcast in 1954, equates fraternal sharing (which included the sharing of belief) with religion itself.[65] But traces of this shift are already evident in *Annihilation of Caste*. The fearless claim for a politics without territory or ground is already present in that lecture. There is no equality, he argues, without the sharing of freedom (and vice versa), no immortality of politics without a collective respect for the immeasurable singularity of every creature's mortality. The irrefutable truth of impermanence alone lends politics its immortal value. The moral sovereignty of democracy over all other political forms and activities (or at least, the lack of adequate alternatives that might take its place) stems only from its promise to establish the everyday, even mundane, realm of "communicated experience" as the ethical and political ground of existence. In such a realm, argues Ambedkar, the social exists "by communication, indeed in communication," and one's failure is considered as justly sharable with others as one's success.[66] In true democracy, then, the sovereignty of the self is always mediated by one's "reverence" toward the neighbor.[67] Any other mediation of the multitude's action by representatives, agents, priests, philosopher-kings, or demagogues of class war, compromises the spiritual sovereignty and task of the revolutionary subject. There was something profoundly insurrectionary and anarchic in this conception of the political. For here, the political subject came into existence only through incandescent acts of force and martyrdom, through its immeasurable freedom to posit a republic unmarked by the logic of transcendence.

I have referred, earlier in the book, to this particular strand in Ambedkar's thought that strives toward an unmediated politics as his attempt to formulate the conditions of an "egalitarian sovereignty." Inasmuch as this neologism bears the marks of classical republicanism of French revolutionary heritage, it is also a contradiction in terms, as Étienne Balibar has pointed out. It certainly captures, within itself, a set of political and moral psychologies that would unfold in the 1930s and 1940s as India began to move irreversibly (if as yet slowly) toward universal adult franchise, with Ambedkar himself at the forefront of those constitutional debates and formulations. *Annihilation of Caste* remains the most unequivocal encapsulation of that complex moment, a fulcrum not merely of Ambedkar's thinking of egalitarian forms of sovereignty—the people's constituent power—but a testimony to his anticipations of the future of democratic politics in modern India. Its timing and tenor may have had something to do with his 1932 Poona Pact with Gandhi, signed under the threatening shadow of Gandhi's fast unto death; the pact had convinced Ambedkar that neither the imminent constitutional reforms nor the elections to be held under their auspices were going to bring any radical transformation in the way franchise, reform, and representation had been arranged until then by the colonial government. The prospect of separate electorates for the "depressed classes" had all but evaporated, and with it, the grounds for consolidated electoral advantage and political voice. The formulation of an unmediated force belonging to the sovereign realm of the multitude, the demand to reclaim the egalitarian foundation of general will shorn of all measure and mediation, the grounding of action in the love of truth alone, emerged in this context.

I return to the question of truth—and the young Ambedkar's striking willingness to see it in action in the *Gita*, a text of which he would subsequently become an uncompromising critic—below. But first, a contextualization of this insurgent thought, which was both deeply indigenous in its sensitivities and global in its theoretical resourcefulness, is necessary. To speak of "unmediated" or "religious" or "revolutionary" force in Ambedkar's thought requires separating these strands carefully from both the purely sacrificial logic of negative theology (which institutes the doctrine of pure groundlessness and immateriality of being, rendering the body immaterial to moral and political life) and the mythic humanism and language of class war such as those developed by the European syndicalists at the beginning of the twentieth century. The syndicalists, after all, were notorious for avoiding programs of reform. Any sort of intermediate reform, they feared, might induce complacency in the proletariat. In fact, reform within the existing structure of capitalist production, they insisted, made the contamination of revolutionary morals by the bourgeoisie nearly certain. The bourgeoisie's only antidote, the French syndicalist Georges Sorel had argued in his influential work *Reflections on Violence* (1908), lay in the divine force of the "general strike." "With the general strike," promises Sorel, "all these fine things disappear; the revolution appears as a clear, simple revolt, and no place is reserved either for the sociologists or for the elegant amateurs of social reforms or for the intellectuals who have made it their profession to think for the proletariat."[68]

There was an immense rhetorical, semantic, and political affinity here between Sorel and Ambedkar. "In any struggle," a young Ambedkar had exhorted in 1927 during a Satyagraha campaign to allow untouchables to enter Hindu temples, "there are negotiations first and then war. I think we have had enough negotiations." Minutes earlier (and still about a decade away from renouncing Hinduism completely), he had invoked a quotation from the *Mahabharata* itself. "Go and show your bravery even for a moment without fearing death," he had paraphrased from the epic, quoting a mother spurring her warrior son to action. "It is better to die in a battle than living slowly de-composing in a bed for hundred years."[69] Notwithstanding this invocation of revolutionary purity, this celebration of fatal force—in which violence of the weakest was posited as unavoidable, excusable, and belonging to the order of truth (*satya*) and sacrifice (*yajna*)—Ambedkar had often worried that the fine lines of exclusion, which Sorel had imagined would dissolve in the pure simplicity of the European strike, might never disappear in India. Was there, he inquires ten years later in *Annihilation of Caste*, a proletariat in India wor-thy of the name, one that would act freely, undeterred by inhibitions of sense and touch that had marred its revolutionary purpose? In their belief that the morals of revolutionary action could be grounded in the transcendental (and mythic) purity of classes, were not the syndicalists showing themselves to be blind to the invisible cleavages, shame, and humiliations among the work-ers themselves? Wasn't the moral law of purity itself an instrument of the op-pressor—indeed, of all regimes of sovereignty—which the oppressed must fight? Could equality be secured without freedom from this cognitive and sensory servitude, merely through the "equalization of property"?[70] But per-haps more fundamentally, Ambedkar asks, doesn't the failure of all theologies of the strike lie in their replication of the mysticism characteristic of religion at its worst? Is not the rhetoric of purity a mystical abstraction, which, speak-ing in the name of God, seeks to simply replace one form of passivity, one form of surrender to the moral law, with another?

Ambedkar very often comes close to suggesting that any rhetoric of quasi-transcendental purity (of concept and action), any invocation of di-vine force in the name of truth, is always already compromised by a perni-cious theologico-political ambition. In fact, in India abstract categories such as "proletariat" and "class," were they to remain blind to that society's peculiar ways of loving and hating democracy, would inevitably lapse into the worst exclusions and violence of its moral law. It was in 1938, two years after *Anni-hilation of Caste*, however, that Ambedkar's critique of syndicalism's political theology acquired its most unequivocal form. The Nazi-Soviet Nonaggres-sion Pact of 1939 was still to come, and Ambedkar's appointment as the Labor Member in the Viceroy's Executive Council was three years away. So the anti-strike tenor of his 1938 presidential speech for the Indian Labor Party is signif-icant, given especially the importance of Indian labor in Britain's war effort to which, by 1940, most Indian nationalists too had reconciled. But there is also a more constitutive impulse at work in Ambedkar's critique of syndicalism, one that I think is irreducible to the pragmatic constraints that might have been imposed by his position in the Viceroy's council. This impulse—the resistance against the mystical—would subsequently surface in an even stronger form in his mature engagement with the *Gita*. "Strikes as a divine means of creating discontent," Ambedkar warns meanwhile, "whether they have created greater discontent or not, they have most certainly destroyed the very trade union organizations which were the source of their strength and power, and now they are practically on the streets seeking to take shelter under all sorts of capitalist organizations." The revolutionary syndicalist or his latter-day communist kin, he suggests, "is like an incendiary who, in his desire to set up a general conflagration, has not taken care to save his own house. As a result, there are no unions in existence to which workers can resort to."[71]

The pure means of European syndicalism's nonprogrammatic, utopian, divine violence, condensed in its otherwise incandescent call for the "general strike," could then lapse not only into an abstention from politics.[72] It could, warns Ambedkar, compromise the free space of the political itself. For in the hands of the conflagrating syndicalist demagogue, he insists, divinity demanded the ultimate sacrifice from the worker even as it burned down the very structure and space of revolutionary reason. It was this radical destructiveness of the general strike—which, he cautions, is most pernicious, indeed effective, when force is most mystical, most convincing, most godlike—that had made him discern a spiritual kinship between syndicalism and capitalism, each sheltering and corrupting the other until one becomes the apparition of the other. One had to always be cautious when lives were taken, spaces occupied, machines burned down, artisanal and manual work privileged, in God's name. "A society which does not believe in democracy may be indifferent to machinery," he exhorted two years before he was nominated to preside over the constitution drafting committee, "but a democratic society cannot. A society that does not believe in democracy may well content itself with a life of leisure and culture for the few and a life of toil and drudgery for the many,"[73] but not democratic society, he warned, for justice would come only when the hand of the weak multitude had been liberated from its historic unfreedom, only when the tyrannical had been restrained and the just had been made the strongest,[74] only when, above all, he declared in a dizzy formulation, "machine takes the place of man."[75]

This utopian dream of the posthuman automaton, which appeared in 1945, is made even more enigmatic by its presence in a text whose dedication page contained a lengthy passage from the Old Testament. I will return to that religious impulse in Chapter 7. My focus now, as a preliminary step toward reconstructing this theologico-political critique of mysticism, is Ambedkar's radicalization of the "general strike" itself, a radicalization that takes syndicalism's principle of generality—the unconditional immeasurability of force (and this includes, in an unmistakable Bergsonian inflection, the force of machinery without limit)—to its spiritual extreme, and yet refuses to renounce the factory. It is not entirely clear from Ambedkar's citations, bibliographies, and annotations that he had read Sorel. But as his direct critique of the theology of syndicalism intimates, he had read the anarcho-syndicalist literature of the time, of which Sorel was the most important theoretical voice. And then there was W. E. B. Du Bois across the Atlantic, whose *Black Reconstruction in America* (1935), published just a year before *Annihilation of Caste*, had placed war and mobilization at the heart of American emancipation, devoting an entire chapter on the "General Strike." Ambedkar and Du Bois would eventually exchange letters in 1946 and express familiarity with each other's works. But perhaps much before that, this encounter had already been mediated by the revolutionary grammar of Sorel's demand to generalize force.[76] Sorel's own debt to Henri Bergson, whom Ambedkar read from the late 1930s onward, was decisive, and explicit traces of Bergson's influence surface not only in the early pages of *Philosophy of Hinduism* but even before that, somewhat obliquely, in the closing passages of *Annihilation of Caste*. Ambedkar would in fact pick key passages from *Annihilation of Caste* and graft them into *Philosophy of Hinduism*, with, as I argue in Chapter 5, much graver consequences. His argument in the presidential lecture, at any rate, was pitched directly against early twentieth-century syndicalist theory of action that the French anarchist had proposed. And yet common to both Ambedkar and syndicalist thought was their attempt to lay bare, in the strongest manner possible, the aura of tradition whose legitimacy was enforced not by divine sanction but by the bourgeois and capitalist phenomenology of spirit that had legitimized itself in God's name. At the heart of both was the attempt to retrieve, beyond all measure and norm, the singularity of the revolutionary act—one might call it the immanence of force as such. In fact, the chronology of texts might suggest that Ambedkar's revolutionary neologism "general mobilization," which appears for the first time in *Annihilation of Caste*, may have indeed been rather directly inspired by Sorel's idea of the "general strike."[77]

Let us note the tension in this neologism. The concepts Ambedkar couples together—"general" and "mobilization"—refer to two very distinct idioms, strategies, and traditions; they pull in directions that were never easily reconciled in his own thought. In fact, Ambedkar was to remain both enduringly partial to the Bergsonian idea of vitality and life, to its claim of singularity and incommensurability, and yet somewhat cautious about the temptation to mysticism that inhered in that tradition of thought. In "general mobilization," then, the term "general," whose Rousseauist antecedents grounded in the theory of general will Ambedkar was deeply drawn to, bore the greatest weight of his revolutionary sensibility and conceptual tact. But in invoking action as generality, Ambedkar does not merely seek to mobilize the quotidian energies of the people against Brahmanic and Kshatriya corruptions of force, as if, he argues, in a society debilitated by the "graded sovereignty" of caste, force is available equally to every subject, as if its presence could be taken for granted, as if the subject itself could be considered fully formed and conscious. Instead, what he calls "the general" summons the force of a negative universality, which is to say, the immortal force of mortals, the infinite freedom of the unfree, the incommensurable equality of unequals whose only commonality lies in the everyday violations of their life and finitude. Individualism is the soul of this theory of action, yet no individual worthy of the name would fail to recognize the shared truth and force of creaturely mortality. Breaking from the classical schemas of access, distribution, and substitution of goods that configure the modern discourse on equality, *Annihilation of Caste* expresses this immanent and immeasurable universality of force. Force does not simply belong to the multitude; rather, claims Ambedkar, it remains so only when it is in their free and equal hands, unmediated by the disciplinary measure of the moral law that institutions such as empire, nation, *kshatriyadharma*, or even class, seek to impose on it. Force, despite its propensities to be corrupted all too quickly by the law, could not be renounced, then. On the contrary, the conditions of justice had to be formulated in the very act of retrieving another force. This belief remained at the heart of Ambedkar's ethical, political, and religious struggle—the point, as we shall see, of his greatest affinity for and resistance against the permanence of the theologico-political. That vertiginous declaration, at once militaristic and egalitarian, spiritual yet just, and, above all, classically republican, had emerged from this paradox. "Everyone must do war. Everyone must be a soldier," he would demand in *Philosophy of Hinduism*.[78]

Ambedkar's complex relationship to republicanism, which lent his thought both an insurrectionary energy and moments of equivocation, is framed most succinctly in *Thoughts on Pakistan*. "Force, it cannot be denied, is the medicine of the body politic and must be administered when the body politic becomes sick," he states without naming Burke, who he is almost entirely rephrasing. "But just because force is the medicine of the body politic it cannot be allowed to become its daily bread. A body politic must work as a matter of course by springs of action which are natural."[79] Compare this with Burke's plea for a force that would be irreducible to its executive and military functions: "God forbid," Burke argues, "that on a worthy occasion authority should want the means of force, or the disposition to use it. But where a prudent and enlarged policy does not precede, and attend it too, where the hearts of the better sort of people do not go with the hands of the soldiery, you may call your constitution what you will, in effect it will consist of three parts, (orders, if you please,)—cavalry, infantry, and artillery—and of nothing better."[80]

It is hardly surprising that among all the later works, Ambedkar echoes Burke most strongly in *Thoughts on Pakistan*, a work profoundly immersed in the language of territory, security, and national culture, a work so uncharacteristically mired in the conservative desire for purity and spirit. And yet the feeble beginnings of Ambedkar's turn away from the science of the state proper—his unwillingness to cede the sovereignty of the multitude to the ambitions of the national state or the rhetoric of national culture—can be discerned even at the center of his most uncompromisingly state-oriented work. Force had to be retained, but only in a therapeutic or healing manner, in a fashion that prevented it from lapsing into an instrument of hostility and oppression; only in a manner that kept it separate from the moral law of obedience and constraint, or worse, from the monastic rituals of nonviolence. Without this vigilance, without a force regulated by the multitude's justness and a justice backed by the multitude's force, without a force whose source lay in the people's action and civility alone, the constitution of a people, as Burke had warned, would consist of only three parts: "cavalry, infantry, and artillery—and of nothing better." The monopolization of force by the executive branches and military orders rendered it destitute, for it killed the morals of difference and disagreement between communities, ceded agency to a unitary and centralized state, always leaving behind in its wake, as Ambedkar evocatively put it, "an impoverished and defeated violence."[81] It was this appropriation of force, the expropriation of the multitude's constituent power by the executive and military orders of the state (an appropriation rendered invisible by its very ubiquity as custom), that Montaigne, and following him, Pascal, had called the "mystical foundation of authority." "Laws are now maintained in credit, not because they are just," writes Montaigne in his essay "On Experience" (1587–1588), "but because they are laws. It is the mystical foundation of their authority; they have none other."[82]

The problem of authority, then, is classical, mystical, implicated in rituals of belief, complicit with systems of rule that people had been forced to hold as being true. There was no authority that did not draw its sustenance from this economy of voluntary trust, voluntary obedience, and in the final instance, voluntary servitude. Hence, the formulation, "Laws are now maintained in credit." Ambedkar would himself see the solution to the problem—the distinctive relationship between authority and acquiescence—in terms of force, a force that by its very constitution, he conceded, oscillates between the incalculable energies of ordinary mortals and the rule-bound, calibrated enforcements of the state. This oscillation is the heart of classical democracy. To recover the authentic truth of politics, to reclaim the incommensurable equality of mortals, was to struggle at once for an incalculably primordial and an incandescently new force. In newness alone lay the originary authenticity of truthful action.

Newness as the Love of Truth

It was in the late 1920s, between 1927 and 1928, and the period especially around the Mahad Satyagraha at which a copy of the *Manusmriti* was publicly burned, that Ambedkar, still in his thirties, made a series of public formulations—much of it published in his newspaper *Bahishkrit Bharat*—on what he would subsequently call the "love of truth." "Anything old becomes virtuous by virtue of customs and everybody believes it to be true," he had announced in a dramatically Pascalian tenor in 1927. "'New' does not have the force of custom and how so ever attractive it may look, people hesitate to accept it." Then, on behalf of untouchables barred by custom from places of civic amenities and worship, he laid claim over a new regime of truthful action (*satyagraha*) itself. "We never went to any temple before this! We never went to any public lake or well before this! Now if we insist on this, will it be right; will it be considered *Satyagraha*?"

Note here Ambedkar's characteristic—and often unresolved—suturing of two incommensurable and inseparable orders. The order of a calculable and human right (to enter temples and use wells) had been braided with a justice whose purity remained incalculable, its truth immanent to the deepest, most primordial recesses of the satyagrahi's belief. "The *Satyagrahi* should know what are the signs of truth and how to identify the truth." Only from this "knowledge and belief that what he is doing is moral and pure truth," Ambedkar exhorts, might the satyagrahi nurture the ground of justice, one that was tethered to "fraternity and brotherhood" alone.[83] So that truthful action was not confined to the sacrificial and solitary practice of the heroic individual. It was aligned with a new order, a new right, a new law, an insurrectionary norm of equality in public spaces, instituted by the "general mobilization" of the weakest, most fallible, most threatened. "Anybody about whom we are certain that he belongs to us, whether he is a Brahmin or Non-Brahmin by caste is acceptable to us and we shall fully cooperate with him."[84] This would be a society of equals proper, then; one where the fraternal and equitable sharing of truth would subsume the demands of individual and communal interest, and where the rigor of truthful action would not be confined to the trained heroics of the few. Civic disobedience at its most truthful was marked by this generality or universalization of force. Its universalism extended beyond the limits of caste and

belonging. "*Satyagraha* is a difficult test of persistence. You will have to observe very strong restraint on yourself while suffering the difficulty in *Satyagraha*," Ambedkar calmed his followers in December 1927 as they took the
decisive step of burning the *Manusmriti* in Mahad. "We are willingly offering our lives to others."[85]

Force was nothing if not this truthful, selfless act of giving death to
oneself in the cause of an equal life. Force was nothing if not a virtuous,
sacrificial, shared, and yet always immeasurable love of truth, an indivisible, free, and unifying faith in equality. Force was the freedom to posit,
found, and constitute a new order. "If you have faith in equality," thus came
Ambedkar's decisive formulation, "you will never attempt to divide the people; you will try to bind them together instead." This indivisibility of the
people nourished not just the republic but the convictions and conditions
of action itself. "Where there is equality, there is fraternity and where there
is fraternity, there is truth. And any action to establish these principles is
Satyagraha!"[86] I want to pause briefly on the simultaneously religious and
humanist dimension of the expression "faith in equality." Far too often, I
think, the faith invoked here is taken lightly, read in its secular sense, as if
it stood for Ambedkar's juridical and legislative commitment. Read closely,
put back in and among the texts that Ambedkar had produced during this
period, a more sustained struggle shows itself. For this neologism, "faith in
equality," had condensed, consciously or otherwise, in a deceptively simple
fashion anyway, an enduring struggle to find an Archimedean point between and belief and truth, between theology and the political. And if this
were already not a formidable task, Ambedkar would find in the *Gita*—the
ancient religious text that he would himself declare to be the most violent
articulation of an oppressive faith and its theology—the unimpeachable articulation of his truth. This was Ambedkar exhorting his followers to truthful action (*satyagraha*) in November 1927, more than two decades before he
would begin composing a history of "counterrevolution in ancient India," at
whose corrupt and immoral center he would place the sacrificial violence of
the *Gita* itself. But the beginnings of this truth were different.

Many people believe that *Satyagraha* is not a subject matter of the Gita; but that is
not a correct understanding. In fact, *Satyagraha* is the basic tenet of the Gita. . . .
When Arjuna climbed down the chariot and sat crestfallen seeing his elders and
teachers in front of him in war, what did Shri Krishna advise him? Shri Krishna
said, "Do not be sad, be determined to fight for your rights with those who have
taken away your kingdom." Upon this, Arjuna asked, "Tell me, how what you tell is
truth and how my demand is *Satyagraha*." And the entire Gita is an answer by Shri
Krishna to this one question by Arjuna. There cannot be any other doctrine but only

Satyagraha in the Gita. And that is why I have taken the Gita as a basis for our demand for equal rights. . . . Violence meaning only killing is a very narrow approach
to distinguish between violence and nonviolence. The meaning of violence includes
hurt to the body or feelings of another person. Therefore, nonviolence means not
to cause pain of any nature to any living being. If we apply this broader definition
of nonviolence, then Mahatma Gandhi's nonviolence also is violence in a way. Because, according to his methods even though nobody is physically hurt, it hurts the
sentiments of opposite parties. . . . In fact *Satyagraha* should adopt nonviolence as
far as possible and may have to resort to violence in case of need . . . that would be
a practical approach.[87]

Note how a fratricidal text is mobilized here in order to reveal the passivity and hurtfulness, even voluntary servitude, that insinuates itself into
civic life—and into the life of warriors—every time nonviolence is given
the form of an unimpeachable moral precept. But Ambedkar does not simply reveal the invisible and psychological violence of nonviolence. He mobilizes the right to force—over oneself or another, through self-sacrifice or in
self-defense, at war or in the city—against a long history of oppression and
hurt itself. This was the great paradox of civic disobedience in the colony
then; that the enthusiasm and civility of its practitioners—the "practical reason" of satyagraha—could never be predicated upon a nonviolence secured
by the law, colonial or religious. Instead, civility here was grounded in a certain transparency of will, in an unapologetic enthusiasm and freedom, even
excess, a civic right to use violence within the limits of justice. Hurt against
hurt, then: never again would Ambedkar publicly stand and speak in greater
intimacy with Gandhi than he does here. Had he seen and read Gandhi's *Discourses on the Gita*, which had been delivered over nine months at the Satyagraha Ashram in Ahmedabad between 24 February and 27 November 1926,
exactly a year before he makes this speech? We do not know, and even though
Ambedkar had taken serious issue with Gandhi's general conception of nonviolence here, he did not go as far as to specifically invoke Gandhi's *Gita* lectures. In fact, Ambedkar would maintain a sustained silence on Gandhi's
interpretation of the *Gita*, even as he would mount a scathing critique of its
other famed interpreters in the nationalist circle.

What was even more striking here, however, was Ambedkar's attempt to
turn the truth of *satyagraha*—and its relationship to justice—against Gandhi
himself, forcing open the door of its spiritual rigor, which entailed the duty
and right to cultivate the virtue of civic disobedience, to those millions whom
Gandhi often considered least prepared. These were the millions who worked
with their hands everyday (in occupations considered not only unskilled but
also degrading and polluting), under oppressive prohibitions, in inhuman

spaces and on brutal wages. And yet this revolutionary multitude, its general will, Ambedkar insists, must never dissolve the incommensurable self, faculty, and individuality of each citizen and non-citizen (that had come together to constitute it) in a vortex of anonymous, abstract equals. Indeed, the moment Ambedkar asserts, "our *Satyagraha* is for regaining our human rights," and simultaneously, "it is also a *Yajna* for our self-introspection and purification," he makes claim over a counterhistory of *satyagraha*, one that might emerge from the unconditional opening of the right to civic disobedience to even the most degraded and unequal, from the democratization of the will to speak the truth forcefully and with civility.[88] It was in this democratization of truth rather than in nonviolence as such that the possibility of justice showed itself to the people.

Even by the high standards of heresy that Ambedkar had set for himself, then, this was a rather heterodox beginning. Why had he posited a text—a text that would come to eventually repel him for its celebration of fratricide as virtue, its institution of war as moral duty—as the wellspring of revolutionary justice? And what might the logic be behind his militant separation of the *Gita* (with its impeccable call, as he puts it, to truthful, virtuous, and egalitarian action) from the *Manusmriti* (that other, equally classical, equally oppressive text whose copy he would burn less than a month later)? What does this early affirmation of the *Gita* give us most to think about Ambedkar's faith in equality? That his claim of Hinduism as a positive religion, "a religion of the book," cannot be viewed as a gesture of Orientalist inspiration, one that, with his purportedly blind faith in Enlightenment categories of European vintage, was geared to frame the heterogeneity of Indic religions in the mirror of Christianity. Ambedkar, more than anyone else in his time, knew there was not one but many Hinduisms to contend with; many ancient books to meticulously translate, silently absorb, and mount resistance against; many classical traditions, republican and theological, to rework for a new language of freedom. His amplification of Hinduism's monotheistic tendencies was more of an ethical and political gesture, one meant to apprehend that which had always remained cryptic in Indic traditions of statecraft and its ancient constitution: the nexus between theological truth and political power, whose force over the citizens of the republic—and their obedience to sovereign power—was maintained through the intermediary universality of the moral law, through the "categorical imperative," as he would call it, of *dharma*. As if rules could be applied universally to every moral person everywhere, as if any act of transgression against the law—or absolute servitude—was a reflection of the person's weakness of will rather than the exclusions of the law itself.

But in 1927, with a decade still to pass before he would compose *Annihilation of Caste*, Ambedkar had indeed sought inspiration in the universality of the *Gita's* theologico-political mandate, with its prescription on truth and action edging out from his view, at least for the time being, its regime of killing and sacrifice instituted around the expediencies of statecraft. What is the nature of the questions that Ambedkar might have been grappling with when he approached the *Gita* as a treatise on truthful action? Only when we probe his thinking of force as immanence, force as inalienable being, force as the irreducibility of justice, does this attraction toward the *Gita*—this interpretive *coup de force* in which the *Gita* is extracted from the injunctions of its own moral law and mobilized by precisely those who were barred from touching the scripture—become understandable. Could not every dogged practitioner of truth, every resolute passive resister, regardless of whether he was Brahmin or Shudra, a young Ambedkar had asked, embody in his person the virtues of the warrior Arjuna? Might Arjuna, with his supreme command over his craft, yet wracked with dilemma and guilt, a person completely human, fallible, and mortal, be the universal exemplar? Might anticolonial nationalism, with its profound interest in defending the *Gita* as a marker of civilizational unity, allow its truth to be democratized, its call of action returned to the realm of popular religion, letting the everyday beliefs and sacrifices of the multitude acquire the heights of an egalitarian sovereignty, the radiance of a freedom unrestrained by the exclusions of the ancient constitution? What would such a political space, where the practice of satyagraha would be open to the weakest and most untouchable, and where resistance would be inscribed at the heart of a democratic constitution, truly look like?

Perhaps the early fascination with *Gita* was an anticipation of what would remain an enduring conundrum in Ambedkar's encounter with the theologico-political. How to think about a virtuous use of force, or put differently, a force that emerged from the everyday virtues of ordinary mortals alone? As Burke, and clearly following him, Ambedkar, often wondered (and this brings us back to the paradox we saw Ambedkar begin with himself early in life), could force, which by its very name remains somewhat inseparable from the institutional, mystical, and pernicious tentacles of power, be rendered pure and given over to an egalitarian sovereignty of the people? Could force be freed from its statist logic, as he had clearly believed in the 1920s, reclaimed from its millennial roots in rituals of mastery, separated from its embodiment in the figure and will of the sovereign, and given over to an ethics and politics of everyday life? Isn't there, as Hegel had proposed in the *Phenomenology*, just one unitary force that makes the world and vanishes into it?[89] How might then force be separated, conceptually and structurally, from itself, from its myriad duplicities and representations? How might it be turned against the constraints of the moral law and realigned with the materiality of social justice? Ambedkar approaches these questions with scruple and reserve, and inasmuch as this was always going to be a question of imagining a sovereignty of a people freed from the rhetoric of territory and nation, it did require a methodological extremism, an embrace of the new and even the terrifying. "I am not staggered by Pakistan; I am not indignant about it" is how he would frame his obligation to truth in the face of the imminent realignments of borders, forces, and sovereignties in the subcontinent.[90]

Misgovernance in Its Classical Roots

It is a remarkable paradox that Ambedkar's relentless pursuit of newness alone explains why so much of his lifework was devoted to classical texts. So immense was his attraction toward the *Gita*, so powerful his repulsion toward its disregard of sharing and autonomy in the spurious name of disinterest (*upekha*), for instance, that not only had it forced in his mature thought a militant turn away from the text, it had forced Ambedkar to plan a book-length study on it. He had tentatively titled it *Essays on the Bhagavad Gita*, not incidentally similar to Gandhi's *Discourses on the Gita*, some written and unfinished parts of which were subsequently collected in *Revolution and Counter-Revolution in Ancient India*. Ambedkar's *Gita* is not, contrary to nationalist common sense, an entirely ancient text. In fact, the integrity of its temporal and philosophical authority is moot. Patches of the *Gita*, he argues, were composed as late as the fourteenth century under the threat of Muslim invasions of the subcontinent. Contrary to the claims made in Tilak's magisterial treatise *Gitarahasya*, it is not even "a single book written by a single author." It is instead a patchwork of contingent improvisations.[91] Concerned in its original form solely with the state's sanction of kin killing in the interest of moral order and general obedience, the great poem is an oddity in the sacred canon, rooted not in the realm of the mystical but in what Ambedkar, rebelling against the Vedic sanctity accorded to mystic speech, frequently calls the "vulgar" and popular.[92]

Were its phenomenal richness, its plebian authenticity, its populist charm, reasons for Ambedkar's enduring fascination with the *Gita*? The *Gita*, like the *Iliad* in Simone Weil's rereading of Homer's classic (a reading itself refracted through Weil's encounter with the *Gita* as she grappled with Nazism), is a brilliant poem on force, saturated with violence and yet, as Gandhi's *Discourses* had argued, not exhausted by it.[93] Its originary enunciation had occurred at the moment of a fratricidal war, at the moment of struggle between armed brothers for sovereignty over territory. And like Weil's *Iliad*, Ambedkar's *Gita* too condensed, in the most poetic if immaculately duplicitous fashion, the moral and political anxieties of struggle. It is a symptom and creation of that originary moment when the violent alliance between theology and the state had insinuated itself at the heart of the Indic doctrine of government. For Ambedkar, however, the *Gita* is morally destitute not on account of this alliance—that is, it is deficient not because it is a theologico-political discourse on statemaking. Rather, it is poor because it is shorn of the kind of love and courage that Weil had associated, in her 1939 essay, with Homer's classic. One might even argue that for Ambedkar the *Gita* is unequal precisely because it had proved incapable of fulfilling its original purpose: the task of formulating a classical ethics of sovereignty and love for India.

It was not that the early twentieth-century nationalist rediscovery of the *Gita* as the definitive Indian text on the epistemology of moral and political action was compromised simply by inaccuracies of fact and history.[94] In fact, Ambedkar resolutely resists turning this argument with liberal and extremist commentators of the *Gita* into one purely of history, canon, and tradition. What was at stake for him was a much more fundamental, even classical, problem at the heart of India's modernity, a problem that was nevertheless transcendental in its historicity, equally ancient and modern, and a problem, conversely, of transcendentalism itself, one that had disappeared from history and become invisible to democratic reasoning. What was the relationship between the power of religious institutions, their authority to endorse and disseminate interpretation, on the one hand, and on the other hand, these theologico-political discourses on action and sacrifice of which the *Gita* had become a galvanizing instance? Where were those moral and political foundations of truth—textual or religious—on which a people's egalitarian sovereignty, its cognitive autonomy, its freedom that included the liberty of reading and heresy, even self-sacrifice (as he had exhorted in 1927 during his own mobilization of the *Gita*), might be imagined? How much authority ought a theology of government have, above all, to regulate the everyday truths, beliefs, and faculties of the multitude?

Refracted through this set of classical problems—the relationship between state and religion; the tension between political (and interpretive) secrecy and the people's right to truth; the contamination of faith by institutional and juridical power—nationalist readings of the *Gita* began to look especially unfaithful to Ambedkar. Mired in an ecclesiastical and territorial logic, he argued, its interpretation by liberals such as Radhakrishnan could barely be separated from those by extremists such as Tilak, the sedimented and agonistic history of the *Gita*'s interpretation and transmission replaced in their readings by a theological unity produced solely by the nationalist need for a classical ethics.[95] In this shift from the study of the *Gita*'s transmissibility (across epochs of foreign invasion and Indic defeat that had lent it its form) to a consolidation of its citability (that could be mobilized, paradoxically, to impart moral thickness to Indic discourses on sovereignty at moments precisely of its greatest crisis) lay a more pernicious, even pacifist secret, that of the *Gita*'s steady mutation from being a poem on force to becoming treatise on duty and nonviolence—a secrecy in which Ambedkar saw nothing short of the death of originality, the "end of criticism," itself.[96]

Note, thus, the dissonance between the young Ambedkar's forceful, public, and intensely sacrificial mobilization of the *Gita* in the 1920s as a treatise on the morals of action and his later turn away from its sacrificial framework. His problem, clearly, had never been with authority. Nor had the religious essence of politics been for him a matter of doubt. His problem, on the contrary, seems to be with the crisis of originality and critique, the crisis of moral authority and legitimacy itself, a crisis that stems from nationalist betrayal of a classical ethics, even as nationalism reduces this ethics to a hermeneutics of false triumph and complacency. Ambedkar's was not a call to purge force but to formulate legitimate and truthful conditions for its critique. It was nationalists, he insists in a brilliant reversal, who had not read the *Gita* honestly. They had not even inherited it faithfully. Perhaps only Ambedkar could have made that accusation, for it was indeed he who, as a child, had inherited the *Gita*—and the epic *Mahabharata* of which it was part—from his soldier father. And this inheritance too is a question of force, a matter of resistance and rejection of history, a new way of dealing with the past, an interminable movement between filiation and dissidence.

My father was a military officer, but at the same time a very religious person. He brought me up under a strict discipline. From my early age I found certain contradictions in my father's religious way of life. . . . I asked my father why he insisted on our reading the Mahabharata and Ramayana, which recounted the greatness of the Brahmins and the Kshatriyas and repeated the stories of the degradation of the Shudras and the Untouchables. My father did not like the question. He merely said, "You must not ask such silly questions. You are only boys; you must do as you are told.". . . After some time, I asked again the same question. This time my father had evidently prepared himself for a reply. He said, "The reason why I ask you to read the Mahabharata and Ramayana is this: we belong to the Untouchables, and you are likely to develop an inferiority complex, which is natural. The value of [the] Mahabharata and Ramayana lies in removing this inferiority complex. See Drona and Karna—they were small men, but to what heights they rose! Look at Valmiki— he was a Koli [tribal population], but he became the author of [the] Ramayana. It is for removing this inferiority complex that I ask you to read the Mahabharata and Ramayana." I could see that there was some force in my father's argument. But I was not satisfied. I told my father that I did not like any of the figures in [the] Mahabharata. I said, "I do not like Bhishma and Drona, nor Krishna. Bhishma and Drona were hypocrites. They said one thing and did quite the opposite. Krishna believed in fraud. His life is nothing but a series of frauds. Equal dislike I have for Rama. Examine his conduct in the Sarupnakha [Shurpanakha] episode [and] in the Vali Sugriva episode, and his beastly behavior toward Sita." My father was silent, and made no reply. He knew that there was a revolt.[97]

Despite the revolt, the early nourishment on the epics left a deep imprint on the son's moral psychology. There is always force in paternity, Ambedkar concedes reluctantly. There was at least "some force" in it, a force that had, over the course of half a century, acted cognitively, psychically, and silently. It had lent shape not only to the world but also to one's place in it. And yet, despite the father's insistence that the epics be revered, there was an enigmatic destitution in the *Mahabharata*'s core, an inequality at the heart of its war, that the son could never come to terms with. It is not the skill of war as such, Ambedkar argues, that is destitute and unequal but rather the morality behind it, which then begs a Bergsonian question, one that Ambedkar would raise in the final pages of *Annihilation of Caste*. Is the practice of mastery, simply because it is skillful, rigorous, and sacrificial, necessarily a religious one? Is an act of timing one's death, playing on the relationship between being and time by, say, fasting unto death, virtuous in itself? Perhaps most important, are all religions that insist on such mastery, all theologies that ground themselves in the immateriality and ephemerality of finite being, equally just? Doesn't morality itself summon the "necessity of discriminating between them?"[98]

Certainly, the most exemplary figures in the *Mahabharata* sacrifice and suffer heroically. Yet founded on self-inflicted procedures of Kshatriya duty (*kshatriyadharma*), on the regicidal and fratricidal procedures of the state, this suffering of warriors is devoid of moral force. Suffering that ensues from interest in domination not only lacks civility, it is shorn of authenticity itself. No warrior in the *Mahabharata*, not even the outcaste and heroic Karna, mounts resistance against the sacrifice-demanding *kshatriyadharma* that so perniciously regulates and keeps guard over everyday life and virtues. None dies resisting its call to guiltless killing. None disengages from the violent rituals of statemaking, which, according to Ambedkar, would have laid the ground for an authentic and essential sacrifice, a sacrifice necessary for a virtuous government. Instead, in the *Gita*'s meticulously cultivated aura, its concealment of those popular and cultic practices of Indian antiquity that had given it its form and content, its willful suppression of those popular orals traditions from which it had itself emerged, its guiltless fratricide legitimized in the interest of the state, its disavowed inheritances (especially the words and lexicon that it had inherited for its own conservation from Buddhism), its destruction of the possibility of a religious revolution, indeed, its betrayal of the multitude's revolutionary belief itself—but above all, in its immaculate and exhaustive construction of rules for everyday duty, obeisance, and obedience so that it might conceal what was actually a moment of violent vacillation—the *Gita* embodies the most exemplary failure of the discourse of sovereignty in the Indian tradition. Any thinker of force, let alone a just force, claims Ambedkar, could not avoid reading this text faithfully. If only in this heretical fidelity, in this attentiveness simultaneous to its universality and failure, Ambedkar was for once in the company of worthy antagonists such as Tilak and Gandhi, who had discerned in the same *Gita* the elements of a timeless ethics.

In the final chapter of this book, I will take up Ambedkar's conceptualization of another, equally exemplary and sacrificial civic resistance, one that was proper to authentic *kshatriyadharma*, which he formulated through his retelling of a strikingly similar episode in another Kshatriya warrior's life. The young Siddhartha, yet to become the Buddha, would show what Arjuna might have become; he would exemplify a sacrifice, a relinquishment of sovereignty, in a manner truly proper to justice. Suffice it is to note now that the paternal authority that had sought to nourish the young Ambedkar on the Indic epics managed to enforce on him neither deference nor guilt nor the imperative, in the manner of the outcaste hero Karna, to suffer in silence. Rather, it is his memory of resistance as a child that returned Ambedkar to the sources and texts of Indic ontotheology, to their mystical discourses on war as duty. One has to only look at Ambedkar's voluminous and unfinished writings on the Indic epics, his rigorous critique of their claims to religiosity and sovereignty, to comprehend how tireless and indefatigable this return was. As if attempting to condense in one forceful passage this immense critique, Ambedkar writes of the secret of *Gita's* mystical endurance:

The first instance one comes across in reading the Bhagavat Gita is the justification of war. Arjuna had declared himself against the war, against killing people for the sake of property. Krishna offers a philosophic defense of war and killing in war. This philosophic defense of war will be found in Chapter II verses 2 to 28. The philosophic defense of war offered by the Bhagavat Gita proceeds along two lines of argument. One line of argument is that anyhow the world is perishable and man is mortal. Things are bound to come to an end. Man is bound to die. Why should it make any difference to the wise whether man dies a natural death or whether he is done to death as a result of violence? Life is unreal, why shed tears because it has ceased to be? Death is inevitable, why bother how it has resulted? The second line of argument in justification of war is that it is a mistake to think that the body and the soul are one. They are separate. Not only are the two quite distinct but they differ in-as-much as the body is perishable while the soul is eternal and imperishable. When death occurs it is the body that dies. The soul never dies. Not only does it never die but air cannot dry it, fire cannot burn it, and a weapon cannot cut it. It is therefore wrong to say that when a man is killed his soul is killed. What happens is that his body dies. His soul discards the dead body as a person discards his old clothes—wears new ones and carries on. As the soul is never killed, killing a person can never be a matter of any movement. War and killing need therefore give no ground to remorse or to shame, so argues the Bhagavat Gita.[99]

Within the text, at the moment of its enunciation, what was actually a willful call to fratricide was in due course transformed through recursive practice into the moral law, rendering life and law inseparable from each other. The moment of encounter between Krishna and Arjuna, which was, in the first instance, a moment of impending fratricide, is thus transformed into a dialogue between an infinite God and a trembling subject, imparting to the moment a theological sanctity. A whole matrix of disciplinary obligations (*kshatriyadharma, maryada dharma, rajadharma*) comes to be founded on one sovereign truth: the groundlessness of the divine. Thus, the spiritualization of the body; the rendering of life into an austere, sacrificial, and immortal soul; the refusal of mortality as a site of any experience, any tragedy, any remorse, and therefore, any politics: these did not simply remain constituents of a momentary theology. Instead, they facilitated the mutation of a reproducible and vulgar-popular myth into rules of voluntary obedience and sacrifice. Justified by divine law, violence toward the body was now transformed into everyday custom. It is this violence toward finitude, the dark possibility of destruction of life, that Ambedkar calls the *Gita*'s will to "murder."

Beneath the lucid flow of the passage lies, then, an immense theological engagement with nondualism (*advaita*). In fact, Ambedkar's critique is as religious as it is politico-ethical and juridical. His concern is not the body, nor blood, nor mere life, above all, in any simple sense, but rather, the betrayal of the spirit of mortality, the spirit that makes humanity in all its vulnerability the space of a shared universality. What he finds so condemnable in the *Gita*, in other words, is the denial of finitude, which is so improper to any classical ethics of civility, liberty, and government, let alone virtuous sacrifice. In fact, his resistance against *advaita* Hinduism's disregard of finite matter, its denial of the materiality of the soul and spirit itself, was so exacting that it would take him a lifetime to give it the form of a proper epistemological critique. In the *Gita* commentary, at any rate, that epistemological-critical charge remains nebulous. Part of the reason for that nebulousness, perhaps even indecision, lies in Ambedkar's own affinity for a certain strand of negative theology drawn from Madhyamika Buddhism. It would take careful thinking to reconcile that negative theological belief in the ephemerality of the distinction between being and nonbeing with the demands of a materialist and revolutionary democracy—a democracy that might be as sensitive to the fact of corporeal and cognitive injury as it might be open to force and war. The bond between the theological and political, between spirit and matter, between conceptuality and empiricism, had thus to be rescued from false dichotomies and mobilized in full force. The method, tone, and vocabulary of the *Gita* commentary, at once ontological and historical, are thus revealing. They anticipate and even prefigure much that was to come in a dramatically different text: Ambedkar's mature engagement with annihilationism (*ucchedvad*) and his elaborations on the materiality of life, which he would undertake over several complex passages in *The Buddha and His Dhamma*. That mature masterwork would ask the question of matter proper; matter not as goods or as mere body but as the irrevocably universal constituent of life as such; matter as the spirit of finite and death-bound existence; matter, above all, as the ground of a radically aware finitude whose force lay in the moral agent's consciousness of the impermanence (*sunnyata*) of self itself. On the consciousness of this mortality—and this is what made *sunnyata* radical—lay the immortality of a revolutionary democracy.

Ambedkar's encounter with nihilism coalesced into a galvanizing impulse in his later thought, to which I will turn in Chapter 7. Meanwhile, in the remainder of this chapter I want to stay with the shared set of moral concerns and framework within which the unfinished *Essays on the Bhagavad Gita* and the rigorously executed *Buddha and His Dhamma* acquired their form. This, I should make clear, was not a project of theological reconciliation; on the contrary, even within this framework, a violent tension was at work. Inasmuch as this yoking of the *Gita* and Madhyamika Buddhism had posited a unity, it was on account of Ambedkar's integrated critique of force alone, his attempt to reclaim it for the multitude again. After all, the *Gita*, which had formulated an intricate mandate for just violence, is not simply another theologico-political text. Rather, it is exemplary among Indic texts because of its transcendental historicity, because it had captured in its purest, ageless, and most stubborn form a "felony" at the heart of a civilization. How did it acquire its nonviolent aura, its deathless endurance? By immunizing itself against all "counterviolence," by reserving the right of force for warriors alone, and, therefore, in a brilliantly dialectical reversal, stabilizing itself as an antithesis of its own violent nature. In its later law-preserving forms, argued Ambedkar, the *Gita* could thus be seen to have instituted the theological law of nonviolence by enunciating, at the very moment of Krishna's monstrous revelation, a set of sacred injunctions and prohibitions, a set of demarcations between those who could sacrifice and those who could not. Sacrifice was banned, then, at the moment of greatest violence.

Krishna says: that a wise man should not by counter propaganda create a doubt in the mind of an ignorant person who is a follower of Karma and which of course includes the observance of the rules of Chaturvarnya. In other words, you must not agitate or excite people to rise in rebellion against the theory of Karma kand and all that it includes. The second injunction . . . tells that every one do the duty prescribed for his Varna and no other and warns those who worship him . . . that they will not obtain salvation by mere devotion but by devotion accompanied by observance of duty laid down for his Varna. In short, a Shudra however great he may be as a devotee will not get salvation if he has transgressed the duty of the Shudra—namely to live and die in the service of the higher classes.[100]

Krishna's law-positing occurs, in other words, at the moment of terror and then turns against its own original form—that is, against its founding violence—to enunciate a statist injunction of nonviolence on those who would henceforth not wield arms. This mystical alliance between sacred theology and civic authority, this exclusion at the heart of government, strongly attracted early twentieth-century nationalists to the *Gita*. But the commandment of war as obligation to God did not merely found a sacrificial ethics. It also stabilized that which, according to Walter Benjamin, is crucial to all law preserving violence: the rhetoric of fate that circumscribes the universal right to go to war, the sequestering of the freedom to mobilize and revolt, the denial, above all, of the inalienable immanence of force that must otherwise belong to every agent equally.[101] For a Shudra was born Shudra by his fate and must aspire to salvation only as Shudra. He must live within the limits of this destiny and serve those he was born to serve. In so doing alone, he would open his person to divine light. In *Chaturvarnya*, and this is the secret of its endurance, fate circumscribes not merely the boundaries of the Shudra's action, his abilities and gestures, his spaces and movements, but also his soul, that singular, immanent, and incorruptible source of virtuous action. The potential of any revolutionary counterviolence is thus efficiently suppressed. Not only is the Shudra barred from insurgency and "general mobilization"; those who provoke him are barred too. Law is thus conserved by outlawing, in advance, any rebellion that might threaten to establish a new law: it is here that the act of burning the *Manusmriti*, beyond all limits, injunctions, and closed doors of the law, belonged to the order of a *coup de force*, the act (at once material and symbolic) of founding a new law of insurrection itself. In the *Gita*, meanwhile, the Indic doctrine of government had finally acquired its mystical foundation, and in Krishna, an all-too-human God that deserved, paradoxically, a rather nonhuman treatment.

A Heretical Empiricism

Was it the Machiavellian humanity of Krishna that sustained Ambedkar's exemplary fidelity to this god, a relationship in which heresy, the active deface-ment of God's groundless existence, promised to open the empirical ground of a new freedom? Krishna, of course, was not the only god worthy of deface-ment. But given the logic that nationalist politics had followed in the decades before Ambedkar, he was the most accessible. In their important studies on the moral psychology of anticolonial resistance, Sudipta Kaviraj and Ashis Nandy have in different ways shown how strategically necessary Krishna's humanity, his Christlike ideality, had been to the theologico-political "imaginaries" of late nineteenth-century nationalisms.[102] A humanist divinity maintained such a potent presence in the politics of the time because, in the emerging realm of the national-popular, a human God helped nationalist theology nourish a politics and ethics in which defining action—rebellion, murder, war—as the colonial subject's sacrificial obligation to the divine made it possible to abstract the bloodletting fanaticism of this sacrifice from the messiness of sedition and street politics, rehabilitating it to the order and imperative of *dharma*, or spir-itual duty. Krishna, the sovereign among humans, the most human among Gods, Ambedkar would argue, was crucial to this translation of theology into a new language of nationalism. In fact, the very purpose of theology, we have seen him argue in Chapter 2, was to nationalize faith.

For Ambedkar, nevertheless, this formula was not so much irreligious as it was against the morals of sacrifice proper; it affected not so much the foun-dations of belief as it did devalued religion's place within the set of moral val-ues, virtues, and mentalities necessary to democratic life and reason. And it was the mentality and virtue proper to democracy he was concerned with re-covering, appropriating, reinstituting. In the unfinished "Analytical Notes," which he had begun to compile on two crucial chapters of the *Mahabharata*, Ambedkar thus institutes a politics of what can only be called defacement, a force beyond measure, mounted against Krishna's already compromised di-vinity, as if he were locked in a struggle to reclaim the immanence (and im-mortality) of human action by inflicting pain on the transcendental figure of God himself. Not just his interpretation, but the very language of the "Notes" attempts to destabilize the nationalist celebration of the *Mahabharata* as an archive of virtuous conduct and just rule. If a properly revolutionary ontol-ogy of force were to be brought into existence, the revolutionary citizen—the citizen who forces the city in order to make it equal—had to annihilate all those fratricidal histories that nationalists' theological humanism—God as human—had marked out as its own. Acts of foundation had to be acts of force and desecration, and if need be, of sacrifice. The monstrosity of this humanism—and Krishna was the exemplar par excellence of this deformed vision of the body politic—that Ambedkar calls in *Thoughts on Pakistan* "half-human and half-animal" became, thus, the chosen subject of his sacrifice.[103] His will to annihilate antiquity coalesced into an ethics of another violence. It is this other violence—revolutionary and just, belonging to the order of the weak and mute, a violence at once interpretive and material beneath which lay an immeasurable desire for freedom—that Ambedkar often calls "force."

The immanent equality and ubiquity (to the point of invisibility, as Gandhi had put it) of this generalized force lent it an ontological essence— that is, an essence of truth that custom and power did not have. Of course, Ambedkar, like Hannah Arendt after him, accepted that power is the imperative of all governance, punitive and consensual alike, perhaps even necessary to the established morality and norms of action. Yet power does not belong to the order of essence, if only for the simple reason that it could be exchanged, usurped, and reclaimed. Force, on the contrary, was irreducible, equally available to the weakest and the strongest, and therefore the only constituent of being that was wholly true and just. In *Annihilation of Caste*, and two decades later in *The Buddha and His Dhamma*, Ambedkar—as a way of claiming that it was its very immanence that keeps force separate from the external (and even transcendental) interests, institutions, and coerciveness of power— would call it "energy." "What makes one interest dominant over another is power," Ambedkar asserts in his "Warning to the Untouchables." "That being so, power is needed to destroy power. There may be the problem," he concedes, "of how to make the use of power ethical."[104] Power would become ethical by proper use of force, for force alone opens the citizen to the moral dimension of revolutionary justice. And a revolutionary's faith could not be one among others. By the very nature of his work, it had to move between belief and annihilation, history and newness.

There is, thus, an entire vocabulary in Ambedkar's painstaking exegeses that amplifies the morbid, the base, and the inhuman in the *Mahabharata*. In his meticulous reconstructions emerge the "brag and boast" of Karna, the tragic antihero of the epic; the "slander" by Karna of Drona, the revered warrior and teacher of the Pandava and Kaurava brothers who had gone to war with one another over their right to the state; an entire lexicon of Kshatriya apology and guilt: ridiculing, arrogance, surrender, and anger; taunts, refusals, illicit liaisons, and bastard origins of legendary warriors;[105] "abuse" heaped by the royal mother on her son Duryodhana, the ambitious prince whose desire for monarchical power lay at center of the epic fratricide; the destruction and cowardly flight of Kshatriya warriors; metaphysical concerns regarding duty put in the "mouth" of Arjuna, the supreme but wavering warrior, precisely when he was resisting Lord Krishna's mandate to war; fainting of an entire army; and corpses, lunatic asylums, and the morbidity of human and horse sacrifice.[106] The heretical responsibility of corrupting the legislative powers of the *Mahabharata* and *Gita* demands an exception to the custom of hospitality, recognition, and respect; thus, inflation, misreading, and misrecognition become instruments of Ambedkar's emancipatory civility. In his essay "Krishna and His Gita," for instance, he denounces Krishna for making a "fool" of himself by defending *Chaturvarnya* on the basis of the *guna* theory of Sankhya philosophy. The angry, yet rigorously precise language is aimed not merely at critique but also at a radical defacement of the scripture itself, a scripture plagued by God's disappointingly ordinary vices: absurdity, stupidity, abhorrence, murder, effeminacy, puerility, childishness, fear, and trembling.[107]

Now, in this gesture of irreverence, this fidelity to religion-as-heresy, this search for a religion without religion, there is more than a little trace of Nietzsche's *Gay Science*, with its will to proclaim God dead and thus break from ontotheology by revealing its basest impulses.[108] In fact, from this "ostensible excess"[109]—which is the soul of any insurrectionary reversal of sovereignty and which functions as an exception itself by bringing the established norms of moral and political conduct into crisis (*aapad dharma*)—it is clear that Ambedkar, by now well immersed and even implicated in the *Gita*'s sacrificial logic and decisions, had gone well beyond the merely corporeal, cognitive, and historicist registers in his readings of the verse. His exactitude had opened the space for an excessive politics, a politics of annihilative responsibility to religion, an act of positing another force beyond all norms, values, and meanings of belief. It is more than fortuitous, thus, that he focuses on the Lord Krishna's face. After all, within the Hindu tradition, Krishna's divinity hinges critically on his face: his devouring of monsters, his revelation of numerous mouths, his horrifying tusks, his bristling fangs, his calm and cosmic resplendence. Ambedkar's defacement of Krishna's aura starts, very strategically and precisely, with the face and passes violently through it, first ravaging it so as to humanize it, and then dehumanize it. In his hands, one might argue, the talkative Krishna mutates into a figure with a mouth but no face.

For Ambedkar, these acts of heresy are more than mere humanistic reversals of negative theology, more than an attitude of anthropological antagonism toward divinity and enchantment that believes religion can be mastered by merely cataloging its practices and manipulations. They are gestures instead of a singular sacrifice, deeply grounded in a religious responsibility. The defacement of Krishna is neither a humanist act that expects the God to be made human, touchable, and seen as face. Nor is it theistic in the theological sense, inasmuch as this will, even autonomy, never desires a God who could be made accessible to the untouchable. The singularity that underlies the defacement, instead, expresses an insurrectionary general will. Inasmuch as it breaks from the ontotheological structure of reverence, to which nationalists of his time were so committed, Ambedkar's defacement manifests an exemplarily free and unconstrained thinking of freedom. And because it manifests itself in that way, waging war on the proper name of God on behalf of religious freedom, rendering the mysticism of the *Gita*'s moral law into the concreteness of a thing (much like Ambedkar's burning of the *Manusmriti* at the 1927 Mahad Satyagraha), such an act makes the presence of general will material and visible to the most oppressed, unequal, and untouchable. It gives a surface, a texture, a body, to the ghostly jurist and his "spirit of inequality" that any revolution must, as its first measure, exorcize.

With all its perils, its rhetorical, performative, and material excesses (whose risks have played out in the much more public spaces of postcolonial India with disconcerting frequency), then, defacement galvanizes the multitude and makes possible a certain sharing of freedom among mortals as equals. For freedom is authentically free only inasmuch as it is capable of being shared in the most quotidian and social sense. It thus becomes unthinkable without *maitri*, without fraternity or friendship. Such freedom could be secured only through an immeasurable force, in a sacrificial and irresponsible excess of means that would render the ends of its own action irrelevant: defacement of God's aura without any desire of replacing that God by another or unconstrained by any will to open up access to that God-as-subject. Ambedkar's responsibility constituted an immeasurable responsibility—indeed, a properly religious one—precisely because it had breached the theological frontiers of all established religious protocols and structures. By defacing Krishna's divinity and humanity, he had violated the theologico-political structure of sacredness and sovereignty alike. As if to resist the *Gita*'s theory of sovereignty and, at the same time, obediently respond to God's call to war, Ambedkar had sacrificed the God himself.

Force against force, religion without religion, then: this insurgent heresy requires that we separate carefully the interpretive, rhetorical, and conceptual dimensions of Ambedkar's religiosity, his simultaneous avoidance of and attraction toward sacrifice, his profound resistance against ontotheology mounted through acts of religious—and often theologico-political—materialism. Some of these impulses would return with even greater force in his masterwork *The Buddha and His Dhamma*. Suffice to note for now that this war on transcendence and sovereignty of God was announced, from the very beginning, out of a sense of an incommensurable religious responsibility. The language of sovereignty that Ambedkar had found so pernicious in *kshatriyadharma* would often touch his own critique of force. But then, he had himself, remarkably early in life, arrived at a recognition of this ineradicable problem of contamination—contamination of responsibility by sovereignty, of faith by force, of newness by return—that often put democratic aspirations and values to risk.

By the late 1920s, at any rate, the conceptual ambitions of this thought had been laid out, if still only in its broad strokes. Resonances of these early struggles were to be heard in works composed and published—as well as many others left unfinished and even fragmentary—until the middle of the 1950s. Even if its futures and features could not be fully anticipated as yet, notwithstanding the immense certitude with which, beginning in the 1930s, nationalist historiography would pass its moralistic judgments on him, Ambedkar had clearly assigned himself an exacting lifework, one in which many strands were to remain enduring, more than a few unresolved, some enigmatic, but all concerned with the relationship between force, faith, and justice. In fact, the New York writings are symptomatic of the young Ambedkar's already deep awareness that a critique of force did not always demand, in the manner of French syndicalism, a utopian or anarchist relinquishment of moral realism and authority, or even the state. On the contrary, to him, such relinquishment smacked of the same affinity for sovereignty, the same contamination of politics by mysticism, the same irresponsibility toward authentic and lived faith, that the people's "direct action" was meant to annihilate in the first place. To struggle against this risk was to struggle against a deathless spirit, an apparition of force; it was to feel the weakness of one's own force, from which came perhaps that paradoxical neologism that Ambedkar coined in a late essay, "weak force."[110] To retrieve force, then, not within the dialectic of violence and counterviolence or within the distinctions between belief and heresy, but force as that which might institute faith itself as the immanent ground of a revolutionary heresy, force as the right to an equal life and the militant freedom to sacrifice it too. This thought acquired its decisively republican inflection in the 1930s, and it is toward that period, which offers a radical prehistory of anticolonial constitutionalism and its relationship to popular sovereignty, that I now turn.

PART II

INTERWAR: SOVEREIGNTIES IN QUESTION

4

Apotheosis of the Unequal
Gandhi's Harijan

When in 1908 he took the decision to rename "passive resistance" *satyagraha* and, a year later, sat down on a ship back to South Africa to compose *Hind Swaraj*, Gandhi was more than two decades away from what would turn out to be the most audacious act of faith in the history of anticolonial thought: his 1931 decision to consecrate the Hindu "untouchable" as *harijan*, literally translatable as "god's people," and in Gandhi's own improvised rendering, "a man of God."[1] Although it was *satyagraha* that had lent linguistic and moral density to Gandhi's grammar of action, condensing in one powerful neologism the demands that he would henceforth make on himself and others, the introduction of *harijan* into the nationalist vocabulary turned out to be an equally pivotal measure, if only more vexed in its meanings, aspirations, and consequences. The *harijan*, as subject and name, and, above all, as a figure of touch, revealed the most constitutive, exacting, and elliptical impulses in Gandhi's thinking of equality. Its institution in 1931 as the ethical locus of his interventions in colonial India's social relations would be no less decisive for the contours of a democracy that was still to come than the composition of *Hind Swaraj* in 1909 had been for the kind of anticolonialism that had yet to be born. In fact, both names and the events around them can be understood in their fullest sense only as knots in one tensile thread along which Gandhi conducted his experiments in truth. But it is to the *harijan* that we need to return in order to grasp fully the meanings, promises, and fate of the collective subject (*praja*), the moral value attached to the category of the people (*jan*) in its simplicity and ordinariness, in non-Western iterations of democracy since the early twentieth century.

There was a profound leap of faith, indeed, an abyssal difference, between *praja* as a spiritual collectivity that Gandhi had mobilized in *Hind*

Swaraj and *jan* as an authentic, ordinary, and incurably mortal way of being (in its ambiguous nearness to God) that, a decade later, he would attach to the *harijan*. In this leap of faith—a faith that would be mobilized simultaneously within the framework of religious heterodoxy inspired by medieval and early modern *bhakti*, on the one hand, and Hindu negative theology (*advaita*) in its classical, even ecclesiastical form, on the other—lay the most attentive, deliberate, and ambiguous steps of Gandhi's turn toward the question of justice. For many impatient nationalists throughout the 1920s and 1930s, Gandhi's obsession with *harijan* life was at best a distraction from the urgent tasks of the anticolonial struggle. Lower caste activists and crusaders for caste equality, on the other hand, discerned in his approach to untouchability a lack of commitment to genuine emancipation. Yet *harijan*, as name and subject, was neither an unjust aberration in satyagraha nor a symptom of a deviant intrusion of social questions—caste legislation, religious reform, ritual rights, and occupational dignity—into the domain of the political. The *harijan*, instead, was the soul of satyagraha, the point of its greatest integrity, intensity, and mastery. It was also, I argue, a disciplinary limit, a *maryada* inscribed at the heart of anticolonial articulations of freedom itself.

A limit at the heart of politics: we need to work through this formula carefully, for Gandhi's thinking of limit was not simply a question of observing measure and civility. Nor was it simply a matter of respecting the unequal's suffering and of placing this respect at the center of his moral ontology. Limit, instituted through the *harijan*'s supposed filiation with divinity, was the making of transcendence and infinitude into politically salient categories. A somewhat cryptic conception of sovereignty, one that invoked the infinite God (or divine force) as frequently as it did the mortal subject, was thus built into Gandhi's choice of neologisms. As a beginning toward understanding the connectedness and integrity of this profound thinking of limit, let us here recall just one instance of a pattern within satyagrahic morals: Gandhi's gesture of limiting and even renouncing, on the most decisive occasions, his own claims to originality. *Hind Swaraj* begins with that iconoclastic confession, "These views are mine, yet they are not mine," and the naming of the *harijan* two decades later repeats that relinquishment of authorial sovereignty.[2] "It is not a name of my coining," Gandhi writes in 1933, two years after having adopted the name. "Some years ago, several 'untouchable' correspondents complained that I used the word *asprishya* in the pages of *Navajivan*. *Asprishya* literally means untouchable. I then invited them to suggest a better name."[3]

In 1931, just as in 1908, Gandhi transforms, indeed inverts, the act of naming—which, by its very nature, institutes and edifies a relationship of hierarchy—into a democratic gesture, into a transaction between equals. On both occasions, his readers respond to his search for a name, and once adopted publicly, it is the people's usage alone, insists Gandhi, that gives the neologisms their general force. He coins *satyagraha* in the wake of his struggle in South Africa, and he arrives at *harijan* during his second mass civil disobedience movement against the British in India. Although the first event monumentalizes an inaugural moment in his engagement with the ethics of popular firmness or resistance (*agraha*), it is the second that develops quickly into the most distinctive torsion within that ethics. A torsion that would impart to satyagraha's conceptual and rhetorical rhythm an unprecedented volatility, a sense of inescapable "fear and trembling" in its encounter with the unequal.[4] And far from being metaphorical, Gandhi would concede, this sense would touch the heart of his phenomenology of everyday life.

In this chapter, I retrace the rhythms of that momentous event, placing its depth, movements, and the activities around it within satyagraha's "spirit of democracy," as Gandhi called it. At the heart of this spirit, I argue, is a fundamental paradox: Gandhi's radical attempt to evacuate the untouchability of the *harijan*—in all its juridical, rhetorical, and phenomenological meanings and effects—from its roots within social relations into a site of political mediation and action. The classical laws of touching and not touching were now not merely issues of legislative redress; they were not part of the social question alone, which might be reduced, as liberal social reformers before and after Gandhi would argue, to issues of stigma, humiliation, and discrimination. Instead, firmly placed within the moral ontology of satyagraha, those theological laws and injunctions on touching were now embraced (juridically, figuratively, physically) and rendered into questions of discipline, obligation, and freedom. Touching, which is hardly an innocent gesture even under the most egalitarian and fraternal conditions, would henceforth become, in an irreversible manner, a theologico-political question.

Gandhi had a reason, he believed, for thinking of figures of untouchability—sacred, inviolable, transcendent, unequal, radiant, alien, and different—as necessarily sacrosanct "limit figures," as figures inhabiting the extremes and even exteriors of political society; as figures of immiscible—and when God was involved, transcendental—difference. If the *harijan*'s proper company was either only God or animal, then it was so simply because the condition of the immeasurably unequal—the existence of those who were unequal or sovereign beyond measure—could be thought about only at the limit of humanity. Gandhi's own decisions, routines, and laws of touching or not touching the untouchable, in other words, were not instituted in the interest of a more humane politics. They also demonstrated satyagraha's willingness to probe the limits of the human (and its own implication in those limits) as such. What was at stake here, as a consequence, was not just the sovereignty of the human at the center of the political, but also—especially when God's transcendence was invoked—satyagraha's own predilection for the moral law, its own search for an morally infinite sovereignty that spoke only to God (often only through the satyagrahi's innermost convictions). When Gandhi named the *harijan*, he not only brought the immeasurable and cruel inequality of untouchable life to bear on the collective moral conscience of colonized Indians. He also exposed satyagraha's unresolved relationship with the classical structures, languages, and institutions of sovereignty. It was this irresolution, at once profoundly egalitarian and exclusionary, at once intimate with the radical *bhakti* traditions of the medieval period and at absolute odds with them, that Gandhi would try to contain within the moral-juridical framework of *shudradharma*.

I end this chapter with an examination of the ethical and political logic behind Gandhi's practice of the "fast unto death," that singular form of individual action in which his moral ontology of force, his ethics of rigorous and truthful practice (*sadhana*), reached its extreme, unilateral, and most material form. Gandhi had begun refining the strategy of atonement through fasting rather early in his career, around 1914 in South Africa, and went on to undertake at least fifteen major fasts before his death in 1948. A majority of these came during a period that might be called, following Tim Pratt and James Vernon, "the golden age" of the hunger strike in the British Empire.[5] The most "epic" of these, however, monumentalized in Gandhi's aide Pyarelal's *The Epic Fast* (1932), was one that Gandhi undertook earlier that year during his confrontation with Ambedkar over the question of separate electorates for *harijan*s (Ambedkar often preferred the term "depressed classes" or simply, playing on the nationalist farce around the fast, "Untouchables," with a capital *U*).

I mine the conceptual and rhetorical features of that epic fast not simply because its consequences for the formation and trajectories of the democratic subject in India remain so inadequately explored.[6] I do so also to trace the means by which anticolonial political thought turned something as inalienably shared as mortality into a site of a sovereign decision (to die or kill), to retrace the measures by which satyagraha transformed something as universal as human finitude into a set of moral distinctions within the human itself— a human partitioned along its faculty, failing, and, in the final instance, its ability to have a relationship to death. Was Gandhi himself struggling against this classical problem, this identification of freedom with death? Is that why he barred less adept hands and souls from the science of sacrifice? Might sacrifice, whether of the self for others or of others that secures—often by force—the interest and privileges of the self, with all its unilateralism and limits, have a place in a society of equals at all?

As late as 1946, less than two years before his assassination, in an essay titled "What Is in a Name?," Gandhi was still forced to explain the *harijan*'s sacred provenance and, with it, his own intent.[7] Indeed, the political and ethical conundrum opened up by that name was to outlive him. Even a passing mention of it in the political arena in postcolonial India tends to generate allegations against those who use it of harboring antidemocratic prejudice against Dalits. What sort of agency, what sense of political and ethical proximity, then, might be imparted a name that would become a mark of exactly its opposite? Was the name's "sacred force," as Gandhi called it, merely a linguistic derivative of Indic exclusions and sacrifices, the modern sound of a classical tongue? Was it someone else's force, a symptom of satyagraha's attraction for classical forms of sovereignty, one that had betrayed what was most unjust in Gandhi's thinking of equality? If he had indeed sought to create a political subject out of the large mass of India's most oppressed people, if justice was for him unthinkable without the divine force of the name, what possibilities of action and intimacy (and risk of self-sacrifice that only a few might take) did this philosophical anthropology produce?

In probing Gandhi's conception and practice of touching the unequal within the framework of distance, his thinking of equality in terms of *maryada dharma*, I trace another sense and sensibility of freedom in the colonial world, one that goes against the grain of treating Gandhi's politics—and his attempt to reform untouchability—as an extension of his religious convictions and practices alone. In fact, we need to carefully trace how Gandhi at decisive moments separates the theological from the ontological, the transcendental from the mythic and superstitious, even as he carefully restores the relevance of faith as uncertainty—indeed, as undecidability and guesswork (*anumaan*)—to the realm of transformative action. The theological source of the name notwithstanding, in other words, it is inadequate to consign the term *harijan* to an unambiguously religious history of satyagraha. Certainly, the name evokes visions of authentic, even innocent, nearness to divinity. Refusing mediation by any scripture, priest, or organized ecclesiastical authority, the very sound of *harijan* calls forth the untouchable's immediate and filial intimacy with God. Rather than simply being a semantic extension of a transcendental and sovereign being, the name also posits in Gandhi's own terms, a "force," one whose truth was available neither unconditionally nor universally but which could be experienced (and its authenticity conserved) through sacrificial action alone. In fact, to truly understand the violence of

untouchable life, Gandhi insisted, one had to become *harijan*. From this ethics of "becoming *harijan*," ironically, satyagraha's deepest exclusions would
emerge.

The naming of the *harijan* condensed not only the satyagrahic norms of
judgment about what constituted rigorous, disciplined, and truthful action.
It marked out an elaborate constellation of faculties and abilities along which
the humility and truthfulness of sacrifice, the moral ontology of being proper
(*sattvik*), would be arranged. This constellation did not simply illuminate—
Ambedkar might have said, "betray"—the moral and juridical limits of truth
within which satyagrahic egalitarianism took form. It instituted the *harijan*
itself as the limit. Within the surreptitious logic of *maryada dharma*, in other
words, the *harijan* became the limit beyond which satyagraha, no matter how
militantly reformist it promised to be, would not venture—a limit beyond
which it could not venture without losing its meaning, its mastery, its very
truth.

Unsurprisingly, the severest questions concerning Gandhi's ability to
imagine the conditions and possibility of justice for India's religious and
caste "minorities" arose not around the everyday practices that formed the
moral crucible of *satyagraha*—a term that even Ambedkar adopted and retained for his movements—but around the effects of the name *harijan*.
And these questions were asked not because Gandhi had broken away from
democracy's intrinsic tendency to deploy those numerical and social categories that render it susceptible to manipulation and division. Rather, they
were asked precisely because it was in the face of the *harijan* that Gandhi's
resistance against democracy's enumerative principle, his cultivated indifference to calculation and measure, his firmness against the majoritarian rhetoric of the greatest good of the greatest number, turned most ambiguous,
most vulnerable to remission. In this chapter I probe both the unconscious
and calculated nature—the economy—of this ambiguity, beginning with its
earliest intimations in Gandhi's thought at the turn of the century. For even
if its effects were to emerge with greatest force in the 1930s, this thought had
begun to take its exemplary form around the composition of *Hind Swaraj*.
Gandhi's elevation of the "untouchable" to divine height and transcendence
in 1931, his epic "fast unto death" and the subsequent pact with Ambedkar
a year later, would make the 1930s the decisive decade in India's struggle to
constitute a just polity. Indeed, it would affect, explicitly or obliquely, the
very vocabulary of moral critique and social justice in modern India. But it
is the depth of certain continuities in Gandhi's thought and procedure, the
suppleness of satyagraha's justness and exclusion, their inseparability, that interest me here.

Subject to Civility

Among the many ironies of *Hind Swaraj* is that it was composed in the shadows of an imperial assassination: the killing of Sir Curzon Wylie by the Punjabi extremist Madanlal Dhingra, who was subsequently hanged in London in 1909. The founding figure of this radical strand of Indian anti-imperialism was the Oxford graduate Shyamaji Krishnavarma, born twelve years before Gandhi, in 1857. Krishnavarma founded the Indian Home Rule Society in 1905 and the India House, both in London.[8] It was at the India House that the Hindutva extremist V. D. Savarkar found his early foothold in anticolonial politics and came in contact with Gandhi, right on the eve of the composition of *Hind Swaraj*, casting his deep shadow over it. Viewed against the backdrop of this insurgent anticolonialism, Gandhi's audacious emphasis on force, both in *Hind Swaraj* and throughout his later writings, is striking not for the way he ties it to the promise of *swaraj* but rather for the way in which he reconstitutes force as a form of civility and patience, indeed as a form of self-sacrificial nonviolence. In response to those extremist nationalists who had, in their pursuit of freedom, decided to resort to political assassinations, Gandhi's rejoinder in *Hind Swaraj* is an exemplary instance of this counterintuitive thinking. Speaking of the difference between Italy and India in the light of Dhingra's action in the fifteenth chapter of the dialogue, Gandhi's "editor" asks the extremist "reader":

Do you not tremble to think of freeing India by assassination? What we need to do is to sacrifice ourselves. It is a cowardly thought, that of killing others. Whom do you suppose to free by assassination? The millions of India do not desire it. Those who are intoxicated by the wretched modern civilization think these things. Those who will rise to power by murder will certainly not make the nation happy. Those who believe that India has gained by Dhingra's act and other similar acts in India make a serious mistake. Dhingra was a patriot, but his love was blind. He gave his body in a wrong way; its ultimate result can only be mischievous.[9]

A sacrifice that involves killing those whose means and ends are unequal to one's own merely underlines the superfluity of empty violence rather than representing an act of heroism. Sacrifice is proper only when one dies in a particular fashion. One could not die using just any method and be called a *satyagrahi*. A death proper to satyagraha must be underpinned by a fearless and militant equality of means, by an attentiveness to *sadhan*. If those who are killed are unequal or unarmed, if the battle is not of equals, then that act is worthy neither of satyagraha nor of *swaraj*. Dhingra had shot dead an unarmed British official in a civil gathering of noncombatants. That was clearly not a battlefield proper to the struggle for *swaraj*, even if the revolutionary had gone to the gallows with a smile. Instead, such sacrifice is simply the wrong way of giving one's body away. An Indian capable of being a satyagrahi, Gandhi writes at the end of *Hind Swaraj*, "will know that no nation has risen without suffering; that, even in physical warfare, the true test is suffering and not the killing of others, much more so in the warfare of passive resistance."[10] Laying down the requisite virtues with the same conviction four decades later, he would declare, "To die without killing is the badge of the satyagrahi."[11]

Satyagrahic nonviolence—its truth and firmness—is thus grounded in the perfectibility of death as equality, in the gesture of giving away one's body with equanimity and civility. The satyagrahi's openness to dying, his willingness to abandon life, opened for Gandhi the possibility of living an equal life. Until the moment of death, to which he ascribed a peculiar perfection, life was necessarily unequal, violent, and impure. "All life in the flesh exists by some *himsa* [violence]," Gandhi wrote in an essay on euthanasia published two decades after *Hind Swaraj*. "None, while in the flesh, can thus be entirely free from *himsa* because one never completely renounces the will to live."[12] Life, even the most peaceful one is constitutively self-threatening, its violence rooted in the most primordial of human desires: the will to live. The very existence and survival of life, dependent on the consumption of grain or acts of procreation is founded on an ineluctable violence. The least violence in the practice of nonviolence might therefore reside in the satyagrahic belief that "sacrifice of self is infinitely superior to the sacrifice of others."[13] Nonviolence might be mastered in its authenticity only in the satyagrahi's embrace of death while refusing to kill. The satyagrahi sacrifices for something that is always worth more than mere life, more than mere body: he sacrifices for sovereignty over himself alone. For the satyagrahi, Gandhi declares revealingly, "it is really the spirit behind" that matters.[14] In this early judgment concerning the right and wrong ways of "giving away," in this suturing of the ability to gift one's mortal self to the other with the spirit of a transcendental and immortal truth, Gandhi anticipates an ontology of force that would enduringly guide and trouble his moral and political practice.

By the early 1930s, having matured in the vicissitudes of the successes and failures of his two mass movements and being faced more squarely than he had ever been with the cruelest prohibitions inflicted on India's untouchables by its Hindu majority, Gandhi felt compelled to reconceptualize the language and practice of satyagrahic sacrifice. Truth is not—indeed, it cannot be—constituted around sacrificial nonviolence alone. "Truth," he now insists, "implies justice."[15] And this justice he had come to associate with *Ramarajya*, the monarchical rule of the god-king Rama, a rule bound in the most exemplary fashion by the disciplinary norms and injunctions of the moral law. In fact, Rama is the *purusha*, the sovereign human and cosmic exemplar of this moral law. He is both the sovereign spirit of the laws and the most disciplined abider of the limits that the law imposes on human affairs. Thus, within the Indic tradition he is the figure of *maryada purushottama*. No term exemplifies this transcendentalism of limits lodged at the heart of Gandhi's attraction to the laws of *Ramarajya* more strongly, more economically, I think, than the concept of *maryada*. In one of his speeches delivered in 1931, Gandhi had the word translated as "discipline."[16] But as we shall see, a very particular kind of disciplinary and surreptitious force comes to be articulated around it, one that is acutely aware of difference, one that probes the "farthest limits" of satyagraha's universalism, one that is bound up with an intricate (and excessive) set of everyday measures and routines. *Maryada* is not simply a regime of exorbitant and external force, an economy of injunctions and discipline instituted in order to conserve moral and social limits that are necessary to an ethics of state. *Maryada* is the constitutive excessiveness of satyagrahic measure itself, the insuperable sovereignty of the limit as such.

Two decades after *Hind Swaraj*, in an extended discussion of the ethical state, Gandhi looped back to the conceptual threads that he had first begun to weave in that early work. Commenting on one of the later chapters from the Hindu epic *Ramayana*, he considers the debate over public morality that ensues after Rama's triumph over the evil king Ravana. The cause of the war was Ravana's abduction of Rama's wife, Sita. After the righteous war that Rama wages to wrest Sita back, the royal couple return to their kingdom in Ayodhya. But fissures and disquiet surface soon thereafter. Given the long period of abduction, war, and return, most of which Sita had been forced to spend in Ravana's custody, Rama's subjects begin to question her chastity. Had she succumbed to temptation and fallen into impurity? Rama, Gandhi argues, responds to public doubt as a just sovereign must:

Ramachandra elicits public opinion and finds that Sita is the object of censure in a particular washerman's home. He was well aware that this adverse criticism was groundless; Sita was dearer to him than his own life, nothing could lead to a difference between him and her; nevertheless, he renounced her, realizing that it was improper to let such criticism continue. . . . Rama honored public opinion in this manner; his rule is called *Ramarajya*. Even a dog could not be harmed in that State, as Ramachandra felt that all living beings were part of himself. There would be no licentious conduct, no hypocrisy, no falsehood in such a State. A people's government would function in such a truthful age. The ruler forsakes his dharma when this age ends. Attacks will then be made from outside the State. Germs from outside attack the body when the blood becomes impure. Likewise when society as a body gets corrupted, people who are like its limbs are subjected to external attacks.[17]

To prevent such external attacks on the state and protect the polity, Rama orders Sita to prove her chastity publicly by walking through fire. The most abiding threads of Gandhi's thought are spun around this episode in a lucid and exorbitant narrative, saturated with the most visceral (and anthropological) visions of sovereignty and power. And it is not only that Gandhi's theory of moral sovereignty—which he deploys to legitimize the sovereign's paramount right of decision to take life in the interest of general will and security of the realm—is exorbitant. His attempt to render this sovereignty amenable to the morals of satyagraha, his willingness to ratify the master's right to violence as the ground of morality and discipline necessary for the cultivation of nonviolence, illuminates Gandhi's somewhat tendentious understanding of popular will itself. But perhaps most important, the passage reveals how strongly given over Gandhi himself was (or could be) to the humanist rhetoric of excess and exception, to the biological and punitive rhetoric of juridical authority, to the liberal discourse on that classical fear of the body politic being wrecked from the inside before it is attacked from the outside. This fear, as we know, following the tradition of modern humanism beginning with Thomas Hobbes's *Leviathan* (1651), has come to justify the state's right to extraordinary, even lawless, measures of safety and security.

Residing inside this body politic since Hobbes, in traditions liberal and revolutionary alike, is the threatening presence of the animal, the figural and rhetorical presence of that which is strange, alien, risky—that is to say, the presence of the immeasurably unequal, the prehensile creature that possesses limbs but not the skill and felicity of the hand, the woman who gifts life but remains sacrificeable because her fecundity invites and exemplifies immoral temptation. These are lives worthy of compassion yet spiritually destitute. Rama's just rule, Gandhi recalls, is exemplary precisely because not even the most unequal remain unprotected in that kingdom. "Not even a dog"— something is constitutively deficient and unequal about this animal, about the animal as such, for the dog comes up again in one of Gandhi's allegories from the *Mahabharata* as a substitute for the *harijan*.[18] There is a terrifying continuity between God, animal, and unequal, a nebulous kinship of unequals in which respect and violence, justice and horror, become inseparable. And yet despite this inequality at the heart of satyagraha, Gandhi's stress on the protection of the unequal, his commitment to guarding the violated and oppressed, remains impeccable. The excess of violence comes to be regulated by an unflinching vow of civility.

How is this impeccable civility, this immense sheen of satyagrahic equanimity, one that was (rightly and wrongly) to become already in Gandhi's own time globally recognizable, maintained? There are two sources of this civility:

one that Gandhi thought through deeply and sensitively, the other that remained suspended and unthought, only to emerge at the most tactical and
fragile moments of satyagrahic intervention in the social. Together these two
sources form the heart of Gandhi's thinking of the limit. The first source institutes the ethical subordination of sovereign will to popular opinion—that
is, civility as an ethical limit enforced by the people on the power and rule,
the *rajya*, of the sovereign. This limit prevents, according to Gandhi, the tyranny of rulers, the kind of tyranny he associated with the British Empire and
which, after the name of the demonic antihero Ravana, he called *Ravanara-
jya*. The second and more pernicious source, the sovereign's sacrificial violence, makes the injunctive authority and civility of the people possible in the
first place. In his innumerable readings of the *Ramayana*, for instance, Gandhi
rarely fails to praise Sita's exemplary resistance against Ravana. Yet once Rama
emerges victorious and brings her back to Ayodhya, the same exemplary Sita
would be emptied of the capacity to resist the sacrificial injunction on her
life enforced by public morality. Instead, she must be sacrificed precisely for
the moral order, for *maryada*, the law of the limit, to be restored. So Sita, the
Shudra, the *atishudra*, the animal—the unequal—were at one moment exemplary of what chaste passive resistance required and at another moment rendered wholly subject to the sovereign's "limitless sacrifice."

One must ask, then, whether in his readings of classical texts, Gandhi
is indeed not betraying his susceptibility to the most punitive impulses of the
moral law. After all, sovereign power in its modern democratic guise is often
exercised on behalf of public morality; its disciplinary regime sustained often
by invocations and endorsements of general will; its absolutism simultaneously
limited and enabled by "the democratic mandate," as it is called in the modern tradition. Had Gandhi broken from what he would himself have considered the worst impulses of republican democracy? Or had he aligned his morals
with precisely those tendencies that render democracy in its executive form so
conducive to strategies of mastery and oppression? These are classical questions,
and they go to the heart of the modern democratic tradition. At the moment,
I want to pick up only one recurrent and constitutive element in Gandhi's discourse, his privileging of "public opinion" as the ontological ground of self-
rule, or *swaraj*, which is a crucial element precisely because it remains, despite
its ubiquity, elliptical in his critique of sovereignty in its various ruses.

Gandhi was deeply aware of the fact that public morality, founded on the
perverse strength of numbers, harbored a pernicious affinity for majoritarian
rhetorics of goodness and safety of the greatest number. This violent convergence of sovereignty and majority, which had begun to speak in colonial India
the language democracy and national security in the most fanatical overtones

(whose most strident exemplar would be Gandhi's own Brahmin assassin), was to enduringly trouble his program of social reform.[19] Gandhi was sensitive to this problem. In his reformulation of *shudradharma* in the 1920s and 1930s, we can discern traces of his attempt to mount a formidable resistance against this tendency within republican democracy to turn against its own limit, its propensity to justify oppression as the instrument of civility, and even liberty, of the masses. The consequences, however, of Gandhi's own attempt to supplement the satyagrahic ethics of firmness with a sense of moral (and juridical) obligation that, for the first time in the history of mainstream Indian nationalism, would mobilize not the skills of the warrior Kshatriya but the abilities of the oppressed Shudra, were to be equally momentous and divisive. And, to anticipate the argument of the rest of this chapter in briefest terms, the problem would not as much be the distinction (or even hierarchy) between *shudradharma* and *kshatriyadharma* that would coalesce around Gandhi's moral ontology. Beyond doubt, his ontology seemed to cleave along the two axes of satyagrahic obligation, one articulated around what Gandhi believed was the *dharma* proper to "Kshatriya spirit" and the other around what he was convinced was immanent to the Shudra's being. There was for him anything but sameness or substitutability between these two orders. And yet it was the unity of their logics, the radical equality that Gandhi would posit between *kshatriyadharma* and *shudradharma*, the moral ontology of force—the ethics of ability and exactitude—that would run through this thinking of equality-in-difference like an integrating thread, which would transform satyagraha's relationship to the political culture of its times.

Force by Another Name

In 1931, under some pressure from lower caste critics, Gandhi invited the readers of his paper *Navajivan* to suggest a substitute for the word *antyaja*, literally meaning "last born" and a pejorative used to refer to "untouchables." *Antyaja* is the spiritual cognate of *asprishya* (literally, "untouchable"). It banishes the "last born" from the theological and moral space of Hinduism, who come, by their very name, at the end (*anth*) and are thus consigned beyond the pale of faith. The terms *asprishya* and its more colloquial (and therefore more insidious) corporeal rendering, *achhoot*, however, carry the marks not only of spiritual exclusion. They also banish the untouchables from the world of sight, touching and contact (*sparsh*) and make the *harijans*, in Gandhi's evocative words, "unapproachables and invisibles."[20] Among several suggestions of a substitute for *antyaja* that Gandhi received in 1931, he decided to retain *harijana*. "The word is not new," he remarked, quoting the correspondent who had sent the suggestion, "but a beautiful one already used by the father of Gujarati poetry. Moreover, as used by him, the word '*Harijana*' can also mean men of God who are abandoned by society. The third advantage of that word is that, probably, *Antyaja* brethren would lovingly accept that name and try to cultivate the virtues which it connotes."[21] Notwithstanding subsequent accusations that he had, by the stroke of a name, robbed the *harijan* of moral and political agency while at the same time imparting to their everyday humiliations the aura of history and virtue, Gandhi had attempted to lend the unequal at once an authority (to reform society) and a responsibility to be virtuous in action. A week later, at a ceremony in Ahmedabad organized to open the gates of a temple to *harijan*s, he clarified the provenance of the name further.

It was a word used by the great saint Narasinha Mehta, who by the bye belonged to the Nagar Brahmin community and who defied the whole community by claiming the 'untouchables' as his own. I am delighted to adopt that word which is sanctified by having been used by such a great saint, but it has for me a deeper meaning than you may imagine. The "untouchable," to me, is, compared to us, really a "*Harijana*"—a man of God, and we are "*Durjana*" (men of evil). For whilst the "untouchable" has toiled and moiled and dirtied his hands so that we may live in comfort and cleanliness; we have delighted in suppressing him. We are solely responsible for all the shortcomings and faults that we lay at the door of these untouchables. It is still open to us to be *Harijana* ourselves, but we can only do so by heartily repenting of our sin against them.[22]

I will return to Gandhi's discourse on the *harijan*'s laboring and soiled hands, for satyagraha's commitment to the spirit of democracy turned most ambiguous around the abilities of the hand as such, around Gandhi's attempt to transform the social meaning of manual labor into the morals of political and spiritual action. Meanwhile, the responsibility for restitution comes to be framed above in the language of choice between saintliness and evil, beauty and monstrosity, belief and oppression. The stakes, thus, are neither simply religious nor juridical. They belong to the order of spirit. Untouchability is first and foremost a spiritual malady, an affliction Gandhi called the "touch-me-not spirit" of Hinduism. It is a destitute spirit, too, a "white ant" that must be "touched at it source."[23] And yet there could be no easy purges because this spirit of Hinduism remained simultaneously religious and irreligious, clean and unclean. It was destitute and yet necessary to the morals of satyagrahic struggle, violent yet fundamental to the sense of mastery without which satyagraha might itself falter.

This affinity with mastery notwithstanding, a critique of domination was not absent here. Hinduism's horrible deviance was caused, Gandhi insisted, by precisely its contamination by sovereignty, its impoverishment by "our collective delight in suppressing them"—the untouchables (*asprishya*) and unequals (*asamaan*). The name *harijan*, inasmuch as it invokes God, then, sought spiritual restitution through another sovereign and another force, brought into the world by the poet-saint Narasinha Mehta. This other sovereign was not just any transcendent sovereign. The *harijan* invokes an exemplary God among gods: Vishnu (Hari), the chosen deity of the Vaishnava sect to which Gandhi's family belonged. "The *Vaishnava* way of life," Gandhi claimed, "had its very origin in compassion, in spiritual knowledge, and in the desire to purify the fallen."[24] In fact, as early as 1908 in South Africa, he had introduced one of Narasinha Mehta's devotional songs into the everyday life of inmates at the Phoenix settlement in Natal. The *bhajan* "Vaishnava Jan To" defines the Vaishnava as a person of infinite humility, a person capable of dissolving the self, open to turning himself into a cipher if compassion with the other's suffering demanded.

Over the next four decades, the *bhajan* became satyagraha's principal hymn. To the satyagrahi, it was the enchanting and sonorous reminder to mobilize *dayabal*, the force of compassion and nonindifference toward another's inequality and suffering, to the extent that the satyagrahi, Gandhi mandated, must not refrain from dissolving even his own "I" in the interest of equality with the poorest and most untouchable. Fidelity to Vishnu, or Hari, was not guided by any pragmatic desire to touch the untouchable, even if the *harijan* was brought into the world right as—and perhaps with an eye on—the colonial debate over franchise was beginning to gain momentum. On the contrary, within the moral fabric of the name *harijan*, the force of satyagrahic reform was to be inextricably woven with acts of healing and self-effacement. Gandhi's disciple Pyarelal wrote of the "haunting refrain" of the *bhajan* with which his master, even as the fast in 1932 had started to rapidly drain the life out of his body, began his mornings in prison. "He alone is the true Vaishnava, / Who knows and feels for another's woe."[25] The memory of Gandhi's own childhood provided the framework in which God's children had to be now tended: through the sacrifice of one's own self in empathy with the suffering of the unequal. And this framework, despite its religiosity that it had inherited from Gandhi's childhood, was not shy of mounting fierce resistance against that past. "I am," Gandhi was unequivocal, "in no way prepared to accept as religion, even though it might have a historical basis, the punishment of pouring molten lead into the ears of the Shudra listening to Vedic recitations."[26]

Other knots in the history of this name, however, would prove more intractable. Vishnu's earthly incarnation is the mythic sovereign, the god-king

Rama of Ayodhya, whose moral exemplarity forms the core of the Gandhi's favorite epic, Tulsidas's *Ramayana*. How, Gandhi recalled thinking as a child when readings of epics were occasions for family gatherings (as they were in Ambedkar's family), "can the *Ramayana* in which one who is regarded nowadays as an untouchable took Rama across the Ganges in his boat, countenance the idea of any human beings being 'untouchables' on the ground that they were polluted souls?"[27] Gandhi had often meditated publicly about the protective force of Rama.[28] This explains his enduring fascination with *Ramaraksha*, a set of hymns that invoke Rama for protection against evil spirits. Weaving beautifully this discourse on immunity with the question of touching and not touching, Gandhi, at the height of his first noncooperation movement in 1921, spoke of his childhood in Gujarat.

After some time we shifted to Porbandar, where I made my first acquaintance with Sanskrit. I was not yet put into an English school, and my brother and I were placed in charge of a Brahmin who taught us *Ramaraksha* and *Vishnu Puja*. . . . Now it happened that I was very timid then, and would conjure up ghosts and goblins whenever the lights went out, and it was dark. The old mother, to disabuse me of fears, suggested that I should mutter the texts whenever I was afraid, and all evil spirits would fly away. . . . I could never believe then that there was any text in the *Ramaraksha* pointing to the conduct of the "untouchables" as a sin. I did not understand its meaning then, or understood it very imperfectly. But I was confident that *Ramaraksha*, which could destroy all fear of ghosts, could not be countenancing any such thing as fear of contact with the "untouchables." . . . I claim to have understood the spirit of Hinduism. Hinduism has sinned in giving sanction to untouchability.[29]

A few days earlier too, Gandhi had claimed, in as many words, "to have understood the spirit of Hinduism, and I hope to die for the defense of my religion at any moment but I should cease to call myself a Hindu if I believe one moment that Hinduism requires me to consider it a sin to touch a single human being."[30] Thus, almost a decade before he would consecrate the untouchable, a prolific discourse on spiritual reparation, the announcement of the need to reclaim the spirit of religion by recovering the extinct ethics of touching, was already underway. It bears repeating that, despite its mythological undertones, the act of faith that had led Gandhi to introduce the *harijan* into his grammar of action did not entail the politicization of a Hindu religious ideal in its conventional sense. Rather, it involved a distinctive ontology of resistance; a precise, limited, and vigilant extenuation of force against empire and religious orthodoxy alike; a radical attempt, above all, to reclaim the lost measure of touching the unequal (attentively and in a way that stayed faithful to the unequal's vulnerability) in the very shadows of the moral law that barred it. This act of faith involved a courageous and militantly original ethics: an ethics of touching within the transcendental injunctions of limit. In other words, it demanded attaching the empirical finitude of the *harijan* to the infinite sovereignty of God, a measure that would project the deepest ambiguities of Gandhi's egalitarianism onto the screen of twentieth-century nationalist politics.

For India's freedom to have any moral meaning, the immeasurable power of touching had to be purified and restored, according to Gandhi, both from the cruelties of Hindu orthodoxy and the legislative measure of liberal reformism. Untouchability had to be purged not in the interest of homogeneous citizenship but in the interest of maintaining a shared world in which difference could be instituted as the ground of moral and political responsibility. Touching, as gesture and faculty, condenses the deepest, immortal, and infinite sense of humanity's shared finitude; one is human inasmuch as one might touch and be touched.[31] And yet, inasmuch as touching is always singular and irreproducible, inasmuch as one touches another in a way, at a time, and at a place that is never reproducible when one touches others at another time and place, one can be faithful to touching only when one is faithful to humanity's immeasurable heterogeneousness, or shall we say, variousness. In fact, among all the senses that constitute the human in its proper form, Gandhi argued, touching alone could be reclaimed for an ethics and politics of absolute difference. It alone had the force proper to self-sacrifice. And it had force because touching touched the law at its limit; it was a threshold, a gesture and transgression, that was both outside the law (because it remained irreproducible and irreducible) and within the law (because it required restraint, measure, and, above all, a "spirit of obedience" that conserved the integrity of the moral law itself).[32]

Among ordinary mortals, then, given the immense differences in their faiths, beliefs, and ways of touching, Gandhi mandated, touching could not be a merely corporeal gesture; it could not be seen as a purely physical act that worked to heighten, simply at the point and moment of contact between two mortals, a degree of sameness between them. Such sameness, brought about without the vigilance of the law, would lack force. Instead, touching must become a *coup de force*, a moment of equality within the incontrovertible truth of difference and distance between mortals. That was also to say, touching was to remain within the norms and rules of measure. It could not be indiscriminate, unreserved, and overenthusiastic. "India's degradation" in the hands of the empire, Gandhi fumed elsewhere the same year, had resulted precisely from its habit of indiscriminate touching, whether out of lust or reverence.[33] Every living species was equally touchable, but this touchability had to thrive within the permissions and injunctions of untouchability. The battle against untouchability demanded nuanced and intricate ways of practicing the ability to touch, the ability to refuse to touch, the right to say no and yes to untouchability, the right to follow the law of untouchability itself, not its absolute annihilation.

At its extreme, as we shall see most powerfully expressed in the series of speeches on untouchability Gandhi delivered around the time of the Bihar earthquake of 1934 (one of the most disastrous in the subcontinent), this battle would take the form of a profound undecidability within satyagraha, one that would refuse—or find itself unable—to separate life from law, measure from mastery (or God) itself.

Untouchability against untouchability, then: this was the moral framework of Gandhi's kinship with unequals, a distinctive universalism and understanding of finitude marked by measure, compassion, and force. Less than six months after he had named the *harijan*, while still lodged in Yeravda Prison in the wake of his second civil disobedience movement, Gandhi established his new paper. He called it, summoning that universalism, *Harijan.* Everyone, but especially the satyagrahi, was expected to aspire to master the exemplary virtues, the godlike impeccability, that the name marshaled. Most important, everyone had to be untouchable by turns because such untouchability, Gandhi believed, was alone the source of the subject's intimacy with the divine. "As God is the help of the helpless, and as it is the helpless who naturally turn to God," Gandhi told a group of *harijan* interlocutors barely a month before Ambedkar published *Annihilation of Caste.*

I thought you deserved the name better than I for instance. For, whilst I have to aspire to become a Harijan you are Harijans in the very nature of things. But you will say, "When your objective is to make Harijans Hindus why don't you start by calling them Hindus straightaway?" What am I to do so long as I have not succeeded in abolishing untouchability? [A *harijan* retorts by asking] But today, sir, it is an opprobrious term. There is a Brahmin who threatens to hammer us if we call him a Harijan. [Gandhi unequivocally reasserts] Then he is no Brahmin. You know the word "Harijan" occurs in Tulsidas's Ramayana? There Lakshmana describes to Parashurama the characteristic of a true Kshatriya. He says:

सुर महसिुर हरजिन अरु गाई| हमरे ̇ कुल इन्ह पर न सुराई||

(It is the trait of our clan never to use force towards a god, a Brahmin, a Harijan or a cow.)

"Harijan" there means a man of God, a devotee, no matter to what caste or varna he belongs. We all have to treasure the beautiful connotation of the word and try to be worthy of the name.[34]

Now, the *harijan* is not merely a subject, if he is a subject at all. Rather, his name institutes a moral ontology of force—an ontology because there is, around the *harijan*, not simply the invocation of force as metaphor, but an entire constellation of related insinuations, instruments, and abilities that separate the being of the properly sacrificial human (*sattvik*) from its failed, narcissistic double (*rajasik*). It is a conflict of faculties: threat, anger, sword, on the one hand, and restraint, virtue, disarmament, immunity, potency, plenitude, on the other. Gandhi institutes the *harijan* not merely as a sacred name. He grants his personhood an intrinsic beauty as well, a beauty that must be kept unscathed and given protection against the force of Kshatriya arms. Inasmuch as this beauty recalls a filiation with God, the *harijan* is now both God's child and satyagraha's exemplar, one whom the satyagrahi must become worthy of and keep sacrosanct. A radical equality, an equality that belongs to the radiance of sacrifice alone, is set to work here. The *harijan* and the Brahmin are now equally proper to *Ramarajya*; one does not contaminate the other. If one is a true Brahmin, one must not only know the provenance of the *harijan*'s name. The Brahmin, to be legitimately identified as a Brahmin, must also know that in that epochal "kingdom of righteousness," he and the *harijan* are equal not only to each other but also with the animal and God.[35] The onus of this knowledge, however, remains with the Brahmin; cognitive freedom, in the most Hegelian fashion, issues from the master, not the bondsman. This may be why Gandhi often pronounces the Shudra incapable, even unworthy, of reading the Vedas. "The injunction against Sudras studying the Vedas is not altogether unjustified," he had said in 1925, because "a person without moral education, without sense and without knowledge would completely misread the Shastras."[36] This cognitive servitude is less a characteristic of the Shudra alone than it is, in a dramatic reversal, a symptom of the Shudra having become a universal name for all destitute existence. Shorn of moral force—and of sense itself—such life, Gandhi confirmed, was "devoid of spirit."[37]

Without being detained by the gratuitous violence of this remark—for after all, the Shudra was a subject without sense precisely because it had been sequestered, by force, from the world of sense as such—let us turn to the pivotal passage from the *Ramayana* that Gandhi cites. In the encounter between Lakshmana and Parashurama, whose force has been rendered spiritual? Who was at war and who was being kept unscathed? What kind of force is it that makes the *harijan*—or the animal—exemplary? Not necessarily their own force, for Rama's warrior-brother Lakshmana cites the *harijan* not as an agent wielding arms but instead as a figure that demands restraint and limit. Inasmuch as his presence suspends the war, the *harijan* is indeed an exemplary counterforce to violence. His name enables the sacrifice of sacrifice—that is, it mandates Kshatriya nonviolence on the battlefield. But in that very injunction to not kill, by way of celebrating the warrior's restraint—and the *harijan's* immunity—the name reveals, at the heart of satyagraha, a theologico-political impulse—a strange failure to think without the language of the state. As Gandhi frequently stated in the 1920s and the 1930s, "swaraj and *Ramarajya* is one and the same thing."[38] And he said this often on behalf of the people themselves. "According to the popular conception swaraj is synonymous with *Ramarajya*—the establishment of the Kingdom of Righteousness on earth."[39] This conception of righteousness, at once circumscribed by an ethical limit (the people's civility) and the exorbitance of Kshatriya obligation (the executive duty to sacrifice the subject for the sake of maintaining that civility), did not mandate that the satyagrahi (or the master/oppressor) must relinquish force. What was required instead was a new measure and discipline, a new ethics of reform, which Gandhi would subsequently call *maryada dharma*.[40]

The Soul of the Master

The concept of *maryada* is not found in Gandhi's early writings. Although *Hind Swaraj* had conceptualized, in the most counterintuitive and audacious fashion, the civility of force and had emphasized the moral value of limit, it had never named it as such. Gandhi adopted the term in the 1920s, during his extensive public meditations on the *Gita* and the *Ramayana*. What had propelled this resurgence of "limit" by another name? Was it the debate over the expansion of colonial franchise that had begun to gather a new sense of urgency in the 1920s and that was now threatening to open the purportedly divisive gates of electoral politics to hitherto marginal religious and caste groups? Was it the fear of excessive—Ambedkar might say "revolutionary"—democracy that had compelled Gandhi to elaborate on the moral value of measure anew? Was it the profound incivility of caste violence sanctioned by Hinduism and the threat it posed to satyagraha itself? Or was this resurgence of the limit linked to something more elliptical, to Gandhi's enduring fascination with a sovereignty that would have been neither imperial nor democratic, but one that would also refuse to remain, despite his good conscience, restricted to the self? Had an abiding fascination with the ethics of mastery, a soft latitude for the oppressor, reemerged in a new form after and between the failures of his two mass campaigns that had ended in 1922 and 1931?

By the 1920s, at any rate, Gandhi could not have continued to conceptualize and put into practice the morals of satyagrahic action in terms of satyagraha's confrontation with the empire alone, as he had in *Hind Swaraj*.

He had to now face—in the wake of his mass movements, which had relentlessly invoked justice and sacrifice—Hinduism's own violence toward the oppressed. He needed to mobilize another force, one that turned inward, toward annulment of pride and cruelty; one that had to be grounded in soulful, ascetic, and immeasurable love for the unequal. Who was the exemplar of this immeasurable force, this love? Gandhi's enduring answer had been, we have seen, the epochal sovereign Rama. And this exemplarity of the mythic monarch was articulated even before Gandhi had launched his first mass movement. Let us take a step back here, 1917 to be precise, in order to grasp more fully the ways in which a political war against the empire comes to be aligned, within satyagraha, along axes of Kshatriya, Shudra, and Brahmin obligations. "Rama stands for the soul and Ravana for the non-soul. The immense physical might of Ravana is as nothing compared to the soul-force of Rama. Ravana's ten heads are as straw to Rama. Rama is a yogi; he has conquered self and pride. This represents the ultimate in satyagraha."[41] Then comes the curious assertion of kinship between satyagrahic mastery and *varnadharma*, the system of obligations structured around *Chaturvarnya*, the classical four-fold division of Hindu society. Note here the return of force as the precondition of a nonviolent and civic polity:

It is certain that India cannot rival Britain or Europe in force of arms. The British worship the war-god and they can all of them become, as they are becoming, bearers of arms. The hundreds of millions in India can never carry arms. They have made the religion of nonviolence their own. It is impossible for the *varnashram* system to disappear from India. The way of *varnashram* is a necessary law of nature. India, by making a judicious use of it, derives much benefit. . . . So long as this institution of *varnashram* exists in India, everyone cannot bear arms here. The highest place in India is assigned to the *brahmana dharma*—which is soul-force. Even the armed warrior does obeisance to the brahmin. So long as this custom prevails, it is vain for us to aspire for equality with the West in force of arms.[42]

In a fashion that otherwise resonates with his brilliant description of "soul-force" in *Hind Swaraj*, Gandhi declares *varnadharma* to be the law of nature. But he now equates this nature neither with one religion nor with the ordinary life and quotidian practices of the multitude. He instead arms it with the force of a spiritual universality that guards not one creed but the sacredness of all life. *Varnadharma* is not merely a ritual obligation of the few; it is, Gandhi insists, an egalitarian ontology of life, a natural law everyone living being must equally respect. Life lived on the principles laid out by *varnadharma* opens the ontological ground of nonviolence proper to Indian's struggle against the empire. A classical matrix of social exclusion is thus inscribed into the struggle for national sovereignty, and by extension, into the matrices and meanings of citizenship that this struggle would give way to. By the end of the passage, at his most rigorous, Gandhi in fact recedes even deeper, setting up a troubled—and no doubt, troubling—equivalence between *brahmanadharma* and soul-force, between exclusion and compassion itself. This *dharma*, with its judiciousness and civility of force, institutes the irrefutable law of priestly sovereignty (to which even the warrior Kshatriyas are subservient) and distributes the multitude's work, labor, and freedom along a thread of reverence he calls "custom." By regulating the right to wield arms and sequestering it away from the ordinary multitude, who lacks the moral discipline necessary for sacrifice proper, Gandhi's *brahmanadharma* thus secures the very possibility of nonviolence for India.

"The vast organization of caste," he had argued less than a year earlier, in 1916, "answered not only the religious wants of the community, but it answered too its political needs. They managed their internal affairs through the caste system, and through it they dealt with any oppression from the ruling power or powers. It is not possible to deny of a nation that was capable of producing the caste system its wonderful power of organization."[43] What would have seemed, just a year later, to be Gandhi's tactless (if decisive) celebration of *varnadharma*'s exclusions, then, had here already mutated into a deliberate, tactical irony. It was a relationship of abjection—a common thread of sacrificial energy that ran like an integrating thread—between satyagraha and the classical injunctions of the moral law (*dharma*). It is as if Gandhi could not despise *varnadharma* without, in the same breath, marveling—not unlike Ambedkar—at its aesthetics of force, its juridical ethics of disarmament, and therefore, its potential to produce the conditions of mass nonviolence. Could nonviolence, Gandhi wondered, ever find a more tactical, more institutional, more political ground than in the land where the majority of the multitude had already been disarmed by religious and natural law? Shouldn't the colonial world, especially its revolutionaries, as Gandhi had demanded in *Hind Swaraj*, emulate this exemplary and nonviolent history of gradation, dispossession, and "willing surrender" that social relations under caste allowed? Was anything more exemplary for *ahimsa* (and more necessary for it) than the institution of *varnadharma*? In another sense, was dispossession, no matter how violent, not the most fertile ground for testing the moral efficacy of satyagraha's ontology of force—force as the vulnerable, self-sacrificial ground of being—as such?

This is, in other words, not simply a question of social nonviolence between caste and religious communities but of the ontology of the political— the making political of being—in itself. Indeed, Gandhi's counterintuitive genius may seem to lie in rendering the rich and divisive particularities of history, the immense difference in social relations between the colonizer and colonized, oppressor and oppressed, absolutely irrelevant to satyagraha's universalism. And yet this institution of weakness and dispossession as the moral ground of firmness has everything to do with the political in its most institutional sense—that is, with the conceptual and rhetorical structures of rule, obedience, and discipline. It has, in fact, everything to do with relations of force between the excluding and the excluded. For what one critiques, regulates, measures, and institutes every time one touches the other, every time one seeks to formulate an ethics of touching as such, according to Gandhi, is the notion and economy of force. To retrieve from the shadows of untouchability a just order of touchability (conceptual and corporeal) would require, then, a *coup de force* in moral relations. "We make them crawl on their bellies; we have made them rub their noses on the ground; with eyes red with rage, we push them out of railway compartments—what more than this has the British Rule done?"[44]

With this 1921 speech, we have returned to the exigencies created by Gandhi's mass mobilization against the empire, one whose successes and failures were to prove no less transformative for satyagraha than they would for debates over citizenship and duty in colonial India. Let us note, for instance, the disappearance of that cruel irony that had so gratuitously, even brazenly, marked the speeches of the late 1910s. In these radical moments now, when the critique of domination is turned inward, the empire is nothing more than an allegory in Gandhi's thinking of force, nothing more than a recent mutation of an old enslavement and cruelty that Hinduism had subjected its unequals to. Empire—or even an earthquake—becomes a legitimate, sometimes divine, punishment for India's inner inequality and cruelty, and the dehumanizing social laws of "not touching" reveal a deeper symptom of Hinduism's own moral blindness, its politically suicidal affinity for colonization by others. Thus emerges the imperative and politics of touching—that is, touching as the question of sovereignty and duty, or *dharma*, one that replaces and exceeds the imperative of mere social reform.

But even a blind man can see that the practice of untouchability is contrary to dharma. Only, in the same way as the *atman*'s inhabiting the body for ages prevents us from knowing it, the long existence of the practice of untouchability does not permit us to see the *adharma* inherent in it. To make the any persons crawl on their stomachs, to segregate them, to drive them to live on the outskirts of the village, not to be concerned whether they live or die, to give them food left over by others—all this certainly cannot be religion. That an untouchable cannot live in our neighborhood and cannot own land, that an untouchable must, on seeing us, shout: "Please keep at a distance, do not touch me," and should not be permitted to sit with us in the train—this is not Hinduism.[45]

Despite the oblique theologico-political impulses in his exhortations, Gandhi's militancy is most apparent in his acute attention to the quotidian violence, the empirical and routine indifference, in which social inequality thrived. But he turns, with a courage that was singular among twentieth-century nationalists, the question of social laws into one of moral imperatives. And in so doing, Gandhi transforms the meaning of *ahimsa* into something more (and as we shall see, something less) than mere nonviolence: namely, nonindifference. Inequality thrives not because of difference among ordinary mortals, he insists, but precisely because of the lack of it—that is, because of a people's indifference toward that which is different. Indifference is the greatest violation of life because it is the most empirical. Letting people die on the boundaries of humanity, denying them the right to be neighbors, banning them from the world of gods and men, is so insidious a habit that it had impoverished Hinduism at its soul, bringing it to the verge of its own death. Thus, even in the mid-1930s, more than a decade after he had begun his program against untouchability, Gandhi would refuse to let go of the question of the right of "temple entry" for the *harijan*s, calling Ambedkar's flagging interest in the temple-entry question, ironically, a symptom of his "comparative indifference."[46]

In temples, Gandhi saw not merely a space for ritual and social mores but a political chance. For Hinduism's indifference to the empirical prohibitions it had imposed on the movements of its own people, around temples or public squares, was the cause not only of its spiritual destitution but also of India's general servitude. "We must reject such verses. I am a great admirer of Tulsidas. And I consider the *Ramayana* to be the greatest work. But I cannot," he put it unequivocally, "subscribe to the idea contained in the couplet: 'The drum, the village-fool, the Sudras, animals, women—all these are fit to be beaten.'"[47] The only antidote to this violent religiosity was rejection and firmness. Indeed, what was required was another force, that of compassion and voluntary poverty, which must be mobilized even at the possible cost of extracting the greatest sacrifice from the satyagrahi. Even and especially if that sacrifice, Gandhi conceded without a qualm, might demand another untouchability.

Against Possessive Individualism

The institution of force as the ground of satyagraha's moral responsibility was not specific to Gandhi's obligation toward the *harijan* alone, even though the *harijan* became the apotheosis of his egalitarian politics. Much before he had turned to the *harijan*, he had trained this force of nonindifference on the satyagrahi himself. After all, the "tentacles" of inequality lay not in one religion or nation, nor in one empire. They emerged from the depth of humanity's unjust passions, not only toward untouchables, unapproachables, and invisibles, but toward animals too.[48] Inequality thrived in infinite greed, in the belief that human life and its needs were limitless. The world became indifferent to inequality and suffering, and therefore unequal itself, the moment humanity's awareness of limit and measure moved out from the realm of morals to the domain of interest. It was this critique of interest that motivated Gandhi's rehabilitation of voluntary poverty (*aparigraha*) and suffering as the truly egalitarian measure of finitude. For only physical suffering touched the masters with the same intensity as it did the oppressed. Suffering, armed with the immediacy of one's own mortality, harbored a uniquely egalitarian sentiment. It nourished the knowledge of life's inevitable perishing, reminding the dominant and unequal alike of their shared humanity, of the "indestructible" equality that stemmed from their finitude alone.

This relationship between satyagraha and voluntary dispossession was given public form in London two decades after the publication of *Hind Swaraj*. "Possession," spoke Gandhi, "seems to me to be a crime. I can only possess certain things when I know that others, who also want to possess similar things, are able to do so. But we know—every one of us can speak from experience—that such a thing is an impossibility. Therefore, the only thing that can be possessed by all is non-possession, not to have anything whatsoever. In other words, a willing surrender."[49] Brilliant in its succinctness and demanding in its ethics, Gandhi's statement on voluntary poverty has something deeply persuasive about it. And yet it marks less a break with liberalism's moral sentiment, from its compassionate empathy even (which has been so crucial to that tradition since at least Adam Smith)[50] than it is a departure from its "possessive individualism," as C. B. Macpherson calls it.[51] While the possessive individual measures equality by what he possesses, gives, and receives, the satyagrahi must consider equality as something that might be accomplished neither in gift nor in possession. Equality for the satyagrahi is secured, instead, in the moral decision of not having—that is to say, in the knowledge that "not having" is the only empirical condition available to all and hence the only mode of being equal.

This understanding of equality explains Gandhi's lack of faith in restitution as a mode of securing justice. For restitution is based fundamentally on an abstraction, on the principle that something has been lost. This loss, in turn, can only be comprehended when someone has an interest in the thing or person or right that is considered as having been lost. In the absence of such desire to possess, restitute, or reclaim, the object of desire might merely be construed as having disappeared. At the same time, an empirical object that might reasonably or unreasonably be construed as having been lost may or may not have existed in the first place. "The only thing the interested party has to 'own' in order to experience loss," asserts Adi Ophir in his book on the ontology of morals, "is the interest itself."[52]

Satyagraha translated this idea of interest grounded in material possessiveness (fundamental to liberal conceptions of property and even liberty) into a problem for moral ontology. The only thing the satyagrahi needed to master was the force of ethical nonindifference. Rather than seeking juridical or legislative redress, he was required to turn dispossession into a question of equality in its ontological sense—that is, as equality between beings in their barest, minimalist, most austere states. The satyagrahi could possess such moral force, Gandhi argued, only from the point of being a cipher, a living being on the point of vanishing, a life that in its very nearness to nothingness became equal with the immeasurably unequal. In *Hind Swaraj*, he had called this force the force of "immeasurable pity."[53] In satyagraha's encounter with unequals, thus, nonviolence was to be practiced as compassion, as "nonindifference"—that is, as love founded on the satyagrahi's attentiveness to the unequal's vulnerable mortality.

Contrary to what sympathetic critics such as C. F. Andrews and Rabindranath Tagore argued, it was not a contradiction but fairly consistent with the nature of this ethics of attentiveness that Gandhi's formulations on equality acquired their greatest—and sometimes gratuitous—force often when satyagraha was faced with lives that were in his eyes most unequal, most violated, most vulnerable, most different. In such instances, force, as attentive and exacting as ever, took the form of a sacrificial radicalism, perhaps even a cruelty toward the self and others in their absolute equality. For only in such extremities of equality, directed as much toward the unequal as toward one's own self, might something as austere, as unilateral, and as remorseless as the practice of self-limiting and self-dissolution (*tapascharya*) be given moral form. The closing pages of Gandhi's *Autobiography* describe this strategy with unwavering clarity.

Identification with everything that lives is impossible without self-purification; without self-purification the observance of the law of Ahimsa must remain an empty dream . . . and purification being highly infectious, purification of oneself necessarily leads to the purification of one's surroundings. But the path of self-purification is hard and steep. . . . To conquer the subtle passions seems to me to be harder far than the physical conquest of the world by the force of arms. . . . I must reduce myself to zero. So long as a man does not of his own free will put himself last among his fellow creatures, there is no salvation for him. Ahimsa is the farthest limit of humility.[54]

Reducing oneself to a cipher was the purest experience, the founding ground of all moral judgment. It entailed slow, rigorous, and contagious dissolution of the self into the humility and inequality of everyday existence. "In English," Gandhi commented during his 1926 lectures on the *Gita*, "'i' is a vertical line with a dot [*shunya*, or zero] above it. Only when this 'I' is done away with can one attain self-realization."[55] Suffering grounded in an austere sense of selfhood and self-dissolution (*tapascharya*), a self rooted in discipline and penance, was especially meaningful, for it allowed the satyagrahi to comprehend his indivisible kinship with the *harijan*'s estrangement and distance. The satyagrahi's own alienation from his blood kin, Gandhi asserted, was most exemplary because it opened the satyagrahi to the corporeal landscape on which to experience for himself the suffering and mortality of the *harijan* at the moment of his own most rigorous isolation.

While I do hold that the institution of untouchability as it stands today has no sanction in Hinduism, Hinduism does recognize "untouchability" in limited sense. For instance, every time that my mother handled unclean things she became untouchable for the time being and had to cleanse herself by bathing. . . . I refuse to believe that anyone can be regarded untouchable by reason of his or her birth, and such untouchability as recognized by religion is by its very nature transitory—easily removable and referable to the deed not the doer. . . . Just as we revere our mother for the sanitary service that she renders us when we are infants, and the greater her service the greater our reverence for her, similarly, the Bhangis [untouchables responsible for removing excrement] are entitled to our highest reverence for the sanitary service they perform for society.[56]

We can discern a distinctive shift in this passage. At its extremity now, the critique of possessive individualism veers into an ironic ethics of untouchability. Note, for instance, the double occlusion: the untouchable scavenger produces his own ontological impurity. It is the intrinsic nature of his work, not the juridical history of the work's degradation by scriptural injunction, that renders him unequal. And thus, Gandhi's incomplete break from historicism surreptitiously rears its ugly head: the scavenger must remain a scavenger, for that is history, a lesson for India's colonial present. "Untouchability in limited sense" is what he prescribes for equality, social and national, then, which is also to prescribe equality as contingency, as reversibility, as simultaneously touchable and untouchable, and, above all, as *maryada*, as limit or constriction, as discipline. The mother is an indelible marker of this limit. Nowhere is Gandhi's thinking more gendered, nowhere does he succumb to a more masculine humanism than when his thought comes to be furtively organized around the subtleties, silences, and excesses of *maryada*. By repeatedly rehearsing his mother's transitory and necessary untouchability, meanwhile, he seeks to create a ground of filial nonindifference toward the unequal. By rendering the mother contingently untouchable, he foregrounds the sacrificial imperative of one's difference and distance from even that which is one's own. One becomes, in those moments, a subject rightfully deserving of untouchability, separated from one's own by an abyss not of violence but indeed of nonindifference. One might even argue that the ethics of *ahimsa* mutates into that of an exclusionary and ontological difference, the morals of limit turn into their own paradoxical excess.

Equality, at any rate, does not subsume the difference and distance between the mother and the satyagrahi, between the satyagrahi and the *harijan*. Equality, on the contrary, constitutes and coalesces around the moral law—and sense—of limit. It comes to be founded on being voluntarily untouchable by turns. By making this move, Gandhi renders untouchability as simultaneously intimate and estranging, disdainful yet necessary, voluntary but enforceable, contingent on practice yet inseparable from one's birth (and thus, history). Within the moral calculus of satyagrahic austerity, everyone was at some point or other meant to be unequal and untouchable, not only to another but also to oneself and one's kin. Within the *ashram*, one was often unequal with oneself; one voluntarily accepted one's own untouchability and impurity, even dissolution, during certain hours of the day. Only then, according to Gandhi, might the satyagrahi experience, in all his finitude and fallibility, the suffering of the *harijan*. In his most proper form, the satyagrahi embodied the figure that possessed this ethical knowledge in all his humility. He was one who embraced *maryada*—the limit and force—of contamination with equal rigor. He was one who turned voluntarily into a cipher when equality so demanded. At other times and other places, Gandhi would declare the *atishudra* to be the sovereign exemplar of this ethical annulment, a figure whom every satyagrahi must emulate and, simultaneously, make the recipient of his compassion and generosity. It was this ethics of gift that he called *shudradharma*.

Maryada—Of Touching

There was a radical paradox involved in Gandhi's rendering of the satyagrahi equal with the *harijan* through rigorous rules of spiritual and corporeal discipline. Gandhi's own name for this paradox was *maryada*, a term used sparingly but one that underpinned his thinking of measure in powerful and surreptitious ways. I have adopted "touchability" as the most intimate rendering of *maryada*, or a rendering that stays closest to Gandhi's formulations on it in the 1920s and the 1930s. Touchability, which might in turn be translated more literally as *sparshyata*, ran along two moral ontological axes. Along the first, we have seen, was Gandhi's instantiation of touching as the sovereign faculty of nonindifference. This was connected to his radicalization of finitude, his privileging of mortality and dissolution, a voluntary zeroness (*shunyata*) as the moment of absolute equality between the satyagrahi and the *harijan*. Along the second axis, to which I now turn, ran the counterforce of restraint and distance—that is, the force that instituted, through the reversal of the first, the ethics and politics of not touching indiscriminately. Within satyagraha, touching the *harijan* required economy and discipline; it demanded a discriminating conviction, patience, and detail.

"It will not be enough," Gandhi warned the satyagrahis, "if you in a flush of enthusiasm go to a Harijan and touch him and embrace him, and then forget all about him. It will not do even if you go to the Harijan quarters every day and make it a point to touch a number of Harijans as a token of your conviction." Rather, Gandhi insisted, "you should regulate your day-to-day conduct in such a manner that you make it absolutely evident to the Harijans whom you come across that a better day has dawned for them all."[57] Touchability, as practice and as the law of satyagrahic reform, involved, then, a resistance against abruptness. It demanded from the satyagrahi a descent from the generalities of polemical and reformist universality into the minute particulars of empirical and finite corporeality. Strongly underpinned by civility and measure, touching, despite all its temptations, was not to be rendered into a relationship of corporeal excessiveness among false equals. On the contrary, it was to remain delimited by moral firmness, by a voluntary curtailment of exorbitance and enthusiasm. But the practice of touchability involved not simply a delimiting of force and hierarchy. It involved *dharma*, the obligation to activate, with greatest care, the irreducible force of the limit as such, hence the neologism *maryada dharma*.

In fact, touchability, in light of Gandhi's counterintuitive insistence, might sometimes have mandated not touching at all. And more often than not, it enforced a limit on caste reform itself. As Gandhi puts it, "The *rishis* of old carried on exhaustive researches through meditation, and as a result of the researches they discovered some great truths, such as have no parallel perhaps in any other religion. . . . Knowing as they did how compelling sometimes the force of social customs of the people among whom men lived was, they promulgated *maryada dharma* to help one in such emergencies." In other words, *maryada* came into effect precisely in an emergency, as an exception. "Though, however, I believe in *maryada dharma*," he continues, "I do not regard it as an essential part of Hinduism. I can even conceive a time when these restrictions might be abolished with impunity. But the reform contemplated in the untouchability movement does not obliterate the restriction as to inter-dining and inter-marriage. I cannot recommend wholesale abolition of these restrictions to the public, even at the risk of being charged with hypocrisy and inconsistency."[58]

I will return to Gandhi's support for the ban on interdining later, a ban in which he would come to see, without irony or sarcasm, a juridical more and exclusion necessary to the "spirit of democracy" itself. Meanwhile, in the thinking of *maryada*, reformist force comes to be mediated as much by an awareness of the unequal's finitude and suffering as by a moral pragmatism that speaks, indeed remains—not in the least because of Gandhi's vigilant sense of fidelity to *dharma*—vulnerable to the oppressors and the theologico-political injunctions of the moral law. The satyagrahi, Gandhi is clear, must be open to relinquishing reform if the force of custom so demanded. After all, *maryada* is, more often than not, guarded by the force of "public opinion" and sometimes by the force of the majority's customary beliefs. It is no coincidence either that so many of Ambedkar's essays in the 1940s and 1950s (most tellingly in *Riddles of Hinduism*), as we have seen in Chapter 2, sought to cut through the coherence and rigor attributed to custom where none existed. The satyagrahi, however, must respect the truth of the custom, its dangerous alliance with tyrannical forms of sovereignty notwithstanding. Gandhi's ethics of touchability is not, then, merely the renunciation of equality, not merely the limiting of touching. Instead, *maryada* demands the exceptional decision to renounce the temporal urgency of justice itself. It might even demand the subordination of justice to the will of the oppressor or to the demands of moral law. The greatest force, Gandhi had argued, must be seen in the unconditional renunciation of force and, if need be, of life. In his elaborations on *maryada dharma*, he finally demands this sacrifice from the untouchable, from the unequals themselves. "One word to the impatient and needy *harijans*," he pleads revealingly.[59]

I began this chapter by suggesting that the moral and juridical framework of *maryada dharma* was not simply a form of religious scaffolding for Gandhi's approach to the social question. Rather, it was a coalescence of an ontological limit within the structure of anticolonial visions of sovereignty (and this vision included the space for internal exclusions of groups construed as subhuman and, by implication, noncitizens). *Maryada dharma*, apart from its moral and juridical axes, was also distinctively political in that its economy, its sense of measure and discipline, touched not merely the untouchable but the unequal and the excluded as such. And there was that classically political issue of immunity lodged here too: the conceptual and rhetorical movements of the Gandhian limit opened an abyss in his egalitarianism right where he had sought to touch and protect the weakest. Asked in 1928, for instance, whether he would take the life of his own daughter had her modesty been outraged, Gandhi dug into the *Ramayana* to underline the moral priority of *maryada* over life. "I would take her life only if I was absolutely certain that she would wish it. I know Sita would have preferred death to dishonor by Ravana. And that is also what I believe our Shastras have enjoined. . . . I am not prepared to admit that the loss of chastity stands on the same footing as the loss of the limb. But I can imagine circumstances in which one would infinitely prefer death even to being maimed."[60]

For a brief moment, it seems as if the unequal has agency, even transformative force, but then the injunction of *maryada* takes over. Satyagraha invites the ethical subject to stare militantly at death without parsing out others' responsibility for her violated life. The responsibility is always her own, and this responsibility always demands something more than mere life. For Gandhi, life is worthy only when it is open to its own groundlessness and perishability.

Within the dictates of *maryada*, therefore, the contingency of an equalizing death is deemed infinitely more preferable than dishonor. In Gandhi's plea against indiscriminate exogamy and collective eating, similarly, satyagraha was compelled not only by the ethics of touching the untouchable, nor only by the imperative of keeping the unequal safe. It also mobilized a counterforce, a resistance against touching recklessly and reforming indiscriminately. Gandhi's phenomenology of measure, thus, cannot be seen merely as the radical negation of untouchability in any simple sense. Touchability shared with its antithesis—that is, with untouchability—a resolute mindfulness of difference and, for Gandhi, the moral imperative of keeping distance from the unequal. One could refuse to eat with the *harijan* and still be within the bounds of *maryada*. Gandhi's problem with untouchability is not that the *harijan* scavenger's child is still a scavenger, for there is, according to him, no problem with the inheritance and transmission of knowledges in spaces where they had traditionally existed. Satyagraha, on the contrary, is unthinkable without fidelity to inheritance itself, no matter how violent, unjust, and unequal its history. "The fault," he wrote in a telling essay, "does not therefore lie in recognizing the law of hereditary transmission of qualities from generation to generation, but it lies with the faulty conception of inequality."[61]

In the section that follows, I return to this expression, "faulty conception of inequality." Suffice it now to note the reversal at work in this phrase. It is not equality that must be blindly embraced. Rather, Gandhi demands, it is inequality that must be restituted, restored, given an ethical salience that untouchability has violently robbed from it. Gandhi was the most rigorous theorist of inequality, one might argue then, not of equality; he loved, tended, corrected, and rescued inequality from its faultiness and raised it to the level of a concept. In 1929, two years before he consecrated the *harijan*, he had made a preliminary correction in this chain of innovations. He renamed the discipline and knowledge of carding—the work of combing fiber to prepare it for spinning—*dhanurvidya*. This was hardly an innocuous move. Indeed, its suppleness hides a radical thinking of equality. For *dhanurvidya* is the Sanskrit term for the art of archery and is reserved within the classical rules of *varnashramadharma* for Kshatriya warriors. Gandhi applies it—he opens its access, even if only in name yet—to the lowest orders, to weavers and manual laborers: "The word pinjan [bow-shaped tool] has become disagreeable in our language," he begins. "Even in figurative language, it is a term implying censure. When a person keeps on pointlessly repeating the same thing, we say of him that he is doing pinjan. This usage of the word has become so established that we do not like the word 'pinjanshastra' or 'pinjanvidya.'" The way out of this impasse is not to disavow the craft practiced by the lower castes, Gandhi insists; the way out is to rename it. This was a singular move, for it was not simply the history of impurity and contamination that had marred the beauty of a craft that was being repaired but its very spirit, and through it, the oppressor's disdain for the unequal's discipline. Most subtly, Gandhi institutes here an ethics of mastery itself, one in which the sovereign warrior learns from the unequal's disciplinary rigor. Newness for the oppressor, at least, if not for the oppressed as yet:

Hence I have made bold to use a word which has become endeared in the terminology of the Kshatriyas, i.e., "dhanurvidya" instead of the word "pinjanshastra." I have given a new definition of the word Kshatriya. The latter is not a person who knows how to kill others but rather one who acquires the art of sacrificing his own life so that others may live. A Kshatriya is one who has well mastered the mantra of never retreating in the battle between gods and demons that is raging in this world. A Kshatriya is one who is the very embodiment of compassion. What knowledge of archery should such a Kshatriya possess? While reflecting on this problem, just as a carpenter invariably thinks of a babul tree, is it any wonder if my mind turns towards carding? This vidya presupposes both physical and spiritual strength. Let anyone who wishes, have a look at a carder's chest. Every carder's chest is something that would make another envious. It is round, expanded, and beautiful. The muscles of his arms too are likewise well developed.[62]

Nowhere is Gandhi's thinking of sacrifice, his understanding of virtue, his awareness of the need to turn the moral ontology of action into an ethics of work, as acute as it is in this passage. Symptomatically, the hand has returned as the exemplary instrument of spiritual action. The hand is not merely an organ among others. It is neither simply an instrument of the warrior Kshatriya's armament and knowledge, his *dhanurvidya*, nor is it simply a limb that makes visible, in its fullness and fecundity, the Shudra's rigorous discipline, his *pinjanvidya*. Instead, the hand defines the exemplary wholeness of the inalienable equality between the Kshatriya and Shudra practitioners. And this wholeness lends a certain beauty to their shared ability to sacrifice for causes greater than their crafts. Rather than letting a decadent and ancient Hindu *dharma* stipulate the everyday rules of *varnashrama*, it was the quotidian rigor of each person's willingness to live according to his *varna*, each living differently yet near to the other, that now opened the ground for *ahimsa*. The universality of *dharma* was to be derived, thus, from the authentic difference of Shudra life rather than from the regime of scriptural rules. This is Gandhi at his most radical, attentive not only to the corporeal elements of the Shudra's disciplined craft but also to its spirit, to those sounds and words that had corrupted in the name of a violent religion (which was, for him, no religion) the rigor and beauty of the unequal's handicraft. It is not fortuitous either that each of the terms that Gandhi had brought into his practice—*dhanurvidya*, *maryada*, *harijan*, *shudradharma*—mobilizes the dexterities of the hand. They are, in fact, inconceivable without Gandhi's tireless imaginings of the hand's masterly movements. And they all marshal, in a strange adjacency with the Indic laws of oppression, the morals only of Kshatriya force and mastery.

There was exclusion at work in this rehabilitation of a manual ethics for satyagraha, even if by introducing and maintaining the lines of difference between practitioners, Gandhi radicalizes all extant understandings of work and justice. For him, justice begins not with restitution, but with reversal. As he argues, the Shudra weaver, spinner, and carder could not be viewed as unequal to the Kshatriya archer simply because they practice disciplines with different names or because the skill demanded in the Kshatriya battlefield is any greater than that required by weaving. On the contrary, the moral and muscular force that characterizes each craft, the ethical compassion of the warrior and the rhythmic strength of the carder, are not only equal but also reversible. One's capacity to sacrifice necessarily brings to mind the humility and roundness of the other. In their shared mastery over specific knowledges, the warrior and weaver are tied in spirit and reversible in the bodies they inhabit. This reversibility opens the ground of touchability between them. Reversibility without sameness, equality without substitution: neither becomes the other forever. Instead, one merely lends another his name at the moment of a contingent equality. It was this reversibility that cleared the ground for what Gandhi called a more truthful, more just, "conception of inequality."

Being Shudra

Which "faulty conception of inequality" was Gandhi revolting against? What new thinking of equality, new relationship to history, new institutions and meanings of craft, above all, might restore inequality to its proper place? What, in other words, did a just conception of inequality look like? For Gandhi, inequality stemmed from the orthodox Hindu's lack of fidelity to the existing knowledges, from his abrogation of moral courage to touch these knowledges in their corporeal authenticity. Inequality lay in the caste Hindu's moral failure to learn from existing disciplines and produce new and more compassionate ones. By introducing new words and sounds into the political discourse of colonial India, Gandhi pushed these disciplines into new conceptual spaces. Rendering them into reversible words and contingent meanings, he realigned the relationship between the purportedly pure and impure disciplines and the sequestered social spaces that their practitioners had historically inhabited. In many ways, as Gandhi unequivocally put it, the Shudra was not the contaminant but instead the master of fidelity to discipline, and therefore an exemplary lesson for the satyagrahi himself. Thus it was that satyagraha responded to Hinduism's denial of streets, wells, and neighborhoods to the *harijan* by transforming the *ashram*, every day, if only for fixed hours, into a spiritual neighborhood, a place where untouchables were to be welcomed and embraced. Far from accepting it as the antithesis of justice, Gandhi had rendered untouchability into its moral foundation.

There was an element of changeability and contingency allowed within the order of *ashram* equality that called for, both on part of the satyagrahi and the *harijan*, measure, restraint, and humility. The *harijan* could be rendered touchable without being forced—and allowed—to purge his vocation and discipline. He and the satyagrahi came to equality in the measured regularity and unconditional humility of everyday life, each being touchable and untouchable by turns. The act of regularly practicing the impure vocations transformed their social meanings and turned the disciplines necessary to their mastery (until now considered degrading) into emblems of knowledge. It made the impurity attached to their practices extrinsic (rather than immanent) to the disciplines and thus rendered, Gandhi believed, the disciplines and their practitioners touchable again. Touchability transformed not merely the *harijan* but the satyagrahi too. For it pushed their knowledges and crafts into new spaces and made those spaces equal. It was from this productive equality, from this equality produced by pushing old crafts into new spaces (and new into old), that the universality of Gandhi's politics was extracted, one that he called *shudradharma*.[63]

What was *shudradharma*? Was it merely a satyagrahic pledge to become a Shudra? Or was it attributing to Shudra life an exemplary fullness? Often Gandhi asked the satyagrahi to reduce himself into the lowest of the low. "If I should be born again," he declares in 1921, "I should do so not as a Brahmin, Kshatriya, Vaishya, or Sudra, but as an *Atishudra*." A few sentences later, he takes this sacrificial desire to dissolve himself a step further. "I love scavenging," he reveals.[64] There is a glorious easiness, luminescence even, that Gandhi attached to the life of the *atishudra*. Stripping it of the irreducible violence that constitutes such existence in the first place, he found in such life an exemplary universality. Through such practices as sweeping and scavenging, he sought to radicalize the very idea of sacrifice, one whose immense knowledge lay in the hands of the *harijan* alone. The *atishudra-as-harijan* was not simply rendered touchable then. With his craft now framed in the language of archery, or *dhanurvidya*, he became a moral exemplar proper to satyagraha. He was, of course, an exceptionally tragic exemplar among satyagraha's exemplars, born from the death of Indic mastery, not from its resplendent sovereignty. I will come to that tragic sense of politics—and the *harijan* as a subject of political tragedy, even defeat—in a moment. There could be no satyagraha meanwhile, and clearly no *swaraj*, Gandhi often declared, without the *harijan*.

Once belonging to the tribe of boatmen who had ferried the god-king Rama across the holy rivers of antiquity, the outcaste had been known to be the trusted host of the Kshatriya warrior. And yet this exemplarity of the unequal, which Gandhi so scrupulously institutes at the center of his politics, does not as much produce an egalitarian universalism (or even autonomy) as much as it sustains an ontological distinction at the heart of satyagraha. Reminding the upper caste Hindu of the exemplary conduct of the Pandava king Yudhishthira, whose usurpation from the throne lay at the fratricidal center of the epic *Mahabharata*, Gandhi warned his followers in 1921: "So long as the mass of Hindus consider it a sin to touch a section of their brethren, swaraj is impossible of attainment. Yudhishthira would not enter heaven without his dog. How can, then, the descendants of Yudhishthira expect to obtain swaraj without the 'untouchables'?"[65]

We have already encountered the fecund place occupied by the animal in Gandhi's writings on spirit and *Ramarajya*. The animal now emerges as a dogmatic provocation. Desertion of the unequal, human or animal, amounts to disavowing the moral law, *maryada dharma*, on which satyagraha's egalitarian edifice was founded. For Gandhi, Yudhishthira's refusal to abandon the dog exemplifies the sovereign's refusal to let go of the unequal. The satyagrahi must touch, protect, respect, and refuse to part with the *harijan*, he argues, in the same spirit that Yudhishthira had refused to part with his dog on the gates of heaven; hence, the equivalence between the animal and *harijan*. Each remains the satyagrahi's exemplary hostage and witness. Neither being himself a master, each becomes a handless, prehensile witness to the ethics of Kshatriya mastery. Satyagraha could not be constituted without the presence of this interlocutor, the coexperimenter, the witness, the reader, the animal— in sum, the unequal. At the same time, it required a scientist of sacrifice, an exemplar of mastery, a tirelessly experimental craftsman, a figure of force. Figures of force would include not only the figure that might wield force, then, but also the witness, the figure subject to force, one whose very existence ensured someone else's (the satyagrahi's, the Kshatriya's, or the sovereign's) craft, one whose passivity secured someone else's action. Satyagraha would not thrive outside this logic of passivity and witnessing, and at its worst, servitude and defeat. By the time of his epic fast in 1932, in fact, Gandhi had come to conceptualize not merely Indic slavery but India's conquest by Britain itself through the figure of the Shudra. "Shudras are those who serve and are dependent upon others. India is a dependency; therefore every Indian is a *Shudra*."[66] Here, the Shudra, whose name institutes an artisanal and ascetic universality, is rendered, in the same stroke, into a symptom of India's colonization; a figure of oneness is reduced into a being emblematic of a whole civilization's defeat, one whose life and death—its ontological essence—reveals India's servile condition at large.

Could the *harijan* ever be a warrior himself? Could he bear arms within the bounds of *maryada*? Could *shudradharma* facilitate the democratization of sacrifice, and therefore, potentially, help overthrow the yoke of foreign rule? Might it clear the ground of what Ambedkar had called, in a militant vein in *Annihilation of Caste*, a "general mobilization"? Gandhi, as he tellingly did seven years later, would often speak of the Shudras mournfully, as if in their collective body (or just spirit) a residue of prehistory had been left behind. "That leaves us the *Shudras*. They possess no learning. They consider themselves slaves. They do not serve with knowledge. That is to say, there are not really even *Shudras* left in India."

We have by the name of the Shudra, as it circulates in Gandhi's discourse between 1932 and 1939, then, a subject at the limit, a cipher for Gandhi's moral ontology of the limit as such, a mystical figure that is at once always present like an emblem of a tragic defeat, and yet a subject that has also, in its absolute lack of knowledge, gone missing, leaving behind an emptiness in the manner of a ghost that can only be mourned. Gandhi's Shudra is simultaneously being and nonbeing, ontologically partitioned from the human at the very moment of its apotheosis. Like the animal—or God— it is being *otherwise*, a being wracked by the undecidability lodged at the very heart of satyagraha, at once exemplary for the nonviolent satyagrahi and spiritually destitute. It is the first subject of satyagrahic obligation and force. Perhaps this is why Gandhi refuses to renounce *varnadharma*, finding in it the ethical reserve of satyagrahic action. But more crucially, he refuses to renounce its laws because *varnadharma* makes possible a framework of obligation in which the Shudra as moral being can be approached, touched, and redeemed for a just conception of inequality, one in which self-sacrifice, even dying for the unequal, might find a moral reasoning for its unilateralism. "Since we believe in *varnadharma*, let us accept the *dharma* of service. Let us adopt *Shudradharma*."[67]

Three months later, Gandhi returned to this argument with even greater force, with a sense of immediacy. "The varna system has just now broken down. . . . There is no true Brahmin or true Kshatriya or Vaishya. We are all Shudras, i.e., one varna."[68] At its best, this affirmation of oneness amplifies the paradox of trying to find exemplary sacrifice precisely in those who are most sacrificeable, of seeking nonviolence in the lives of the most violated, of finding equality in the most unequal. The Shudra reminds Gandhi, in this very antinomy, of India's conquest and weakness. "All of us cannot become Kshatriyas," he warns. "Some will remain weak."[69] In such moments, *shudradharma*, Gandhi's substitute for "equality," instead becomes the perverse ground for mourning the death of classic *varnadharma*, or worse, a trope for India's more recent colonization. "Brahmins are a rarity these days," Gandhi responded to a questioner in 1939. "As for the Kshatriyas there are none left in India. If there had been any, the country would not have lost its freedom. India would not remain in her present condition if great learning and great valor could be found here."[70]

This is yet another gesture of sequestering the privilege of war and confining its sacrificial art, its capacity to resist colonization, to one *varna*. Here, for instance, Gandhi attributes India's loss of sovereignty not to the disarming of the majority of its people by the natural law of *varnadharma*; instead, he blames the conquest of India on the extinction of that one valorous *varna* whose business by birth it was to go to war. Just as the Shudra is the exemplary figure of mourning and conquest, the Kshatriya embodies India's will to resistance. Despite the ambiguous equality between the Brahmin, Kshatriya, Vaishya, and Shudra that Gandhi had sought in *shudradharma*, then, he consistently refuses the idea of equality in which one's abilities, rights, and even ethics, might be substitutable by another. On the contrary, he had grounded *shudradharma* in the logic of an insurmountable, even necessary, difference. "Inter-drinking, inter-dining, intermarrying," he had insisted in 1921, "are not essential for the promotion of the spirit of democracy. I do not contemplate under a most democratic constitution a universality of manners and customs about eating, drinking and marrying. We shall ever have to seek unity in diversity, and I decline to consider it a sin for a man not to drink or eat with any and everybody."[71]

It is in this affinity for difference, this respect for measure and limit, even exclusion, that Gandhi's break with the excesses of majoritarian democracy reveals itself in its greatest ambiguity. In representative democracy, whose logic is far from being free of routine violence, each person is countable and each counts equally. But Gandhi, trying tirelessly to keep satyagraha separate from this democratic principle, stated in 1928, "public opinion cannot be measured by counting of heads or raising of hands. I would not regard this as a measure of public opinion."[72] For him, the modern enumerative principle, the law of democratic counting, violated the morals of empirical difference in the same manner as forcing people to eat together by law did. Both abstracted the person, reducing his materiality and finitude into a mere number. If the modern conception of equality was impossible without this calculus, Gandhi was not for it. But he was not for it in different ways for different subjects. Thus, satyagraha was less inegalitarian, I think, than it was exclusionary in an egalitarian way. When a Brahmin reformer suggested in 1915 that everyone ought to be called Brahmin because there is only one *varna* left, Gandhi resisted. Recalling this incident nearly two decades letter, he wrote: "I could not reconcile myself to that proposition then and I could do so less now. Whilst we can all serve and hence be called Shudras, we do not all possess learning nor do we possess divine knowledge. Therefore it would be untruthful to regard ourselves as Brahmins."[73] It was not contamination that troubled Gandhi; rather, it was an unconditional equality, equality without limit, a reversibility of identities without measure that did.

Within this radical conservatism of the limit, one might become a Shudra or *atishudra*, but the Brahmin's virtues remain exceptional and unattainable. The *harijan* and satyagrahi might thrive in the contingency of mutual sacrifice and contamination, but the Brahmin remains untouchable. Not simply the source of transcendental truth, he is the theologico-political master of injunctions, rendered sovereign at the moment of what otherwise would appear to be the untouchable's apotheosis. In ontological terms, the Brahmin does not simply guard satyagrahic limit, he exemplifies the limits of the limit itself. If Gandhi's touchability entails a conscious sharing of space and mortality between unequals who are tied by nothing else but their inevitable death, then the Brahmin is the limit figure, the abyss of untouchability. Neither the satyagrahi nor *harijan* could emulate, resemble, name, or touch the Brahmin across that abyss.

The foundation of *shudradharma*, then, is not the Shudra but rather the Brahmin; its founding obligation is neither contact nor touch but a sensitive recovery of untouchability appropriate to modern India's egalitarian politics. But neither is *shudradharma* antidemocratic in any straightforward, tyrannical sense. Instead, curiously in line with the most classical framework of democracy, it harbors a tendency to resort opportunistically to the language of counting and enumeration, a tactical readiness to mobilize the will of the greatest number. "The case against untouchability," Gandhi wrote in 1939, "has to be supported by purity of character, industry, and strictest honesty of reformers, and a limitless capacity for sacrifice." Preparing the satyagrahi for the resistance that such reform would inevitably encounter, especially from the knowledgeable Brahmins, he warns that "the wrath of the opponents" may take "a heavy toll of the lives of reformers." Even so, "no sacrifice, however great, will deter the reformers from pursuing the God-given mission of ridding Hinduism of the curse of untouchability. For I must repeat for the thousandth time that Hinduism dies, as it will deserve to die, if untouchability lives."[74] The emphasis on patience and sacrifice, patience as sacrifice, comes a decade after Gandhi had most explicitly relinquished, in the name of *Ramarajya*, the enumerative principle of parliamentary democracy.[75] But the desire to conserve *brahmanadharma*, the need to vouchsafe the purity of religious reason, more often than not forces Gandhi to adopt the tone and language of measure. In such moments he inevitably lapses back into the grammar of numbers. "Only let the reformers know that impatience will be fatal to success," he continues. "They must not open a single temple where a clear majority of temple-goers to a particular temple are demonstrably opposed to its opening. Untouchability will not be removed by the force even of law. It can only be removed when the majority of Hindus realize that is a crime against God and man and are ashamed of it. In other words, it is a process of conversion, i.e., purification, of the Hindu heart."[76]

The lapse into numerical rhetoric couched in the language of spiritual conversion and penance, the hopeful and patient wait for that time in the future when a majority of Hindus might realize that untouchability had been a crime, would seem to be a deferral at best, inequitable and retrograde at worst. In this sense, Uday S. Mehta's argument that Gandhi's emphasis on patience as virtue epitomized his unflagging concern with time—one that was distinctively at odds with the hurried world of political activity where patience is seen to have no rational content and value[77]—takes on a radical dimension. But this dimension, which shines through in Gandhi's writings and speeches of the 1930s with undeniable constancy, acquires moral and political import not because Gandhi had broken away from the temporal imperatives, hurries, and exigencies of modern politics as such, but precisely because satyagrahic patience had now begun to take the form of a profoundly instrumental slowness, a moral and political procrastination, a tactical wait for the majority to make up its mind. Either way, Gandhi's purported break from the calculus of classical liberal democracy here shows itself to be susceptible to a certain turn in his thought toward its own worst (if calculation and instrumentality were for Gandhi the worst of modern politics). Indeed, he falls back on that very calculus when it comes to temple entry for the lower castes.

Maryada dharma, in such moments, was sequestered from the proclaimed obligation that satyagraha owed the unequal and hitched onto a conservative public morality. Its disciplinary limit coalesced not around nonviolence but around measure. But were nonviolence and measure, satyagraha and limit, ever separate? Why could the sages and wise men of past eras, whom Gandhi frequently invoked, not mandate equal and uninhibited access to sacred spaces? Why not mobilize their millennial wisdom now rather than wait until the soul of the majority had been converted? Why this sudden return to the normative language of "clear majority" and "patient conversion"? Was this an instance of satyagraha's routine compromise of democracy, the contamination of its ethics by the moral law? Or was this lapse into measure precisely a resort to the norms of classical democracy on Gandhi's part, an indecision toward its law of numbers, at the very moment when an unconditional responsibility would demand that exception against the majority will be made and the force of satyagrahic sacrifice be mobilized against the majority itself? Why had Gandhi recoiled into the worst of democracy as such, one in which power and might are confused with right?

One can discern here the conservatism of *maryada* at the point of its greatest resilience. And it was Ambedkar who, in the manner proper to a rigorous thinker of satyagraha, in the manner of an insurgent, even insubordinate practitioner who despite all political acrimony called his movements by that name, offered the most radical critique of this conservatism. "I can understand that in organizing resistance to injustice," he wrote in a probing appreciation of Gandhi, "the problem is to find forms of resistance that will not destroy the meagre resources for rational and moral action." But is not satyagraha or passive resistance precisely such a weapon? "He asked the people of India to offer Satyagraha against British Imperialism." And one may add to this Gandhi's notorious 1938 advice to the German Jews to offer satyagraha against the Nazis, or his willingness to see in Adolf Hitler the figure of *sadhana*, a spiritual exemplar who, like a virtuous satyagrahi, had come to master his means (*sadhan*) unconstrained by any moral anxiety

over the consequences of his war (on which more below).[78] So then, Ambedkar probes, "why does [Gandhi] not want to use the same means against
the caste Hindus in the interest of Untouchables?"[79] The problem is not as
much with the satyagrahic ethics of action and force, which, despite their
being grounded in sacrificial practices of a very specific religious provenance,
might still, Ambedkar obliquely concedes (and desires), be universally appli-
cable. The problem lies, he insists, in the satyagrahic economy of judgment
and constraint, its moral theology of disciplinary limit and measure, which
mars its (and religion's) emancipatory promise and gives it a form identical
to those very institutions of domination it promises to resist. Perhaps it is its
obsessive and solipsistic pursuit of measure, its intensification of limit, that
renders satyagraha incapable of separating itself from the laws of mastery.
"To a slave," writes Ambedkar in his "Reply to the Mahatma," composed in
response to Gandhi's critique of *Annihilation of Caste*, "his master may be
better of worse. But there cannot be a good master. A good man cannot be a
master and a master cannot be a good man."[80]

I will take up Ambedkar's conception of goodness and virtue, which
was inseparable from his attempt to conceptualize another mastery, one that
would be grounded in the right to universalize force—to open it to "general
mobilization"—in Chapter 5. But the early radicalism of *Hind Swaraj* seems
stark and instructive in light of these criticisms and turns in Gandhi's own
thought, which explains why it was Ambedkar, more than Nehru and other
acolytes, who continued to return to the work. "It is a superstition and ungodly thing to believe," Gandhi had written in that 1909 manifesto, "that an
act of a majority binds a minority. Many examples can be given in which acts
of majorities will be found to have been wrong and those of minorities to have
been right. All reforms owe their origin to the initiation of minorities in opposition to majorities. . . . So long as the superstition that men should obey unjust laws exists, so long will their slavery exist. And a passive resister alone can
remove such a superstition."[81] The militancy of this urge to resist tyranny, to
counter the force of the majority, to refuse to obey unjust laws, to pay heed to
nothing but truth, is striking. Thirty years later, faced with an insurgent critic,
this early radicalism had recoiled and mutated into the language of counting
and conversion. The birth of the *harijan* in 1931, inasmuch as it had revealed
satyagraha's unambiguous commitment to justice, had also exposed an undecidability, or what Gandhi might call his guesswork, with respect to the distinction between life and law, truth and norm. And this undecidability was
not an exception but the foundation of satyagrahic rigor.

The Rigorous Undecidability of *Sadhana*

Before I turn to the rigor of Gandhi's commitment to justice, I want to focus on that one word against which Gandhi mounts in *Hind Swaraj* the firmness of passive resistance most strongly: superstition. In the passage taken above from his dialogue with the militant nationalist, for instance, Gandhi mentions superstition twice, calling it "ungodly." Superstition, he insists, cannot be a function of people's faith or religion; it is, contrary to what rationalists usually believe, not even related to people's enchantment with the divine or their belief in mythic, natural, and supernatural forces (which Gandhi distinguishes from God's law). Superstition, unlike faith, on the contrary, is a function of "unjust laws" and blind beliefs and commitments (*andhvishwas*), and therefore belongs to the order of "feud" and "slavery."

Blindness, as we have seen, is a running thread in satyagrahic phenomenology. The extremist Dhingra (with his violent and futile way of giving away his life), Gandhi had announced in *Hind Swaraj*, was blind. So are those who see untouchability all around them and yet refuse to see it. And then, there are the blind among his own followers, who undertake a fast without understanding its logic, reason, and principles (*shastra*). There is a remarkable integrity to the firmness that Gandhi displays against the blind majoritarian belief that it is always right because it has might. In fact, he returns to this theme repeatedly. But never does he return to it more creatively than in his critique of untouchability in the 1930s. Here is Gandhi writing in his newspaper *Harijan* about the Bihar earthquake of 1934, placing untouchability at the center of his moral ontology of being (and belief).

Nature has been impartial in her destruction. Shall we retain our partiality—caste against caste, Hindu, Muslim, Christian, Parsi, Jew, against one another—in reconstruction, or shall we learn from her the lesson that there is no such thing as untouchability as we practice it today? . . . I share the belief with the whole world—civilized and uncivilized—that calamities such as the Bihar one come to mankind as chastisement for their sins. When that conviction comes from the heart, people pray, repent and purify themselves. I regard untouchability as such a grave sin as to warrant divine chastisement. I am not affected by posers such as "why punishment for an age-old sin" or "why punishment to Bihar and not to the South" or "why an earthquake and not some other form of punishment." My answer is: I am not God. Therefore I have but a limited knowledge of His purpose. Such calamities are not a mere caprice of the Deity or Nature. They obey fixed laws as surely as the planets move in obedience to laws governing their movement. Only we do not know the laws governing these events and, therefore, call them calamities or disturbances. Whatever, therefore, may be said about them must be regarded as guess work. But guessing has its definite place in man's life. It is an ennobling thing for me to guess that the Bihar disturbance is due to the sin of untouchability. It makes me humble, it spurs me to greater effort towards its removal, it brings me nearer to my Maker. That my guess may be wrong does not affect the results named by me. For what is guess to the critic or the skeptic is a living belief with me, and I base my future actions on that belief. Such guesses become superstitions when they lead to no purification and may even lead to feuds. But such misuse of divine events cannot deter men of faith from interpreting them as a call to them for repentance for their sins. I do not interpret this chastisement as an exclusive punishment for the sin of untouchability. It is open to others to read in it divine wrath against many other sins. Let anti-untouchability reformers regard the earthquake as a nemesis for the sin of untouchability. They cannot go wrong, if they have the faith that I have.[82]

It is difficult to overestimate the originality of this passage. What finds the clearest expression here is Gandhi's belief that, at its most perfect and "ennobling," convictions of the heart (immanence) are rarely at odds with divine will (transcendence). If that were the case, as Ambedkar asks in many different ways (but especially in his scattered remarks on Kant's "categorical imperative"), what would prevent the mortal subject—"priestly" or "secular," faithful or faithless—from becoming a mere "arm" of—or one with—the law?[83] What would separate life from the moral formalism, the invisible prison, of the norm? How would one judge between good laws and bad?

Let me, within this framework, mark out two shifts that occur in Gandhi's essay—initially delivered as a speech—on the Bihar earthquake and that are relevant to our larger discussion about the relationship between justice and norm, life and law. First, the suggestion that Gandhi had made (more than once) just a few weeks earlier as he toured southern India in order to raise funds for *harijan* uplift has been tempered here. In separate meetings in Tinnevelly and Tuticorin on January 24, Gandhi had expressed firm belief that the massive earthquake was an act of "divine will," God's "chastisement," even punishment (*saja*) delivered by a transcendental force against those who practice the sin of untouchability.[84] In an important essay, Ajay Skaria cautions against judging these statements on the basis of classically secularist distinctions between immanence and transcendence, reason and enchantment, secularism and faith, which often lead to easy conclusions about Gandhi's religious idiosyncrasies. Such judgments, I think, deplete the richness of Gandhi's ability to see the chance of equality in the strangest corners of human sociality, his willingness to make a case for egalitarianism in the unlikeliest of places and moments. They also undermine the moral effects of Gandhi's turns of phrase and rhetoric, even polemic, which he knew might be judged as a symptom of his being "uncivilized" and yet used them with great temerity.[85] That such a reading would be unfair, even hasty, is also made clear in Gandhi's subtle recoil above. The issue that presses upon any study of his morals and politics, however, is not his merging of the transcendent and the immanent grounds of being. As Skaria rightly suggests, this happens frequently in Gandhi's thought. The issue instead is: what gives this merging of the immanent and transcendent its immense resilience? If the faith that emanates from such merging leaves a space for Gandhi's guesswork, then what does that guess become—or stand in for—in his thinking of action? Was what Gandhi calls "guess" actually a rigorous undecidability, the ability to suspend decision (and therefore break from ideals of individual will and collective sovereignty)?

Clearly, the passage raises questions that touch the fundamental concerns of classical moral and political philosophy. They touch especially strongly those concerns that acquired greater salience in the wake of Europe's first modernity (even among its later critics, such as Adorno and Horkheimer).[86] For humanist proponents and radical critics of the Enlightenment alike, these concerns emerge from their indignation against the persistence of premodern tastes for myth and mythologization in modern consciousness. Gandhi anticipates these anxieties brilliantly in the passage, giving voice to questions such as "why would God choose to punish innocents?" or "was every person who became a victim of the earthquake guilty of practicing untouchability?" or "was the earthquake not simply a calamity caused by laws of nature and planetary movement?" or, most important, "why make suffering bearable by citing it as the will and rule of the highest law?" These questions, he then argues, in a gesture that a humanist might call Gandhi's "temptation to theodicy," are hardly relevant to a person who chooses to retain faith in the ruins of greatest catastrophe.[87] For such a person, God's guilt, his punitive violence (that kills innocents too), matters less than God's indications, the paths he suggests for the curing of sin. When a catastrophe is approached in this fashion, what becomes relevant is the nature of redemptive duty (*prayshchit*) that the ordinary mortal decides to make his own with humility and patience (*sanyam*), the ground of practice (*abhyasa*) he vows to pursue in responding to God's will and decision. Gandhi leaves it "open to others" to read in the earthquake a divine punishment for various sins they believe they commit most. In other words, contrary to his earlier certainties about the direct relationship between untouchability and the Bihar earthquake as God's wrath for it, he now clears the ground for multiple sins, leaving it to the oppressor to decide what he is being punished by God for.

A fissure opens at this juncture, a fissure precisely at the point where Gandhi has cleared the space for individualism, choice, openness, perhaps even agency. It is a fissure in which Gandhi seems to renounce not just decision but also the moral edifice of measure he otherwise shapes with such care. After all, a decision (the ability and authority to decide) can be a manifestation of will, a temporary moment of autonomy, but rarely does a decision break out of the law—unless it is God's or a sovereign's—and announce the agent's freedom. One might even argue that there is autonomy in a decision without freedom; there is agency in it without equality. For as we shall see in Chapter 6, when we approach Gandhi's critique of *Annihilation of Caste*, even this decision— say, the decision to read the divine basis of human laws and authority—is not open to everyone equally. Within the larger argument that Gandhi makes for the centrality of decision, occurs, then, the second turn of thought toward that which he calls, contra superstition, skepticism and decision itself, the work of guess or "guess work."

Guesswork is not blind, indecisive, or wavering; it is, Gandhi suggests, rooted in the deepest convictions of the heart. Its force comes from the abso- lute belief that when the satyagrahi's actions are given their everyday form with firm faith in divine law, then the imperative to take decisions, or the right to freedom, becomes redundant. Guess is the act of unmooring life from the cer- tainties of principles and resituating it in a world where distinctions between decision and indecision, belief and skepticism, freedom and unfreedom, are suspended in order to accomplish a unity with the highest law. The law that Gandhi has in mind does not operate tyrannically or unilaterally. It functions precisely within the cultivated space of undecidability (or as we have seen, *un- touchability*), in a space where the very difference between decision and guess, reason and doubt, are relinquished. On the one hand, then, guesswork refuses the certainty of reason and the authority to take decisions that sustain the vio- lence of sovereign power (including the violence of divine wrath). In fact, it is precisely the authority to make a decision that marks all—and often unjust— exercises of power and domination, especially, as Gandhi reminds his follow- ers, those that are sustained by blind majoritarian will. On the other hand, in its refusal of certainty and decision, in turning—or looking—away from the feuds generated by majoritarian fallacies and superstitions, satyagraha opens it- self to a radical undecidability, one in which the distance between nonviolence and law, life and norm, autonomy and servitude, the very measure between means and ends that Gandhi posits as being central to the satyagrahi's *sad- hana*, are put to risk.[88] In this renunciation of measure, in this undecidability or guesswork, we discern what I have called the excessiveness of the Gandhian limit, or *maryada*.

What can, after all, this limit be that is at once within and in excess of the quasi-transcendental law (*dharma*), a law whose reach is no longer confined to individual precepts, principles, and actions but extends, with godlike force and precision, and most important, with godlike uncertainty, to the totality of the agent's existence? What would this limit be, other than being a deeply private norm and *self*-rule that has rendered the separateness between self and other, oppressor and oppressed, fate and law, undecidable, placing them within a moral order in which guesswork alone offers the sense of agency or autonomy? No event would amplify this undecidability, this immense force of guesswork, more starkly than Gandhi's telling fascination in the early years of the Second World War with Hitler, a figure of limitless mastery in whom Gandhi would disconcertingly find satyagraha's spiritual exemplar. Undecidability, to reemphasize the point, refers in this case not to Gandhi's failure to come up with a coherent or decisive theoretical response to fascism. Undecidability refers instead to Gandhi's inability—or his refusal—to separate norms from life; his failure to distinguish the rules of ascetic practice (*tapascharya*), the ethics of spiritual and manual exactitude (*sadhana*) on which satyagraha had been founded, from the juridical norms and structures of mastery into which the satyagrahi's love for monastic rules was susceptible to lapse. It was fascism that exposed in satyagraha's moral ontology—its vision of fearless self-sacrifice as the foundation of truth (*satya*) and being (*sat*)—a profound indecision toward sovereign power, its cultivated undecidability in the face of a new form of mastery of the law over life. In 1940, at the crest of Hitler's victories in Europe, Gandhi tells his followers:

No one knows my imperfections better than I, but what little power I possess is derived from my ahimsa. What is it but my ahimsa that draws thousands of women to me in fearless confidence? But neither you nor I can trade on our capital. We have to be up and doing every moment of our lives and go forward in our sadhana. We have to live and move and have our being in ahimsa, even as Hitler does in himsa [violence]. It is the faith and perseverance and single-mindedness with which he has perfected his weapons of destruction that commands my admiration. That he uses them as a monster is immaterial for our purpose. We have to bring to bear the same single-mindedness and perseverance in evolving our ahimsa. Hitler is awake all the 24 hours of the day in perfecting his sadhana. He wins because he pays the price. His inventions surprise his enemies. But it is his single-minded devotion to his purpose that should be the object of our admiration and emulation. Although he works all his waking hours, his intellect is unclouded and unerring. Are our intellects unclouded and unerring? A mere belief in ahimsa or the charkha [spinning wheel] will not do. It should be intelligent and creative. If intellect plays a large part in the field of violence, I hold that it plays a larger part in the field of non-violence.[89]

The paradox here is obvious. The possibility of nonviolence and limit is formulated, using the exemplary figure of Hitler, in the idiom of their opposite, in the language of limitlessness and exorbitance. The search for mastery seems to have appropriated into itself, through the monstrous figure of Hitler, satyagraha's scrupulous vigilance over measure. There are continuities here too.

Two decades earlier in *Hind Swaraj*, in a page-length chapter on "Discontent and Unrest," Gandhi had associated sleep with nothing less than servitude, a "comatose state" from which India was slowly "twisting free."[90] Sleep is antithetical to knowledge and ability, but more threateningly for Gandhi, it marks the annihilation of measure. Wakefulness, on the other hand, exemplifies a measure of true force, one that is at once vigilant and indifferent to the normative conundrums and moral judgments in which its exercise during war often gets embroiled. Let us separate for a moment, Gandhi suggests (in the interest of edification), Hitler from his war. For, as this passage shows, mere belief in nonviolence is inadequate to *sadhana*. In fact, the *sadhak* can be distinguished from any other person neither by his taste for violence nor his committment to nonviolence but only by his ability to surprise his enemies, by his perfection of means in their purity, by his ability to master and transcend the normative relationship between means and ends itself.

Thus, just six months before beginning his 1932 "fast unto death," Gandhi had unhesitatingly written, "I think that the sadhak will not trouble himself with deciding what is and what is not for general good."[91] In other words, the *sadhak* eschews general principles of goodness and embodies the science of sacrifice in his personhood; he amplifies the unity between his life and the moral law through the single-minded intensification of his finitude (even and especially in face of death). If *sadhana* is grounded in the empiricism of this act of self-intensification and self-dissolution, then the *sadhak* is one who has renounced the idealistic universalism of categories such as equality and freedom and mastered the concrete specificity of his own place, moment, and mortality. If one were willing to countenance this moral empiricism, this formidable theory of personhood in which the person *becomes* the law in its absolute singularity (this singularity would be *sat*, or the absolute truth of being), then Hitler's mastery, the autonomy of his act from the instrumentalism and bloodshed that surrounded him, his single-mindedness (by which Gandhi means the unity between his pursuit of moral perfection and his faithfulness to duty), is indeed exemplary.

In fact, at the extremities of his thought now, Gandhi has suspended the very need to distinguish between an act that is exemplary (or deviant) and an act that ensues from the deepest convictions about moral duty, so that autonomy would reside in the ability to not decide, the capacity to rely on guess, the radical openness to undecidability between autonomy and obedience, between means and ends. It was, in other words, not simply that a person took fatal blows or went to prison or even sacrificed his life, as a satyagrahi did during "civil disobedience," for freedom from the oppression of colonial law. It was that, within the structure of undecidability, sacrifice had been rendered inseparable from the law as such. For one can only guess, according to Gandhi, what one is being punished for by God, one can only guess whether the punishment—"divine event"—was in truth derived from the law of nature, from human laws, or God's will. One can only be attentive to God's indications. And in this attentive guesswork, in this suspension of certainty and decision alone lay the moral agent's inalienable autonomy, one that accrued from his ability to learn from the sacrifice of others and give his own self to duty. Giving oneself in the right way, as we have seen earlier in the chapter, was crucial. It required a purity of means, but it also required a rigorous ability to not decide. "I do not want to see the Allies defeated," wrote Gandhi as he guessed about Hitler's early blitzkrieg in Europe. "But I do not consider Hitler to be as bad as he is depicted. He is showing an ability that is amazing and he seems to be gaining his victories without much bloodshed."[92]

The most that can be said of this terrifying guess about Hitler's bloodlessness is that Gandhi firmly believed that guess offered autonomy of the self, not freedom from the law. And not everyone was equally capable of mastering the law of the guess. He was being only partly metaphorical when, in a letter to Narandas Gandhi, he concedes, "as we cannot do without a ruler or general, the name God is and will remain more current." Undecidability, then, had a law, a truth, a God that was inseparable from one's innermost being (*sat*), indifferent to the finitude of the perishable body (*deha*). "The quest of Truth," Gandhi writes in the same letter, "involves *tapascharya*, self-suffering, sometimes even unto death. . . . The pursuit of Truth is true *bhakti*, devotion. Such *bhakti* is 'a bargain in which one risks one's very life.'"[93] It is to this risk (and its immeasurable inequality) as it mediated Gandhi's science of fasting unto death, that I now turn.

Saving Death for Oneself

It was to remain a perennial source of perplexity for Ambedkar that in Gandhi's opportunistic resorts to numbers and majorities, in his lapse into the language of sacrifice precisely when he seemed farthest from the radiant universality that sacrifice (when it is opened up and insurgently democratized) grants to every mortal being, it was a certain ideal of political civility that Gandhi claimed to be protecting. He claimed to be saving a people's collective capacity to understand the transformative force of measure and restraint. He claimed to be immunizing through this ethics of limit, above all, the life of the *harijan* against the outbursts of orthodox anger. Thus, during the extreme politicization of suffering brought about by his 1932 fast unto death against separate electorates for untouchables—in the extreme and hyperbolic politicization that is entailed in any act of proposing and acting out one's own public death—Gandhi directed the force of his mortality toward friends and equals alone, not against the *harijan*. The fast was not against those, he reiterated, "who have no faith in me, whether they be Hindus or others; but it is against those countless Indians (no matter what persuasion they belong) who believe that I represent a just cause." But it was not only the direction of the sacrificial missive toward friends and away from the unequal that was crucial to the satyagrahic struggle for justice. It was the fast's attentive, discriminating, and mystical science that concealed its moral firepower.

By the fast I want to throw the whole of my weight (such as it is) in the scales of justice pure and simple. Therefore, there need be no undue haste or feverish anxiety to save my life. . . . If the Hindu mass mind is not yet to prepared to banish untouchability root and branch, it must sacrifice me without the slightest hesitation. . . . Any betrayal of the trust can merely postpone the day of immolation for me and henceforth for those who think with me. . . . Moreover, to the best of my light, I have reduced it to a science. As an expert, therefore, I would warn friends and sympathizers against copying me blindly or out of false or hysterical sympathy. . . . In so far as I know myself this fast is being undertaken with the purest of motives and without malice or anger to any single soul. For me it is an expression of, and the last seal on, non-violence. Those, therefore, who would use violence in this controversy against those whom they may consider to be inimical to me or the cause I represent will simply hasten my end. Perfect courtesy and consideration towards opponents is an absolute essential of success in this case at least if not in all cases.[94]

With its references to feverishness, immolation, and hysteria, with its hyperbolic discourse on the science of mastery and purification, the corporeal and rhetorical violence of the 1932 fast—an act that Gandhi strangely calls "the last seal on non-violence"—pushes humanist understandings of finitude to their limit.[95] And despite warning his followers of the dangers of hysteria as he lay in prison slowly dying, all the while negotiating over numbers, seats, and percentages with remarkable doughtiness, there was a very familiar kind of hysteria at work in his own proclamations as well, one that was generated around the fast's technique, the secretive force that enabled its perfect enactment, the exclusivity and mysticism of true mastery itself. The epistemology of the Gandhian fast was singular for another reason. Its force was directed only toward the reformist-nationalist equal and the imperial sovereign, not toward the unapproachable *harijan*. By its sheer disengagement from the *harijan*, Gandhi succeeded in irking Ambedkar and forcing him into bouts of political sarcasm. By the end of the year, he had begun to call Ambedkar's bewildered responses to the fast "taunts" and to speak, without irony, of "Dr. Ambedkar's comparative indifference" toward the question of justice.

Clearly, he was seeking to reclaim for Hinduism, even to usurp from Ambedkar, the revolutionary will that Ambedkar had found Hinduism to be incapable of producing.[96] "To me at any rate," Gandhi wrote after the Yeravda Pact with his opponent, "votes were no consideration. To me the question was one of undoing the harm that had been done to Harijans by the declaration of the British cabinet [to grant them separate electorates]."[97] Ambedkar is silenced here, barred not as much from nationalist accounts of negotiations that eventually led to the pact between him and Gandhi as much as from the unilateral world and gift of Gandhian sacrifice. It is not simply Ambedkar's politics, not simply the manipulation of the British cabinet that Gandhi obliquely accuses him of, but his vision of politics and ethics, which Gandhi has in mind as he walls in his antagonist within the mystical discourse of the fast. But then, the satyagrahi must address only the sovereign, not the unequal, only the imperial cabinet, not the disbelieving antagonist.

This silence—or exclusion of the unequal—is not simply solipsism in the classical sense, sequestered from practical reason. On the contrary, satyagrahic silence is maintained through a very intense, very audible, very precise science, an ontology of means (*sadhan*) and ends. "Even a small thing like the charkha has a philosophy," Gandhi argues. "Fasting, similarly, has its shastra. Fasting not governed by a philosophy does not conform to dharma. If someone says he will fast so long as God does not appear before him, he may well die but God will not appear before him."[98] In other words, truth has to be embedded in the principled purity of means, in the sacredness of the satyagrahi's vow (*vrat*), rather in the obsession with ends. Writing to Nehru just a year after the fast, Gandhi expresses this law of purity in the clearest terms since *Hind Swaraj*. "I have concerned myself principally with the conservation of means and their progressive use. I know that if we can take care of them, attainment of the goal [swaraj] is assured. I feel too that our progress towards the goal will be in exact proportion to the purity of our means."[99] There is no space for cowardice or anxiety, sleep or defeat, in this intensification of the rule, in this actualization of the vow as law that acts upon the body (which includes moral agent's vow of fasting unto death). In fact, the vow becomes the law—the transcendental rule or even truth—in its very actualization. Gandhi shows a remarkable awareness of this quasi-transcendentalist trait, this inseparability of—and undecidability between—life and law, within satyagraha. And yet only in a figure of godlike sovereignty, in the example of a *sadhak*—a practitioner who has mastered the nothingness of sleep and fear and acquired the unmediated purity of means—does he identify the apotheosis of satyagrahic measure. In the spirit of this moral ontology (or ontotheology) of *sadhana*, he had written in 1925: "Even God is full of sleepless and selfless activity."[100]

Gandhi's willingness to die for percentages and numbers (of seats, electors, representatives), in any case, complicates the longstanding nationalist claim that votes were not the consideration behind his extreme measure. But we have been more concerned in this chapter about a particular moment in the genealogy of anticolonial political thought, a moment that is symptomatic of Gandhi's scrupulous thinking of equality within the framework of distance. Within this framework, the impasse opened up by his fasts, especially during the two decades of expanding imperial franchise leading up to India's independence in 1947, acquired a form that well exceeded the question of mere caste reform. If untouchability was, as Gandhi had remade it, now inseparable from the question of sovereignty, could fasting unto death—with its undeniable predilection for mastery, its willingness to speak with the sovereign alone—be a ground for its eradication? Gandhi's answer to this question was unconditionally affirmative. To him fasting, an art that was unfathomable both within the religious and humanist compulsions of keeping life safe, was the irreducible ground of cultivating nonindifference toward the unequal. Fasting entails an accommodation with one's own death; it is an act of staying fearlessly with one's own mortality. Only in that strange ground between life and death could one's knowledge of finitude be perfected with humility, and the capacity for nonindifference toward one's unequals aroused.

But this ethical dimension of fasting, centered on the sacrificial capacities of the self, was never unconnected to Gandhi's understanding of the political community. In fact, ethics and politics here seem to have been rendered inseparable, the priority of one over the other rendered into a zone of undecidability; or, one might argue, the 1932 fast marked, in an unprecedented and irreversible sense, the making political—indeed, theologico-political—of the vow. After all, the most vital element in Gandhi's thinking of the fast, precisely because of its emphasis on solitary effort, was his deployment of the language of democracy and representation, even collective interest. He was, he claimed, representing a cause, a popular and moral one. If this representation was geared toward the equality of the unequal, if the fast was mounted in the interest of democratization of humility and reason alone, why was sacrifice itself kept private and privative? Why was the science of suffering still consumed by hierarchy, by a sacrosanct sovereignty, by a sense of mastery and opacity that increasingly resembled those very institutional structures that it had committed itself to resisting? Why was sacrifice disengaged from the *harijan* at the very moment its force—rhetorical and performative—was deployed, as a very public performance indeed, for his emancipation? Why enforce another ban on the unequal under the ruse, yet again, of protection? This is, as I suggested at the beginning of the chapter, not merely the question of the *harijan*. It reveals an affinity for the spirit of the law lodged inside satyagraha, a disciplinary limit that predated the birth of the *harijan* and only found its most rigorous social form in it. The *harijan*, one might argue, was not simply a name. It was a *place* between being and nonbeing, one that exemplified the simultaneous condescension and love of the people inscribed at the heart of Gandhi's thinking of action.

Revealing, both for its timing and content, its condescension and love, was Gandhi's silence on the socialist revolutionary Bhagat Singh's decision in 1929 to fast until death in prison. Singh, who was arrested along with comrades from the Hindustan Socialist Republican Army after they threw a bomb in the Central Legislative Assembly, was demanding better living conditions for colonial prisoners. The fast was observed in order to bring moral force to bear on the British government. Even as he continued to refuse food, Singh was charged with murdering a British official in an earlier conspiracy. He was hanged in March 1931. Gandhi, a self-proclaimed critic of the death penalty, came under fierce criticism for not doing enough to save the life of the 23-year-old hero. It was widely believed that he had failed to try hard enough to secure—at the height of his influence over the British Government during the second civil disobedience movement in 1931—the commutation of Singh's and his comrades' death sentences, trying instead to defer the hanging only until the session of the Indian National Congress had passed in peace. In response to that criticism, Gandhi wrote equivocally of the militants' sacrifice. "These heroes had conquered the fear of death. Let us bow to them a thousand times for their heroism." But, he warned, "we should not imitate their act."[101]

Among the pronouncements he made during those weeks, Gandhi's celebration of the revolutionaries' fearless disregard of pain (which he admired) is not as suggestive as his absolute silence on that one mode of sacrifice that Bhagat Singh had come to share with him and, by all accounts, even mastered: the art of fasting nonviolently unto death. Singh survived the hunger strike that lasted for 116 nonviolent days, but his comrade Jatin Das died on the sixty-third day. "My motive," Gandhi clarified a month later, "was plain enough. The deed was condemned. The spirit of bravery and sacrifice was praised." However, "every murder" and retaliation, he wrote, indicting the young revolutionaries for their actions, "has hampered me in my pursuit."[102] Even in this instance, Gandhi recalls Singh's assassination of Saunders, a British official posted in the Punjab, not the martyr's subsequent hunger strike in prison.

Just five months after Singh was hanged, Gandhi, in a seemingly unconnected gesture, inducted the *harijan* into the grammar of India's anticolonial struggle. But the pattern is uncanny. The urgency of this act bears the same imprint that Dhingra's assassination of Wylie and his subsequent trial and hanging in London in 1909 had borne on the frantic tone of *Hind Swaraj*. On both occasions, Gandhi had instituted a new category, a new name, and with each had been activated a constellation of sacrificial practices around which in turn, would take form an audacious moral ontology of force. Both *satyagraha* and *harijan* bore the semantic, performative, and often visceral imprint of this force. And yet unlike 1909, when a militant universality had been discernible in Gandhi's thinking of a people in its promising collectivity (*praja*), it was a people within and apart from that early sense of people who were constituted in 1931—a people endowed not as much with the faculty of sacrifice themselves as with a capacity to bear witness to that of others. Viewed especially in the light of imperial events and activities around it, the naming of the *harijan* thus seems anything but fortuitous (or even circumstantial). Instead, as figure, subject, and place, the *harijan* epitomized satyagraha's enduring attempt to engage the social question in its mundane, corporeal, and everyday form. It touched the disciplinary core of what Gandhi believed was a sense of measure proper to anticolonial sovereignty. Lodged as a mystical place between being and nonbeing, God and animal, force and nonforce, the *harijan* embodied satyagraha in its greatest proximity to the moral law. Who but God (or God's own child), after all, could occupy that place, that groundless abyss, that immeasurable depth of inner being, from which the law of satyagrahic measure emerged?

Thus we return to the paradox with which I began tracing the history of satyagraha in this chapter—the transcendentalism of limits at the heart of Gandhi's thinking of equality, the indifference at the heart of his nonindifference. Throughout the 1930s and 1940s, Gandhi remained oblivious to the oppressive religiosity of his many fasts, famously arguing that unlike revolutionaries and other practitioners whose target was a hostile colonial state or an antagonist, he was targeting—and atoning for—only his friends.[103] The sphere of the fast was circumscribed by this insuperable friendship of equals. It made little difference to Gandhi whether his friends were able to contain their insinuations toward his antagonists, whether his friends and disciples were, in a perverse reversal of moral responsibility, prone to blaming his opponents for his impeccably executed plans for death. Like the Kshatriya warrior Lakshmana, the fast circumscribed satyagraha, its craft of restraint and sacrifice, solely around equals. Like the limit at work in the classical ethics of *kshatriyadharma*, the fast consecrated the unequal as silent witness of the satyagrahi's elusive sacrifice. If one sacrifices only one's equals, if one sacrifices only those whose means are equal to one's own, as Gandhi had stipulated in *Hind Swaraj*, then the presence of the *harijan* required the satyagrahis to unconditionally disarm. The satyagrahis, Gandhi stipulated, "should approach them [the *harijan*] not in a militant spirit but as befits their nonviolence, in a spirit of friendliness."[104]

This formula of equality, constituted at once by rules of friendship and untouchability, was clearly not a call for assimilating the untouchable into the humanist regime of substitution. On the contrary, it recalls a classical problem within democratic humanism, one that in *Democracy in America* (1835–1840) de Tocqueville—and following him, Lefort among others—identifies as reversibility, a co-creative relationship between servitude and freedom,[105] a risk in which one mutates seamlessly into the other right at the heart of democracy—a swift shift, in Gandhi's case, between satyagraha's radical touching and its disinterested abandonment of the untouchable. Thus, where the craft of satyagrahic *tapascharya*—fasting until death—could have politicized that ambiguous zone between life and death in which the untouchable too dwelled (if only under much more punitive and involuntary force), satyagraha merely reaffirmed its own unambiguous mastery over pain. Where it could have politicized the unequal's routine violation and vulnerability by treating them as equal to the satyagrahi's own practiced nearness to death, it instead lapsed into the language of sacrifice on behalf of the unequal. Such intense folding of *dharma* into oneself, such unforgiving sovereignty over oneself that only death could actualize, demanded discipline and resolve. Perhaps it is this disciplinary sovereignty, this wait for equality until death, that Gandhi calls "patience."[106]

The Freedom of Others

Annihilation of Caste *and Republican Virtue*

In May 1936, just about a month after Gandhi clarified in a brief essay the sacred origins of the term *harijan* (which he insisted he had extracted from an episode in the *Ramayana*), Ambedkar published his censored lecture, *Annihilation of Caste*. The treatise, it was immediately clear to those who read it in any depth (as it would have earlier been to those who had prevented its delivery as a lecture) was no ordinary pamphlet on caste reform. Instead, in both its substance and rhetoric, *Annihilation of Caste* had achieved something unthinkable in its time, inscribing the genesis, endurance, and ubiquity of social cruelty in India at the heart of the moral and political rules of her very struggle for freedom from colonial domination. Anticolonial nationalism, in all its weakness and violence, had been critiqued before, most notably in Gandhi's *Hind Swaraj*. But never before had the pernicious innocence of nationalism been stripped, its silent complicity with the laws of caste cruelty and domination revealed, its failure to conceptualize a freedom proper to a just republic laid threadbare, as rigorously and fearlessly as it was in *Annihilation of Caste*. Classically republican in its understanding of freedom as the founding principle of an egalitarian citizenship—equality first as foremost as every individual's equal right to freedom from domination in civic and private spaces—*Annihilation of Caste* was no less unequivocal in its belief that freedom as such, indeed, sovereignty in its essence, needed to be emancipated from nationalist interest in the state. "Annihilation" stood for this freedom without measure, a purity of force as means extracted from the instrumental calculations and constraints of ends. "I have emphasized this question of the ways and means of destroying caste," Ambedkar makes it clear, "because I think that knowing the proper ways and means is more important that knowing the ideal."[1] At the center of the undelivered lecture, then, was the struggle to formulate an ethics of responsibility and justice unconstrained by the moral law; the principle, as Ambedkar called it, of an egalitarian sovereignty; a shared love of truth, above all, that was at once closest to the language of classical republicanism—indeed, one might argue, the language of republican constitutionalism—and at greatest distance from it.

"Annihilation," or *ucched*, was also a tradition-defying concept in Ambedkar's ethical, religious, and political thought. On the one hand, its etymological and conceptual roots were immersed in the classical recesses of Buddhist negative theology and Indo-European nihilism (*ucchedvad*). On the other hand, it was called upon to perform a rhetorical and interpretive *coup de force*, aligning the insurrectionary threads of Ambedkar's conception of freedom along the axis of his revolutionary constitutionalism, an axis around which his moral and political engagements during the decade between 1936 and 1945 would take their singular form. Bookended by *Annihilation of Caste* and the second edition of *Thoughts on Pakistan* (1941), revised and reissued under the title *Pakistan, or the Partition of India* (1945), this was the period during which Ambedkar's vision of politics, his struggle to navigate the distinction between constitution and insurrection, between justice and force, would acquire its greatest depth and difficulty. I juxtapose *Annihilation of Caste* with *Thoughts on Pakistan* not simply because of their temporal proximity, but because, despite the immense tension between these works, there is a conceptual and rhetorical integrity in Ambedkar's republican ethics that shines through in all its emancipatory promise and extremism during this period. It was within this ethics that the expression he borrowed from Henry Sidgwick's *Elements of Politics* (1891), "right of insurrection," referring to the constituent power of the people to proclaim their autonomy and will beyond the constraints of the law—an autonomy he rendered most often as "force," sometimes as "crisis," and in his later works as "virtue"—emerged as the unifying thread running through all of his major works in this period.

Apart from resisting the temptation to approach *Annihilation of Caste* as an isolated if revolutionary treatise that intervenes in the social question alone (or intervenes in it in a manner that can be judged as being devoid of ethics, or worse, constrained by its author's love of law), there is another way in which the task of understanding the extremist—even anarchic—richness of the text demands that it be not read: by placing it within the unfolding sequence of events that together constitute the formidable history of the Indian nationalist movement. For contextualized thus, it might be argued that Ambedkar's radical accentuation of means over ends, one that made his titular concept (and his call for) annihilation operative, was impelled by his recognition that the configuration of popular franchise under the Government of India Act of 1935 had left little room for him to gain a consolidated electoral advantage of the kind other religious minorities, such as Muslims, might have after the general elections that were scheduled for 1937. And so, wedged between those two crucial years, *Annihilation of Caste* revealed Ambedkar's nihilistic urge to destroy not only scripture but also divinity, his openness to doubt not only the legitimacy of the nationalist demand for freedom from empire but also his cognitive inability to understand the meaning of a democratic national social state itself.

But nationalists' general assessment of Ambedkar's infidelities had neither begun nor ended with *Annihilation of Caste*. Their revulsions against his terse prose and speech dated back to the London Round Table conferences convened in the early 1930s by the British government to discuss the future of Indian franchise, which were followed by his clash with Gandhi and their compromise in Poona in 1932. Whatever Gandhi's motives were, in purely strategic terms, aided by his remarkable ability to prepare for and embrace in full public view his own death, he had emerged from this confrontation victorious, forcing Ambedkar to withdraw his demand for separate electorates for the "untouchables." Accounts of the Poona Pact negotiations not only illuminate Gandhi's immense capacity for numerical calculation and his fortitude in sticking to them down to their minutest percentages (a strategy intrinsic to modern politics from which, it is claimed, he had broken); they also reveal the numerical foundations of his deeper moral claims themselves—indeed, his willingness to fast and die for them.[2] The strategy paid off. The Congress Party went on to sweep the general elections in 1937, gaining absolute majorities in five out of eleven provinces of British India, demolishing along the way, even if temporarily, the Muslim League's claim to speak for the subcontinent's largest religious minority. Ambedkar's Independent Labor Party won decisively in Bombay, where it claimed 13 out of 15 reserved seats. This provincial triumph, however, marked not the beginning of Ambedkar's electoral ascendancy but its apex, followed by a long, slow, and steady phase of decline caused by his inability to muster the tactical advantage that in a democracy only the strength of numbers bestows.

Placed solely within this electoral context, *Annihilation of Caste* is reduced to a symptom of an unfortunate division in the anticolonial front against the empire that its author had willfully opened, its tenor more a sign of Ambedkar's divisive contrarianism and recalcitrant approach to the caste question than a sign of a more fundamental rift in anticolonial conceptions of the political itself. This explains why, beginning in Ambedkar's own time with the Gandhian nationalist C. Rajagopalachari's polemical tract *Ambedkar Refuted* (1946), and within the massive historiography on twentieth-century anticolonialisms at large, *Annihilation of Caste* (when mentioned at all) is barely approached as a text located in the interstices—and engaged with the problematic relationship—of republicanism, religion, and sovereignty. Valuable beginnings have been made by Upendra Baxi, Partha Chatterjee, Anupama Rao, and Kamala Visweswaran, with Baxi having pointed out two decades ago that there was always a "moral logic" at work in the choices we make when grappling with Ambedkar's thought.[3] But despite Baxi's call to understand the heterogeneous elements and pressures that mediated Ambedkar's moral and political trajectory, the scholarly consensus on the matter remains fairly well entrenched. Ambedkar's incendiary thoughts on Pakistan, grounded in his conviction about the ineradicable nature of Muslim social and religious difference, his demand for Muslim excision from Indian society as the only solution to the subcontinent's minority and "communal problem," his purportedly blind love of the state typical of conservative nationalists of the interwar period, and his decision to convert to Buddhism rather than to one of the Abrahamic faiths he otherwise greatly admired, all had something to do, we are told, with the man's secretive attachment to the idea of an Indian civilization (or tradition) within which alone he envisioned the redemption of the "untouchables."

The oblique, gradual, almost furtive, effect of such historiography is a delimitation of the recalcitrant movements of a thought whose rhythms, perhaps too uncomfortably, traverse the outer extremities of nationalist discourse on periodization and sovereignty. In fact, the insurrectionary elements of any such thought, even before its outermost boundaries have been probed, might come to be circumscribed almost immediately by the certitude of national origins and individual biography, or more frequently, by laws of historical context (contexts whose frames are themselves surreptitiously predetermined by narratives of what Ambedkar had in 1943 wryly called—distinguishing it from authentic "martyrdom"—nationalist "heroics").[4] It is indeed easy to forget, as Ambedkar seems to be suggesting in his separation of martyrdom from mere heroics, that historical truth and memory have never been innocent of the desires, anxieties, and fears of the nationalist imagination,[5] each of which predetermines the contexts, contours, and topography of what can be called—or must be excluded from—the properly political.[6] In this chapter, my concern is less with Ambedkar's relationship with nationalist historiography per se (although this relationship does mediate his attempt to write a classical counterhistory of citizenship and freedom for India) than it is with his struggle to make the social foundations of citizenship *political*; or rather, with his attempt to render the ethics of social justice and civic responsibility *insurrectionary*, liberated from the injunctions of the moral law and grounded in the virtuous and positive freedom of principles. "Annihilation," I argue, encapsulated this radical democratic gesture, marking at once Ambedkar's exit from the nationalist framework of reform and his reclamation of autonomy as the immeasurable potentiality—faculty, force, reason—of the unequal.

The Autonomy of Principles

How could this other freedom (which was also the freedom of others before it was of the self) be conceptualized—this freedom as force, freedom as intelligence and faculty of the most unequal and outcaste (*atishudra*), freedom as a just and virtuous sovereignty, without lapsing into mastery, interference, and domination? This freedom had to be thought, argued Ambedkar, in the interstices between faith and action, between religious responsibility and civic insurrection. Freedom must be an act of faith. In its truest form, in fact, it could be (before every measure, foundation, and rule) grounded only in the autonomy of "principles." The autonomy of the principle—and principle within the limits of autonomy alone—was not the demand for abstract moral norms, a search for the categorical imperative. Instead, principle, according to Ambedkar, was that which contained the seeds of a discriminating intelligence (*pradnya*), and if need be, insurgent force; it was the will to break the rule (even of nonviolence), one whose ethics would be given its most rigorous form two decades later in *The Buddha and His Dhamma*. "Man has Pradnya and he must use it," Ambedkar writes in his discussion of the Buddhist conception of nonviolence (*ahimsa*). "A moral man may be trusted to draw the line at the right point. . . . To put it differently the Buddha made a distinction between Principle and Rule. He did not make Ahimsa a matter of Rule. He enunciated it as a matter of Principle or way of life. . . . A principle leaves you freedom to act. A rule does not. Rule either breaks you or you break the rule."[7]

If principle opened for the virtuous citizen a realm of autonomous action, then rule—as an instrument of mastery—was that which interfered with the citizen's autonomy. Rule was that which corrupted the very possibility of an authentic sovereignty. Faced with a rule, the citizen had no moral choice but to break it. Without being detained here by Ambedkar's understanding of nonviolence as a principle that could be grounded only in a responsible and just practice of autonomy, a principle that could be legitimized only by the shared and free will of mortals—an understanding from which his critique of the death penalty would subsequently emerge—let me simply note here that this strain of thought appears for the first time (and in its most insurrectionary form) in *Annihilation of Caste*. For if the nationalist desire for an independent state had instituted a separation between political struggle and social reform, privileging the former and deferring the latter, then *Annihilation of*

Caste had not simply inverted the nationalist rule. It had sought a new principle of sovereignty itself, one in which neither the religious nor the ethical could henceforth be separated from the insurrectionary force of an egalitarian citizenship. "The moment it degenerates into rules," goes that decisive passage in the treatise, "it ceases to be Religion, as it kills responsibility, which is the essence of a truly religious act." Then, comes Ambedkar's pivotal formulation: "I have, therefore, no hesitation in saying that such a religion must be destroyed and I say, there is nothing irreligious in working for the destruction of such a religion."[8] Religion, then, must be destroyed the moment it is recognized that it has turned into a structure of rule—(rule both as a disciplinary injunction (*maryada*) and rule as domination by the force of law (*dharma*). This rule of religion must be destroyed, most importantly, in the very name of a religious responsibility. Or rather, argues Ambedkar, religion becomes religious in its essence only when it is opened to destruction and rebirth in the hands of the mortal citizen. And this imperative of annihilation is, for Ambedkar, not the question of just one religion. Instead, he is speaking of religion in its singularity. One can, as he argues, never and nowhere separate the mortal subject's insurrectionary force—the "essence of a truly religious act"— from the civic duties, responsibilities, and virtues of the citizen.

Perhaps most crucially, *Annihilation of Caste* crystallizes—in less than a hundred small pages divided further into twenty-six parts—Ambedkar's attempt to formulate the conditions of a new politics in which justice can be conceptualized without the fear of illegitimate authorities and corrupt foundations, a space for civic action where the right to belief is available to everyone, liberated from nationalist expectations of reverence and laws of ecclesiastical interference alike. *Dhamma* was the later Ambedkar's name for this principle of freedom, this religion without religion, in which faith was at once freed from the need of human mediation—"the authority of man"—and its transcendence secured in the everyday responsibilities and autonomies of the citizen. "The Dhamma must be its own successor," says his Buddha in *The Buddha and His Dhamma*. "Principle must live by itself, and not by the authority of man. If principle needs the authority of man it is no principle. If every time it becomes necessary to invoke the name of the founder to enforce the authority of Dhamma then it is no Dhamma."[9] *Dhamma*, then, was the call for an immanent faith in which freedom—in its transcendence and immortality—was secured in the act of surrendering to the will precisely of one's mortal others. This will was, by its very nature, simultaneously transcendent and immanent. On the one hand, it owed no obedience to artificial, unjust, and illegitimate powers that interfered with the virtuous conduct of everyday life. On the other hand, it only thrived in responsibility toward principles whose universality transcended the interests of the self; hence, in Ambedkar's view, the Buddha's refusal to appoint even his own successor. "Twice or thrice the Buddha was requested by his followers to appoint a successor," he recounts. "Every time the Buddha refused." *Dhamma* did not simply eschew or resist foundations. *Dhamma* was the absence of foundation (including the foundation of the self) itself. It was the absence of foundations even of the founders. There was something profoundly insurrectionary, and indeed anarchic, about this autonomy, even and especially when it is formulated, as it is in *The Buddha and His Dhamma*, in the name of justice for vulnerable and mortal lives.

Keeping for Chapter 7 the relationship that the mature Ambedkar would forge between responsibility, justice, and finitude, I want to focus in this chapter on an earlier and connected moment in this insurrectionary trajectory, one during which Ambedkar's political and ethical conception of citizenship—his vision of a citizen who might be governed but not mastered[10]—began to acquire its enduring attributes. What was *Annihilation of Caste*, one might ask, if not an attempt to achieve a just—if still a classically republican—balance between revolutionary action and moral obligation, between freedom and equality, between constituents and their constitution? In its essence, after all, the question of religion (and its destruction) has always been the question of the relationship between sovereignty (whether of God or the state) and the people. For Ambedkar, in fact, there is a fundamental relationship between the constitution and insurrection. "The constitutional questions are in the first instance not questions of right but questions of might," he argues, reproducing a decisive passage from Ferdinand Lassalle's widely circulated 1862 speech, "On the Essence of Constitutions." "The actual constitution of a country has its existence only in the actual condition of force which exists in the country: hence political constitutions have value and permanence only when they accurately express those conditions of forces which exist in practice within a society."[11] Equality, then, must be made equal to freedom: this was at once the revolutionary Ambedkar's most insurrectionary demand and the source of the constitutionalist Ambedkar's most enduring difficulty. But are these two identities, one pulling Ambedkar into the everyday ethics of revolutionary fraternity and love of truth, the other into the juridically measured, anonymous, and abstract republic of equals, so easily separable? Does not Ambedkar's pursuit of virtue, his "faith in equality," gather its force precisely around his struggle to free freedom from the internal exclusions of the republic for which he would be called to provide the founding document? And if such indeed are the tensions of this struggle to rescue sovereignty from its appropriation by nationalism and secure it as the virtuous, shared, and public use of reason, what conception of freedom did this struggle yield?

For a concept that is seen to establish the moral and ontological distinctiveness of human life, setting the human apart from the multitude of other life forms, freedom has proved to be a notoriously elusive attribute to define and delimit. This is not the least because of the risk—and great violence—that, since its consolidation as the sovereign ideal and governing principle of political community, has troubled all attempts to realize and secure freedom. If anything, the liberal conception of freedom—in which liberty is defined negatively as freedom from interference—has proved to be as violent as freedom defined in any other tradition of modern political thought. Even a quick reading of *Annihilation of Caste* makes it amply clear that Ambedkar is writing against liberty as it is defined in classical liberalism. Mere absence of interference is not only no guarantee of freedom, he argues; such absence of legal interference is precisely the precondition of a form of domination that works less through visible apparatuses than it does through the insidious force of rumor. The brilliance of caste sovereignty lies not in its indivisibility (which is the defining attribute of sovereign power as such) but in its infinite gradation, dispersal, and deterrence. Every right and authority (*adhikara*), every responsibility and sacrificial rite (*samskara*), has more above and below it. "Now this gradation, this scaling of castes makes it impossible to organise a common front against the caste system," writes Ambedkar in part 21 of *Annihilation of Caste*. "If a caste claims the right to inter-dine and intermarry with another caste placed above it, it is frozen the instant it is told by mischief-mongers—and there are many Brahmins amongst such mischief-mongers—that it will have to concede inter-dining and intermarriage with castes below it! All are slaves of the caste system. But all slaves are not equal in status."

For Ambedkar, this divisible and pernicious form of mastery, one that employs fear and deterrence, one that feigns noninterference precisely by freezing the desire for social mingling, movement, and resistance the moment they become genuine possibilities, is not the ideal form of sovereignty. But what suffers under this law of noninterference—under the vision of freedom as mere noninterference—is not as much sovereignty as the ordinary virtues that make an ethics of a just sovereignty possible. Freedom in its true sense—and here Ambedkar is as close to early modern republicanism as he is to Gandhi—means not a negative liberty, not simply noninterference, but the freedom to cultivate positive virtues, the physical space to nourish skills, the cognitive space to educate the mind, the collective and shared space, above all, to mobilize, act, and touch.[12]

One is human, which is to say, political, only inasmuch as one is corporeally and cognitively free, only inasmuch as one is capable of comprehending and defending this freedom as the inalienable liberty of self and others. But whenever deployed and let loose without a moral constraint or calculus, freedom's radical immeasurability—the "thing, force, and gaze" of freedom[13]—threatens to veer off into the realm of prejudice, meaninglessness, and evil itself. There is a suggestive moment in *Pakistan, or the Partition of India*, for instance, in which Ambedkar expresses regret over his own lapse into inflammatory rhetoric. He regrets the force of his prose—and how else might freedom be understood, expressed, and grasped without this interpretive force that constitutes it—but he has, he insists, no remorse. I will return to this ethics of regret without remorse—humility without guilt and subordination—later in this chapter. Suffice it to recall, from our discussion in Chapter 3, the relationship Ambedkar forges in "Ranade, Gandhi, and Jinnah" (1943) between love and force. In *Partition*, he conjures a similar expression, "love of politics." In a passage on the uneven distribution of wealth maintained by force under the classical laws of *Chaturvarnya*, he examines the continuities of those old exclusions in the new nationalist dispensation centered on money. "Spread of religion or acquisition and promotion of culture do not interest him," Ambedkar claims, pointing toward the defining attribute of the Bania caste of moneylenders to which Gandhi belonged (obliquely targeting Gandhi's immense skill as a fundraiser for the Indian National Congress). "Only one new service, on the expenditure side, has found a place in his budget. That service is politics. This happened since the entry of Mr. Gandhi as a political leader. . . . Here again, the reason is not love of politics. The reason is to make private gain out of public affairs."[14]

In its negative sense, clearly, "love of politics" is that which nationalism and its money-minded practitioners lack, their conduct marred by an inability to grasp the relationship between wealth and corruption. But what is "love of politics" in its positive sense (which Ambedkar leaves undefined here)? It is that in which, he would write almost two decades later, virtue and autonomy, love and insurrection, equality and freedom have equal share. It is that in which one's deepest truths, one's most inalienable will, are restrained only by the ethics of quotidian skill and fraternal responsibility. "Come, thou brother! Be virtuous," Ambedkar retells the story of the Buddha speaking to a Brahmin, reminding the latter of the masterful hands of a "clever horse-trainer," a person who works with animals and may have never read the scripture. "Abide, be constrained by the restraint of the obligation."[15] It is in this inseparability of the transcendent and immanent, this democratization of virtue in which the absolute freedom and rhythm of the self—the skills of the hand—is constrained only by a higher obligation to mortal others, that a positive love of politics thrives. Even the slightest conflation of freedom and autonomy with such concepts as mastery, decision, rule (concepts that belong to the domain of moral law)—indeed, even a little mediation of its immeasurability by injunctions and measures of the law—tends to render freedom morally empty, its emancipatory promises and its quotidian and fraternal possibilities imprisoned by the jurisdictions of the (often illegitimate) norms and effects of sovereign power. This chapter examines how in choosing *Annihilation of Caste* as the title of his manifesto, deploying a particular configuration of words and metaphors, Ambedkar intervenes in this long history of religious and republican risk, seeking to imagine another, more just, possibility for a freedom beyond nature.

It is true that even the most conservative liberals—many of whom Ambedkar had often taken head on over matters both political and theological—shared the argument that republicanism in India had roots in its ancient constitution. But rhetorical resonance cannot, in this instance, be read as conceptual, let alone ideological, continuity. S. Radhakrishnan, speaking in the Constituent Assembly in January 1947, for instance, had famously claimed: "We cannot say that the republican tradition is foreign to the genius of the country. We have had it from the beginning of our history. . . . Panini, Megasthenes and Kautilya refer to the Republics of Ancient India. The Great Buddha belonged to the Republic of Kapilavastu." But this was a republicanism, "sometimes governed by assemblies, sometimes by kings," always already given over to the moral law of *dharma*. "Much has been said about the sovereignty of the people. We have held," argued Radhakrishnan, "that the ultimate sovereignty rests with the moral law, with the conscience of humanity. People as well as kings are subordinate to that. Dharma, righteousness, is the king of kings."[16] The nuances of Ambedkar's own reading of Kautilya's *Arthashastra* (variously translated as *Science of Statecraft* or *Science of Material Gain*), his admiration for the Brahmin theorist's commitment to public safety on which came to be founded his intricate theory of sovereignty, is expressed most fervently in *Who Were the Shudras?* (1946).[17] The *Arthashastra* is possibly the greatest text on republican government and power composed in the Indic tradition, although Ambedkar's affinity with its author need not detain us here. But clearly, for a thinker so attuned to everyday restrictions on physical movement and psychological humiliations that were the norm in colonial India's public places, there were elements of republican thought—liberty of movement, freedom of association, freedom of public use of reason—that Ambedkar just could not have disavowed.

At least since the English Civil War, out of whose vicissitudes emerged the form and content of Thomas Hobbes's *Leviathan* (1651), freedom in its most fundamental sense has meant the sovereign state's guarantees on the physical security of its citizens. It has meant, in Hobbes's terms, "absence of all impediments to action that are not contained in the nature and intrinsic quality of the agent."[18] Only in minimizing the constraints on the subject's action and securing his freedom of movement does a republic find its own reason to exist, its legitimacy measured by the success it achieves in safeguarding the everyday activities and practical reasons of civic life. It is precisely because of this unitary emphasis on security and safety—an emphasis that had never been far, Hannah Arendt would caution in the 1950s, from the dangerous conflation of freedom with the belief in the prolongation and infinitude of human life[19]—that republican ideals of liberty have remained difficult to separate from the immoral excesses that the sovereign state invested with powers to maintain that security inevitably lapses into. To understand this risk inherent in republicanism, one can go back further to Machiavelli, for whom "a small part of the people wish to be free in order to command, but all the others who are countless, desire liberty in order to live in safety."[20] Freedom, Machiavelli insinuates in chapter 16 of his *Discourses on Livy* (1531), is thus won—and even invented—almost by accident, its real promise being security and prolongation of life rather than liberty. In calling the chapter "A People Accustomed to Living under a Prince Maintains Its Freedom with Difficulty If, by Some Accident, It Becomes Free," Machiavelli was not being ironic in the least. He was setting in motion a fundamental paradox of republican concerns with freedom: freedom tends to dissolve the moment it is born. To exist, it must be swallowed by the very state whose legitimate authority alone it is to protect it. And yet, Machiavelli insists, there is no freedom greater and more inalienable than the freedom to refuse oppression, to create legitimate counterpowers, to mobilize insurgent force if need be.

　In the works that he composed during the decade and a half between the publication of *Annihilation of Caste* in 1936 and the formal founding of the Indian republic in 1950, Ambedkar assigns himself the task of parsing out this insurrectionary subject: the sovereign citizen whose existence might be given a moral form separate from the norm of mastery and domination; the free citizen whose autonomy must be imagined beyond the concerns of republican safety and unity alone. And while this task was inseparable from the struggle to annihilate caste, it was precisely the work of annihilating caste that pushed Ambedkar's thought deeper into classical territory, forging a relationship between his emancipatory commitments and early modern republican and constitutional traditions. In 1950, India's Constituent Assembly finally ratified the constitution whose drafting Ambedkar had presided over for three years since India's independence. The moment of independence itself, 15 August 1947, was euphoric and unprecedented, Nehru famously calling it, in the Constituent Assembly, India's "tryst with destiny."

But the task was daunting, at once exceptional and classical. The task—which Ambedkar had seen emerging in its full paradox since at least 1940 in ways few others had—of bringing into existence, from the remains of a religious genocide that would soon leave more than a million dead and two new republics, the figure of a "republican citizen," one whose freedom would somehow, at once, redeem and exceed the strictures of the state—and the "categorical imperative" of *dharma*—and thrive in the citizens' shared love of truth alone. This republican citizen, in other words, was one who might be governed within the limits of moral constraints and virtuous conduct and yet not mastered. Beyond doubt, Ambedkar's relationship with this tradition, which I call, following Martin van Gelderen and Quentin Skinner, the tradition of "republican constitutionalism," remained elliptical.[21] In fact, there was a tension between his awareness of the value of the liberal conception of negative liberty (liberty as noninterference) and his belief in the positive and transformative force of shared moral virtues (to be cultivated, secured, and affirmed, without fear of domination, in the autonomous pursuits of the citizen). On the one hand, republicanism pulled Ambedkar into an unequivocal desire for the mobility, safety, and unity—in classical parlance, an indivisible sovereignty—of the people. On the other, it nourished his attentiveness to the tyrannical excesses of power that have historically, in the name of liberty, put the very legitimacy of democratic ethics—democracy's responsibility toward the freedom of others—at risk. The most rigorous, difficult, and demanding lines of Ambedkar's moral and political thought would follow this latter direction and align themselves—as they move from the 1940s onward through the thought of Rousseau and Nietzsche—with a decidedly insurrectionary, even anarchic, theory of justice. A theory that would in turn institute, in Ambedkar's thought and rhetoric alike, force as the seed of emancipation, incorruptible by the apparatuses and injunctions of the moral law. And this force is the strongest, most just, most positive, argues Ambedkar, when it is in the hands of the republic's weakest, wielded by its "spent and sacrificed people" alone.[22]

In the final part of this chapter, I examine Ambedkar's conception of ordinary virtues, which he sought out not only to repair an authentic "love of politics" but also to imagine a freedom, a shared liberty, which might thrive at the limits of—if never fully beyond—the state. Anticipations of this thought had appeared much earlier, as his dissatisfaction with the nationalist approach to caste reform grew. By the middle of 1930s, Ambedkar had lost much of his early interest in claiming the "untouchables' right" to enter temples, those quintessentially confined spaces of ritual reverence and control. Instead, it was now the right to the polis as such, the shared spaces of work and assembly, the collective right to life and sacrifice, that he wanted to be opened to those barred from it. His use of the term "general mobilization," which appears for the first time in *Annihilation of Caste* and whose militant—and at times militaristic—extremism I probe in this chapter (in the context of his relationship to revolutionary republicanism), must be seen as the call to this egalitarian presupposition; that is to say, as his registration of the unequal's irreducible "right to have rights," a right preceding all foundation and law, and one that was therefore fundamentally anarchic in its essence.[23] One was not free because one had the right to go to war; rather, argued Ambedkar, there was no war worthy of the name in the first place without the unconditional freedom to mobilize—and the equal right to sacrifice oneself freely—for a cause greater than one's interest. There was no equality, and certainly no sacrifice and action adequate to justice, without the citizen's autonomy to master the skill and instruments of war, without his freedom to perfect the lessons and techniques of struggle. The term "general mobilization" concealed this insurgent dimension of Ambedkar's revolutionary thought. In fact, so uncompromising was his conceptualization of the principle of revolutionary generality (on which more below) that one might mistake Ambedkar's moral perfectionism for hostility if one does not carefully follow his formidable attempt to subordinate the pernicious desire for mastery (that inheres in all republicanisms ancient and modern) to the force of obligation and virtue, which had come to saturate his rhetoric and theory of justice in the late 1930s and early 1940s. It was in this sense that works as varied as *Annihilation of Caste* and *Thoughts on Pakistan*, not to leave out *Philosophy of Hinduism*, carried a common insurrectionary strain fundamental to Ambedkar's politics and ethics.

The tension between justice and force lies at the very foundation of any thinking, republican or otherwise, that can be called "modern." Beginning with Montaigne and Pascal, down to those figures that Ambedkar read and absorbed more directly in the interwar years (especially Rousseau, Burke, Marx, Nietzsche, Dewey, and Bergson) the relationship between "just force" and "brute force" has been a precarious one.[24] The political philosopher Jacques Rancière, following the work of Hannah Arendt, has recently tried to work through this classic tension in a counterintuitive fashion. Rather than seeing it as a goal whose pursuit should be as fair and just as possible, Rancière imagines equality as an irreducible presupposition of a just politics.[25] Equality for Rancière is not a category that might be placed within the teleological pursuit of the greatest good, as it is within the liberalism. In fact, it is neither an ambition nor an end. Equality is just there, inalienable and fundamental, at the foundation of any moral and political principle, made visible during the people's autonomous—and at times, precarious—acts of breakage and force, which he associates with the productive power of disagreement. Any regime or society needs to draw, in howsoever superficial a form, its legitimation from this irrefutable "egalitarian presupposition," this precariousness of force that the people, even the most disenfranchised, rightfully contain within themselves. In Ambedkar, there was in such enunciations of force always an acute awareness of vulnerability, always a deep resolve to resist the wrong committed precisely by institutions and structures that claimed in spirit to be egalitarian (in their distribution of goods or ordering of spaces); a resolve he expressed by claiming the "weak force" of the most unequal, most excluded, and which lent his thought a rather singular energy, one that was never afraid to question the over-constitutionalization of the political itself. This is also a chapter, then, on the methodological extremism central to Ambedkar's difficulty with the concept and rhetoric of constitutional authority.[26]

As an event that inaugurated this strand of thinking, perhaps every word, every sentence in *Annihilation of Caste* demands a careful archeology. By "archeology," I do not only mean recovering the motivations behind the prophetic or even intermittently apocalyptic language of the treatise, a feature that *Annihilation of Caste* shares strongly with a work considered radically heterogeneous to it, the explicitly political philosophical *Thoughts on Pakistan*. Rather, by archeology, I mean tracing those extremities that Ambedkar's moral and political thought traversed—sometimes in ways unknown to him—in the period between 1936 and 1945. One of my intentions is to provide a genealogy of the Indian political slightly different from what C. A. Bayly has called, in a reading that privileges a fundamental consensus—even deep intellectual unity—over radical dissent, the "advent of constitutional liberalism in India."[27] But in what follows, I am concerned not as much with the resonances and departures of Indian liberalism from its European roots and countercurrents, a capacious tradition to which Ambedkar has been consigned for a long time. Rather, I explore the material, cognitive, and moral nuances of Ambedkar's thinking of freedom as such. In the process, I hope, will emerge not only a more global genealogy of radical democracy but also a more inclusive (and textured) understanding of the relationship between force and justice, insurrection and constitution.

Touched by Law

Certainly, the complete failure by the middle of the 1930s of his conversation with liberal reformers and nationalists, which made his conversion to another religion only a matter of time, had been politically disappointing for Ambedkar. But conceptually, the failure only intensified his fearless approach to politics, spurring him into probing the limits of anticolonial political thought and practice and pushing its moral certitude to its breaking point, forcing him to craft a new language of action that would be alive, as he put it, to the silences and exclusions that even a mention of caste produced in what was otherwise the greatest mobilization in the history of anticolonial struggles. The question, in the aftermath of the Poona Pact with Gandhi, was not merely of his recent defeat but of its prehistory, one that transcended the dialectic of nation and empire. In fact, as we have seen, Ambedkar brilliantly radicalizes his own defeat by positing it as yet another symptom of the defeatism built into India's ancient constitution itself. The question, in other words, was not just of the colonial-nationalist betrayals of the present but the historicity of their sovereignty over the past. For him, it had become urgent to reveal not merely the sovereignty of one tradition over another, the rule of one nation over another, but the invisible operations of sovereignty as such. It was this urgency that imparted to *Annihilation of Caste* its exemplary grammar of force.

All are slaves of the Caste System. But all the slaves are not equal in status. To excite the proletariat to bring about an economic revolution, Karl Marx told them "You have nothing to lose except your chains." But the artful way in which the social and religious rights are distributed among the different castes whereby some have more and some have less, makes the slogan of Karl Marx quite useless to excite the Hindus against the Caste System. Castes form a graded system of sovereignties, high and low, which are jealous of their status and which know that if a general dissolution came, some of them stand to lose more of their prestige and power than others do. You cannot, therefore, have a general mobilization of the Hindus, to use a military expression, for an attack on the Caste System.[28]

For a work considered to be so militantly egalitarian in its logic, it is striking that *Annihilation of Caste* also establishes, in the most unequivocal fashion, its author's profound disinterest in abstract conceptions of equality and substitution. What makes such conceptions inadequate to a spiritual revolution, Ambedkar argues, is the careful juridical gradation of equals and unequals, the free and unfree, within the moral law of four *varnas* (*Chaturvarnya*). The magic of this system is that nobody except the most damned and untouchable, the *atishudra*, is denied liberty, and yet nobody is not enslaved either. *Chaturvarnya* is not a merely vertical regime of force; it is a sly nexus of inducements, alliances, and obligations. And it is this mystical enslavement, this moving web of jealousies, complicities, and dependencies between the oppressor and the oppressed, man and woman, animal and human, that makes a general mobilization of the multitude at once difficult and imperative. The solution to the problem of caste lies, then, not in simply substituting a regime of juridical untouchability with that of a rule-bound and measured touchability between virtuous persons. For touching, which is each time singular and irreproducible, which always changes more than just one's own self and is therefore always under the purview of the law (implicated in the obligations, autonomies, and boundaries between oneself and others), is not merely a mode of contact, not merely one sense among others. In India since antiquity, it has been the axial sense around which all other senses and relationships, all laws of contact and distance, has been organized. Touching here was not simply a gesture or force; it was that which made experience intelligible. It was that which gave experience over to language— social, ethical, juridicial—as such. It was the tongue in which all social and ethical relationships were experienced and expressed. Not confined simply to tactile encounters, the corporeal and moral empiricism of touch has come to condense within itself an entire universe of sensations, one in which not simply sight but even breathing—indeed, utterances and words (*vach*) that spread with one's breath—have come to be seen as "means of contact." This is why the classical ban on touching, Ambedkar insists, belonged neither to the order of sensations and social relations nor to the regime of legal permissions and injunctions regulated by the government. Instead, its laws (of sight, smell, and breath)—and any attempt, such as Gandhi's, to reform it through a new phenomenology of everyday life—belonged to the moral law of sovereignty alone. Touching belonged to the unimpeachable order of rules and commands that could be comprehended (and critiqued) only by grasping the force of theological metaphors and transcendental truths.

If contact in the Indic traditions cannot be reduced simply to flesh touching flesh, if even breathing and sight are sensory extensions of touching, then, how could touching as such, Ambedkar asks, be reduced to the logic— and reformed merely through an ethics—of presence and proximity? How could emancipation from untouchability be accomplished merely by a new sociality and routine of touching, or worse, simply by another name? On the contrary, the "untouchable," insists Ambedkar, must be called *untouchable* in order precisely to render unconditionally audible the "wrong" that this figure, sound, and word stood for, every time it was uttered. "There is also the feeling that the name Harijan is indicative of pity," he writes in his critique of Gandhi's gesture. "If the name meant 'chosen people of God' as the Jews claimed themselves to be it would have been a different matter. But to call them 'children of God' is to invite pity from their tyrants by pointing out their helplessness and their dependent condition."[29]

This was not the only instance in which Ambedkar had mobilized the allegory of the Old Testament against Gandhi's preference for the New. Nor was it the only instance of his invoking freedom of movement and exodus against Gandhi's rhetoric of civilization and dwelling. But before we turn to exile, escape, wandering, and visa, I want to stay a little longer with the relationship—or rather, the absolute nonrelation—between Ambedkar's conception of freedom and the theologico-political laws of touching. How could one be free to touch, he asks, without the emancipation of freedom itself from the constraints and measures of the law? After all, to touch in India—that is to say, to belong to a caste—is not merely a matter of inhabiting (or being barred from) the world of senses. It is to implicate oneself in the "categorical imperative" of the transcendental law. It is to invite on oneself the wrath of sovereign power. The truly untouchable, in fact, is not the untouchable person, argues Ambedkar, but the moral law, *dharma*, that renders him as such. It is the sacred authority of the law, its punitive and disciplinary limits, *maryada dharma*, which is the absolute untouchable. "The interdictions relating to the sacred are binding on all," whether "touchable" or "untouchable," citizen or noncitizen, Ambedkar writes in a striking passage in *The Untouchables* (1948). "They are not maxims. They are injunctions. They are obligatory but not in the ordinary sense of the word. They partake of the nature of a categorical imperative. Their breach is more than a crime. It is a sacrilege."[30]

This remains the clearest exposition of Ambedkar's resistance against the Kantian "categorical imperative" (an expression he often used in a disapproving sense). His resistance, that is, against Kant's notion that the faculty of obedience to the law—the moral person's ability to answer the call of duty without exception—stems from the universality of moral being, one that must be the same everywhere, autonomous of the sensuous world of passion, anger, and temptation; and that the failure to follow this transcendental call of duty—the failure to not just identify in law an unimpeachable call of obligation but to make law the extension of one's very own will (over and above personal opinion)—suggests a failure of a person's moral imagination. For Ambedkar, categorical imperatives that manage, through legal injunctions, the everyday proximity and distance between people in civic spaces, the imperatives of *dharma* that render millions sacred and untouchable, belong to the domain of legal violence and authority, not the shared spaces of moral virtue and responsibility. For they regulate the everyday relationship of citizens to sovereign power through the mediating force of the moral law. And this law is transcendental; its regulative ideal touches everyone (but differently); its strictures have to be respected and revered as if they were untouchable. "The Sacred," writes Ambedkar elsewhere, "creates the sentiment of Reverence. It also creates the sentiment that it is inviolate. When a belief becomes consecrated as a sacred thing"—that is, when belief turns irreligious and insinuates itself as the law—"it is forbidden to touch it, to deny it or to contest it. There is a prohibition of criticism of the Sacred. The Sacred is 'untouchable' and above discussion."[31]

This critique of the law as categorical imperative returns with even greater force in *The Untouchables*, when Ambedkar finally takes up the most material, most political, most modern, example among the exclusions of *dharma*. If "the sacred is untouchable in that it is beyond the pale of debate," he writes (paraphrasing and then going immediately beyond Durkheim), then such a law secures, equally tightly, its own punitive and anthropological reversal: the juridical apotheosis of the untouchable human as sacred.[32] Gandhi's consecration of the untouchable as *harijan*, then, was not simply a gesture of contact, the sign of an everyday ethics of touching. Instead, it belonged to the world of discipline (*maryada*) and obedience, to the practice of tact, measure, and the law. Note, for instance, the sensitivity with which Ambedkar distinguishes between religious sacrilege and secular crime, only to quickly reveal their insidious connection forged by the law that moves between them, so that, in his own account of legal violence, theological metaphors relentlessly jostle with juridical ones. Indeed, any rigorous critique of violence, Ambedkar suggests, must first and foremost eschew the (secularist) distinction between civil and sacred religion, between the immanent and transcendent. For this was a world in which civic ban had been lent the sacred aura of a punishing law, where crime in the "ordinary sense of the word" was seen to transgress against nothing less than transcendental will and thus threatened with disproportionate force, and where religious injunctions on movement and contact had been instituted not merely as corporeal interdictions in the republican sense but as laws of cognitive servitude—a strange servitude, as Ambedkar argues in "Krishna and His Gita," for its blame and shame were put on the unequal's own failure to cultivate in his person the faculty of obedience to the moral law.

In revealing the juridical foundations of the unequal's guilt and placing it at the center of his own attempt to formulate another sovereignty, the later Ambedkar also begins to move toward a distinctive conception of autonomy, one in which one's own freedom could be had, authentically, guiltlessly, immeasurably, only in relation to—and through one's responsibility toward—the freedom of others. There was a lesson for conservative nationalists and theorists of *dharma* here, especially those who were all too willing to put the responsibility—and guilt—for Gandhi's death (during his epic fast in 1932) on Ambedkar's sense of autonomy, his ability to conceptualize another freedom, another justice, itself. Guilt at once secured the legitimacy of illegitimate powers and sustained the conditions of voluntary—cognitive and corporeal—servitude of citizens. In placing its operations in the interstices between power and consent, in revealing guilt as the zone of inseparability between corporeal oppression and the psychological acquiescence (of the oppressed) that made it possible, Ambedkar makes a radical break from those strands of classical philosophy—Platonism and *advaita* Hinduism, for instance—that separate the domain of spirit from that of matter, the realm of the intelligible (of moral faculty and duty guided by transcendental ideals, autonomous of the messiness of everyday life) from the domain of the sensible (which harbors everyday experiences, senses, desires, passions, and fallibilities). And it was in his struggle against this anthropological separation of the sensible from the intelligible—a separation that the unequal, the outcaste, the noncitizen is purportedly unable to make and thus gives himself voluntarily to domination—that the seeds of Ambedkar's irreconcilable difference with revolutionary socialists and nationalist reformers of his time were sown.

Those who most strongly defend the public use of reason, Ambedkar argues, are often most strategically blind to the punitive exclusions of everyday experience, often cognitively unfree to rebel against barriers erected by the invisible functioning of customary reason. To these liberal reformers and theorists of class warfare alike, the exercise of reason somehow seemed to transcend, even justify, the hierarchical laws—violent or nonviolent—that regulated their own inhuman conduct. Before every other measure and calculation, reason itself, Ambedkar insists, must be freed from these arrogant exclusions of higher truths, from these hierarchies of categorical imperatives and abstract universals such as class, nation, property, and state. Before a republic of equals could be born, reason's internal partitions and injunctions (encrusted on public consciousness as moral law) must be subjected to the free, shared, and if need be, sacrificial, morals of everyday life.[33] Sacrilege, heresy, sacrifice, conversion, escape, exodus: these words appeared so frequently, so forcefully, in Ambedkar's writings, then, not because he had an instrumental relationship with religion, as if, imprisoned by the framework of a secular theology, he could see the usefulness of faith only because it secured the ground for civic liberties and restitution. On the contrary, these words appeared precisely when he was most religious, unsure, on the one hand, whether religion could be ever freed from its complicity with republican forms of sovereignty, and yet, on the other, unwilling to concede the ethical ground—and the language of vulnerability and sacrifice common to religion and republican democracy—too easily to majoritarian fanatics. Like Rousseau, perhaps, Ambedkar wanted to have the people at once annihilate by force the intermediary nature and interest of the law and yet have them retain a touch of their vulnerability and virtue, even weakness.

After all, the passage on slavery in *Annihilation of Caste* I quoted earlier had provoked its readers precisely because of its radical combination of militaristic energy and moral virtue, its republican language of citizenship, sovereignty, and mobilization rarely straying too far from religious invocations of fraternity, sacrifice, and belief. What makes *Annihilation of Caste* such a singular text—and a text on "singularity," as Gandhi might have said—is not simply its egalitarian ethics. Instead, the nationalist reader wonders, why freedom from caste servitude, which could be as easily formulated in the liberal language of freedom as noninterference, must be proclaimed in the language of such immense and intense force (especially when it is mobilized against the very idea of domination and mastery), delivered through the parables of sacrificial virtue and fraternal mobilization so unreconcilable with the kind of restitutive politics—the humanism that bases itself in the desire to prolong life—with which Ambedkar is often hastily associated. "You cannot, therefore," Ambedkar warns, "have a general mobilization of the Hindus, to use a military expression, for an attack on the Caste System."

This is indeed the classically republican—or, shall we say, theologico-political—bond between an armed (and free) citizenry and the everyday possibilities of virtuous conduct, between life that is fraternally shared and death that is fraternally gifted, that often compels both Ambedkar and Gandhi to discern in the struggle for equality something of a warlike condition: a condition in which equality, to become worthy of equals, has to be at war with its own meanings, at war with those abstract laws that confine equality to citizens and brothers alone. Unconditional equality—equality in the sharing of freedom—requires, on the other hand, an absolute respect for the autonomy of incommensurable others, different and indifferent strangers alike. Only in fulfilling its moral obligation toward neighbors, strangers, and enemies as equals—that is, in absolute relinquishment of mastery, as Ambedkar would come to subsequently insist in *The Buddha and His Dhamma*—could the citizen open the ground for the constitution and science of a sovereign republic. Thus, the proclamation during the Constituent Assembly debates in 1949, "fraternity can be a fact only when there is a nation"—or even more unequivocally, "caste is anti-national"—renders the social cruelty and exclusion sanctioned by caste into a political problem; hierarchy is now a matter not of social reform but of the republic's sovereignty. In fact, for Ambedkar, the moral integrity of the republic depends on ensuring the autonomy of the most vulnerable and excluded constituents among those who bring it into existence.[34]

There were, of course, others whose republicanism came to be instituted, in the 1920s and 1930s, around an equally revolutionary critique of the relationship between formal freedom and material exclusions, between religious obligation and voluntary servitude that lay at the core of India's ancient constitution. Among them was the young Bhagat Singh of the Hindustan Socialist Republican Army, who placed colonial property relations (as opposed to the problem of India's religious diversity) at the center of his revolutionary war against the empire. "Let us declare," Singh wrote in a letter to the British governor of the Punjab, "that the problem of war does exist and shall exist so long as the Indian toiling masses and the natural resources are being exploited by a handful of parasites."[35] Singh's internationalist equanimity refused to distinguish these capitalist parasites by their nationality. "They may be purely British capitalist or mixed British and Indian or even purely Indian," he argued. But it was precisely this militant anti-capitalist universalism that obscured for Singh and other socialists the most material of truths: that even the laws and forces of capital touched the multitude in India differently, divisively, unequally. In fact, here law touched the weakest by *not* touching. For in India, touching was neither an innocent gesture, nor was it merely an expression of desire. Instead, it was a question of life and death, a feeble dividing line between civility and cruelty across which one quickly, insidiously, gave way to the other.

Touching, we have seen Gandhi insist, was also a craft, a force marked by discrimination, judgment, and precision around which lay a whole web of disciplinary limits and responsibilities. Unlike any other society, there was in India a spiritual and material density attached to touching that far exceeded the bounds of mere life. Touching could not simply be a gesture that might help bridge the immense difference and hierarchy within an ancient civilization. Touching was itself an abyss of difference, an act of separation. "The Hindu," Ambedkar writes in his unfinished autobiography, "would prefer to be inhuman rather than touch an untouchable."[36] It was this juridico-theological ban on touch, that most irreducible, originary, even primordial of senses, that made a new moral ontology necessary; an ontology that might yield a citizen capable of cultivating virtue and autonomy, willing to see force where there was only oppression and forcelessness; an ontology that might bring into view a new freedom that held the promise to transcend, through a singular act of faith, the juridico-theological distinctions between caste and outcaste, self and nonself.

In Chapter 7, we shall see this critique of the self mature in Ambedkar's later writings into a morally thick conception of justice, one that would come to be grounded in the citizen's awareness of the finitude of human and nonhuman others. Here, I want to follow the thread that connects this theory of justice with that other concept that mediates for Ambedkar the relationship between oneself and another most intimately, namely, freedom. Within this

non-nationalist conception of freedom—which has been shaped, in all revolutionary and constitutional traditions, by the desire to solve social questions
by political means, by the need to narrow the distance between the everyday
life of the people and the state, by the general will to bridge the separation of
equality from freedom—the multitude's demand for justice was never easily
separable from the practices and rhetoric of sovereignty of the republic. The
weakest, Ambedkar argued, have always had to take advantage of the revolutionary possibilities that the republic and its contradictions have offered,
transforming, as in Rome, the laws of mastery into formulae of an egalitarian freedom. If the multitude's "right of disruption," its duty of fraternal and
civic disobedience against illegitimate laws, was for Ambedkar always a question of a national state, then it was so only inasmuch as shared freedom—
the positive freedom (and, indeed, sovereignty) of equals—could be framed
in terms of republican virtue alone; in terms, that is, of the obligations and
truth of those vulnerable citizens and noncitizens for whom freedom is not
simply a material and corporeal necessity that secured their liberty of movement, activity, and life (free from domination by others). Freedom is for them
the inalienable ground for leading an ethical life; it is a space where even the
outcaste and unequal live by principles; it is their way (and right) of forging
a moral and physical relationship with others. There was little work that an
internationalism of Communist vintage could do for this conception of sovereignty rooted in moral virtues, desires, and responsibilities of everyday life.
The vision of this politics was irrefutably republican, but only in the most insurrectionary sense of the term, lodged between the demand for social citizenship on national scale (franchise being its least important if most easily visible
and identifiable institutional expression) and an anarchic refusal to be governed by the hierarchical norms and laws of Hindu *dharma*. It was precisely
for the most vulnerable citizens of the republic, citizens who could be quickly
reduced to outcastes and noncitizens, citizens who could be turned from millions to fractions, neighbors to strangers, just by a turn of divine mood or an
evidence of theological statute, that freedom could not simply be a plea for
nondomination. Freedom for them had to be an anarchic—indeed, annihilative—principle, a moral duty, an act of faith, grounded, one might argue following Hannah Arendt, in the right to have rights.

Only a citizen secure in this anarchic principle, in the immeasurable
autonomy of will, could refuse to be governed by unjust laws and choose, as
Ambedkar threatens, to exit the republic itself. "The injustice and suffering
inflicted upon us by this land are so enormous," Ambedkar had told Gandhi
tersely in 1931, "that if knowingly or unknowingly we fall prey to disloyalty to
this country, the responsibility for that act would be solely hers." There was

not a hint of apology here, just a resolute, even fierce, reclamation of moral responsibility from the corruptions of nationalism. "If at all," Ambedkar finished, with Gandhi reportedly forced to listen as the moment of rare moral defeat—and Ambedkar's refusal of his moralizing benevolence—dawned on him, "I have rendered any national service as you say . . . to the patriotic cause of this country, it is due to my unsullied conscience and not due to any patriotic feelings in me."[37] It should not be surprising, then, that Ambedkar, even as he emerged as the foremost constitutionalist of his time, would remain forever at odds with the dominant institutional structures of those times, especially large political parties designed for electoral success in large republics, while Gandhi, the solitary practitioner, would never be more dependent on those institutions than when he spoke of the rules and practices of the self. For Ambedkar, at any rate, to think of the republic was not the same as delimiting the political within the boundaries of the nation; and to formulate the conditions of constituent power—that is, of sovereignty at its most popular, most insurrectionary, most anarchic—not necessarily the same as celebrating just any constitution. It certainly did not entail celebrating the constitution received as gift from masters and oppressors.[38] "Let the consent of the people," he exhorted at the London Round Table Conference just months before his first meeting with Gandhi, "and not the accident of logic be the touchstone of your new constitution, if you desire it should be worked."[39]

By the time of the Poona Pact, which was negotiated and signed with Gandhi just over a year later, the myth of Ambedkar's divisiveness had come to be so deeply entrenched among nationalists that any possibility that *Annihilation of Caste* might be approached from outside the framework of caste, any openness to the crisis of faith (and thus, to the death of virtue and civility) in India it was trying to warn against, was defeated in advance. In return, Ambedkar, rather than following the course of a remorseful politics, raised the intensity of his language further, fashioning his rhetoric around the language of crisis itself. In 1945, for instance, he placed "crisis" among the most potent cognitive and material levers of revolutionary force. "The salvation," he declared in a religious vein, "will come only when the Caste Hindu is made to think and is forced to feel that he must alter his ways. For that you must create a crisis by direct action against his customary code of conduct. . . . The great defect in the policy of least resistance and silent infiltration of rational ideas lies in this that they do not compel thought, for they do not produce crisis."[40]

There was more than a trace of Romanticism here, one that impelled Ambedkar, in a tendency borrowed from Marx's own Romanticist affinities, to see in spiritual and material crisis the opportunity of a revolutionary strike, a potential for usurpation of apparatuses of domination, the state even, and a moment of radical appropriation of the political by highlighting the rifts in its founding norms and social alliances. The redemptive value of a crisis, Ambedkar believed, lay in the unequal's not having to wait for an external force to unleash an annihilative strike against systems of exclusion and domination. On the contrary, crisis, whether moral, political, or cognitive—such as the one that he foresaw taking form around the Pakistan question (and was proven tragically right six years later)—allowed the "harnessing" of insurrectionary and disruptive force from within the material contradictions and forces of civilizational and religious structures. During such revolutionary conjunctures, means rather than the pursuit of ends were alone integral to the act. "I have emphasized this question of the ways and means of destroying caste," let us recall again that crucial proposition, "because I think that knowing the proper ways and means is more important that knowing the ideal."[41]

The temptation to see freedom in the purity of means was not the sole cause of the nearly apocalyptic turn in *Thoughts on Pakistan*, in which a militant and remorseless conception of popular sovereignty is aligned with the corporeal discourse reminiscent of classical republicanism. Freedom within this early modern discourse is defined first and foremost as the freedom of corporeal movement. For Hobbes especially (and the political tradition that has since followed him), freedom has often simply meant the absence of physical interference and restraints on the mobility of the human subject.[42] Pakistan, Ambedkar prophesizes, just six years before the violent partition of the subcontinent would take over a million lives and displace close to ten million, was the territorial and "spiritual destiny" of Muslims, who must be granted the right to move there as soon as they had formulated their desire to do so. In the revised edition, published four years later, he added an additional fifth part with three new chapters. Tempering his initial suggestion, which had been couched in a vocabulary drawn from Renan and Toynbee, he now concedes that there was nothing inevitable about the foundation of a separate Muslim homeland in the subcontinent. Such a homeland, however, was no less necessary now, he argues, than it was when he had first published *Thoughts on Pakistan*. Indeed, a homeland must still be granted to the Muslims, if only because respect for (and an ineradicable mutual fear generated by) the religious differences that divided the two communities—and even more crucially, the safety of the republic against the threat of a potentially catastrophic civil war—demanded it.[43] Otherwise, went the unbridled warning, formulated in a manner not very different from Gandhi's discourse on *Ramarajya*,

The spread of that virus of dualism in the body politic must some day create a mentality which is sure to call for a life and death struggle for the dissolution of this forced union. If by reason of some superior force the dissolution does not take place, one thing is sure to happen to India—namely, that this continued union will go on sapping her vitality, loosening its cohesion, weakening its hold on the love and faith of her people and preventing the use, if not retarding the growth, of its moral and—material resources. India will be an anemic and sickly state, ineffective, a living corpse, dead though not buried.[44]

We are now, clearly, in the vicinity of a rather different approach to the relationship between touching and law, body and sovereignty. But there are continuities too. For this motif of a body dead but not buried, haunting the republic like a deathless ghost, which invariably emerges around Ambedkar's struggle with the laws of force, we have seen in Chapter 3, dates back to his formative days in New York. And the amplification of the symbolic dimensions of the multitude's energy is as integral a part of this struggle as the emphasis on the material dimensions of everyday exclusion; it is a strategy in which the promise of the emancipated future comes to be wagered on an apocalyptic and corporeal diagnosis of the crisis-ridden present. Equality and freedom might be unified in such moments, according to Ambedkar, neither by recourse to the established norms of "government's civility," as Gandhi terms it, thereby rendering civility (*sadachar*) itself innocent of the invisible hierarchies and cruelties on which its rules were founded,[45] nor by offering platitudes of formal pluralism, which, for Ambedkar, only weaken rather than strengthen "the love and faith of a people." Instead, equality and freedom might be rendered inseparable only by revealing those mystical spaces where rules of civility had themselves been used to conceal the marks of greatest fear, violence, and unfreedom. Indeed, freedom could thrive only under conditions in which difference, with all its centrifugal tendencies, was truthfully restored to the theater of the political, the diversity of the multitude's lives allowed to thrive together by nothing other than their shared finitude, the heterogeneity of their beliefs arbitrated only in a battlefield of equally prepared neighbors.

This way of conceptualizing freedom, as Ambedkar himself concedes in the preface to the second edition of *Thoughts on Pakistan*, was clearly untimely. It was bound to wound the sensitivities of friends and opponents alike, not to mention its potential to stoke those nationalist conservatives who had always seen in Ambedkar a theorist of division as opposed to a thinker of difference. Yet *Thoughts on Pakistan* was untimely not simply because its grammar and syntax had tried to interweave the gloom of crisis and partition with that of life and equality between neighbors, the imminence of war with the hope for authentic civility between nations, the blood-spilling transcendence of sacrifice with the authentic freedom of vulnerable mortals.

It was untimely also because its notion of freedom itself had broken away decisively from the framework of nationalist and imperial sovereignty, away from those sovereignties that were grounded, as Ambedkar believed, in visions of a centralizing juridical state.

"If the Hindus are hoping that the British will use force to put down Pakistan, that is impossible," he writes, dismissing the morality of arbitrations and decisions initiated by any party other than the two religious communities that were going to be most affected by a new Muslim homeland in the subcontinent. "Coercion, as an alternative to Pakistan, is therefore unthinkable. Again, the Muslims cannot be deprived of the benefit of self-determination." Thus, he declares, "the matter must, therefore, be decided upon by the Muslims and the Hindus alone. The British cannot decide the issue for them."[46] This must be a freedom, whenever it comes, without measure and mediation, one whose risks, Ambedkar confesses, have always haunted the modern political tradition. After all, this freedom seeks a foundation for the social state grounded in the unmediated sovereignty—which is to say, decision—of a fraternal, armed, and perennially war-ready council of equal citizens alone. The inspiration behind this vision of the armed citizen, this grammar of "general mobilization" of the multitude, especially of the most unequal within it, let us recall, is familiarly Rousseauist. And its perils, as they have stalked republican constitutionalisms of various inspirations since the Jacobin experiment, are fairly substantive, perils that are most strongly evident to Ambedkar himself. For all the passion that his vision of the armed republic marshals, in fact, *Thoughts on Pakistan* is no less sensitive to the vulnerability of ordinary people in Muslim-majority provinces of British India; people who, caught in the web of colonial and nationalist machinations, were soon left in a legal limbo, a space where they might count neither as citizens of a republic nor otherwise. Thus, that striking turn later in the book toward unmediated decision, referendum, direct democracy. "It must be left to be decided by the people who are living in those areas and who will have to bear the consequences of so violent, so revolutionary and so fundamental a change in the political and economic system."[47] Now, this is not the only thread running through the vast swath of Ambedkar's interwar writings. It is certainly not the only thread running through *Annihilation of Caste*. And yet the methodological extremism, the passion to take freedom, beyond all norms and limits, to its ontological extremities, an impulse that *Thoughts on Pakistan* would come to exemplify in all its risk and violence, would never be easily separable from the revolutionary energies of *Annihilation of Caste* that had given it birth.

A Methodological Extremism

Perhaps more than any other concept, perhaps unknown to Ambedkar himself, by the late 1930s, it is "annihilation" as the figure, trope, and word for radical autonomy that seems to most effectively represent the heterogeneous, tensed, and inseparable elements of Ambedkar's moral and political thought. On the one hand, there is the Burkean formula "the use of force is but temporary," which underlines, as early as his Round Table speeches in London in 1930–1931, Ambedkar's commitment to freedom as nondomination, centered on the authority and security of a constitutional republic.[48] On the other hand, the word reveals in no uncertain terms his belief in revolutionary sovereignty grounded in the constituent power of the multitude alone, in a people's responsibility to annihilate all rules, injunctions, and laws that bar them from the world of sense, in the citizen's right to nourish, freely and equally, the principles of a virtuous life. Annihilation was, in that sense, the soul of an immeasurable faith, the "essence of a truly religious act."

One discerns in Ambedkar's thought at this time a radical circularity, often entailing a movement of concepts and arguments from one center of ostensible excess to another. One might begin anywhere in this circle, but I have suggested beginning with an examination of that inflammatory classic, *Thoughts on Pakistan* (1941), because it is there that Ambedkar gives his principle of autonomy and virtue its most unbridled republican form. This republicanism was influenced by dramatically different texts, from the utilitarian Henry Sidgwick's *Elements of Politics* (1891), with its theory of the "right of disruption," to Rousseau's *The Social Contract, or Principles of Political Right* (1762), with its incandescent formulation of the general will as the sole ground of individual freedom (an idea that had itself marked the most galvanizing eighteenth-century reversal of classical liberalism).[49] What Ambedkar truly inherits from Rousseau and gives it his singular energy, however, is the latter's conviction that it needs just one religion and its pernicious theologico-political power, just one faith and its mystical capacity to intrude into the moral and social relations of the people, to destroy the possibility of an egalitarian citizenship. Hinduism becomes for Ambedkar what Christianity had been for Rousseau, or for that matter, for Hobbes. A third horizon was opened around the nineteenth-century radical liberalism of George Grote, whose *History of Greece* (1856) and affinity for direct democracy, crucial to Ambedkar's elaborations on "constitutional morality," would further amplify his difficulty with the negative conception of freedom (that is, with freedom understood simply as noninterference).

I will return to Ambedkar's elaborations on the insurrectionary aspects of constituent power later in the chapter. In this section, I want to stay with the excessive dimensions of his political thought. And it is in *Thoughts on Pakistan*, along with certain parts of *States and Minorities* (1947), where a historic tension within classical republicanism comes to be articulated in Ambedkar's own relationship with that tradition in full force: the tension between the universalist/federalist "rights of citizen" and the conservative/centripetal logic of territorial security. Ambedkar's prophetic if incendiary warning about a perennial civil war and police action in free India had emerged from this moment in his encounter with republican theory. "So long as the hostility to one Central Government for India, which is the ideology underlying Pakistan, persists," he warns in a moment that captures the centripetal logic of *Thoughts on Pakistan* in the most vertiginous fashion, "the ghost of Pakistan will loom, casting its ominous shadow upon the political future of India."[50]

And yet, for all its warnings about the specter of Muslim difference, this logic never ceased to be haunted by Ambedkar's own dramatic formulation of popular force, one in which the indivisible sovereignty of republican vintage was replaced by a call for divisibility, division, and insurrection. Force divided itself further—divisibility was its very essence—separating, for instance, the multitude's "right of insurrection" from its "right of disruption." The right of insurrection, Ambedkar argues, is geared toward government reform and might be associated with civic revolution, civil disobedience, or civil war. The right of disruption, potentially catastrophic, belongs to the order of eviction or annihilation and so demanded another state altogether. Only through the right of disruption might a people's "spiritual essence"—the "invisible hand" of their national and geopolitical destiny—be restored in a truly republican form. Pakistan, insists Ambedkar, deserves this right to disrupt India; indeed, it has the moral obligation to do so. Its excision from India alone might ensure that all future antagonisms are resolved, even and especially at war, within the bounds of civility befitting two equals. Such egalitarian war between neighbors, each safe within its own territory even if each was at perennial risk from the outside, would be more ethical, truer to the logic of fidelity and sacrifice, than the ceaseless specter of distrust, deterrence, and civil war that might otherwise haunt from within a polity kept united by little else than governmental (soulless and illegitimate) force.[51]

Viewed through the lens—or placed solely within the context—of the interwar minority problem, let alone within the framework of anticolonial nationalism, *Thoughts on Pakistan*, it is not surprising, shows itself to be remorselessly divisive. But context cannot substitute for the fullness (and irresolutions) of meaning. And when we seek out meaning, there emerges a much more enduring, painstaking, and (despite the rhetorical hyperbole) even hesitant engagement with the ethics of sovereignty. Ambedkar tries at once to contain this ethics within his principle of autonomy as responsibility, within his idea of virtuous citizenship grounded in the liberty of noncitizens—that involves, we have seen, an insurrectionary, interpretive *coup de force* against territorial and juridical norms of politics—and yet, ineluctably, gives this sovereignty over to an equally classical republican discourse on sacrifice, security, and war.

Sovereignty, Ambedkar argues, is reducible neither to geopolitical interest nor indivisible states. It is neither a spiritual monopoly of nationalism nor simply a theory of governmental unity. Rather, sovereignty belongs to the order of incommensurability and difference; it belongs to divisibility and imperfection. "Notwithstanding the efforts made to bring the creeds together by reformers like Akbar and Kabir," he recalls, "the ethical realities behind each have still remained, to use a mathematical phrase, which nothing can alter or make integers capable of having a common denominator."[52] An uncompromising critic of discrimination had turned, then, toward the power of a discriminating politics, deploying what appears to be a prejudice against the Muslim neighbor with a peculiarly mathematical vehemence. And yet, in the same stroke, as if in a virtual circle, Ambedkar attempts to replace the history of two warring religions with an ethics of militant neighborliness between them. This argument of neighborliness never veers too far from concerns about the security of the republic. If the Muslim warrior could not be trustfully deployed in the troublesome, Muslim-majority areas of the republic's northwestern frontiers, Ambedkar asks, for instance, wasn't his expulsion from the armed forces key to the future security of the state?

To understand the longevity—and classicism—of this precarious logic within which history Ambedkar had placed himself, let us simply recall Bentham, who appears in a quotation in the newly added chapter 14 of the second edition of *Thoughts on Pakistan*.[53] "What is liberty?" Bentham had asked a hundred years earlier in his *Rationale of Judicial Evidence* (1843). "Security is the political blessing I have in view, security as against malefactors on the one hand, security as against the instruments of government on the other."[54] Note the fragile balance between autonomy and safety. In fact, Bentham's proposition exemplifies the near impossibility of freedom—its ultimate founding and loss—whenever it has been posited, as it has been in all humanistic traditions, in relation to political power; freedom has suffered every time its permanence has been wagered on the struggle for or against the state, on the security and infinitude of life that the sovereign promises to guarantee.

As he expresses his discomfort with the idea of continuing with Muslim regiments in the armed forces of free India, Ambedkar nearly paraphrases

Bentham, "A safe army is better than a safe border."[55] When deployed in the "troublesome" Muslim majority provinces of India's northwest, the loyalty of these regiments would always remain vulnerable against the mutinous call of their faith.[56] Safer, he advises then, to separate the armies too, safer to have an identifiable and hostile neighbor—indeed, it would be ethical and egalitarian to let a scenario of war among free equals unfold periodically along India's western borders—than to harbor a perennial threat of mutiny led by religiously susceptible soldiers from within. How much of Ambedkar's reasoning had been inherited from the deep British distrust of the armed Muslim magnates of colonial north India—that decadent and dying feudal nobility that had led in 1857 one of the most violent uprisings known to the British empire, and which was then systematically punished and excluded by the colonial government well until the end of the nineteenth century—we cannot clearly tell.[57] He certainly did not believe in the colonial myth that Muslims were any more skillful as warriors—even if they were less faithful—than the Mahars, the western Indian "untouchable" community to which he belonged and whose regiment had helped the East India Company quell the rebellion of 1857. At any rate, freedom's propensity to lapse into (or be confused with) an absolutist concern with security, a problem that has plagued the republican political tradition since its Greek and Roman inception, could not have been given a more sacrificial, war-bound form than it is in these arguments about immunizing the Indian armed forces.

With this grave prescription on security as the foundation of that potentially "explosive substance" called self-determination, in fact, we have arrived at the heart of Ambedkar's methodological extremism, a place where sovereignty is wagered at once on the tightening of republican indivisibility—framed within the discourse of a moral and militarized absolutism that brooks no interference, internal or external, in the liberty of its subjects—and on the insurrectionary right of the people to partition the commonwealth, their autonomy grounded in the fundamental and liberating divisibility of the republic itself.[58] If, as conventional readings of *Thoughts on Pakistan* might suggest, Ambedkar was prone to viewing sovereign power as necessarily indivisible and centralizing, there was an equally frequent reverse movement in his thought, one that posited the obligation to civic disobedience, and if need be, the right of insurrection, as the constitutive principle of citizenship. This was Ambedkar circling between potential extremes, then, oscillating between conservative excess and revolutionary austerity, refusing to let one overpower the other. I call this ethics "conservative" not because he seems invested in conserving the spiritual purity of the state, which is undeniably one impulse among many that seem to have vitiated the rhetoric of *Thoughts on Pakistan*.

Rather, I do so because at the center of this ethics is an attempt to conserve a semblance of freedom, even a radiant commonality between enemies, one which thrives precisely beyond the split, divided, and autonomous boundaries of the state. This revolutionary fraternity, this vision of brothers as warriors, which is never far from the imminence of war, is not predicated on civility as nonviolence. Instead, fraternal civility between equals thrives on a moral ontology of force, an ontology whose knowledge, skill, and craft lies—or has to be granted to—the weakest, most unequal, most defeated subjects of the republic. This was perhaps why Ambedkar displays an enigmatic sympathy for the defeated Hindu, while perversely imputing to the Muslim "hordes," throughout *Thoughts on Pakistan*, a spiritual exemplarity worthy of true warriors. It is clear that Ambedkar is drawn to the figure of the warrior citizen—another republican motif, even if it is not a solely Rousseauist one (one thinks of the Machiavellian construction of an armed citizenry)—as a transformative force. And yet, it is this very affinity that pushes him to set up the paradoxical equivalence between the world-making Islamic invader of medieval history and the static, reactionary, and rebellious oddity that was the modern Muslim subject.

Before I return to *Annihilation of Caste* in the sections that follow, let me lay out the emerging contours of what I have called Ambedkar's struggle to formulate the conditions of radical autonomy. This is necessary to understanding the full force of his conception of virtue, lest the idea of war he works with is mistaken with his predilection for hostility and conflict. Within this struggle, the possibility of virtuous rule is premised on the fragility and weakness, even illegitimacy, of sovereignty rather than on its permanence, its force —at its most just—drawn from the immanence of shared, equal, imperfect, and incommensurable lives rather than from the transcendence of civilizational rules and exclusions. What remains immortal, indivisible, and immanent to a people is neither their ineradicable difference nor their contingent syncretism. What remains immortal, amidst all their weakness and difference, instead, is force. This immortal force, conversely, stems from an unconditional equality of free citizens, which only an inalienable and shared autonomy of mortals is capable of nourishing. It is equality grounded, in other words, in the equal freedom of all to affirm and sacrifice life, out of which emerges that formula of an egalitarian sovereignty, and whose risk reappears in *Philosophy of Hinduism* with even greater effect around the expression "Indian wars." War here is that primordial activity, that sacrificial test of virtue, that space to craft one's sense of responsibility, within which freedom is gained (and lost) in its purity. To rethink the political, Ambedkar tells us, requires not merely the

reformulation of the rules of war but its reinstatement as the very principle—
a higher truth—of a sovereign collective.

To take a catastrophe like war, society must mobilize all its resources for militarization. Every one must do war. Every one must be a soldier. Is this possible under the
theory of caste? Obviously not. Indeed, the destiny of a defeat which has been the
lot of India throughout history is due to caste. Caste prevented general mobilization.
Or the extent of mobilization was of a very limited character. Only the Kshatriyas
were expected to fight. The rest the Brahmins and the Vaishyas were not armed and
the Shudras who formed the large majority of the country were disarmed. The result
was that once the small class of Kshatriyas were defeated by a foreign foe the whole
country fell at his feet. It could offer no resistance. It was not capable of resistance.
Indian wars have been mostly wars of single battles or single campaigns. This was due
to the fact that once the Kshatriyas fell everything fell. Why? Simply because there
was no general mobilization and the theory deeply imbedded in the psychology of
the people.[59]

Let us keep the richness of the expression "general mobilization," elsewhere reformulated as "direct action," for later. True civilizations, meanwhile,
Ambedkar insists, must survive without retreat. When beaten back, they do
not settle down into their newfound slavery. Instead, they regroup, mobilize,
and resist, indomitably if secretively, even after their subjugation. This perennial and fearless resistance wins great republics (like Rousseau, Ambedkar has Rome in mind)[60] the love of the stranger and respect of the enemy.
Battles, therefore, must be transformed into wars, brittle and meek confron-
tations replaced by prolonged resistances. Now this theory calls for multi-
plication of conflict, certainly, but only if, cautions Ambedkar, "every one
[is] a soldier," only if everyone could do war. This was republican ethics reconstituted around a radical renunciation of measure, with its force, reason,
and craft unconditionally generalized, its limits collectively annihilated. In
fact, an immortal and sovereign people, an authentic love of politics, could
be constituted, asserts Ambedkar, only when justice is rendered inseparable
from force; only when freedom includes in its ambit, beyond all calculus
and restraint, the physical and cognitive rearming of immediate neighbors,
brothers, unequals, and outcastes; only when equality, above all, is grounded
in a "general mobilization." It was as if, in a radical inversion of hierarchy, the
untouchable's justice is made possible only when it responds to the needs of
his immediate, defeated, and unfree Hindu oppressor.

Caste, then, is not merely a question of social relations. Instead, in its
annihilation lies the possibility of a new moral ontology. "Goats and sheep
are sacrificed, not tigers," Ambedkar would declare in Nagpur in July 1942 to
a crowd of 75,000 Mahars, the outcaste community to which he belonged.[61]

"We will give our life for the blue flag. . . . We will sacrifice all for the blue flag! Whatever Bhim wants we will do," ran a revolutionary poem chanted by members of Ambedkar's Samata Sainik Dal (Soldiers for Equality) in the 1940s, "We see our blood flow for the blue flag!"[62] I will return to the intriguing nature of Ambedkar's demand to generalize war later in this chapter. *Thoughts on Pakistan*, even a quick skim would have told its incensed readers, meanwhile, is an attempt to think through this force of the unequal, the force of those barred from its very economy, at its extremities. Ambedkar's quotation from chapter 3 of book 1 of *The Social Contract*, extracted from precisely those passages in which the limits of force as concept and instrument are most explicitly addressed, is even more edifying. "As Rousseau said," Ambedkar quotes, "the strongest is never strong enough to be always master, unless he transforms his might into right, and obedience into duty."[63] Then, immediately after this antiliberalism is mobilized (quoted cryptically but appropriated in great depth), comes his prescription: "Only ethics can convert might into right and obedience into duty. The [Muslim] League must see that its claim for Pakistan is founded on ethics."[64]

What might this separatist ethics, one that would transform the oppressive moral laws of obedience into a virtuous realm of civic duty, be? Ambedkar's expectation from the Muslim League, its gangsterism and politics of the street, was rather low, even if it was not as low as the expectation he had often had from the majoritarian fanatics of the Hindu Mahasabha and the Congress. So clearly, it was less the problem of Pakistan and more the fragile relationship between obedience and duty that was on his mind, less the unbridled show of strength by forces and more the antinomy of force central to the republic that lay at the core of this ethics. Was not the antinomy itself fairly Rousseauist? Just a little later in the same passage of *The Social Contract* that Ambedkar had quoted from, Rousseau himself clarifies: "Force is a physical power; I fail to see what morality can result from its effects. To yield to force is an act of necessity, not of will . . . in what sense can it become a duty?" There was a reason for Ambedkar's not quoting these lines: their flow would have been disrupted by his demand of ethics from the Muslim League. But perhaps more crucially, the "philosopher of Pakistan" realized he was at once the closest and farthest from Rousseau—farthest because his force, unlike that of the philosopher from Geneva, was not simply reducible to physical potentiality. Rather, it belonged to the order of constituent power—material, cognitive, and symbolic—of a multitude ready to become citizens, and so, closest to Rousseau too, because it was through this insurrectionary force that the possibility of a justice unconstrained by the interest of nationalist unity, property, and security had to be given form.

"Nationality," writes Ambedkar in a decisive formulation in *Partition*, "is not such a sacrosanct and absolute principle as to give it the character of a categorical imperative, over-riding every other consideration."[65] And a decade later, in his *Thoughts on Linguistic States* (1955), he mounts a careful critique of linguistic majoritarianism, tempering even more radically what had seemed just a decade earlier to be his affinity for a centralized republican state. "One State can never be a categorical imperative."[66] There were a series of tensed relationships contained in this republican ethics: tension between general will and individual liberty, between constitution and insurrection, between security and freeedom. "Let us agree then, force does not make right, and that one is only obliged to obey legitimate powers," Rousseau had proposed. And with this deceptively lucid proposal, he had opened an irresolvable puzzle in republican theory. "Thus, my original question keeps coming back," he concedes as much.[67] It was that difficult balance between virtue and necessity, justice and force—that impossible possibility that Rousseau calls "legitimate powers"—whose conditions of possibility *Annihilation of Caste* would try to probe (and reinstitute) in a manner few other works of its time would.

The Principle of Generality

Few in modern India were more troubled by democracy's propensity to harbor morally illegitimate powers, more awake to the risk of granting democracy's rule of numbers the status of an unimpeachable system, than Ambedkar. Only when it allowed an insurrectionary subject to prosper at its heart, only when it granted the citizen's right to rebel against lawless powers the status of a moral universality, available everywhere and to everyone, without measure and limits, in civic assembly or private homes, might democracy be rendered truly radical, generalized to include the whole of humanity. In that sense, Ambedkar's idea of rights was grounded in the moral universality (and autonomy) of principles, but rarely ever bound by a foundationalist view of politics, by limits and categories of birth, region, and nation. "Annihilation," I have argued, was his expression for this ethics of generality. Before taking up the principle of generality as such (with its theology-inflected love for negation, sacrifice, and void), let us note its relationship to Ambedkar's positive conception of freedom, freedom as freedom to reason and think without the fear of domination. For given the rhetorical negativity, given his suspicion of rights promised by liberal reformers, given, above all, his belief that rights by themselves do nothing to alleviate the fragility and vulnerability of right-bearing subjects, all of which was in full display in *Annihilation of Caste*, it is easy to miss—Gandhi certainly missed—the immense rigor, thoughtfulness, and exactitude that is at work in the more affirmative arguments that the treatise makes. And despite the nascent forms in which these insurrectionary affirmations appear in *Annihilation of Caste*, they would have a decisive impact on Ambedkar's ruminations on constitutions and constituent power just over a decade later.

The unifying thread running through these deliberations is Ambedkar's enduring concern with the liberty of others, liberty of those left behind, left untouched, consigned to the shadows of virtue. For him, there is no radical democracy without a freedom that is available to citizens and noncitizens, neighbors and strangers, one's own and others, equally. This generalization—indeed, this anonymous universality, a universality freed from attributes inherited by birth, caste, and community—required a positive conception of freedom. This would be a freedom understood not simply as noninterference or even nondomination, not simply as the liberation of the citizen from the "multitude of commands and prohibitions"[68] but rather freedom as the autonomy to forge a new relationship between sovereignty and justice, a new relationship between reason and truth. This freedom would open a space where the citizens' incommensurable energies and beliefs, the contest of their faculties, could be played out equitably, competitively, graciously, truthfully.[69] The opening itself was less a matter of constitutional norms, in fact, than it was of a moral ontology of individual and collective action. For Ambedkar, authentic freedom dwells within those social bonds and activities of everyday life—fertility, nourishment, reproduction, care, and obligation—that might be secured only in shared virtues, or what he would call in *Philosophy of Hinduism*, the common "love of truth."[70] But most important, for him, freedom dwelled in a radical autonomy of skill, craft, and ability—an autonomy that was available to anyone who might virtuously turn a social and moral crisis into an opportunity for regeneration of ethics, anyone who might take the crisis to its meaningful resolution. Freedom is not learning and mere intellect, insists Ambedkar, then; it is "the combustible stuff of reason and morality,"[71] a revolutionary "dynamite" made of virtue and force that turns crisis into a possibility of justice. "If the intellectual class is honest, independent, and disinterested it can be trusted to take the initiative and give a proper lead when a crisis arises," but, Ambedkar pointedly concedes, "it is true that intellect by itself is no virtue. It is only a means and the use of means depends upon the ends which an intellectual person pursues."[72]

Two crucial, and often misunderstood, terms appear in these declarations, both of which are inscribed at the heart of Ambedkar's principle of generality: reason (which is frequently confused with Ambedkar's purported instrumentalism, even hyperrationality; and virtue (which is rarely approached as a locus of his moral psychology of dissidence, if at all). I think there is a fundamental relationship between these two, one that coalesces around—and gives form to—Ambedkar's understanding of sovereignty. In this section, I want to explore this relationship at some length, focusing especially on the consequences of those moments when reason and virtue—transcendent and immanent—become inseparable from the force of an insurrectionary citizenship: a citizenship not only rooted in resistance to sovereign power but one in which resistance was the moral foundation of sovereignity itself, indeed the sovereign virtue of the ethical right-bearing subject. Reason, as such, has a polyvalent status in Ambedkar's thought. But in *Annihilation of Caste*, it means, in the most unequivocal sense, a virtue—that is, an obligation to truthful conduct and performance of duty—constituted solely by its commitment to the immeasurability, even tactlessness, of freedom. "Can you," he inquires in the opening sentence of part 22 of the treatise, "appeal to reason and ask the Hindus to discard Caste as being contrary to reason? That raises the question: Is a Hindu free to follow his reason?" Annihilation becomes operative at this critical juncture, at once invoking a freedom without foundation and measure: freedom (in the negative sense) from any constraint on a people's right to force, mobilization, and movement, and freedom (in its positivity) to create conditions (or crisis) through revolutionary action for a new form of sovereignty. But what kind of action is Ambedkar considering? And who is this call for generalizing force addressed to? To understand this recursive and potent use of the "general," this principle of generality, let us go back a few passages in the text where nonhereditary military service is lent the status of an exemplary virtue in Ambedkar's theory of government. This exemplarity, it is almost immediately clear, belongs to resistance rather than rule, to the moral sovereignty of the citizen rather than his political mastery over others.

It is true that even in Europe the strong has not shrunk from the exploitation, nay the spoliation of the weak but in Europe, the strong have never contrived to make the weak helpless against exploitation so shamelessly as was the case in India among the Hindus. Social war has been raging between the strong and the weak far more violently in Europe than it has ever been in India. Yet the weak in Europe has had in him freedom of military service his physical weapon, in suffrage his political weapon and in education his moral weapon. Three weapons for emancipation were never withheld by the strong from the weak in Europe. All these weapons were however denied to the masses in India by Chaturvarnya. There cannot be a more degrading system of social organization than Chaturvarnya. It is the system, which deadens, paralyses and cripples the people from helpful activity. This is no exaggeration. History bears ample evidence. There is only one period in Indian history, which is a period of freedom, greatness and glory. That is the period of the Maurya Empire. At all other times the country suffered from defeat and darkness. But the Maurya period was a period when Chaturvarnya was completely annihilated, when the Shudras, who constituted the mass of the people, came into their own and became the rulers of the country. The period of defeat and darkness is the period when Chaturvarnya flourished to the damnation of the greater part of the people of the country.[73]

Force, while it attains its greatest amplitude in war, is not synonymous with war. On the contrary, force, always groundless, anarchic, and primordial, resides with the weakest, the most excluded, and the socially "damned." For Ambedkar, it encapsulates, in a word, their right to resistance. He invariably places its truth in the realm of mundane, invisible, and, very often, pedagogical pursuits. For a people constituted by its collective power to refuse *and* legislate, to obey *and* govern, for a people in whom individual interest had been sacrificed at the altar of the shared truth and immediacy of the general will, there could be no force, and certainly no sovereignty, without ordinary virtues, which he calls, in a moment of uncharacteristic understatement, "helpful activity." It is virtue alone that prevents collective might, whether mobilized in the name of national struggle or class war, from turning into rituals of mastery and oppression. And this virtue demands the ability at once to think in terms of sovereign action and immeasurable capacity—radical autonomy—to relinquish the state itself. Unless the sovereignty of the citizen is secured in his commitment to the freedom of others (which is the heart of a religious sense of responsibility), unless it is grounded in the principle of truthful resistance against the corruptions of the moral law, there is every chance that force will mutate into—or be reduced to—mere mastery. It was this perversion, Ambedkar believed, which had culminated in fascism's global war and revealed the seeds of antidemocracy that parliamentary representation contains within itself. In fact, to him, the fate of Europe had come to exemplify the deepest malaise of representative democracy, whose perversion had found only its most brutal form in fascism. Fascism had simply revealed, with terrifying effectiveness, the hidden and repressed tendencies of the liberal contract on which modern democratic practice is founded; a sinister result, Ambedkar put it in a Nietzschean vein, of liberal democracy's privileging of the "idea of freedom of contract" over equality.[74] In fact, in Germany and Italy, Ambedkar insists, parliamentary democracy had failed because its "movements are very slow. It delays swift action."[75] Two years before the end of the Second World War, in a lecture on "Labor and Parliamentary Democracy" at the All-India Trade Union Workers' Study Camp, he would caution: "Beware of Parliamentary Democracy, it is not the best product as it appears to be."[76]

The principle of generality that undergirds Ambedkar's "general mobilization," then, is at once antirepresentation and antimastery, and not to forget, intermittently suspicious of the parliament itself. But along with this anarchic energy, this predilection for justice that is shared in a groundless commonality, generality has always had, as Pierre Rosanvallon has shown in his careful recovery of the concept, a strangely democratic quality to it too.[77] In this instance, it displays a deep urgency that, while rooted in the French revolutionary inspiration of Ambedkar's thought, also recalls his equivocation concerning the masculine and colonizing impulses of European humanism within which that revolutionary tradition in its broad contours had emerged. I will return to his turn away from that humanist heritage in Chapter 7, a turn perhaps best captured in Ambedkar's shift away from the language of "general mobilization" to that of "measureless whole."[78] At the moment, I want to point out that inasmuch as the actions and effects of this generality are grounded in the immediacy and finitude of social life—which is to say, in the material conflicts, everyday antagonisms, and minutiae of shared sacrifices of the masses—generality, which is in essence a fundamental renunciation of all measure, alone creates the conditions of the rule of the people, a society of equals. It alone makes possible a freedom, in other words, which required no—and defied all—representation.

This perhaps explains why, through three years of Constituent Assembly deliberations (1947–1950), right until the moment that he unveiled the preamble of the Indian constitution—which begins, of course, with the classic declaration "We, the people of India," a people who promise themselves justice, liberty, equality, and fraternity, in that order—Ambedkar had resolutely refused to speak in the name of the people themselves. There was not a moment in his writings and speeches—many prepared, quite a few delivered extempore to an often-hostile body of lawmakers—in which he seems to have assumed the role of a representative. Inasmuch as he was a legislator, his mandate, he frequently repeated, was simply to give the general will a moral-legal form, not only because the Constituent Assembly of India was not yet an elected body or a parliament (which would replace the Constituent Assembly only after the first general elections in 1951–1952), nor only because Ambedkar was a notorious stickler—in nationalist constructions of him—for legal proprieties and nuances. The reason for this, I think, was that Ambedkar remained profoundly ambivalent about the idea that in a world that lacked conscience, the multitude, especially the most vulnerable and unequal within it (many of whom, it was undeniable, were prone to obey the *dharma* of voluntary servitude) might ever be adequately represented without further violence and disenfranchisement. This was the limit of democracy, its infidelity to the people, which is fundamental to democracy as such, a violent limit—indeed, a ventriloquism without which democracy could not survive. Perhaps *Thoughts on*

Pakistan had condensed, in the most inflammatory form, Ambedkar's struggle with this limit: the extreme equivocation toward representation that lay at the heart of his own militant republicanism. But then, has this antinomy between immediacy and mediation, between the people in its immanence and the state in its transcendence, striving for the life and security of the very people without whose sacrifice—and sanction—it is quickly reduced to an instrument of lawless authority, not insinuated itself in all formulations on constituent power since at least 1789?

It is Ambedkar's struggle for immanence, his striving for a moral ontology in which a mortal's subject's deepest belief might be rendered inalienable, his conception of responsibility toward others—"the essence of a truly religious act"—as the first (and groundless) principle of freedom that leads him to impute an ontological generality to the act of mobilization. At once singular and shared, "general mobilization" captures for Ambedkar the essence of Rousseau's famously difficult "general will": "each, by giving himself to all, gives himself to no one."[79] This would have, as we have seen in *Thoughts on Pakistan*, grave implications. And yet this generality alone can produce the conditions of an egalitarian and virtuous sovereignty, or rather, a radical equality that might be grounded in the unconditional autonomy of a citizen's deepest convictions and truths, and yet, always resist lapsing into private interest and solipsism. Generality introduces not only the conceptual and polemical scenario of war as the common space of ethical action. It also posits mobilization as an act of faith, the sovereign truth, which brings the multitude into existence. This generality of force is the Machiavellian foundation, not an antithesis, to civic virtue.[80] If the Hindu is unfree, cognitively incapable of thinking reasonably and freely, unconscious of the immanence of force that constitutes even the weakest and most unequal of subjects, then by what means other than an unconditional freedom of force, by what means other than putting dynamite to scripture, could the virtue of action be secured? After all, the war on caste was not a struggle against a regime of "barbed wire" and "mere mercenary soldiers"; it was a struggle not for property and control of means and machinery. Instead, it entailed a battle against cognitive servitude, one that required recovering the moral psychology of action from the treason of India's intellectuals themselves.[81] This struggle for freedom would have to be singular, beyond all measure and ground, beyond all pragmatic unities and constraining interests imposed by the nationalist struggle against the empire. The purity of the people's means alone would lend this freedom its positive and virtuous force.[82]

Where does the source of this means unfettered by the teleology of ends, freed from the anxiety of consequences, lie? It lies in the democratization of force (which is also Ambedkar's name for inner faculties and internal reasons), in the purity of "direct action," in the outcaste's anarchic refusal of the laws and foundations of *maryada dharma*. And *Annihilation of Caste* is not the only time Ambedkar uses the notion of direct action—a term possibly taken during his early days in New York from the 1912 essay "Direct Action" by the American anarchist Voltairine de Cleyre (1866–1912)—or the rhetoric of "general mobilization" to describe his revolutionary ethics. In fact, "general mobilization" appears at decisive moments in his intellectual itinerary, notably in *Philosophy of Hinduism* and *What Congress and Gandhi Have Done to Untouchables* in 1945. Its meanings are not always the same, its tact and energies, its radical desires and conserving impulses, shifting over time. But its driving logic remains by and large truthful to its revolutionary origins. And that logic had been set in motion much earlier. In that incipient form, general mobilization had suggested the imperative of thinking force as an immanent generality, as that which lies beyond the transcendental prohibitions of the moral law, or *dharma*, and is therefore, at once groundless and inalienable from the obligations of the weakest. In Ambedkar's mature thought, which I take up in Chapter 7, there are two pivotal turns—involving his reworking of the concepts of *maitri*, or friendship, and *sunnyata*, or emptiness, which he renders as "impermanence"—around which this vision of egalitarian sovereignty, a sovereignty anchored in the ethics of responding justly, would be given their fullest form.

Virtue, that is to say, the capacity and duty of a people to hold something just as being true, which is the essence of an authentic love of politics, had always been for Ambedkar a question of a religious responsibility, just as virtuous conduct (*sila*)—rooted in reason and truth—had been for him the only ground of an inclusive, free, and egalitarian republic. In fact, virtue was another name for what Ambedkar perceives as a moral commitment to "principles": the irreducible obligation of the citizen toward the freedom of strangers, an act of faith that thrives in the inseparability between the immanent and transcendent, between one's own autonomy and that of another. This conception would acquire its highest resolution in *The Buddha and His Dhamma*. But *Annihilation of Caste* already makes a radical separation in the political, ethical, and conceptual unity of religion as it had until then been formulated in twentieth-century India, refusing precisely this nationalist-theological separation between the immanent and transcendent, between the ethical and political, between justice and sovereignty. If anything, Ambedkar's galvanizing 1935 declaration in Yeola—that he was born a Hindu but would not die as one—had already cleared the ground for a rather insurrectionary separation of faiths.[83] For Ambedkar, this separation was not merely a question of moving away from the deceptive resonance between Hindu *dharma* and Buddhist *dhamma*. Nor was this separation a prelude to claiming spiritual proximity or theological equality between classical Hinduism and Buddhism—a counter-intuitive way, as some saw it, of establishing commensurability between two religions. Such commensurability, on the contrary, was Gandhi's dream, which he had often tried to realize by inscribing Buddhism as an episode of anguish and insubordination within the inescapable universality of Hindu *dharma*. Within that satyagrahic understanding of religion, as we have seen in Chapter 2, India's religious difference could be formulated in the nonhierarchical, even egalitarian, language of spiritual concentricity, of which Hinduism forms the outermost, all encompassing orbit of faith and citizenship—an orbit within whose boundaries every other belief falls, excluded but absorbed.

For Ambedkar, however, the separation was an abyss between two heterogeneous and sovereign (if neighborly) faiths, a separation that mere pluralist rhetoric—false tolerance—and geopolitical manipulation of communities might never bridge. For this difference was not social, confined simply to anthropological variations of ritual and practice. The difference belongs to the realm of sovereign power, grounded in the incommensurable logics of each faith's singular and irreproducible relationship to sovereignty as such. And only one gives itself to the autonomy—autonomy within the framework of sovereignty—of its practitioners. Between *dhamma* and *dharma*, then, lies for Ambedkar not simply the question of virtue but the very possibility of autonomy. Buddhism—and with it, its doctrine of annihilationism (*ucchedvad*)—was for Ambedkar at once more and less than a classical religion. It was certainly not a secular theology. Instead, it was a way or path to grasp and reformulate, in a classically theologico-political sense, the relationship between force and justice, between the radical autonomy ingrained in a people's constituent power and their responsibility toward a just republic. I now turn to that republican moment, especially as it shaped Ambedkar's interventions in the Constituent Assembly debates of the late 1940s. The moment would reveal, once again, the enduring significance of *Annihilation of Caste*: not merely for Ambedkar's own relationship with republicanism but for the ethics of insurrection that he would make fundamental to anticolonial constitutionalism itself.

An Insurrectionary Constitutionalism

"Revolution is the mother of philosophy," Ambedkar insists in *Philosophy of Hinduism*, "and if it is not the mother of philosophy it is a lamp which illuminates philosophy."[84] Nothing but the gleaming sword of revolutionary light, an absolute generality of force (which swerves every now and then, as it does in *Thoughts on Pakistan*, into a celebration of republican mastery and centralization): this had been the guiding moral principle of *Annihilation of Caste*. But "annihilation" was also an act that cleared the ground for political virtue and restraint—the ground for an authentic "constitutional morality"—to emerge. Now, with this expression, which appears for the first time in the late 1940s, we arrive most directly at that productive space between constitution and insurrection, between civic virtue and civic disobedience, at work in Ambedkar's political thought. There are two ways to understand this expression. One might argue that working through the potential possibilities and perils of republican government in India during his defense of the draft constitution at the Constituent Assembly debates in November 1948, Ambedkar (quoting from George Grote's *History of Greece* (1856), from which he had taken the expression "constitutional morality") amplifies the tension central to what I have called, following Rosanvallon, "the principle of generality," one on which his enduring engagement with force had been instituted. Or, alternatively, recomposing this idiom of republican constitutionalism (which begins to gather in the 1940s a new kind of salience in Ambedkar's moral and political thought) in the language of *Annihilation of Caste*, one might argue that by conjoining constitution with morality, Ambedkar attempts to reclaim force itself—the constituent power of the multitude—from the throes of sovereignty (the state) and rehabilitate it within the realm of ordinary virtues, moralities, and obligations. Was this reclamation, especially given some of the conservative threads that had been woven a few years earlier in *Thoughts on Pakistan*, as easily accomplished?

While everybody recognizes the necessity of the diffusion of Constitutional morality for the peaceful working of a democratic Constitution, there are two things interconnected with it, which are not, unfortunately, generally recognized. One is that the form of administration has a close connection with the form of the Constitution. The form of the administration must be appropriate to and in the same sense as the form of the Constitution. The other is that it is perfectly possible to pervert the Constitution, without changing its form by merely changing the form of the administration and to make it inconsistent and opposed to the spirit of the Constitution. It follows that it is only where people are saturated with Constitutional morality such as the one described by Grote the historian that one can take the risk of omitting from the Constitution details of administration and leaving it for the Legislature to prescribe them. The question is, can we presume such a diffusion of Constitutional morality? Constitutional morality is not a natural sentiment. It has to be cultivated. We must realize that our people have yet to learn it. Democracy in India is only a top dressing on an Indian soil which is essentially undemocratic.[85]

Before I turn to the question of morality, let me attend to two oblique, even contradistinctive, propositions that serve as the basis for Ambedkar's more legalistic arguments in this passage. First, any constitutional ethics—indeed, any theory of action and obligation—that excludes the weakest, most vulnerable, and most unequal of the republic opens itself to perversion, even violence. Such constitutions—like India's own ancient constitution, its Hindu *dharma*—were merely a rule of "police power." Whether constitutional or revolutionary (and Ambedkar, let us reemphasize, rarely considers these as separate), responsibility as such—which alone would qualify as virtue—is owed, first and foremost, to the minority, neighbor, friend, stranger, enemy, and the animal, rather than to the state. Second, in the absence of such a theory and practice of obligation, democracy itself, with its intrinsic tendency to ride on the back of constitutional authority and representative institutions, mutates into the most monstrous form of antidemocracy. If democracy has made humanity politically modern, then its success needs not simply the laws of modern representation but also the theologico-political ethics of classical, even ancient, constitutions.

With this tension in mind, let me return to the passage in a more direct fashion. Ambedkar's extremely strained faith in representative institutions—rendered even more striking when juxtaposed with the extended lawmaking mandate he tended to grant the executive and parliament (over the judiciary) during the Constituent Assembly debates—shines here in all its polyvalence. And the term "constitutional morality" only aggravates this strain. Representation in itself, as he makes it amply clear, is neither the sovereign foundation nor the irrevocable guarantee of democracy. On the contrary, when constitutional morality stands on deficient ground, elected legislatures are bound to act no differently from the people they represent; their legislative life is no less corrupted by hierarchy and exclusion than the electoral configurations, calculations, and manipulations that bring them into positions of lawmaking authority in the first place. For those who remain socially excluded and morally violated, being represented under such conditions, by such legislators, becomes yet another dimension—even extension—of their familiar, perpetual, and often voluntary servitude. This thought had distilled, as we shall see later in the chapter, Ambedkar's extreme wariness of authoritarian tendencies that interwar democracies sometimes nourished, in opposition to which he would place the unconditional generalization of mastery—that is, the right of everyone to be a master—as the only ground for freedom. By way of gradually approaching this perilous conception of freedom as mastery, or rather, this theory of freedom that swerves (once in a while) into a theory of mastery, let us retrace Ambedkar's equivocation in relation to the foundations of republican constitutionalism.

Who are the people who have failed to cultivate a constitutional morality, thereby perverting the "spirit of the constitution"? Not ordinary citizens, not subjects excluded from the domain of citizenship itself, insists Ambedkar; instead, these are people who lack an authentic love of politics and reduce it to fiscal manipulation and private interest. In a suggestive reading, the political theorist Pratap Bhanu Mehta identifies both the nonviolent satyagrahis often ready to fast unto death until their demands were met and violent and armed revolutionaries willing to spill blood for their cause as the target of Ambedkar's criticism.[86] In Ambedkar's view, Mehta argues, both forms of action, despite their differing modalities, jeopardized (in equal measure) the propriety of constitutional procedure and its redistributive mechanisms, thereby stymieing the moral foundations—the Indian soil—of egalitarian citizenship and social justice. Interpreted thus, according to Mehta, it becomes possible to see Ambedkar as an even greater proponent of nonviolence than Gandhi.

I find Mehta's reading illuminating. But I also find it overdetermined by the boundaries of the liberal heritage—and the kind of nonviolence Mehta has in mind is undeniably guided by a liberal construction—if not by the certitude of the liberal belief that measure, restraint, and contractual mediation—"freedom of contract" as Ambedkar disapprovingly puts it—can by themselves create conditions for a just society, one where agonistic pursuits and conflicts might be resolved through legislative mediation. In fact, Ambedkar's invocation of Grote—or for that matter, his treatment of Mill elsewhere—has often exposed him to widespread belief and interpretation that he had placed himself decisively within the lineage of procedural democracy.[87] Mehta himself takes Grote's "paramount reverence for the forms of the Constitution" to heart, identifying the same logic to be at work in Ambedkar's deployment of the term "constitutional morality." This, again, is an important interpretive gesture. But it does make light of the fact that Grote was, in the final instance, speaking in the classical spirit of direct democracy, which Ambedkar, even in the unlikeliest of scenarios, often tended to prefer over its parliamentary corruptions. And while the language of constitutional morality establishes an undeniable kinship between traditions (who can deny, least of all Ambedkar himself, his immense affinity with the American pragmatist heritage), a shared vocabulary does not always suggest a shared logic, let alone shared moral commitments and meanings.

Anglophone liberalism, even the most radical variations within it, is not the only inspiration that had during those years come to mediate Ambedkar's political thought, let alone his understanding of constituent power. Nor was he decisively on the side of pacifism over force. Just a minute further into his defense of the draft constitution, for instance, Ambedkar warns, "Minorities are an explosive force which, if it erupts, can blow up the whole fabric of the state. The history of Europe bears ample and appalling testimony to this fact."[88]

Now this force, as presented in *Thoughts on Pakistan*, we have seen, is at once symbolic and real, generous and vehement, egalitarian and masculine. And yet it mobilizes not only the threat of violence—whose blame, Ambedkar warns, must lie with the desire of nations to create and retain their own states by force—but also the explosive, disruptive, freeing power of generality, one whose potency lies not in virility but virtue, not in masculinity but civility, not in the sovereign and indivisible state but the multitude that founds it. If one takes out of Ambedkar's constitutionalist thought such bursts of rhetorical and conceptual energy around force, if one makes light of his immense distaste for juridical moralities and obligations enforced by the police power of nationalist *dharma*, one effectively erases the radical energies of "annihilation" (and *Annihilation of Caste*): annihilation as the insurrectionary escape of the unequal from theologically sanctioned servitude. As for Ambedkar's nonviolence, I think its ethics and politics are so distinct from Gandhi's, their moral commitments grounded in such different orders of belief, action, and sacrifice, that neither gives itself easily to be measured against the other.

I return to these incommensurable commitments to nonviolence in the third part of the book, placing their irreconcilability within Ambedkar's and Gandhi's shared attempt to make finitude the moral foundation of a just form of sovereignty. There is, of course, much in Ambedkar's vigorous defense of proposed features in the constitution in the years leading up to its ratification by the Constituent Assembly in 1950 that might tempt us to assume that he was concerned solely with the matrices of social citizenship. Yet it is equally clear, since at least *Thoughts on Pakistan* (1941), if not *Annihilation of Caste* (1936) itself, that for him social justice is unthinkable without probing the most mystical, cryptic, and religiously kept secrets of sovereignty. His immense interest in spaces of resistance available at the center of the modern state, his radical (one might call it, if somewhat inadequately, republican) faith in freedom, is imprinted no more indelibly by his belief in civic virtue as the ground of constitutional morals than it is by his belief in the citizen's right of insurrection in public spaces (and full governmental view) as the foundation of a sovereignty faithful to the people. After all, if there are no moral or even transcendental principles, then no constitution, and certainly no representation, would be adequate to securing a society of equals. Such a society, corrupted as it would already be by executive excess—an excess of force whose moral legitimacy and value, it is important to note, Ambedkar never relinquishes either—would but be a mirror of "police control."[89]

The dilemma that runs through Ambedkar's remarks on constitutional morality, then, does not seem to be about the moral constraints that a constitution might place, legitimately or otherwise, on solitary or collective action of its subjects, satyagrahic or revolutionary. The more important question for Ambedkar is: What might those moral foundations be on which the depth and limit of constitutional authority—which, despite all its claims to neutrality, speaks the language of the majority, the mighty, the strongest—itself must be judged? What might prevent a constitutional (that is, elected) government that rules without an ethics of responsibility, without a regard for the freedom of the weak, the unequal, and the stranger, from quickly mutating into an extra-constitutional tyranny? The emphasis, let us note, is not on "morality," which is already contaminated by the exclusions of *dharma* (as we shall see in the Nietzschean inspirations of Ambedkar's mature thought). For Ambedkar, the emphasis, instead, must be on the "constitutional": on the authorities and powers that operate at the threshold between the constitutional and extra-constitutional, legal and illegal, patronizing and punitive domains of democratic government. For it is not solely the constitutional foundation of social citizenship that is put at risk when law and non-law are rendered inseparable. After all, in a society in which democracy is simply a top dressing, the moral and political legitimacy of the constitution itself (let alone of the constituted state) can never be assumed, according to Ambedkar, as given. The question, to ask it in a slightly different way then, was: under these conditions of democratically sanctioned illegitimacy and servitude, what equilibrium of obedience and insurrection, what balance of virtue and resistance, must the citizen retain in his relationship with the constitution? Must the citizen choose freedom over equality? Or, in a revolutionary reversal of this liberal dilemma, must equality itself be rendered equal to freedom? On what grounds, in sum, might the always imperiled, always risky, legitimacy of democracy be secured?

"Sir, my friends tell me that I made the Constitution," Ambedkar announced in 1953, just three years after India's constitution had been adopted by its Constituent Assembly. "But I am quite prepared to say that I shall be the first person to burn it out. I do not want it. It does not suit anybody."[90] Or in a more theologico-political vein, reportedly, "the Constitution was a wonderful temple for the gods, but before they could be installed, the devils have taken possession."[91] I will let the more obvious fact about Ambedkar's recalcitrant fearlessness—and the ethics of courage it exemplifies—which shines through in these moments pass. But it is worth mentioning that there has rarely been in the annals of modern republican constitutionalism a figure so close to the authoring of a constitution whose moral courage, whose demand for justice, whose perennial search for ways to reclaim the freedom of ordinary citizens (and noncitizens) to produce their own equality, whose rhetorical, interpretive, and conceptual *coup de force*, above all, has spared not even the sanctity and self-righteousness of the foundational document he has himself helped author. Rarely has there been a more insurrectionary constitutionalist who is perfectly willing to annihilate that which he has helped found. Constitutionalism, inasmuch as it has for Ambedkar any value at all, has it only as long as it belongs to the domain of ordinary and inclusive virtues. It requires belief, comportment, and civility rather than juridical rules and injunctions. Although it does embody the norms and values necessary for the maintenance of a sovereign state, constitutionalism is not reducible to it. On the contrary, its force—constituent power—is mightier than the spirit of the laws, its purposes higher than mere security of the republic.

This force is immanent, attuned to the lives of the weakest. When this force is lost, the constitution loses not merely its legitimacy but its immortality as well. To burn such a constitution would be no less just than burning away the hierarchical, punitive, and ancient *Laws of Manu* (*Manusmriti*), which, we have seen in Chapter 3, Ambedkar had indeed publicly burnt in 1927.[92] There was something profoundly insurrectionary about this vision of constituent power that Ambedkar imputed to the weak force of the masses, something irreducibly anarchic about this ethics of civic disobedience that brooked no interference from the procedural norms of state power (or its hagiography of constitutional triumph). It was this kinship of faith with insurrection, this extremity of constitutionalism that allowed the architect of the constitution to dream of burning that foundational document, which Ambedkar had tried to condense in that militant concept: general mobilization.

With this formulation of general mobilization, this rebellion against the constraints on the manual and cognitive abilities of the multitude, this exacting attentiveness to the materiality of revolutionary action, we are back to the most difficult passage of Ambedkar's movement through classical republicanism. Certainly, what makes *Annihilation of Caste* a revolutionary—if not in itself also a deeply republican—text is its attempt to reclaim the material fabric of freedom from the invisible rules of nationalist *dharma* (which has always been, as Radhakrishnan reminds the Constituent Assembly, the *dharma* of kings). Freedom, for Ambedkar, on the other hand, lies in the symbolic and physical openness of neighborhoods and cities, factories and hospitals, utterances and gestures. Freedom lies in the autonomy to nourish quotidian skills, faculties, and instruments freed from hierarchies and distinctions between the manual and cognitive. Freedom, above all, lies in the right to expose the untouchable to the mundane richness of the social bond and educate him in the virtues of force, one whose moral and political wholeness—its immeasurability and immortality—might accrue from the unequal's mastery over his fear alone.

And yet there is no force, conceived in even the most minimalist sense, that is not already implicated in operations of mastery and sacrifice. Any thinker of faith who evades this perilous theologico-political bond (and what else was the "ghost of Pakistan" if not the reared head of this repressed kinship)[93], any thought that claims to have escaped this pernicious logic had actually lost its love of politics, its sense of virtue. In fact, such a thought had failed in its love of truth itself.[94] Ambedkar, thus, insists that "it is necessary to separate religion from theology. . . . Theology is secondary. Its object is merely to nationalize [the religious]."[95] As it turned out, by the time he writes the preface to *The Buddha and His Dhamma* in 1956, theology especially in its monotheistic sense, would not be secondary anymore. Its force would be aligned with the ethics of shared finitude and justice, a principle of autonomy for the "measureless whole," of which every citizen was equal and incommensurable part.

The Antinomies of Virtue

The emphasis on incommensurability, which alone secured a world of free and responsible citizens, was not a feature of Ambedkar's later works. Nor did the language of immeasurable wholeness—the virtuous and constituent power of the citizenry—acquire its religious inflection in the 1950s. Note already, for example, how the following passage in *Annihilation of Caste* begins with the theme of social revolution and justice, then blends seamlessly into a critique of moral relations, before returning to that most enduring of problems in classical political philosophy: voluntary servitude enforced as the unequal's fate. It is in these engagements with the question of theologico-juridical domination that Ambedkar's conception of republican virtue acquires its extreme form, pushing his desire to formulate the conditions of a revolutionary democracy itself to its limit.

Why have there not been social revolutions in India is a question which has incessantly troubled me. There is only one answer, which I can give and it is that the lower classes of Hindus have been completely disabled for direct action on account of this wretched system of Chaturvarnya. They could not bear arms and without arms they could not rebel. They were all ploughmen or rather condemned to be ploughmen and they never were allowed to convert their ploughshare into swords. They had no bayonets and therefore everyone who chose could and did sit upon them. On account of the Chaturvarnya, they could receive no education. They could not think out or know the way to their salvation. They were condemned to be lowly and not knowing the way of escape and not having the means of escape, they became reconciled to eternal servitude, which they accepted as their inescapable fate.[96]

So the reclamation of force for the multitude required a study of their everyday rhythms and social prohibitions. But it also demanded an examination of the pernicious kinship between the customary discourse on duty and the theological laws of fate and servitude. For, it was precisely the rhetoric of eternity that had for centuries diverted the attention of the multitude away from the truth. What is this truth, which the multitude must master again in order to break the web of voluntary reverence and enslavement? The truth of transformative action, the "love of truth" itself, insists Ambedkar, which thrives only when the senses are educated, faculties roused, and virtue sought in the materiality of everyday rhythms and movements. In fact, if it were not to be prevented from lapsing into mere fiction or fallacy, equality and equal-ness (or, to use Ambedkar's term, *samata*)—that is, the virtue necessary to become equal and which everyone had the ability to nourish in equal measure—must be cultivated as technique and technology with greatest care, in greatest autonomy. The responsibility to produce equal-ness is the unequals' too, which begins with the knowledge that what seems eternal, a gift of fate, is actually the force of law. Responsibility, the essence of a truly religious act, thus demands, by its very nature, an act of faith against faith. It demands, insists Ambedkar, grasping, handling, turning, holding, smelting, and apprehending the "spirit of inequality."[97] What is virtue, after all, if not the cultivation of the craft of being sovereign, a sharing of freedom across gender and species? Thus reconstituted—in the language of an insurrectionary empiricism—ploughshares, bayonets, swords, and machinery would not simply remain the tools of production. They would, in their very physicality and rhythm, come to be imbued with a spiritual force in whose reclamation the unequal might open the space (physical and cognitive) of another freedom. There remained in Ambedkar's conceptual innovations till the very end this immense emphasis on the virtues of everyday solidarity, one that would, as we have seen in Chapter 3, mediate his encounter with a series of religious texts in the 1940s and 1950s.

Virtue, however, could not be predicated on nonviolence alone; on the contrary, it might sometimes necessitate war. To make that point, Ambedkar resorted as frequently to modern political thought as to ancient ethics. In a remarkable passage in *The Buddha and His Dhamma*, for instance, his Buddha assuages disciples worried over their master's ambivalence toward nonviolence. "It is not I, o disciples, that quarrel with the world, but the world that quarrels with me. A teacher of the truth does not quarrel with anyone in the world." The almsmen, trained to be truthful, remain perplexed. They probe further. "Warriors, warriors, Lord, we call ourselves. In what way then are we warriors?" The sermon takes a suggestive turn. "We wage war, o disciples, therefore we are called warriors," Ambedkar's Buddha replies. "Wherefore, Lord, do we wage war?" they persist, now anxious whether an authentic love of truth requires them to sacrifice themselves or demands nonviolence.

In return, the Buddha shifts the accent, attaching truth to absolute disinterest (*upekha*) in disciplinary and sacrificial rules, whether of war or nonviolence. Instead, truth is grounded in the empiricism of action—it is *sila*, a mode of conduct—that is organized around the freedom of others; it calls for belief in the contingency of life—indeed, an intensification of life in its materiality. One attains truth—and equality with oneself—when one becomes capable of making a decision to sacrifice life by oneself; in fact, one attains equality only when one has made such a decision to go to war (or refrain from it) freely. "For lofty virtues, for high endeavor, for sublime wisdom—for these things do we wage war: therefore we are called warriors. Where virtue is in danger," mandates the Buddha, "do not avoid fighting, do not be mealy-mouthed."[98] An incommensurable equality thus, equality not of measure but of immeasurable freedom of the self called forth truthfully and masterfully—this is where Ambedkar was most Nietzschean, never shying away from the language of force, never renouncing the value of sovereignty, even mastery, in the institution of a just politics.

It is suggestive, therefore, that while his repulsion toward Nazism's claim to spiritual mastery remains unambiguous throughout the 1940s, his responsibility toward Nietzsche and nihilism carries the strain of a distinctive equivocation. There certainly is, Ambedkar concedes, an affinity between Nietzsche's *Anti-Christ* and the *Manusmriti*, just as there is between Nazism and nihilism, and for that matter, between liberalism and fascism. Yet, Ambedkar qualifies, "Manu's degraded and degenerate philosophy of Superman as compared with that of Nietzsche is far more odious and loathsome."[99] Indeed, inasmuch as he thought that warriors in the Indic tradition had obligations toward the ordinary masses, the good radical Nietzsche may have misread the *Manusmriti*—and the exclusions of *kshatriyadharma*—entirely. But at the very least, the mad philosopher, whose absolute rejection of equality as sameness Ambedkar admires, truly believed that in the soul of every revolution worthy of the name there lies a commitment to immeasurable and incommensurable equality—that is, equality that does not subsume difference within existing rules of morality and unfreedom.[100] Ambedkar's Nietzsche was a thinker of the future, one who "took comfort [and perhaps gave Ambedkar himself some comfort] by placing himself among the 'posthumous men,'" a thinker in whose ideas virtue and force were emancipated from their petty cruelties and hierarchical perversions.[101]

Can there be any doubt that Zarathustra is a new name for Manu and that *Thus Spoke Zarathustra* is a new edition of the Manusmriti? If there is any difference between Manu and Nietzsche, it lies in this. Nietzsche was genuinely interested in creating a new race of men, which will be a race of Superman as compared with the existing race of men. Manu, on the other hand, was interested in maintaining the privilege of a class who had come to arrogate to itself the claim of being Superman. Nietzsche's Supermen were Supermen by reason of their worth. Nietzsche was a genuinely disinterested philosopher. Manu, on the contrary, was a hireling engaged to propound a philosophy which served the interests of a class, born in a group and whose title to being Superman was not to be lost even if they lost their virtue.[102]

Even as he finds deplorable resonances of the *Manusmriti* in *Thus Spoke Zarathustra*, Ambedkar refuses to deny the insane genius of Nietzsche's ambition—imagining an ethics of mastery for the future founded in disinterest and authentic virtue. One discerns here Ambedkar's own predilection for the immeasurable virtuosity of war between those who were equal in force and courage. The promise of equality that comes by way of mastery, even militarized sovereignty, never ceased to attract him. But this mastery was not of one over another; instead, this was a relational mastery, mastery without domination, one that forged a certain kinship between sovereign equals. Everyone must dutifully and concertedly prepare for such an "equalitarian" war. In fact, nonviolence, and in the final instance, love of politics itself, might be construed as being truthfully established only when everyone is equally an agent of transformation, only when everyone has the freedom to act, only when every subject has mastered the virtue of war and nonviolence alike. Fascism's language of spiritual ancestry had thus contaminated what might have been, at its center, its authentic "leveling force."[103]

Let us pause briefly to consider the term "leveling force," which is a peculiar way of describing equality. In a related formulation, again in *Philosophy of Hinduism*, Ambedkar describes "unfettered slavery," which is the equal right of everyone to own slaves, as an "equalitarian principle." As long as everyone is a master, as long as one class (Shudra) alone is not enslaved and devoid of mastery, slavery retained its "leveling force." Barely three paragraphs earlier, Ambedkar had already declared, "in short, justice is simply another name for liberty, equality, and fraternity."[104] The problem of whether general (and generalized) slavery, while it might be egalitarian inasmuch as everyone could be a master, is also just, whether mastery could ever be a ground for justice, whether the slave and his master could be brothers, Ambedkar does not resolve (and certainly does not address directly until his final writings in the 1950s). It is an obstacle his own thought creates for him. However, it is clear that for him justice within the system of generalized slavery ensues from the fact of equality in virtue, in the free access to experience and subjectivity. There is justice, in other words, if each is equally allowed the right, space, and faculty to hone his skill, master his craft, be a master. Within the precincts of such radical autonomy, everyone, without discrimination although not without competition, would be seen as equally deserving of owning a slave (and taking care of his property). Rather than being grounded in charity or compassion of one dominant community toward another, general slavery thus universalizes—no, radically frees—responsibility and moral action. Each now touches the other freely, each is obliged to care for the other, and each defends his neighbor and slave equally; everyone—and not the benevolent abolitionist alone—above all, is equally responsible for freedom. If it were not for Ambedkar's exacting critique of social and moral hierarchies, whether under slavery or democracy, this enigmatic privileging of general slavery as the ground of freedom would have been a terrifying formula. Here was one form that this concern with the freedom of others took, once the revolutionary equivalence between freedom-as-equality (the social demand for "equal opportunity") and freedom as the right to bear arms (the foundation of republican virtue, the defense of liberty in its classical sense) had been established. Let us be attentive to the equivalence Ambedkar sets up between knowledge and arms, sense and force, freedom and insurrection.

Assuming there is a grievance, assuming there is consciousness of grievance; there cannot be a rebellion by the lower orders against the Hindu social order because the Hindu social order denies the masses the right to use arms. Other social orders such as those of the Muslims or the Nazis follow the opposite course. They allow equal opportunity to all. They allow freedom to acquire knowledge. They allow the right to bear arms and take upon themselves the odium of suppressing rebellion by force and violence. To deny freedom of opportunity, to deny freedom to acquire knowledge, to deny the right of arms is a most cruel wrong. It mutilates and emasculates man. The Hindu social order is not ashamed to do this. It has, however, achieved two things. It has found the most effective, even though it be the most shameless method of preserving the established order. Secondly, notwithstanding the use of most inhuman means of killing manliness, it has given to the Hindus the reputation of being very humane people. The Nazis had indeed a great deal to learn from the Hindus. If they had adopted the technique of suppressing the masses devised by the Hindus they would have been able to crush the Jews without open cruelty and would have also exhibited themselves as humane masters.[105]

This is an alarming passage by any standard of ethics and rhetoric. The Jew, even in the shadows of the Nazi officer, claims Ambedkar, retains his consciousness, his experience and mortality, and, above all, his force. And this retention of the insurrectionary attribute—even if the Jewish revolt against Nazism never materialized—has left behind a semblance of existence, a moral psychology of freedom that might be brought to life again, a consciousness of Jewish being at its limit that might slowly claw back and reclaim its old virtues. The *atishudra*, however, is wholly sacrificed, his very sense of being annihilated, his personhood reminiscent of what Rousseau had called "total alienation."[106] And yet, at the same time, only by making this absolute alienation of the individual person—his indignity, humiliation, and violation—visible, by giving the experience and knowledge of suffering the force of radical autonomy and disinterest, would the general will of unequals and untouchables find its collective realization in the republic (thus the oxymoron in Rousseau, the "common me"). Without this productive tension between insurrection and alienation, this exchanging of place between force and weakness, this often heroic balance between sharing and solitude that republican virtue demands, there might be no freedom proper to justice.

There is, it is undeniable, something radically conservative in a thought that seeks to redraw the world according to a hierarchy of sufferers—Jew, *atishudra*, animal—whose fates, Ambedkar knew fully well, are incommensurable; their perishing is equal only inasmuch as their existence was saturated, equally, by an immeasurable suffering. Why, then, had Ambedkar felt compelled to conserve this global hierarchy of incommensurable sufferers and unequals? Does such a hierarchy of sufferers not reduce equality precisely to that which he had come to abhor, which is measure? Why does the untouchable have to be the most sovereign unequal, most unequal among the world's unequals? Measuring the violence of untouchable life against the servitude of the slaves of antiquity, he would write elsewhere: "To enslave a person and to train him is certainly better than a state of barbarity accompanied by freedom. Slavery did mean an exchange of semi-barbarism for civilization, a vague enough gift but real."[107] The argument for radical incommensurability of *atishudra* experience, the desire to amplify the exceptional cruelty of untouchability (a desire in which freedom must be denounced as a juridical form more repressive than slavery itself) leads Ambedkar into the language of violent measure and hierarchy. It propels him into seeing elements of liberty even in Roman bondage, in ways he found unavailable to the Hindu untouchable. It forces him into describing slavery as a "vague gift" for the slave, and in more religious moments, as a "saving grace," turning the insurrectionary force of his thought every now and then into republican exceptionalism.[108]

One cannot end this section without remarking on the risk of this emancipatory thought, then, one that has troubled republicanism, ancient and modern, Indian and European, since its inception. It is a thought that strives to generalize virtue, struggles to render every citizen's ability to love truth equally autonomous of their birth, religion, and race, and precisely in doing so, pushes itself to an extremity where it becomes difficult, even for its most scrupulous practitioners, to separate this radical autonomy of the citizen from his desire for mastery, even domination, over others. And yet, when one places this risk, this radicalization of autonomy—this conception of justice within the framework of sovereignty—within the revolutionary wholeness of Ambedkar's oeuvre, it becomes immediately clear that focusing on the risk by itself yields a rather incomplete interpretation of his moral and political commitments. Ambedkar's relationship with classical republicanism, especially his relationship with constitutionalism, was crucial his intellectual history, but it was never reducible to it.

Belief in Truth

Annihilation of Caste turned out, thus, to be anything but an anticipation either of a secular theology of government or of Ambedkar's restitutive constitutionalism.[109] Instead, it marked the most insurgent moment in his enduring struggle to formulate the conditions of a revolutionary faith beyond the limits of religion alone. Inserting himself into a classical debate on the relationship between force and justice, Ambedkar, one might argue, had attempted to transform the relationship between philosophy and revolution itself. In fact, the treatise, published despite conservative attempts to obstruct its delivery and dissemination, was itself an act of faith—a democratization of force—that had inscribed the right of insurrection at the heart of the social question in India. And "annihilation," or *ucched*, at once in the theological and republican sense of that word, was the making political of the void (I will take up in Chapter 7 Ambedkar's radicalization of the Buddhist notion of void or emptiness) that lay at the center of nationalist conceptions of freedom. If Ambedkar's frequent recourse to the republican Buddhism of Mauryan antiquity was any indication, this politicization of the void was not simply a gesture of responsibility toward the freedom of those left out by nationalism; it was also what he calls the "essence of a truly religious act," the obligation to reclaim belief. The desire for mastery that is so immanent to religion, he argues thus, cannot be overcome by turning away from religion. Such desire can be overcome only by forging another relationship between belief and sovereignty, another bond between religion and autonomy. It was a relationship that pushed classical republicanism—from which Ambedkar had no doubt learned a good deal—to its limit.

I would have no hesitation in attributing to Ambedkar's heretical approach to religion a kind of radical secularity but for the fact that the designation "secular" (and the many attitudes, commitments, and institutions that it is attached to within humanist conceptions of public life) raises for Ambedkar more questions about the pernicious attributes of the theologico-political than it answers. The least one can say is that for him, "secularism"—especially as a transcendental norm that ends up not only resembling the absolutist and sacrificial values of the "religious" but also begins to quickly develop a self-serving, insidious, and parasitic relationship with religion's enchanting and mystical power—was no less prone to interfering in the private lives of citizens than religion itself had been in the not so distant past. The claim that religion could be safely consigned to citizens' private lives, while a secular government could be left to manage public affairs, was a false one. In fact, the secularist distinction between public and private, between transcendent and immanent, Ambedkar believed, smacked of the same will to dominate everyday life that had sustained nonsecular political systems. "Is it reasonable," he asks in *Annihilation of Caste*, "to expect that the Brahmins will ever consent to lead a movement, the ultimate result of which is to destroy the power and prestige of the Brahmin caste?" His answer is unequivocal. "In my judgement, it is useless to make a distinction between the secular Brahmins and priestly Brahmins. Both are kith and kin. They are two arms of the same body, and one is bound to fight for the existence of the other."[110]

It was of paramount importance that mastery, domination, and interference be resisted. But untouchability was a counterintuitive form of interference. For it worked precisely through distancing and noninterference. Noninterference, nontouching, keeping distance, privacy and privation, invisibility and silence were, in fact, the juridical foundations of untouchability. Interference in India, in other words, worked through laws of noninterference; humiliation worked through practices of abandonment. Resistance against such laws could not be mounted simply through a negative (and secular-restitutive) conception of liberty, through the liberal notion of liberty as noninterference. Resistance, instead, had to be mounted around the principle of positive autonomy (which would also be an *equal* autonomy, an egalitarian sovereignty of citizens, granted to everyone for the pursuit and formulation of principles), a skillful cultivation of virtue, a collective reclamation of faculty and force, a shared love of truth. It is this democratization of autonomy, one that made virtuous pursuits available to even the weakest, poorest, and most untouchable of the republic, one that made reason accessible even to those barred from the world of Gods, scriptures, and men, that Ambedkar, in a public speech in 1927, calls "truth." "Whatever is for fraternity and brotherhood," he insists, "is truth."[111]

The fraternal sharing of freedom, making one's deepest personal convictions and truths political, acting with the sense that any action was truly responsible and autonomous only inasmuch as it was a resource for the freedom of others, the making transcendent of the immanent, in other words, was crucial to Ambedkar's religion. A faith freed from the injunctions of *dharma*, then; a religion grounded not in rules but principles: in the final years of his life, this striving for a religion without religion, a religion sensitive to sovereignty, even intimate with it (yet never subordinate to it), would culminate in Ambedkar's militant rearticulation of the Buddhist notion of *dhamma*. What new genealogy of radical democracy in the modern non-West might come into view, I ask in Chapter 7, if Ambedkar's turn to Buddhism—and his momentous conversion along with 500,000 followers just seven weeks before his death—is viewed not as a step taken by a melancholic man whose republican dreams lay shattered but actually as a revolutionary measure that marked the highest point—the immeasurable freedom—of his republican ethics? Perhaps "annihilation," as concept, figure, and force, was the first step, a means without measure, a strike without foundation, toward that freedom. It was certainly the mediating category in the revolutionary dialectic of freedom and equality, the "organic filament," the "integrating force" around which the unequal's demand for justice had finally revealed its insurrectionary form.[112]

PART III

RECONSTITUTIONS: OF BELIEF AND JUSTICE

6

Gandhi, the Reader

The decisive measure in Ambedkar's intellectual history, one that perhaps made his difference with Gandhi insurmountable, was the introduction of "annihilation" into his moral and political thought. Appearing for the first time in *Annihilation of Caste*, the term "annihilation," while used sparingly, quickly becomes the conceptual and rhetorical center of Ambedkar's elaborations on the morals of revolutionary action. One might even argue that *Annihilation of Caste*, by the sheer provocation of its title, lays the foundations of its author's singular call: the cognitive, material, and spatial universalization of force; the democratization (and dramatization) of its moral intensity and energy—general mobilization—as the precondition for equality in modern India. But this militant formulation of equality apart, "annihilation" also encapsulates, in a word, Ambedkar's demand that anticolonial thought reconceptualize the meaning of that very category for which it was mobilizing the people: freedom. Imagining equality without freedom, a freedom that must include the unmediated space to transform both freedom and equality in their very materiality, remained not only insufficiently political. Such an imagination, argued Ambedkar, was counterrevolutionary and irreligious in a distinctively Indian way. It was an imagination that sought to speak for the people even as it left them voiceless. "Let there be no repetition of the old method when the reformer claimed to know more of the requirements of his victims than the victims themselves," Ambedkar had told Gandhi in 1932 during their negotiations leading up to the Poona Pact.[1]

Force emerged as a mediating category in this inseparable relationship between freedom and equality, and, insisted Ambedkar, it could be thought only with them together. In the preceding chapters I have traced his struggle to formulate in the theologico-political shadows of *kshatriyadharma* the conditions of this egalitarian sovereignty: a moral and political order in which the annihilation of caste might not only reconstitute the society of equals but also, by destroying the structure of transcendence on which *Chaturvarnya* was founded, institute the people in its immanence as the sovereign locus of all action. In its purest form, Ambedkar argued, force belongs to the incommensurability, even singularity, of ordinary and mortal life, to the order of infinite difference and immeasurable freedom of civic activity, each shaped by the often conflicting yet inalienable liberties of the people, its authenticity secured by their quotidian energies, commonalities, and civility in shared spaces. This awareness of shared mortality within the richness of human difference, this everyday materiality—Ambedkar might call it the "generality"—of force, alone produces the constituents of a truly democratic sovereignty; it alone nurtures a genuine love of politics. Made with such provocative intensity in *Annihilation of Caste*, this proposition could not have resonated more strongly with the moral and political impulses of *Hind Swaraj*. But it was precisely this vision of politics that led Gandhi in 1936 to exclaim of Ambedkar, "Thank God. . . . he is singularly alone!"[2] Let us go straight to Gandhi's first response to *Annihilation of Caste*, in which a series of gathering thoughts takes the form (in quick sequence) of summarization, admiration, relief, and then, a subtle reprimand, even exclusion, one whose full force, at this point, is still to come.

The author of the address has quoted chapter and verse in proof of his threefold indictment—inhuman conduct itself, the unabashed justification for it on the part of the perpetrators, and the subsequent discovery that the justification was warranted by their scriptures. No Hindu who prizes his faith above life itself can afford to underrate the importance of this indictment. Dr. Ambedkar is not alone in his disgust. He is its most uncompromising exponent and one of the ablest among them. He is certainly the most irreconcilable among them. Thank God, in the front rank of the leaders he is singularly alone and as yet but a representative of a very small minority. But what he says is voiced with more or less vehemence by many leaders belonging to the depressed classes. Only the latter . . . not only do not threaten to give up Hinduism but find enough warmth in it to compensate for the shameful persecution to which the vast mass of Harijans are exposed.[3]

Ambedkar's fault is not that he highlights, with such incandescent brilliance, the exclusion and cruelty that is intrinsic to *Chaturvarnya*. His inadequacy lies, according to Gandhi, in his inability to find enough warmth in the divine glow of his own faith. By threatening to give up Hinduism altogether, by refusing, unlike other reformers, to partake of Hinduism's immeasurable spiritual reserves, which are enough to "compensate for the shameful persecution to which the vast mass of Harijans are [otherwise] exposed," Gandhi argues, Ambedkar's grasp not only of the meaning of freedom but of the meaning of faith as such—his understanding of the very relationship between faith and freedom—reeks of a terrifying lack of measure. In Chapter 7, I will return at length to how Ambedkar, with increasing vigor in his later works, comes to formulate the relationship between belief and autonomy, religion and will. But here, let us stay with the context of this developing disagreement over the ethics of reading and interpretation itself.

Gandhi published his response to *Annihilation of Caste* in two parts within a week in July 1936 in his newspaper *Harijan*. There was, apart from *Annihilation of Caste*, another thread of ontological concerns running through these essays. I call this thread "ontological" because responding to *Annihilation of Caste* was not simply, for Gandhi, a matter of immunizing Hinduism or *varnashramadharma* from Ambedkar's rebellious critique. Rather, responding to Ambedkar's treatise seems to have become for Gandhi a matter of reconceptualizing the foundations of responsible personhood. It involved—and coalesced around—his enduring search for a style and skill of reading proper to belief and being. And it quickly transformed, well beyond the duty to respond to a brilliant critic, into a moral task of emphasizing the value of manner (over matter) of truth. For it was in the means used to realize truth, Gandhi insists, that the possibility of justice lay. "Out of the Gita and the Ramayana, read carefully, one can get everything," he had written to a correspondent a decade before Ambedkar published *Annihilation of Caste*. "Purifying the heart and concentration of mind, reading of the above mentioned books and meditation on them, as also repetition of *Ramanama* [Rama's name] while not busy with benevolent activities, are very helpful. We should keep on trying and have faith that our efforts shall not go unrewarded. The only means of self-realization is total annihilation of the six-fold passion."[4]

It is not simply Gandhi's contention, then, that readings and meditations organized around certain religious texts bring the satyagrahi closer to realizing his self. Rather, it is his belief that reading, when mastered as a means (*sadhan*) and freed from the pressure of ends (*sadhya*), has an inalienable, indissoluble, and ontological relationship with one's very being. This emphasis on attentiveness toward the means of reading over the obsession with its ends extended well beyond Gandhi's early years (whose significance and sensitivities Isabel Hofmeyr has recently demonstrated in her history of the Gandhian printing press).[5] Indeed, by the 1930s, the focus on the purifying properties and proprieties of reading had acquired the form of a rigorous moral ontology. In what follows, I examine this ontological—or rather, ontotheological—framework within which Gandhi's relief at Ambedkar's aloneness took its form. I juxtapose the formidable exchange triggered by the publication of *Annihilation of Caste* with Gandhi's related meditations on what it meant, ontologically and phenomenologically, for a person to have

faith. What kind of person, as Gandhi often asked, was capable of cultivating the abilities and beliefs proper to a religious and ethical life? What
was the nature of that personhood around which—and in whom—an honest and sympathetic critique of religion might thrive? In ways more than
one, perhaps, *Annihilation of Caste* had cleared an unprecedented ground for
Gandhi's meditations on the relationship between faith and meaning, fidelity
and truth, and given them their most intense political form.

The Failure of Faith

It takes a reader little time to discern that at the heart of the disagreement between Ambedkar and Gandhi, particularly as it developed around
Annihilation of Caste, was the question of an ethics of reading. Reading here
did not involve just a person's encounter with texts. Rather, for both, reading
was an act of (keeping) faith. Reading was the sovereign among means to respond justly and faithfully to the other (master or unequal, God or untouchable). It was, above all, a phenomenological awareness of the relationship (and
place) between belief and meaning, verse and force, word and justice. This was
probably the reason why, among all the early twentieth-century public per-
sonalities who may have had equally strong commitments to—and engagement with the demanding realities of—mass politics, it was Ambedkar and
Gandhi who spent so much of their time reading, even and especially before
they responded in writing (and they wrote prolifically). "Caste has a divine
basis," Ambedkar had declared. "You must therefore destroy the sacredness
and divinity with which Caste has become invested. In the last analysis, this
means you must destroy the authority of the Shastras and the Vedas."[6]

Note, beneath the rhetoric of rebellion against the Shastras and Vedas,
the subtle intimations of force contained in the expression "in the last analysis."
Its use here seems to suggest that there are, for Ambedkar, at least two analytic
and performative dimensions of "annihilation." There is, in the first instance,
the annihilator's insurrection against the sacred foundation of the moral law
(*dharma*) that lends caste its social meaning and mystical power. In its negative sense, his destructive force is directed against this divine, transcendental,
and ontotheological foundation of meaning. And yet, in the second instance,
annihilation, when pushed to the limits of its own meaning, when pushed beyond its etymological and theological roots in nihilism and annihilationism
(*ucchedvad*)—from which Ambedkar would separate his own Madhyamika
Buddhist theology two decades later—also institutes a positive measure of autonomy. In fact, annihilation posits a principle of autonomy as such, one that
is available to even the most excluded, untouchable, unread, and unequal.

This autonomy, moreover, can come only through the act of reading the scripture in a sovereign way, unconstrained by the disciplinary rules, injunctions, and laws that prevent one from reading them. As Ambedkar demonstrates repeatedly, especially in his later works, the task of the annihilator was very similar to the task of the reader. Indeed, if there was a moral lesson in Ambedkar's exacting and exemplary readings of the verses from the *Manusmriti* in the *Annihilation of Caste* itself, it was that there was no annihilation without faithful, close, and intimate reading. The call for the annihilation of scripture, then, was provocative, intentionally performative, but it was for that reason no less sensitive to the ethical demands of keeping (and responding to) faith. On the contrary, there could be no annihilation in Ambedkar's terms without a certain religiosity, without a rigorous and revolutionary faith that kept vigil over the people's force and conduct.

It is clear in light of Gandhi's own extensive meditations on laws of proximity and distance (which often came to be organized around the surreptitious logic of *maryada dharma*) that he was no less resistant to Hinduism's injunctions underwriting untouchability. He was no less repelled by their cruel everyday forms than Ambedkar was. So it is all the more striking that, responding to *Annihilation of Caste* four years after their epic clash over the issue of minority representation and separate electorates, Gandhi, often only interested in the spirit of ancient texts, takes refuge in the notion of authenticity. Here is his second and lengthier response to the treatise, published a week later in *Harijan*.

The Vedas, Upanishads, *Smritis* and Puranas including *Ramayana* and *Mahabharata* are the Hindu scriptures. Nor is this a finite list. Every age or even generation has added to the list. It follows, therefore, that everything printed or even found handwritten is not scripture. The *Smritis*, for instance, contain much that can never be accepted as the word of God. Thus many of the texts that Dr. Ambedkar quotes from the *smritis* cannot be accepted as authentic. The scriptures properly so called can only be concerned with eternal verities and must appeal to any conscience, i.e., any heart whose eyes of understanding are opened. Nothing can be accepted as the word of God which cannot be tested by reason or is not capable of being spiritually experienced. And even when you have an expurgated edition of the scriptures, you will need their interpretation. Who is the best interpreter? Not learned men surely. Learning there must be. But religion does not live by it. It lives in the experiences of its saints and seers, in their lives and sayings. When all the most learned commentators of the scriptures are utterly forgotten, the accumulated experience of the sages and saints will abide and be an inspiration for ages to come. . . . Arrogation of a superior status by any of the varnas over another is a denial of the law. And there is nothing in the law of varna to warrant a belief in untouchability. (The essence of Hinduism is contained in its enunciation of one and only God as Truth and its bold acceptance of ahimsa as the law of the human family.). . . . In my opinion the profound mistake that Dr. Ambedkar has made in his address is to pick out the texts of doubtful authenticity and value and the state of degraded Hindus who are no fit specimens of the faith they, so woefully misrepresent. Judged by the standard applied by Dr. Ambedkar, every known living faith will probably fail . . . . Can a religion that was professed by Chaitanya, Jnyanadeva, Tukaram, Tiruvalluvar, Ramakrishna Paramahamsa, Raja Ram Mohan Roy, Maharshi Devendranath Tagore, Vivekanand and host of others who might be easily mentioned, so utterly devoid of merit as is made out in Dr. Ambedkar's address? A religion has to be judged not by its worst specimens but by the best it might have produced. For that and that alone can be used as the standard to aspire to, if not to improve upon.[7]

Gandhi's strategy of assimilating even the most insurgent among Hinduism's critics into its capacious fold emerges from a set of theoretical convictions that had begun to take shape more than a quarter of a century earlier in South Africa. But here, moving away from Gandhi's rather weak understanding of the relationship between mainstream and dissenting religious traditions of the subcontinent, I want to focus on his grasp of the relationship between faith and autonomy, or, in a more recognizable parlance, religion and reason. Every faith, according to Gandhi, must be judged within the limits of reason alone—that is, within the means and measure afforded by the faith to only those who reasonably believe in it. A truly religious critique turns only inward. For a religious critique to not turn into either empty idealism or dangerous nihilism, one must stand inside the faith to measure its true spiritual depth and richness, and only then obtain, if need be, the means to faithfully renounce it. One must, in other words, open oneself to religion at its best; one must give it a chance, even risk one's life for it.

This act of opening oneself to the best (and riskiest) of religion involves a distinctive measure, a profound restraint—namely, to refuse to judge a faith, especially a faith that one had not oneself experienced, by its worst. This may explain why Gandhi never himself argues in any substantive way for the reform of any religion, Judaism or Islam or Christianity, which he was not born into. It certainly explains why he strategically fails to recognize that *Annihilation of Caste* was composed by a Hindu as the parting act of faith, that its rebellious plea for investigating religion's meanings was indeed instigated from the inside, and that scrutinized closely, there could not have been a greater act of fidelity to truth, a more faithful gesture of responsibility toward religion, than an individual's decision to opt out of one in which he had lost faith. To concede that much, however, would amount to conceding that Ambedkar possessed the means and measure proper to a faithful destruction of religion, that he had mastered the revolutionary rigor and authenticity of sacrifice itself.

We have already, in the earlier chapters, explored the place of measure and means, or *sadhan*, in Gandhi's considerations on spiritual and manual rigor. Let me only note at this point that one can discern in the discriminating integrity of his thought—his refusal to denounce any religion he did not have faith in—the first visible marks of a sensitive thinker of agency coming close to a relinquishment of autonomy, indeed, to a renunciation of freedom in its most religious sense. If one can never stand outside existing religious traditions, if one cannot turn away religiously from one's own or another's faith to formulate a new one, if all one can do is reform that which was already given (the retrograde analogue of which is Hindu nationalism's perennial suspicion and appropriation of Buddhism as heresy or dissent within its own fold rather than conceding that it was a religion outside and autonomous of it), then what of the revolutionary promise that religion makes to the faithful and faithless alike: the promise of newness in their world? What of the gift of infinite regeneration, fecundity, and movement (Ambedkar might say "exodus" and escape), the affirmation of the immanent freedom and shared equality of life? What, as *Annihilation of Caste* demands, of the most sovereign of all religious obligations: the duty to destroy religion itself?

Gandhi was too careful a reader, too supple a theologian, to have missed the force of this religiosity, this call for a revolution in the ontology of faith, this demand for a religion without religion. So it is even more instructive that while Ambedkar questions the meaning of sacredness, Gandhi turns toward defending—as if this were a battle with a nihilist—the sacredness of meaning. From this defense follows a series of conservative gestures and contradictions, which express a desire to immunize not only faith but also reason. What is this immunization of belief, this rhetoric of authenticity—after more than a decade of interpretive liberty whose sovereign example was Gandhi's own *Discourses on the Gita*—mounting a resistance against? And what is it seeking to conserve? Not scripture itself, and in this Gandhi is consistent, but a certain religion of measured and practiced sacrifice, a religion that must be protected from hasty reading, from unreasonable rhetorical, conceptual, and performative force. Gandhi does not even momentarily confine the right of reading to learned men alone. There is, in these moments, a deep commitment to the democratization of scripture. But there also is, at the heart of this democratization, a supple and sensitive institution of limit on faith (and this includes limits on the craft of keeping faith). In fact, one might argue, that in reducing the mortal believer's experience of God to a phenomenology of experience and *place* (vision, touch, eye, heart, conscience, scripture)—as if God can be accorded a theoretical clarity, a reasonable and practical state of nature that can be mastered through infinite experimentation—it is Gandhi who makes a profoundly secularist gesture. And it is Ambedkar, who, in positing incandescent and annihilative force as the "essence of a truly religious act," opens himself to the gift (at once) of religion and autonomy, a faith, as he would put it, unbound by the law. I will take up the rhythms of the immense movement of religion in Ambedkar's thought in Chapter 7. In this chapter, I want to stay with Gandhi's moral ontology, especially that aspect of it that mediates his reading of *Annihilation of Caste* most strongly.

An Ambiguous Finitude

Six years before *Annihilation of Caste*, in a letter composed after his Tuesday morning prayers, Gandhi formulates in an extended fashion the crucial elements of his theory of being, of a life truthful and proper to religion.

The Satyagraha Ashram owes its very existence to the pursuit and the attempted practice of truth. The word "*satya*" is derived from *sat*, which means that which is. *Satya* means a state of being. Nothing is or exists in reality except Truth. That is why *sat* or *satya* is the right name for God. In fact it is more correct to say that Truth is God than to say that God is Truth. But as we cannot do without a ruler or general, the name God is and will remain more current. On deeper thinking, however, it will be realized that *sat* or *satya* is the only correct and fully significant name for God. . . . But how is one to realize this Truth, which may be likened to the philosopher's stone or the cow of plenty? By *abhyasa*, single-minded devotion, and *vairagya*, indifference to all other interests in life—replies the *Bhagavad Gita*. . . . Truth is the right designation of God. Hence there is nothing wrong in every man following Truth according to his lights. Indeed it is his duty to do so. Then if there is a mistake on the part of anyone so following Truth, it will be automatically set right. For the quest of Truth involves *tapascharya*, self-suffering, sometimes even unto death. . . . The pursuit of Truth is true *bhakti*, devotion. Such *bhakti* is "a bargain in which one risks one's very life." It is the path that leads to God. There is no place in it for cowardice, no place for defeat. It is the talisman by which death itself becomes the portal to life eternal.[8]

The reversal of conventional religious and theological discourse in this passage is decisive, at once reminiscent of early modern *bhakti*'s radical mysticism and yet brilliantly Gandhian in its rigor. It is not the sacrosanct name of God that secures the quotidian empiricism—or even the ontological essence—of the subject's truth and being. Rather, it is truth, one's very mode of being, which lends God his name and form. Only that which is experimental yet rigorous, contingent yet insoluble, finite yet transcendental, accessible to every being equally yet always understood unequally, Gandhi argues, is worthy of being called "faith." Apart from the ironic fact that God's transcendence is secured only in the subject's sacrificial rigor, in his *tapascharya*, in his conscious decision to risk his mortal life in the pursuit of eternal truth or being—as if one's death is a solitary experience that touches only one's own self, as if one's death does not touch precisely the others who remain behind to mourn it, as if death is anything but incommensurable and shared—there is a distinctive if oblique satyagrahic tendency at play here, one that takes this entire passage (and satyagraha itself) toward that zone of inseparability between life and law, measure and mastery.

Let us focus on two explicit and obverse gestures that Gandhi makes in this passage: one, rendering God into a figure of empirical finitude and worldly sovereignty whose commands—rules of propriety—now regulate the material and everyday spaces of the subject's being; and two, rendering the mortal subject itself into a mythic figure of infinitude—in the manner of classical humanism—that is deathless precisely because it could be given over to the transcendental logic of sacrifice. Between these two gestures, we can discern in Gandhi's thinking a peculiar insinuation of sovereignty—but sovereignty without autonomy—that often expresses itself in his writings through the name of "God" (and sometimes, as here, in the surreptitious guise of a mortal "general" or "ruler").

Beyond doubt, Gandhi's experiments in truth, as he called them, were marked by a radical universalism, by an egalitarian inclusion of the faithful and faithless alike, sometimes without any discrimination between the human and animal even. But in its perfect fullness and warmth, truth revealed itself only through privation, practice, and sacrifice. Indeed, it became inseparable from the sacrificial laws of nonviolence, and at its extremes, from the innermost desire to embody the law-as-self itself. "I often feel," Gandhi writes, reemphasizing satyagraha's commitment to the law as innermost voice, "that ahimsa is in Truth, not vice versa. What is perceived by a pure heart at a particular moment is Truth to it for that moment. By clinging to it, one can attain pure Truth. And I do not imagine that this will lead us into any moral dilemma."[9] Thus, a nonviolent life, a life of measure, can be attained only through a pure and unmediated pursuit of truth rather than the other way round. In this sense truth or *satya*, rather than being a means to some material end, becomes being or *sat*. The form and effects of this truth are autonomous—or indifferent—to moral judgments and consequences.

It is at this point that the accent shifts to the second sense of "being," and the ontology becomes more dogmatic. For this other being that Gandhi invokes is not always human and finite. In fact, Gandhi often swerves into invocations of the infinite and transcendent. "If it is possible for the human tongue to give the fullest description of God," he tells an audience in Europe in 1931, "I have come to the conclusion that for myself, God is Truth. But two years ago I went a step further and said that Truth is God."[10] The satyagrahi recovers truth (and therefore God) in quotidian forms of constantly improvised (but always truthful) devotion and obligation. Truth thus comes to be shaped by the satyagrahi's theistic style, private conviction, and, above all, by *sadhana*, the measured mastery of means. The laws of *sadhana* turn so profoundly inward here, their truth so incontrovertibly obeyed, that the life of the satyagrahi—the immanence of being—becomes inseparable from the transcendentalism of the moral norm.

This is why *niti dharma*, moral obligation grounded in the empirical knowledge of finitude, Gandhi can insist, is at once deeply private, almost secretive, and yet ameliorative and universal. For the consciousness of death alone, the need to forge a relationship with it and master one's fear of it, which sustains the practice of sacrifice in all religious traditions, transcends the specificities of the social or human world's myriad rituals, scriptures, and histories. The universality of mortal life, in other words, is constituted by the ironic awareness of the divine force that exists only in human guesswork (*anumaan*) and exceeds local peculiarities of species life and death. Inasmuch as one is human and distinct from other species, one's very being is shaped by this faith. Otherwise, one's life and death, an existence devoid of being, might merely resemble "the thoughtless annihilation of the moth in flame."[11] In its very universalism then, satyagrahic faith comes to be marked by a distinctive humanism, an anthropological exclusion even. Sacrificial agency, posits Gandhi, is characteristic of the human alone; death touched by faith is constitutively distinct from the acts of annihilation characteristic of other species. One even mourns the death of someone intimate faithfully, Gandhi writes, only inasmuch as one sees in that loss the source of force, an inspiration to duty, a resistance against annihilation through one's awareness of measure.

Finitude, the knowledge of death, thus, is the foundation of Gandhi's moral ontology (and the antithesis of annihilation, or *ucched*). It is only by mastering the secret of living by dying, in accord with the negative theology of the Upanishads, that the unequal, Gandhi argues, must seek equality. He writes of this fatal asceticism in the most unequivocal terms at the beginning of his final—and beyond any doubt his most heroic—endeavor, mounted in the winter of 1947–1948 against the genocide unleashed in northern India by the country's partition. "A pure fast, like duty, is its own reward. I do not embark upon it for the sake of the result it may bring. I do so because I must." The courage that flows from such self-knowledge runs deep, touching the nerve of one's very mortality. "Let me die, if I must," Gandhi demands, "in peace which I hope is ensured. Death for me would be a glorious deliverance rather than that I should be a helpless witness of the destruction of India, Hinduism, Sikhism, and Islam."[12] This is a heroic universalism. And yet it is also Gandhi's final statement on the primacy, indeed sovereignty, of means over ends, means that coalesce, in their very purity, around satyagraha's moral limits and anthropological exclusions. Less than three weeks later, he was shot dead by a Hindu fanatic on the lawn of Birla House in New Delhi. The universalism of this moral strategy is audacious. It was celebrated, even by Jewish writers such as Isaac Rosenfeld, as that singular gesture through which Gandhi revolutionized not only the practice of "self-realization" but also offered an escape from the violent idealism of modern politics.[13] Grappling in the aftermath of the war with the question of German guilt and the residues of his own nation's terrifying spirit of obedience, the German existentialist Karl Jaspers viewed this sacrificial politics, however, in a more ambivalent light. "Every sacrifice would be secret," wrote Jaspers on satyagraha's ontological privacy; it would be "rendered without publicity, untouchable in its metaphysical substance, to be sure, but unknown to men. Because no echoes would reach the public, no political consequences would result. Against a terror that knows no restriction by legal or conscientious qualms, sacrifice is futile insofar as it remains outside the communication of human activities."[14]

Perhaps in Ambedkar's call for annihilation, Gandhi had detected a force that was not so much an antithesis to life as it was an antithesis to the metaphysical substance and secrets of a proper death, and therefore, within satyagraha's moral ontology, antithetical to the meaning and truth of being. Annihilation, as that which was proper only to a moth, was antimeasure, its purported faithlessness a threat to satyagrahic measure. Which is perhaps why, wary of the visions of destructive reading (and collective faithlessness) that Ambedkar's lecture had conjured—and there was certainly a performative *coup de force* in *Annihilation of Caste*—Gandhi the reader lapsed into an immunizing mode, attempting, in a deeply nonreligious gesture, to delimit religion as religion within the limits of reason alone. In his turn toward *dhamma*, on the other hand, as we shall see in the final chapter of this book, Ambedkar opens himself to a gift of religion without religion, one grounded in the shared finitude of species life, rooted in an affirmation of life over death. Gandhi, at any rate, remained untouched by the most empirical of truths: finitude, like being, is irreducibly plural, and sacrifice infinite in its variety, logics, modes, and consequences. Innumerable and often involuntary forces shape the subject's experience of life and mortality, so that the conditions under which beings encounter their death are not only heterogeneous but also profoundly unequal. There can be no essence, no death as such. And inasmuch as there can be no proper, universal, or even truthful way of dying, there can be no politics founded on its mastery—on the sacrificial perfection of a people—that does not jeopardize the possibility of justice, and that is itself not unjust.

Responding Justly

Ambedkar, Sunnyata, *and Finitude*

Gandhi's death on 30 January 1948, six months after the British departure from India, marked a curious moment in Ambedkar's enduring engagement with the question of mortality. As the news of Gandhi's assassination by a Hindu fanatic spread and people crushed past the fences and lawns of the Birla House in New Delhi for one last view of the Mahatma, Ambedkar hurried to Gandhi's temporary residence in New Delhi. There is an archived photograph of Ambedkar, visibly perplexed and distraught, holding someone's hand for support while speaking with the Congress leader Shankarrao Dev at the Birla House that fateful evening.[1] He joined the funeral procession for a brief stretch, it is reported, before receding into his official residence in central Delhi.[2] As obituaries and tributes for the man who in Jawaharlal Nehru's words had been "loved beyond measure" began to flow in, however, Ambedkar went silent, moved but perhaps still gathering his thoughts, delimiting the impact that the event might possibly have on him. For both him and Gandhi, after all, civility toward the adversary had been inseparable from the unrelenting agonism of their exchanges. Punctuated by bouts of rhetorical excess, it was a relationship otherwise given to studied reserve, a reticent admiration even. Perhaps Ambedkar's silence was meant to prevent a lapse of this reserve, which would have been legitimate in its own right, given the momentousness of the event. But such a lapse might have also compromised his sense of his own irreducible obligation: interminable critique and sustained difference, even distance from the adversary who was now gone. Or perhaps after years of antagonism, the silencing of Gandhi and the end of India's struggle for freedom had also opened between them the possibility of another relationship, one constituted simultaneously by equanimity and avoidance, by a kind of equality that perhaps only the death of one might have established.

After all, in these years the language of compassion (*karuna*) and friendship (*maitri*)—and, above all, nonviolence (*ahimsa*), even though incommensurably different from Gandhi's—had also begun to acquire force in Ambedkar's own thinking. Gandhi's death, one might argue, had revealed to him the moral richness of the adversary in a way no other event might have.

Yet like all revelations, this too brought not as much a closure for Ambedkar or his final conversion to the idea of Gandhi's saintliness and luminosity as it inaugurated a new epoch of questioning the foundations of revelation itself. Only a few days later, breaking his silence on the assassination, Ambedkar offered a peculiar antiobituary (at once deeply private and unambiguously political), dramatically reversing the opening words of the address that Nehru had delivered to the nation on All India Radio the evening of the assassination. "Friends and comrades," the prime minister had announced, "the light has gone out of our lives and there is darkness everywhere." Even as he absorbs the demise of his antagonist, Ambedkar radicalizes, indeed inverts, the spiritual equivalence between Gandhi and luminescence that would henceforth be inscribed on all future histories of nationalism. "My real enemy has gone," Ambedkar is reported to have said. "Thank goodness the eclipse is over now."[3]

What kind of mourning was this? And where did its sudden force, its extremism and intensity, its strange sense of freedom even, come from? Why had Ambedkar ended his silence on Gandhi's assassination with this pronounced (if private) relief? Was this because, as the standard narrative goes, Gandhi's death had finally cleared the ground for a more urgent and purely political approach to questions of redistribution, militarization, and social security? Had Ambedkar's respite merely betrayed what was otherwise already a deep sense of discontent among Gandhi's followers perturbed by the lack of urgency in their leader's approach to the social questions that faced the new republic? Or did the antiobituary, on the contrary, reveal an insurrectionary ethics now beginning to take even firmer form within Ambedkar's moral ontology, within his "philosophy of life," as he called it, an ethics of survival that required him to keep distance and silence—even and especially when Gandhi's death had been consecrated in the annals of nationalism as an instance of the Mahatma's final and greatest self-sacrifice—from satyagraha's sacrificial politics? Was there at work in this act of distancing, in this desire to be neither moved nor touched by the adversary's death, in other words, a will to inscribe another ethics into politics, an attempt to retrieve justice and autonomy, indeed freedom itself, from the burdens of the political (a politics that includes rampant memorialization and appropriation of the past)? Beginning with these possibilities (and risks), this chapter brings together the religious, political, and ethical dimensions of Ambedkar's conception of radical democracy within the history of his final engagements with the theologico-political tradition (Indian and European). It is a history of Ambedkar's attempt to retrieve justice and freedom—indeed, autonomy as such—from the absolutism of the political and rehabilitate it into the richness of social life, or into that which, placing his thought somewhere between the religious and revolutionary, between justice and force, Ambedkar would call "the fraternal."

Death Penalties

Less than six months after Gandhi's assassination, at the height of the murder trial that would eventually end in November 1949 with the death by hanging of the Mahatma's assassin (and his co-conspirator), Ambedkar formulated in the newly formed Constituent Assembly of India a brief yet radical critique of the death penalty. Ethical and astute, affirming the sovereignty of life—the sovereignty of its vulnerable finitude—over all classical laws of sacrifice, death, and transcendence that had been arranged since antiquity under that pernicious juridico-religious category called *dharma,* he recalled India's ancient relationship with nonviolence instead, eloquently contrasting it with the violent theology that had come to sustain its modern state's right to take life. "This country," Ambedkar argued in an act of unprecedented concession, "by and large believes in the principle of nonviolence. It has been its ancient tradition, and although people may not be following it in actual practice, they certainly adhere to the principle of nonviolence as a moral mandate which they ought to observe as far as they possibly can and I think that, having regard to this fact, the proper thing for this country to do is to abolish the death sentence altogether."[4]

What had prompted this momentary lapse into the language of "ancient tradition," this peculiar combination of two categories, one referring to antiquity and the other to a canon, both of which Ambedkar had always approached with greatest scruple and suspicion? Was Ambedkar simply attempting to formulate another politics and ethics of sovereignty, one in which the state might voluntarily renounce its right to take the life of its subjects, which it often does in the very name of keeping them safe? Or was he trying to retrieve another prehistory of nonviolence, one that would be untouched by the monumental shadows of Gandhi's satyagraha against the empire (a satyagraha whose own rules of nonviolence, to say the least, were marked by a profound exclusion)? I say untouched by Gandhi, for just as Ambedkar had gone into silence in January 1948, he had again left unmentioned the name of the man who had so tirelessly insisted that such a spiritual tradition of nonviolence had indeed existed in India since antiquity.[5] But then, unlike Gan-

dhi, Ambedkar, even before invoking this classical history in the Constituent
Assembly, had always thought of nonviolence differently. He had never conceptualized it as mastery, as an ability to adhere to a transcendental norm or
rule of self-sacrifice, as an index of the spiritual strength and exemplarity of
a civilization. Instead, he spoke of nonviolence in the language of the weak,
those who had been victims of civilization's felony, violated by the lawlessness
of its *dharma*. And this violent illegality of the law, Ambedkar had always argued, was not contrary to *dharma*. Instead, lawlessness was the very foundation of its police power, felony lodged at the heart of its nonviolent ethics of
strength and mastery.

Yet a more constitutive aspect of Ambedkar's critique of capital punishment, certainly more significant than just his desire for another history
of nonviolence, and undeniably stronger than his desire for an *ahimsa* untouched by Gandhi, was his resistance against the rhetoric of exemplarity; his
opposition to rules of exemplary sacrifice, exemplary punishment, exemplary
norms and limits; his resistance, above all, against the exclusions of exemplarity as such. The earliest expression of this resistance had appeared more than
a decade earlier in *Annihilation of Caste*, where a critique of the violence that
perniciously sustained the rule of *maryada purushottama* Rama, that most exemplary of sovereigns, had been integrated with a critique of the death penalty. Note that the critique is not simply mounted against the laws of caste
(*Chaturvarnya*). Instead, it gets quickly woven around a critique of the exemplary violence of the norm, here exemplified by what even Ambedkar conceded was a work of genius, the *Manusmriti*.

Chaturvarnya cannot subsist by its own inherent goodness. It must be enforced
by law. That without penal sanction the ideal of Chaturvarnya cannot be realised
is proved by the story in the Ramayana of Rama killing Shambuka. Some people
seem to blame Rama because he wantonly and without reason killed Shambuka.
But to blame Rama for killing Shambuka is to misunderstand the whole situation.
Ram Raj was a raj based on Chaturvarnya. As a king, Rama was bound to maintain
Chaturvarnya. It was his duty therefore to kill Shambuka, the Shudra who had transgressed his class and wanted to be a Brahmin. This is the reason why Rama killed
Shambuka. But this also shows that penal sanction is necessary for the maintenance
of Chaturvarnya. Not only penal sanction is necessary, but the penalty of death is
necessary. That is why Rama did not inflict on Shambuka a lesser punishment. That
is why the Manusmriti prescribes such heavy sentences as cutting off the tongue, or
pouring of molten lead in the ears, of the Shudra who recites or hears the Veda.[6]

Ambedkar returns to Rama's murder of Shambuka in greater detail in
appendix 1 of his mature (and posthumously published) work, *Riddles of Hinduism*. There, he translates *dharma* as "sacred law," inscribing, in the process,

the death penalty at the punitive center of Indic religious and ascetic practices (*tapasya*). Shambuka was killed not simply because he was a Shudra; he was sacrificed, Ambedkar insists, because he had sought to perfect a form of mastery whose very law barred him from trying to touch its rules and practices. At the foundation of *Ramarajya,* then, is the inseparability between violence and norm, sacrifice and life, one that is given its most lawless, sovereign, and juridical form in the death penalty. It is in *The Buddha and His Dhamma,* as he integrates his critique of violence with a new prehistory of nonviolence, that Ambedkar ponders: "In the course of ancient past someone must have raised the question. Is the fittest (the strongest) the best?"[7] Nonviolence worthy of the name would belong, then, not to the realm of ascetic masters who had learned "the secret of living by dying," as Gandhi called it in a nondualist vein.[8] Rather, it would belong to the everyday life of those who live and die under the shadow of force. Nonviolence would belong to those ordinary mortals whose knowledge of suffering and death permits them to do nothing but affirm life. In this other conception of nonviolence, one that he had tried to reclaim in the Constituent Assembly, one in which life, even community, is affirmed in its finitude rather than in its immortal transcendence (to be secured by rules of self-sacrifice), a finitude wrested back from the anxieties of nothingness for a shared ethics of justice (rather than returned to the privacy of self-knowledge), Ambedkar perhaps felt Gandhi had no place.

If Ambedkar did not cultivate a taste for nationalist hagiography of spirit, immortality, and civilization, it was not only because he believed that categories such as civilization are deeply colonizing and shorn of civility, especially when they speak in the language of transcendence and infinitude. It was also because he never developed an affinity for death, either as concept, as institution, as a punitive rite monopolized by the state, or as a spiritual threshold in the life of a mortal that could be seen (as it is in many faiths and philosophies) as but a passage toward his absorption into the transcendental, groundless, and imperishable being (*purusha*). For Ambedkar, the immensity of death could be grasped neither by attending the rituals of mourning (for every death was mourned differently, or rather, the very institution of mourning was marked by inequality). Nor could death be grasped by viewing it as a perfectible route to mastery and transcendence, an outlook that reduced it to an "essence," as if there was a proper, universal way of approaching death as such. To understand death, one did not need to master *advaita* Hinduism's *mantra* of living by dying, especially if one had been born and condemned by the "force of law" to inhabit even the most public and shared spaces as "untouchable" and "invisible" in the perennially imminent shadows of one's own death.

It was precisely in those philosophical and theological traditions in which death had been elevated to the art of sacrifice and self-sacrifice, Ambedkar noted with a hint of sarcasm, that the most neighborly common, most civic elements of everyday life, the awareness of mortality that emerged only from the commonality of social life, the shared finitude of being—which together made possible a fraternity of equals—had been disavowed. For Ambedkar, this sharing of finitude did not simply involve sharing the rites of death and mourning. What I call finitude, on the contrary, was Ambedkar's awareness of the phenomenological richness, texture, and intricacy of creaturely life, each element in this intricate journey being singular and yet shared, each mutation in one's life incommensurable with another's, and yet conjoined by pacts of responsibility, attentiveness, and sympathy. "The condition for the growth of this sentiment of fraternity," Ambedkar argues, "lies in sharing in the vital processes of life. It is sharing in the joys and sorrows of birth, death, marriage and food."⁹ Barred by law from the equal sharing of these incommensurable and irreplaceable experiences, he asks, "Is there any wonder that the sentiment of fraternity is foreign to the Hindus?" Note how sensitive this formulation remains to the incurability of life's finitude, its slow mutation and inevitable dissolution, its constitutive perishability and impermanence (which Ambedkar would call *sunnyata*). And yet he remains farthest from renouncing its vitality, its energy, its force. Indeed, around *sunnyata* would coalesce Ambedkar's distinctive thinking of justice as responsibility. Suffice it to note here that "fraternity," which he sometimes substitutes with *maitri* in his later works, is not a masculine extension of brotherhood. On the contrary, fraternity is a form of autonomy grounded in responsibility toward that which Ambedkar had called in *Annihilation of Caste* the "incommensurability" of every individual.

Even rendered as *maitri*, its revolutionary force mediated by the ethics of Madhyamika Buddhism, "fraternity," as we shall see, remained nevertheless the point of greatest convergence and distance between Ambedkar and Rousseau. Shared between them was their enduring concern with the relationship between autonomy and will. Each life is singular, each is constituted by its difference from the other, and each that is born perishes in its own way. This awareness alone, for Ambedkar, serves as the foundation of a just autonomy, a responsible will. And yet, inasmuch as each life is equally perishable, vulnerable, finite, and new, each is also irreducibly equal to the other, an equality that is accomplished through the merging of the autonomous self in the authentic (and unmediated) sovereignty of the general will. Do rituals of mourning for only a few, do rhetorics of sacrifice and self-sacrifice, especially when they are institutionalized, allow for this incommensurable equality?

Unlike Gandhi, whose memorial speeches and obituaries for friends and dissenters alike came to constitute a thick compendium, it is thus revealing that Ambedkar wrote little about and in mourning.[10] "I shall die pretty soon," he had declared nonchalantly, as if to congratulate the legislators hostile to him in the middle of a parliamentary debate in 1956, just six months before his death.[11] This public nonchalance toward mortality, even his own, was balanced by a supreme, almost mystical, reserve toward the finitude of others. His most shattering losses—the deaths of his own children—remained guarded, preserved in poignant sentences of private correspondence, and shielded from public commentary.[12] Ambedkar simply refused to cultivate the kind of self-affection, the love of oneself cloaked in disinterest, that a genre like autobiography demands, which may be why, unlike so many nationalists of his time—among which Gandhi's *Experiments with Truth* was the most magisterial—he abandoned his own altogether after producing a few fragments between the late 1930s and early 1940s. And the least that can be said of those fragments is that only two—even in his projected autobiography—were about Ambedkar himself.

The irreconcilable resonance—simultaneity and separateness—between these two approaches to the self (self understood both as an ontological category and the phenomenological locus of being), becomes even starker when Ambedkar's preface to *The Buddha and His Dhamma* is juxtaposed with Gandhi's preface to *Hind Swaraj.* The similarity between the two masterworks is uncanny. Both appeared in their preliminary form as articles, Gandhi's in *Indian Opinion* in 1909, Ambedkar's as a smaller essay that had been commissioned by the *Journal of Mahabodhi Society* in Calcutta in 1951. Both were composed in dramatic frenzy, in a race against time (indeed, in a race against death), in a state of inflamed possession, with an equal mix of hope and pessimism. "I have written," Gandhi confessed to his Gujarati readers, "because I could not restrain myself."[13] In both *Hind Swaraj* and *The Buddha and His Dhamma,* authorial originality had been renounced straightaway, each text prefaced with expressions of debt to those who had come before, thought similarly, and kept faith. But where *Hind Swaraj* was composed by a man whose self-restraint and self-knowledge—whose self alone—seemed to be at stake (and at fire), Ambedkar writes with scruple and care deserving of what he calls the principle, even essence, of a religious responsibility. "On the publication of this article" he writes, "I received many calls, written and oral, to write such a book. It is in response to these calls that I have undertaken the task."[14] Writing is not an act of purifying the self (or it is not only that). It is rarely solitary, even in the greatest depths of solitude and aloneness. It is the act of responding justly to the other, nourishing that attentiveness, that faith, that memory, that shared place and refuge where justice might thrive.

I will take up in this chapter each of these moments in which Ambedkar's self appears fleetingly in that indecisive and inseparable knot between the private and public, the ethical and political, the immanent and transcendent, as he struggles to formulate, even liberate, the right to survive, the ethics of care and finitude—his term would be fraternity, or *maitri*—beyond the norms of the moral law. It was perhaps this affirmation of life in face of the profound exclusion that marks public rites of mourning, this affirmation of survival in face of the inequality that marks all rituals of life-taking (sanctioned either by the state or by the fanatic majority that acts in its name) and which themselves precede, necessitate, and enable (in a strangely circular logic) the rituals of mourning themselves, that Ambedkar's taciturnity around Gandhi's assassination had amplified.

Two suggestive silences on the adversary separated by less than six months, then, each shadowed by Ambedkar's own worsening illness and hardening resolve, amplify this unfolding responsibility to finitude. And this responsibility would concern not the vulnerability of the human alone. It would attempt to reconceptualize nonviolence as that which is owed to every living being susceptible to injury, whether woman or untouchable, human or animal, brother or enemy. It is toward this distinctive radicalization of finitude—a concept that often appears in Ambedkar's later writings as *sunnyata*, or "impermanence," and includes human and nonhuman others as equals—within his conception of justice as the principle of attentiveness and responsibility toward the other (and the principle itself as freedom from interference of rules and injunctions in which such responsibility might be nourished), as he put it in a Rousseauist vein in *Annihilation of Caste*, that this chapter turns. At its center is neither the question of Ambedkar's proximity and faithfulness to a particular religion among religions, nor an attempt to judge whether *The Buddha and His Dhamma* was a work of positive or negative theology (or of theology at all).[15] At the center of the chapter instead is an attempt to trace the movements of Ambedkar's theory of justice—his thinking of the "principle"—at the moment of its greatest distance and greatest proximity with religion as such, religion in the singular, or what Ambedkar calls "faith."

In contravention of his own will to scripture then—his desire that *The Buddha and His Dhamma* be seen as filling the void that is felt in Buddhism because it has no unitary foundation as Christianity has in the Bible[16]—I approach Ambedkar's masterwork not simply as a theological (or even religious) treatise. Nor do I take it as a treatise whose rhythms and impulses might be delimited and approached at a remove from Ambedkar's more political works, such as

Annihilation of Caste, Philosophy of Hinduism, or even the unfinished *Essays on the Bhagavad Gita.* Instead, I approach *The Buddha and His Dhamma* as a work in which the relationship between Ambedkar's ethics and politics, his understanding of the social in the shadows of the state, is illuminated in its greatest tension and fecundity. I approach it as a treatise in which his relationship to the theologico-political itself finds its most magisterial and promising form. *The Buddha and His Dhamma* is a testimony, I propose, to Ambedkar's keeping his faith in the fullest sense of the expression: keeping faith that beyond, without, and before its juridical and sacrificial perversions within particular traditions—beyond, that is, its "flaccid latitudinarianism," its false "spirit of toleration," its feigned "catholicity," as he had described them in response to Gandhi's critique of *Annihilation of Caste* in 1936[17]—religion as such has an immanent place in democracy; keeping faith, more crucially, that democracy will survive but only when it responds justly to religion.

One can, of course, argue that democracy, both before and after the birth of Christianity, has always had a co-creative relationship with "civic religion."[18] Ambedkar himself veers toward such a position when he quotes Burke's argument: "True religion is the foundation of society, the basis on which all true Civil Government rests, and both their sanction."[19] But neither in Ambedkar's early works nor in his later, more explicit religious writings, is democracy's relationship with faith reduced to the language of civic religion and municipal functions alone. In its truest form, Ambedkar argues instead, democracy involves an antifoundational annihilation of precisely those theologico-civic norms that prescribe and impose a false civility (and silence) rooted in exclusion and violence. "When I urge that these ancient rules of life be annulled, I am anxious that their place shall be taken by a religion of principles, which alone can lay claim to being a true religion."[20] Democracy demands, then, a repositing of virtue, a radical newness that can emerge only after an unconditional annulment, after an immeasurable act of faith, has transformed a people's moral psychology. But most crucially, these gestures and potentialities that democracy makes possible can be accessed through the irreducibility—Ambedkar's "essence"—of religious obligation alone. One can discern in these moments, especially as Ambedkar tries to think of religion as such, his profound ability to think of the immanence of belief—the ability to keep a faith that is equal and intrinsic to the constitution of every moral agent—itself opening out to a transcendental notion of religion.

In chapters 3 and 5, especially in light of his readings of Rousseau and Bergson, I argued that Ambedkar might be placed within that tradition of revolutionary thought in which force is seen not as an antithesis but as an irreducible constituent of acts of popular imagination and moral judgment, constitutive of a people's moral responsibility toward autonomy and free-dom (their own and others'). I called this Ambedkar's conceptual, rhetorical, and performative *coup de force*, the anarchic and antifoundational element in his moral ontology of action and belief, whose intensity was perhaps most immaculately arrested in his use of the word "annihilation." In the wake of *Annihilation of Caste* and its critique by Gandhi, Ambedkar tries to grasp and reconstitute this belief again. This is a difficult and distinctive task, for it re-quires him to think of belief in its essence in the midst precisely of his un-compromising annihilation of whatever remains of it in Hinduism. In this passage, he takes up the law of *varnashramadharma*, which stipulates that the mortal subject follow, in the interest of civic order, only the occupation that is mandated by the *varna* he is born into.

That a man is ready to render homage to many gods and goddesses may be cited as evidence of his tolerant spirit. But can it not also be evidence of an insincerity born of a desire to serve the times? I am sure that this toleration is merely insincerity. If this view is well founded, one may ask, what spiritual treasure can there be within a per-son who is ready to be a priest and a devotee to any deity that it serves his purpose to worship and to adore? Not only must such a person be deemed to be bankrupt of all spiritual treasures, but for him to practice so elevating a profession as that of a priest simply because it is ancestral—without faith, without belief, merely as a mechanical process handed down from father to son—is not a conservation of virtue; it I really the prostitution of a noble profession which is no other than the service of religion.[21]

Three crucial and related categories of Ambedkar's moral and politi-cal thought appear here: faith, tolerance, and virtue. But each is defined only negatively, in terms of features and elements that have come to compromise the possibility of belief rather than constitute it. The tension is thus palpa-ble, with Ambedkar negating—indeed, making a case for annihilating—what has come to be called (but is not) faith. And in this very instantiation of force—indeed a revolutionary intolerance—against faith, there is the attempt to think faith in its absolute singularity and autonomy, one that might come before any law and norm, grounded in the will and sovereignty of the "prin-ciple," worthy of people's belief. There is, on the one hand, then, Ambedkar's resistance against the moral law of ancestral calling. Such a law incurably blights the possibility of movement and newness, tying people's abilities and faculties to the immovable and indelible burden of birth. But more crucially, such law compromises the virtue of faith as such, its authenticity ruined by those lawgivers who reduce the practice of religion to a matter of inherited of-fice, duty, and occupation. This ruin, as Ambedkar unsparingly writes, leaves behind a spirit of personhood "without faith, without belief," incapable of "conservation of virtue." There is, on the other hand, in this resistance against the perversions of one religion, Ambedkar's struggle to reclaim precisely that which he thinks exists in its essence—and must be grasped—before the law and beyond religion: belief. There are glimpses here of what he has already called, a couple of months earlier in *Annihilation of Caste,* "responsibility," or rather, "the essence of a truly religious act." Here he calls this responsibility, somewhat obliquely, "sincerity." Rephrased thus, faith becomes both radically secular and irreducibly religious. In its secular sense, faith would involve the ability to keep a word, a promise, a secret (as, for instance, Ambedkar would keep the grief of burying his children private and secret) as the first gesture of responding justly to the other; an ability, at any rate, to be sincere and truthful to one's words. In its religious sense, faith would entail for Ambedkar an act of absolute belief (here, this belief is expressed negatively, as a ruin and exclusion), a belief that there are "spiritual treasures" and virtues that everyone must be allowed to cultivate, hone, and disseminate freely and responsibly. The question for Ambedkar, as it permeates his prolific final decade, was: Where could this faith, worthy of a citizen's belief, founded in citizen virtue, be found? In a stronger ontological sense, what would this faith, this religion without religion, be? It is this set of questions that he is seized by as he rushes to finish *The Buddha and His Dhamma* in his final months.

This struggle with religion, which acquires in the final years the language of love and nonviolence, coalescing around Ambedkar's critique of law and capital punishment, rarely ever strays far from the enduring political theoretical questions of freedom and force. In fact, these continuities would become even more strongly discernible in essays and writings of the same period, such as "Buddha or Karl Marx" and *Revolution and Counter-Revolution in Ancient India.* In "Buddha or Karl Marx," for instance, Ambedkar, in the footsteps of Dewey, posits "force as energy," one that makes possible a truly radical democracy, even annihilates evil. In more insurrectionary moments, he makes force the means to revolutionary justice, rendering the religious inseparable from the political. Indeed, the inseparability of the religious and the political, justice and force, is precisely what Ambedkar calls "responsibility." In the Mauryan Empire that had ruled over much of the Gangetic north three centuries before Christ, the same geographically and spiritually fertile landscape from which Buddhism emerged as a revolutionary critique of Brahmanism, not just law but ethics itself, after all, had been the business of sovereigns. Especially under the converted Mauryas, whose greatest exemplar was Asoka, the emperor who took shelter in Buddhism after his bloody and victorious campaign against a defiant state in peninsular India, religiosity was inseparable from the sovereign's right to disseminate, punish, and enforce moral conduct.[22] In renouncing violence after a necessary war, "Did not [the sovereign]

Asoka set an example?" Ambedkar asks in his essay on Marx.[23] Radical equality, he insists, is never free from the moral imperative of sovereignty; it renounces violence but never the faith in—faith as—force.

And yet, this was a very distinctive thinking of sovereignty, a struggle to grasp sovereignty without letting it lapse into mastery: sovereignty of the principle over the laws of solipsistic autonomy. In even the most political writings in the 1950s, thus, it is not the notion of a political self but rather an extremely vigilant sense of selflessness—a selfless self aware both of the threats of narcissism and temptation to nihilism that inheres in the negative theological determinations of the self (*atman*)—that Ambedkar places at the center of responsibility. And this ethics of responding justly and selflessly, which was the essence of an authentic faith, did not preclude war. "War there may be," we hear the Buddha conceding in the essay "Buddha or Karl Marx." But, the master cautions, "It must not be for selfish ends."[24] In *The Buddha and His Dhamma*, a few months earlier, not just war but love itself is inscribed within a responsibility to the other's life, a firmness of sincerity toward his finitude. The Buddha's principle, we are told, is, "Love all, so that you may not wish to kill any."[25] "From this it appears," concludes Ambedkar, "that the doctrine of Ahimsa [nonviolence] does not say, "Kill not." It says, "Love all."[26] It is at the extremities of this love, a love that thrives in the interstices between force and justice, between annihilation and care, between autonomy and equality, above all, that Ambedkar's radicalization of finitude, his thinking of *maitri* as responsibility beyond the human, would appear in its greatest promise.

The Principle of Responsibility

By way of retracing the movements of this thought in Ambedkar's later works, let us begin by posing a more limited question. What unifies the two moments of silence that punctuate Ambedkar's speeches and writings in 1948, a year otherwise important not only for the vigorous debates in the Constituent Assembly (where he raises the issue of death penalty) but also of prolific scholarly output (with *The Untouchables* published later that year)? The reply would be: both silences occur around Ambedkar's problem with the right to take life (and give death), a theme that saturates *The Untouchables* itself. There were, no doubt, differences here. The first silence was prompted by a Hindu fanatic's violent punishment to a "saint" who had purportedly let India's majority down. The second had developed around Ambedkar's critique of the alacrity of the theological tradition that sanctions the state's right to award capital punishment to its citizens (and indeed to those were less than citizens), a tradition of which he saw Gandhi—the punished saint himself—as being an important part. And yet both punishments—one executed by a fanatic, the other by the state—were inseparable, conjoined by what Ambedkar had discerned, as early as *Annihilation of Caste*, was their shared adherence to the punitive injunctions of *dharma*. Now himself in the final decade of his life, Ambedkar had entered a phase in which his enduring concern with the relationship between citizenship and force, justice and autonomy—not to mention his awareness of finitude itself—would acquire its most searching form. The silence on Gandhi's death, one might argue, had only expressed, albeit taciturnly, this emerging ethics. For no matter how close one is to one's own mortality, no matter how preoccupied one is with imagining an alternative universe of belief, the manner of one's condolence for the other, one's generosity or withholding of mourning, one's timing and untimeliness are never simply reducible to behavioral aberration, political motivation, or personal habit. Rather, as Partha Chatterjee shows, the work of mourning, silently or otherwise, may bring to surface deeper tensions at the heart of an entire constellation of reasons and responsibilities—tensions, for instance, between civility and antagonism, faith and heresy, cultures of living and dying, tensions, above all, between the ethical, political, and religious foundations of community.[27] How one mourns death is never innocent of how sovereign a condition—or precondition of sovereignty—one considers death (or the art of dying) to be.

In speaking of Ambedkar's silence, his resistance against offering condolence on Gandhi's demise in haste and in public, then, we are already in the vicinity of his enduring critique of sovereignty, whether this sovereignty, as he saw it, is instituted around the norm and rhetoric of a transcendental and deathless civilization or founded on a nationalist theology of spirit and immortality of soul. Theology, Ambedkar insists, even as he prepares to himself write one in his final years, is always already touched by the political. The discourse of religion is inseparable from the interest of nationalism and from the spirit of the state itself.[28] And yet religion also opens the possibility of justice and responsibility beyond all norms, laws, and rules of sacrifice and correctness. "A religious act may not be a correct act," he points out in *Annihilation of Caste*, "but at least it must be a responsible act."[29] What would this religious act, aware of its responsibility toward oneself and the other, grounded in the freedom of the principled believer, be? Or rather, as Ambedkar tirelessly asks in the 1940s and 1950s (in the wake of the catastrophic religious genocide that accompanied the partition of India), what would a responsible religion itself look like, a religion given over to virtue beyond (and before) the law, a religion in which faith and norm, life and rule, ethics and politics, would be restrained from lapsing into one another, a religion in which sacrifice would not compromise the principle of justice? A religion that would be, above all, aware of incommensurability and finitude (of its mortal practitioners), and yet "truly universal"?[30]

Such universality would be grounded not in the assumed sameness and homogeneity of world's religions, as if all religions were equal. "A force," writes Ambedkar categorically of religion in *Philosophy of Hinduism*, "which shows such a strange contrast in its result can [not] be accepted as good without examining the form it takes and the ideal it serves. Everything depends upon what social ideal a given religion as a divine scheme of governance holds out. This is a question that is not avowed by the science of comparative religion. Indeed, it begins where comparative religion ends."[31] Religion as such, religion in the singular then—by which Ambedkar means the principled and virtuous force of faith in its essence—unites not the gods of world's religions irrespective of their time, deed, and place (as if these differences did not matter), nor even gods of the same religion, who, for Ambedkar, are themselves grossly unequal (and must be welcomed or annihilated differently). Instead, religion (inasmuch as it can be spoken of in the singular) unites only the mortals who practice it; religion is morality grounded in finitude. Of this religion without religion (*dhamma*), Ambedkar writes in *The Buddha and His Dhamma*: "In Dhamma morality takes the place of God, although there is no God in Dhamma. In Dhamma there is no place for prayers, pilgrimages, rituals, ceremonies, or sacrifices. Morality is the essence of Dhamma."

Note that universal moral principles such as love and compassion are not abrogated. Instead, their irreducible, essential, and nonsubstitutable transcendence—which is what makes the fundamental obligation of one mortal toward another infinite, which gives finitude its universality across nations, races, and traditions, and which, therefore, gives *dhamma* its force—is grafted into the immanent and inalienable autonomy of the subject. In his religion without religion, or as Ambedkar calls it, following Bergson (if not only Bergson), "morality as religion," the transcendent supplements the immanent without being fully displaced by it. "Be good to your neighbour, because you are both children of God. That is the argument of religion. Every religion preaches morality, but morality is not the root of religion." On the other hand, separating those nonmoral religions from his own, he argues, "Morality is the essence of Dhamma. Morality in Dhamma arises from the direct necessity for man to love man. It does not require the sanction of God. It is not to please God that man has to be moral. It is for his own good that man has to love man."[32]

With this formulation, we have arrived at Ambedkar's predefinition of religion in the singular, a religion that comes before all religions, one in which religion's immeasurable force is unmoored from the transcendence of God and given over to an infinite responsibility and love between finite beings. Ambedkar calls this infinitude of responsibility amongst mortals "fraternity," positing it as the antidote not only to the sacrificial violence of organized religions but also to the classic liberal solution of "liberty for some" and "equality for a few," which in turn works as the foundations of the utilitarian theory of greatest good for the greatest number. "What is Fraternity?" he asks, before inscribing religion—indeed, the sacred—back into this revolutionary term. "It is nothing but another name for the brotherhood of men—which is another name for morality. This is why the Buddha preached that Dhamma is morality; and as Dhamma is sacred, so is morality."[33] Religion, if it exists at all, then, is that which brings mortals closer in a sacred moral pact that might be consummated only in their shared freedoms and responsibilities, forged only by their shared temperament and respect for autonomy. This autonomy requires force. For it requires, says Ambedkar, the destruction of religion in order to recover the essence of religion as such. In fact, one becomes religious only with the belief that like the mortal subject, religion too is finite, responsible to something other than itself. And only in this act of becoming responsible toward—responding justly to—the other (the other in its vulnerable finitude and immeasurable freedom) does a religion becomes "religious." Thus that "formula of impermanence," or *sunnyata*, that is eventually posited in *The Buddha and His Dhamma*: "being is becoming."[34] Let us first return, however, to that passage in *Annihilation of Caste* in which this moral ontology of responsibility as autonomy, a belief inalienable yet shared, principled yet insurrectionary, is given its most explicit form.

This difference between rules and principles makes the acts done in pursuit of them different in quality and in content. Doing what is said to be good by virtue of a rule and doing good in the light of a principle are two different things. The principle may be wrong, but the act is conscious and responsible. The rule may be right, but the act is mechanical. A religious act may not be a correct act, but must at least be a responsible act. To permit of this responsibility, religion must mainly be a matter of principles only. It cannot be a matter of rules. The moment it degenerates into rules it ceases to be religion, as it kills the responsibility which is the essence of a truly religious act. . . . I have, therefore, no hesitation in saying that such a religion must be destroyed and I say, there is nothing irreligious in working for the destruction of such a religion. Indeed, I hold that it is your bounden duty to tear the mask, to remove the misrepresentation that as caused by misnaming this Law as Religion.[35]

In ways more than one, this is a decisive passage in *Annihilation of Caste*. And it is so not simply because Ambedkar thinks religion has lost its soul to rules, but because he insists—in a moment of simultaneous negation and affirmation—that religion must be saved from itself. That there is, beyond all laws and rules of religion, an essence of belief, a faith that thrives only in the radical freedom of (destructive) action. This is a faith that might be expressed only (and before everything else) in an interpretive and cognitive *coup de force* against the law. This gesture must, in fact, be considered the most insurrectionary, most anarchic aspect of Ambedkar's annihilation (*ucched*): the belief that only when religion is shown to be complicit with the law can it be opened up for destruction. But Ambedkar also goes further here (and this is the moment of an unconditional, methodological annihilation): an irreligious religion, a norm, a rule, can be broken only when it is shown to be the law. "What," he asks earlier in the text, "will move men to such an action? It seems to me that, other things being equal, the only thing that will move one man to take such an action is the feeling that other men with whom he is acting are actuated by feelings of equality and fraternity and—above all—of justice."[36]

Responding justly to the other, then, requires that one exceed rules and norms. For responsibility is either in excess of the law or it is not a responsibility at all. It is a principle of radical autonomy, the essence of justice grounded in the sovereignty of will, one that joins the revolutionary force of fraternity—the shared force that is ingrained in the modern history of that word—with the attentiveness and respect toward the other that only the life force of religion as morality makes possible. "Law is secular, which anybody may break," Ambedkar would declare unequivocally in 1954, "while fraternity or religion is sacred which everybody must respect."[37] Note here the use of "must": religion must have the force of principle behind it; it must be respected; respect, even obligation, must be grounded in a shared moral ontology that imparts a just commonality to acts of individual will. This commonality is both the precondition of faith and the gift of religion to mortals (that every mortal must equally receive). No justice without force, then; and no force without justice. I will return later in the chapter to examine how deeply inflected Ambedkar's conception of religion is by the Rousseauist vision of the "general will," which he grafts on to the classical notion of *maitri*.

Here, meanwhile, autonomy involves revolutionary force—that is, the freedom (and will) to break from norms and injunctions. This is a freedom at once universal (because it must be given to everyone) and immanent (because on it rests an irreducible duty to respond justly to the finitude of being as such). "The Religious Revolution," Ambedkar writes in *Philosophy of Hinduism*, "was a revolution in norms," the norms that "enable us to judge what is right and wrong." As a result, "justice became appropriate to the modern world in which individual being the end, the moral good was held to be something which does justice to the individual." If, he hypothesizes, "it is said that these norms are not transcendental enough," then his own response to such a critique might be "that if a norm whereby one is to judge the philosophy of religion must be Godly, it must also so be earthly."[38]

Two parallel but inseparable gestures are thus made in *Annihilation of Caste, Philosophy of Hinduism,* and *The Buddha and His Dhamma.* First, Ambedkar proposes to think of religions in their immeasurable difference, religions at the outer limit of any possible comparativism and commensurability. He does not refute the great advances made by comparative religion, a discipline that has "abrogated the capricious distinctions between true and false religions" for good.[39] But in their social effects and force, religions must be thought discriminatingly and differentially. Not all religions, after all, place equal emphasis on morality; not all religions gift their believers an equal life (or, more importantly, an equal death). This gesture of differentiation makes possible the second measure, which shifts the analytical focus from the differences between religions to their singularity, from their incommensurability to the essence of religion. In fact, only when grasped in its infinite and immeasurable difference, insists Ambedkar, can religion be separated and thought in its absolute singularity; that is, in terms of what it gives the world rather than what it takes or demands from it, in terms of an immortal, sacred—indeed a quasi-transcendental—faith grounded in the knowledge of the limits and finitude of its practitioners rather in the groundless transcendence and infinitude of God. This would be a "religion of principles," one in which moral responsibility would entail not simply following rules but also securing a shared freedom, a justice grounded in the ordinary virtues and autonomy of mortals. This would be, above all, Ambedkar argues, religion in its "essence."

In *The Buddha and His Dhamma,* Ambedkar returns to the immortality of this virtue of mortals in three different places, each time through the classical Buddhist term *sila,* one of the ten virtues, among which were also *karuna* (love) and *maitri* (or friendship), that the Buddha laid out for his followers. I will return to these two terms below. Note here, meanwhile, how *sila* is rendered at once singular to a person's deepest temperament and yet can be thought through only in terms of shared moral values, and, indeed, shared places of refuge. "*Sila,*" Ambedkar quotes in the first instance, "is moral temperament, the disposition not to do evil and the disposition to do good; to be ashamed of doing wrong. To avoid to do evil for fear of punishment is Sila, Sila means fear of doing wrong."[40] But perhaps most important, *sila* is virtue grounded in the refusal to take life. It is an act of responding to the mortal other beyond all faith and knowledge, intuition and intelligence (*pradnya*). In fact, "the use of knowledge [itself] depends upon a man's Sila. Apart from Sila, knowledge has no value." Just a little earlier, in an even more unequivocal fashion, he affirms (and this is, let us note, Ambedkar's formulation, before he returns to the Buddha's own), "Pradnya is necessary," he confirms. "But Sila is more necessary. Mere Pradnya is dangerous. Pradnya is like a sword in the hand of man. In the hand of man with Sila it may be used for saving a man with danger. But in the hand of a man without Sila it may be used for murder. That is why Sila is more important than Pradnya. Pradnya is Vichar Dhamma or thinking aright. Sila is Achar Dhamma, acting aright."[41]

This is one moment in *The Buddha and His Dhamma* when Ambedkar uses his own voice not simply for a summation of Madhyamika Buddhist lessons but for deepening a classical concept, a moment (among many others) when he reorients classical metaphors in order to respond justly both to religion and to those mortals who practice it. In fact, it almost seems, here as elsewhere in *The Buddha and His Dhamma*, that he is addressing the oppressors, even as he wants the "depressed" and excluded to keep faith in their own virtues. It is important to pause here, then, for two main reasons. Firstly, because the question of responding to the other's vulnerability, the refusal to take life, the will to renounce all mastery over the other—or as Ambedkar says, in a word that he draws from his essay on the *Gita*, the principle against injury and "murder"—is made central to a life of virtue. Secondly, and more crucially, because the act of keeping faith, the quotidian gestures of sincerity and sympathy, are given unequivocal moral priority over acquiring knowledge and capacities of the soul and hand. Now the latter, which Ambedkar calls *pradnya*, and which can also refer to gnosis, or awareness, is by many accounts a notoriously difficult term within Indian traditions. In Gandhi's *Discourses on the Gita*, for instance, we have seen it rendered as moral and cognitive stability, an indifference to the vicissitudes of circumstance (*stithiprajna*) that Gandhi associates with those masters who have learned the "*mantra* of living by dying."[42]

In Ambedkar's writings, as in Buddhism at large, however, *pradnya* takes rich and varied meanings at different places, ranging from the "faculty" that helps overcome doubt to the capacity for analytical discrimination to the ability to balance faith with skepticism. Ambedkar's *pradnya* does not refer, in other words, simply to the power of concentration. In his reading of tradition, as we have seen above, it is likened, as Robert E. Buswell and Donald S. Lopez also remark, "to a sword that cuts through the web of ignorance."[43] This is the classical sword or faculty—which Gandhi associates with the *kshatriyadharma* of the warriors of the *Mahabharata*—that perhaps Ambedkar resists while privileging *sila* over *pradnya*. Knowledge without a commitment to keeping faith, without the resolve to keep the other safe, does not simply yield a swordlike knowledge susceptible to turning into an instrument of violence. It yields a body or person with knowledge intrinsically unsuitable to a religious responsibility toward the unequal. *Sila*, as remedy to this violence of learning, is not simply an ethics of virtuous action; it is a moral ontology, a place, a refuge of being otherwise. It is, Ambedkar now quotes the Buddha, "incomparable in this world. Sila is the beginning and the refuge."[44] It is a refuge of equality especially for those whose capacities and capabilities are deemed unworthy of modern social scientific knowledge, whose daily sacrifices—which demand sweat and blood—are so immeasurable that they escape the logic of modern economics and its laws of calculation, measure, and distribution.

Sila, then, is at once a profoundly political and ethical virtue—that is, at once concerned with a just renunciation of mastery (refusal to take life) and a place of civic refuge for mortals (a home away from sacrifice, prosecution, and calculation). From this mediation of politics by ethics, from the inseparability of Ambedkar's insurrectionary citizenship (that relinquishes mastery unconditionally) from his religious convictions, from his refusal to grant law a higher privilege than faith, emerges in his final years a distinctive theory of justice, one grounded not in measurable capacities of the multitude but in its immeasurable virtues and ability to keep faith. The mediation and inseparability also explain why in his final decade Ambedkar is able—no, compelled, he says—to work (using the best that comparative religion and theories of morality of the time had to offer) on his most intensely political critique of religion, namely, *Philosophy of Hinduism*, and simultaneously, frantically, finish work on his magnum opus, *The Buddha and His Dhamma*, which speaks of nothing other than religion in its singularity and incomparability, a religion of principles proper to justice, a religion that possesses "a philosophy of life." The assembling of this philosophy, this affirmation of virtue as a responsibility toward life, involved a long, melancholic encounter with death itself.

An Affirmative Finitude

It is not that death, as concept and experience, did not touch Ambedkar or that he did not desire or believe in condolences. On the contrary, he often ascribes a transformative force to mortality and mourning, a force that changes one's relationship to the world every single time, leaving in its wake a vacancy and emptiness that one can never prepare for well enough, let alone master. It is this irreducible nothingness that death leaves behind that a younger Ambedkar finds himself unable to celebrate. As he puts it in a poignant 1926 letter written after burying his own children,

I thought you had ceased to care for me. That it is not so and that at least on occasions of grief and sorrow you feel bound a line of condolence is some evidence that the flame is not yet wholly out. There is no use pretending that my wife and I have recovered from the shock of my son's death and I do not think that we ever shall. We have in all buried four precious children three sons and a daughter, all sprightly, auspicious, and handsome children. The thought of this is sufficiently crushing . . . let alone the future which would have been theirs if they had lived. We are living no doubt in the sense that days are passing over us as does the cloud. With the loss . . . the salt of our life is gone and as the Bible says, "Ye are the salt of the earth, if it leaveth the earth, wherewith will it be salted?" I feel the truth of this every moment in my almost vacant and empty life. My last boy was a wonderful boy the like of whom I have seldom seen. With his passing away life to me is a garden full of weeds. But enough of this, I am too overcome to write anymore. With best regards of a *broken man.*[45]

Death breaks. Death is always cloudy, elusive, impossible to experience for oneself, not available to everyone in the same way, and profoundly unequal. There is, then, no death as such—that is, death in its essence. There is in its place only a silent nothingness and nonbeing, left behind when the other has departed. And yet, despite this nonbeing, death always takes something irreversibly away from everyone it touches. Cultural differences in rituals, rites, and mourning are subsumed in the universal finality of loss, which is the same everywhere. It is only for the worse that mortals left behind, mourners who survive, never experience this crushing revelation in their own death (for one's own death never arrives, at least not in the form in which one might ever experience it oneself) but only in another's demise. One possesses the knowledge of death, then, only by being forced to live through another's departure, waiting, in the most unequal and futile way, for one's own. But perhaps most irreparably, death takes away a finite being, a child or an adversary, who can never be replaced. Death changes the earth irreplaceably, every single time, revealing a new corner of nothingness in the life of those left behind; a place of nonbeing that those who must survive, those who must live on, tend like gardeners tend a garden full of weeds, in the shadows of an absent hope that their children (or flowers) will spring back to life.

And yet, note the almost abrupt resistance that emerges precisely from being overcome by death; the resistance that enables the broken man—as it must all broken men—to stop grieving, to resist putting more of the self on paper, to desist from words that speak of oneself alone and thus consume it. Here, finitude is experienced as—transformed into—authentic force, even a primordial one; impermanence, or *sunnyata*, shines as a revolutionary potentiality that belongs to—and anchors the resistance of—the most vulnerable, most unequal, most silent. Ambedkar's poignant endeavor to affirm such force, his acute awareness of the incompleteness opened by another's demise, is inimitably captured in the long dedication that appears in what is otherwise his most strident work of political critique. This dedication is striking not simply for Ambedkar's ethics of firmness and, at times, frantic resistance against death. Instead, it is his belief that life must be affirmed, politically and publicly, even and especially when one stands in the inalienably private shadows of loss and mortality. In *What Congress and Gandhi Have Done to the Untouchables*, completed in June 1945 as the Second World War was coming to an end, a very different Ambedkar writes this tribute to "F." Extracting a pivotal passage of dialogue between Naomi, Orpah, and Ruth from the Hebrew Bible, he reminisces:

I know how, when we used to read the Bible together, you would be affected by the sweetness and pathos of this passage. While you will be glad to read it again you will, I am sure, ask me what made me recall it in this connection. . . . Ruth's statement "Thy people shall be my people and thy God my God" defined ancient society by its most dominant characteristic namely that it was a society of man plus God while modern society is a society of men only (pray remember that in men I include women also). My view was not then acceptable to you. But you were interested enough to urge me to write a book on this theme. I promised to do so. For as an oriental I belong to a society which is still ancient and in which God is a much more important member than man is. The part of the conversation which is important to me at this stage is the promise I then made to dedicate the book to you if I succeeded in writing one. . . . The chances of developing the theme in a book form are now very remote. I am drawn in the vortex of politics, which leaves no time for literary pursuits. I do not know when I shall be out of it. The feeling of failure to fulfill my promise has haunted me ever since the war started. Equally distressing was the fear that you might pass away as a war casualty and not be there to receive if I were to have time to complete it. But the unexpected has happened. There you are, out of the throes of Death. Here is a book ready awaiting dedication. This happy conjunction of two such events has suggested to me the idea that rather than postpone it indefinitely I might redeem my word, by dedicating this book which I have succeeded in bringing to completion. . . . Will you accept it?[46]

Joy, sweetness, gift, struggle, pathos, death, haunting: these form a complex of sentiments that anticolonial historiography generally refuses to identify with Ambedkar, just as it refuses to concede that such sentiments might have been part of his distinctive approach to the question of justice— a justice at odds with the norms of the political itself. Earlier that year, in the preface to *Pakistan, or the Partition of India*, Ambedkar had characterized the nature of his true commitments even more unequivocally. "I cannot help recalling with regret how much of my time it has consumed," he writes, without irony, about his most important work of political philosophy, "when so much of my other literary work of greater importance to me than this is held up for the want of it."[47] So political philosophy—the method and practice of grasping politics in its essence—distracts Ambedkar from his more important literary commitments. The distraction, he wants the reader to know, is irresistible and deeply felt. For it is mentioned, without a hint of irony and with great seriousness, in the preface of his most voluminous (and, he says, distracting) treatise on politics itself. We have already seen in Chapter 3 Ambedkar's attribution to religion a certain love of truth that philosophy lacks. And yet as this confessional statement about the failure, even frustrating inability, to pull oneself decisively away from one toward the other shows, religion and philosophy, private convictions and public commitments, self and the political remain indissociable, even unthinkable, without each other. Ambedkar thinks of literature even as he writes philosophy; or perhaps it is precisely his literary commitments that give his philosophy its religious soul, its truth and love. Here again, in this memory of friendship that has coalesced around the Bible, we see the religious, indeed the theological, aligned with the political, each at once at cross-purposes and woven inseparably into the other. This is not a disenchanted, cynical, nihilistic conception of justice, then, one shorn of moral values such as patience and love, let alone a temperament suitable for reading, as Gandhi had insinuated in his critique of *Annihilation of Caste*. It is a poetic plea for justice imagined in the shadow of scripture, formulated, as if Ambedkar were pointedly responding to Gandhi's accusation that he was a reader without faith, in an act of careful and dedicated reading of scripture itself. An exceptional Ambedkar comes out of the cloud in this dedication to "F." Yes, he admits, the vortex of politics does not leave time for literary pursuits; yes, death awaits us all as a "throe" that must be crossed; yes, in the shadows of war, life (one's own and the other's) is but mere a "casualty," another number, another haunting, another corner of emptiness; yes, one does not know when one might come out of the web of politics to finish writing. For there is justice only in relentless, frantic writing.

The book Ambedkar had promised to write would be, if he finished it, a treatise on the question of God's existence. It would outline the distinction between Oriental and Occidental theologies and their different attitudes toward transcendence and being. It would revolve around those past conversations about Ruth's statement: "Thy people shall be my people and Thy God my God." It would include, as he had always done, women as citizens and not merely men, women as mortals, equal parts of a finite world, women as citizens who retain the freedom to choose whether they might leave their people for foreign lands or stay behind. Just within five years, Ambedkar would begin pushing for his antipatriarchal Hindu Code Bill in the parliament. And yet politics, he confesses, has cast a long shadow on his engagement with questions that had mattered equally if not more to him: questions of home and dwelling, questions of life and its ephemerality. Now he hurries to reclaim life in the gesture of this gift, in the act of keeping his word, in the fulfillment of the promise of a book he had made.

For Ambedkar, keeping faith, keeping the word, sincerity to one's vow—and this ability to keep the word, to be resolute in the vow, which involved a distinctive accentuation of will—was the predefinition of religion. Just as the reclamation of life (one's own and another's), especially when one was confronted with its ineradicable impermanence, was the precondition of a religious responsibility. Ambedkar would return repeatedly in one genre or another (in the dedication inspired by ancient Israel, in a fragment on Shelley elsewhere) to this affirmation of life as the assertion of will, a will given not to mastery but one that was formed out of obligation to the other alone. Shorn of such sense of responsibility and bound instead by rules, "The Hindus," writes Ambedkar in 1936, quoting Mathew Arnold, "are wandering between two worlds, one dead, the other powerless to be born."[48] To be bound by rules, to be devoid of responsibility, was equal to being not born at all. But even as he describes the powerlessness of this community he sees as being devoid of will (the tragedy of a society that is neither alive nor dead, grounded neither in general will nor in the freedom of self-autonomy), Ambedkar's affirmation has taken a radically negative form. In fact, affirmation here involves a very firm and sensitive task of what in Chapter 1, following Hent de Vries, I called Ambedkar's "non-negative negation" of religion, one that appears at its most supple, most oblique, and precisely therefore, one might argue, closest to classical negative theology, in his struggle with the category of the self. In a small autobiographical fragment written the same year that he published *Annihilation of Caste,* Ambedkar recalls a few perilous events that occurred right after his return from London in 1918. He begins by writing about the time, when, after having just found employment with the princely state of Baroda, he had managed to arrange, with considerable difficulty given his social status as an "untouchable," for a place to live. Two decades later, he recounts his kinship with that "dungeon" situated somewhere between life and death thus:

The idea of returning to the inn to spend the night therein was most terrifying to me and I used to return to the inn only because I had no other place under the sky to go for rest. In this big hall on the first floor of the inn there were no fellow human beings to talk to. I was quite alone. The whole hall was enveloped in complete darkness. . . . The caretaker used to bring up for my use a small hurricane lamp. Its light could not extend beyond a few inches. I felt that I was in a dungeon and I longed for the company of some human being to talk to. But there was none. In the absence of the company of human beings I sought the company of books and read and read. Absorbed in reading I forgot my lonely condition. But the chirping and flying about of the bats, which had made the hall their home, often distracted my mind and sent cold shivers through me reminding me of what I was endeavoring to forget, that I was in a strange place under strange conditions. Many a time I must have been angry. But I subdued my grief and my anger by the feeling that though it was a dungeon, it was a shelter and that some shelter was better than no shelter.[49]

The fear of returning every evening not to a prison but rather to that which one must call shelter (and feel fortunate for it too)—Ambedkar here forces his readers to think the conditions of such life: a life constituted in its very alienation from other lives, human and animal; a life in which distinctions between homelessness and being-at-home, between longing for sleep and the risk of sleeping for too long, between solitude and death, are rendered meaningless by the void at which the subject must stare every night. There is the void, of course, that separates the human from the animal, a separation Ambedkar would subsequently renounce by way of introducing the concept of *maitri* into his moral and political thought. But more crucially, there is the void that partitions the human itself: the void of silence, the unavailability of speech, the absence of touch, the inadequacy of a vision constantly imperiled by the darkness of the dungeon (and the unreliability of the lamp); life at the limit of experience, in other words, where all that remains is an exemplary awareness of finitude. This finitude would not simply mean life's mortality. Instead, in this passage, which we must approach not simply as a passage on the memorialization of suffering but also as a passage on Ambedkar's struggle against self-memorialization, Ambedkar gives us perhaps a different meaning of finitude—a finitude grounded not as much in life's fickle intimacy with death as much a finitude grounded in its abyssal difference from that which surrounds it (and yet in that very abyss, constitutes its meaning). There is in this passage, after all, both the fierceness of prose, the lingering memory of anger, and, at the same time, the will to get past that memory, the will to get past *any* memory that concerns the masteries and exclusions of the self alone. Such relinquishment of the self is not a critique of individual will or even individualism. On the contrary, what seems to be at work here is precisely a will grounded in singularity, a will that separates one from the other. And yet this singularity—"incommensurability"—of the self is constituted and becomes visible only in its relationship to—and proximity with—the absolutely other (enemy, animal, Brahmin, God).

Let us note three related threads that run, then, through this autobiographical fragment. First, the inalienable source of will, one that every person possesses, lies in the indestructibility of individual courage. This is the will, for instance, that lends Ambedkar the courage to make his own solitude meaningful by clinging on to the small patch of light, the commitment to read voraciously, the resolve to respond to his alienation by freeing, indeed alienating himself from the strangeness of conditions itself and losing himself in books. Second, this will thrives in its absolute incommensurability; one can neither nourish it for others nor claim to possess and vouchsafe its *mantra* on behalf of others. Third (and this is where the Rousseauist conception of general will inflects Ambedkar's engagement with the self most strongly), one comes to an awareness of this will only in sharing the vital processes and struggles of life and death. One's will is only as strong as one's awareness of the other's loneliness and injurability, one's freedom only as meaningful as one's ability to respond justly to the other's finitude. Perhaps Ambedkar's attempt to write an autobiography and then his abandonment of the project was reflective of this awareness. Perhaps he imagined, for a brief moment in the years immediately following the publication of *Annihilation of Caste,* that the story of his encounter with the nothingness of a dungeon was an exemplary one that needed to be shared. And then this conviction was replaced by his reticence about making himself the moral exemplar of those millions who followed him (as if, like a mystic, he had a secret).

Virtue lies, then, not in exemplarity but in affirming forcefully the shared mortality of life instead. Rarely has the desire to be exemplary, indeed the zeal to be exceptional, not involved the exclusion of others; rarely has exclusion worked without grounding itself in exemplarity. Ambedkar resisted such gestures fiercely, especially when his detractors unleashed sarcastic refrains of his greatness. "Do not pray for my soul," he would interject in the middle of a parliamentary debate some months before his own death. "I do not believe in God. I have no soul. I have spared you that trouble."[50] To live on despite life's destructibility; to nourish the knowledge of one's finitude in which no soul, no spirit, no remainder, no homage to God, nothing except nothingness is left behind; to temper, above all, the irreducible sovereignty of will that accrues from this self-knowledge (without falling to the temptation to mastery and domination over others) is where the seeds of justice lie. Mastery has no place in such a conception because ascetic mastery, even and especially over oneself, merely mocks, despite its best intentions, the suffering of those who bear that experience of privation involuntarily and under force. A just life, on the contrary, must inhabit the world of neighbors, owing responsibility to those as yet unborn. For Ambedkar, the ethical and political value of impermanence, or *sunnyata,* would emerge from this imperative of justice for those still to come. In fact, *sunnyata* was nothing but finitude turned radical, with its classical negative theology of emptiness given the charge of a revolutionary faith that belonged to the people alone. This charge was produced through quotidian sacrifices, from the infinitesimal force of ordinary mortals. It emerged from everyday vulnerabilities of the self rather being grounded in the metaphysics of self-sacrifice. *Sunnyata* was the foundation of shared will, the will to sharing and responsibility beyond the infinite difference of species life. It was the autonomy of mortals without the desire for transcendence, their sovereignty without theology.

Sovereignty *Otherwise*

In *The Buddha and His Dhamma*, compared to any other of Ambedkar's works, of course, this affirmation of survival, this ethics of living virtuously without giving in to sacrifice in its many ritual, theological, and institutional forms, is at its most resolute; Ambedkar's alignment of life's impermanence with the immortality of justice, at its most religious. Neither the ineluctability of war nor the imperative of punishment, as we shall see, however, is renounced there. Yet even if contemporary concerns appear to be only obliquely connected to the nature of the Madhyamika Buddhist materials that Ambedkar chooses for summation, commentary, and interpretation, his engagement with the pernicious presence of the theologico-political in the republican imagination of modern India is at its most sensitive around the time he begins work on *The Buddha and His Dhamma*. Indeed, this engagement with republicanism, one might argue, can appear so oblique precisely because it is at its most sensitive and careful. It was from this sensitivity to the possible (and perennial) corruption of faith by the law, from this awareness of the inability of law to even comprehend the value of life, in fact, that Ambedkar's mature critique of the death penalty—and some of the most fascinating pages of commentary in *The Buddha and His Dhamma*—emerged. The critique of law and its violent "police power" was not a gesture toward renouncing force, let alone relinquishing will, or even sovereignty. Ambedkar's resistance against rites and institutions of death—a resistance whose earliest and most unambiguous expressions had emerged in *Annihilation of Caste*—involved, on the contrary, a distinctive approach to the principle of sovereignty, a sovereignty otherwise, which was in its truest form, he argued, inseparable from those precepts of moral conduct (*achar dhamma*) and everyday virtue that regulate one's citizen's responsibility toward another. True autonomy or sovereignty (a sovereignty worthy of being called human), involved an unconditional brotherliness, a selfless attentiveness toward the needs of the neighbor and brother. It involved a privileging of responsibility and humanity over abstract conceptions of equality. In his 1952 All India Radio speech, breaking away in the most unequivocal fashion from the French revolutionary triad of "liberty, equality, fraternity," Ambedkar would call this other humanity "religion."[51]

Let no one, however, say that I have borrowed my philosophy from the French Revolution. I have not. My philosophy has roots in religion and not in political science. I have derived them from the teachings of my Master, the Buddha. In his philosophy, liberty and equality had a place: but he added that unlimited liberty destroyed equality, and absolute equality left no room for liberty. In His Philosophy, law had a place only as a safeguard against the breaches of liberty and or equality. He gave the highest place to fraternity as the only real safeguard against the denial of liberty or equality or fraternity which was another name for brotherhood or humanity, which was again another name for religion. . . . My philosophy has a mission. I have to do the work of conversion; for, I have to make the followers of *Triguna* theory to give it up and accept mine. Indians today are governed by two different ideologies. Their political ideal set out in the Preamble to the Constitution affirms a life of Liberty, Equality, and Fraternity. Their social ideal embodied in their religion denies them.[52]

Without any risk of overstressing the point, we can immediately acknowledge that Ambedkar sees in the act of conversion—from one faith to another (in the religious sense) and from one set of beliefs and attitudes to another (in a secular, constitutional sense)—not a divisive strategy but a potential force that possesses the capacity to touch and transform the majority and minority, oppressor and oppressed, evil and good, *equally.* Conversions happen, of course, only because religions are different and unequal; they happen because an autonomous person, a person with will and force, is able to discriminate between them while choosing one over the other. But the act of conversion itself does not divide; it only responds to the imperative of justice beyond all religious, political, social, and ontological distinctions. In fact, so firm is Ambedkar's moral conviction—which acquires here, it is true, the form of an anthropological universalism—that he takes it as his ethical duty to convert even those Hindus whose belief in *Triguna*, a strand of the classical Sankhya philosophy within which he places the violence of the *Bhagavad Gita*, has led them to compromise their own constitution. Their religion denies them their constitution, and yet it is not the constitution but religion alone—a religion without religion—that might redeem whatever humanity is left in the oppressor.

The annihilation of one religion in order to recover religion as such: this would be an act of faith at once profoundly religious and secular, a vow and duty—"I have to do the work of conversion," insists Ambedkar—that responds at once to religion and constitution. But even more crucially, conversion itself has been radicalized here with utmost sensitivity, given a moral firmness that resists both the Christian (and colonial) missionary exceptionalism (which saw in its own religion alone the route to emancipation for the colonized) and the majoritarian nationalist insecurity (which felt threatened by the potential decline of its own numbers every time those oppressed within the Hindu fold chose to convert). In Ambedkar's universalism, instead, conversion has been imparted a transformative and, in fact, sovereign force that responds, beyond any constitutional precedent or norm, beyond all existing exclusions and divisions, to the brother and enemy, master and unequal, alike. Like a *coup de force*, conversion has come to stand in for that moment when force and justice, sovereignty and responsibility, become inseparable. It is an act without foundation and measure, an anarchic demand for justice meant to explode—in *Annihilation of Caste*, the metaphor was the use of "dynamite" in order to destroy[53]— the mythic and violent conflation of life with the moral law. And it is anarchic precisely because it refuses to abide by any existing law of social, moral, and ontological distinctions, any hierarchy of virtues, capabilities, and faculties. Conversion is force at its most just, most universal, most life-affirming.

We have dealt with Ambedkar's critique of the conflation between life and norm, justice and law, in Chapter 3. But it bears recalling here the anthropological sensitivity of that enduring critique, if only to highlight the radical affirmation of life as justice (and justice as critique of the law) at work in his conception of conversion. This is what he says in an unpublished speech in May 1936, twenty years before he would eventually convert to Buddhism, publicly and with nearly 500,000 followers, in the greatest act of insurrection of faith against faith known in the annals of non-Western religions (indeed, in the history of religion as such). Note how, uncomfortable with its masculine resonance, Ambedkar has already substituted sympathy for fraternity.

Three factors are required for the uplift of an individual. They are: Sympathy, Equality, and Liberty. . . . Can you say by experience that any of these factors exist for you in Hinduism? A religion in which man's human behavior with man is prohibited, is not religion, but a display of force. A religion which does not recognize a man as man, is not a religion but a disease. A religion in which the touch of animals is permitted, but the touch of human beings is prohibited, is not a religion but a mockery. A religion which precludes some classes from education, forbids them to accumulate wealth and to bear arms, is not a religion but a mockery of human beings. A religion that compels the ignorant to be ignorant, and the poor to be poor, is not a religion but a punishment.[54]

A religion unaccompanied by humanity does not simply reduce itself to a "display of force." Its law itself is rendered inadequate to the task of protecting its subjects against breaches of equality and autonomy (including the liberty to bear arms). In fact, the law is complicit in those breaches. In its place, Ambedkar proposes, as he formulates his "philosophy of life" two decades later (following the Buddha), a fraternity of autonomous and virtuous equals. And this fraternity, he still insists, can be understood only in a religious sense. Indeed, religion in the singular, religion as such, religion as the sovereign life force, can be grasped only as one's responsibility toward the other, a responsibility whose principles thrive at the interstices between force and nonforce, singularity and universality. To this place between force and nonforce, Ambedkar, as we have seen and will see below, gives several names: awareness of one's inalienable capacities (*pradnya*); refuge (which Ambedkar associates in the classic Buddhist sense with *sila,* or virtuous action); sympathy and love (which he calls *karuna*); and fraternity and fellowship (which he begins to render from the late 1940s onward as *maitri*).

This was a thought, in other words, struggling to imagine the conditions of a sovereignty without mastery, freedom without domination, equality without indifference, a conception of civic and political life, above all, whose foundations lay not only in opposition to the punitive aspects of the moral law. It came before the law. How could such sovereignty, in such primordial and ontological form, be imagined? Was such a sovereignty, grounded in force, rooted in virtue and nonindifference toward the other, even sacrifice, and yet free of the risk of domination, especially the domination of the majority by minority, possible? That this approach to sovereignty intensified in the 1940s and 1950s was hardly surprising. In the final decade of their lives, after all, both Ambedkar and Gandhi had to contend not only with their own mortality but also with the communal bloodbath of the subcontinent's partition. In its wake, a responsibility to justice needed to be formulated religiously, truthfully, and justly. Justice for Ambedkar was always a question of collective responsibility, a shared obligation to finitude. The difference between Gandhi and him lay not so much in their willingness to hinge their politics and faith on the incurable impermanence of all existence, their understandings of which had been inflected by the negative theologies of *advaita* Hinduism and Madhyamika Buddhism, respectively. Rather, the difference emerged from their complex relationship to the possibilities opened by this awareness of finitude, from their translations of this awareness into the matter and craft of politics (which, in turn, made these translations even more irreconcilable), from their distinct ways, most fundamentally, of grasping the utterances, structures, and varieties of religious experience in relation to the demands of political and ethical action.

Times aggravated this division further. For Ambedkar it became imperative to engage more deeply with relations between Hindus and Muslims, Muslims and untouchables, the untouchables and a majoritarian postcolonial state, which had always been prone to speak in the language of Brahmanism.[55]

The most momentous act of individual violence in modern Indian history, committed in the name of the security of the national state (but saturated by the Hindu ascetic ethics and language of sacrifice) had already consumed his adversary at the beginning of 1948.[56] Even as Ambedkar began to formulate his critique of the alliance between religion, state, and languages of majoritarian sovereignty, much of which would find its way into his later works, he had never been more estranged from or closer to the state itself. Appointed the first minister for law in the Nehru cabinet, a position to which he came after serving as the minister of labor in the British Viceroy's wartime council, Ambedkar was elected in August 1947 to serve as the chairman of the Drafting Committee of what would soon become the world's longest written constitution. The proceedings of the Constituent Assembly, spread over a period of three daunting years of debate that began right after India's independence, testify to the deep prejudice that Ambedkar battled in his momentous effort, often shielded only by Nehru's interventions from the derogatory slights of representatives in the House (the most frequent among them aimed not at his "untouchability" but at his nihilistic renunciation of faith, his godlessness). Nehru himself remained deeply ambivalent about Ambedkar, even in mourning. As free India's first prime minister, he rarely doubted the justness, intensity, and value of Ambedkar's convictions. But he still found in him a sort of unbearable reactiveness, a "certain manner of utterance and language," as he put it in his obituary for the Ambedkar in the parliament, that in his own conception of civility he construed as "overdoing."[57]

If Nehru had tried to intimate that Ambedkar was insufferable yet indispensable, he was only partly right. Rarely had such a master of agonistic rhetoric been entrusted with the responsibility of founding—or anchoring in a document—a sovereign and inclusive republic of such intractable diversity. Even more rarely had a jurist's supreme mastery of his sources been so indispensable for a democracy and yet so hard to fathom for its grudging statesmen and hostile parliamentarians.[58] But Ambedkar persisted in defiant style, at least until 1950, often asserting his fidelity to the state and even the nation. Hurt by nationalist hostility yet cultivating a studied distance from it, he succeeded in giving the republic its formative substance. An unparalleled document emerged after months of daunting labor. In a measure unprecedented in the global history of democracy, the Indian constitution abolished untouchability and granted universal adult franchise to all its citizens from the moment of the republic's founding. The Constituent Assembly ratified the constitution of India, which had been drafted largely by Ambedkar, in November 1949, almost two full years after Gandhi's death.

A sovereign republic, by no means ready for *swaraj* in Gandhi's sense, had affirmed and brought itself into existence.[59] Whatever early promises Gandhi's closest followers had made in the immediate aftermath of their leader's assassination, committing themselves to his cherished pursuit of small-scale industry, constructive work, and refugee relief, were soon overtaken by plans for massive industrialization and militarization, a trajectory Gandhi had warned against as early as the Congress resolutions of the late 1920s and the early 1930s.[60] Although the republic eventually betrayed Ambedkar too, the conservative sections of its parliament thwarting decisively his attempt in the late 1940s to reform the patriarchal tenets of Hinduism through the revolutionary Hindu Code Bill, Ambedkar rarely curbed his own rhetorical habits. If only in anticipation, his antiobituary for Gandhi had established that neither his rhetorical force nor ethical convictions had dimmed with the demise of the adversary. On the contrary, the extremism of his relief had only intimated to the skeptics that the most exacting threads of his mature thought, at once religious and ethical, theological and political—indeed, his most painstaking attempt at a reconceptualization of justice—was still to come. This would not only be a justice not shy of religion, as we have seen. It would be a justice inscribed at the heart of an unyieldingly theologico-political, even monotheistic imaginary.

What might have been the purpose of that prolific deployment of the category of "fraternity" in those innumerable passages in Ambedkar's later works? "Fraternity is the name for the disposition of an individual to treat men as the object of reverence and love and the desire to be in unity with his fellow beings," he writes in *India and the Prerequisites of Communism*. "This statement is well expressed by Paul when he said 'Of one blood are all nations of men. There is neither Jew nor Greek, neither bond nor free, neither male nor female; for yet are all one in Christ Jesus.' Equally well was it expressed when the Pilgrim Fathers on their landing at Plymouth said, 'We are knit together as a body in the most sacred covenant of the Lord. . . . by virtue of which we hold ourselves tied to all care of each others' good and of the whole.' These sentiments are of the essence of fraternity."[61] Here, fraternity is another name for life itself; not the same life everywhere, but life appreciated in its infinite difference, innumerable virtues, conjoined by its universal need of (and ability to) care; life in its finitude as such. It is not simply the function of privileging the religious over the political, the ethical over the juridical, that the concept of fraternity serves in these instances.

Certainly, the language of sacred covenant (or what I call above a quasi-transcendental pact of faith), the mobilization of love and desire unrestricted by ties of nation and blood, and the reclamation of freedom unconstrained by gender, caste, and bondage, reveal the struggles of a thinker profoundly committed to inscribing ethics, perhaps even a civic religion, at the heart of the postimperial social question. And yet there is an unambiguously political, irreducibly revolutionary, an almost mystical if not anarchic impulse in this conception of fraternal love that remains attached to Ambedkar's commitment to the virtues of an alternative sovereignty. This tension is condensed most productively in *Philosophy of Hinduism*, not least in the title of the work itself, which subtly expresses, on the one hand, Ambedkar's conviction that Hinduism had no moral philosophy proper, and on the other hand, his faith that no moral philosophy engaged with the religious could ignore its force either. The challenge was to think another force. Of this other force, he can speak only in the language of a dissidence without hostility, a fraternity without sacrifice.

Fraternity is a force of opposite character. Fraternity is another name for fellow feeling. It consists in a sentiment that leads an individual to identify himself with the good of others whereby the good of others becomes to him a thing naturally and necessarily to be attended to like any of the physical conditions of our existence. It is because of this sentiment of fraternity that the individual does not bring himself to think of the rest of his fellow-creatures as struggling rivals with him for the means of happiness, whom he must desire to see defeated in their object in order that he may succeed in his own. Individualism would produce anarchy. It is only fraternity, which prevents it and helps to sustain the moral order among men.[62]

The tension between individualism and shared life comes closer in this passage than anywhere else in Ambedkar's writings to the theory of general will that Rousseau had proposed in *The Social Contract*. We have already traced in Chapter 5 the oscillations of this thought between constituent power and popular sovereignty and Ambedkar's affinity for individual virtue, his predilection for a mastery grounded in the self-legislation of the conscientious soul. Suffice it to add here that even for Rousseau, the deep respect for the law that every citizen must share with another and which makes possible citizenship as such—the civil profession of faith—emerges only in the shadows of virtue. General will, in fact, is nothing but a *coup de force*, the becoming-political of virtue and love. It is this transformation of love into force that takes in this passage from *Philosophy of Hinduism* a decisively ethical—or, in Rousseauist terms, "social"—turn. If fraternity is force of an "opposite character," what is it opposed to? It opposes rivalry and anarchy, Ambedkar claims, but also rules and interest, privacy and possessiveness. By the early 1950s, this conception of fraternity had also moved decisively away from notions of abstract equality. "In producing equality," Ambedkar writes in his essay on Marx, "society cannot afford to sacrifice fraternity."[63] On the contrary, *maitri*, he would begin to insist, is owed to precisely those who are enemies, hostile, suffering, or belong to another species altogether. Ambedkar's critique of the *Gita* emerges from this turn toward *maitri* as the everyday conduct of difference, the infinite responsibilities and obligations of shared life as the ground of justice, and perhaps most decisively, the recasting of autonomy as the equal right to belief and heresy. The *Gita's* fratricidal ethics, as I have argued in Chapter 3, not only compromises for Ambedkar the conditions for love between brothers and enemies. It also annuls the possibility of a just force necessary for a truly classical discourse on sovereignty.

It is not a coincidence, then, that *Revolution and Counter-Revolution in Ancient India,* which now includes the unfinished portions of the planned *Essays on the Bhagavad Gita,* and *Philosophy of Hinduism* are the most formidable among those later works that Ambedkar was working on during the years that his most explicit turn toward religion occurred. *The Buddha and His Dhamma* itself—with its complex oscillations between questions of justice, force, and obligation (each inseparable from the other) and its often poetic attempts to rehabilitate such quotidian figures as the monk, bandit, and soldier as political subjects imbued with the highest virtue—remains incompletely illuminated unless it is placed right next to Ambedkar's other mature works. And inasmuch as it remains a magisterial example of his late style, it is also a work that resists, like other works of that period, easy religious or secularist overdeterminations. One passage was even formulated in its early form in the essay on Marx and the problem of means and ends.[64] *The Buddha and His Dhamma* can be best approached only in this space of intertextual complexity and fecundity, placed between Ambedkar's enduring engagement with the relationship between sovereignty and religion, justice and belief.

In the rest of this chapter, I retrace these often labyrinthine turns of thought—especially as they occur in "Buddha or Karl Marx" and *The Buddha and His Dhamma*—by which Ambedkar, beyond all laws and theologies of war and mastery (whose sacrificial entailments he could never renounce), came in the final years of his life to institute such classical Buddhist concepts as *sunnyata* and *maitri* as the foundation of his insurrectionary politics. Faith was throughout the key to this immense intellectual and social labor. And to reemphasize the point I have been making, faith is invoked in the singular because it serves as the "predefinition" and thus comes before it is given the proper name of this religion or that.[65] Faith, rendered in Ambedkar's terms, is that which every moral agent has the innate capacity and faculty—or in more classical terms, insight (*pradnya*)—to nourish. It is both the shared ontological resource that Ambedkar knew well sustains all religions (violent or nonviolent) *and* that singular force, that insurrectionary faculty given to freedom, that separates his religion of principles, his religion without religion, from all the others. As we have seen (and shall see below) in his many gestures of extending, deepening, and diversifying the meanings of concepts such as *sila*, *sunnyata*, and *maitri*, pushing them into the moral psychological realm of the political, while at the same time wresting back conventionally political categories (rooted by their very name in privileges and exclusions of birth, family, and tribe) such as fraternity for his ethics, this religion without religion was not a search for what Martin Fuchs has called Ambedkar's "post-religious religion."[66] Instead, it was a search for religion in the most classical sense of the term, one that involved— as religion as such, everywhere, in its essence, always has—a distinctive conception of freedom and autonomy of the mortal subject in the ineluctable shadows of sovereignty. Ambedkar's decisive contribution was to speak politically (and theologico-politically) of this ethics of the mortal subject and thus radicalize its finitude in the manner no thinker of his time—certainly no figure engaged so closely with the state, with law and norms at large—had.

Making Room for Impermanence

It is in one of his final essays that Ambedkar gives a sense of what it would mean—and take—to formulate an ethics of sociality and citizenship that might break away from the norms and rules of the political, an ethics of shared belief and common struggles that would renounce both the calculative impulses of liberal self-interest and the Marxist rhetoric of collective interest. This would involve, Ambedkar argues, the task of imagining a citizenship in which measure would be renounced and the unity of moral purpose grounded in the universality of shared vulnerability alone. "Only when his eyes have been opened to the fact that he is but a tiny part of a measureless whole," Ambedkar writes of the virtuous citizen in "Buddha or Karl Marx" (1956), "only when he begins to realize how impermanent a thing is his temporary individuality can he even enter upon this narrow path." Note that this citizen leaves no space for equivocation or self-pity, for self-interest or narcissism cannot be replaced by mere self-effacement. It has to be replaced, on the contrary, by a decisive struggle, in the very face of one's dispensability and mortality, against the self itself.

Without being detained by Ambedkar's notion of the self, whose reticence and will—especially in its confrontation with the dungeonlike void of caste violence—we have examined earlier in this chapter, I want to pause here on his emphasis on the "measureless whole," for this is the one conceptual and rhetorical thread that most sensitively joins the moral realism of "Buddha or Karl Marx" with the almost oblique theologico-political sensitivities of *The Buddha and His Dhamma.* In fact, Ambedkar's emphasis on the immeasurability of the whole (a whole that is itself ephemeral), his attentiveness to infinite variations in finite life and, simultaneously, its ineluctable impermanence, together form the crucial vector for that narrow path of virtue (and citizenship) that he tries to grasp in his mature writings. And together, these two paradoxical elements—immeasurability and impermanence— involve a distinctive radicalization of finitude. I say radicalization because Ambedkar—immersed deeply by now in Buddhist negative theology—must at once carefully confront (and embrace) Buddhism's ontotheological ethics, perhaps even its nihilism, and affirm the social conditions under which one citizen, his immeasurable difference with another notwithstanding, must still respond justly to the other's need. He lays out this difficulty with great clarity in "Buddha or Karl Marx" again, as if already responding to critics who have not yet spoken. "When a man's eyes are opened to the great mystery of existence, the impermanence of every individuality, he is likely to be assailed by doubt and indecision as to his action. To do or not to do, after all my individuality is impermanent, why do anything, are questions, which make him indecisive or inactive. But that will not do in life. He must make up his mind to follow the teacher, to accept the truth and to enter on the struggle."[67]

The awareness of impermanence, or *sunnyata,* Ambedkar cautions in categorical terms, is no ground for indecision and abstention from action. On the contrary, *sunnyata* means that one's intrinsic nature, or *swabhava,* which seems to secure the structure of one's feelings (*bhavana*), one's indecisions and deliberations, can be spoken of neither in terms of the presence and absoluteness of the corporeal self nor in terms of its self-negating absence and spiritual transcendence. Instead, inasmuch as there is an intrinsic self, or *swabhava,* at all, it becomes one only in the process of responding justly to the suffering, injury, and death that surrounds it. "Impermanence of the living individual," writes Ambedkar in a crucial pair of passages in *The Buddha and His Dhamma,* "is best described by the formula: being is becoming."[68] Simply put, his *sunnyata* dissolves the very place where indecisions and temptations—sentiments that arise as much from a false sense of mastery as they do from weakness of will—might thrive. Authentic responsibility, or shall we say, following the language of *Annihilation of Caste,* "the essence of a truly religious act," is so radically oriented toward justice, so resolutely measureless and opposed to rule or domination, so pure in its love of community, that it might be apprehended only as a void or emptiness of the nonself, that is to say, as the absolute lack of intrinsic self and mastery. Only within the order of ethical comportment and temperament (*sila*), in which one gives oneself unconditionally to a just conduct toward the other, in which one absolves oneself from the desire for self-presence and control, might the awareness of *sunnyata* be nourished.

This is the gesture that irreconcilably separates Ambedkar from Gandhi's ethics of mastery. The imperative of justice, Ambedkar would say, is not exhausted by mastery over finite life. One cannot simply claim to be truthful and loving, let alone just, by mastering the knowledge of one's mortality or conquering (like a satyagrahi) the fear of one's own death. For the mastery over death is itself impermanent, its means (*sadhan*) and even ends (*sadhya*) mutating with time, its form irreproducible and constituted differently in every person, the knowledge of this mastery accessible unequally. The immortality of justice could therefore be founded only on the belief that even finitude, even the impermanence of finite life (whose knowledge can never be given a permanent form) is wholly impermanent. The absolute meaning of *sunnyata*, if there can be one, is that there is not even *sunnyata*. We get, thus, in a moment of seemingly nihilistic doubling, the radical impermanence of impermanence and, relatedly, the classical notion of a selfless nonself, a nonself that has in its nonbeing rendered itself autonomous from the desire for autonomy itself. "It is on account of sunnyata that everything becomes possible," writes Ambedkar in an uncharacteristically mystical vein in *The Buddha and His Dhamma*. "It is on the impermanence of the nature of all things that the possibility of all other things depends."[69]

Inasmuch as Ambedkar institutes an affirmative impermanence as the foundation of his mature moral and political thought, invoking nothing short of an impossible emptiness as the "possibility of all things," we might ask whether his formulation is itself not a curiously mystical framing of the possibility of justice. He is clearly working within the Madhyamika tradition of Buddhist negative theology. Three exhaustive volumes belonging to that speculative strand within Buddhism, whose most skillful practitioner was the philosopher Nagarjuna (who lived sometime between the second and third century CE), appear in the original bibliography of *The Buddha and His Dhamma*.[70] And if all that remains, in the true spirit of that tradition of negative theology, is impermanence of the nonself (*anatta*), and if, in fact, only a void remains where there is neither self nor nonself (the "emptiness of emptiness" elucidated in the Madhyamika tradition), then on what ground might the possibility of justice for mortals be founded?[71] If mortality—and with it, suffering—is forever elusive, what might the immanent ground of any value and judgment (indeed, any moral reflection necessary for a democratic life) be? Is this a moment when Ambedkar has moved decisively toward a mystical theology in the classical sense of the term? Or is it a gesture that involves, through a turn toward the empiricism of matter and life, his distinctive politicization of theology itself? Let us turn to that passage in *The Buddha and His Dhamma* in which he takes up the formidable task of conceptualizing the materiality of *sunnyata*, the finitude of finitude in its living, phenomenological sense.

The Buddhist Sunnyata does not mean nihilism out and out. It only means the perpetual changes occurring at every moment in the phenomenal world. Very few realize that it is on account of Sunnyata that everything becomes possible; without it nothing in the world would be possible. It is on the impermanence of the nature of all things that the possibility of all other things depends. If things were not subject to continual change but were permanent and unchangeable, the evolution of all of life from one kind to the other and the development of living things would come to a dead stop. If human beings died or changed but had continued always in the same state what would the result have been? The progress of the human race would have come to a dead halt. Immense difficulty would have arisen if Sunnya is regarded as being void or empty. But this is not so. Sunnya is like a point which has substance but neither breadth nor length.[72]

Sunnyata, argues Ambedkar, is not the same as the classical notion of a void. Which is to say, despite their apparent similarities, it is not the same state as that which ensues from the concept of self-dissolution, one that so strongly mediates the notion of self-sacrifice within the Hindu tradition. This Hindu and satyagrahic negative theology, Ambedkar writes in *The Buddha and His Dhamma,* derives from the mystical doctrine of "not this, not that" (*neti neti*). The transcendental self, according to this doctrine, is neither this nor that. Instead, it is grounded in ontological negation, so much so, insists Ambedkar, that this theology of formless and groundless Being cancels the possibility of knowledge itself. Thus, with a hint of playfulness, he would render the *advaita* doctrine of *neti neti* as "I know not! I know not!" In such a rendering, *advaita*'s negation turns into a failure of knowledge, into an inability to make judgments, and thus, into the impossibility of justice itself.[73] In his own conceptualization of *sunnyavad* as well, he concedes, what remains in the world is "neither breadth nor length," neither space nor dimension. And yet substance, matter, property, a body constituted by its finitude and vulnerability survives the world in its indestructible form, even transcends it by force. *Sunnyata* is this empirical inscription of force on finite matter, this moment of the body's exhaustion and demise as the source of a spiritual affirmation (rather than its disappearance into the nothingness of Being). In his long reconstruction of a classic Buddhist dialogue on death, Ambedkar returns again to this heretical empiricism:

Maha-Kotthita asked, "What is the difference between a lifeless corpse and an almsman in trance, in whom perception and feelings are stilled?" Sariputta replied. "In the corpse not only are the plastic forces of the body and speech and mind stilled and quiescent but also vitality is exhausted, heat is quenched and the faculties of sense broken up; whereas in the almsman in trance vitality persists, heat abides, and the faculties are clear, although respiration, observation and perception are stilled and quiescent." This probably is the best and most complete exposition of Death or Annihilation. There is only one lacuna in this dialogue. Maha-Kotthita should have asked Sariputta one question: "What is heat?" What answer Sariputta would have given it is not easy to imagine. But there can be no doubt that heat means energy. Thus amplified, the real answer to the question, "What happens when the body dies?" Is: "The body ceases to produce energy." But this is only a part of the answer. Because death also means that whatever energy had escaped from the body joins the general mass of energy playing about in the Universe. Annihilation has therefore a two-fold aspect. In one of its aspects it means cessation of production of energy. In another aspect it means a new addition to the stock of general floating mass of energy. It is probably because of this two-fold aspect of annihilation that the Buddha said that he was not an absolute annihilationist. He was an annihilationist so far as soul was concerned. He was not an annihilationist so far as matter was concerned.[74]

His reasons for choosing this dialogue (and indeed staying rather long with the question of death and annihilation) are obvious. Force, energy, heat, vitality, faculty, perception: the lexicon of this ancient passage resonates strikingly with that memorable (and profoundly modern) moment in *Annihilation of Caste* in which, two decades earlier, Ambedkar had taken up, evaluated, and disavowed the unjust structure of Plato's republic. With an exception: here is finally an attempt to grasp the philosophical root, meaning, and risk of "annihilation." Ambedkar now seems to be approaching the word with greater reserve. In fact, he warns, it has a "two-fold aspect." As if it were a revolutionary paradox, as if it were a force that might annihilate itself, the very idea must be used with care, saved from the misappropriation and nihilism toward which certain revolutionary theologies (such as syndicalism) often tend to veer. What, then, happens to life after death if it neither melts away in absolute disappearance (as the nihilist argues) nor merges into the transcendental soul (as the theologian claims)? How does one recover the force of annihilation (*ucched*) as the force of justice? The stakes are high; the very legacy and future of an insurrection—its defining concept—are at issue. Ambedkar clarifies in his own voice:

The Eternalist said that the soul knows no death: therefore life is eternal. It is renewed by rebirth. The thesis of the Annihilationists was summed up in one word, Ucchedvad, which meant that death is the end of everything. There is nothing left after death. The Buddha was not an eternalist. For it involved a belief in the existence of a separate, immortal soul to which he was opposed. Was the Buddha an annihilationist? With his belief in the nonexistence of the soul, the Buddha would naturally be expected to be an annihilationist. But in the Alagaddupamma-Sutta the Buddha complains that he is called an annihilationist when as a matter of fact he is not.[75]

This is the one passage in *The Buddha and His Dhamma* that might give anyone familiar with *Annihilation of Caste* an intrigued if not the longest pause. Taking Ambedkar on his word alone, we can see a sense of discernment, a reserve perhaps, toward the language of "annihilation," that word without which his legacy itself might look different. What is happening here? Was Ambedkar writing in an allegorical mode,[76] especially when, barely sentences later, he quotes the Buddha: "Though this is what I affirm and what I preach yet some recluses and Brahmins, wrongly, erroneously and falsely charge me in defiance of facts, with being an annihilationist and with preaching the disintegration, destruction and extirpation of human beings. It is just what I am not, and what I do not affirm, that is wrongly, erroneously, and falsely charged against me by these good people who would make me out to be an annihilationist."[77] Is Ambedkar responding, two decades later, to criticisms lodged by nationalist reformers and Gandhi against the recklessness and cynicism of *Annihilation of Caste*? Is he carefully separating his revolutionary call to destroy religion from the temptation of nihilism that had given that lecture its inflammatory candor? Why this reserve toward the concept, morals, and semantics of annihilation? What new meaning of finitude, what new conception of newness and life, has been set to work?

It is in framing the central questions of *The Buddha and His Dhamma* in this way that it emerges as a treatise among Ambedkar's other political philosophical works of the period, one in which his struggle to grasp the relationship between justice and force, democracy and finitude, is revealed to be still underway at its fullest powers and sensitivity. *Sunnyata*, Ambedkar states categorically, meanwhile, is neither a nihilistic belief in destruction of all things for its own sake nor, in the sense of negative theology, is it a mystical belief in a deathless and transcendental being that glorified asceticism. Instead, there lies in the emptiness of *sunnyata* a force that coheres and creates an ethical bond between oneself and others. Even in its own vanishing, this force works as an enabling agent, producing a "phenomenal" energy, an invisible and immeasurable potency that makes justice and "all other things" among ordinary mortal, possible. *Sunnyata* is not a dogma that nihilistically valorizes the impermanence of moral values; it is a plea for lending immortal force to humanity's impermanence itself. For Ambedkar, the value of *sunnyata* emerges from this imperative of justice for those still to come. It is nothing, to reiterate then, but finitude turned radical, or even better, making-political of the void that lies at the heart of the human, its hierarchies and exclusions, its concept as such. Rather than being grounded in the metaphysics of self and soul, *sunnyata* emerges from the hospitality offered by one citizen toward another alone, and only when both are equally sovereign.

Maitri, in the Shadow of War

In later essays such as "Their Wishes Are Laws unto Us," in which Ambedkar takes up "the difference between *civics* i.e. citizens and *preregenis* or *hostis* i.e. non-citizens in the early Roman Law"[78] most explicitly (as the most appropriate juridical framework, he insists, to understand the equally classical logic of *Chaturvarnya*), he has already begun to give a sense that it is not simply the manifest violence against noncitizens, say in times of war, but rather the conditions of internal exclusions of citizenship itself—indeed, its founding hostility—that he is trying to grasp and develop a theoretical critique of. Classical republicanism gives him both a legal awareness of the distinctions between a citizen and noncitizen, and, at the same time, a mindfulness of the risky porousness of those distinctions through which hostility toward the enemy, beyond all laws of containment, quickly seeps back into the moral fabric of everyday life of nationals and citizens themselves. The task, then, could not simply be limited to drawing firmer and more abstract moral distinctions between war and peace, violence and nonviolence (especially when everyday life and civic spaces were themselves a perennial battleground). The task, instead, was to seek (and formulate) the conditions of hospitality in the ineradicable shadows of hostility.

Often in his later writings, but most persistently in *The Buddha and His Dhamma*, Ambedkar calls his demand for hospitality *maitri*, a term that in its conventional sense might be translated as "friendship." But Ambedkar himself frequently renders *maitri*, for the first time in his essay on Marx, as "fellowship." "Maitri or fellowship towards all must never be abandoned. One owes it even to one's enemy."[79] In deploying *maitri* in such a fashion, finding the conditions of its possibility in the quotidian sacrifices and actions of the soldier, bandit, magistrate, and even the executioner, the mature Ambedkar departs from usual renderings of *maitri* as "friendship" in two ways. First, he posits *maitri* categorically as that which, in the act of being offered, exceeds the conventional distinctions between the ethical realm (constituted around friendship, self-sacrifice, and civility) and the more political domain (which refers to or is organized around relationships of competition, security, and, if need be, war). *Maitri* exceeds these limits because, Ambedkar insists, it is a gesture that one makes especially toward the enemy and stranger, the aggressor and offender. "You Bhikkhus," he cites the Buddha telling the almsmen, "must bear all insults and injustices inflicted on you, and continue to bear Maitri towards your offenders." But the practitioner of *maitri* is not a passive recipient of whatever comes his way. He is the active, loving, and sovereign annihilator of measure. "Let the ambit of your Maitri," says the Buddha elsewhere in the same work, "be as boundless as the world, and let your thought be vast and beyond measure, in which no hatred is thought of."[80] *Maitri* must not simply exceed the dictates of friendship and neighborliness, then. It must be antimeasure and incalculable, its practitioner unwilling to discriminate between brother and foe, defender and offender. It is in this sense, Ambedkar points out, that Buddhism refuses to foreclose the moral and political value, indeed virtue, of force, even if it denies sacrifice and violence the centrality that they are accorded in other religious and political traditions. This is not only because sacrifice is irreconcilable with *maitri* but also because one can never safely separate the ethical imperative of hospitality—the time and place of welcome—from the ineluctability of sacrificial force, perhaps even war. In "Buddha or Karl Marx," Ambedkar imparts to this conception of force a distinctive moral meaning and realism.

As to violence there are many people who seem to shiver at the very thought of it. But this is only a sentiment. Violence cannot be altogether dispensed with. Even in non-communist countries a murderer is hanged. Does not hanging amount to violence? Non-communist countries go to war with non-communist countries. Millions of people are killed. Is this no violence? If a murderer can be killed, because he has killed a citizen, if a soldier can be killed in war because he belongs to a hostile nation why cannot a property owner be killed if his ownership leads to misery for the rest of humanity? There is no reason to make an exception in favor of the property owner, why one should regard private property as sacrosanct. The Buddha was against violence. But he was also in favor of justice and where justice required he permitted the use of force.[81]

It is not simply a critique of private property and the possessive individualism that sustains its political economy—not to leave out, a critique of the individual who might refuse to let go of his love for things until death—that Ambedkar mounts here. There is a critique of force in its positive sense that runs through the passage as well, one that takes the final sentences of the passage decisively toward a moral ontological register, clearly away from the more juridical and political concerns with which it had opened. Ambedkar begins, for instance, with the violence that characterizes institutions such as the death penalty, moves to the violence that is involved in the killing of citizens and soldiers of hostile nations at war, nods gently and hesitatingly toward the moral legitimacy of class struggle, and ends by underlining the ethical imperative of force, force in its primordial essence, which must be responsibly extracted from precisely such acts of excessive, if not illegitimate, violence. There are many moments in Ambedkar's later writings in which force is given this preethical status, as if it comes before the law. Force becomes in those moments a category integral to violence and yet separate from—indeed contaminated by—it. As an originary energy and faculty constituted by its irreconcilable difference from acts of inhuman cruelty that compromise its purity and purpose, its primordial authenticity, force becomes, through Buddhism, Ambedkar's name for an inalienable autonomy, the ability to keep faith. Here, drawing an unequivocal distinction between the violence and force, meanwhile, Ambedkar goes much further. Violence contaminates force, he suggests, while justice sanctions it. There is no revulsion against the death penalty here, nor is there a defense of its murderous nature. Instead, and rather single-mindedly, there is an attempt to carefully separate the pernicious nature of violence from virtuous and just forms of force. Perhaps Ambedkar is trying to grasp force in its essence, force as such, which makes virtues such as *sila* and *maitri* possible. Perhaps the Buddha is a figure in whose name, in whose historical existence, Ambedkar's struggle to formulate an originary ethics, one that would be separate from the burdens of the political, comes to acquire its most immanent form.

Is this one of those moments—and there are many others apart from "Buddha or Karl Marx"—in which the tension in Ambedkar's (theologico-political) republicanism has appeared in greatest clarity and sensitivity? Is it his desire to conceptualize a form of sovereignty without mastery, force without violence, the conditions of an insurrectionary citizenship, in short, that has led him to Buddhism? Or is it Buddhism that has brought him to classical republicanism's idea of a citizen who must be ruled but cannot be mastered? Ambedkar's Buddha, after all, is a citizen-saint, one who neither retreats in the face of the state nor accepts its norms and injunctions, but one who asks, according to Ambedkar, both the state to retreat from the cruelty of its violent practices and the citizens from the moral emptiness of their nonviolence, so that an ethics of virtue and responsibility might be created. Thus comes, in *The Buddha and His Dhamma*, even as his work on "Buddha or Karl Marx" continues, this formulation of force as virtue. It is now the Buddha who is given direct voice, as he carefully distinguishes for his followers the principle of noninjury from that of responsibility. One, he clarifies, is not predicated upon the other.

He who deserves punishment must be punished, and he who is worthy of favor must be favored. Yet at the same time [the Buddha] teaches to do no injury to any living being but to be full of love and kindness. These injunctions are not contradictory, for whosoever must be punished for the crimes which he has committed suffers his injury not through the ill-will of the judge but on account of his evil-doing. His own acts have brought upon him the injury that the executor of the law inflicts. When a magistrate punishes, let him not harbor hatred in his breast, yet a murderer, when put to death, should consider that this is the fruit of his own act. As soon as he will understand that the punishment will purify his soul, he will no longer lament his fate but rejoice at it.[82]

Religiosity thrives in the world of mortal and fallible beings, even evil ones, as it must, but it never does so in denial of the state (as if the monster did not exist). Inasmuch as the soldier, magistrate, and executioner fulfill their obligations without hostility, they do not contaminate the virtues of—and their own ability to cultivate the ethics of—*maitri*. Rather, by purging hostility from the lethal relationship that joins them with their victims, they extricate force from the cold will of the state and rehabilitate it in the quotidian world of love and equality. They make truth and justice possible. The antithesis of justice, according to Ambedkar, then, is neither force nor sacrifice. The antithesis of justice is hostility, or worse, indifference, both of which lead to a disregard for vulnerability of others. This desire for just force, force *as* justice, partly explains the tension between the ethical and political, the religious and juridical, in Ambedkar's mature writings, whose movements we have examined in this chapter. I am thinking here of the tension that arises from Ambedkar's struggle to formulate an ethics of autonomy for the weak, indeed, their sovereignty, which must, at the same time, save itself from becoming a justification for mastery of the weak. This is the fundamental problem, after all, which plagues not only the various ontotheological traditions but their critiques too, not only majoritarianism nationalism but emancipatory humanisms too.

This struggle illuminates Ambedkar's recourse to the concept of *maitri*. In his final years, immersed in formulating a religious critique of ontotheology, he deepened the concept further, including in its ambit not merely the human (and its sovereignty over other life forms) but also the animal: "*Maitri* is extending fellow feeling to all beings, not only to one who is a friend but also to one who is a foe: not only to man but to all living beings."[83] Humans express love and compassion (*karuna*) only toward other human beings, whereas *maitri* includes all living beings and makes both the adversary and the animal the subject of compassion. "The Buddha wanted man not to stop with Karuna," Ambedkar writes later in the text, "but to go beyond mankind and cultivate the spirit of Maitri for all living beings." *Maitri*, then, is radically inclusive in a way that *karuna* and nonviolence (*ahimsa*) are not. Unlike the latter two, which, despite their best intentions, harbor an anthropological notion of sovereignty (not unrelated to the hierarchical exclusions and partitioning of the human itself) at their source, *maitri* is by its very constitution antisovereignty and nontheological.

Let us recall, from our discussions in Chapter 3, Ambedkar's perennial suspicion of love as duty as it is formulated in the *Ramayana* and *Mahabharata*, which, he argues, is morally empty because that love, precisely when it takes on the humanist or human-centered language of nonviolence, implicates itself in the murderous interest of statemaking. Shorn of commitment to correct thinking (*vichar dhamma*) and awareness (*pradnya*), given over to the metaphysics of duty, and rendered inseparable from the rules of war, such love easily lapses into evil. "Without Prajna," Ambedkar's Buddha says in a rather audacious reversal, "Karuna may end in supporting evil."[84] Mere compassion, without proper temperament and awareness might as well be an extension of evil, a will to mastery shorn of selfless friendship. To be a practitioner of *maitri* worthy of the name, then, one must be able to discern which love is selfless and which is not, whose love is given over to mastery and whose is not. One must be able, above all, to distinguish one's own love from charity and to separate authentic nonviolence from mere promise of immunity. "Man has Pradnya and he must use it. A moral man may be trusted to draw the line at the right point."[85] *Maitri* can thus be understood as a search for an Archimedean point of force, a sovereignty not yet contaminated by the will to mastery, a sense of hospitality toward creaturely life that comes before the law. "When Ram came from Lanka," Ambedkar chides during the parliamentary debate on the States Reorganization Bill barely months before his death, "Bharat [Rama's brother, who had been complicit in Rama's exile from his kingdom] embraced him. What for—for brotherly love and affection. Nothing more than that."[86] It is this betrayal of *maitri*, this emptiness of fraternity within Hinduism—indeed, the institution of fratricide as fraternal duty in Indic ethics and epics—that, for Ambedkar, finds its most pernicious form in the *Gita*. In *The Buddha and His Dhamma*, however, Ambedkar keeps aside this negative critique of violence (which he had been sharpening around the same time in related works) and attempts to recover another prehistory of nonviolence and care, one in which violence is renounced not by a Kshatriya sleight of hand but by affirming a hospitality that is given unconditionally, irresponsibly, unexpectedly, and, in fact, through an act of betrayal.

Before examining this revolutionary prehistory, let me make three brief points about Ambedkar's turn toward Buddhism. First, ascribing instrumental reasons—a tendency so commonplace, so predetermined, that it hardly bears citation—to Ambedkar's choice of this classical faith in itself explains nothing about his formidable desire and decision to write a treatise as demanding as *The Buddha and His Dhamma* turned out to be, especially in the final months of his life, which were already plagued by disappointment and illness. The decision to write itself was an act of faith beyond measure, one marked by a profound expression of freedom, an unconditional sovereignty that, to reiterate the point I made at the beginning of this chapter, perhaps only an awareness of finitude, one's own and another's, only equality of finitude—equality as finitude—brings. Second, we lose the force of Ambedkar's mature ethics unless we recognize that his profound attraction to the *Gita* and to Buddhism, both of which he began to conceive as matters appropriate to book-length studies roughly around the same period—and his strengthening desire in the final decade of his life to separate (as clearly as possible) the originality of Buddhism from the expropriating tendencies of nationalist Hinduism—were equal parts of his interminable struggle to reconstitute a tradition of insurrectionary republicanism. Third, and in a much more fundamental way, Ambedkar's will to rethink a faith proper to justice, his struggle to retrieve a political subject grounded in belief, and his striving, above all, to renew a moral ontology of force, were inseparable from his conviction that religion, a religion with a book even, was immanent to a democratic ethics that might potentially break from all existing norms and traditions that take birth, family, paternity, even language, to be their founding principle. With this intertextuality in view, does the question "Why turn to Buddhism?" give us another answer? Could Ambedkar have found, after all, a more exemplary figure of antitradition, a more civil and defiant Kshatriya, a more heretical thinker of faith than Siddharth Gautama, the warrior by birth who purifies the morals of force at the very moment he renounces, in the most unconditional fashion, the exclusions and violence of *kshatriyadharma*? The sustained manner in which Ambedkar reconstructs at the beginning of *The Buddha and His Dhamma* the moment of Siddhartha's renunciation of the state reveals how important this event is for his desire to formulate a new yet classical, a foundational yet heretical, ethics.

In the year when Siddharth was twenty-eight, there was a major clash over the waters between the servants of the Sakyas and the servants of the Koliyas. Both sides suffered injuries. Coming to know of this, the Sakyas and the Koliyas felt that the issue must be settled once for all by war. The Senapati of the Sakyas, therefore, called a session of the Sakya Sangh to consider the question of declaring war on the Koliyas. . . . Siddharth Gautama rose in his seat and said, "I oppose this resolution. War does not solve any question. Waging war will not serve our purpose. It will sow the seeds of another war. The slayer gets a slayer in his turn; the conqueror gets one who conquers him; a man who despoils is despoiled in his turn". . . . The Senapati encountered the plea urged by Siddharth Gautama. He stressed that in war the Kshatriyas cannot make a distinction between relations and strangers. They must fight even against brothers for the sake of their kingdom. Performing sacrifices is the duty of the Brahmins, fighting is the duty of the Kshatriyas, trading is the duty of the Vaishyas and service is the duty of the Shudras. There is merit in each class forming its duty. Such is the injunction of our Shastras. Siddharth replied, "Dharma, as I understand it, consists in recognizing that enmity does not disappear by enmity. It can be conquered by love only." The Senapati, getting impatient, said, "It is unnecessary to enter upon this philosophical disquisition. The point is that Siddharth is opposed to my resolution. Let us ascertain what the Sangh has to say about it by putting it to vote." Accordingly the Senapati put his resolution to vote. It was declared carried by an overwhelming majority. . . . "You have a majority on your side, but I am sorry to say I shall oppose your decision in favor of mobilization. I shall not join your army and I shall not take part in the war."[87]

In the days following this act of defiant civility, Siddhartha prepares for voluntary statelessness and wandering (*parivraja*), opening the way to his becoming the enlightened Buddha. But there is something else in this event, apart from Siddhartha's exemplary renunciation, that gives Ambedkar pause. What kind of ethics does an outnumbered Siddhartha formulate by standing up to the tyranny of the majority and its endorsement of mobilization and war? Ambedkar is interested here in something that does not happen in the *Gita*, something that Arjuna fails to do when he lets himself be seduced by Krishna's luminous and monstrous face. He is interested in Siddhartha's resolute refusal to blur the distinction between brothers and enemies, friends and rivals, neighbors and aliens, humans and nonhumans. In the *Gita*, Krishna reduces war to a question of duty, of the warrior's moral imperative to stand up for good against evil in a world where abstract norms (and divine will) have rendered all other differences and complicities immaterial, while here Siddhartha turns the imminence of war into an occasion to question the abstractness of the division of good and evil itself. The question, for Ambedkar, is not simply whether the majority (especially in a democracy) is more prone to moral deviance than those who are already outnumbered, vulnerable, minor. Nor is the question simply whether evil in others is always more visible to us than the evil in ourselves, a deceptively obvious possibility that Siddhartha wants the Sakya assembly to consider. The question instead is, should any justice worthy of the name not address the absolutely other, the finite mortal in its irreconcilable difference, rather than those who belong to one's own family, tribe, kingdom, and nation?

There is, then, a more fundamental limit here that pertains to the moral ontology of the political, namely, that a relationship between brothers, whether nonviolent or at war, whether given to charity or mutual annihilation—a field of action in which brothers united by their shared lineage and privilege of birth alone participate—cannot ever be a political relationship. Or perhaps, Ambedkar might argue, it can only be a political relationship rather than an ethical and religious one. For both ethical and religious relationships (in their essence), unlike a political one, must be constituted by the will to respond justly to the absolutely other. Harping on the good and evil that separates the brothers alone, Krishna's ethics of duty thus fails, leaving behind a theory of action that is morally empty, reduced to mere cacophony of ritual, and addressed only to those who are in the end the same. It's a theory of sameness, blind to exclusion and difference.

One calls on the moral reserve of *maitri*, on the other hand, when combat is imminent, directing it toward those who are as—and no more—prone to evil as oneself. This is the originary ground of *maitri*, which Ambedkar returns to in another key moment in *The Buddha and His Dhamma*, that of the encounter between the Buddha and the dreaded bandit Angulimala. In that legendary encounter, Angulimala, the Brahmin bandit (so named because he must furnish a garland made of thousand fingers to redeem himself in the eyes of his Brahmin teacher), runs frantically after the Buddha, sword in hand, to kill him and cut off a finger. But no matter how hard his chase, Angulimala fails catch up with his thousandth victim who, it seems to him, is merely strolling along. Amazed, Angulimala finally calls out and asks the Buddha to stop. The Buddha replies, "I have stopped Angulimala, by forever renouncing violence against all creatures. You are unrestrained towards living beings. So I have stopped and you have not stopped."[88] The violent bandit is not converted to nonviolence because of the sudden dawning of guilt or his momentary exposure to the Buddha's enlightened luminescence.[89] There is no metaphysical expectation, no invocation of spirit here. Instead, Angulimala's evil is converted to renunciation by the empirical truth, the finite body and knowledge manifest in the mortal figure of the Buddha himself.[90] This revolutionary moment establishes the possibility of a faith that exceeds the theological vision of territory and right and instead grounds itself in an ethics of discernment and judgment. Thus, the Buddha could forgive, without fear or punishment, his assailant in a manner the state might never have. "Love is not enough," Ambedkar quotes the Buddha again. "What is required is Maitri. It means fellowship with not merely with human beings but will all living beings. . . . Is not such Maitri necessary? What else can give to all living beings the same happiness which one seeks for one's own self, to keep the mind impartial, open to all, with affection for every one and hatred for none?"[91]

What does Ambedkar's forceful affirmation of finitude and difference, a shared finitude within the framework of difference, his plea for the empiricism and impermanence of life as opposed to its spirit and transcendence, ask us to pay most attention to? That what is living, what exists, and most irreducibly, what *is*, is not that which is same but rather that which is wholly other, wholly unequal, and, above all, wholly mortal. Already in *Annihilation of Caste*, in the midst of his critique of the antidemocratic structure of Plato's republic, Ambedkar had called authentic equality a responsibility toward the incommensurable. This equality would be heterogeneous to calculation, substitution, and measure. It would take into account the uniqueness of each mortal who lived and died in an irreproducible and singular way.[92] In this making-political of finitude, which already anticipates years in advance his mature emphasis on the impermanence of life, Ambedkar does not valorize death or sacrifice in the manner of a satyagrahi, even though he never renounced the imperative of war and "general mobilization." Instead, he locates the awareness of finitude in the irreplaceable lives and everyday vulnerabilities of ordinary mortals who are denied even the basic senses of experience. Finitude emerged from this void of experience (and the experience of void). But this void, this place of impermanence (*sunnyata*), Ambedkar insists, is not as much a groundless dungeon of negativity as it is an affirmative dwelling for a self that must be given over, justly and responsibly, to the other. It is a place where the will to life—the inalienable force of justice—must subsume the fears of that being that is pushed toward death, everyday, slowly but surely, by cruelties seen and unseen. In fact, the possibility of a shared and just responsibility, the unconditional obligations and freedoms of the weakest could be grounded only in this will, in this sovereignty of the selfless self.

Perhaps the proper rendering of the mature Ambedkar's *maitri*, then, is neither "fraternity" nor "friendship" nor even "fellowship," understood in their anthropological sense, even though he often used each of these interchangeably throughout the 1940s and the 1950s. Rather, the proper (and I am not saying literal) rendering of *maitri* might be "justice," an immeasurable justice, an ethics of sociality and universality stemming from shared finitude, one that might respect if not bridge the irreparable abyss of species difference. For only in the belief that mortality and impermanence touch all lives collectively, in the faith that the truth about being is accessible equally to everyone, that the morals of action proper to justice might be forged. This action, conversely, might itself require a *coup de force*, an act of faith in its essence, an act where force and justice become inseparable. The act must not only exceed all existing measures and laws of belief but also destroy religion in its very name. Ambedkar was probably the quickest to recognize the risk of such a conception of faith at the extremities of the law. "Some may not understand," he had prophetically cautioned as early as *Annihilation of Caste*, "what I mean by the destruction of religion."[93] Within this grammar of destruction was an insurrectionary faith open to the weakest of mortals alone.

Epilogue

Citizenship and Insurrection

Among the greatest, most monumental images in modern Indian political life is one of Ambedkar standing majestically tall with his left hand
resolutely folded, holding the constitution of India close to his heart, even
as his right hand, stretched fully outward in a committed synchrony with his
piercing and sweeping vision, scans the horizon in front, index finger gestur-
ing toward a future, a place, a democracy that, notwithstanding the apparent triumph of India's Constituent Assembly, he would never stop insisting,
was still to come. It would be a democracy founded not in sameness, mastery, and even indivisibility of the republic, but one rooted in the virtues and
autonomies of the citizen unconstrained by the punitive laws of *dharma*; a
democracy grounded in the friendship and responsibility of equals alone,
one in which every citizen would belong to a fraternity of shared truth, reason, and faculties. It would be a democracy, even more important, which
would refuse to be reduced to mere representation and franchise. For nothing destroys the possibility of democracy more quickly (and from within),
Ambedkar warned in 1952, than its conflation with consensus, acquiescence,
and "majority rule as the rule of decision."[1] His would be a democracy to
come, then, in which the reason of the weakest might carry as much force
as that of the strongest, and in which resistance rather than obedience to the
lawless foundation and police power of law (juridical and theological) might
form the dissident soul of citizenship.

The image of Ambedkar, his hands speaking two heterogeneous but inseparable languages, one holding the constitution in reserve as the other gestures toward an organized minority of dissent and disobedience, is by now
etched indelibly into Indian democratic consciousness. It has been carved
into statues and disseminated throughout the young republic. Its ubiquity (in

legislative assemblies, parliamentary forecourt, city councils, town squares, and Buddhist temples), fueled by Dalit mobilization and electoral triumphs over the last two decades, undergoes a cycle of competitive intensification and appropriation every time the nation goes to polls. For long a Dalit icon and theorist of social citizenship for the marginalized and oppressed, Ambedkar suddenly finds himself snatched away (in acts of ideological calculation) and placed on the flyers and posters even of the Indian National Congress, a party whose conservative antagonism toward him had proved backbreaking for Ambedkar's political and moral endeavors in the 1940s and 1950s. In fact, the Congress and communists in India have been historically hostile to Ambedkar's "general mobilization" of the virtuous and oppressed, not to say to his language of affirmative action, which they have seen as undercutting both the meritocratic integrity of the nation and the theoretical supremacy of class. But to a broad coalition of secularists, traditionalists, social democrats, and liberals long suspicious of caste mobilization, embracing the memory of Ambedkar now offers the last line of electoral hope and social legitimacy, not to mention a little sheen of moral commitment that they can gleam toward those who, despite being in millions, still exist in caste servitude and whose life still remains a fraction of itself—a gesture this ideologically porous coalition hopes will help reconsolidate a national liberalism (grounded from the very beginning in the sanctity of private property and business interest) that has signally failed to grow out of the warm glow of the anticolonial struggle. It was a struggle against the empire that the coalition believes it had led—and the Indian National Congress lays claim to the largest share of this credit—but whose future, it refuses to see, may soon be long past.

It is undeniable that a wilfull, selective embrace of Ambedkar opens new possibilities for calibrating the discourse on social citizenship within which he can be safely placed, even as Ambedkar's own refusal to dissociate the question of republican sovereignty from the struggle for justice, his attempt to inscribe the right of civic insurrection at the heart of citizen virtue, can be safely circumscribed (and is indeed accomplished by other means). This is perhaps why Ambedkar's fierce attack on the authenticity of the *Gita*, a sacred text that he argued was in part composed as late as the fourteenth-century Muslim invasions of India, was seen to be as problematic, as distinctively anticanonical and antinationalist, as worthy of silence and noncommentary in its own time as it has been since then.[2] After all, this critique, grounded in no small measure in Ambedkar's own hypercritical faith in religion, had complicated the sovereign foundations of Indic antiquity itself, revealing what was classical to have been in fact medieval, what was mystical and disinterested to have been punitive and statist, what was secure in its polytheistic transcendence to be have been perennially threatened by defeat in the hands of a monotheistic "horde," what was, above all, posited as theological to have been in truth the political.

Nothing, as this study suggests, could be more interested than this appropriation of Ambedkar into the grand narrative of nation. For it was in fearlessly conceptualizing a moral ontology of action disengaged from the dialectic of nation and empire, a commitment to virtue and sovereignty that placed itself in the interstices between the just and unjust (rather than in the difference between colonizer and colonized) as its primary site of intervention, that Ambedkar's radical democracy took its greatest risk. In *Pakistan, or the Partition of India*, Ambedkar calls this risk, in a turn symptomatic of a thought that moves often very quickly from insurrection to constitution and back, the "love of politics." And this classical risk—which rebels against the theologico-juridical and, if need be, constitutional foundations of the nation-state, which tries to create more plural, more heterogeneous, more autonomous conditions of citizenship through the very act of insubordination (recall Ambedkar's expression of desire to burn the constitution in the manner that he had burned the *Manusmriti* in 1927)—has never been free of its own tragic paradoxes. It is a risk that yields, on the one hand, the aggressively republican, excessively virtuous, even self-righteous *Thoughts on Pakistan*. It is a risk, on the other hand, that could have given modern India *Annihilation of Caste*. But in the forced universalization of Ambedkar, in the appropriation of his confrontational counteruniversality, there now lies a greater risk to that tradition of insurrectionary democracy in the postcolonial world.

"It has always been the case against the classical citizen," J. G. A. Pocock writes, "that he is at heart a tragic hero, unsafe to associate with, who insists he is living in the realm of freedom and not that of necessity. This is why he is concerned with nondistributable goods like equality and virtue, and it is also why he is constantly confronted with *fortuna*."[3] We cannot be entirely certain that Ambedkar was familiar with the Florentine classic, Machiavelli's *The Prince* (1515), around which Pocock reconstructs the Atlantic history of republicanism.[4] What we can be certain about, however, is that despite his own isolation (which had by the 1950s acquired tragic proportions), silence, lying, idolatry, sycophancy, and dishonesty, to say nothing of cruelty and snobbery—everything that Judith Shklar calls "ordinary vices"—remained for Ambedkar the principal vices of the republic, irreconcilable with the virtues that create the conditions of an egalitarian and just sovereignty.[5] This is perhaps why his republic, unconditionally given over to the freedom of equals alone, never becomes one with the nation. Instead, it remains a republic

grounded in a shared love of truth, one where the ethics of justice and responsibility sometimes demand wounding the sensitivities of the nation itself. In the preface to second edition of *Thoughts on Pakistan*, Ambedkar gives
this conception of virtue its most distinctive form. The sense of tragic (yet
never short of heroic) isolation is palpable here.

This book is more than a mere treatise on Pakistan. The material relating to Indian
history and Indian politics contained in this book is so large and so varied that it
might well be called Indian Political: What is What. . . . That it is disowned by the
Hindus and unowned by the Muslims is to me the best evidence that it has the vices
of neither and that from the point of view of independence of thought and fearless
presentation of facts the book is not a party production. Some people are sore because
what I have said has hurt them. I have not, I confess, allowed myself to be influenced
by fears of wounding either individuals or classes, or shocking opinions however re-
spectable they may be. I have often felt regret in pursuing this course, but remorse
never. Those whom I may have offended must forgive me, in consideration of the
honesty and disinterestedness of my aim. I do not claim to have written dispassion-
ately though I trust I have written without prejudice. It would be hardly possible—I
was going to say decent—for an Indian to be calm when he talks of his country and
thinks of the times.[6]

Fearless civility—indeed, a citizenship grounded in insubordination
and independence—cannot be predicated on false decency, let alone remorse.
In fact, a civility proper to citizenship necessitates a relationship of forgiveness between citizens—an ethics of regret without remorse, a relationship of
disinterest without dispassion—only to the extent that this citizenship also
demands an unconditional, unbridled, and virtuous love of truth. It requires
a will to democratize truth without inhibitions and injunctions, the will to
share it and set it free through an absolute transparency of intentions. That
this formulation on passion, indeed enthusiasm—and within it, the expression "Indian Political"—appears in what is also Ambedkar's most republican
treatise is no coincidence. For insurrection, the passionate pursuit of freedom
unbound by interest and prejudice, the search for a radical autonomy unconstrained by laws of nationalist fidelity and transcendental theology alone
provides a republic of equals with its moral foundation. And this pursuit of
virtue by the citizen, Ambedkar concedes somewhat autobiographically, has
always involved a political and ethical risk, one that he fearlessly took, during the high noon of anticolonial struggle for sovereignty, in face of gravest
attacks on his fidelity and convictions. But the risk Ambedkar hints toward
here does not stem from the anxiety of being secluded, defamed, or punished
for holding on to what the citizen believes is his truth. The risk he gestures
toward accrues from an act of faith as such, which is by its very nature re-

sistant to norms, rules, and measures; it accrues from any gesture of making one's innermost convictions and truths unconditionally sharable and public, a gesture that is susceptible to hurting and wounding fellow citizens. And yet, argues Ambedkar, this risk of transparency must be taken; internal reasons, if they are not to be reduced to exercises in solipsistic self-sacrifice (which are no less violent and exclusionary), must be democratized. For there is no democracy without this risk of hurt—this risk of force—through which alone an egalitarian sovereignty of citizens might emerge.

If, as this book has argued, Ambedkar was a thinker of freedom in the most classical sense of the term—that is, a thinker of freedom as nondomination, as the liberty to cultivate a virtuous life, as the right to a life of activity, action, and speech, nourished in shared spaces as equals—then he was so only inasmuch as his critique of domination, like Gandhi's, eschewed the moral universalism of the nation and set to work a theory of interminable dissidence. Indeed, it renounced, sometimes in terrifying tones, any notion of abstract equality between sufferers. It renounced the vacuous unity of humanity even, seeking to focus the struggle for freedom among the noncitizens and oppressed of the city—that is, civic right as the equal right to civic disobedience—alone. The task of a critique of servitude began with the critique of violence of the nation-state. It began for Ambedkar (even if it did not end there), I have argued, with the act of separation from the laws of theological nationalism and its civilizational certitude. The work of formulating the conditions of a freedom *free* from all physical interference and cognitive limits involved a critique as much of external domination as of internal exclusions, weakness of will, and disciplinary limits enforced by the moral law.

"The English," it is Gandhi who writes in *Hind Swaraj* in a moment of unflinching lucidity, "have not taken India; we have given it to them. They are not in India because of their strength, but because we keep them."[7] And yet, within the moral logic of his *kshatriyadharma*, Gandhi's immense generosity and immeasurable pity would not have given the minor, the untouchable, or the *atishudra* (who is absent in *Hind Swaraj* altogether) this right of decision to keep and host the invader, let alone resist him. It is precisely this right of decision in its virtuous purity, a radical autonomy freed from the disciplinary constraints of *maryada dharma* and juridically enforced rituals and pretenses of civility (*sadachar*), that Ambedkar associates with the moral psychology of a citizen of the city who is, regardless of his birth, family, and caste, as he puts it in *Annihilation of Caste*, "free to follow his reason." *Radical Equality* has brought Ambedkar and Gandhi together, then, not because they were both equally suspicious of liberal nationalist—which has more often than not been dangerously porous with majoritarian—enunciations of sovereign power, but because Ambedkar and Gandhi exemplified two incommensurable ways of forging a relationship between sovereignty and justice, force and disobedience, itself.

In this sense, the social question for Ambedkar remained inseparable from political and ethical ones. His understanding of justice—or what he calls in *Annihilation of Caste* "responsibility" as the "essence of a truly religious act"—was always already and indelibly inscribed at the heart of sovereignty. The challenge was to give this justice the force of virtue and the nourishing ground of fraternity. We have examined the singularity of this insurrectionary democracy, one grounded in Ambedkar's distrust of foundations, rooted in an anarchic conception of autonomy, which can be defined as the right to resist immoral laws and reclaim the city. In fact, only in the city, where the vertical relations of force that operate in the countryside dissolve and give way to newer associations and languages of community and revolt—community as revolt—can this autonomy exist. Of this anarchic ethics, which is founded in an indifference toward foundations, which makes possible a true republic (and prevents its degeneration into a regime of mere laws), Ambedkar never refrains from speaking in the most insubordinate terms. In fact, to return to a point made earlier in the book, no figure in the annals of modern republican constitutionalism so closely associated with the drafting of a national constitution has ever forged such a rebellious relationship with a document to which he has given the most productive and crucial years of his political life. History abounds with instances of republicans sending people to the gallows in order to defend the revolution (or, in our own time, the law). But rarely have revolutionaries openly declared their openness to burning the constitution they have themselves written. A singularly revolutionary democracy, then, a democracy that revolutionizes citizen virtues, even armed preparedness and confrontation with neighboring states, without still ever subscribing to the idea of hostility and bloodshed. "That," says Ambedkar of his vision of revolutionary democracy, "is the real test. It is perhaps the severest test. But when you are judging the quality of a material, you must put it to severest test."[8]

It has, of course, concerned us throughout this study that these are exactly the terms in which Ambedkar speaks of religion too. "Religion," he says in a Rousseauist vein in *Philosophy of Hinduism*, "must be put on its trial."[9] If the conceptual and rhetorical structure of radical democracy that I have traced in the preceding pages is taken as a framework to understand at once the emancipatory power and pernicious limit that the logic of representation imposes on the everyday activities and actions of the weakest among the citizens of the city (a dualism inscribed at the heart of representation that a young, Shakespearean Ambedkar had already begun grappling with in New York in the 1910s), then the iconic and statuesque image with which I began this epilogue—the constitutionalist's two hands speaking in two heterogeneous but inseparable languages—points forcefully toward that other genealogy of democratic ethics that Ambedkar's and Gandhi's politics, often irreconcilably, seemed to craft. Viewed in terms of this genealogy, what becomes striking in the representation and monumentalization of Ambedkar is not his holding of the constitution in one hand but instead the insurrectionary warning that he seems to be issuing with the other. It is as if his raised hand is resisting illegitimate powers from corrupting the constitution. It is as if the architect of the constitution is cautioning that the republic, for all its impatience, is not ready for a true constitution. It seems he is signaling that even the constitution is not enough to save the republic yet. Or perhaps the image, in all its revolutionary and messianic intensity, captures an Ambedkar who must remind the citizens of the republic that the virtues of true gift— here, the constitution that a people gives itself—remain incomplete without a shared love of truth; that justice, which is by its very nature insurrectionary (especially when it is thought through in an annihilative, indestructible, and anarchic autonomy), remains inadequate without force; that the constitution is rendered quickly immoral—and in turn renders itself thoroughly deserving of being burned—if it does not secure the freedom of the republic's incommensurable equals, who become equal only through a shared resistance against unjust laws.

"It is for the majority to realize that its duty not to discriminate against minorities," Ambedkar cautions in November 1948 as he introduces the draft constitution to the Constituent Assembly. "Whether minorities will continue or will vanish must depend upon this habit of the majority. The moment the majority loses the habit of discriminating against the minority, the minorities can have no ground to exist. They will vanish."[10] But equality can survive, he insists on other occasions, not merely by dissolving inequality, let alone by dissolving difference, but by retaining precisely those within the community of citizen-warriors who must remain its radical others. Fraternity, or *maitri*, was nothing if not the egalitarian sharing among citizens and noncitizens, neighbors and strangers, ascetics and bandits, of this "incommensurability." This equality within incommensurability is what the mature Ambedkar attaches in *The Buddha and His Dhamma* to the "risk of conversion"; the risk of opening oneself to even the most violent (and violated), most alien, most unjust, and most intimate others in an unconditional and soverign act of faith; a risk the citizen must take if democracy, which is also Ambedkar's name for a revolutionary nonviolence, is to have a chance.[11] But silence (at once political and methodological) on this antinomic conception of responsibility, this fecund thought that thrives in the inseparability between force and justice, mastery and *maitri*, this rigorous imagination that refuses, above all, to measure democracy within the limits of the nation-state alone (and yet relinquishes neither the dissident's right to the republic nor the unequal's right to the city as such), has not only impoverished the history of democratic ethics in the modern non-West. It has given us a destitute history of citizenship itself.

If the relationship between freedom and citizenship, sovereignty and justice, constituent power and constitutional principles, remains far from settled today, then Ambedkar's struggle only reminds us that the problem is neither new nor simply postcolonial, one whose origins, edifice, and endurance can be safely blamed on the empire alone. On the contrary, these tensions and exclusions were lodged at the foundation of nineteenth and twentieth-century anticolonial experiments with truth and self, morality and sacrifice. Against these, Ambedkar had sought to institute another truth, another awareness of finitude, one rooted in a dissident practice of citizen virtue and creative action, anchored in a demanding balance between reciprocal rights and unconditional freedom (indeed the groundlessness and inalienability of the right to have rights), and pegged in an uncompromisingly just—possibly impossible—point between measure and immeasurability. It was in this sense of justice as immeasurability that Ambedkar critiqued the notion that equality (or inequality) could be a matter of "mathematical exactitude", reducible to the procedural mechanisms of the national social state, as if the promise of distributive, normative, and even constitutionally secured equality could ever be separated from the invisible corruptions, cruelties, and stigmata of aristocratic, majoritarian, and welfarist privilege that smugly promote it.

The results of this critique—this positing of equality as autonomy and incommensurability—were often paradoxical, frequently misunderstood, and invariably radical. From this very struggle to reclaim the sovereign spaces, senses, and techniques of civic action, this ethics of inalienable sovereignty—the craft of force—as such, which Ambedkar mounted with such courage against the majoritarian and nationalist grammar of his times, emerged what I have called his sensitivity toward the theologico-political; a sensitivity that remained inseparable, until the end, from his insurrectionary search for the society of equals. *Radical Equality* has tried to return history to the heart of that insurrectionary past of citizenship, the soul of that responsibility beyond measure that Ambedkar had called, in a moment of revolutionary clarity (and irreducible risk), "the essence of a truly religious act."

Abbreviations

BAWS   B. R. Ambedkar, *Dr. Babasaheb Ambedkar: Writings and Speeches*, 24 vols. (Bombay: Education Department, Govt. of Maharashtra).

BRAP   B. R. Ambedkar Papers, Microfilms Division, Nehru Memorial and Museum Library, New Delhi.

CAD   *Constituent Assembly Debates: Official Report, 9 December 1946–24 January 1950*, 12 vols. (1950; New Delhi: Lok Sabha Secretariat, 1999).

CWMG   M. K. Gandhi, *The Collected Works of Mahatma Gandhi Online*, 98 vols. (New Delhi: Publications Division, Government of India, 1999); available online at gandhiserve.org/e/cwmg/cwmg.htm.

EWBRA   B. R. Ambedkar, *The Essential Writings of B. R. Ambedkar*, ed. Valerian Rodrigues (New Delhi: Oxford University Press, 2002).

MPWG   M. K. Gandhi, *The Moral and Political Writings of Mahatma Gandhi*, 3 vols., ed. Raghavan Iyer (Oxford: Oxford University Press, 1986).

NVPW   M. K. Gandhi, *Nonviolence in Peace and War*, 2 vols. (Ahmedabad: Navajivan, 1942).

PD   *Parliamentary Debates* (New Delhi: Parliament Secratariat, Government of India).

Notes

1. On Ambedkar's use of the expression "faith in equality," see his "Presidential Address at Second Conference of Untouchables from Berar Province," in *Ambedkar Speaks: 301 Seminal Speeches*, 3 vols., ed. Narendra Jadhav (Seattle: Konark Publishers, 2013); hereafter cited as *301 Seminal Speeches*; 1:84; originally published in *Bahishkrit Bharat*, 25 November 1927. I return to this formulation in Chapter 3.

2. For an incisive discussion of what such a mentality might mean, one whose substantive elements and genealogies might be common to a host of post-Enlightenment traditions of dissent in Europe and India, see Akeel Bilgrami, "Value, Enchantment, and the Mentality of Democracy: Distant Perspectives from Gandhi," *Economic and Political Weekly* 44, no. 51 (2009), 47–61.

3. The argument has a distinguished pedigree that goes back to the nineteenth-century metropolitan thought, coalescing around a set of philosophical attitudes and apparatuses that Uday S. Mehta calls "liberal strategies of exclusion." See Mehta, *Liberalism and Empire: A Study of Nineteenth-Century British Liberal Thought* (Chicago: University of Chicago Press, 2000).

4. The term "spirit of democracy" is Gandhi's. See, for one instance, his speech on reforms resolution at Amritsar Congress, 1 January 1920, in *CWMG* 19:201.

5. I draw the expression from Pierre Rosanvallon's *The Society of Equals*, trans. Arthur Goldhammer (Cambridge, MA: Harvard University Press, 2013).

6. "Thank God, in the front rank of the leaders, he is singularly alone and as yet but a representative of a very small minority." Gandhi, "Dr. Ambedkar's Indictment," in *CWMG* 69:206; originally published in *Harijan*, 11 July 1936.

7. See Ambedkar, *Annihilation of Caste: Speech Prepared for the 1936 Annual Conference of the Jat Pat Todak Mandal of Lahore But Not Delivered*, 3rd ed. (1944; Jalandhar: Bheem Patrika Publications, 1968), 1–15; hereafter cited as *Annihilation of Caste*.

8. "*Annihilation of Caste*," wrote Dhananjay Keer, one of Ambedkar's earliest biographers in English, "was logic on fire, pinching and pungent, piercing and fiery, provocative and explosive. It was to the minds of the caste Hindu leaders what silver nitrate is to gangrene." Keer, *Dr. Ambedkar: Life and Mission* (Bombay: Popular Prakashan, 1954), 269.

9. On the relationship between sacrifice, family, and the state, see Georg Wilhelm Friedrich Hegel, *The Philosophy of Right*, trans. T. M. Knox (1821; Oxford: Oxford University Press, 1967).

10. I draw this expression from J. C. Heesterman, *The Broken World of Sacrifice: An Essay in Ancient Indian Ritual* (Chicago: University of Chicago Press, 1993).

11. See Ambedkar, "Conditions Precedent for the Successful Working of Modern Democracy," Pune, 22 December 1952, in *301 Seminal Speeches* 1:287 (emphasis in original).

12. Ambedkar, "Ranade, Gandhi, and Jinnah," in *BAWS* 1:209–212

13. Thomas Nagel, *Mortal Questions* (Cambridge: Cambridge University Press, 1979).

14. See Milind Wakankar, *Subalternity and Religion: The Prehistory of Dalit Empowerment in South Asia* (New York: Routledge, 2010), 4.

15. Ambedkar, *Annihilation of Caste*, 97.

16. Ibid., 63.

17. Ibid., 76.

18. Ibid., 87–88.

19. See Gandhi, *Hind Swaraj, or Indian Home Rule*, in *CWMG* 10:245n1 (originally published in 1910) hereafter cited as *Hind Swaraj-CW*.

20. Gandhi, Ibid., 283.

21. See ibid., 270–306.

22. Ambedkar, *Annihilation of Caste*, 76.

23. Gandhi, "Working of Nonviolence," in *CWMG* 75:48; originally published in *Harijan*, 11 February 1939.

24. See Nehru to Mahatma Gandhi, Allahabad, 4 October 1945, in *Gandhiji's "Hind Swaraj" and Select Views of Others* (New Delhi: National Gandhi Museum, 2009), 241–245. Fewer outside the Congress engaged seriously with *Hind Swaraj*, with the exception of the socialist Rammanohar Lohia, who later wrote *Marx, Gandhi, and Socialism* (Hyderabad: Samata Vidyalaya Nyasa, 1963).

25. Ambedkar, *What Congress and Gandhi Have Done to Untouchables* (1945; Lahore: Classic, 1977), 230; hereafter cited as *Congress and Gandhi*.

26. See Isabel Hofmeyr, *Gandhi's Printing Press: Experiments in Slow Reading* (Cambridge, MA: Harvard University Press, 2013), 132–133.

27. Gandhi, "Dr. Ambedkar's Indictment," in *CWMG* 69:206; originally published in *Harijan*, 11 July 1936.

28. Gandhi's propensity to measure, his susceptibility around Ambedkar to betray the worst form of calculation—fiscal prudence—was revealed in 1931 during their first ever meeting. "I have been thinking over the problem of Untouchables ever since my school days—when you were not even born," Gandhi pointed out to Ambedkar. And as if the question was merely of calculable effort, he persisted: "The Congress has spent not less than rupees twenty lakhs [2,000,000 rupees] on [their] uplift." See Keer, *Dr. Ambedkar: Life and Mission*, 165.

29. See Richard Sorabji, *Gandhi and the Stoics: Modern Experiments on Ancient Values* (Chicago: University of Chicago Press, 2013); Akeel Bilgrami, *Secularism, Identity, and Enchantment* (Cambridge, MA: Harvard University Press, 2014). Two important counterpoints are Tanika Sarkar, "Gandhi and Social Relations," in *The Cambridge Companion to Gandhi*, ed. Judith M. Brown and Anthony Parel (Cambridge: Cambridge University Press, 2011), 173–195, and Ashwini Tambe, "Gandhi's

'Fallen Sisters': Difference and the National Body Politic," *Social Scientist* 37, nos. 1–2 (2009), 21–38.

30. See esp. Eleanor Zelliot, *Ambedkar's World: The Making of Babasaheb and the Dalit Movement* (New Delhi: Navayana, 2013); Gail Omvedt, *Cultural Revolt in a Colonial Society: The Non-Brahman Movement in Western India, 1873–1930* (Bombay: Scientific Socialist Education Trust, 1976) and her *Dalits and the Democratic Revolution: Dr. Ambedkar and the Dalit Movement in Colonial India* (New Delhi: Sage, 1994).

31. This assessment remains the implicit thrust of Perry Anderson's *The Indian Ideology* (New York: Verso, 2013).

32. Ambedkar, "Frustration," in *BAWS* 12:733.

33. See Ambedkar, *Waiting for a Visa*, in *BAWS* 12:661–664. The autobiographical fragment was drafted around the same time that the question of statelessness began to find its global (and moral psychological) charge in Hannah Arendt's essays, especially "We, the Refugees" (1943), "The Jew as *Pariah*" (1944), and "Nightmare and Flight" (1945), which were subsequently collected in *The Jew as Pariah* (New York: Grove Press, 1978). The word "pariah" derives from the name of a community of South Indian "untouchables," an indication perhaps of Arendt's attempt to amplify the experience of exile and unbelonging that European Jews shared with the "untouchables" of the Hindu caste order. The history of the community (and its name) receives probing attention in Rupa Viswanath, *The Pariah Problem: Caste, Religion, and the Social in Modern India* (New York: Columbia University Press, 2014).

34. Keer, *Dr. Ambedkar: Life and Mission*, 166.

35. Ambedkar, *Thoughts on Pakistan* (Bombay: Thacker & Co., 1941), 344; hereafter cited as *Thoughts*.

36. See Renan's 11 March 1882 lecture at the Sorbonne, "What Is a Nation?"; rpt. in *Nation and Narration*, ed. Homi Bhabha (New York: Routledge, 1990), 8–22.

37. Ambedkar, *Thoughts*, 328–329.

38. On Ambedkar's place in the history of minority rights, see Christophe Jaffrelot, *Dr. Ambedkar and Untouchability: Analyzing and Fighting Caste* (London: Hurst, 2005).

39. Partha Chatterjee's "A Modern Science of Politics for the Colonized," in *Texts of Power: Emerging Disciplines in Colonial Bengal*, ed. Partha Chatterjee (Minneapolis: University of Minnesota Press, 1995), 93–117, remains the only sustained treatment of the problem of general will (*sadharan mat*) in both its militant and conservative dimensions within Indian traditions.

40. On the indecisions that lie at the heart of sovereignty, or at the center of what has been called, following Montaigne, "the mystical foundation of authority," see *Sovereignty in Fragments: The Past, Present, and Future of a Contested Concept*, ed. Hent Kalmo and Quentin Skinner (Cambridge: Cambridge University Press, 2010).

41. See Hannah Arendt, *On Revolution* (New York: Penguin, 1963).

42. See Eric Voegelin, *The New Science of Politics: An Introduction* (Chicago: University of Chicago Press, 1952).

43. V. D. Savarkar, *Hindutva: Who Is a Hindu?* (1923; Delhi: Hindi Sahitya Sadan, 2009), 3. For a genealogy of this ideological formation, see Jyotirmaya Sharma, *Hindutva: Exploring the Idea of Hindu Nationalism* (New Delhi: Penguin, 2006).

44. On Savarkar's fondness for Ambedkar, see "Message to Dr. Ambedkar's Golden Jubilee Committee," 15 April 1942, in V. D. Savarkar, *Historic Statements*, ed. S. S. Savarkar and G. M. Joshi (Bombay: Popular Prakashan, 1967), 43. There was mutual respect, certainly, but the relationship between the two remained ambiguous. Ambedkar's personal bibliography, "Books for 1943" (in a note dated 22 September 1943), suggests he was reading S. L. Karandikar's biography, *Savarkar Charitra*. See BRAP, file 3, reel 1. Two years earlier, in *Thoughts on Pakistan*, however, Ambedkar unequivocally denounces the politics of the Hindu Mahasabha as "gangsterism." On the imperial scale of Savarkar's politics, see Janaki Bakhle, "Savarkar (1883–1966), Sedition and Surveillance: The Rule of Law in a Colonial Situation," *Social History* 35, no. 1 (2010), 51–75, and Vinayak Chaturvedi, "Rethinking Knowledge with Action: V. D. Savarkar, the Bhagavad Gita, and Histories of Warfare," *Modern Intellectual History* 7, no. 2 (2010), 417–435.

45. The term is suggested by Karuna Mantena's "Another Realism: The Politics of Gandhian Nonviolence," *American Political Science Review* 106, no. 2 (2012), 455–470.

46. Ambedkar, *Pakistan, or the Partition of India* (Bombay: Thacker & Co., 1945), x; hereafter cited as *Partition*.

47. Dominic Vendell, "Jotirao Phule's *Satyashodh* and the Problem of Subaltern Consciousness," *Comparative Studies of South Asia, Africa, and Middle East* 34, no. 1 (2014), 52–66, offers an important perspective on the local traditions of emancipatory historiography that Phule's thought has inspired, at the same time drawing attention to Phule's much deeper epistemological concerns.

48. Ambedkar is more frequently cited in discussions of the national question now than he was about twenty-five years ago, when Partha Chatterjee published his groundbreaking study, *Nationalist Thought and the Colonial World: A Derivative Discourse?* (Minneapolis: University of Minnesota Press, 1994), a work completely silent on Ambedkar's critique of the ideological, indeed thelogical, foundations of the Indian nationalist imaginary. Chatterjee devotes important passages to Ambedkar's thoughts on citizenship in his more recent work, especially *Politics of the Governed: Reflections on Popular Politics in Most of the World* (New York: Columbia University Press, 2006), ch. 1.

49. Ananya Vajpeyi, *Righteous Republic: The Political Foundations of Modern India* (Cambridge, MA: Harvard University Press, 2012), 238–240.

50. Arendt, *On Revolution*, 102.

51. Ambedkar, *Annihilation of Caste*, 70.

52. Phule established the social reform organization Satyashodhak Samaj (Society for Seekers of Truth) in 1873, which, as the name suggests, was much more concerned with the transformation in moral psychologies of the self than it was with mere social change.

53. Fanon's *Black Skin, White Masks*, trans. Richard Philcox (1952; New York: Grove Press, 2008), and *The Wretched of the Earth*, trans. Richard Philcox (1961; New York: Grove Press, 2004) became canonical texts in the period following the disciplinary consolidation of postcolonial studies in the English-speaking world. His reception in France, however, has been much more stratified.

54. The phrase is Leela Gandhi's, from *Postcolonial Theory: An Introduction* (New

York: Columbia University Press, 1998), 17–18. Gandhi herself draws from Gyan Prakash's introduction to *After Colonialism: Imperial Histories and Postcolonial Displacements*, ed. Gyan Prakash (Princeton, NJ: Princeton University Press, 1994), 9, which credits, among the many "nameless" colonized intellectuals, Gandhi and Fanon for making possible "new forms of historical imagination." Within a decade, this important gesture was turned into a practice so rife that questioning the logic of its selectiveness began to appear beside the point.

55. See Uday S. Mehta, "The Social Question and the Absolutism of Politics," *Seminar* 615 (2010), 23–27, and Sudipta Kaviraj, *The Trajectories of the Indian State: Politics and Ideas* (New York: Columbia University Press, 2011).

56. See Ambedkar, *Annihilation of Caste*, 20–22.

57. See Gopal Guru, "Archeology of Untouchability," in Gopal Guru and Sundar Sarukkai, *The Cracked Mirror: An Indian Debate on Experience and Theory* (New York: Oxford University Press, 2013), 200–222.

58. Dipesh Chakrabarty, *Provincializing Europe: Historical Thought and Postcolonial Difference* (Princeton, NJ: Princeton University Press, 2000), 4.

59. Hannah Arendt, *Between Past and Future* (1961; New York: Penguin, 2006), 14.

60. See Gandhi, *Hind Swaraj-CW*, 290.

61. I draw the term "egalitarian sovereignty" from Étienne Balibar, *Masses, Classes, Ideas: Studies on Politics and Philosophy before and after Marx* (New York: Routledge, 1994), 43.

62. Antonio Negri, *Insurgencies: Constituent Power and the Modern State*, trans. Maurizia Boscagli (Minneapolis: University of Minnesota Press, 1999).

63. An exception is C. A. Bayly's *Recovering Liberties: Indian Thought in the Age of Liberalism and Empire* (Cambridge: Cambridge University Press, 2011), which places Ambedkar, for the first time, within the longue durée of Indian liberal jurisprudence.

64. Romain Rolland's *Mahatma Gandhi: The Man Who Became One with the Universal Being* (New York: Century, 1924) marks a crucial moment in Gandhi's celebrated reception in Europe. Also see Richard Gregg, *The Power of Nonviolence* (Philadelphia: Lippincott, 1935). The important political theoretical studies after India's independence include Joan Bondurant, *Conquest of Violence: The Gandhian Philosophy of Conflict* (Princeton, NJ: Princeton University Press, 1958), and Raghavan Iyer, *The Moral and Political Thought of Mahatma Gandhi* (Oxford: Oxford University Press, 1973). Recent works include Akeel Bilgrami, "Gandhi, the Philosopher," *Economic and Political Weekly* 38, no. 39 (2003), 4159–4165; Faisal Devji, *The Impossible Indian: Gandhi and the Temptation of Violence* (London: Hurst, 2012); Karuna Mantena, "Gandhi's Critique of the State: Sources, Contexts, Conjunctures," *Modern Intellectual History* 9, no. 3 (2012), 535–563; Uday S. Mehta, "Gandhi on the Common Logic of War and Peace," *Raritan* 30, no. 1 (2010), 134–155; and Ajay Skaria, "Gandhi's Politics: Liberalism and the Question of the *Ashram*," *South Atlantic Quarterly* 101, no. 4 (2002), 955–986.

65. In a slightly different form, Gopal Guru registers this demand in "How Egalitarian Are the Social Sciences in India?," *Economic and Political Weekly* 37, no. 50 (2002), 5003–5009.

66. Étienne Balibar has most recently condensed the inseparable relationship between freedom and equality into the term "equaliberty," whose theoretical institution

he traces to the Rousseauist heritage of the French Revolution. See Balibar, *Equaliberty: Political Essays*, trans. James Ingram (Durham: Duke University Press, 2014).

67. I take the phrase from Sudipta Kaviraj, *The Imaginary Institution of India* (New York: Columbia University Press, 2010).

68. It was around this time that Ambedkar helped found the radical fortnightly *Samata*, which was launched in June 1928 under the editorship of Devrao Vishnu Naik and remained in circulation until March 1929.

69. Gandhi, *Hind Swaraj-CW*, 282.

70. An interesting encapsulation of the distinctions between these terms appears in Hannah Arendt, *On Violence* (New York: Harcourt & Brace, 1969), 35–56.

71. The phrase comes from Gopal Guru's "Rejection of Rejection," in *Humiliation: Claims and Context*, ed. Gopal Guru (Delhi: Oxford University Press, 2009), 209–225.

72. For a genealogy of the term *dalit*, see Oliver Mendelsohn and Marika Vicziany, *The Untouchables: Subordination, Poverty and the State in Modern India* (Cambridge: Cambridge University Press, 1998), 2–4.

73. See Rosalind O'Hanlon, *Caste, Conflict, and Ideology: Mahatma Jotirao Phule and Low Caste Protest in Nineteenth-Century Western India* (Cambridge: Cambridge University Press, 1985). On the politics of narrative form and content within local patriotisms, see Prachi Deshpande, *Creative Pasts: Historical Memory and Identity in Western India, 1700–1960* (New York: Columbia University Press, 2007).

74. Anupama Rao, *The Caste Question: Dalits and the Politics of Modern India* (Berkeley: University of California Press, 2009).

75. Dwaipayan Sen, "Representation, Education and Agrarian Reform: Jogendranath Mandal and the Nature of Scheduled Caste Politics, 1937–1943," *Modern Asian Studies* 48, no. 1 (2014), 77–109, and Ramnarayan Rawat, *Reconsidering Untouchability: Chamars and Dalit History in North India* (Bloomington: Indiana University Press, 2011). Rawat's study offers a thoughtful counterpoint to tendencies within historical and sociological studies that reduce Dalit politics to an ensemble of electoral interest.

76. The expression "non-negative negation" is Hent de Vries's, formulated in *Religion and Violence: Philosophical Perspectives from Kant to Derrida* (Baltimore: Johns Hopkins University Press, 2002), 209.

77. I have discussed this mode of fidelity to religion with reference to Ambedkar's simultaneous appropriation and defacement of the Gita in my essay "Ambedkar's Inheritances," *Modern Intellectual History* 7, no. 2 (2010), 391–415.

78. Ambedkar to Dattoba, 16 August 1926, BRAP, file 5, reel 2.

79. See Gopal Guru, "The Language of Dalit-Bahujan Political Discourse," in *Dalit Identity and Politics*, ed. Ghanshyam Shah (New Delhi: Sage Publications, 2001), 97–107.

80. On the construction of religion as universal category, see Tomoko Masuzawa, *The Invention of World Religions: Or, How European Universalism Was Preserved in the Language of Pluralism* (Chicago: University of Chicago Press, 2005).

81. On the connections between imperial expansion and the philosophical foundations of universal history, see Ranagit Guha, *History at the Limit of World History* (Cambridge, MA: Harvard University Press, 2003).

82. Ambedkar, *Philosophy of Hinduism*, 17.

83. See Claude Lefort, "The Permanence of the Theologico-Political," in Lefort, *Democracy and Political Theory*, trans. David Macey (Minneapolis: University of Minnesota Press, 1988), 213–255.

84. This has imparted a remarkable porousness to the analytically rigid distinctions between "civil society" and "political society" usually attributed to modern liberal thought. See John Dunn, "The Contemporary Significance of John Locke's Conception of Civil Society," in *Civil Society: History and Possibilities*, ed. Sudipta Kaviraj and Sunil Khilnani (Cambridge: Cambridge University Press, 2002), 47.

85. See Pierre Manent, *An Intellectual History of Liberalism*, trans. Rebecca Balinski (Princeton, NJ: Princeton University Press, 1995), 3–9.

86. See, for instance, Webb Keane, *Christian Moderns: Freedom and Fetish in the Mission Encounter* (Minneapolis: University of Minnesota Press, 2007); Parna Sengupta, *Pedagogy of Religion: Missionary Education and the Fashioning of Hindus and Muslims in Bengal* (Berkeley: University of California Press, 2011).

87. For an interwar treatment of the continuity between older conceptions of divine will and secularized, sovereign power of the modern type, see Carl Schmitt, *Political Theology: Four Chapters on Sovereignty*, trans. George Schwab (1922; Chicago: University of Chicago Press, 2006).

88. See Georg Wilhelm Friedrich Hegel, *The Philosophy of Mind*, trans. William Wallace (New York: Oxford University Press, 1971), 156–157.

89. Ambedkar, *Philosophy of Hinduism*, 17.

90. I use the term "Indo-European" both in its geographical and linguistic sense, as developed in Émile Benveniste's classic work *Indo-European Language and Society*, trans. Elizabeth Palmer (Florida: University of Miami Press, 1973).

91. See Ambedkar, *Philosophy of Hinduism*, in *BAWS* 3:13–17; hereafter cited as *Philosophy of Hinduism*. On Ambedkar's engagement with the theological content of everyday humiliation under Hinduism, see V. Geetha, "Bereft of Being: The Humiliations of Untouchability," in *Humiliation*, ed. Gopal Guru, 95–107.

92. See D. R. Nagaraj, "Gandhi and the Dalit Question: A Comparison with Marx and Ambedkar," "Self-Purification vs. Self-Respect," and "Two Imaginary Soliloquies," in Nagaraj, *The Flaming Feet and Other Essays: The Dalit Movement in India*, ed. Prithvi Datta and Chandra Shobhi (New Delhi: Permanent Black, 2010), 75–89.

93. On Gandhi's formative encounters in Britain, see Leela Gandhi, *Affective Communities: Anticolonial Thought, Fin-de-Siècle Radicalism, and the Politics of Friendship* (Durham, NC: Duke University Press, 2006).

94. Gandhi, *An Autobiography, Or the Story of My Experiments with Truth*, in *CWMG* 44:127 (originally published in 1929); hereafter cited as *Autobiography-CW*.

95. On this resurgence, see Prathama Banerjee, "Chanakya/Kautilya: History, Philosophy, Theater, and the Twentieth-Century Political," *History of the Present* 2, no. 1 (2012), 24–51.

96. Interestingly, both read the redoubtable T. W. Rhys Davids's late nineteenth-century works on Buddhism. Gandhi read his *Lectures*; Ambedkar pursued his 3-volume *Dialogues of the Buddha*. See Gandhi, "My Jail Experiences," in *CWMG* 29:90 (originally published in *Young India*, 4 September 1924), and Ambedkar, "Bibliography," in

The Buddha and His Dhamma: A Critical Edition, ed. Aakash Singh Rathore and Ajay Verma (1956; New Delhi: Oxford University Press, 2011), 313–314; hereafter cited as *Buddha and His Dhamma-CE*. For a genealogy of vernacular cultures of literary and philosophical speculation in the period preceding Gandhi and Ambedkar, see Tridip Suhrud, *Writing Life: Three Gujarati Thinkers* (New Delhi: Orient BlackSwan, 2009) and G. P. Deshpande, *The World of Ideas in Modern Marathi: Phule, Vinoba, Savarkar* (New Delhi: Tulika, 2010).

97. Gandhi to Esther Faering, 30 June 1918, in *CWMG* 17:109.

98. Ambedkar, *Philosophy of Hinduism*, 71.

99. On some Deweyan resonances in Ambedkar, see Arun P. Mukherjee, "B. R. Ambedkar, John Dewey, and the Meaning of Democracy," *New Literary History* 40, no. 2, (2009), 345–370.

100. Ambedkar, "Buddha or Karl Marx," in *BAWS* 3:444. The title of the essay anticipates a book-length study Ambedkar promised to publish soon after his frantic completion of *The Buddha and His Dhamma* in April 1956, but which remained unfinished at the time of his death in December 1956. See "B. R. Ambedkar's Preface" in Ambedkar, *Buddha and His Dhamma-CE*, xxviii. Apart from the book on *Buddha and Karl Marx*, Ambedkar also promised a treatise on *Revolution and Counter-Revolution in Ancient India*, of which his exegeses of the *Gita* were to become part.

101. Ambedkar, "Labor and Parliamentary Democracy," All Indian Trade Union Workers' Study Camp, New Delhi, 8–17 September 1943, in *301 Seminal Speeches* 1:276.

102. "The religious reflex of the real world," writes Marx in *Capital*, "can . . . only then finally vanish, when the practical conditions of everyday life offer to man none but perfectly intelligible and reasonable relations with regard to his fellow men and to nature." See *The Marx-Engels Reader*, ed. Richard Tucker (New York: Norton, 1978), 327.

103. For a similar argument (with a slightly different emphasis), see Ajay Skaria, "Relinquishing Republican Democracy: Gandhi's *Ramarajya*," *Postcolonial Studies* 14, no. 2 (2011), 203–229.

104. Gandhi, *Hind Swaraj-CW*, 256.

105. Ibid., 294.

106. Gandhi, *Ethical Religion (Niti Dharma)*, in *CWMG* 6 (originally published in 8 installments in *Indian Opinion*, 5 January 1907–23 February 1907), and *Sarvodaya: A Paraphrase of "Unto This Last,"* trans. Valji Govindji Desai (Ahmedabad: Navajivan, 1951) (originally published in 9 installments in *Indian Opinion*, 16 May 1908–1918 July 1908).

107. See Gandhi, "My Jail Experiences," 89–90.

108. See Georges Sorel, *Reflections on Violence* (1908; Cambridge: Cambridge University Press, 1999).

109. For his reading of Durkheim's *Elementary Forms*, see Ambedkar, *Essays on Untouchables and Untouchability*, bks. 1–4, in *BAWS* 5:179–81; hereafter cited as *Essays*.

110. See, for one example, Ambedkar, *Revolution and Counter-Revolution in Ancient India*, in *BAWS* 3:321–322; hereafter cited as *Revolution and Counter-Revolution*.

111. The initial pages of *Philosophy of Hinduism* are evidence of Ambedkar's perennial fascination with the way in which religion and morality come together to apprehend—even formalize the laws of—life at its very source. "Religion consecrates

these life processes while morality furnishes rules for their preservation," he remarks; and just a little earlier: "It is wrong to suppose that [fetishism and magic] form the source of religion . . . these are only the means. The end is life and the preservation of life." The distaste for its violent, fetishistic, and magical constituents notwithstanding, there is an attempt even here to distinguish a religion—indeed, a religious ontology—that might be aware of finitude, a faith given over to morality and life, grounded in the love of truth. See Ambedkar, *Philosophy of Hinduism*, 10–12.

112. On Sorel's reworking of Bergson, especially around the question of "psychological spontaneity" as it is developed in Bergson's *Time and Free Will, Matter and Memory*, and *Creative Evolution*, see John L. Stanley, *The Sociology of Virtue: The Political and Social Theories of Georges Sorel* (Berkeley: University of California Press, 1981).

113. Henri Bergson, *Two Sources of Religion and Morality*, trans. R. Ashley Cloudesley and Laura Brereton (1932; Notre Dame: University of Notre Dame Press, 1977), 266.

114. See esp. Ambedkar, *Philosophy of Hinduism*, 44–45.

115. See Jean-Jacques Rousseau, *The Social Contract and Other Later Political Writings*, ed. Victor Gourevitch (Cambridge: Cambridge University Press, 1997), 49–50.

116. On his engagement with William Robertson Smith's *Religion of the Semites* (1889; New Brunswick, NJ: Transaction Publishers, 2002), see Ambedkar, "Away from the Hindus," *Essays*, 406–407. Robertson Smith appears again, just before the crucial discussion of the Abrahamic tradition in *Philosophy of Hinduism*, 13–17. *Religion of the Semites* strongly inflects Ambedkar's understanding of sacrifice as an economy of force, as a set of ancient practices that he increasingly sees, from the 1930s onward, not simply as an encrusted ritual routine in its anthropological sense—caste, of course, being its most malignant form—but also as a spatial and territorial doctrine formed out of the pernicious alliance between sovereignty and theology, a nexus between holy lands, sacrificial feasts, and military "hordes," one that gave monotheistic religions (and Hinduism) their geopolitical spirit. This understanding finds its extreme resolution in the theory of citizenship and security that is advanced in *Thoughts on Pakistan*.

117. See Émile Durkheim, *Elementary Forms of Religious Life*, trans. Carol Cosman (1912; Oxford: Oxford University Press, 2001), 140–152.

118. Ambedkar, *Buddha and the Future of His Religion* (1951; Jalandhar: Bheem Patrika Publications, n.d.), 11.

119. Gandhi, *Discourses on the Gita*, in *CWMG* 37:211–212.

120. Ambedkar, *Annihilation of Caste*, 74.

121. See Vasant Moon, *Growing up Untouchable in India*, trans. Gail Omvedt (New York: Rowman & Littlefield, 2000).

122. Ambedkar, "Speech at the All Bombay Province Depressed Classes Conference," Yeola, 13 October 1935, in *Dr. Babasaheb Ambedkar*, ed. Vasant Abaji Dahake (New Delhi: Planning Commission, Govt. of India, and Mumbai: Department of Cultural Affairs, Govt. of Maharashtra, 2007), 271; hereafter cited as *Babasaheb Ambedkar*.

123. See *BAWS* 10:166.

124. See Pierre Rosanvallon, "Towards a Philosophical History of the Political," in Rosanvallon, *Democracy Past and Future*, ed. Samuel Moyn (New York: Columbia University Press, 2006), 59–76.

125. See, for instance, Dario Castiglione and Iain Hampsher-Monk, eds., *The History of Political Thought in National Context* (Cambridge: Cambridge University Press, 2001).

126. Partha Chatterjee, *Lineages of Political Society: Studies in Postcolonial Democracy* (New York: Columbia University Press, 2011), 2.

127. Quentin Skinner, *Machiavelli* (Oxford: Oxford University Press, 1981), 1–2.

128. Keith Michael Baker, *Inventing the French Revolution* (Cambridge: Cambridge University Press, 1990); Bayly, *Recovering Liberties*.

129. Quentin Skinner, "Meaning and Understanding in the History of Ideas," in Skinner, *Visions of Politics*, vol. 1: *Regarding Method* (Cambridge: Cambridge University Press, 2002).

130. See Lefort, "Rereading *The Communist Manifesto*," in Lefort, *Democracy and Political Theory*, 149–150.

131. Jeremy Waldron, *God, Locke, and Equality: Christian Foundations in Locke's Political Thought* (Cambridge: Cambridge University Press, 2003); Elizabeth Pritchard, *Religion in Public: Locke's Political Theology* (Stanford, CA: Stanford University Press, 2013) have meticulously problematized the secularist consensus on Locke.

CHAPTER 2

1. Gandhi, "Johannesburg Letter," before 10 January 1908, in *CWMG* 8:80–81.

2. Gandhi, "Price of Freedom," in *MPWG* 3:225–226; originally published in *Young India*, 9 December 1926.

3. Thus, in his 1973 study, Raghavan Iyer translates *agraha* not as "firmness" but as "firmness of grasp." Iyer, *The Moral and Political Thought of Mahatma Gandhi*, 424.

4. Gandhi, "Satyagraha—Not Passive Resistance," 2 September 1917, in *CWMG* 16:9–10. On Gandhi's early interventions on indentured labor, see *The South African Gandhi: An Abstract of the Speeches and Writings of M. K. Gandhi, 1893–1914*, ed. Fatima Meer (Durban: Madiba Publishers, 1996), 959–990.

5. Gandhi, "Satyagraha," in *MPWG* 3:63; originally published in *Navajivan*, 14 September 1919.

6. Gandhi, "Speech at AICC Meeting," Patna, 19 May 1934, in *CWMG* 63:507; originally published in *The Bombay Chronicle*, 20 May 1934.

7. M. K. Gandhi, *Satyagraha in South Africa*, trans. Valji Govindji Desai, in *CWMG* 34:1.

8. Gandhi, *Hind Swaraj-CW*, 293.

9. Gandhi, "Civility," in *CWMG* 25:287–290; originally published in *Navajivan*, 18 December 1921.

10. Gandhi, "Limits to Freedom," in *MPWG* 3:230–231; originally published in *Navajivan*, 31 May 1931.

11. Gandhi, *Hind Swaraj-CW*, 279.

12. Gandhi to Esther Faering, 25 January 1919, in *CWMG* 17:263–264.

13. Gandhi, "Five Great 'Yajnas,'" in *CWMG* 23:401; originally published in *Navajivan*, 10 July 1921.

14. I examine these distinctions in greater detail in my essay "*Satyagraha* and the *Place* of the Animal: Gandhi's Distinctions," *Social History* 39, no. 3 (2014), 359–381.

15. Gandhi, "Speech at Public Meeting," Dakor, 27 October 1920, in *CWMG* 21:399–402; originally published in *Navajivan*, 3 November 1920.

16. Gandhi, "Answers to Questions at Gandhi Seva Sangh Meeting, Brindaban—II," 6 May 1939, in *MPWG* 3:491; hereafter cited as "Answers to Questions."

17. *M. K. Gandhi's Hind Swaraj: A Critical Edition*, ed. Suresh Sharma and Tridip Suhrud (New Delhi: Orient BlackSwan, 2010), 18–19; hereafter cited as Gandhi, *Hind Swaraj-CE*.

18. See Savarkar, "Swadharma and Swaraj," *The Indian War of Independence: 1857*, in *The Selected Works of Veer Savarkar*, 4 vols. (1909; Chandigarh: Abhishek Publication, 2007) 1:5–16.

19. Gandhi, *Hind Swaraj-CE*, 9.

20. See Sharma and Suhrud, "Editors' Introduction," in Gandhi, *Hind Swaraj-CE*, xiii.

21. Gandhi, "May God Help," in *CWMG* 29:374; originally published in *Young India*, 27 November 1924. On the complexities of this statement, see Ajay Skaria, "No Politics without Religion: On Secularism and Gandhi," in *Political Hinduism: The Religious Imagination in Public Spheres*, ed. Vinay Lal (New York: Oxford University Press, 2009), 173–210.

22. See, among his other works, Jacques Derrida, *Rogues: Two Essays on Reason*, trans. Pascale-Anne Brault and Michael Naas (Stanford, CA: Stanford University Press, 2005).

23. Gandhi, *Hind Swaraj-CW*, 279.

24. Gandhi, "Speech at Hindu College," Delhi, 25 February 1931, in *CWMG* 51:183–184; originally published in *Hindustan Times*, 27 February 1931.

25. Gandhi, "Speech at Public Meeting," Dakor, 401.

26. See Michel de Certeau, *The Mystic Fable: The Sixteenth and Seventeenth Centuries*, trans. Michael B. Smith (Chicago: University of Chicago Press, 1995); Sumit Sarkar, "Kaliyuga, Chakri, and Bhakti: Ramakrishna and His Times," in *Writing Social History* (New Delhi: Oxford University Press, 1997), 282–357; Eleanor Zelliot, "Chokhamela and Eknath: Two *Bhakti* Modes of Legitimacy for the Modern Age," in *Tradition and Modernity in Bhakti Movements*, ed. Jayant Lele (Leiden: Brill, 1981), 136–156; and Eleanor Zelliot and Rohini Mokashi-Punekar, eds., *Untouchable Saints: An Indian Phenomenon* (New Delhi: Manohar, 2005).

27. Jyotirmaya Sharma, *Cosmic Love and Human Apathy: Swami Vivekananda's Restatement of Religion* (New Delhi: Harper Collins, 2013).

28. See Ambedkar, "Away from the Hindus," 407.

29. Ambedkar, *Philosophy of Hinduism*, 7.

30. Albert O. Hirschman, *The Passions and the Interests: Political Argument for Capitalism before Its Triumph* (Princeton, NJ: Princeton University Press, 1977), gives a succinct and still unsurpassed account of capitalism's intellectual prehistory.

31. Gandhi, Interview to *Le Monde*, 20 February 1930; available online at http://www.cse.iitk.ac.in/users/amit/books/lewis-1965-gandhi-maker-of.html.

32. See Susan Buck-Morss, *Hegel, Haiti, and Universal History* (Pittsburg, PA: University of Pittsburg Press, 2009).

33. See esp. Paul Valéry, "The European," in *The Collected Works of Paul Valéry*, vol. 10: *History and Politics*, trans. Denise Folliot and Jackson Mathews (New York: Pantheon Books, 1962), 307–323; Edmund Husserl, *The Crisis of European Sciences and Transcendental Phenomenology: An Introduction to Phenomenological Philosophy*, trans. David Carr (1954; Evanston: Northwestern University Press, 1970); and Oswald Spengler, *The Decline of the West* (New York: Knopf, 1926). On the terrifying resolutions of spirit in the thought of Martin Heidegger, Jacques Derrida's *Of Spirit: Heidegger and the Question*, trans. Geoffrey Bennington (Chicago: University of Chicago Press, 1987), remains indispensable.

34. Edmund Burke, *Reflections on the Revolution in France* (1790; Oxford: Oxford University Press, 2009), 86–87.

35. Valéry, "Freedom of the Mind," in *Collected Works* 10:194.

36. Gandhi, "Meaning of the Gita," in *MPWG* 1:79–80; originally published in *Navajivan*, 11 October 1925.

37. A brilliant examination of Valéry's thinking is offered in Jacques Derrida, *The Other Heading: Reflections on Today's Europe*, trans. Anne-Pascale Brault and Michael B. Naas (Bloomington: Indiana University Press, 1992). Also see Rudolphe Gasché, *Europe, or the Infinite Task: History of a Philosophical Concept* (Stanford, CA: Stanford University Press, 2008).

38. Leela Gandhi, *The Common Cause: Postcolonial Ethics and the Practice of Democracy* (Chicago: University of Chicago Press, 2014), 29–54.

39. Martin Heidegger, "Postscript to 'What Is Metaphysics?' (1943)," in Heidegger, *Pathmarks*, ed. William McNeill (Cambridge: Cambridge University Press, 1998), 236–237.

40. Montesquieu, *The Spirit of the Laws* (1748; Cambridge: Cambridge University Press, 1989), 48.

41. See Uday S. Mehta, "Gandhi on Democracy, Politics, and the Ethics of Everyday Life," *Modern Intellectual History* 7, no. 2 (2010), 355–371.

42. Gandhi, "A Tissue of Misrepresentations," in *CWMG* 36:279; originally published in *Young India*, 9 September 1926.

43. Gandhi, "Interview to Nirmal Kumar Bose," in *CWMG* 65:318; originally published in *Hindustan Times*, 17 October 1935.

44. I draw this expression from Étienne Balibar, *Identity and Difference: John Locke and the Invention of Consciousness* (New York: Verso, 2013).

45. But for an influential interpretation of Gandhi as a philosophical anarchist, see Ashis Nandy, *Traditions, Tyranny and Utopias: Essays in the Politics of Awareness* (Delhi: Oxford University Press, 1993).

46. Gandhi, "Interview to Nirmal Kumar Bose," 318.

47. Gandhi, *Hind Swaraj-CW*, 292.

48. Gandhi, *Hind Swaraj-CE*, 60.

49. Gandhi, *Hind Swaraj-CW*, 282.

50. Gandhi, "Speech at Morvi," 24 January 1928, in *CWMG* 41:138–143; originally published in *Navajivan*, 29 January 1928.

51. Gandhi, *Hind Swaraj-CE*, 73.

52. Gandhi, *Hind Swaraj-CW*, 292.

53. Gandhi, "Speech at Mirzapur Park," Calcutta, 21 January 1921, in *CWMG* 22:250.

54. Ibid., 249.

55. Gandhi, *Lectures on Religion*, in *CWMG* 4:244; originally published in *Indian Opinion*, 15 April 1905.

56. Gandhi, "Ethics of Destruction," in *Young India 1919–1922, with a Brief Sketch of the Non-Cooperation Movement by Babu Rajendra Prasad* (New York: B. W. Huebsch, 1924), 556–557; originally published in *Young India*, 1 September 1921.

57. Gandhi to C. F. Andrews, 18 July 1921, in *CWMG* 23:453.

58. Gandhi, "The Secret of It," in *CWMG* 25:17; originally published in *Young India*, 27 October 1921.

59. Gandhi to Esther Faering, 11 May 1918, in *CWMG* 17:24.

60. Gandhi, "Speech at Prayer Meeting," Delhi, 2 January 1948, in *CWMG* 98:161.

61. Gandhi, "Interview with Members of Self-Respect Party," in *CWMG* 63:39; originally published in *Harijan*, 9 February 1934.

62. See, for example, Gandhi to Sri Prakasa, 6 May 1934, in *CWMG* 63:469.

63. Gandhi, "What Is Education?," in *MPWG* 3:378; originally published in *Navajivan*, 28 February 1926.

64. Gandhi, "A Tissue of Misrepresentations."

65. Gandhi, "All about the Fast," in *CWMG* 61:219–222; originally published in *Harijan*, 8 August 1933.

66. Gandhi, "Notes," in *CWMG* 61:136–137; originally published in *Harijan Sevak*, 12 May 1933.

67. Gandhi to H. S. L. Polak, 14 October 1909, in *CWMG* 10:169–170.

68. Ibid., 171.

69. See Ambedkar, *Congress and Gandhi*, ch. 11.

70. Gandhi, *Hind Swaraj-CW*, 289–290.

71. As Gandhi said of the empire, "there is advantage in seeing the virtues even of an enemy. There certainly is goodness in it." Gandhi, "Government's Civility," in *CWMG* 26:32–33; originally published in *Navajivan*, 29 January 1922.

72. Gandhi to Prabhudas Gandhi, 16 January 1931, in *CWMG* 51:35, and Gandhi to Kashinath Trivedi, 17 January 1931, in *CWMG* 51:39.

73. Gandhi, "Meaning of the Gita," in *MPWG* 1:82; originally published in *Navajivan*, 11 October 1925.

74. For a discussion of this anthropology, see Aishwary Kumar, "*Satyagraha* and the *Place* of the Animal," esp. 377–381.

75. Gandhi, Ibid., 83.

76. Gandhi, *Discourses on the Gita*, in M. K. Gandhi, *The Selected Works of Mahatma Gandhi* (Ahmedabad: Navajivan, 1968, 5 volumes), 3:226.

77. Gandhi, "Message to Jawahar Jain Jyoti," in *CWMG* 86:277; originally published in *Bombay Chronicle*, 1 May 1945.

78. Gandhi to Esther Faering, 30 June 1919, in *CWMG* 17:109.

79. For a classic account of that event, see Shahid Amin, *Event, Metaphor, Memory: Chauri Chaura 1922–1992* (Berkeley: University of California Press, 1995).

80. Gandhi, "My Jail Experiences."

81. Gandhi to Mathurdas Trikumji, 1 November 1921, in *CWMG* 25:37.

82. Gandhi, "Ashram Notes," Segaon, 22 January 1940, in *CWMG* 77: 241–242.

83. Gandhi, *Hind Swaraj-CW*, 273.

84. For a post-Kantian genealogy of "touchability" as manipulability by hand, see Adi Ophir, *The Order of Evils: Toward an Ontology of Morals*, trans. Rela Mazali and Havi Carel (New York: Zone Books, 2005).

85. Gandhi, "Story of a Soldier of Truth," pts. 1–5, *CWMG* 8.

86. Simona Sawhney, "Allegory and Violence: Gandhi's Reading of the *Bhagavad Gita*," in Sawhney, *The Modernity of Sanskrit* (Minneapolis: University of Minnesota Press, 2009), 86–124.

87. Gandhi, "Message to the Nation," in *CWMG* 49:52–53; originally published in *Young India*, 8 May 1930.

88. Gandhi, "Speech at Bhimrad," 9 April 1930, in *CWMG* 49:56.

89. Gandhi, "Working of Nonviolence," 49.

90. Gandhi to Amrit Kaur, 1 June 1940, in *CWMG* 78:274.

91. Gandhi to Maheshdutta Mishra, 30 April 1947, in *CWMG* 95:1.

92. Varsha Das, "Introduction to *Gandhiji's Hind Swaraj*," xi.

93. Gandhi to Esther Faering, 1 April 1919, in *CWMG* 17:369.

94. Gandhi, "Speech on Ashram Vows," YMCA Madras, 16 February 1916, in *CWMG* 15:174.

95. Gandhi, "Satyagraha," *MPWG* 3:63; originally published in *Navajivan*, 14 September 1919.

96. Gandhi, "Speech at Public Meeting," Dakor.

97. Gandhi, "Discussion with Teacher Trainees," 3 and 4 February 1939, in *CWMG* 75:30; originally published in *Harijan*, 18 February 1939 and 4 March 1939.

98. On the exclusions of "thinking-with" the hand in humanist thought, see Jacques Derrida, "Heidegger's Hand (*Geschlecht II*)," in Derrida, *Psyche: Inventions of the Other*, trans. Peggy Kamuf and Elizabeth Rottenberg (Stanford, CA: Stanford University Press, 2008), 27–62.

99. Gandhi, "Five Great '*Yajnas*,'" 400–401.

100. See Uday S. Mehta, "Patience, Inwardness, and Self-Knowledge in Gandhi's *Hind Swaraj*," *Public Culture* 23, no. 2 (Spring 2011), 417–429.

101. Gandhi, *Discourses on the Gita*, in *CWMG* 37:82.

102. See Sumit Sarkar, *Swadeshi Movement in Bengal: 1903–1908* (1973; New Delhi: Permanent Black, 2012).

103. Ambedkar, *Annihilation of Caste*, 123.

104. Gandhi, "All about the Fast."

105. Gandhi, "Atomic Warfare," in *NVPW* 2:94; originally published in *Harijan*, 10 February 1946.

106. Cited in Raja Sekhar Vundru, "From Marathi to English," *The Hindu*, 3 June 2013.

CHAPTER 3

1. Ambedkar, *Administration and Finance of the East India Company*, M.A. thesis, Columbia University, May 15, 1915, in *BAWS* 6.

2. I take the phrase "freedom of beginnings" from title of chapter 11 of Akeel Bilgrami's *Secularism, Identity, and Enchantment*.

3. Ambedkar, "Mr. Russell and the Reconstruction of Society," in *BAWS* 1:487; originally published in *Journal of the Indian Economic Society* 1 (1918).

4. Ibid., 486.

5. This polyvalence has been reconstructed with great care in Claude Lefort's *Machiavelli in the Making*, trans. Michael B. Smith (Evanston: Northwestern University Press, 2012).

6. Here, the classical notion of force as a potentiality that is always already turned against itself—and it is this *turning-against-itself* (and vanishing) that separates it from the unilateralism of violence—remains instructive. "The Notion of Force," writes Hegel, "becomes *actual* through its duplication into two Forces. . . . These two Forces exist as independent essences; but their existence is a movement of each towards the other, such that their being is rather a pure *positedness* or a being that is *posited by an other*, i.e., their being has really the significance of a sheer *vanishing*." See Hegel, *Phenomenology of Spirit*, 85.

7. Ambedkar, *Thoughts*, 340.

8. Ambedkar, *Partition*, xix.

9. Ambedkar, *Thoughts*, 344.

10. The classic work on the imperative to maintain the distinction between political means and the social question is Hannah Arendt, *The Human Condition* (Chicago: University of Chicago Press, 1958).

11. Rosanvallon, "Revolutionary Democracy," in *Democracy Past and Future*, ed. Samuel Moyn (New York: Columbia University Press, 2006), 79–97.

12. Gandhi, "May God Help."

13. Ambedkar, *Riddles of Hinduism*, in *BAWS* 4:18.

14. Ambedkar, *Thoughts*, 6.

15. Ambedkar, "Their Wishes Are Laws unto Us," in *Essays*, 283.

16. The theme saturates Ambedkar's writings, but the most exegetically rigorous critique of custom appears in *Annihilation of Caste*, 85–86.

17. Ambedkar, "From Millions to Fractions," in *EWBRA*, 332–333.

18. Pascal, *Thoughts*, trans. Moritz Kaufmann (New York: Collier, 1910), 31.

19. Ambedkar, *Riddles of Hinduism*, 24.

20. Ambedkar, *Essays*, 35–74.

21. On the vicissitudes of immortality in the modern tradition, see Lefort, *Democracy and Political Theory*, 256–282.

22. On the paradoxical place of the military and military service in twentieth-century nationalist and emancipatory politics, whose moral and theological commitments he distinguishes from militarism as doctrine, see Jacques Derrida, "Interpretations at War: Kant, the Jew, the German," in *Acts of Religion*, ed. Gil Anidjar (New York: Routledge, 2002), 135–188.

23. Ambedkar, "Ranade, Gandhi, and Jinnah," in *BAWS* 1:209.

24. Ambedkar, "Away from the Hindus," in *Essays*, 407.

25. Ambedkar, *Philosophy of Hinduism*, 86.

26. Ambedkar, "Civilization or Felony," in *Essays*, 138.

27. Ambedkar, *Philosophy of Hinduism*, 86.

28. Ambedkar, "Ranade, Gandhi, and Jinnah," 208.

29. Ambedkar, *Administration and Finance*, in *BAWS* 6:13.

30. Ambedkar, *Congress and Gandhi*, 205.

31. Ambedkar, *Castes in India: Their Mechanism, Genesis, and Development*, appended in *Annihilation of Caste*, 147.

32. Ambedkar, *Thoughts*, 377.

33. For a genealogy of the Rousseauist tradition, see Patrick Riley, *The Popular Will before Rousseau* (Princeton, NJ: Princeton University Press, 1988).

34. This understanding of politics as scene—and the political as implicated in the logics of theater and representation—proved enduring. In 1943, Ambedkar would describe the deadlock between Gandhi and Jinnah as a "personal feud," an instance of their "colossal egotism," an example of the skill of "wonderful stagecraft" the two had mastered. Ambedkar, "Ranade, Gandhi, and Jinnah," 227.

35. Ambedkar, *Thoughts*, 125.

36. Ambedkar, *Annihilation of Caste*, 77.

37. On the significance of Shakespeare for conceptual innovations around which the modern political tradition developed, see *Shakespeare and Early Modern Political Thought*, ed. David Armitage, Conal Condren, and Andrew Fitzmaurice (Cambridge: Cambridge University Press, 2009).

38. See, for example, Walter Benjamin, *The Origin of German Tragic Drama*, trans. John Osborne (1928; New York: Verso, 1998); Carl Schmitt, *Hamlet or Hecuba: The Introduction of the Time into the Play*, trans. David Pan and Jennifer Rust (1956; New York: Telos Press, 2009); and Ernst Kantorowicz, *The King's Two Bodies: A Study in Mediaeval Political Theology* (Princeton, NJ: Princeton University Press, 1957).

39. On philosophy's fascination with Shakespeare's treatment of political and juridical themes, see Paul A. Kottman, *Philosophers on Shakespeare* (Stanford, CA: Stanford University Press, 2009), 126–127.

40. Jotirao Phule, *Slavery*, in *Selected Writings of Jotirao Phule*, ed. G. P. Deshpande (New Delhi: Left Word, 2002), 33.

41. Gandhi, *Hind Swaraj-CW*, 262.

42. On Bengal, Burke, and Hastings, see Ambedkar, "India on the Eve of the Crown Government," in *BAWS* 12:65–66.

43. Ambedkar, *Thoughts*, 4, and "Buddha or Karl Marx," 453–454.

44. Ambedkar, *Castes in India*, in *BAWS* 1:16.

45. The classic work on the material life of Indian religion is D. D. Kosambi, *Myth and Reality: Studies in the Formation of Indian Culture* (Bombay: Popular Prakashan, 1962).

46. It is of this mystical function that Michel de Certeau writes, "It is as though the function of mysticism were to bring a religious *episteme* to a closure and erase itself at the same time." See Michel de Certeau, *Heterologies: Discourse of the Other*,

trans. Brian Massumi (Minneapolis: University of Minnesota Press, 1986), 37, 80–87.

47. Ambedkar, "Interview with T. V. Parvate," cited in Keer, *Dr. Ambedkar*, 106.

48. Ambedkar, "The Revolt of the Untouchables," in *Essays*, 225.

49. Ambedkar had most possibly derived this insight on contingency from his reading of Friedrich Nietzsche's *The Anti-Christ*. See, for a suggestion of this influence, Ambedkar, *India and the Prerequisites of Communism*, 116–121.

50. For a shared concern with the relationship between sacrifice and friendship, see esp. Georges Dumézil, *Mitra-Varuna: An Essay on Two Indo-European Representations of Sovereignty*, trans. Derek Coltman (New York: Zone Books, 1990), published the same year as Ambedkar's *The Untouchables: Who Were They and Why They Became Untouchables* (New Delhi: Amrit, 1948). *The Untouchables* was itself a sequel to his painstakingly exegetical work published in 1946, *Who Were the Shudras? How They Came to Be the Fourth Varna in the Indo-Aryan Society* (Bombay: Thacker, 1946).

51. Ambedkar, "Ranade, Gandhi, and Jinnah," 222.

52. On the nonexistence of the soul, see Ambedkar, *Buddha and His Dhamma-CE*, 266.

53. Ambedkar, *Annihilation of Caste*, 52.

54. Ibid., 53.

55. Ambedkar, "Ranade, Gandhi, and Jinnah," 240.

56. The formulation "waiting room of history" is drawn from Dipesh Chakrabarty, *Provincializing Europe*, 8–10.

57. Ambedkar's difficult relationship with historicism has been explored in Debjani Ganguly, *Caste, Colonialism and Counter-Modernity: Notes on a Postcolonial Hermeneutics of Caste* (New York: Routledge, 2005).

58. Ambedkar, *Annihilation of Caste*, 35–36.

59. On reason and *sadachar*, see esp. ibid., 81.

60. Ibid., 60.

61. Ambedkar, *Philosophy of Hinduism*, 24.

62. Ambedkar, *Annihilation of Caste*, 60.

63. Ibid., 30.

64. One notices in this understanding of democracy the unmistakable imprint of Dewey. In quintessentially Deweyan terms, for instance, Ambedkar calls the sharing implicit in democracy the morals of "associated living." *Annihilation of Caste*, 54–55.

65. Ambedkar, "My Philosophy of Life," All India Radio Broadcast Speech, 3 October 1954, in *BAWS* 17, pt. 3, 503.

66. Ambedkar, *Annihilation of Caste*, 44.

67. Ibid., 55.

68. Sorel, *Reflections on Violence*, 129.

69. Ambedkar, "Amravati Address," in *301 Seminal Speeches* 1:88–92; originally published in *Bahishkrit Bharat*, 25 November 1927.

70. Ambedkar, *Annihilation of Caste*, 35–36.

71. Ambedkar, "Capitalism, Labor, and Brahmanism," Presidential Address of the Indian Labor Party, 12 and 13 February 1938, in *Thus Spoke Ambedkar: A Stake in the Nation*, 2 vols., ed. Bhagwan Das (New Delhi: Navayana, 2010), 1:58–59.

72. On this risk of abstention from politics, one that plagued the most radical strands within interwar revolutionary thought, see Werner Hamacher, "Afformative, Strike: Benjamin's Critique of Violence," in *Walter Benjamin's Philosophy: Destruction and Experience*, ed. Andrew Benjamin and Peter Osborne (New York: Routledge, 1994), 108–136.

73. Ambedkar, *Congress and Gandhi*, 295.

74. See Ambedkar, *The Buddha and His Dhamma*, in *BAWS* 11:324; cited hereafter as *Buddha and His Dhamma-WS*.

75. Ambedkar, *Congress and Gandhi*, 295.

76. See Ambedkar to Du Bois [undated] and Du Bois to Ambedkar, 31 July 1946, *South Asian American Digital Archive*, available online at http://www.saadigitalarchive .org/tides/article/20140422-3553.

77. Ambedkar, *Annihilation of Caste*, 81.

78. Ambedkar, *Philosophy of Hinduism*, 71.

79. Ambedkar, *Thoughts*, 362–363.

80. Edmund Burke, *The Correspondence of Edmund Burke, vol. 8: September 1749– April 1796*, ed. R. B. McDowell (Chicago: University of Chicago Press, 1969), 255.

81. Ambedkar, *Partition*, xviii–xix.

82. For an exemplary discussion of this tradition, see Jacques Derrida, "Force of Law: The "Mystical Foundation of Authority," in Derrida, *Acts of Religion*, 238–242.

83. Ambedkar, "Amravati Address," in *301 Seminal Speeches* 1:84.

84. Ambedkar, "Speech No. 7," Mumbai, 25 September 1928, in ibid., 67.

85. Ambedkar, "Speech No. 4," Mahad, 26 December 1927, in ibid., 67.

86. Ambedkar, "Amravati Address," in ibid., 83–84.

87. Ibid., 84–88.

88. Ibid., 91.

89. See Hegel, *Phenomenology of Spirit*, 79–103.

90. See Ambedkar, *Partition*, xv.

91. Ambedkar, *Revolution and Counter-Revolution*, 376.

92. See, for instance, Ambedkar, *Castes in India*, appended in *Annihilation of Caste*, 147. Thirty years later, he pitches even more forcefully the "vulgar" (as that which is not so much closer to truth as it is necessary to establishing a democratically acceptable value of truth in political life as such) against the "mystical" (as that which is shrouded in secrecy). "I have been guided by the best tradition of the historian who treats all literature as vulgar—I am using the word in its original sense of belonging to the people—to be examined and tested by accepted rules of evidence without recognizing any distinction between the sacred and the profane and with the sole object of finding the truth." See Ambedkar, "Preface" to *Who Were the Shudras*.

93. "Force is its sole hero," Weil wrote of *Iliad*. "No ambiguous, complex, or anxious feeling appears in it; courage and love alone have a place there." *Simone Weil's The "Iliad" or the Poem of Force: A Critical Edition*, ed. and trans. James P. Holoka (1939; New York: Peter Lang, 2003), 62.

94. On the *Gita* as a "ballad" and "historical saga," see Ambedkar, *Revolution and Counter-Revolution*, 376. On the twentieth-century life of the *Gita*, see *Political Thought in Action: The Bhagavad Gita and Modern India*, ed. Shruti Kapila and

Faisal Devji (Cambridge: Cambridge University Press, 2013); and Sanjay Palshikar, *Evil and the Philosophy of Retribution: Modern Commentaries on the Bhagavad-Gita* (New Delhi: Routledge, 2013).

95. Hannah Arendt, from whom I draw here, had discerned a similar problematic in Benjamin's relationship to authority. "Walter Benjamin knew," writes Arendt, "that the break in tradition and the loss of authority which occurred in his lifetime were irreparable, and he concluded that he had to discover new ways of dealing with the past. In this he became a master when he discovered that the transmissibility of the past had been replaced by its citability and that in place of its authority there had arisen a strange power to settle down, piecemeal, in the present and to deprive it of 'peace of mind,' the mindless peace of complacency." See Arendt, *Men in Dark Times* (New York: Harcourt Brace & Company, 1968), 200.

96. "To Telang, as to every Hindu—how much so ever enlightened—it is an article of faith to believe in so high an antiquity of the *Bhagavat Gita*," Ambedkar argues, "and where such necessities are powerful criticism indeed comes to an end." *Revolution and Counter-Revolution*, 366.

97. Ambedkar, *Buddha and His Dhamma-CE*, xxvi.

98. Ambedkar, *Philosophy of Hinduism*, 24.

99. Ambedkar, *Revolution and Counter-Revolution*, 361.

100. Ibid., 365.

101. See Walter Benjamin's 1921 essay, "Critique of Violence," in *Selected Writings, vol. 1: 1913–1926*, ed. Michael W. Jennings, Howard Eiland, and Gary Smith (Cambridge, MA: Harvard University Press, 1996), 236–252.

102. Ashis Nandy, *The Intimate Enemy: Loss and Recovery of Self Under Colonialism* (New Delhi: Oxford University Press, 1985). Also see Sudipta Kaviraj, *The Unhappy Consciousness: Bankim Chandra Chattopadhyay and the Formation of Nationalist Discourse in India* (Delhi: Oxford University Press, 1995).

103. Ambedkar, *Thoughts*, 3.

104. Ambedkar, "A Warning to the Untouchables," in *Essays*, 399.

105. Ambedkar, *Revolution and Counter-Revolution*, 390.

106. Ibid., 381–387.

107. Ambedkar, "Krishna and His Gita," in *EWBRA*, 193–204.

108. See Nietzsche, *The Gay Science*, trans. Walter Kauffman (New York: Vintage, 1974).

109. I draw the term "ostensible excess" from Benjamin, *The Origin of the German Tragic Drama*, 47.

110. Ambedkar, "Held at Bay," in *Essays*, 259.

CHAPTER 4

1. Gandhi, "Why 'Harijan'?," in *CWMG* 59:234; originally published in *Harijan*, 11 February 1933.

2. Gandhi, *Hind Swaraj-CW*, 246.

3. Gandhi, "Why 'Harijan'?," 234.

4. The expression appears in Gandhi, "My Attitude towards War," in *NVPW* 1:79; originally published in *Young India*, 13 September 1928.

5. Tim Pratt and James Vernon, "'Appeal from this fiery bed . . . ': The Colonial Politics of Gandhi's Fasts and Their Metropolitan Reception," *Journal of British Studies* 44 (January 2005), 94.

6. But for a thoughtful attempt to rescue the Gandhian fast as the site of political contest (beyond its solitary ethics), see Sudhir Chandra, "Gandhi's Twin Fasts and the Possibility of Nonviolence," *Economic and Political Weekly* 46, no. 23 (4 June, 2011).

7. Gandhi, "What Is in a Name?," in *CWMG* 90: 189; originally published in *Harijan*, 14 April 1946.

8. For an early biography, see Indulal Yagnik, *Shyamaji Krishnavarma: Life and Times of an Indian Revolutionary* (Bombay: Lakshmi Publications, 1950).

9. Gandhi, *Hind Swaraj-CW*, 285.

10. Ibid., 310.

11. Gandhi, "Speech at AICC," 314.

12. Gandhi, "The Fiery Ordeal," in *MPWG* 2:274; originally published in *Navajivan*, 30 September 1928.

13. Gandhi, *Hind Swaraj-CW*, 292.

14. Gandhi, "Speech at Guildhouse Church," London, 23 September 1931, in *CWMG* 53:398.

15. Gandhi, "Of Princes and Paupers," in *CWMG* 51:285; originally published in *Navajivan*, 22 March 1931.

16. Gandhi, "Speech at Hindu College," Delhi, 182.

17. Gandhi, "Speech at Morvi," 141–142.

18. See Gandhi, "Speech at Suppressed Classes Conference," Ahmedabad, 27 April 1921, in *CWMG* 23:44; originally published in *Young India*, 27 April and 4 May 1921; hereafter cited as "Suppressed Classes."

19. See Nathuram Godse, *Why I Assassinated Gandhi? And the Events, the Accused, and the Epilogue by Gopal Godse* (Delhi: Surya Bharati Prakashan, 1993).

20. Gandhi, "Interview to the Press," in *CWMG* 57:362; originally published in *Bombay Chronicle*, 8 November 1932.

21. Gandhi, "My Notes: Harijana," in *CWMG* 53:166; originally published in *Navajivan*, 2 August 1931.

22. Gandhi, "Speech at Ahmedabad," 2 August 1931, in *CWMG* 53:168–171; originally published in *Young India*, 6 August 1931.

23. Gandhi, "The Right Way and the Wrong Way," in Pyarelal Nair, *The Epic Fast* (Ahmedabad: Navajivan, 1932), 320.

24. Gandhi, "Purifying Flame," in *CWMG* 32:30; originally published in *Navajivan*, 21 June 1925.

25. Pyarelal, *Epic Fast*, 40.

26. Gandhi to Habibur Rahman, 5 November 1932, in *CWMG* 57:338.

27. Gandhi, "Suppressed Classes," 43.

28. Gandhi, *Autobiography*, 114–116.

29. Gandhi, "Suppressed Classes," 42–44.

30. Gandhi, "Speech at Public Meeting," Madras, 8 April 1921, in *CWMG* 23:19–20; originally published in *The Hindu*, 9 April 1921.

31. This humanism finds its twentieth-century apotheosis in Maurice Merleau-Ponty's unfinished classic, *The Visible and the Invisible*, trans. Alphonso Lingis (Evanston, IL: Northwestern University Press, 1969).

32. On his mobilization of the "spirit of obedience" in the context of mass politics, see Gandhi, "Quit India Speech, 1942," in M. K. Gandhi, *Hind Swaraj and Other Writings*, ed. Anthony Parel (Cambridge: Cambridge University Press, 1997), 181.

33. Gandhi, "Speech at Meeting in Sangamner," 22 May 1921, in *CWMG* 23:168; originally published in *Navajivan*, 9 June 1921.

34. Gandhi, "Discussion with Harijan Sevaks," in *CWMG* 68:327; originally published in *Harijan*, 4 April 1936.

35. Gandhi, "Suppressed Classes," 45.

36. Gandhi, "Meaning of the Gita," in *MPWG* 3:79; originally published in *Navajivan*, 11 October 1925.

37. Ibid., 79.

38. Gandhi, "Speech at Morvi," 140.

39. Gandhi, "Suppressed Classes," 45.

40. Gandhi, "Speech at Untouchability Conference," Belgaum, 27 December 1924, in *CWMG* 30:16–17; originally published in *Young India*, 22 January 1925.

41. Gandhi, "Satyagraha—Not Passive Resistance," 11.

42. Ibid., 11.

43. Gandhi, "Speech on Swadeshi at Missionary Conference," Madras, 14 February 1916, in *CWMG* 15:160–161.

44. Gandhi, "Suppressed Classes," 44.

45. Gandhi, "Who Is a 'Sanatani' Hindu?," in *CWMG* 22:316; originally published in *Navajivan*, 6 February 1921; reprinted in *Hindu Dharma* (Delhi: Orient Paperbacks, 1978), 47.

46. Gandhi, "Interview to the Press," 362.

47. Gandhi, "A Difficult Question," in *CWMG* 36:63; originally published in *Navajivan*, 18 July 1926.

48. Gandhi, "Interview to the Press," 362.

49. Gandhi, "Speech at Guildhouse Church," London.

50. See, for a resonance, Adam Smith, *The Theory of Moral Sentiments* (Indianapolis: Liberty Fund, 1974), 9. On the intricacies of Gandhi's conception and practice of voluntary poverty, see Rajeswari Sunder Rajan, "Refusing Benevolence: Gandhi, Nehru, and the Ethics of Postcolonial Relations," in *Burden or Benefit: Imperial Benevolence and its Legacies*, ed. Helen Gilbert and Chris Tiffin (Bloomington: Indiana University Press, 2008), 136–159.

51. C. B. Macpherson, *The Political Theory of Possessive Individualism: Hobbes to Locke* (Oxford: Oxford University Press, 1962).

52. Ophir, *The Order of Evils: Toward an Ontology of Morals*, 106.

53. Gandhi, *Hind Swaraj-CW*, 291.

54. Gandhi, *Autobiography*, 468–469.

55. Gandhi, *Discourses on the Gita*, in *CWMG* 37:87.

56. Gandhi, "Speech at Untouchability Conference," 14–18.

57. Gandhi, "Speech at Harijan Workers' Conference," Kengeri, 10 June 1939, in *CWMG* 69:105; originally published in *Harijan*, 20 June 1936.

58. Gandhi, "Speech at Untouchability Conference," 16–17. Also see Gandhi, "Speech at Bhusaval," 21 May 1921, in *CWMG* 23:168; originally published in *Aaj*, 29 May 1921.

59. Gandhi, "Limitation of Reformers," in *In Search of the Supreme*, 3 vols., ed. V. B. Kher (Ahmedabad: Navajivan, 1961), 3:79; originally published in *Harijan*, 21 March 1936.

60. Gandhi, "Implications and Interpretations of *Ahimsa*," in *MPWG* 2:220–222; originally published in *Young India*, 25 October 1928.

61. Gandhi, "'Varnashrama' and Untouchability," in *CWMG* 32:285; originally published in *Young India*, 13 August 1925; reprinted in *Hindu Dharma*, 82.

62. Gandhi, "Carding or Archery," in *CWMG* 47:1–3; originally published in *Navajivan*, 1 September 1929.

63. Gandhi, "Answers to Questions." In thinking about equality as production, I follow Jacques Rancière's lead in *Dis-agreement: Politics and Philosophy*, trans. Julie Rose (Minneapolis: University of Minnesota Press, 1999).

64. Gandhi, "Suppressed Classes," 45.

65. Ibid., 44.

66. Gandhi, "Ashram Observances in Action," 11 July 1932, in *MPWG* 2:600.

67. Gandhi, "Answers to Questions."

68. Gandhi to Haribhau Pathak, 6 October 1932, in *CWMG* 57:180.

69. Gandhi, "Speech at Kathiawar Political Conference," 30 October 1921, in *CWMG* 25:30.

70. Gandhi, "Answers to Questions."

71. Gandhi, "The Caste System," in *CWMG* 22:68; originally published in *Young India*, 8 December 1920.

72. Gandhi, "Speech at Morvi," 141.

73. Gandhi to Satis Chandra Das Gupta, 5 November 1932, in *CWMG* 57:335–336.

74. Gandhi, "Temple Entry," in *CWMG* 76:335; originally published in *Harijan*, 23 September 1939.

75. For his lengthiest meditation on the distinction between *Ramarajya* and democracy, see Gandhi, "Speech at Morvi," 141.

76. Gandhi, "Temple Entry," 335.

77. Mehta, "Patience, Inwardness, and Self-Knowledge in Gandhi's *Hind Swaraj*."

78. Gandhi, "The Jews," 26 November 1938, in *NVPW* 1:172. For a response, see Martin Buber to Mohandas Gandhi, Jerusalem, 24 February 1939, in *The Letters of Martin Buber: A Life of Dialogue*, ed. Nahum N. Glatzer and Paul Mendes-Flohr, trans. Richard and Clara Winston and Harry Zohn (New York: Schocken, 1991), 476–482.

79. Ambedkar, "Gandhi and His Fast," in *Essays*, 375.

80. Ambedkar, *Annihilation of Caste*, 116.

81. Gandhi, *Hind Swaraj-CW*, 294.

82. Gandhi, "Bihar and Untouchability," in *CWMG* 63:82–83; originally published in *Harijan*, 2 February 1934.

83. Ambedkar, *Annihilation of Caste*, 77.

84. Gandhi, "Speech at Public Meeting," Tinnevelly, and "Speech at Public Meeting," Tuticorin, 24 January 1934, *CWMG* 63:38–41; originally published in *Harijan*, 2 February 1934.

85. Skaria, "No Politics without Religion," 192–194.

86. Theodor Adorno and Max Horkheimer, *Dialectic of Enlightenment: Philosophical Fragments* (1966; Stanford, CA: Stanford University Press, 2006).

87. "Theodicy," Emmanuel Levinas writes, "effectively succeeds in making God innocent or in saving morality in the name of faith or in making suffering bearable." And, he adds, "it is impossible . . . to underestimate the temptation of theodicy." Levinas, "Useless Suffering," in *Entre Nous: Thinking-of-the-Other*, trans. Michael B. Smith and Barbara Harshav (New York: Columbia University Press, 1998), 96.

88. Coming from a different perspective, Karuna Mantena gives the problem of means and ends sustained attention in her unpublished paper "Gandhi, Weber, and the Means-Ends Question in Politics."

89. Gandhi, "Speech at Meeting of Gandhi Seva Sangh and Charkha Sangh," Wardha, 22 June 1940, in *CWMG* 78:349.

90. "When a man rises from sleep, he twists his limbs and is restless. It takes some time before he is entirely awakened. . . . Rising from sleep, we do not continue in a comatose state, but according to our ability, sooner or later, we are completely restored to our senses. So shall we be free from the present unrest which no one likes." Gandhi, *Hind Swaraj-CW*, 253.

91. Gandhi to Narayan M. Khare, 10 February 1932, in *MPWG* 2:171.

92. Gandhi to Amrit Kaur, Wardha, 15 May 1940, in *CWMG* 78:219.

93. Gandhi to Narandas Gandhi, 22 July 1930, in *CWMG* 49:383–384; originally published in *Mangal Prabhat* (Ahmedabad: Navajivan, 1930).

94. Gandhi, "Statement to the Press," 16 September 1932, in *CWMG* 57:39–42.

95. Ibid., 42.

96. Gandhi, "Interview to the Press," 362–366.

97. Gandhi to Habibur Rahman, 5 November 1932, in *CWMG* 57:338.

98. Gandhi, "Speech at Prayer Meeting," New Delhi, 17 June 1947, in *CWMG* 95:293

99. Gandhi to Jawaharlal Nehru, 14 September 1933, in *CWMG* 61:393.

100. Gandhi, "A Correspondent's Dilemma," in *CWMG* 31:376; originally published in *Young India*, 21 May 1925.

101. Gandhi, "Bhagat Singh," in *CWMG* 51:316; originally published in *Navajivan*, 29 March 1931.

102. Gandhi, "The Cult of Violence," in *CWMG* 51:385–387; originally published in *Young India*, 16 April 1931.

103. Gandhi, "Coercive Fast," in *NVPW* 2:45; originally published in *Harijan*, 3 March 1946.

104. Gandhi, "Constructive Program: Its Meaning and Place," 13 December 1941,

in *Mahatma Gandhi: The Essential Writings*, ed. Judith Brown (Oxford: Oxford University Press, 2008), 167.

105. Alexis de Tocqueville, *Democracy in America*, trans. Gerald E. Bevan (New York: Penguin, 2003), 806. Also see Lefort, "Reversibility," in *Democracy and Political Theory*, 165–182.

106. Gandhi, *Hind Swaraj-CW*, 255.

CHAPTER 5

1. Ambedkar, *Annihilation of Caste*, 76.

2. For an account of the exhausting evenings spent over seats and percentages during the Poona Pact negotiations, see Pyarelal Nair, *Epic Fast*; Ambedkar, *Congress and Gandhi*; and Keer, *Dr. Ambedkar*, 208–216.

3. See Baxi, "Emancipation and Justice: Babasaheb Ambedkar's Legacy and Vision," in *Crisis and Change in Contemporary India*, ed. Upendra Baxi and Bhikhu Parekh (New Delhi: Sage, 1995), 124; Chatterjee, *Politics of the Governed*, ch. 1; Rao, *The Caste Question*; and Kamala Visweswaran, *Un/Common Cultures: Racism and the Rearticulation of Cultural Difference* (Durham, NC: Duke University Press, 2010), ch. 6.

4. There are suggestive passages on the distinction between false heroism of the nationalist epoch and what he seems to consider authentic martyrdom of the classical type in Ambedkar's 1943 essay "Ranade, Gandhi, and Jinnah." The attempt to reclaim the language of "martyrdom," the struggle against nationalists over the true meaning of sacrifice, was hardly casual. But the completion of this movement of thought would take more than a decade of experiments in religious and moral psychology.

5. See the essays in *The History of Political Thought in National Context*, ed. Dario Castiglione and Iain Hampsher-Monk.

6. Although it presents problems of a somewhat different order than contextualism, periodization is no less implicated in the rules and practices of republican sovereignty. See Kathleen Davis, *Periodization and Sovereignty: How Ideas of Feudalism and Secularization Govern the Politics of Time* (Philadelphia: University of Pennsylvania Press, 2008). Nicholas Dirks, *Castes of Mind: Colonialism and the Making of Modern India* (Princeton: Princeton University Press, 2011) traces a similar political and disciplinary impulse behind the assembling of what he calls the "biography of an archive" in colonial and postcolonial India.

7. See Ambedkar, *Buddha and His Dhamma-CE*, 183.

8. Ambedkar, *Annihilation of Caste*, 87–88.

9. Ambedkar, *Buddha and His Dhamma-CE*, 118.

10. The axiomatic principle in post-Renaissance republican theory, as Van Gelderen and Skinner put it, was that "republican citizens could be governed, but not mastered." See Martin van Gelderen and Quentin Skinner, eds., *Republicanism*, vol. 2: *Republicanism and Constitutionalism in Early Modern Europe* (Cambridge: Cambridge University Press, 2005), 3.

11. Ambedkar, *Annihilation of Caste*, 27.

12. For perspectives on the republican conception of freedom, especially in its

difference from the liberal construction, see Quentin Skinner and Martin Van Gelderen, eds., *Freedom and the Construction of Europe*, 2 vols. (Cambridge: Cambridge University Press, 2013).

13. The expression is Jean-Luc Nancy's. See Nancy, *The Experience of Freedom*, trans. Bridget McDonald (Stanford, CA: Stanford University Press, 1993), 96.

14. Ambedkar, *Partition*, 119–120.

15. Ambedkar, *Buddha and His Dhamma-CE*, 119.

16. S. Radhakrishnan, "Speech to the Constituent Assembly," New Delhi, 20 January 1947, in *CAD* 1:272.

17. Ambedkar, *Who Were the Shudras?*, 117.

18. Hobbes, "Of Liberty and Necessity," in *The English Works of Thomas Hobbes*, 11 vols., (London: John Bohn, 1890), 4:273.

19. "Security remained the decisive criterion," wrote Arendt of the nineteenth- and twentieth-century mutation in the idea of freedom, "but not the individual's security against 'violent death,' as in Hobbes (where the condition of all liberty is freedom from fear), but a security which should permit an undisturbed development of the life process of society as a whole." Arendt, "What Is Freedom?," in *Between Past and Future* (New York: Penguin, 1954), 148–149.

20. Niccolò Machiavelli, *Discourses on Livy*, trans. Julia Conaway and Peter E. Bondanella (1531; Oxford: Oxford University Press, 1997), 64.

21. Van Gelderen and Skinner, *Republicanism* 2:3.

22. Ambedkar, *Frustration*, in *BAWS* 12:733.

23. The expression "right to have rights" is Hannah Arendt's. See Arendt, *The Origins of Totalitarianism* (1951; New York: Schocken, 2004), 376.

24. Also see Martin Heidegger, *Aristotle's Metaphysics θ 1–3: On the Essence and Actuality of Force*, trans. Walter Brogan and Peter Warnek (Bloomington: Indiana University Press, 1995).

25. The classic work on the subject is John Rawls, *Justice as Fairness: A Restatement* (Cambridge, MA: Harvard University Press, 2001).

26. I draw the term "methodological extremism" from Samuel Weber, *Benjamin's—Abilities* (Cambridge, MA: Harvard University Press, 2008), 179–180.

27. See Bayly, "Rammohan Roy and the Advent of Constitutional Liberalism in India, 1800–30," *Modern Intellectual History* 4, no. 1 (2007): 25–41.

28. Ambedkar, *Annihilation of Caste*, 81.

29. Ambedkar, "Gandhi and His Fast," in *Essays*, 363–364.

30. See Ambedkar, *The Untouchables*, ch. 14, which uses key passages from the first chapter of Durkheim's *Elementary Forms*.

31. Ambedkar, "The Rock on Which It Is Built," in *Essays*, 181.

32. "The sacred thing," writes Durkheim, "is, par excellence, that which the profane must not and cannot touch with impunity." Durkheim, *Elementary Forms*, 38. But it is Derrida who most explicitly connects the untouchability of the sacred—and thus, the rendering sacred of the untouchable—with the operations of sovereignty and the law. "One should understand tact, not in the common sense of the tactile," writes Derrida, "but in the sense of knowing how to touch *without* touching, without touching *too much*. . . . Tact touches on the origin of the law. Just barely. At the limit."

See Derrida, *On Touching—Jean-Luc Nancy*, trans. Christine Irizarry (Stanford, CA: Stanford University Press, 2005), 67.

33. On the freedom to use reason, see Ambedkar, *Annihilation of Caste*, 81.

34. See Ambedkar, "Discussion on the Draft Constitution," 25 November 1949; in *CAD* 11: 11; available online at http://parliamentofindia.nic.in/ls/debates/vol11p11.htm.

35. Bhagat Singh, "Letter to the Punjab Governor," available online at *Marxist Internet Archive*, http://www.marxists.org/archive/bhagat-singh/1931/x01/x01.htm.

36. Ambedkar, *Waiting for a Visa* (New Delhi: Navayana, 2003), 27.

37. Keer, *Dr. Ambedkar*, 167.

38. For a genealogy of "constituent power" within the modern political tradition, see Andreas Kalvyas, "Popular Sovereignty, Democracy, and the Constituent Power," *Constellations* 12, no. 2 (2005), 223–244; Martin Loughlin and Neil Walker, eds., *The Paradox of Constitutionalism: Constituent Power and Constitutional Form* (New York: Oxford University Press, 2008). Also see Philip Pettit, *On the People's Terms: A Republican Theory and Model of Democracy* (Cambridge: Cambridge University Press, 2012), which highlights the distinction between Anglo-American and continental thinking on the relationship between popular sovereignty, freedom, and domination.

39. Keer, *Dr. Ambedkar*, 151.

40. Ambedkar, *Congress and Gandhi*, 136.

41. Ambedkar, *Annihilation of Caste*, 76.

42. For an incisive treatment of the Hobbesian conception of freedom, see Quentin Skinner, *Hobbes and Republican Liberty* (Cambridge: Cambridge University Press, 2008).

43. See esp. Ambedkar, *Partition*, 362.

44. Ambedkar, *Thoughts*, 342.

45. Gandhi, "Government's Civility," 32.

46. Ambedkar, *Partition*, xviii–xix. The resonance in this statement with a younger Gandhi is unmistakable. "The fact is," the editor in *Hind Swaraj* had argued, "we have become enslaved and, therefore, quarrel and like to have our quarrels decided by a third party." See Gandhi, *Hind Swaraj-CW*, 271.

47. Ambedkar, *Partition*, 164.

48. Keer, *Dr. Ambedkar*, 151.

49. On Sidgwick, see *Thoughts*, 328–329. On Rousseau, see *Partition*, 377.

50. Ambedkar, *Thoughts*, 5.

51. Ibid., 328–329.

52. Ambedkar, *Partition*, 322–324.

53. Ibid., 370.

54. Jeremy Bentham, *The Works of Jeremy Bentham*, 11 vols. (Edinburgh: John Bowring, 1843), 7:522.

55. Ambedkar, *Thoughts*, 95.

56. Ibid., 92–95.

57. We do know, however, that Ambedkar tended to celebrate the quelling of the rebellion more than he was prone to mourning its defeat. "The Mutiny of 1857 was an attempt to destroy British Rule in India," he writes in a passionate 1930 speech

composed for the London Round Table Conference. "It was an attempt to drive out the English and re-conquer India." This was a war, in other words, not between empire and nation but between two equally treacherous conquerors. But the Mutiny led by native feudal oppressors failed, Ambedkar argues, thanks to the valor, loyalty, and sacrifice of the Bombay and Madras Armies of the British East India Company, both of which were predominantly composed of the "untouchable" multitude of India, the Mahars of the west and the Pariahs of the south. Surrounded by nationalist memory and monumentalization of the event, with V. D. Savarkar's *The Indian War of Independence: 1857*, published in 1909, quickly becoming the paradigmatic work in that genre, Ambedkar's own lecture, "The Untouchables and *Pax Britannica*," provides one of the most audacious counterhistories of the Indian Mutiny. See Ambedkar, "The Untouchables and the *Pax Britannica*," in *BAWS* 12:86–87.

58. On self-determination as an explosive substance, see Ambedkar, *Partition*, 368.

59. Ambedkar, *Philosophy of Hinduism*, 69–71.

60. See esp. Ambedkar, *Ancient Indian Commerce*, in *BAWS* 12:2–3. For his enduring attraction to Roman republicanism, see Ambedkar, "Presidential Speech, Mahad Satyagraha," Mahad, 25–27 December 1927, in *301 Seminal Speeches* I: 96–97; and again, a decade later, in *Annihilation of Caste*, 29–30.

61. Gail Omvedt, *Ambedkar: Towards an Enlightened India* (New Delhi: Penguin, 2004), 103.

62. Quoted in Moon, *Growing Up Untouchable in India*, 65.

63. Rousseau, *The Social Contract and Other Later Political Writings*, trans. Victor Gourevitch (Cambridge: Cambridge University Press, 1997), 43.

64. Ambedkar, *Partition*, 377.

65. Ibid., 371.

66. Ambedkar, *Thoughts on Linguistic States* (1955; Aligarh: Anand Sahitya Sadan, 1989), 20.

67. See Rousseau, *The Social Contract*, 44.

68. Ambedkar, *Annihilation of Caste*, 87.

69. Ibid., 60.

70. Ambedkar, *Philosophy of Hinduism*, 86.

71. Ambedkar, *Annihilation of Caste*, 85.

72. Ibid., 79.

73. Ibid., 65.

74. See Ambedkar, *Congress and Gandhi*, 203–209.

75. Ibid., 205.

76. Ibid., 205.

77. Pierre Rosanvallon, *The Demands of Liberty: Civil Society in France since the Revolution*, trans. Arthur Goldhammer (Cambridge, MA: Harvard University Press, 2002), chs. 1–4.

78. See esp. Ambedkar, "Buddha or Karl Marx," 444–446.

79. Rousseau, *The Social Contract*, 50.

80. On the tradition of the armed citizen, see Louis Althusser, *Machiavelli and Us* (New York: Verso, 1999). On the creative relationship between force and civic virtue, see Lefort, *Machiavelli in the Making*; J. G. A. Pocock, *The Machiavellian Moment:*

Florentine Political Thought and the Atlantic Republican Tradition (Princeton, NJ: Princeton University Press, 1975).

81. Ambedkar, *Annihilation of Caste*, 86. One can do worse than recall the revolutionary heritage of the word "dynamite," conjured in Walter Benjamin's essay published the same year as *Annihilation of Caste*. See Benjamin, "The Work of Art in the Age of Mechanical Reproduction" (1936), in *Illuminations: Essays and Reflections*, ed. Hannah Arendt (New York: Schocken, 1968), 236.

82. Ambedkar, *Annihilation of Caste*, 76.

83. See Ambedkar, "Speech at the All Bombay Province Depressed Classes Conference," 271.

84. Ambedkar, *Philosophy of Hinduism*, 8.

85. Ambedkar, "Motion on the Draft Constitution," 4 November 1948, in *EWBRA*, 484–485.

86. Pratap Bhanu Mehta, "What Is Constitutional Morality?," *Seminar* 615 (November 2010), 17–22.

87. On Mill, see Ambedkar, *Philosophy of Hinduism*, 44–65.

88. Ambedkar, "Motion on the Draft Constitution," 4 November 1948, in *EWBRA*, 487.

89. Ibid., 489.

90. Keer, *Dr. Ambedkar*, 499.

91. Cited in G. Sampath, "B. R. Ambedkar, Arundhati Roy, and the Politics of Appropriation," *Livemint*, 19 March 2014.

92. Keer, *Dr. Ambedkar*, 499.

93. Ambedkar, *Partition*, xix.

94. Ambedkar, *Thoughts*, 125.

95. Ambedkar, "Away from the Hindus," in *Essays* 407.

96. Ambedkar, *Annihilation of Caste*, 64–65.

97. Ambedkar, *Philosophy of Hinduism*, 32.

98. Ambedkar, *Buddha and His Dhamma-CE*, 237.

99. Ambedkar, *India and Communism*, 124.

100. Repelled by the principle of equality as mere sameness, Nietzsche renders it into a creaturely metaphor. "All thought, judgment, perception, considered as comparison, has as its precondition a '*positing* of equality,' and earlier still a '*making* equal.' The process of making equal is the same as the process of incorporation of appropriated material in the amoeba." Friedrich Nietzsche, *The Will to Power*, trans. Walter Kaufmann and R. J. Hollingdale (New York: Vintage, 1967), 501.

101. Ambedkar, *India and Communism*, 117.

102. Ibid., 123.

103. Ambedkar, *Philosophy of Hinduism*, 26.

104. Ibid., 25.

105. Ambedkar, *India and Communism*, 126–127.

106. Étienne Balibar traces this expression to the influence on Rousseau of Hobbes himself. See Balibar, "The Reversal of Possessive Individualism," in Balibar, *Equaliberty*, 80.

107. Ambedkar, *Miscellaneous Notes*, in *BAWS* 12:754.

108. Ambedkar, "Hindus and Want of Public Conscience," in *Essays*, 92.

109. Gauri Viswanathan, whose work *Outside the Fold: Conversion, Modernity, and Belief* (Princeton, NJ: Princeton University Press, 1998) remains an indispensable study on the place of Ambedkar's 1956 conversion to Buddhism in South Asia's complex entry into the "secular age," is only partly right in suggesting that *The Buddha and His Dhamma* might have been a text of secular theology. For Ambedkar, as I argue above, the designation "secular" itself, in the sense that someone like Charles Taylor approaches it, remains unfit—too immanent, or rather, too inadequately transcendent—to a politics without God. See Taylor, *A Secular Age* (Cambridge, MA: Harvard University Press, 2007).

110. Ambedkar, *Annihilation of Caste*, 77.

111. Ambedkar, "Presidential Address at Second Conference of Untouchables from Berar Province," in *301 Seminal Speeches* 1:84; originally published in *Bahishkrit Bharat*, 25 November 1927.

112. Ambedkar, *Annihilation of Caste*, 69.

CHAPTER 6

1. Gandhi, "The Right Way and the Wrong Way," 320.

2. Gandhi, "Dr. Ambedkar's Indictment-I," in *CWMG* 69:206; originally published in *Harijan*, 11 July 1936.

3. Ibid., 206–207.

4. Gandhi to Chimanlal B. Patel, 3 April 1926, in *CWMG* 35:14.

5. See especially Hofmeyr, *Gandhi's Printing Press*, ch. 5.

6. Ambedkar, *Annihilation of Caste*, 76.

7. Gandhi, "Dr. Ambedkar's Indictment-II," in *CWMG* 69:226–227; originally published in *Harijan*, 18 July 1936.

8. Gandhi to Narandas Gandhi, 22 July 1930, in *CWMG* 49:383–384; originally published in *Mangal Prabhat* (Ahmedabad: Navajivan, 1930).

9. Gandhi to Jamnalal Bajaj, 16 March 1922, in *CWMG* 26:364.

10. Gandhi, "Speech at Meeting in Lausanne," 8 December 1931, in *CWMG* 54:268.

11. Gandhi, "Speech at Prayer Meeting," Sevagram, 24 August 1946, in *CWMG* 92:60; originally published in *Harijan*, 8 September 1946.

12. Gandhi, "Speech at Prayer Meeting," New Delhi, 12 January 1948, in *CWMG* 98:218.

13. See Isaac Rosenfield, "Gandhi: Self-Realization through Politics," in *An Age of Enormity: Life and Writing in the Forties and Fifties*, ed. Theodore Solotaroff (Cleveland: Ohio University Press, 1962).

14. Karl Jaspers, *The Future of Mankind*, trans. E. B. Ashton (1958; Chicago: University of Chicago Press, 1961), 39.

CHAPTER 7

1. *Dr. Babasaheb Ambedkar*, 193.

2. Ibid., 63.

3. Bhagwan Das, "Introduction," in Ambedkar, *Gandhi and Gandhism* (Jaland-har: Bheem Patrika Publications, 1970), vii.

4. "Draft Constitution: Article 110," in *BAWS* 13:640; extracted from *CAD*, 3 June 1948, 612–614.

5. Ibid.

6. Ambedkar, *Annihilation of Caste*, 60–61.

7. Ambedkar, *Buddha and His Dhamma-WS*, 324.

8. Gandhi, "To the People of Kheda," in *CWMG* 49: 176; originally published in *Navajivan*, 4 May 1930. Ajay Skaria explores the sensitivity of this expression in his essay "Living by Dying: Gandhi, *Satyagraha*, and the Warrior," in *Ethical Life in South Asia*, ed. Anand Pandian and Daud Ali (Bloomington: Indiana University Press, 2010), 211–231.

9. Ambedkar, *Philosophy of Hinduism*, 64–65.

10. Gandhi, *Homage to the Departed* (Ahmedabad: Navajivan, 1958).

11. "States Reorganization Bill," 1 May 1956, in *PD* 12A: 834–845; reprinted in *BAWS* 15:969.

12. Ambedkar to Dattoba," Bombay, 16 August 1926, BRAP, file 5, reel 2.

13. Gandhi, *Hind Swaraj-CE*, 9.

14. Ambedkar, *Buddha and His Dhamma-CE*, xxvii.

15. Scholars rarely pose questions about authenticity and fidelity in their engage-ment with Gandhi's *Discourses on the Gita*, taking, more often than not, his commen-taries on classical texts as reflections of the turns in his own thought. What matters most in these encounters between a modern thinker and classical texts is not the thinker's fidelity to the works at hand (nor certainly the authenticity of a text itself) but the turns in the thinker's methodological and ideological priorities, the turn as such (in the moral and political vocabulary of the times) induced by the encounter. Aakash Singh Rathore and Ajay Verma, in their introduction to the critical edition of Ambedkar's *Buddha and His Dhamma*, have done great service by clarifying some of these implicit inequalities, the "void" as they call it, that frame the reception of Ambedkar's works.

16. Ambedkar, Preface to *Buddha and His Dhamma-CE*, xxvii.

17. Ambedkar, *Annihilation of Caste*, 119.

18. See Jean-Luc Nancy, "Finite and Infinite Democracy," in Giorgio Agamben et al., *Democracy in What State?* (New York: Columbia University Press, 2012), 58–75.

19. Ambedkar, *Annihilation of Caste*, 89.

20. Ibid.

21. Ibid., 119–120.

22. In *Annihilation of Caste*, Ambedkar even calls the monarch Chandragupta Maurya a political revolutionary of the Lutheran kind, one who built on the Bud-dha's religious and social revolution. See Ambedkar, ibid., 31.

23. See Ambedkar, "Buddha or Karl Marx," 459.

24. Ibid., 451. In this essay Ambedkar deploys John Dewey's intervention, "Means and Ends," which was first published in *New International* in August 1938. Dewey's text is a response to Leon Trotsky's *Their Morals and Ours* (New York: Pathfinder

Press, 1969), composed in exile in Mexico and subsequently published in *New International* in June 1938.

25. Ambedkar, *Buddha and His Dhamma-CE*, 183.

26. Ibid., 183.

27. See Partha Chatterjee, "On Civil and Political Society in Postcolonial Democracies," in *Civil Society: History and Possibilities*, ed. Kaviraj and Khilnani, 165–178.

28. See, for instance, Ambedkar, "Away from the Hindus," in *Essays*, 407.

29. Ambedkar, *Annihilation of Caste*, 87.

30. Ibid.

31. Ambedkar, *Philosophy of Hinduism*, 23–24.

32. Ambedkar, *Buddha and His Dhamma-CE*, 171–172.

33. Ibid., 173.

34. Ibid., 130.

35. Ambedkar, *Annihilation of Caste*, 87–88.

36. Ibid., 35.

37. Ambedkar, "My Philosophy of Life," All India Radio Broadcast, 3 October 1954, in *BAWS* 12:503.

38. Ambedkar, *Philosophy of Hinduism*, 22.

39. Ibid., 23–24.

40. Ambedkar, *Buddha and His Dhamma-CE*, 72.

41. Ibid., 158.

42. Gandhi, "Doctrine of the Sword," in *CWMG* 21:160; originally published in *Navajivan*, 15 August 1920.

43. Robert E. Buswell Jr. and Donald S. Lopez Jr., *The Princeton Dictionary of Buddhism* (Princeton, NJ: Princeton University Press, 2014), 655.

44. Ambedkar, *Buddha and His Dhamma-CE*, 158.

45. Ambedkar to Dattoba, 16 August 1926.

46. Ambedkar, Dedication to *Congress and Gandhi*.

47. Ambedkar, *Partition*, ix.

48. Ambedkar, *Annihilation of Caste*, 127.

49. Ambedkar, *Waiting for a Visa*, in *BAWS* 12:675–676.

50. "States Reorganization Bill." This refusal to be prayed for after death is strikingly reminiscent of Ambedkar's resistance two decades earlier against another prayer: Gandhi's naming of the *harijan*.

51. Ambedkar, "My Philosophy of Life," 503.

52. Ibid.

53. Ambedkar, *Annihilation of Caste*, 86.

54. Ambedkar, "Speech at Bombay Presidency Mahar Conference," Bombay, 31 May 1936; available online at: http://www.columbia.edu/itc/mealac/pritchett/00ambedkar/txt_ambedkar_salvation.html#19

55. For a probing study of Ambedkar's linguistic anthropology, see Kamala Visweswaran's *Un/Common Cultures*, ch. 6.

56. Gandhi's assassin devoted considerable time during his trial to asserting the spiritual sovereignty of Hindi as the language for a modern India. See Godse, *Why I Assassinated Gandhi?*

57. Nehru, "Obituary Reference," 6 December 1956, in *PD* 10C: 1769–1770; reprinted in *BAWS* 15:974.

58. See, for one example, the debate on the "States Reorganization Bill."

59. Apart from the constitution, the Hindu Code Bill was the most ambitious legislative project that Ambedkar undertook in the late 1940s. He resigned from Nehru's cabinet on 27 October 1951 after conservatives mounted resistance against the bill's more radical provisions. See "Ambedkar and the Hindu Code Bill," in *BAWS* 14, pts. 1 and 2, which brings together, from the *CAD*, his interventions in the Parliament between November 1947 and October 1951. On the question of women's rights, see *Against the Madness of Manu: B. R. Ambedkar's Writings on Brahmanical Patriarchy*, ed. Sharmila Rege (New Delhi: Navayana, 2013).

60. See Gopalkrishna Gandhi, ed., *Gandhi Is Gone. Who Will Guide Us Now? Nehru, Prasad, Azad, Vinoba, Kriplani, JP, and Others Introspect, Sevagram, March 1948*, trans. Gopal Gandhi and Rupert Snell (New Delhi: Permanent Black, 2007).

61. Ambedkar, *India and Communism*, 97–98.

62. Ambedkar, *Philosophy of Hinduism*, 44–45.

63. Ambedkar, "Buddha or Karl Marx," 462.

64. See esp. ibid., 450–451; compare this with the dialogues in *Buddha and His Dhamma-CE*, 262–264.

65. "However little may be known of religion *in the singular*," writes Derrida in his "pre-definition" of religion, "we do know that it is always a response and responsibility that is prescribed, not chosen freely in an act of pure and abstractly autonomous will. There is no doubt that it implies freedom, will and responsibility, but let us try to think this: will and freedom *without autonomy*. Whether it is a question of sacredness, sacrificiality, or of faith, the other makes the law, the law is other: to give oneself back, and up, to the other." See Derrida, "Faith and Knowledge: The Two Sources of 'Religion' at the Limits of Reason Alone," in *Acts of Religion*, ed. Gil Anidjar (New York: Routledge, 2002), 47.

66. See Martin Fuchs, "Ambedkar's Buddhism," in *Indian Religions*, ed. T. N. Madan (Delhi: Oxford University Press, 2004), 307–325.

67. Ambedkar, "Buddha or Karl Marx," 444–446.

68. Ambedkar, *Buddha and His Dhamma-CE*, 130.

69. Ibid.

70. Ambedkar, *Buddha and His Dhamma-CE*, 313. Also see Jan Westerhoff, *Nāgārjuna's Madhyamaka: A Philosophical Introduction* (Oxford: Oxford University Press, 2009).

71. See, for instance, C. W. Huntington Jr. and Geshé Namgyal Wangchen, *The Emptiness of Emptiness: An Introduction to Early Indian Madhyamika* (Honolulu: University of Hawaii Press, 1989); Geshé Rabten, *Echoes of Voidness*, trans. Stephen Batchelor (London: Wisdom, 1983). On *anatta*, see Steven Collins, *Selfless Persons: Imagery and Thought in Theravada Buddhism* (Cambridge: Cambridge University Press, 1982).

72. Ambedkar, *Buddha and His Dhamma-CE*, 130.

73. Ibid., 59.

74. Ibid., 175.

75. Ibid., 173–174.

76. On the allegorical strategies in *The Buddha and His Dhamma*, see Simona Sawhney's "Ambedkar: The Inheritance of Buddha" (unpublished paper). Also see *Engaged Buddhism: Buddhist Liberation Movements in Asia*, ed. Christopher S. Queen and Sallie B. King (New York: SUNY Press, 1996); *Reconstructing the World: B. R. Ambedkar and Buddhism in India*, ed. Surendra Jondhale and Johannes Beltz (New Delhi: Oxford University Press, 2004).

77. Ambedkar, *Buddha and His Dhamma-CE*, 174.

78. Ambedkar, "Their Wishes Are Laws unto Us," in *Essays*, 278.

79. Ambedkar, "Buddha or Karl Marx," 442.

80. Ambedkar, *Buddha and His Dhamma-CE*, 159–160.

81. Ambedkar, "Buddha or Karl Marx," 450.

82. Ibid., 264.

83. Ambedkar, *Buddha and His Dhamma-CE*, 72–73.

84. Ibid., 74.

85. Ibid., 183.

86. "States Reorganization Bill."

87. Ambedkar, *Buddha and His Dhamma-CE*, 17–19.

88. This version of the dialogue appears in *Angulimala Sutta*. See Richard F. Gombrich, "Who Was Angulimala?," in *How Buddhism Began: The Conditioned Genesis of the Early Teachings* (London: Athlone, 1996), 140–141.

89. Ambedkar, *Buddha and His Dhamma-CE*, 112–114.

90. Ibid., 113.

91. Ibid., 73.

92. See esp. Ambedkar, *Annihilation of Caste*, 60.

93. Ibid., 86.

EPILOGUE

1. Ambedkar, "Conditions Precedent for the Successful Working of Modern Democracy," *301 Seminal Speeches* I: 287.

2. Note the silences, for instance, in Richard Davies's *The Bhagavad Gita: A Biography* (Princeton, NJ: Princeton University Press, 2014), and Sanjay Palshikar's *Evil and the Philosophy of Retribution*.

3. Pocock, *Virtue, Commerce, and History* (Cambridge: Cambridge University Press, 1985), 44.

4. Yet the dramatic way in which Ambedkar puts to use the metaphor of the torrential river (that appears as the emblem of *fortuna* in chapter 25 of *The Prince*) to describe the logic of force—does give the reader pause. See Machiavelli, *The Prince*, ed. Quentin Skinner and Russell Price (Cambridge: Cambridge University Press, 1988), 85, and Ambedkar, *Thoughts*, 340 (I discuss this passage in Chapter 3). A closer resemblance appears between *Thoughts on Pakistan* and the 1908 translation of *The Prince* by W. K. Marriott, now available online at constitution.org.

5. Judith N. Shklar, *Ordinary Vices* (Cambridge, MA: Harvard University Press, 1984).

6. Ambedkar, *Partition*, x–xi.

7. Gandhi, *Hind-Swaraj-CW*, 262.

8. Ambedkar, "Conditions Precedent for the Successful Working of Modern Democracy," *301 Seminal Speeches* I: 287.

9. Ambedkar, *Philosophy of Hinduism*, 17–18.

10. Ambedkar, "Introduction to the Draft Constitution," 4 November 1948, in *EWBRA*, 487.

11. Ambedkar, *Buddha and His Dhamma-CE*, 115.

Index

251; and freedom, 224–29, 230–31, 235,
239–40, 242–44, 245, 252–53, 265, 270,
372n46; and "general mobilization," 252,
254–58, 259–60; and historiography,
221–22; in independent India, 339–
40; and Indian constitution, 256, 260,
264–65, 342; and insurrection, 231, 246;
and justice, 239–40; and liberalism, 134,
226, 232; and moral law, 235–36; and
Platonism, 136, 326, 336; and reason,
237, 253–54, 258–59; and rejection of
Hinduism, 258–59; and religion, 225, 237–
38, 272, 314; and Romanticism, 241–42;
and security, 246, 247–48, 372–73n57;
and Social Question, 22; and sovereignty,
223–24, 247, 248, 249–50, 254, 263; and
theologico-political problem, 266, 272–73;
and touching/touchability, 234, 235, 239;
and violence/nonviolence, 267–68; and
virtue, 253–54, 258–59, 266–72, 340
Ambedkar-Gandhi affinities: and classical
thought, 51–52; and equality, 2, 43–44;
and force, 6, 12, 27–28, 29; intellectual
influences, 353n96; and ontology, 26–27;
and sacrifice, 6–7; and sovereignty, 3, 13,
35–36; and suffering, 6–7; and theologico-
political problem, 13; and truth, 147
Ambedkar-Gandhi differences: and classical
thought, 37; and enumeration, 13–14;
Gandhi's critique of *Annihilation of Caste,*
106, 204, 277–87, 297, 310; and Gandhi's
death, 289–90; and religion, 116, 317–18,
324
Ambedkar on caste: and annihilation, 9;
and *Bhagavad Gita,* 152–53; and classical
thought, 36–37; and cognitive servitude,
257, 374n81; and custom, 193; and equality,
47–48; and force, 31, 135, 143, 233; and
freedom, 226; and "general mobilization,"
199, 233–34; and moral law, 235–36;
and ontology, 250–51; and rejection of
Hinduism, 49; and republicanism, 229,
234–36, 238; Rousseau's influence on, 126;
and *samata,* 48–49; and temple entry,
139, 145, 230; and terminology, 33; and
touching/touchability, 234; and truth, 145.
See also Annihilation of Caste
Ambedkar on force, 109–62; and Ambedkar-
Gandhi affinities, 6, 12, 27–28; and
annihilation, 156; and authority, 36,
129–31, 144–45, 151; and *Bhagavad
Gita,* 146–47, 148, 150–57, 160, 364n92,
365n96; and caste, 31, 135, 143, 233; and
constituent power, 26, 134, 135, 251; and

constitutionalism, 225; and constitutional
morality, 263; and custom, 118, 119–
20; and democracy, 137–39, 363n64;
and Durkheim, 43; and education, 110;
elements of critique, 117–25; and equality,
114–15, 143; and extremism, 251; and
freedom, 121–22, 124–25; and Gandhi's
critique of *Annihilation of Caste,* 277–78;
and heresy, 158–62; and Hindu-Muslim
relations, 113–14; and historicity, 120;
and insurrection, 112–13, 114, 124; and
intellectual influences, 16–17, 231, 268;
and language, 110–11, 114; and law, 118–
19, 129–30, 131–32, 133, 135–37, 143; and
Manusmriti, 129–31; and military service,
121; and mysticism, 115, 122, 140–41;
and ontology, 115; and power, 159; and
religion, 121–24, 297–98, 299, 330–31; and
republicanism, 136, 143–44, 231–32, 233,
250, 251; and Rousseau, 42; and *samata,*
29, 121; and *satyagraha,* 146–48; and
Shakespeare, 125–26; and soul, 132–34,
137; and sovereignty, 127–28, 138, 162;
and state, 144; and statelessness, 16; and
syndicalism, 139–43; and theater, 126–27,
362n34; and theologico-political problem,
10, 36, 117, 119–20, 129–31, 148–49, 151,
158–59; and truth, 124, 140, 145–50; and
violence/nonviolence, 111–12, 147, 155,
156–57, 159; and virtue, 268; and war, 143,
249–50
Ambedkar on religion, 32, 289–336; and
Ambedkar-Gandhi differences, 116, 317–
18, 324; and annihilation, 10–11, 224,
326–27; and authenticity of *Bhagavad
Gita,* 338–39; and autonomy, 303–5, 315;
and Bergson, 42; and conversion, 315–16,
343; conversion to Buddhism, 222, 274,
332–33; and death, 293–95, 300–301, 307–
9; and egalitarian sovereignty, 10, 122;
and empiricism, 122, 123; and finitude,
296, 313–14, 336; and force, 121–24, 297–
98, 299, 330–31; and fraternity, 294, 303,
304, 316–17, 319–20; and Gandhi's death,
289–91, 319; and heresy, 158–62; Hinduism
as "religion of the book," 34, 36, 72, 148;
and humanism, 158, 238; and Indian
constitution, 318; and law, 304; and *maitri,*
294, 304, 320–21, 328–36; and measureless
whole, 322–23; and morality, 354–55nIII;
and moral law, 298–99; and mysticism,
116–17, 122, 130–31; and negative theology,
139, 155–56, 311, 313–14, 317, 323, 324, 325;
and Partition, 301–2, 317; and philosophy,

Cultural Memory in the Present

Gyanendra Pandey, *Routine Violence: Nations, Fragments, Histories*

James Siegel, *Naming the Witch*

J. M. Bernstein, *Against Voluptuous Bodies: Late Modernism and the Meaning of Painting*

Theodore W. Jennings, Jr., *Reading Derrida / Thinking Paul: On Justice*

Richard Rorty and Eduardo Mendieta, *Take Care of Freedom and Truth Will Take Care of Itself: Interviews with Richard Rorty*

Jacques Derrida, *Paper Machine*

Renaud Barbaras, *Desire and Distance: Introduction to a Phenomenology of Perception*

Jill Bennett, *Empathic Vision: Affect, Trauma, and Contemporary Art*

Ban Wang, *Illuminations from the Past: Trauma, Memory, and History in Modern China*

James Phillips, *Heidegger's Volk: Between National Socialism and Poetry*

Frank Ankersmit, *Sublime Historical Experience*

István Rév, *Retroactive Justice: Prehistory of Post-Communism*

Paola Marrati, *Genesis and Trace: Derrida Reading Husserl and Heidegger*

Krzysztof Ziarek, *The Force of Art*

Marie-José Mondzain, *Image, Icon, Economy: The Byzantine Origins of the Contemporary Imaginary*

Cecilia Sjöholm, *The Antigone Complex: Ethics and the Invention of Feminine Desire*

Jacques Derrida and Elisabeth Roudinesco, *For What Tomorrow . . . : A Dialogue*

Elisabeth Weber, *Questioning Judaism: Interviews by Elisabeth Weber*

Jacques Derrida and Catherine Malabou, *Counterpath: Traveling with Jacques Derrida*

Martin Seel, *Aesthetics of Appearing*

Nanette Salomon, *Shifting Priorities: Gender and Genre in Seventeenth-Century Dutch Painting*

Jacob Taubes, *The Political Theology of Paul*

Jean-Luc Marion, *The Crossing of the Visible*

Eric Michaud, *The Cult of Art in Nazi Germany*

Anne Freadman, *The Machinery of Talk: Charles Peirce and the Sign Hypothesis*

Stanley Cavell, *Emerson's Transcendental Etudes*

Stuart McLean, *The Event and Its Terrors: Ireland, Famine, Modernity*

Beate Rössler, ed., *Privacies: Philosophical Evaluations*

Bernard Faure, *Double Exposure: Cutting Across Buddhist and Western Discourses*

Alessia Ricciardi, *The Ends of Mourning: Psychoanalysis, Literature, Film*

Alain Badiou, *Saint Paul: The Foundation of Universalism*

Gil Anidjar, *The Jew, the Arab: A History of the Enemy*

Jonathan Culler and Kevin Lamb, eds., *Just Being Difficult? Academic Writing in the Public Arena*

Jean-Luc Nancy, *A Finite Thinking*, edited by Simon Sparks

Theodor W. Adorno, *Can One Live after Auschwitz? A Philosophical Reader*, edited by Rolf Tiedemann